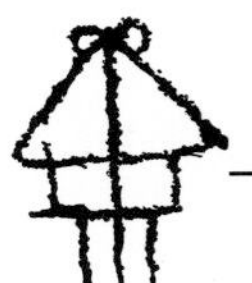

Pictures in Place

A companion to *The Archaeology of Rock-Art* (Cambridge, 1998), this new collection edited by Christopher Chippindale and George Nash addresses the most important component around the rock-art panel – its landscape. *Pictures in Place* draws together the work of many well-known scholars from key regions of the world for rock-art and for rock-art research. It provides a unique, broad and varied insight into the arrangement, location and structure of rock-art and its place within the landscapes of ancient worlds as ancient people experienced them. Packed with illustrations as befits a book about images, *Pictures in Place* offers a visual as well as a literary key to the understanding of this most lovely and alluring of archaeological traces.

CHRISTOPHER CHIPPINDALE is a curator for archaeology collections and Reader in Archaeology at the Cambridge University Museum of Archaeology and Anthropology. He is also affiliated to the School of Archaeology and Anthropology, Australian National University, Canberra, and the Rock Art Research Institute, University of the Witwatersrand, Johannesburg, South Africa. He is the author of the prize-winning *Stonehenge Complete* (1st edition 1983; now in its 3rd edition) and the editor of *The Archaeology of Rock-Art* (with Paul S. C. Taçon, Cambridge 2001) and *European Landscapes of Rock-Art* (with George Nash, 2001).

GEORGE NASH is a part-time lecturer at the Centre for the Historic Environment, Department of Archaeology, University of Bristol. He is also the technical director of a commercial consultancy, Border Archaeology. Previous publications include *Semiotics of Landscape: Archaeology of Mind* (edited, 1997), *Status, Exchange and Mobility: Mesolithic Portable Art of Southern Scandinavia* (1998) and *Signifying Place and Space: World Perspectives of Rock-Art and Landscape* (edited, 2000).

'The grave-digger': sixteenth or seventeenth century AD, engraved image carved into clunch chalk wall, Harlton Church, Cambridgeshire.

Although rock-art, as images made on exposed bed-rock, is rare in the western cultural context, there is much in the way of imagery that is 'rock-art' more broadly defined. This figure was carved into the clunch wall of a Cambridgeshire parish church, an artificial open rock surface.

Appearing to show a man in Tudor dress holding a spade, it depicts a human being and the physical means by which he shaped and modified his landscape – but it is not an image of a landscape as such.

Photograph by Gwil Owen; reproduced with his permission and by courtesy of Harlton Parochial Church Council.

Pictures in Place

The Figured Landscapes of Rock-Art

edited by

Christopher Chippindale

and

George Nash

CAMBRIDGE
UNIVERSITY PRESS

PUBLISHED BY THE PRESS SYNDICATE OF THE UNIVERSITY OF CAMBRIDGE
The Pitt Building, Trumpington Street, Cambridge CB2 1RP, United Kingdom

CAMBRIDGE UNIVERSITY PRESS
The Edinburgh Building, Cambridge CB2 2RU, UK
40 West 20th Street, New York, NY 10011-4211, USA
477 Williamstown Road, Port Melbourne, VIC 3207, Australia
Ruiz de Alarcón 13, 28014 Madrid, Spain
Dock House, The Waterfront, Cape Town 8001, South Africa

http://www.cambridge.org

First published 2004

Printed in the United Kingdom at the University Press, Cambridge

Typefaces Bembo 10/13.5 pt and Futura   *System* LaTeX 2ε [TB]

A catalogue record for this book is available from the British Library

ISBN 0 521 81879 6 hardback
ISBN 0 521 52424 5 paperback

For Ruth

For John Oddie

Contents

Figures

Tables

Contributors

Andrea Arcà
Cooperativa Archeologica Le Orme dell'Uomo, Piazza Donatori di Sangue 1 – 25040 – Cerveno (BS), Italy
aarcat@inrete.it

Daniel Arsenault
Départment d'histoire de l'art, Case postale 8888, succursale Centre-Ville, Montréal (Québec), Canada H3C 3P8
arsenault.daniel@ugam.ca

Geoffrey Blundell
Rock Art Research Unit, University of the Witwatersrand, Private Bag 3, PO WITS 2050, Johannesburg, South Africa
107geoff@cosmos.wits.ac.za

Christopher Chippindale
Cambridge University Museum of Archaeology and Anthropology, Downing Street, Cambridge CB2 3DZ, England
cc43@cam.ac.uk

Bruno David
Department of Geography and Environmental Science, Monash University, Clayton 3168, Australia
Bruno.David@arts.monash.edu.au

Josephine Flood
Ffynnon Bedr, Llanbedr-y-Cennin, Conwy, Gwynedd LL32 8YZ, Wales
josephineflood@compuserve.com

Don Hann
Bear Valley Ranger District, 528 East Main, John Day OR 97845, USA

Knut Helskog
Tromsø Museum, University of Tromsø, 900 Tromsø, Norway
knut@imv.uit.no

William D. Hyder
Social Sciences Division, 117 Social Sciences 1, University of California Santa Cruz, 1156 High Street, Santa Cruz CA 95064, USA
bill@zzyx.ucsc.edu

James D. Keyser
US Forest Service, Pacific Northwest Region, Portland (OR), USA
jkeyser@fs.fed.us

Tilman Lenssen-Erz
Heinrich-Barth-Institut, University of Cologne, Jennerstraßpte 8, D-50823 Köln, Germany
lenssen.erz@uni-koeln.de

Lawrence Loendorf
Department of Sociology and Anthropology, PO Box 30001, New Mexico State University, Las Cruces NM 88003-8001, USA
lll@loendorf.net

Jannie Loubser
New South Associates, 6150 East Ponce de Leon Avenue, Stone Mountain GA 30083, USA
jhnl@hotmail.com

George Nash
Centre for the Historic Environment, University of Bristol, 43 Woodlands Road, Bristol, England
georgejayne@lineone.net

Lindsey Nash

Sven Ouzman
Anthropology Department, University of California, Berkeley CA 94720–3710, USA
svenouzman@hotmail.com

George Poetschat
Oregon Archaeological Society, PO Box 13293, Portland OR 97213, USA
cgpoet@pcez.com

Benjamin W. Smith
Rock Art Research Unit, University of the Witwatersrand, Private Bag 3, PO WITS 2050, Johannesburg, South Africa
107bws@cosmos.wits.ac.za

Paul S. C. Taçon
Anthropology Division, Australian Museum, 6 College Street, Sydney, NSW 2010, Australia
pault@amsg.austmus.gov.au

David Whitley
W&S Consultants, 447 3rd Street, Fillmore CA 93015, USA
huitli@impulse.net

Editors' acknowledgements

The editors thank the contributors for the speedy, good-humoured and efficient way in which they have worked with us. We thank also Mary Baxter, Frances Brown, Jessica Kuper, Neil de Cort and Eva Walderhaug Saetersdal for their assistance in several ways.

Note on radiocarbon dating

Dates given as BC, AD, BP ('Before Present') are in calendar years, however they have been arrived at. Dates given as 'bp' are uncalibrated radiocarbon determinations, and are measures of 'radiocarbon years' that do not equate exactly with calendar years.

1

Pictures in place: approaches to the figured landscapes of rock-art

Christopher Chippindale and George Nash

Pictures in place (Fig. 1.1)

Each class of archaeological material has its own character, and with each character comes the special strengths and weaknesses of that personality. Animal bones from Pleistocene sites give precise information about the biology of these ancient creatures, but leave uncertain the human role; the creatures may have occupied the caves in lives and deaths to which the human element contributed nothing. Lithics can be studied as technical objects, but they consistently prove hard to translate from their own world of stone and mechanics into realms of human meaning. Rock-art, seen as an engaging but obscure class of archaeological material, seems to offer an interesting paradox. It gives a direct record, made by ancient people, of ancient worlds as those ancient people saw and experienced them. Its central point is in the meaning of things, inviting an archaeology of human perception, of world-view and of religion. But the means to do this, starting with systematics of dealing with its shapes, are weak: 'Is this wiggly line a picture of a rattlesnake?' 'If it is, then what did a picture of a rattlesnake mean?' Its best strength may be in it being simply *art on rock* – an image made on an unmovable surface which is set in a certain place. Unlike portable artefacts of every kind, rock-art is fixed in landscape. These are pictures in place.

That immovability is a central strength. It is shared among archaeological materials only to a limited extent with buildings, themselves rock-art of an artificial kind and in truth movable; certainly buildings are not permanent markers within the landscape (or townscape) in the way rock-art provides pictures in place. Naturally, some aspect of location has a part in most rock-art research (e.g., among very many, Morris 1988; Swartz and Hurlbutt 1994; Bradley 1997; Nash 1997). A very few full-length studies deal with landscape and rock-art as a research question (e.g. Hartley 1992). What is lacking are good and focused studies of location as a *central* concern, addressing both specifics and the – again underdeveloped – potential of cross-cultural responses (Taçon 1990).

Immovability usually applies on a macro-scale – where rock-art is placed in an expansive landscape. It can also apply on a smaller scale – for example, the area in and around the panel. Again this fixed quality of rock-art sets it apart from other kinds of archaeological material. Portable artefacts of all kinds, on the other hand, move around a landscape, to and from and within sites for all sorts of reasons; during occupation, whilst a site is going out of use, subsequent to its abandonment, or in consequence of symbolic exchange and contact (Nash 1998).

One of us entitled a preceding and companion book *The* ***archaeology*** *of rock-art* (Chippindale and Taçon 1998b), in order to emphasize the archaeological aspect. Likewise, we offer a matching attitude in the present volume, shown by its matching *subtitle, The figured* ***landscapes*** *of rock-art.*

Fig. 1.1. Figures on a landscape: a defining character of rock-art is that its images are fixed in place on the land.

Ochre rock-painting on sandstone, western Arnhem Land, Northern Territory, Australia. Although these figures, characteristically for western Arnhem Land painting, are equipped with various artefacts, and painted as if standing or walking in a group of five, there is nothing painted which appears to show the landscape.

Photograph by Christopher Chippindale.

Fig. 1.2. The 'hand on the land'.

Lily Gin.gina, Wardaman elder, holds her hand alongside a hand-stencil in a sandstone rock-shelter of her traditional country in north Australia, 1998.

Images of human hands and feet – often of adults, sometimes of children, occasionally of babies – seem to run through the long sequence of rock-painting in north Australia. The images thought to be earliest are printed, from ochre put on the hand then pressed on to the rock. Subsequent ones are usually stencilled, and the present-day bark painters sometimes put hand-stencils on their new paintings.

Photograph by Christopher Chippindale.

Again, this is an archaeological book (Fig. 1.3) but with an emphasis on landscape and the relationship landscape has with the art, the artist and the audience. Our team of contributors is aware of the beauty of these images, and we are often moved by them. Who could fail to be struck, for example, by the human force of an ancient hand stencil (Fig. 1.2), its image of a human being's hand and fingers on a smooth rock surface? However distanced is one's own life from that of the person whose hand made that mark – and there are hand-stencils in Palaeolithic old Europe as well as in ancient and in modern Australia – one feels there is common experience. At the physical level, each of us knows our own hand and each of us knows how it works and feels, and each of us can move our own thumb and fingers to make just that pattern recorded in enduring red ochre on the rock face. At the mental level, one supposes, there must be *something* held in common with that distanced human being who placed a hand against the rock, as each of us can now, and who made that ochre mark, as each of us can now.

Uncertainty in time

Change over time is so fundamental to archaeology that it is famously hard to make an effective study of undated material. Most rock-art is weakly or imprecisely dated.

The ubiquitous basis of archaeological dating for half a century now has been radiocarbon, but we know of only one body of rock-art which is now comprehensively and well dated directly by radiocarbon. This is the beeswax art of western Arnhem Land, north Australia (Nelson *et al.* in press), made in the unusual material and technique of *appliqué* dots, lines and sheets of beeswax placed on rock surfaces in designs of characteristic form (Fig. 1.4). Beeswax is a first-rate material for radiocarbon study, lasting surprisingly well: a component of beeswax is a variety of chemicals which make it resistant to biological attack and decay. The oldest of these Australian beeswax figures is dated to 4000 years ago (Nelson *et al.* 1995), and a suite of 142 dating determinations makes for a full picture. Another body of rock-art with some radiocarbon chronology is the painted art of the Palaeolithic deep caves in Europe, where we now have sufficient dates – a couple of score – by which to sketch an absolute chronology for such a long-enduring body of art (Clottes 1997, the work having started with e.g. Clottes *et al.* 1992). Those Palaeolithic dates are on charcoal, an ideal material for radiocarbon work; in the caves it unusually survives from the Pleistocene painted on a rock wall because it is in such protected places.

Fig. 1.3. Figures in a landscape: a defining character of the archaeologist's approach to rock-art is learning from its place on the land.

(*upper left*) Diepkloof Rock Shelter, on the Verlorenvlei near Elands Bay, South Africa, shelter with rock-painting; (*upper right*) Red Tank Draw, V-Bar-V Ranch, Coconino National Forest, Arizona, USA, shelter with rock-engraving; (*lower left*) Nuttall's Shelter, Drakensberg mountains, Kwa-Zulu Natal, South Africa, shelter with rock-painting; (*lower right*) Little Petroglyph Canyon, China Lake Naval Air Station, Coso Range, California, USA, shelter with rock-engraving.

Photographs by Christopher Chippindale.

Most rock-art is painted with an earth pigment, or engraved into a rock surface. Most rock-art is therefore not immediately datable by radiocarbon as a bone or a chunk of charcoal is; more ingenuity is required in the dating procedure, and there is more risk of error. If painted, then likely it was applied as a paint combining inorganic colour with a binder of some kind, likely

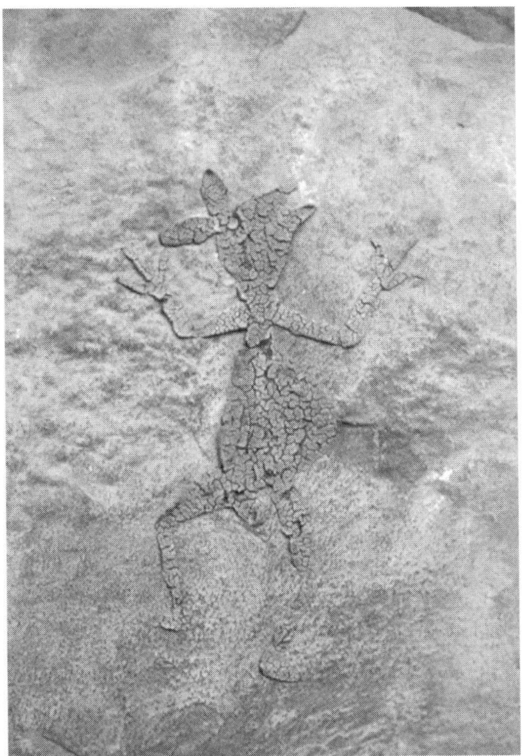

Fig. 1.4. A well-dated class of rock-art: the Aboriginal beeswax art of north Australia.

Beeswax figure from Djarrng, western Arnhem Land, north Australia.

The common design in the beeswax art is an array of dots, set in single or double lines, or extending over an area. This animal-headed being is a more unusual subject.

Photograph by Christopher Chippindale.

an organic proteinaceous or other material with a contemporary carbon component: dating the organic material in the binder would date the art itself. If engraved, then often the figure has developed some kind of patina, surface coating, skin or crust, to which again a contemporary radiocarbon component contributes: that would date events subsequent to the art itself.

Since van der Merwe *et al.* (1987), direct carbon dates have been reported for rock-art (Ilger *et al.* in press), some of them gratifyingly old, and others gratifyingly consistent with researchers' expectations. But the field remains new and uncertain. A rock-shelter wall is the interface between two physical zones: the solid rock within, stable in its conditions and often saturated with water, and the atmosphere without, often dry and fluctuating much in temperature and humidity. That frontier at the rock surface is a zone of intense biological and biochemical activity, much of it involving micro-organisms whose nature is little understood (see Soleilhavoup 1995 for a rare study of what happens on that rocky support for the art; also Dorn 2001, especially 172–3). So it is hard to know if the carbon one can extract from a pigment sample – and AMS radiocarbon dating can give a determination on a few milligrams of the element – *does* derive from that organic element to the original paint; it may instead derive in whole or in part from some other source, which according to its nature may give a younger date (from subsequent activity, e.g. algae on the rock face) or an older date (from earlier material, e.g. old carbon in the rock) (Rowe 2001).

The dating of engravings is yet harder, and these will be dates not for the act of engraving but of an event related to it, such as a patination or varnish that forms after the engraving is made, and so gives a minimum age for the engraving; or the dated material forms before the engraving, and so gives a maximum.

Seeing the care with which the technical problems are addressed (e.g. Watchman and Lessard 1992; Watchman 1993), and the cautious optimism expressed (e.g. Ilger *et al.* 1995; Rowe in press), we also notice where direct-dating studies are contradictory and confused in their findings, whether for Lawrie Creek, north Australia (Loy *et al.* 1990; Nelson 1993; Loy 1994), or the Foz Côa, Portugal (e.g. Bahn *et al.* 1995; Bednarik 1995a; 1995b; Clottes *et al.* 1995; Dorn 1995; Oliveira Jorge 1995; Watchman 1995; 1996; Zilhão 1995; 1997; Phillips *et al.* 1997; and now IPA 1999). Dismayingly, Dorn – one of the very few researchers in the direct dating of engravings – has expressed doubt about his collected results

(Dorn 1996; see also Beck *et al.* 1998, for critical comment), work which is a substantial proportion of all the studies done. This caution puts into question some remarkably early dates obtained, e.g. those for engravings in the Olary province of South Australia (Dorn *et al.* 1988; and see now Dorn 1997) and in the far western USA (Dorn and Whitley 1984; Whitley and Dorn 1987; 1993) – dates on which much has depended.

A second approach to dating is indirect: 'bridging' across from the art to a dated archaeological or geological context. When engravings are stratified within an archaeological deposit, then the age of the covering sediment is, arguably, a minimum age for the engravings; an instance is the 'Early Man' site in north-east Australia, where engravings are thereby dated to before several thousand years ago (Rosenfeld *et al.* 1981). With less security – the paintings themselves on the rock walls often seem to perish when buried – one can link a distinct mass of pigment in the deposits below, to an intense episode of painting on the rock surface above (David *et al.* 1994). In these contexts the chronological relationship between the event to which the radiocarbon determination refers and the rock-art date which may interest us must always be kept in mind.

Also of note are the potentially insecure attempts to 'bridge' from rock-art to broader regional sequences of archaeology: for example, the paintings of western Arnhem Land, with a good relative chronology, have been linked across to the well-defined palaeo-ecological sequence in the region (Chippindale and Taçon 1998a), by thinking that the changes in ecology will be reflected in subjects of the art (and see Faulstich 1997). It has long been found that the distribution of Scandinavian rock-engravings near the sea-shore is consistent with the notion that figures were made close to the shore, even in the zone where the salt keeps the rock surfaces clear of vegetation and perhaps the surfaces themselves are splashed by the sea; so the date of the rock-art will be a close, even a very close function of changing post-glacial sea-levels, whose chronology is known with good accuracy (e.g., among many studies, Helskog 1986).

A more archaeological kind of 'bridging' relates the rock-art to the known absolute age of distinctive subjects depicted; the daggers, halberds and other characteristic objects of the early metal age in Alpine Europe are the main means by which that phase of the Alpine and of the Iberian rock-engravings is defined and dated (e.g. Costas and Novoa 1993; Lumley *et al.* 1995). Shared iconography will also be helpful: the boats ubiquitous in Bronze Age Scandinavian rock-engravings also occur engraved into razors and other portable bronze artefacts, whose date is reliably known (Kaul 1998), and the subjects of Palaeolithic mural art recur on the portable artefacts – *art mobilier* – in the deposits (Bahn and Vertut 1998). Similarity in other aspects of design have also proved useful (e.g. Christensen 1994; Cole 1994).

With absolute dating itself so uncertain and often indirect, relative dating has special value, using the established and not wholly satisfactory techniques commonplace in archaeology. It is entirely premature to declare those methods obsolete or dead in the face of novel and unproved approaches to absolute dating, as has been argued for some years now (by e.g. Lorblanchet and Bahn 1993; Bednarik 1995). In that respect rock-art studies resemble the later prehistory of a generation ago, before routine radiocarbon dating determined regional absolute chronologies, and the painstaking approaches to relative chronology that are in other sub-fields out of fashion, even obsolete, remain important for rock-art (see Bradley *et al.* 2001 for these chronological issues and approaches to them for later prehistoric rock-art in Europe). Distinctive aspects in subject-matter and/or in the manner in which subjects are depicted are taken as indications that figures with those common elements will be of the same age, broadly: variability should vary in some coherent relation to time. Sequence between the entities so recognized can then be discerned by stratigraphic sequence – often not easy reliably to observe in faded paintings or in worn engravings. The more systematic approach of Harris matrices, applying that algebraic technique developed for complex stratigraphies in the ground, is proving useful (e.g. Chippindale and Taçon 1993; Mguni 1997; Chippindale *et al.* 2000).

Chronology is not the subject of the present volume, but it must be taken note of – along with its uncertainties. When chronology is uncertain or absent, it is barely possible to acquire any sense of change over time: this is a difficulty with our research knowledge for the southern African rock-paintings – and for many other bodies of rock-art. Often the basis for chronology is tenuous, as it is for the 'cup-and-ring' marks that amount to most of the rock-art of the British Isles; efforts therefore to report change over time cannot be more secure than the precarious dating evidence they depend on. And in the absence of independent dating evidence, overstrong and oversimple models are naturally resorted to. The painted Bradshaw figures of north-west Australia are an instance (Walsh 1994); it being supposed that their variability will be a straightforward function in time, an enormously subdivided chronology is proposed, with each small variant of these intricate human figures taken to represent a corresponding distinction in time. The Australian beeswax study and the set of absolute determinations for Palaeolithic Europe, noted above, point to a more complex relationship, in which variability *is* indeed a function of time but not in a conveniently simple way: figures of decisively different 'style' may be nearly or even contemporary, whilst figures of the same or decidedly similar 'style' prove to be of unquestionably different dates. This finding, not encouraging one to have confidence in the simple model of variability in relation to time, is consistent with what has often been discovered in other archaeological studies of the 'style' concept (see e.g. Conkey and Hastorf 1990).

Arguably, if one had little confidence in absolute chronologies, one could simply consider phases – which image came first? It was probably the intention of the artist, one could think, that the art was to be a permanent fixture within the landscape. (But there has to be caution as to that, for the Australian ethnography tells one that the point may be in the act of *making* the image, not that once made it shall endure.) Philosophically speaking, both the landscape and the rock-art are timeless. It is the curious mind of the scientist that insists on precise dating. One could argue that the intention of the artist (and the audience) was not to produce images for scientific deconstruction, but to produce an art that would last a generation or two.

Certainty in place

This insecurity in time is compensated for by security in place. Rock-art, by definition, is made in or on a fixed surface of the earth, rather than on a portable artefact. This fact gives a secure starting-point for one theme to rock-art research, the theme which is the topic of this book. That said, there are traditions of rock-art which extend beyond fixed rock surfaces to mark boulders which may be and have been moved, and/or which are applied also to elements of monuments. The cup-and-ring rock-engravings of the British Isles are a case in point, usually occurring in earth-fast surfaces but also extending to the stone lids of graves (Beckensall and Laurie 1998), as well as to the stone surfaces inside built monuments (Bradley 1998a). They share features with the 'megalithic art' (Shee Twohig 1981) on the very large but certainly portable kerbstones and slabs of stone-built structures. Where this is the case, dividing study arbitrarily as regards the 'fixed' and the 'movable' elements in a single tradition has no merit.

Even the rock of the Earth can occasionally move, and so can human access to rocky places. The blocking of one access-way to a cavern and the opening of another may shift a Palaeolithic painted panel from a place close by the entrance into the farthest depths. The Réseau René Clastres with modern access-ways is the remote portion of the painted cavern of Niaux in the Pyrenees, reachable only by pumping out flooded tunnels (Clottes and Simonnet 1972); but we are sure it was approached by a more direct way in Pleistocene times through an entrance now blocked and lost.

More often, the rock itself has not physically moved, nor the routes of human access to it, but the topographic landscape is transformed. We know, from falling local sea-levels, that many Scandinavian rock-art panels that now lie among the trees above flat ploughed fields of barley (Fig.1.5) were made close by the sea-shore, when those grain fields were the sandy bays of the beach and the rocks defined the coves above the beaches. Closer than just 'near the shore', they may have been splashed by the waves or submerged by the tide in the era of their engraving. And this propinquity to the sea may be a key to understanding their rationale and meaning (Helskog 1999).

At the same time, in some cases one can think of the rock-art locales as being 'stationary sites in a moving environment'. This concept also applies to south Scandinavia, where the land slopes gently: the Bohuslän sites above the barley fields are now a few kilometres from the modern shore. So one needs to go away to that present sea-shore to see a topography that echoes in its relation of sea to rocky shore to woodland what took place at the higher level some 3000 years ago.

Fig. 1.5. 'Stationary figures in a moving landscape.'
Rock-engraving panel of later prehistoric date near Tanums, Bohuslän, Sweden.
Now in a typical location, amongst the woods and between the cultivated fields, in its time it was on the rocky shore at or just by the beach and the sea shallows. The engraved figures, like the circles in the foreground, have been painted with red to make them more visible, as is customary in Scandinavian management of rock-art.
Photograph by Christopher Chippindale.

In western Arnhem Land, north Australia, the once-remote sea came decidedly closer to the rock-art regions in the later post-glacial era, and we think that dwindling distance is reflected in the subject-matter as it changes over time. Fish are depicted (Taçon 1988) more often in the recent rock-paintings than they are in the old ones. A high proportion of the fish in the older paintings are species of upper creek systems, the eeltail and salmon-tail catfishes which are tolerant of smaller streams; a high proportion of the fish in the newer paintings are those like barramundi, which flourish in the lower rivers and their broad swamplands nearer the sea. In the Arnhem Land bird paintings, one sees the magpie goose, whose habitat is the recent freshwater swampland, only appearing late in the art. As is the case for more direct palaeo-ecological records, offered by the bones and seeds in archaeological deposits, we are seeing in the rock-art a record of changing environment. Alongside that – and not always easy to distinguish from it – is record of how human beings responded to that environmental change. Again, in western Arnhem Land, that time when the sea-level rose and moved rapidly over an extended continental shelf is strikingly coincident both with a marked occurrence of fighting scenes showing large-scale battles (Taçon and Chippindale 1994) and with the first images of Rainbow Serpents, which in their distinctive early form have elements of a fish in their make-up (Taçon *et al.* 1996).

Very often, the landscape will have been transformed by modern impacts. A few rock-art sites are now under water or in towns – there is (or perhaps now, was) a rock-engraving of a fish in central Sydney, Australia, to which access is secured by a trapdoor through the floor of a city garage (Stanbury *et al.* 1990: 24–7) – and many are in farmland. In Scandinavia, and surely very generally across Europe, the landscape is more open now; there is much less in the way of trees than there was in the time of early prehistoric farmers.

The visibility both of a rock-art site from its surroundings and of the surroundings from the rock-art site has decisively changed. In Europe, that long-term change is in many regions nowadays being reversed: as marginal farmland in the Alps and in Scandinavia is now given up, and grazed or ploughed land reverts to woodland, so the rock-art sites are becoming less visible. On Mont Bego, high in the French Alps, timber-cutting at the turn of the century took out the large trees in the rock-art zones; now the mountain is protected within a national park, the larch trees are recolonizing the slopes. A global warming may decisively encourage that by lifting the tree-line. As this happens, the rock-engravings will begin to 'move downhill' from the rocky heights of the bare mountain and into the shelter of the larch-forest. At the same time, the dwindling of the mountain flocks means the understorey is less grazed; now the forest is rather less open below the canopy of larches. Many of the rock-engravings of Valcamonica, at a lower elevation in the Alps, are on rock slabs recently disinterred amongst the trees. They were made when the valley was more a land of bare rock than of chestnut woodland as it is today; if not kept clear, they now accumulate leaf litter and begin again to go underground. In north Australia, and in arid far western North America, different fire regimes may have decisively changed the vegetation. Our judgements of how open or how hidden rock-art sites are may be false if based on visual circumstances today. These are pictures which do remain fixed in place, but the contexts of those places are not fixed.

Very often, a rock-art pattern we can now clearly see in the landscape has much to do with differential survival alongside the original order. It was long suspected that the Palaeolithic rock-art of Europe was not confined to the caves, and open-air sites were finally discovered in Iberia (Bahn 1995); but without any grounds to estimate comparative survival rates, one cannot usefully guess what proportions of the original ensemble were in each type of locale. These open-air sites are all engravings, rather than paintings; yet, since European weather is absolutely opposed to the long-term survival of rock-paintings, one cannot conclude the open-air figures were originally *only* and *always* engraved. To the handful of sites first reported have been added the many engravings from the Côa Valley – but, not atypically for rock-art research, doubts and debates about dating (above) make it hard clearly to see the pattern. In north Australia, where we have a reasonable chronology, one can see a striking correlation between rock-art patterns and geology. Those regions with a long sequence extending to the survival of paintings evidently over 6000 or so years old are those regions with cliffs and shelters of the harder quartzites within the Kambolgie sandstone formations on which the far northern rock-art is mostly made. Regions with a short sequence are those with the softer sandstones; one can conjecture that erosion rates are there so much greater that no surface survives now from 6000 or so years ago. That pattern of occurrence of old paintings today will be a matter of differential survival more than of original structures.

Since patterns in the landscape occupy the rest of the book, we need here only point to a few aspects in respect of landscapes for rock-art.

First, the immovability of rock-art applies not just to location of rock-art in the landscape, but to location on the smaller scales, of where rock-art panels occur within a site or rock-shelter, and of where individual figures occur on a panel. A fundamental weakness in studying spatial order within an archaeological site is the way objects are moved, either by human or by non-human means, subsequent to its use. Even strong patterning may be due to those later disturbances, rather than to the spatial regularities of the site as an active and lived-in space. The immovability of rock-art is an asset in this respect. Some cautions will apply. Ground levels may change, portions of wall or ceiling may split or collapse, rock-art – especially painting – may differentially perish, so that the present pattern of occurrence may not be the whole story.

Finally here in respect of location, one must remember that the first factor defining the occurrence of rock-art is the occurrence of rock! There is no rock-art in the English county of Cambridgeshire, where one of us lives, because it is a low landscape of swamp, boulder-clay ridges, sands and gravels – lacking entirely caves, rock-shelters or outcrops of sturdy geology. Our nearest rock-art, across the county boundary into Hertfordshire, is predictably enough on chalk, the nearest we have to a robust rock in the region, and just strong enough as a material to support an unusual cave (perhaps natural, perhaps artificial, perhaps part each) at Royston, whose walls bear singular medieval and post-medieval rock-engravings (Beamon 1992).

In north Australia, alongside the likely differential survival according to the occurrence of the robuster quartzite (above), one can see another pattern in the pattern. In the Alligator Rivers region, especially in its higher 'stone' country, the rock-art is rather dispersed, with a great many sites scattered across the areas surveyed in detail. To the south, in Wardaman country, the rock-art occurrences are noticeably concentrated, with clusters of up to scores of sites in a focused patch, and large areas in between the concentrations which lack rock-art. Why so? A matter, first, of where the rock is! The 'stone' country – hence its name – is largely exposed rock; it is full of rock-shelters and overhangs; the rock-art is ubiquitous. Wardaman country is less rugged, with very large areas of surface sand and alluvium. There are defined and rather restricted areas of rocky outcrops; even the more extensive do not often provide good overhangs and shelters where rock-art can be made and will survive. So the striking distinction between a 'stone' country pattern of dispersed rock-art and a Wardaman pattern of concentrated rock-art no more than reflects, to start with, the foundation difference, between a pattern of dispersed rock occurrence and a pattern of concentrated rock occurrence. An exploration of human choice will need to demonstrate human patterning beyond that arising from the natural pattern of opportunity.

That kind of rationale for a spatial order must always be kept in mind when noticing patterns in the occurrence of rock-art.

In northern England, hilly but not abruptly rough or mountainous, there is slight exposure of rock. An attractive place there to look for rock-art is at the top of the valley-slope, where the hill-side breaks back on to flatter moorland. It is in this zone that there may indeed be found rock-art, the distinctive cup-and-ring marks of later British prehistoric times. But notice that this zone is a characteristic place in a soft and earth-cloaked landscape to find bare rock. It will *not* be significant if, simply, there is rock-art in this topographic location. It will be significant if there is *more* and if there is *more often* rock-art in that topographic location than one would anticipate by extrapolating from the high proportion of such exposed rock as exists in the landscape which occurs there.

Another characteristic prehistoric trace on the upper hillsides of English valleys is the round burial-mounds of the Bronze Age, similarly located such that they appear on the profile of the horizon, as that is seen from the valley below (Ashbee 1960). Since an earth mound or stone cairn can be placed in the landscape nearly anywhere and at will, their matching pattern of occurrence in itself *does* have evident significance in a way that the comparable rock-art occurrence on its own does not.

One could point to many other instances. In the lower Alpine valleys with open-air rock-engravings, Valtellina and Valcamonica, the art was pecked into the sandstone and schist surfaces which were scraped smooth by the glaciation. Since the glacial retreat, those surfaces have been covered by accumulating soil and vegetation, whilst the valley floor is now covered by post-glacial alluvium. The rock-art reflects this. The surfaces already covered when the prehistoric habit of rock-engraving began in the post-glacial era will not have been available, and they will not have been used. Of the surfaces used and bearing rock-engravings, many will now be covered. A characteristic pattern of discovery in Valcamonica is for a few figures to be found on a rock exposure, poking out of the soils in the mixed deciduous woodland which blankets much of the valley; explored, that small exposure turns out to be the tip only of an extensive slab, of which much the greater portion has been covered over. The 'Rupe Magna' in Valtellina, its 5454 figures spread over a great many square metres making it the single Alpine surface bearing most figures, was detected and brought to light in that way; its notice began with just a handful of cup-marks visible above the turf and through the moss in 1966 (Fossati 1995: 11). So the pattern of occurrence in those Alpine valleys, as we know it, is an intricate consequence of where the rock was available for rock-engraving in prehistoric times, of where those rock surfaces that were used have and have not been covered over, of where chance observations and systematic surveys have led to their notice, and of where the effort to clear and expose surfaces has been made.

The concept of landscape in archaeology, and its application to rock-art

From the fixity of rock-art in the location it was made there follows the concept expressed in this introductory essay's subtitle, 'approaches to the figured landscapes of rock-art': we can approach rock-art as figures in a landscape, as marks in and on the land, that have been made by human beings, by human figures. Initially, we *must* approach the rock-art that way, because that is where we find it – though once there we may choose immediately to close our eyes to its surroundings, and to address, say, the form of the figures alone. Richard Bradley's good and influential study of prehistoric rock-art in Atlantic Europe (1997) talks of the rock-engravings as 'signing the land'; other Bradley studies have addressed the 'shaping of human experience' as that was directed by the monuments (1998b), those key elements to the human structure and knowledge of place (see e.g. Barrett *et al.* 1991). 'Landscape' has been a fashionable word in archaeological theory over the last decade (see e.g. Rossignol and Wandsnider 1992; Bender 1993; Tilley 1994; McGlade 1995; Kirch and Hunt 1997; Ashmore and Knapp 1999; Bowden 1999; Edmonds 1999; Fisher and Thurston 1999; Ucko and Layton 1999), alongside a matching mode for landscape studies in other social sciences (e.g. Cosgrove 1998). Wagstaff's pioneering book, which presents some geographical and archaeological perspectives on landscape and culture, is not so many years old (Wagstaff 1987). To an extent, all systematic field archaeology has been landscape archaeology, and this is not the place even to outline the full diversity of landscape archaeology; instead, we report recent trends which are pertinent to rock-art studies of the kind that make this book.

Why is landscape proving so popular an analytical framework in archaeology?

A first cause is that a landscape approach evades the concept and word 'site', perhaps a useful notion only when the archaeological traces are unusually confined to more-or-less small 'spot' occurrences, each localized, separated by more-or-less large vacant areas without traces. The concept of 'off-site archaeology' (Foley 1981) helps if there is something in between the rich spots, but often the archaeological traces are more nearly continuous. Then it is hard to define sites or their edges in a fair way, and the number of 'sites' is multiplied or reduced according to what is taken to define a 'site' – which seems altogether too arbitrary a business.

In the study of archaeological landscapes, rather than spot sites, Willey's (1953) study of the Viru Valley, Peru, was a key American pioneer, and the landscape approach of Vita-Finzi (1969) influential in the Mediterranean lands. Nowadays in archaeological research some kind of a landscape approach is routine, even ubiquitous (e.g. among many: Barker and Lloyd 1991; Barker *et al.* 1995; Mee and Forbes 1997; Tolan-Smith 1997; Jochim 1998) – to the point that the Scottish Royal Commission, charged in its name with recording the 'Ancient and Historical *Monuments*' of its nation, chooses nowadays to report on those monuments in terms of '*an archaeological landscape*' of Scotland (RCAHMS 1997). Outside archaeology, the idea of landscape is now repeatedly called on to articulate relations of land to human experience (e.g. among many: Arnold 1998 for architectural history; Picot 1997 for British poetry; Labbe 1998 for gender and romanticism).

Obvious though a landscape approach may now be, it is useful to remember that the idea of 'landscape' is neither ubiquitous nor any kind of human universal. The history of the English word 'landscape' is striking; it comes into some common use only about 1600, and then as a technical term in painting. Only later is it extended in its meaning from a 'picture of scenery' to become a name for the scenery itself. In particular, this should warn us away from presuming that a prehistoric conception of place and land necessarily would take a form broadly like the modern western concept of landscape. There are *no* good grounds to say, as a European often will who lives after the Romantic era: 'Prehistoric people at this place *must* have noticed the great cliff, and *must* have been awed by the narrowness of the valley and *must* have responded to the rush of the great river over the falls.'

Rock-art itself provides a reminder of this. Whilst images in the form of human beings and animals are commonplace in rock-art of many regions and periods, views of landscape are rare – vanishingly so. Not a single rock-art image comes to our mind that is an unambiguous picture of

Fig. 1.6. A rare unambiguous rock-art image of a building, part of the humanly created landscape.

Rock-engraving depicting a building, Foppo di Nadro, Valcamonica, Italy, Iron Age; and Jack Belmondo's reconstruction of the structure it depicts, also at Nadro.

If groups of these building images are taken to be a collected composition, rather than a palimpsest of individual images, then they make a landscape image of a village.

Photographs by Christopher Chippindale, that of the rock-engraving taken by night with slanting artificial light.

a landscape in the modern painterly sense. The Alpine traditions of rock-engravings are most unusual in containing designs that can be interpreted as maps. In the Alps there are also, again unusually, images of buildings (Fig. 1.6), some so grouped that one wonders if they might perhaps be images of grouped buildings, and therefore of village landscapes.

Alongside a landscape approach to archaeological patterning there have developed the various mathematical techniques of studying spatial distribution in standard archaeological use (Hodder and Orton 1976), further advanced with GIS methods (Savage 1989; Allen *et al.* 1990). Aspects which may be of special concern to rock-art studies, such as orientation, have their own specialized formal methods (e.g. Pick and Acredolo 1983).

In the USA, landscape studies in archaeology have often used an ecological framework (Bender 1999), with the environment as a dynamic and historically contingent frame for human existence (for that issue see e.g. Sanders *et al.* 1979; Ball and Taschek 1991; Binford *et al.* 1997; Erickson 1999). Some rock-art studies have taken this approach with evident success (e.g. Hartley and Wolley Vawser 1996; 1998).

In anglophone Europe, landscape archaeology has now taken a rather different course (Bender 1993), in which the distinctive feature has been the emphasis on the ancient or prehistoric actor. The central point here is a concern for worlds as ancient people themselves experienced them, a more 'embodied' view of landscape. In its most physical form, it attempts to repeat and rediscover ancient human experience by re-enacting views, movements, actions in the landscape through repetition of what ancient people may have done or by some other act which seems equivalent in its feeling (Bender *et al.* 1997). That is a characteristically 'post-modern' venture also in its self-regarding focus and in its naïve confidence in some universal of human experience: for how is one to know that what strikes *me* today must have anything in common with what ancient people felt and found telling? Like other aspects to the study of prehistoric Europe, it suffers – by comparison with other temperate zones such as North America – from the near-complete absence in Europe of any direct report of its societies equivalent to the riches of the immediate contact and post-contact period ethnography and ethnohistory of North America. Nevertheless, there is no higher – and therefore no better – ambition for archaeological study than an understanding of ancient life as ancient people experienced it. And no better starting-point exists than rock-art, images of that world in some way directly representing what ancient people experienced and chose to record from what was in their lives and surrounding them. And so one sees landscape and rock-art brought together as a collected archaeological topic, in individual papers (e.g. Sognnes 1994; Swartz and Hurlbutt 1994), in conference sessions, and now in the present collected book.

Art and landscape are currently of special interest beyond the small worlds of rock-art and of archaeology. Simon Schama, most successful English historian of our time, has chosen for successive books a subject in landscape and a subject in art (Schama 1995; 1999).

Informed methods and formal methods in studying rock-art

Whichever direction of study one chooses to take, the question follows: by what means can we study the rock-art so as to learn about its ancient nature, context and meaning? With landscape in mind, how can the methods used in studying the archaeology of landscape from other evidence be adopted and adapted to the special character of archaeological evidence? With the same theme in mind, what can we learn from and with rock-art that has not been possible on the basis of those other types of archaeological materials?

A frame of reference found useful before is again used here. This is the distinction between *informed methods* and *formal methods* (Taçon and Chippindale 1998).

By *informed methods* we mean those that depend on some source of insight passed on directly or indirectly from those who made and used the rock-art – through ethnography, through ethnohistory, through historical record, or through modern understanding known with good cause to perpetuate ancient knowledge; then, one can hope to explore the pictures from the inside, as it were. Since iconographic meanings seem to be variable and historically idiosyncratic – rather than standardized and accessible by some generalizing rules in a universal anthropology of art – that inside insight into an informed knowledge appears nearly essential to that developed kind of understanding.

Practically no rock-art traditions continue into the present, and there are precious few of which there is a good ethnographic or ethnohistoric record (but see Morwood and Hobbs 1992; Chippindale *et al.* in press); so for much prehistoric art, we have no basis for informed knowledge. There we must work with *formal methods*, those that depend on no inside knowledge, but which work when one can come to the stuff 'cold', as a prehistorian does. The information available is then restricted to that which is immanent in the images themselves, or which we can discern from their relations to each other and to the landscape, or by relation to whatever archaeological context is available.

Often, then, we have formal methods only. Where a basis for insight exists, we can have both informed and formal methods.

Informed methods and the landscape of rock-art

A, or *the*, obstacle to rock-art studies is the paucity of ethnographic and ethnohistoric referents. Practically nowhere in the world is there a continuing and vigorous habit of rock-art being routinely made today which without doubt links smoothly and unbrokenly on from an ancient tradition of archaeological interest. There is rock-art in the modern western world – a great deal if one defines contemporary rock-art widely enough – but it takes singular forms that seem rather specific to our own cultural context. Intriguing though the iconography, social context and meaning of urban graffiti may be (Castleman 1982), they will be equivalent to the rock-paintings of ancient hunter-gatherers only in an indirect way.

Nevertheless, as interest in rock-art grows, so – it seems – does the availability of ethnographic sources by which one can gain some insight. There was a breakthrough in southern Africa (Lewis-Williams 1981), where contact-era records of Bushman lore and knowledge were found to have a few direct references to rock-painting, and some indirect hints which permitted the development of a strong school of confident interpretation (Chippindale *et al.* in press). In far western North America, following that African example, basis for insight again has been found in a close reading in the ethnohistoric records and its broad application (Whitley 1992; 1994). Elsewhere in North America, sufficient clues are coming to light to permit some kind of understanding that learns from insiders' insight, whether for Ojibway petroglyphs (Conway and Conway 1990), for cup-marks in the Southeast (Loubser in press) or for rock-art in the desert Southwest (Young 1985; 1988). There remain other regions where there is – or at present appears to be – no such relevant record; one instance would be central India, where the informed research approach does not seem possible despite the promising combination of a rich rock-art tradition, an acute interest in history, and the existence of 'tribal peoples'.

Indigenous people are also showing a renewed interest in their own rock-art traditions. A singular instance is the revival of rock-paintings by a Bushman group in South Africa who now paint as part of their role in a tourist game-park (de Jongh 1999). They have painted both on small portable stones and in some rock-shelters (Fig. 1.7). They are far from their modern lands, but in country full of Bushman paintings. It is certain that Bushmen painted there in the past; it is equally certain that this is neo-Bushman painting, a conscious taking-up again of the old ways, rather than a simple continuing of old ways. Rock-art, strikingly visual and fixed in place, is an immediate way to remember, to revive and to remake links with land once lost and now recovered from alienation to indigenous ownership, recognition and control. Under Australian land-rights legislation, an Aboriginal community is granted land if it can demonstrate close and continued relation to the land and knowledge of it; for that reason the existence of rock-art of which the community is aware and knowledgeable has a new importance in present-day Aboriginal society.

It is certainly a singular experience to spend time – as one of us has been fortunate to – at a California rock-art site in the company of a knowledgeable Native American, an elder who knows the meaning of the pictures, who knows what people should do to look after this sacred place, and who knows how the sacred place can look after people by healing their pains. One often finds at a North American rock-art site the offerings left by Native Americans, commonly money and tobacco. One also finds the offerings left by visitors of 'New Age' persuasion, characteristically flowers and incense sticks, whose feeling response is from outside the indigenous tradition.

A research concern then becomes the degree of continuity or of change between the attitudes to rock-art today and those that prevailed in the past. The meaning of rock-art, and of pictures in general, appears to be idiosyncratic and particular to the history of a certain cultural

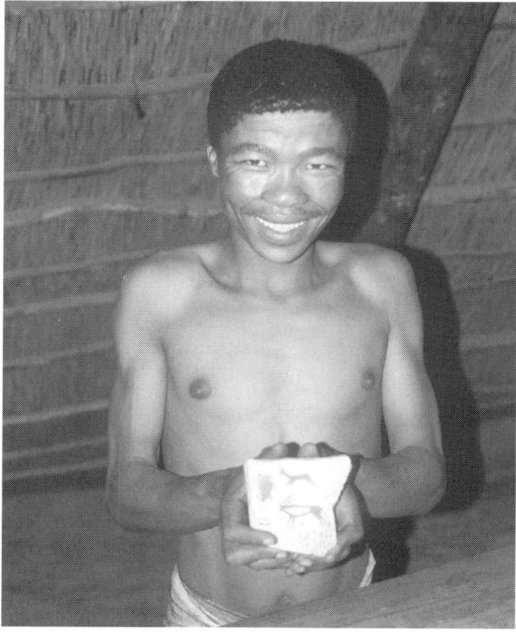

Fig. 1.7. A rock-painting tradition newly revived.

The Kagga Kamma Bushman group are now painting again, in the Cedarberg region of Western Cape Province, South Africa.

(*left*) Some painting is on small stones of a size the tourists can take away.

Isak Kruiper says of his painting (de Jongh 1999: 49): 'We paint on the small rocks not to forget those times. It sometimes comes as a dream and many of those dreams become true. To remember the dreams you put it on a rock and then it will always be a memory. You depict it in that way. It is not every day that you can paint on the stones. When I wake up in the morning and I have the right feeling, and I feel happy, then I will leave the tasks I wanted to do that day, and I will paint on the little rocks. I depict stories on stone. Say I am walking in the field and I see the animals chasing each other. This will bother me. I go to sleep. I get up and I see how they move and paint that on rock-pieces.'

(*right*) Neo-Bushman paintings in a Kagga Kamma rock-shelter.

Photographs by Joané de Jongh.

context. One cannot decide by applying some general principles, and then know what a figure means. Deer are a common motif in the prehistoric rock-engravings of Valcamonica but one cannot deduce from that fact alone just *why* deer should be imaged so often, and just *what* they stand for. Bighorn sheep are ubiquitous in the rock-engravings of the Coso Range, south-east California; there, from pertinent ethnography, Whitley (1998) can offer a meaning for the sheep, in terms of rain and rain-making. Demonstrably, in the case of 'New Age' responses to rock-art and to other archaeological places like Chaco Canyon or Stonehenge (Chippindale 1986c), there is no direct continuity or connection. The rock-art itself may give clues. South African researchers can point to the very close resemblance between the recent images in classic rock-art regions like the Drakensberg and the ancient painting on a stratified slab from the Apollo 11 Cave, Namibia (Wendt 1976): such a consistency in image implies a consistency in meaning, so the contact-era ethnography would indeed apply to the collected rock-paintings of varied ages, even back to the Pleistocene.

There exists another respectable view of rock-art and society, advanced in the work of Emmanuel Anati (1983): societies move through a characteristic set of successive stages in their social evolution, and each stage is conducive to a characteristic kind of rock-art imagery. Pictures of hunting will belong to a Mesolithic, the era of bow-hunters; pictures of farming to the Neolithic or Bronze Age, eras of farming. Accordingly, one can observe salient characteristics of a body of rock-art not seen before, and deduce from it with confidence the social stage it represents and its approximate relative chronology. We disagree with this approach, which we see as placing too much faith in unproven social universals and having too little respect for the particular course of social change in any place or region. That is why the *specific* insights that informed methods may offer are the key.

For the particular subject of the present book, rock-art in its landscape, our better examples of informed methods will be those contexts where we have a good ethnohistoric knowledge of *rock-art*, a good ethnohistoric knowledge of attitudes to and concepts of *landscape*, and a good ethnohistoric knowledge of how these two relate together. Whitley (1998) provides a rare study where the ethnohistory appears to offer sufficient information for the two themes to be explored alongside each other in this spirit. Are these studies rare because the ethnohistoric information rarely exists? Or because rock-art researchers have not sufficiently sought it? Since we are concerned, as archaeologists always are, with long-term change, our best example of informed methods will add another element, a good ethnohistoric knowledge of how attitudes to and concepts of landscape and of rock-art *change* over time.

Fig. 1.8. Australian Aboriginal rock-art without an ethnohistoric context.

Rock-engraving on open sandstone bedrock exposure, undated, Sydney, NSW, Australia.

Around Sydney Harbour, landing-place of the colonizing First Fleet in 1788, we have slight basis for an approach through informed methods, and therefore the rock-art comes to be studied through formal methods.

Photograph by Christopher Chippindale.

The example of Aboriginal north Australia

Fortunately, there exists one zone of the world where we have reasonably full, reasonably well-documented and contemporary evidence of rock-art as an active medium today and in a direct continuity with a tradition extending back many centuries. This is sufficiently remarkable and precious it is worth briefly noticing here.

In some parts of Australia, we have no contact-era ethnohistory or any direct guide by way of informed insight. The Aboriginal rock-engravings on the Sydney sandstone (Fig. 1.8: Stanbury *et al.* 1990) were noticed by the First Fleet settlers of 1788; their early colonial accounts in words and paintings tell us a little of Aboriginal artefacts and life-ways in the region – but nothing of the rock-art. In that respect, studying and interpreting the Sydney sandstone rock-art today is a research question matching that of, say, later prehistoric Europe; the Roman sources, in documents and inscriptions, tell us a tantalizing little about the other European societies the Romans encountered, and usually conquered – but nowhere is there even a single word about their rock-art.

Elsewhere in Australia, we are more fortunate. In several regions, there is still knowledge of rock-art handed down the traditional way, so that the figures are still alive with meaning. In respect of a certain number of paintings, one even knows the name of the person who painted it, the date it was painted, and just what kind of event it depicts (Chaloupka 1982). From time to time new rock-images are made (Smith 1994) – though many of these seem to be in response to some request or interest external to the Aboriginal community. In many places, Aboriginal art is lively and flourishing for a tourist and collecting market, transformed and contemporary to be sure from its role in past times but very much continuing the iconography of the rock-art. The regions celebrated for this new and traditional Aboriginal art are Arnhem Land (on the tropical north coast of the Northern Territory) and the dry land of the continent's desert centre. In Arnhem Land, pictures continue to be painted in traditional earth pigments applied to eucalyptus bark and now to fine-art papers (Caruana 1993: 21–96); they follow and develop the iconography, colours and conventions of the later rock-art. In the desert country, painters use synthetic acrylic paints, but the iconography with its celebrated convention of coloured dots derives from and perpetuates traditions evident also in the rock-engravings of the region (Caruana 1993: 97–152).

This is not the place even to sketch the essentials of Australian Aboriginal society and knowledge pertinent to rock-art research: the topic needs a book in itself. Fortunately, Robert Layton's *Australian rock-art: a new synthesis* (1992) is that, taking as its subject 'the part which rock-art plays today, and has played in the past, in indigenous Australian communities' (Layton 1992: 1). A great worked example is George Chaloupka's *Journey in time* (1993), an illustrated account of the western Arnhem Land rock-art which is founded in Aboriginal perceptions. Equivalent accounts could be given for some other regions, such as Wardaman country that lies between the full tropical north and the desert centre (see Flood *et al.* 1992a; 1992b; Flood and David 1994).

Fundamental in Aboriginal society in the north today is the idea of 'country', a sense of personal place and more than that: 'Country is a place that gives and receives life. Not just imagined or represented, it is lived in and lived with' (Rose 1996: 7). Part of 'country' is territory, the portion of land where your forebears lived, where you were born and where you grew up and where you live now – the place you belong. That aspect to 'country' is emphasized today when land rights recognize a defined area as the country of its traditional Aboriginal owners and they have legal power over it. But this is territory which 'owns' people, the people who owe it allegiance and care, rather than territory as land owned and possessed for the benefit of the proprietor in the modern western sense. As 'country' is the justification of land rights for Aboriginal people, through a demonstrated connection to land proved by a legal procedure, so it links to and leads to ownership in the western sense. Rose (1996: 7) continues: 'Country in Aboriginal English is not only a common noun but also a proper noun. People talk about country in the same way that they would talk about a person: they speak to country, sing to country, visit country, worry about country, feel sorry for country, and long for country. People say that country knows, hears, smells, takes notice, takes care, is sorry or happy.' Importantly for ideas of landscape, the attachment to 'country' is specific to the individual kin group. One has connections, obligations, knowledge in that area. So 'country' expresses an intense and special attachment to place, in its practical matters – the right to hunt and fish and dig ochre – and in feelings.[1]

Like other fundamentals of Aboriginal knowledge, 'country' – how it is and whose it is – has always been there. Its enduring state is an aspect to what is nearly always now called the Dreaming or the Dreamtime, not the most happy term (Wolfe 1991): the English word 'dreaming' has connotations of something fantastical and unreal that passes in a transient present of sleep, not the Aboriginal notions at all. There are alternative words. Of them we like the word 'law', as a Gunjepmi elder taught one of us in western Arnhem Land, because the Dreaming is about when the world was made as it is and must be in all its aspects, with its rocks and creeks, and its plants and creatures, and its people and their tongues and clans. The Dreaming is the great and permanent putting into rightful order everything that is. It is also the 'law' because to break the law is to upset that proper order. An Anyuwa elder from south-east Arnhem Land uses the same metaphor (Mussolini Harvey, in Bradley 1988: xi):

> White people ask us all the time, what is Dreaming? This is a hard question because Dreaming is really a big thing for Aboriginal people. In our language, Yanyuwa, we call the Dreaming *Yijan*. The Dreamings made our Law or *narnu-Yuwa*. This Law is the way we live, our rules. This Law is our ceremonies, our songs, our stories; all of these things come from the Dreaming. One thing that I can tell you though is that our law is not like European Law which is always changing – new government, new laws; but our Law cannot change, we did not make it. The Law was made by the Dreamings many, many years ago and given to our ancestors and they gave it to us.

[1] One of us, who grew up in the honest and hard country of north England, now lives in the soft south of the country – happily enough but knowing it can never really be Home with a capital H: his heart lifts when he goes back up to the real country of the north. He finds the notion of 'country', as he has learnt it in Australia, expresses well for him that nagging feeling of emotional distance from his own proper place on the English land.

When it comes to rock-art, the Wardaman people are typical of north Australian Aborigines in their understanding. Some images in rock-art they acknowledge as their own, made in recent times by Wardaman people. Some images they know to have been made in and of the Dreaming. Those are not pictures made by ancient human beings. Rather these are places where in the Dreaming the creator-beings painted themselves on to the rocks as they travelled across and made the country. And Wardaman people want to keep safe and fresh the great striped images of Ancestral Beings that are scattered across their country, as part of their caring for it. The great shelters with their varied rock-art each have their names and stories; those stories relate to the rock-art images they are told from. And those stories are specific to place, and they need to be told in place, in front of the paintings and engravings which they illustrate, record and hold in place.

(If one were to talk with Shoshonean Native Americans about their country and its rock-art, one might hear a strikingly similar account.)

So here is a set of relationships: between landscape, creation and the order of things; between rock-art as pictures in the landscape and the circumstances under which that rock-art came to be; between the pictures, the people and the stories of the land; between time future and time present and time past. In its rich intricacy, echoing the complexity that surrounds present-day painting and ceremony (Morphy 1991), it hints at how much knowledge can surround and structure images which – on the uninformed face of it – will appear just as simple paintings of animals or anthropomorphs.

Is Aboriginal north Australia typical of communities world-wide in which rock-art was important? We cannot know. We may fear that the rock-art of agricultural societies will be different at base from that of hunter-gatherers. The heart of the problem is that we do not have a good number of well-documented comparative examples; if we did, then we would be able to discern what is common across the group, and what is confined to each instance. Nor is the story either simple or uniform within Australia. And one does not know if the perceptible differences in how different north Australian communities today relate to rock-art perpetuate ancient distinctions, or more reflect the loss and violence of harsh times since contact as different communities have experienced it. But Australia does provide two precious benefits. First, these are reliable accounts of events which actually do happen and have actually happened, a better source of exemplars and models than theoretical propositions as to what *might* have happened in the abstract suppositions of social theorists. Second, these actual accounts of indigenous arts are complex, conditional, layered, elaborate in their meaning: they offer a richer kind of narrative than the simplified sketches which for prehistoric rock-art, as for other remote and opaque archaeological materials, may be the fullest account the material remains permit us to give.

A good way forward, then, may be to use these Australian examples as a starting-point for some more general ideas, but always with an awareness of what may be singular to Australia, and with special concern for how its distinctive features are or are not specific to Australian experience (Taçon 1994; 1999b; Taçon *et al.* 1997).

Formal methods and the landscape of rock-art

Alongside the informed methods run the formal methods: any method of study which does not depend on inside knowledge, but works by the features that can be observed in the rock-art itself, or in its physical and landscape context; arguably, all prehistoric rock-art can only be observed in this way. Where informed methods can apply, the formal methods complement the informed. Where the informed methods do not apply, we have the formal alone, complemented by approaches through analogy and inference.

Among the most formal approaches to landscape are the more analytical techniques, those dealing with spatial distributions as they can be mathematically described and algorithmically expressed. These do not figure in the present book, which we would as editors have liked, and they are not numerous in rock-art studies. Indeed, quantitative methods in rock-art are not much developed (see e.g. Maggs 1967; Tokioka 1992), in part because we do not sufficiently grasp what the entities are that are to be counted and statistically explored.

Among those less fully formal in their methods will be comparative studies. A case in point is the rock-art of deep caves, not the ubiquitous shallow overhangs and shelters, but those deeper caverns where one moves into a 'dark zone' beyond reach of natural light. As landscapes, these have some uniting factors. Nearly always sited in limestone, they show the features of calcareous geology, with its sinks, squeezes and pot-holes, its soft muds and shiny surfaces, its stalagmites and stalactites. These elements alone are cause of some unity. It is not entirely surprising that the soft wet walls of calcareous muds invite human beings to run their fingers across them; but it is striking how similar are the 'meander' marks so made in caves in Pleistocene Europe and in Pleistocene Australia (Bednarik 1986). What is the human response to deep caves? Is it consistent or recurrent in its forms? Do these strange kinds of enclosed spaces evoke similar human reactions? How can spatial study, analysis of where in a deep cave-system rock-art is located and what form it takes, indicate its structures and meanings? How much is there held in common between 'dark-zone' rock-art in the south-western United States (Greer and Greer 1997), in the eastern and south-eastern United

Fig. 1.9. Built monuments: a different kind of created art in the human landscape.

The megalithic tomb ('portal-dolmen') of Pentre Ifan, south-west Wales.

Photograph by George Nash.

States (Faulkner *et al.* 1984; Faulkner 1986; 1988; 1996; Crothers and Watson 1993; Faulkner and Simek 1996a; 1996b; in press; Simek *et al.* 1998; in press; Simek and Cressler in press), in North America generally (Greer and Greer 1998), in the Maya realm (Stone 1995)? And in what usefully comparable relation to the better-known dark-zone cave-art of Palaeolithic Europe? Are there indeed uniting systematics, and do they extend to rock-art outside the caves through other linking themes and determinants (Clottes and Lewis-Williams 1998)?

We have mentioned above the fitting combination of landscape, of rock-art and of change over time in an approach defined as the 'landscape archaeology of rock-art'. Tilley in his *Phenomenology of landscape* (1994) has attempted to draw out the landscape in this spirit when looking at the siting of megaliths within various landscapes around southern Britain (Fig. 1.9). Yet these deliberate arrangements of stone within the landscape say much less of ancient perceptions than can representational rock-art. The rock-art can provide a number of avenues for valid interpretation purely in the sense of what is present within its design coding. Is there a formal link between, say, Norwegian red deer depictions and coastal rock-art sites? Can it be proven to exist by suitable formal study? Likewise, do the fighting or 'war' scenes from the Levantine Gasulla Gorge frescoes in south-eastern Spain relate to the surrounding landscape? Other (invisible) mechanisms are surely at work which relate indirectly to landscape. It could be the case, for instance, that the 'warring' scenes at Gasulla Gorge were painted because of a territorial dispute (that involved landscape); or a painting may depict not war, but a dancing scene that bonded together through contact and exchange two neighbouring groups, and so on. The scenarios are numerous, too numerous.

Landscape appears a fundamental constraint when dealing with prehistoric, historic and contemporary rock-art. Rock-art is there to be seen but, at the same time, to be unseen. All rock-art was initially created or caused to be created by someone for someone; its landscape position would have been most important. We know this from the large number of studies world-wide that report strategic orientation and siting of the rock-art. So one can apply some kind of a formal analysis, such as a series of grammatical rules to describe explicitly the systematics of rock-art location that involve both the micro-landscape and the macro-landscape – what Nash (2002) terms 'micro-scape' and 'macro-scape'.[2] What we mean by micro- and macro-landscape is the spatial

[2] See Stiny (1975; 1987; Stiny and Gips 1978) for early work in rule-based systems in generating art and artefacts, Knight (1994) for an archaeological case-study of a design-system grammatically described and defined, Chippindale (1986b; 1992) for an archaeological view of the approach.

Chippindale (1986a) gives an instance of a study of spatial order in rock-art exploring a set of generative rules of location, at the 'micro-scape' level.

landscape dimensions which determine a rock-art site. It could be the case that the panel and the surrounding cave/rock-shelter walls represent the micro-scape, whereas the landscape represents the macro-scape. We see both micro- and macro-scapes as negotiable and reliant on what architects term 'a sense of occasion': how a human being – be it the artist, the audience, the voyeur, even the archaeologist – views the world, in this case the corner of the world which is the rock-art site. And we must remember that landscape is very much an artificial process, socially constructed within our minds. Although landscape is around us, in the mountains, streams, forests, the imagination and cognitive construction of that landscape is controlled by ourselves (Children and Nash 1997: 2). Tilley's phenomenological ideas (1994), and before this the work of Merleau-Ponty (1962), have placed space, place and landscape into part of an historical/geographical discourse focusing on personal perception. The mechanics of perception incorporate such human emotions as power, time, memory, social interaction and politics. These mechanics help us to organize the landscape into a personal perception; therefore no two interpretations will be exactly the same.

Definitions and research practicalities

'Rock-art' as a term is sometimes disputed, but we are content with it.

'Rock' is clear enough, provided it is extended from the hard materials to encompass the soft – the sand and earth of shaped mounds and 'geoglyphs', the cave sediments and muds of and in which art is made, for example in the 'mud glyph' limestone caves of the south-eastern United States (Faulkner 1986).

'Art' can be more disputed, but its overlapping meanings point to representational images and to skilled craftwork, with indications of a world of symbolism: all these are fitting.

We prefer to hyphenate 'rock-art' (also 'rock-painting', 'rock-engraving') as a gesture towards these being united in a portmanteau concept, more than just 'rock' and 'art' placed adjacent (Taçon and Chippindale 1998; Taçon 1999a).

Linking rock, art and the landscape is more problematic. 'Rock-art' in its modern conception is, to the casual 'on-looker', something which is first an aesthetic phenomenon – a red deer or a ploughing scene *is* a picture of that naturalistic subject which is seen. (And if no subject is recognized, then it is 'abstract' art.) However, it is more than probable that the art on a rock panel represented something more complex when seen through the eyes of our prehistoric ancestors. Moreover, it represents a medium that is more than just art; it ventures beyond the realms of mere and idle graffiti. The same can be said of those 'mere and idle graffiti' in contemporary cities. These spray-painted 'tags' and 'pieces' appear to the naïve outsider to be placed at casual hazard on inviting surfaces along city streets. Not so; in the US cities where they began (Phillips 1999), the graffiti are specific to the individuals and the gangs who make them. Their placing is an expression and statement of territorial possession. In the portions of cities like Los Angeles where gang culture is famously strong, the placing of graffiti can have most serious consequences; placing it just a city block further on amounts to a claim to a rival gang's turf.

Perversely, one can witness this with the 'vandalism' that is found on many a rock-art surface. The rock-art of the western USA, and of those parts of Australia close to its southern cities, has not only undergone changes to the panel through indigenous ideology, but has also often been defaced by usually white settlers. By placing 'our' signs – initials, names, dates, explicit statements of 'I was here' – the 'graffiti artists' are also making their mark on the landscape, placing their identity over and through an older art form which they do

Fig. 1.10. A rock-art panel: defining units of landscape study. A single entity? Or just a small unit within an extensive site?
Little Petroglyph Canyon, China Lake Naval Air Station, Coso Range, California, USA.
Photograph by Christopher Chippindale.

not understand and see as a memory of another possession.

Placed within a landscape setting, rock-art becomes a more complex and expressive visual language. We the on-lookers can only begin to comprehend the reason why an artist should want to paint on a particular rock, at a chosen time and in a certain place. More importantly, that this artist should be either influencing other artists or being influenced to place similar images elsewhere in identical landscape settings.

The same defining issues, and more so, apply to rock-art landscapes as they do in landscape archaeology generally. A case in point is the usefulness of the concept of 'site', and its definition. Variability within the range of definitions that can be applied to comparable material is illustrated by Little Petroglyph Canyon (Fig. 1.10) in the Coso Range of eastern California (Moore and Younkin 1992; Baird and Younkin 1998). That is just one of the many celebrated places where rock-art occurs more-or-less continuously over an area to be measured by distances of hundreds to thousands of metres: is it one site, or several, or many? Nämforsen, the great Scandinavian rock-engraving site, is another place which can be reasonably treated as a single place, or reasonably divided into sixteen separate areas (Ramqvist 1992).

This is perhaps a small matter, a difference in definition between researchers who work at a distance from each other. We mention it because it seems to us symptomatic of the doubts about units, entities and approaches that pervade rock-art study even more than they do archaeology in general. One can contrast this with the established procedures of lithic study, where cores and flakes, retouched pieces and formal artefacts are – for the most part – accepted concepts, routinely used in record and analysis.

Lithics and other kinds of portable artefact have been, over the past, subjected to rigorous typological study. Certainly, prior to the introduction of sound radiocarbon dating, typologies were based – rightly or wrongly – on idiosyncratic developments that were both spatially and temporally motivated; a point in case is the development of Scandinavian Neolithic and Bronze Age pottery and metalwork (Müller 1918). Typologies, rather out of fashion when they attempt to place into chronological order some form of development in style and form, nevertheless do apply to the development of rock-art.

One can see this with the lines of development of Spanish Levantine hunting art, for which the major researchers of the early and mid twentieth century have constructed dates for its emergence and demise; these are based on consistent changes in form, in particular of human and animal figures. Also included within these chronologies has been the schematic phase which followed the decline of the hunter's art (Nash 2000b). The earlier date, promoted by the Abbé Henri Breuil, placed Levantine art at the Aurignacian/Gravettian transition, around 26,000 BC (1935), whereas Pericot (1952) promoted a Magdalenian date, about 15,000 BC. Both chronologies merge the hunter's art into the schematic phase around the Mesolithic/Neolithic transition. But Almagro Basch (1965) and Ripoll (1965) had the earliest art starting in the Mesolithic and merging with the schematic during the Neolithic/Bronze Age transition. The two later chronologies had the benefit of dates for cave sediments from a number of painted rock-shelters. A newer account derives from Dams (1984: 10) who recognizes four chronological sequences based on stylistic changes (Styles I, II, III and IV): in it, Levantine art appears in the twelfth millennium BC and terminates by about 4000 BC. Within the earliest phase no human figures are present, whilst Style II includes large bovids, horse, red deer and human figures. Style III involves numerous human figures usually involved in hunting scenes. Apart from human figures, the red deer and wild boar suggest woodland environs; also present are caprids including chamois and goat. These Style III elements date from 8000 to 5500 BC. The final Style IV is represented by the emergence of schematic figures and abstract motifs as well as combat scenes (especially within the Gasulla and Valltorta gorges). Schematic panels tend to be located within the far eastern regions, between Malaga and Cadiz. It is at this point that farming groups emerge, and new artefact assemblages take precedence. These dates roughly correlate with the Almagro chronology (1965). Dams' chronology, based on the typological development of painted figures, does not correlate with any of the cultural phases expressed by the general texts covering this period previously; not surprisingly the development is based on stylistic change or typology. In the same region, typology has also been used to argue a diffusionary relation between warrior images from Gasulla Gorge and warriors in north Africa (Muzzolini 1995).

Many painted rock surfaces show stylistic change as an act of simple retouching, overpainting and slight subject modification. In the case of carved panels, change is more blatant and permanent. Again, looking to the Spanish Levantine hunter/gatherer rock-art, there appears to have been a need to change the identity of certain figures. (See also on this issue Chippindale in press.) The application and reapplication of design formulate two criteria: one of time and the other of an established socio-symbolic order,

Fig. 1.11. Changing ideology: from bulls to deer.
The Spanish Levantine rock-painting panel of Cueva de la Vieja, Alpera, Albacete, Spain (after Beltrán 1982).

highlighted in this case by certain animals. In the red deer and wild cattle designs, there appear to be phases dictated by changes in fashion: hence the defacement and metamorphic changes from red deer to something else. The process of design-change is evident from a number of panels within this assemblage, in particular, at the Cueva de la Vieja fresco, Alpera, Albacete. Here, four naturalistic bulls (within the central group) have been changed into deer; with horns becoming antlers (Fig. 1.11) (Beltrán 1982). Similarly, carved art too undergoes changes based on, most probably, fashion and the introduction of new ideology. At the complex panel at Bardal, Nord-Trøndelag, there are two clear changes in design morphology (Gjessing 1932; Hallström 1938).

At Bardal, as with other sites in this central part of Norway, a change at a socio-economic transition is seen with the defacement of earlier naturalistic zoomorphic carvings by farming-style long boats and warriors of the Bronze Age (Fig. 1.12). The boats, by far the largest and most imposing of the panel designs, appear to be an act of vandalism over the old order. Both sets of designs are also creating a chronology, an historical sequence that establishes a beginning (the original carving), a middle (the point of transition) and an ending (the act of defacement). In producing new rock-art, it would seem more obvious to carve on a new rock surface than to use an older already carved surface. One can possibly see a chronological build-up of designs which may interact, even though the later design obliterate the earlier ones. It could be that hunter/gatherer and farming economies are working alongside each other, one form of art taking precedence over another at one particular point in time (Nash 2003). Although changes to a rock-art panel are fixed at moments in time (Fig. 1.13), they nevertheless constitute a chronological sequence which cannot be looked at in complete isolation. It is more probable that changes in rock-art style are synchronic with other forms of material culture.

Rationale and structure of the present book

The present book approaches landscapes of rock-art in varied ways consistent with this overall view. With two exceptions – one survey of theory and one essay in method – each is a substantive study building on field observation. No systematic survey of regions or techniques is planned as such, but the range covered includes many of the major

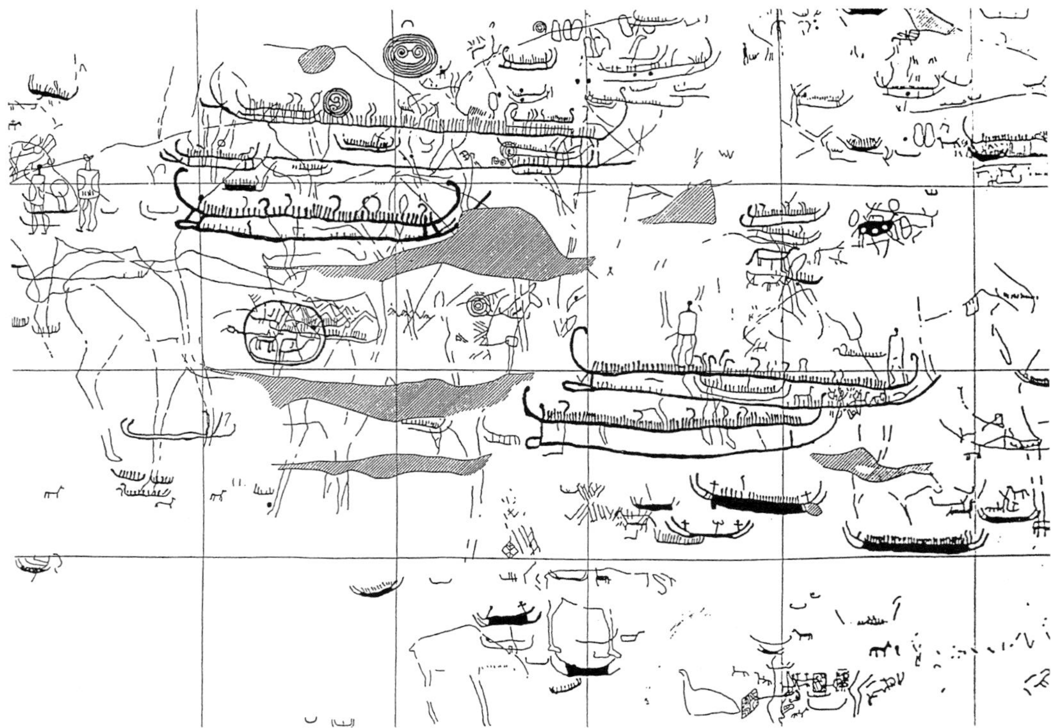

Fig. 1.12. A confusing palimpsest: graffiti-ing an older panel.
Hunting and farming art at Bardal, Nord Trøndelag, central Norway (Gjessing 1932).

rock-art traditions, many of the research traditions by which archaeologists approach the major rock-art traditions, and aspects special to the techniques of painting and of engraving. Some use informed methods in conjunction with formal, some use formal methods alone.

We have signalled in this introductory essay some central issues which run through the book and unite it. There exist many more than these we have flagged in this chapter. The chapters were initiated in various ways, some given at conference sessions, some written especially for the book; nearly, each has been written independently of the others. We are struck by how much they have in common. We took notice of common elements in ordering the book, but a linear order permits each paper to have only two neighbours, when often they deserve more.

These are research papers, whose purpose is not to give a rounded and general account for a certain body of rock-art material. But there is always some kind of introduction, however brief, and some indication of where more may be discovered. When more than one chapter addresses the same or a similar body of material, the introductory remarks may overlap each other; this means any single chapter may be read on its own without loss.

The essays collected in this book are divided into three parts, each in truth entwined to an extent with its separately presented neighbours.

In Part I, entitled 'Principles of landscape and rock-art in practice', six chapters address fundamentals of rock-art in landscape and show by worked examples how their nature can be grasped. Paul S. C. Taçon and Sven Ouzman,

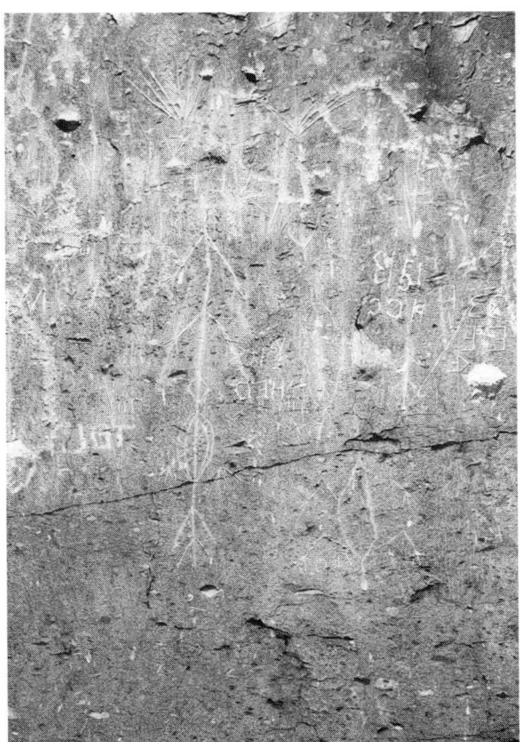

Fig. 1.13. Rock-art: a continuing habit of making an enduring mark in the landscape.

Early-settler twentieth-century rock-art over Native American rock-art of the Buena Vista rock-painting site, French Glen, south-east Oregon, USA.

Photograph by George Nash.

'Worlds within stone: the inner and outer rock-art landscapes of northern Australia and southern Africa', explore dimensions common to rock-art in northern Australia and southern Africa, two great regions of rock-art rarely considered together. These dimensions are common to so much rock-art they fairly constitute first principles. Daniel Arsenault surveys 'Rock-art, landscape, sacred places: attitudes in contemporary archaeological theory', attitudes which turn out to address some helpful concepts and miss others. William D. Hyder reports the more specific and sometimes technical studies that amount to 'Locational analysis in rock-art studies'. Christopher Chippindale proposes a framework of scales of study, stepping up by orders of magnitude in physical dimension in 'From millimetre up to kilometre: a framework of space and of scale for reporting and studying rock-art in its landscape'; illustrated by prehistoric figures in the French Alps, its nesting scales will apply to nearly all bodies of rock-art. James D. Keyser and George Poetschat address one of those scales, that of the rock-art panel, as 'The canvas as the art: landscape-analysis of the rock-art panel'. Part I closes with Tilman Lenssen-Erz's systematic approach to 'The landscape setting of rock-painting sites in the Brandberg (Namibia): infrastructure, *Gestaltung*, use and meaning'. All these studies use informed methods or formal methods or both in combination; we place them together in this first part because they address issues clearly of wide application – hence 'principles'.

Part II explores a more specific circumstance – occasions when 'Informed methods: opportunities and applications' are specially applicable, thanks to a secure point of departure in present-day knowledge or in recorded ethnohistory. Each chapter here has a regional focus, for a distinctive feature of rock- and other art (above) is its being embedded in the specifics of a local experience. At the same time, each study is concerned with wide issues. First, Bruno David, 'Rock-art and the experienced landscape: the emergence of late-Holocene symbolism in north-east Australia', combines knowledge of a Queensland landscape today with its distinctive archaeological pattern to document changing perceptions of landscape over time. Josephine Flood explores aspects of the wider pattern of 'Linkage between rock-art and landscape in Aboriginal Australia', another element in the singular shape of Aboriginal Australian societies. Lawrence Loendorf, in analysing 'Places of power: the placement of Dinwoody petroglyphs across the Wyoming landscape', finds a striking pattern to which elevation is the key, explicable in terms of indigenous knowledge of where special and sacred places are found. David S. Whitley, Johannes H. N. Loubser and Don Hann, in 'Friends in low places: rock-art and landscape on the Modoc Plateau', explore the making and meaning of shamanistic landscapes. In the closing paper to this part, Benjamin W. Smith and Geoffrey Blundell go on to 'Dangerous ground: a critique of landscape in rock-art studies'; they see good cause in indigenous perceptions of the landscape in northern South Africa to mistrust the habitual expectations which researchers unthinkingly impose when they use seemingly 'common-sense' or neutral frames for rock-art.

Part III is devoted to the other circumstance, where we have thought we have had no immediate basis for direct insight, and instead use an approach through 'Formal methods: opportunities and applications'. First, Knut Helskog looks at 'Landscapes in rock-art: rock-carving and ritual in the old European North', where a link can nevertheless be made between the old rock-carvings and the knowledge continuing today in the knowledge of Sami people, itself within the broader cultural pattern of the circum-polar lands. Daniel Arsenault, in 'From natural settings to spiritual places in the Algonkian sacred landscape: an archaeological, ethnohistorical and ethnographic analysis of Canadian Shield rock-art sites', finds a patterning in rock-art sites in Québec which is strikingly consistent with that of the Algonkian sacred landscape. For prehistoric Europe, where surely we have no basis of informed insight, Andrea Arcà examines 'The topographic engravings of Alpine rock-art: fields, settlements and agricultural landscapes', and finds them indeed to have the characteristics of maps – maps informative of prehistoric human attitude.

Everything up to this point in the book is primarily made of words, as if pictures were enigmatic things which would be made clearer or even transparent if only that graphic meaning were to be translated into textual terms through the idiom of letters. So we close our book with a reminder that pictures are pictures *sui generis*; they have a meaning to be addressed in terms of images: George Nash, Lindsey Nash and Christopher Chippindale, 'Walking through landscape: a photographic essay of the Campo Lameiro valley, Galicia, north-western Spain'. That is a place where we have no basis for informed methods, so this essay would belong in Part III. Since the point it makes, of the differences between words and images, is fundamental, we instead give it a part of its own, Part IV, 'Pictures of pictures' (cf. Chippindale 2001).

Overall, then the balance of the book strongly favours informed methods, rather than being divided equally into formal and informed methods. Why is this – if the times and places where we have good present-day, ethnographic or ethnohistoric insight into the social meaning of rock-art are rather fewer than we would like? True; but it is also true that our formal methods are rather underdeveloped. And the proven way in developing archaeological method is this: first, look at those cases and conditions where we do have some insight on which to base *informed methods*. Then, see the systematic patterns and regularities that emerge from those informed studies taken collectively. If any patterns and regularities do emerge – and they always do, even though there is no *a priori* reason why they must exist – then use those to build robust uniformitarian *formal methods* which are broadly applicable.

References

Allen, K. M. S., S. W. Green and E. B. W. Zubrow (eds.). 1990. *Interpreting space: GIS and archaeology*. London: Taylor and Francis.

Almagro Basch, M. 1964. El problema de la cronológia del arte rupestre levantino Español, in Luis Pericot Garcia and Eduardo Ripoll Perello (eds.), *Prehistoric art of the western Mediterranean and the Sahara*: 103–11. New York: Wenner-Gren Foundation for Anthropological Research. Viking Fund Publications in Anthropology 39.

Anati, E. 1983. *Gli elementi fondamentali della cultura.* Milan: Jaca Book.

Arcá, A., A. Fossati, E. Marchi and E. Tononi/ Cooperativa Archeologica 'Le Orme dell'Uomo'. 1995. *Rupe Magna: la roccia incisa piú grande delle Alpi.* Sondrio: Consorzio per il Parco delle Incisioni Rupestri di Grosio.

Arnold, D. (ed.). 1998. *The Georgian country house: architecture, landscape and society.* Stroud: Sutton.

Ashbee, P. 1960. *The Bronze Age round barrow in Britain: an introduction to the study of the funerary practice and culture of the British and Irish single-grave people of the second millennium BC.* London: Phoenix House.

Ashmore, W. and A. B. Knapp (eds.). 1999. *The archaeology of landscape: contemporary perspectives.* Oxford: Blackwell.

Bahn, P. G. 1995. Cave art without the caves, *Antiquity* 69: 231–7.

Bahn, P. G., R. de Balbín, M. Lorblanchet, S. Ripoli, D. Sacchi and V. Villaverde. 1995. Avis de la Commission Internationale d'Experts [on the standing and age of the Côa petroglyphs], reprinted in J. Zilhão (ed.), *Arte rupestre e pré-história do Vale do Côa: trabalhos de 1995–1996: relatório científico ao governo da República Portuguesa elaborado nos termos da Resolução do Conselho de Ministros N° 4/96, de 17 de Janeiro*: 452–3. Lisbon: Ministério da Cultura (1997).

Bahn, P. G. and J. Vertut. 1998. *Journey through the Ice Age.* 2nd edition (1st edition 1988). London: Weidenfeld and Nicolson.

Baird, J. and E. Younkin (eds.). 1998. *New perspectives on the Coso petroglyphs.* Ridgecrest, CA: Maturango Museum.

Ball, J. and J. Taschek. 1991. Late Classic lowland Maya political organization and central place analysis, *Latin American Antiquity* 2: 149–65.

Barker, G., R. Hodges and G. Clark. 1995. *A Mediterranean valley: landscape archaeology and* Annales *history in the Biferno Valley.* London: Leicester University Press.

Barker, G. and J. Lloyd (eds.). 1991. *Roman landscapes: archaeological survey in the Mediterranean region.* London: British School at Rome. Archaeological Monographs of the British School at Rome 2.

Barrett, J. C., R. Bradley and M. Green. 1991. *Landscape, monuments and society: the prehistory of Cranborne Chase.* Cambridge: Cambridge University Press.

Beamon, S. P. 1992. *The Royston Cave: used by saints or sinners? Local historical influences of the Templar and Hospitaller.* Baldock: Cortney.

Beck, W., D. J. Donahue, A. J. T. Jull, G. Burr, W. S. Broecker, G. Bonani, I. Hajdas and E. Malotki. 1998. Ambiguities in direct dating of rock surfaces using radiocarbon measurements, *Science* 280: 2132–9.

Beckensall, S. and T. Laurie. 1998. *Prehistoric rock art of County Durham, Swaledale and Wensleydale.* Durham: County Durham Books.

Bednarik, R. G. 1986. Parietal finger markings in Europe and Australia, *Rock Art Research* 3: 30–61, 159–70.

1995a. The age of the Côa valley petroglyphs in Portugal, *Rock Art Research* 12(2): 86–103.

1995b. The Côa petroglyphs: an obituary to the stylistic dating of Palaeolithic rock art, *Antiquity* 69: 877–83.

Beltrán, A. 1982. *Rock art of the Spanish Levant.* Cambridge: Cambridge University Press.

Bender, B. (ed.). 1993. *Landscape: politics and perspectives.* Oxford: Berg.

Bender, B. 1999. Introductory comments, *Antiquity* 73: 632–4.

Bender, B., S. Hamilton and C. Tilley. 1997. Leskernick: stone worlds, alternative narratives, nested landscapes, *Proceedings of the Prehistoric Society* 63: 147–78.

Binford, M. *et al.* 1997. Climate variation and the rise and fall of an Andean civilization, *Quaternary Research* 47: 235–48.

Bowden, M. (ed.). 1999. *Unravelling the landscape: an inquisitive approach to archaeology.* Stroud: Tempus.

Bradley, J. 1988. *Yanyuwa country: the Yanyuwa people of Borroloola tell the history of their land.* Richmond: Greenhouse Publications.

Bradley, R. 1997. *Signing the land: rock art and the prehistory of Atlantic Europe.* London: Routledge.

1998a. Incised motifs in the passage-graves at Quoyness and Cuween, Orkney, *Antiquity* 72: 387–90.

1998b. *The significance of monuments: on the shaping of human experience in Neolithic and Bronze Age Europe.* London: Routledge.

Bradley, R., C. Chippindale and K. Helskog. 2001. Post-Palaeolithic Europe, in David Whitley (ed.) *Handbook of rock art studies*: 482–529. Walnut Creek, CA: AltaMira Press.

Breuil, H. 1933–35. *Les Peintures rupestres schématiques de la péninsule ibérique*. Lagny: Fondation Singer-Polignac.

Caruana, W. 1993. *Aboriginal art*. London: Thames and Hudson.

Castleman, C. 1982. *Getting up: subway graffiti in New York*. Cambridge, MA: MIT Press.

Chaloupka, G. 1982. *Burrunguy, Nourlangie Rock*. Darwin, NT: Northart.

1993. *Journey in time: the world's longest continuing art tradition*. Chatswood, NSW: Reed.

Children, G. and G. H. Nash. 1997. Establishing a discourse: the language of landscape, in G. H. Nash (ed.), *Semiotics of landscape: archaeology of mind*: 1–4. Oxford: British Archaeological Reports. International Series 661.

Chippindale, C. 1986a. A microcomputer simulation of variable forms in prehistoric rock art, in A. Voorrips and S. Loving (eds.), *'To pattern the past': proceedings of Amsterdam conference on mathematical methods in archaeology*: 160–87. Brussels: PACT.

1986b. Archaeology, design-theory and the reconstruction of prehistoric design-systems, *Planning and Design (Environment and Planning B)* 13: 445–85.

1986c. Stoned Henge: events and issues at the summer solstice, *World Archaeology* 18: 38–58.

1992. Geometry, generative grammars, and 'meaning' in artefacts, in Christopher Peebles and Jean-Claude Gardin (eds.), *Representations in archaeology*: 251–76. Bloomington, IN: Indiana University Press.

2001. Prehistoric rock-art: studying ancient pictures as pictures, in David S. Whitley (ed.), *Handbook of rock art studies*: 247–72. Walnut Creek, CA: AltaMira.

In press. Pictures and stories, stories and pictures: a model from Aboriginal north Australia today for the prehistoric meanings of rock-art, in Marcia-Anne Dobres and Christopher Chippindale (eds.), untitled book on approaches to rock-art. Washington, DC: Smithsonian Institution Press.

Chippindale, C., B. Smith and G. Blundell (eds.). In press. *Knowing and seeing*.

Chippindale, C. and P. S. C. Taçon. 1993. Two old painted panels from Kakadu: variation and sequence in Arnhem Land rock art, in J. Steinbring *et al.* (eds.), *Time and space: dating and spatial considerations in rock art research (papers of Symposia F and E, AURA Congress Cairns 1992)*: 32–56. Melbourne, Vic.: Australian Rock Art Research Association. Occasional AURA Publication 8.

1998a. The many ways of dating Arnhem Land rock-art, north Australia, in C. Chippindale and P. S. C. Taçon (eds.), *The archaeology of rock-art*: 90–111. Cambridge: Cambridge University Press.

Chippindale, C. and P. S. C. Taçon (eds.). 1998b. *The archaeology of rock-art*. Cambridge: Cambridge University Press.

Christensen, D. D. 1994. Rock art, ceramics, and textiles: the validity of unifying motifs, in Ken Hedges (ed.), *Rock art papers* 11: 107–16. San Diego, CA: San Diego Museum of Man. Museum Papers 31.

Clottes, J. 1997. New laboratory techniques and their impact on Paleolithic cave art, in Margaret W. Conkey, Deborah Stratmann and Nina Jablonski (eds.), *Beyond art: Pleistocene image and symbol*: 37–52. San Francisco, CA: California Academy of Sciences. Memoir 23.

Clottes, J., J. Courtin, H. Valladas, M. Cachier, N. Mercier and M. Arnold. 1992. La Grotte Cosquer datée, *Bulletin de la Société Préhistorique Française* 89(8): 230–4.

Clottes, J. and D. Lewis-Williams. 1998. *The shamans of prehistory: trance and magic in the painted caves*. New York: Harry Abrams.

Clottes, J., M. Lorblanchet and A. Beltrán. 1995. Are the Foz Côa engravings actually Holocene?, *International Newsletter on Rock Art* 12: 19–21.

Clottes, J. and R. Simonnet. 1972. Le réseau René Clastres dans la caverne de Niaux (Ariège), *Bulletin de la Société Préhistorique Française* 69(1): 293–323.

Clottes, J., H. Valladas, M. Cachier and M. Arnold. 1992. Des dates pour Niaux et Gargas, *Bulletin de la Société Préhistorique Française* 89(9): 270–4.

Cole, S. J. 1994. Roots of Anasazi and Pueblo imagery in Basketmaker II rock art and material culture, *The Kiva* 60(2): 289–312.

Conkey, M. W. and C. A. Hastorf (eds.). 1990. *The uses of style in archaeology*. Cambridge: Cambridge University Press.

Conway, T. and J. Conway. 1990. *Spirits on stone: the Agawa pictographs*. San Luis Obispo, CA: Heritage Discoveries.

Cosgrove, D. E. 1998. *Social formation and symbolic landscape*. New edition. Madison, WI: University of Wisconsin Press.

Costas Goberna, E. J. and P. Novoa Alvarez. 1993. *Los grabados rupestres de Galicia*. La Coruña: Museo Arqueolóxico e Histórico.

Crothers, G. and P. J. Watson. 1993. Archaeological contexts in deep cave sites: examples from the Eastern Woodlands of North America, in P. Goldberg, D. Nash and M. Petraglia (eds.), *Formation processes in archaeological context*: 53–60. Madison, WI: Prehistory Press.

Dams, L. 1984. *Les Peintures rupestres du Levant Espagnol*. Paris: Picard.

David, B., I. McNiven, V. Attenbrow, J. Flood and J. Collins. 1994. Of Lightning Brothers and White Cockatoos: dating the antiquity of signifying systems in the Northern Territory, Australia, *Antiquity* 68: 241–51.

de Jongh, J. 1999. Ethnography in archaeological interpretation of southern African and northern Australian rock-art. Unpublished MPhil dissertation, Department of Archaeology, University of Cambridge.

Dorn, R. I. 1995. Constraining the age of the Côa valley (Portugal) engravings with radiocarbon dating, *Antiquity* 71: 105–15.

1996. A change of perception, *La Pintura* 23(2): 10–11.

1997. Uncertainties in the 14C ages for petroglyphs from the Olary province, South Australia, *Archaeology in Oceania* 32(3): 214–15.

2001. Chronometric techniques: engravings, in David S. Whitley (ed.), *Handbook of rock art studies*: 168–89. Walnut Creek, CA: AltaMira.

Dorn, R. I., M. Nobbs and T. A. Cahill. 1988. Cation-ratio dating of rock engravings from the Olary province of arid South Australia, *Antiquity* 62: 681–9.

Dorn, R. I. and D. S. Whitley. 1984. Chronometric and relative age determination of petroglyphs in the western United States, *Annals of the Association of American Geographers* 28: 38–49.

Edmonds, M. 1999. *Ancestral geographies of the Neolithic: landscape, monuments and memory*. London: Routledge.

Erickson, C. L. 1999. Neo-environmental determinism and agrarian 'collapse' in Andean prehistory, *Antiquity* 73: 634–42.

Faulkner, C. H. 1988. A study of seven Southeastern glyph caves, *North American Archaeologist* 9(3): 223–46.

1996. Rock art in Tennessee: ceremonial art in this world and the underworld, in C. H. Faulkner (ed.), *Rock art of the Eastern Woodlands*: 111–18. San Miguel, CA: American Rock Art Research Association.

Faulkner, C. H. (ed.). 1986. *The prehistoric Native American art of Mud Glyph Cave*. Knoxville, TN: University of Tennessee Press.

Faulkner, C. H., B. Deane and H. H. Earnest, Jr. 1984. A Mississippian period ritual cave in Tennessee, *American Antiquity* 49: 350–61.

Faulkner, C. H. and J. F. Simek. 1996a. Mud glyphs: recently discovered cave art in eastern North America, *International Newsletter on Rock Art* 15: 8–13.

1996b. 1st Unnamed Cave: a Mississippian period cave art site in east Tennessee, USA, *Antiquity* 70: 774–84.

In press. Variability in the production and preservation of prehistoric mud glyphs from southeastern caves, in P. Drooker (ed.), *Fleeting identities: perishable material culture in archaeological research*. Carbondale, IL: Southern Illinois University Press.

Faulstich, P. (ed.). 1997. *Rock art as visual ecology*. Tucson, AZ: American Rock Art Research Association. IRAC Proceedings 1.

Fisher, C. T. and T. L. Thurston. 1999. Special section: Dynamic landscapes and socio-political process: the topography of anthropogenic environments in global perspective, *Antiquity* 73: 630–88.

Flood, J. and B. David. 1994. Traditional systems of encoding meaning in Wardaman rock art, Northern Territory, Australia, *Artefact* 17: 6–22.

Flood, J., B. David and R. Frost. 1992a. Dreaming into art: Aboriginal interpretations of rock engravings: Yingalarri, Northern Territory (Australia), in Mike J. Morwood and D. R. Hobbs (eds.), *Rock art and ethnography*: 33–8. Melbourne, Vic.: Australian Rock Art Research Association. Occasional Publication 5.

1992b. Pictures in transition: discussing the interaction of visual forms and symbolic contents in Wardaman rock pictures, in Mike J. Morwood and

D. R. Hobbs (eds.), *Rock art and ethnography*: 27–32. Melbourne, Vic.: Australian Rock Art Research Association. Occasional Publication 5.

Foley, R. 1981. *Off-site archaeology and human adaptation in eastern Africa: an analysis of regional artefact density in the Amboseli, southern Kenya*. Oxford: British Archaeological Reports. International series 97. Cambridge Monographs in African Archaeology 3.

Fossati, A. 1995. La scoperta e la storia delle ricerche, in Andrea Arcá, Angelo Fossati, Elena Marchi and Emanuela Tononi/Cooperative Archeologica 'Le Orme dell'Uomo', *Rupe Magna: la roccia incisa più grande delle Alpi*: 11–13. Sondrio: Consorzio per il Parco delle Incisioni Rupestri di Grosio.

Francis, J. E., L. L. Loendorf and R. I. Dorn. 1993. AMS radiocarbon and cation-ratio dating of rock art in the Bighorn Basin of Wyoming and Montana, *American Antiquity* 58: 711–37.

Gjessing, G. 1932. *Arktistic Halleristninger i Nord-Norge*. Oslo: H. Aschehoug.

Greer, J. and M. Greer. 1997. Dark zone rock art in Surratt-Cave, a deep cavern in central New Mexico, in Steven M. Freers (ed.), *American Indian rock art* 23: 25–40. Tucson, AZ: American Rock Art Research Association.

1998. Dark zone rock art in North America, in Ken Hedges (ed.), *Rock art papers* 13: 135–44. San Diego, CA: San Diego Museum of Man.

Hallström, G. 1938. *Monumental art of northern Europe from the Stone Age* 1: *The Norwegian localities*. Stockholm: Almqvist and Wiksell.

Hartley, R. J. 1992. *Rock art on the northern Colorado plateau: variability in content and context*. Aldershot: Avebury.

Hartley, R. J. and A. W. Vawser. 1996. Wayfinding in the desert: evaluating the role of rock art through GIS, in Paul Faulstich (ed.), *Ecology of rock art*. Proceedings of the International Rock Art Congress, Flagstaff, AZ, 1994.

Hartley, R. J. and A. M. Wolley Vawser. 1998. Spatial behaviour and learning in the prehistoric environment of the Colorado River drainage (south-eastern Utah), western North America, in Christopher Chippindale and Paul S. C. Taçon (eds.), *The archaeology of rock-art*: 185–211. Cambridge: Cambridge University Press.

Helskog, K. 1986. *Helleristningsfeltene i Hjemmeluft/Jiebmaluotka: a guide*. 4th edition. Alta: Alta Museum.

1999. The shore connection: cognitive landscape and communication with rock carvings in northernmost Europe, *Norwegian Archaeological Review* 32(2): 73–94.

Hodder, I. and C. Orton. 1976. *Spatial analysis in archaeology*. Cambridge: Cambridge University Press.

Ilger, W. A., M. Hyman, J. Southon and M. W. Rowe. 1995. Dating pictographs with radiocarbon, *Radiocarbon* 37: 299–310.

Ilger, W. A., M. Hyman, J. Southon and M. W. Rowe. In press. Dating pictographs with radiocarbon, *Radiocarbon* 37(3).

IPA [Instituto Português de Arqueologia]. 1999. Archaeologically-dated Paleolithic rock art at Fariseu, Côa valley, at http://www.ipa.mincultura.pt/news/noticias/fariseu/Fariseu_uk, September 2000.

Jochim, M. A. 1998. *A hunter-gatherer landscape: southwest Germany in the late Paleolithic and Mesolithic*. New York: Plenum Press.

Kaul, F. 1998. *Ships on bronzes: a study in Bronze Age religion and iconography*. Copenhagen: National Museum. Publications from the National Museum, Studies in Archaeology and History 3.

Kirch, P. V. and T. L. Hunt. 1995. *Historical ecology in the Pacific Islands: prehistoric environmental and landscape change*. New Haven, CT: Yale University Press.

Knight, T. W. 1994. *Transformations in design: a formal approach to stylistic change and innovation in the visual arts*. Cambridge: Cambridge University Press.

Labbe, J. M. 1998. *Romantic visualities: landscape, gender, and romanticism*. Basingstoke: Macmillan Press.

Layton, R. 1992. *Australian rock art: a new synthesis*. Cambridge: Cambridge University Press.

Lewis-Williams, J. D. 1981. *Believing and seeing: symbolic meaning in southern San rock paintings*. London: Academic Press.

Lorblanchet, M. and P. G. Bahn (eds.). 1993. *Rock art studies: the post-stylistic era or, Where do we go from here?* Oxford: Oxbow. Monograph 35.

Loubser, J. H. N. In press. In small cupules forgotten: rock markings, archaeology, and ethnography in the Deep South, in Christopher Chippindale, David Whitley and Lawrence Loendorf (eds.), *Picturing the American past*.

Loy, T. H. 1994. Direct dating of rock art at Laurie Creek (NT), Australia: a reply to Nelson, *Antiquity* 68: 147–8.

Loy, T. H., R. Jones, D. E. Nelson, B. Meehan, J. Vogel, J. Southon and R. Cosgrove. 1990. Accelerator radiocarbon dating of human blood proteins in pigments from Late Pleistocene art sites in Australia, *Antiquity* 64: 110–16.

Lumley, H. de *et al*. 1995. *Le Grandiose et le sacré: gravures rupestres protohistoriques et historiques de la région du Mont Bego*. Aix-en-Provence: Edisud.

McGlade, J. 1995. Archaeology and the eco-dynamics of human-modified landscapes, *Antiquity* 69: 113–32.

Maggs, T. 1967. A quantitative analysis of the rock art from a sample area in the western Cape, *South African Journal of Science* 63: 100–4.

Mee, C. and H. Forbes (eds.). 1997. *A rough and rocky place: the landscape and settlement history of the Methana Peninsula, Greece: results of the Methana Survey Project sponsored by the British School at Athens and the University of Liverpool*. Liverpool: Liverpool University Press.

Merleau-Ponty, M. 1962. *Phenomenology of perception*. London. Routledge and Kegan Paul.

Mguni, S. 1997. The evaluation of the superpositioning sequence of painted images to infer relative chronology: Diepkloof Kraal shelter as a case study. Unpublished BA (Hons.) thesis, Department of Archaeology, University of Cape Town.

Moore, D. and E. Younkin. 1992. *Little Petroglyph Canyon tour guide*. Ridgecrest, CA: Maturango Museum of Indian Wells Valley.

Morphy, H. 1991. *Ancestral connections: art and an Aboriginal system of knowledge*. Chicago, IL: Chicago University Press.

Morris, D. 1988. Engraved in place and time: a review of variability in the rock art of the Northern Cape and Karoo, *South African Archaeological Bulletin* 43: 109–21.

Morwood, M. J. and D. R. Hobbs (eds.). 1992. *Rock art and ethnography: proceedings of the Ethnography Symposium (H), Australian Rock Art Research Association Congress, Darwin 1988*. Melbourne: Australian Rock Art Research Association. Occasional AURA Publication 5.

Müller, Sophus 1918. *Stenalderens Kunst i Danmark*. Copenhagen: I Kommission hos C. A. Reitzel.

Muzzolini, A. 1995. *Les Images rupestres du Sahara*. Toulouse. Collection Préhistoire du Sahara 1.

Nash, G. H. 1997. Symbols in space: rock carvings of the Campo Lameiro region, southern Galicia, Spain, in G. H. Nash (ed.), *Semiotics of landscape: archaeology of mind*: 46–58. Oxford: British Archaeological Reports. International Series 661.

1998. *Exchange, status and mobility: Mesolithic portable art of southern Scandinavia*. Oxford: British Archaeological Reports. International Series 710.

2002. The landscape brought within: a re-evaluation of the rock-painting site at Tumlehed, Torslanda, Göteborg, west Sweden, in G. H. Nash and C. Chippindale (eds.), *European landscapes of rock-art*. London: Routledge.

2003. Conceptualising a landscape: discovering and viewing on Bronze Age rock art of the Campo Lameiro Valley, southern Galicia, Spain, in Kalle Sognnes (ed.), *Rock art in landscapes – landscapes in rock art*. Trondheim: University of Trondheim. VITARK: Acta Archaeologica Nidrosiensia 3 (forthcoming).

Nelson, D. E. 1993. Second thoughts on a rock-art date, *Antiquity* 67: 893–5.

Nelson, D. E., G. Chaloupka, C. Chippindale, M. S. Alderson and J. Southon. 1995. Radiocarbon dates for beeswax figures in the prehistoric rock art of northern Australia, *Archaeometry* 37(1): 151–6.

Nelson, D. E., C. Chippindale, P. S. C. Taçon, G. Chaloupka and J. Southon. 2000. *The beeswax rock-art of Arnhem Land, Northern Territory, Australia: field records, archaeology, anthropology, dating, chronology and interpretation*. CD-ROM publication. Burnaby, BC: Simon Fraser University, Department of Archaeology.

Oliveira J. V. (ed). 1995. *Dossier Côa*. Oporto: Sociedad Portuguesa de Antropologia e Etnologia.

Pericot Garcia, L. 1952. *L'Espagne avant la conquête romaine*. Paris: Payot.

Phillips, F. M., M. Flinsch, D. Elmore and P. Sharma. 1997. Maximum ages of the Côa valley (Portugal) engravings measured with Chlorine-36, *Antiquity* 71: 100–4.

Phillips, S. 1999. *Wallbangin: graffiti and gangs in LA*. Chicago, IL: University of Chicago Press.

Pick, H. L. and L. P. Acredolo. 1983. *Spatial orientation: theory, research, and application*. New York: Plenum Press.

Picot, E. 1997. *Outcasts from Eden: ideas of landscape in British poetry since 1945*. Liverpool: Liverpool University Press. Liverpool English Texts and Studies 28.

Ramqvist, P. H. 1992. Hällbilder som utgångspunkt vid tolkningar av jägarsamhället, *Arkeologi i norr* 3 (1990): 31–53.

Ripoll Perello, E. 1964. Para una cronologia relativa del arte levantino español, in Luis Pericot Garcia and Eduardo Ripoll Perello (eds.), *Prehistoric art of the western Mediterranean and the Sahara*: 43–61. New York: Wenner-Gren Foundation for Anthropological Research. Viking Fund Publications in Anthropology 39.

Rose, D. B. 1996. *Nourishing terrains: Australian Aboriginal views of landscape and wilderness*. Canberra, ACT: Australian Heritage Commission.

Rosenfeld, A., D. Horton and J. Winter. 1981. *Early man in north Queensland*. Canberra, ACT: Department of Prehistory, Research School of Pacific Studies, Australian National University. Terra Australis 6.

Rossignol, J. and L. Wandsnider (eds.). 1992. *Space, time, and archaeological landscapes*. New York: Plenum.

Rowe, M. W. 2001. Dating by AMS radiocarbon analysis, in David S. Whitley (ed.), *Handbook of rock art studies*: 139–66. Walnut Creek, CA: AltaMira.

In press. Chronometric studies of prehistoric rock-paintings in North America, in Christopher Chippindale, David Whitley and Lawrence Loendorf (eds.), *Picturing the American past*.

Sanders, W. T., J. R. Parsons and R. S. Santley. 1979. *The Basin of Mexico: ecological processes in the evolution of a civilization*. New York: Academic Press.

Savage, S. H. 1989. *Late Archaic landscapes: a Geographic Information Systems approach to the late Archaic landscape of the Savannah River valley, Georgia and South Carolina*. Charlotte, SC: University of South Carolina. Occasional Papers of the South Carolina Institute of Archaeology and Anthropology, Anthropological Studies 8.

Schama, S. 1995. *Landscape and memory*. London: HarperCollins.

1999. *Rembrandt's eyes*. London: Allen Lane.

Shee Twohig, E. 1981. *The megalithic art of western Europe*. Oxford: Clarendon Press

Simek, J. F. and A. Cressler. In press. Images in darkness: prehistoric cave-art in southeast North America, in Christopher Chippindale, David Whitley and Lawrence Loendorf (eds.), *Picturing the American past*.

Simek, J. F., S. R. Frankenburg and C. H. Faulkner. In press. Towards an understanding of Southeastern prehistoric cave art, in S. Prezanno and L. Sullivan (eds.), *Integrating Appalachian Highlands archaeology*. Knoxville, TN: University of Tennessee Press.

Simek, J. F., J. D. Franklin and S. C. Sherwood. 1998. The context of early southeastern prehistoric cave art: a report on the archaeology of 3rd Unnamed Cave, *American Antiquity* 63: 663–77.

Smith, C. 1994. Situating style: an ethnoarchaeological analysis of social and material context in an Australian Aboriginal artistic system. Unpublished PhD thesis, University of New England, Armidale.

Sognnes, K. 1994. Ritual landscape: toward a reinterpretation of Stone Age rock art in Trondelag, Norway, *Norwegian Archaeological Review* 27: 29–50.

Soleilhavoup, F. X. 1995. Les supports rocheux: altérations et bioconstructions: témoins d'archéo-environnements, in H.-P. Francfort and J. A. Sher (eds.), *Répertoire des pétroglyphes d'Asie centrale, fascicule 2, Sibérie du Sud* 2: *Tepsej I–III, Ust'-Tuba I–IV (Russie, Khakassie)*: xli–lxviii. Paris: Diffusion de Boccard. Mémoires de la Mission Archéologique Française en Asie Centrale 5.2.

Stanbury, P., J. Clegg and D. Campbell. 1990. *A field guide to Aboriginal rock engravings with special reference to those around Sydney*. Sydney: Sydney University Press.

Stiny, G. 1975. *Pictorial and formal aspects of shape and shape grammars*. Basel: Birkhäuser.

1987. *Computing with form and meaning in architecture*. Los Angeles, CA: UCLA Graduate School of Architecture and Town Planning.

Stiny, G. and J. Gips. 1978. *Algorithmic aesthetics: computer models for criticism and design in the arts*. Berkeley, CA: University of California Press.

Stone, A. J. 1995. *Images from the underworld: Naj Tunich and the tradition of Maya cave painting*. Austin, TX: University of Texas Press.

Swartz, B. K. and T. S. Hurlbutt. 1994. Space, place and territory in rock-art interpretation, *Rock Art Research* 11(1): 13–22.

Taçon, P. S. C. 1988. Identifying fish species in the recent rock paintings of western Arnhem Land, *Rock Art Research* 5(1): 3–15.

1990. The power of place: cross-cultural responses to natural and cultural landscapes of stone and earth, in J. Vastokas (ed.), *Perspectives of Canadian landscape: Native traditions*: 11–43. North York, Ont.: York University, Robarts Centre for Canadian Studies.

1994. Socialising landscapes: the long-term implications of signs, symbols and marks on the land, *Archaeology in Oceania* 29(3): 117–29.

1999a. Andrée Rosenfeld and the archaeology of rock-art, in Ursula Frederick, Meredith Wilson and J. Peter White (eds.), *Making a mark: papers on rock art for Andrée Rosenfeld*: 95–102. Sydney: Oceania Publications. *Archaeology in Oceania* 34(3).

1999b. Identifying ancient landscapes in Australia: from physical to social, in Wendy Ashmore and A. Bernard Knapp (eds.), *Archaeology of landscapes: contemporary perspectives*: 33–57. Oxford: Blackwell.

Taçon, P. S. C. and C. Chippindale. 1994. Australia's ancient warriors: changing depictions of fighting in the rock art of Arnhem Land, N.T., *Cambridge Archaeological Journal* 4: 211–48.

1998. Introduction: an archaeology of rock-art through informed methods and formal methods, in Christopher Chippindale and Paul S. C. Taçon (eds.), *The archaeology of rock-art*: 1–10. Cambridge: Cambridge University Press.

Taçon, P. S. C., R. Fullagar, S. Ouzman and K. Mulvaney. 1997. Cupule engravings from Jinmium-Granilpi (northern Australia) and beyond: exploration of a widespread and enigmatic class of rock markings, *Antiquity* 71: 942–65.

Taçon, P. S. C., M. Wilson and C. Chippindale. 1996. Birth of the Rainbow Serpent in Arnhem Land rock art and oral history, *Archaeology in Oceania* 31: 103–24.

Tilley, C. 1994. *A phenomenology of landscape: places, paths and monuments*. Oxford: Berg.

Tokioka, K. 1992. Rock art of Escalante Canyon: quantitative analysis of rock art elements of Glen Canyon. MA thesis, Department of Anthropology, Northern Arizona University, Flagstaff.

Tolan-Smith, C. A. 1997. *Landscape archaeology in Tynedale*. Newcastle upon Tyne: Department of Archaeology, University of Newcastle upon Tyne. Tyne-Solway Ancient and Historic Landscapes Research Programme Monograph 1.

Ucko, P. J. and R. Layton. 1999. *Shaping your landscape: the archaeology and anthropology of landscape*. London: Routledge.

van der Merwe, N. J., J. Sealy and R. Yates. 1987. First accelerator carbon-14 date for pigment from a rock painting, *South African Journal of Science* 83: 56–7.

Wagstaff, J. M. (ed.). 1987. *Landscape and culture: geographical and archaeological perspectives*. Oxford: Basil Blackwell.

Walsh, G. L. 1994. *Bradshaws: ancient rock paintings of north-west Australia*. Carouge-Geneva: Edition Limitée.

Watchman, A. 1993. Perspectives and potentials for absolute dating prehistoric rock paintings, *Antiquity* 67: 58–65.

1995. Recent petroglyphs, Foz Côa, Portugal, *Rock Art Research* 12(2): 104–8.

1996. A review of the theory and assumptions in the AMS dating of the Foz Côa petroglyphs, Portugal, *Rock Art Research* 13(1): 21–30.

Watchman, A. and D. Lessard. 1992. Dating prehistoric rock art by laser: a new method for extracting trace organic matter, *International Newsletter on Rock Art* 2: 14–15.

Wendt, W. E. 1976. 'Art mobilier' from the Apollo 11 Cave, South West Africa: Africa's oldest dated works of art, *South African Archaeological Bulletin* 31: 5–11.

Whitley, D. S. 1992. Shamanism and rock art in far western North America, *Cambridge Archaeological Journal* 2: 89–113.

1994. Ethnography and rock art in far western North America: some archaeological implications, in David S. Whitley and Lawrence L. Loendorf (eds.), *New light on old art: recent advances in hunter-gatherer rock art research*: 81–93. Los Angeles, CA: Institute of Archaeology, University of California, Los Angeles. Monograph 36.

1998. Finding rain in the desert: landscape, gender and far western North American rock-art, in Christopher Chippindale and Paul S. C. Taçon (eds.), *The archaeology of rock-art*: 11–29. Cambridge: Cambridge University Press.

Whitley, D. S. and R. I. Dorn. 1987. Rock art chronology in eastern California, *World Archaeology* 19: 150–64.

1993. New perspectives on the Clovis versus pre-Clovis controversy, *American Antiquity* 58: 626–47.

Willey, G. R. 1953. *Prehistoric settlement patterns in the Viru Valley, Peru*. Washington, DC: US Government Printing Office. Bulletin (Smithsonian Institution, Bureau of American Ethnology) 155.

Wolfe, P. 1991. The Dreamtime in anthropology and in Australian settler culture, *Comparative Studies in Society and History* 33: 197–224.

Young, M. J. 1985. Images of power and the power of images: the significance of rock art for contemporary Zunis, *Journal of American Folklore* 98(387): 2–48.

1988. *Signs from the ancestors: Zuni cultural symbolism and perceptions of rock art*. Albuquerque, NM: University of New Mexico Press.

Zilhão, J. 1995. The age of the Côa valley (Portugal) rock-art: validation of archaeological dating to the Palaeolithic and refutation of scientific dating to historic or proto-historic times, *Antiquity* 69: 883–901.

Zilhão, J. (ed.). 1997. *Arte rupestre e pré-história do Vale do Côa: trabalhos de 1995–1996: relatório científico ao governo da República Portuguesa elaborado nos termos da Resolução do Conselho de Ministros N°4/96, de 17 de Janeiro*. Lisbon: Ministério da Cultura.

Part One

Principles of landscape and rock-art in practice

The principles developed in this part take account of two central issues.

First, landscapes are matters of human perception and of cultural experience. Following from that, our observations and measurements should not depend on unsupported expectations and suppositions as to what human beings of other cultural experiences would have done.

Second, from the principles there need to follow practical and robust methods which can be effective in the field.

2

Worlds within stone: the inner and outer rock-art landscapes of northern Australia and southern Africa

Paul S. C. Taçon and Sven Ouzman

The hunter-gatherer rock-arts of northern Australia and southern Africa have much in common: an abundance of engraved and painted rock-art occurs at topographically comparable locales. Though northern Australian and southern African hunter-gatherers had no contact, their world-understandings have tended to find expression in similar ways – ways which often involve rock-art imagery. In the case of northern Australia and southern Africa, rock-art points the way, often literally, to multiple landscapes that co-exist but which do not seem to have been equally accessible to all hunter-gatherers. In both regions the notion is pervasive that inner worlds of extra-ordinary experience simultaneously and immanently exist alongside and intertwined with the outer world of 'ordinary' existence. Rock-art sites represent places where these worlds connected. As important as the rock-art imagery in this respect is the rock itself; by no means a neutral support for imagery, it was and it is an active, a living and sometimes a dangerous entity. Ethnography, rock-art imagery and a consideration of rock and place, taken together, allow exploration of the nature of landscape perception and use among the hunter-gatherers of northern Australia and southern Africa.

Worlds within stone

In many parts of the world it is still commonly believed that spirits, human-like beings and fantastic creatures live deep inside the planet, sometimes within rock-worlds with connections to the earth-plane of existence. Indeed, an almost universal theme of death via descent to an underworld and resurrection through a journey to the sky-world can be found among highly diverse peoples, past and present (Eliade 1974: 43; 1975). More complexly, these worlds of extra-ordinary experience are sometimes believed to exist simultaneously with and parallel to the world of ordinary experience. These extra-ordinary worlds, everywhere immanent, can become manifest at any time or place if certain socio-symbolic conditions are met. We categorize these extra-ordinary worlds as 'inner' worlds, for they belong to a differentially experienced scape of land and mind (e.g. Ouzman 1998a; 1998b). The world of ordinary experience thus becomes an 'outer' world. Many of these 'inner' worlds are believed to be similar to the ordinary world of human existence; in other cases, the inner worlds are perceived or constructed as dark, dangerous places where one would not feel welcome or comfortable. Cultures with shamanistic orientations often have visions of the inner world with many points in common; those with organized religions may be quite different.

Eliade (1996: 216–38, 437–40), exploring notions about underworlds, rock and stone among hunter-gatherer societies in depth, has argued that the properties inherent in rock are interpreted as reflective of another dimension, world or realm (Eliade 1996: 216):

> And nothing was more direct and autonomous in the completeness of its strength, nothing more noble or more awe-inspiring, than a majestic rock, or a boldly-standing block of granite. Above all, stone *is*. It always remains itself, and exists of itself; and, more important still, it *strikes*. Before he even takes it up to strike, man finds in it an obstacle – if not to his body, at least to his gaze – and ascertains its hardness, its roughness, its power. Rock shows him something that transcends the precariousness of his humanity: an absolute mode of being. Its strength, its motionlessness, its size and its strange outlines are none of them human; they indicate the presence of something that fascinates, terrifies, attracts and threatens, all at once. In its grandeur, its hardness, its shape and its colour, man is faced with a reality and a force that belong to some world other than the profane world of which he is himself a part.

Fig. 2.1. Men-an-Tol, Cornwall, England. For centuries, children and adults have been passed through the rock hole in the belief that certain illnesses could be cured.

Particular notions about rock leading to another dimension of being can be found all over the world, past and present. The painted caves of Upper Palaeolithic Europe have been described as religious and magical contexts; often their passageways or chimneys are adorned with specific subjects and with objects such as antlers, bear teeth, shells and stone tools which are deposited on ledges and in cracks in walls (Clottes 1995: 52–3). Clottes and Lewis-Williams (1998) have argued that Upper Palaeolithic hunter-gatherers considered the cave wall a permeable 'membrane' that both separated and connected the outer and inner worlds. More recently and globally, many people have marked human grave sites with significant stones or built rock cairns, crypts or mausoleums over and around human remains – western cemeteries are prolific contemporary examples.

A connection between different states of existence and rock as a substance can also be found in a variety of other contexts. One example lies in Cornwall, England. The site of Men-an-Tol consists of two column-like standing stones set either side of a standing stone with a circular hole in it (Fig. 2.1). These standing stones were originally part of a Neolithic tomb, the pierced stone forming the entrance, now some four or five millennia old. In recent centuries, long after they were placed in their current arrangement, there has been a traditional belief that by passing through the hole one could be cured of various afflictions through symbolic rebirth (Bord and Bord 1988: 21; Taylor 1997: 222–3). One could be transformed from one state (sickness) to another (wellness), the pierced rock acting as the enabling and transformative mechanism. Among many peoples it was or is still believed supernatural creatures, such as Medusa, Australian Rainbow Serpents or the North American Northwest Coast double-headed snake, Sisiutl (see Boas 1966: 307; Stewart 1982: 70), could turn people into stone; at hundreds of locations throughout the world it is said humanly placed or naturally positioned standing stones are the petrified remains of once living individuals and beings (e.g. the 'Merry Maidens' of Cornwall, England: Grinsell 1976: 90; or a petrified woman in Arnhem Land, Australia: Taçon 1994: 125).

There are also beliefs related to rebirth or release from stone. Among the Inuit of the Canadian Arctic, for instance, ivory and soapstone carvers contend that the act of carving releases rather than creates creatures; already existing deep inside the ivory, if not immediately apparent to the artist, they will reveal themselves during seemingly aimless carving (e.g. Carpenter 1961). In the Pacific, among the Kanakas of New Caledonia, large holes through rock are a symbol of rebirth. At the Tjibaou Cultural Centre, Noumea, this is expressed in a contemporary context with a large sculpted stone containing a prominent hole through which one can pass one's gaze to the surrounding sea (Fig. 2.2). An accompanying interpretation sign relates the story of the rebirth of Téâ kanaké, the local Ancestral Hero associated with such stones:

> Like the shoots which sprout from a cut tree-trunk, Téâ kanaké, the eternal bearer of the Kanak message, passes through the hole in the rock, the symbol of rebirth. He breathes his solemn words into the twigs of the ironwood tree, where they will sing on forever. From these words a new era begins.
>
> The snake, and particularly the striped sea-snake, is the image of the dead person who wishes to come back to the world of the living. He rises from the sea and leaves his skin on the beach as he regains human form.

Fig. 2.2. A contemporary Kanaka rock sculpture telling the story of the rebirth of the Ancestral Hero, Téâ kanaké, Tjibaou Cultural Centre, Noumea, New Caledonia.

Among the Seneca (People of the Stone) Iroquois of North America, a large boulder was held to be responsible for imparting knowledge to humans and initiating the mythic tradition (Jacobs 1975: 26–9). For the near-by Ojibwa, rocky areas of the landscape were traditionally considered to be particularly charged with spiritual energy or *manitou*, the same as is found in living creatures. As Vastokas and Vastokas note, 'boulders, rocky hills, and outcroppings with unusual dimensions or character, such as clefts, holes, or crevices, were especially charged with *manitou* and often conceived as the dwelling-places of mythological creatures' (1973: 48). At the Peterborough Petroglyph site (Ontario, Canada), depictions of snakes and other creatures seem to emerge from cracks in the rock surface (Vastokas and Vastokas 1973: 99–101). Among the Maya, mountains are thought to be hollow and home to a variety of creatures: 'The "heart of the mountain" is said variously to contain the home of the Earth Lord, the corrals where he keeps wild animals, or repositories of valued resources, including maize, treasure, and – significantly – water' (Brady and Ashmore 1999: 126). In many parts of Africa people use 'ringing rock' – naturally occurring 'rock gongs' – to communicate with their ancestors (e.g. Fagg 1997). The ancestors are believed to be everywhere immanent and influential; by beating certain rocks, a resonant, ringing sound is released which appeases the inner-world ancestors who, satisfied that they are not forgotten, will not interfere negatively in the lives of outer-world inhabitants (Ouzman 2001).

Strikingly similar ideas about spirits and supernatural beings that live in inner rock-worlds can be found among some San Bushfolk[1] of southern Africa and Australian Aboriginal peoples. Although we do not argue for any direct connections and/or transmission of ideas or belief between peoples of northern Australia, southern Africa and elsewhere in recent or even ancient times, we note a number of similarities between these two areas in terms of inner and outer rock-art landscape beliefs, as they can be gleaned from ethnography, rock-art depictions and placements. In this comparative study we explore similarity, as well as some differences, in order better to understand the nature of landscape perceptions, conceptions and usage in each region. We also see if the evidence supports ideas about ancient origins for such beliefs or, alternatively, if the pattern simply reflects common concerns of those living in hunter-gatherer physical and social environments. We consider only rock-art, as it is currently the most theoretically informed class of material culture, though we acknowledge the valuable collaborations between rock-art and excavation-centric archaeologists in northern Australia and southern Africa (e.g. David *et al.* 1994; Ouzman and Wadley 1997).

[1] Following the lead of Walker (1996) we use the term 'Bushfolk' to refer to the 'San' or 'Bushman' hunter-gatherers responsible for much of southern Africa's rock-art. We reject any pejorative connotations 'Bushfolk' may have and use it as an 'honest' term that approaches the character and texture of much of hunter-gatherer life and thought. We also acknowledge that 'Bushfolk' runs the risk of homogenizing spatially and temporally separate individuals, communities and achievements.

Northern Australia

Australia has over 100,000 surviving rock-art sites (Flood 1997), with the largest portion in the northern half of the continent (see Fig. 2.3 for rock-art regions). The imagery found at these sites ranges from finger flutings, stencils, prints, peck-marks, cupules and crude charcoal drawings to elaborate paintings, engravings, and figures made out of pressed beeswax. In northern Australia, used pieces of ochre have been found in the bottom of excavated rock-shelter deposits, radiocarbon- and luminescence-dated to between 40,000 and 60,000 years ago (Roberts *et al.* 1990; 1993). The earliest rock-painting fragment has been dated to about 39,000 years ago (O'Connor 1995) but most of the rock-art is believed to be less than 20,000 years of age, with much being produced in the past 10,000 years (Lewis 1988; Lewis and Rose 1988; Taçon 1989; Chaloupka 1993; David *et al.* 1994; Taçon and Chippindale 1994; Mulvaney 1996; Flood 1997; Roberts *et al.* 1997; Chippindale and Taçon 1998). There is much historic and contemporary Aboriginal knowledge about rock-art of the past few thousand years across northern Australia, sometimes extending to much older material.

Aboriginal ethnography – stories of the *Mimi*

In northern Australia we are fortunate to be able to approach the study of the past, including rock-art, with both formal and informed

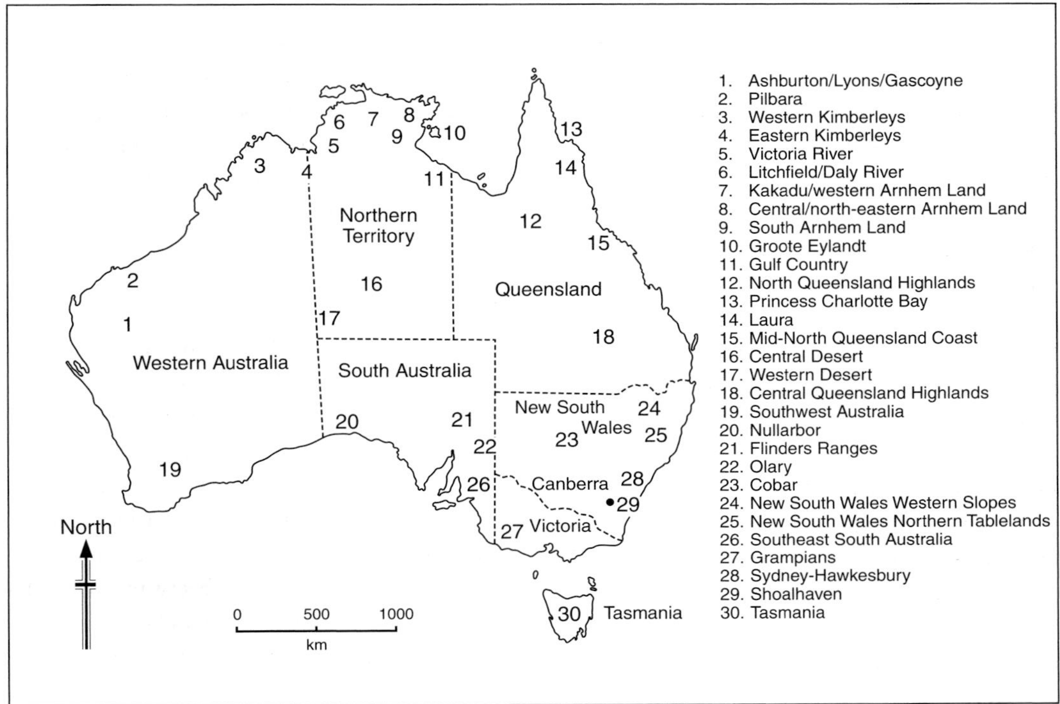

Fig. 2.3. Australian rock-art regions including those mentioned in the text.

methods. Formal methods are those which rely on no inside knowledge; information and meaning is restricted to what can be discerned by analysis of the verifiable material elements that constitute landscapes, artefacts and images. Though subjective to a degree, formal methods operate best when applied to a rock-art region. This extensive approach results in a network of mutually constraining and enabling strands of evidence that provide a strong degree of confidence in the formal method. Alternatively, there are informed methods which 'depend on some source of insight passed on directly or indirectly from those who made and used rock-art – through ethnography, through ethnohistory, through the historical record, or through modern understanding known with good cause to perpetuate ancient knowledge' (Taçon and Chippindale 1998: 6).

Across Australia, orally transmitted stories about spirits or supernatural creatures that live deep inside rock, stony landscapes or great boulders abound (e.g. Mountford 1978; 1981: 37; Chaloupka 1993). In northern Australia they are prolific, especially in the greater Arnhem Land region where stories of the *Mimi* beings form an important part of past and present oral history. The *Mimi* are significant for many reasons; said to populate large landscapes and to have the ability to move in and out of rock, they are timeless, for they played a significant role during the early creation period of human existence. And they are active today as spirits that visit in dreams or may be 'encountered' in more remote parts of the 'stone' country. Aboriginal elders will call out to them when visiting those areas, introduce guests (including visiting researchers) and point out significant locations where the *Mimi* live in their inner rock-worlds.

There are a number of origin stories that Aboriginal people use to describe how the world came into being, how it changed, and what gave rise to populations of plants, animals, people and places. Details vary between language groups but there are many common, unifying features, such as the powerful Rainbow Serpents who continue to transform landscapes and people's lives (Taylor 1990; Taçon *et al.* 1996) or the general structure of change over time (Taçon 1993). Across Arnhem Land, Aboriginal people will tell you the *Mimi* once had human-like form and resided on the land in ways similar to those of Aboriginal people before contact with Europeans (Mountford 1956: 181–2; Carroll 1977; Edwards 1979; Taylor 1987; Taçon 1989; Chaloupka 1993). It is said the *Mimi* taught the first Aboriginal people how to hunt and butcher kangaroos, gave them certain songs and ceremonies and, significantly, showed them how to paint on shelter walls and ceilings (Taçon 1989: 396; Chaloupka 1993: 64; Taçon and Garde 1995: 33). Later, during a period of great change, the *Mimi* became tall, thin spirits with the ability to slip through cracks in the rock. There they still reside in a rocky inner world where landscapes are much like those outside. There are plants and animals to gather and hunt, sources of water to drink and other supernatural creatures to encounter, including Rainbow Serpents, benevolent beings and dangerous demons. Differences include the fact that the *Mimi* have certain kangaroos and other native animals as pets (but not dingos or dogs). Sometimes these pets, like the *Mimi* themselves, leave the rock-world to venture on the Earth's surface. Pity the poor hunter who mistakenly kills such a creature; invariably some misfortune follows. However, the *Mimi* are generally not dangerous; they are more curious and mischievous than anything else and are desirous of human company. But occasionally, the *Mimi* might entice or capture a human, taking him or her to their inner rock-world for a journey that will irrevocably change both of them. 'Young people are warned not to follow the Mimi because they would never come back' (Chaloupka 1993: 66).

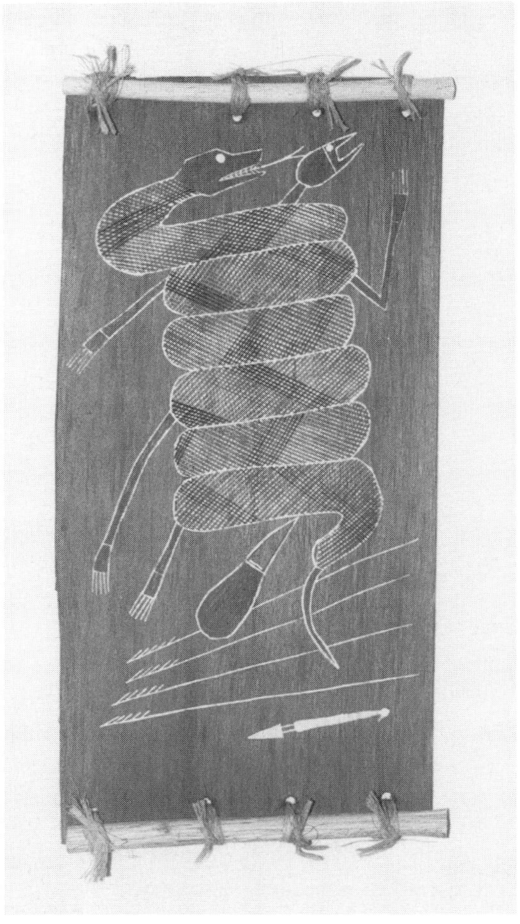

Fig. 2.4. This 1991 bark-painting by Jerimiah Garlngarr shows a *Mimi* being suffocated by a Rainbow Serpent inside a rock-world.

Stories continue to be told about the *Mimi* and they are a frequent subject in contemporary painting (e.g. see Brody 1984; Dyer 1994; West 1995; Fig. 2.4). Many rock-painting sites are attributed to the *Mimi*, with most of the older red paintings of humans and animals said to have been done by them rather than by Aboriginal people (Chaloupka 1993: 64):

> As the majority of the early rock-paintings were executed, or remain, as images in red, depicting subjects no longer portrayed or even present in their environment, and as they are in many instances situated beyond the reach of man's hand, the Aborigines consider they were executed by the Mimi spirits. They say that the Mimi can magically bring a rock wall down within the reach of their hands, paint on it, and then raise it again.

Fig. 2.5. This group of Dynamic Figures, from Kakadu National Park, appears to glide across the rock wall. Aboriginal elders claim they are depictions of the *Mimi*, who now live inside the rock, painted by and of themselves. Archaeologists believe they are at least 10,000 years of age.

Rock-painting and the inner world

In contrast to recent and contemporary painting on bark and paper, there are very few recent depictions of the *Mimi* in rock-art (Taçon 1989; Chaloupka 1993: 64), although a one-legged *Mimi* called *Daddubbe* was sometimes depicted near the Mann River of Central Arnhem Land (Taçon 1993). This may be partly because human figures in the widespread 'Dynamic Figure' manner of depiction, a distinctive manner of painting which falls early in the regional sequence and is found at over 250 sites, are invariably said to be depictions the *Mimi* made of themselves. Dynamic Figure paintings are at least 10,000 years of age (Taçon and Chippindale 1994), possibly older (Chaloupka 1993). Dynamic human figures are shown engaged in various activities, from hunting to fighting, from intercourse with partners to interaction with animal-headed supernatural creatures (Chaloupka 1984; 1993; Taçon and Chippindale 1994; 2001; Chippindale *et al.* 2000). A recent analysis of Dynamic Figure imagery has concluded that some of it is related to shamanistic activities, including experiences resulting from trance or other ritually induced altered states of consciousness (Chippindale *et al.* 2000). This is supported by an analysis of composite creatures from the Dynamic and subsequent periods of art production, as both formal and informed methods show these creatures to be of the sort that one encounters in altered states of consciousness (Taçon and Chippindale 2001). The practice called broadly 'shamanism' spanned an enormous variety of experiences and practices; the 'clever men' of Arnhem Land have a body of knowledge and skills with its own distinctive character, alongside elements shared with other cultural groups.

Dynamic Figures were not painted in such a way that they appear to move into or out of the rock surface; instead they glide and move across the rock with grace and elegance (Fig. 2.5). They do not emerge or enter into cracks or crevices; occasionally they were painted across cracks. Sometimes they hold weapons; limbs or other body parts wrap around the rock, extending over vertical, sloping and horizontal surfaces. For example, a Dynamic Figure painted on a vertical surface may appear to lack feet when seen from the front, but a closer look shows that the feet are painted on the underside of a horizontal surface where the vertical face turns in.

Subsequent to the Dynamics is a different manner of depiction, called 'Simple Figures with Boomerangs'; in this, male figures with large head-dresses often appear to 'float' up to prominent ceiling cracks. Sometimes parts of the head-dress disappear inside these cracks (e.g. Chaloupka 1993: fig. 126) and there are rare depictions of animals with heads that disappear into cracks and crevices (e.g. Chaloupka 1993: fig. 129). At one extraordinary site, two groups of Simple Figures are depicted as if in combat on either side of a large vertical crack that divides the wall surface (Taçon and Chippindale 1994: 244). This has its counterpart in a more recent battle scene, near the East Alligator River, again arranged around a prominent vertical crack (Taçon and Chippindale 1994: fig. 10).

During the period in which Simple Figures were painted, about 4000–6000 years ago (Taçon and Chippindale 1994; Taçon and Brockwell 1995), the first depictions of Rainbow Serpents were made (Taçon *et al.* 1996). In Aboriginal oral history, it is said these powerful creatures can travel through rock, across the land and through the sky. They first emerged from the sea and their journeys shaped and formed many Australian landscapes, especially those composed of rock. At several locations, they entered into the rock, leaving their image behind at the point of entry in the process (such as at Ubirr, near the East Alligator River – see Taçon 1992: fig. 10). Sometimes an early depiction of a Rainbow Serpent was placed inside a natural, circular hollow of the rock wall (e.g. Taçon *et al.* 1996: fig. 19), suggestive of the creature emerging from or entering into stone.

At dozens of locations across the Top End of the Northern Territory other Ancestral Beings also entered into the rock, leaving blazing depictions of themselves on rock walls and ceilings at the points of contact. Elsewhere, large holes or tunnels are said to have been made where Ancestral Beings emerged from their rocky domains. A large number of Ancestral Beings turned to stone at their final resting place. At several locations within 'stone' country traditional Aboriginal elders can point to where people are said to have been locked inside the rock, when caves were sealed by Ancestral Beings such as *Namarodo*, sometimes depicted as a giant fisherman in rock-paintings (Taçon 1989: 251; Chaloupka 1993: 60). On occasion, it is said, one can still hear the people pounding on the inside of the rock, trying to get out.

In the most recent period of rock-art production, from about 4000 years ago to the present, it was important to renew paintings in order to tap into the Ancestral power believed to be retained within the rocky landscapes the Ancestral Beings created (Taçon 1989; 1991: 197):

> The retouching and repainting changed the shelter art back from dull to brilliant, and allowed Aborigines to make contact with the continuing cycle of spiritual and physical existence. In the process it reaffirmed the Aboriginal past and present for the artists and their extended families. It also helped ground them in both time and space. Through painting, as well as myth and ritual, Aboriginal creativity became united with natural creativity, and Aborigines intensified their links and bonds with the larger natural and supernatural world.

Rock-engraving and evidence from the earliest landscapes

The oldest evidence of some sort of concern with inner rock-worlds comes from rock-engravings rather than rock-paintings. Across northern Australia, from the Kimberleys through to Arnhem Land, there are hundreds of sites with panels, clusters or arrangements of cupules – cup-like indentations 2.5–7.0 cm across and of varying depth but usually quite shallow (< 4 cm). Cupules are among the oldest surviving forms of rock-markings not only in Australia but also in the Americas, Asia, Europe and, significantly, southern Africa. However, they were also made in recent periods; some sites were periodically re-marked and cupules renewed.

The first intensive study of these marks in Australia, which resemble similar forms from other continents, focused on the Keep River region, where twenty-six sites were documented in detail (Taçon *et al.* 1997). A number of patterns were noted in terms of how cupules were arranged at sites; it was concluded that in northern Australia one function of cupules was to mark places, to define boundaries, to link localities, to highlight natural features, and to define spaces within shelters. In other words, cupules were used not only to mark components of landscapes but also to accentuate particular types of spaces and places within landscapes. The most common pattern noted, at almost half the sites, was that cupules were used to mark or accentuate the *outside* edges of natural holes, tunnels and passageways through the rock but not the *insides* (Taçon *et al.* 1997: 95): 'Cupules were not placed inside holes or passageways but rather mark their boundaries or limits. "Inside *versus* outside *versus* other side" is a common, repeated theme.'

Of course, many other sorts of meaning could have been attached to cupule arrangements; those are not accessible to us, owing to the antiquity of most sites (in the order of tens of thousands of years for the oldest cupule sites, substantially pre-dating Dynamic Figures) and a corresponding lack of informed insight. What is important to note in the context of this study is that people were concerned with 'space' and 'place' (cf. Tilley 1994) – highlighting or drawing attention to aspects of the insides of rocky locations in long-lasting ways from soon after initial colonization of an area, region or continent. The ways in which this was done changed or were added to tangibly in the form of rock-art and by intangible ways such as stories, beliefs, ceremonies and so forth. Thus, at the time of contact with Europeans and Asians, a rich artistic and oral history had developed that marked, described and emphasized not only outer landscapes familiar to living humans but also connections to the inner rock-worlds of spirits. This concern with inner and outer landscapes and with marking them is remarkably similar to the hunter-gatherer rock-art of southern Africa.

Southern Africa

Southern Africa has a wealth of many different rock-art traditions such as the finger-painted 'protest art' of the Northern Sotho Bantu-speaking farmers, the geometric motifs of Khoe-speaking herders and the militaristic images of Afrikaans- and English-speaking Boer and British soldiers. But southern Africa is best known for its hunter-gatherer 'Bushman' or 'San' – whom we call 'Bushfolk' in this chapter – rock-engravings and rock-paintings. It is on this rock-art tradition that we focus. Through the work of Wilhelm Bleek (1874), Patricia Vinnicombe (1976), David Lewis-Williams (1981) and subsequent researchers, it is now clear that Bushfolk rock-art is dominantly shamanistic in inspiration and character. Bushfolk rock-art is also enormously variable and nuanced: capable of providing information on aesthetics (Skotnes 1994), economics (Maggs 1971), gender relations (Solomon 1992; Stevenson 1995; Ouzman 1997a), politics (Dowson 1994), long-distance geographic and conceptual relations (Prins and Lewis 1992; Ouzman 1995a; Jolly 1998), and landscape perception and construction (Deacon 1986; 1988; 1997; Ouzman 1996a; 1998a; Solomon 1997).

Rock-art types and distribution

It is useful here to consider the appearance and distribution of rock-engravings and rock-paintings in southern Africa. As a general rule – albeit with exceptions – rock-paintings are found in the more mountainous parts of southern Africa, whilst rock-engravings occur in the dry, relatively flat central interior (Fig. 2.6). These two art forms do not often co-occur in the same region or site.

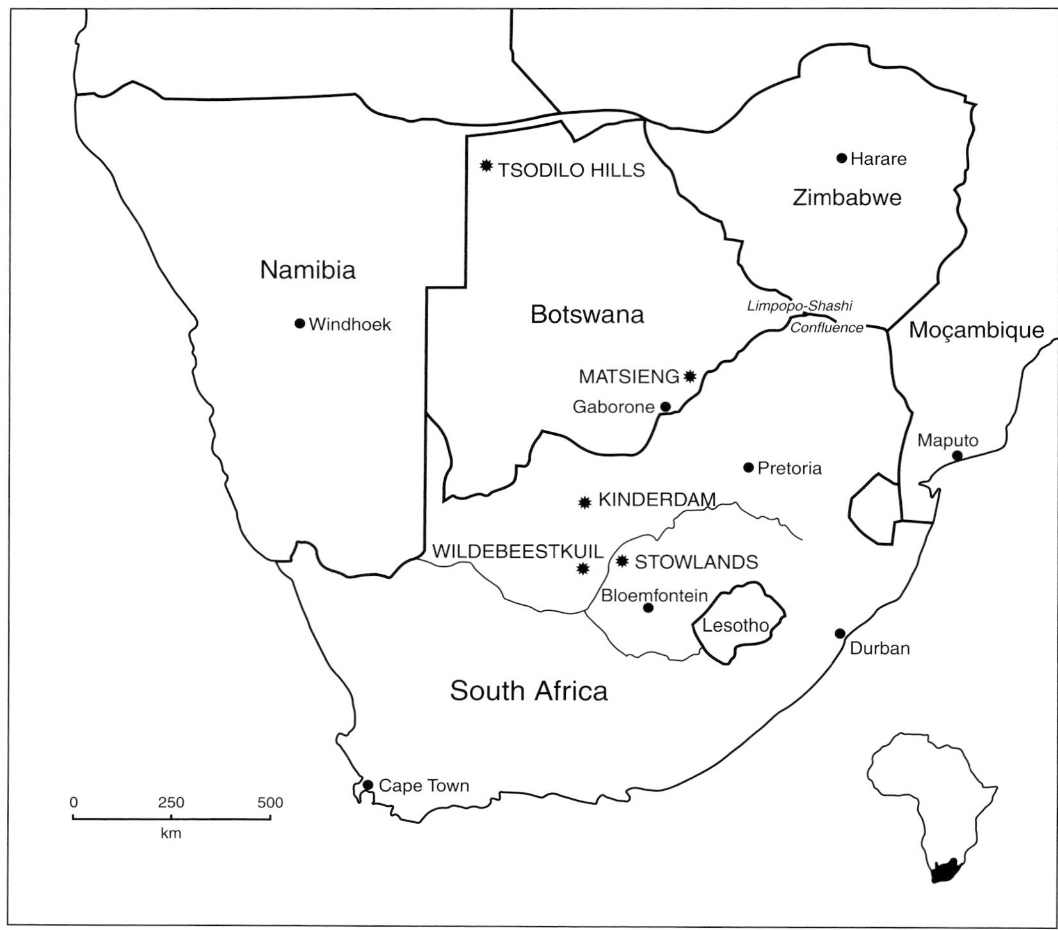

Fig. 2.6. Southern African rock-art sites mentioned in the text.

Rock-paintings are easily located in shallow rock-shelters. These paintings may, in extreme cases, cover a length of over 50 m along a shelter wall; they are more typically clustered in smaller areas, often discontinuously 'pulsed' at intervals on the shelter wall and, very rarely, on the shelter roof. Reds, ochres, blacks and whites are the dominant colours used. These colours are applied to the rock in monochrome, bichrome and polychrome techniques; shading of colours is sometimes employed. Painted images often exhibit fine details and regularly occur in complex panels or 'scenes' that depict a wide variety of imagery. Imagery typically includes: human figures in a variety of postures and contexts, often with items of material culture; frequent animal images; and fantastic hallucinatory spirit-world beings. Plant and landscape features are very rarely depicted. There is also a small percentage of demonstrably entoptic geometric motifs (see Smith and Ouzman in press for discussion of non-Bushfolk, non-entoptic painted and engraved motifs).

Rock-engravings, on the other hand, are typically found on low and iron-rich hills, ridges and rocks in the drier, relatively featureless central interior of southern Africa where there are few rock-shelters. 'Sites' may consist of a single engraved rock or they may consist of over 10,000 engravings that sprawl discontinuously over hundreds of metres, even kilometres – raising serious problems for archaeologists trying to define the 'site' (Ouzman 1998a: 37–9). Imagery tends to be pecked, incised and scraped into the lighter, honey-coloured rock beneath the dark outer cortex of the doleritic diabase. Engraved motifs seldom occur in large, complex panels; it is often difficult to know which images relate to each other, even for those that occur on the same rock. Imagery typically includes human figures, though they are less commonly depicted than in the rock-paintings and seldom occur in group contexts. In the animals, there is a preference for antelope such as eland and gemsbok, and for mega-herbivores such as rhinoceros, elephant and giraffe. Other animals such as baboon, birds, felines, wildebeest and so on occur. Footprints and animal tracks constitute a significant and widespread image class – as is the case in Australia – and there is also a very small percentage of entoptic geometric motifs in the rock-engravings. A great many non-representational marks are encountered at almost every rock-engraving site.

Bushfolk ethnography – conversations about 'being in the world'

Bushfolk ethnography – problematic as it and ethnographic analogy may be – is an unavoidable cornerstone of southern African rock-art research (e.g. Bleek 1874; Vinnicombe 1976; Lewis-Williams 1981; Dowson 1992; Solomon 1992; Deacon and Dowson 1996; Ouzman 1996a). The way in which ethnography and rock-art have been brought together has been achieved through a parallel process of carefully using an informed ethnographic perspective (cf. Lewis-Williams 1991; see also Bernstein 1983) and by analysing the art using formal methods (cf. Chippindale and Taçon 1998).

Though not as explicitly articulated as in Aboriginal Australia – possibly because we non-Bushfolk miss many metaphors, nuances and inflections contained in Bushfolk ethnography – inner and outer landscapes were important concerns for Bushfolk, as they are for most people. They focused their attention on 'the rock' – in particular on rocks, hills, mountains and waterholes (e.g. Deacon 1986; 1988; 1997; Dowson 1992; Solomon 1992; Ouzman 1996a; 1998a) – and on how people from the outer world related to each other, to the outer landscape and to the places and beings of the inner, spirit world. Consider, for example, the following conversation of the /Xam Bushfolk man Dia!kwain in 1875 (in Bleek and Lloyd 1911: 399–401):

> The wind does thus when we die, our [own] wind blows; for we, who are human beings, we possess wind; we make clouds, when we die. Therefore, the wind does thus when we die, the wind makes dust, because it intends to blow, taking away our footprints, with which we had walked about while we still had nothing the matter with us; and our footprints, which the wind intends to blow away, would [otherwise still] lie plainly visible. For, the thing would seem as if we still lived. Therefore, the wind intends to blow, taking away our footprints.

The pathos and bathos in this are moving, speaking of the transience of human life and the place of people in the universe. The philosophy certainly presages Heidegger's concept of 'being in the world' (Heidegger 1962; Haar 1993: 35–42). But lurking beneath and between the words is an overriding concern with place – with the inner place to which one goes after death, with the inner 'mindscape' of humanity (cf. Ouzman 1998b) and with the people, places and relations one leaves behind. A contemporary of Dia!kwain, //Kabbo (literally 'Dream' – he was a shaman) conversed with the ethnographers Wilhelm Bleek and Lucy Lloyd, telling them of his intended journey home. This conversation, like Dia!kwain's, has pathos but also irony as //Kabbo's 'home' – especially the social nexus of which he was once part – no longer existed (//Kabbo 1873, in Bleek and Lloyd 1911: 300–1):

> My fellow men are those who are listening to stories from afar, which float along; they are listening to stories from other places. For, I am here [Cape Town prison]; I do not obtain stories; because I do not visit, so that I might hear stories which float along.

Either in jail or in the custody of his ethnographers-cum-pupils, in the Cape, far from his home country, //Kabbo was unable to 'obtain stories', unable to function as a full member of Bushfolk society. By not being able to visit people, to maintain and renew relationships with favourite places, to tell and to listen to 'stories', //Kabbo lost his identity. This tense process of alienation and dis-connection is more explicitly voiced in one of Dia!kwain's conversation-poems known as 'The Broken String'. In this piece the 'string' is used as a metaphor to describe one's sense of rootedness and empathy within a social and geographic nexus. With the arrival of black and then white colonists into southern Africa, this nexus altered fundamentally; though Bushfolk often adapted successfully at times in places, even to the extent of fundamentally altering the nexus of the colonists, ultimately the rock-art-producing Bushfolk communities succumbed to genocide, assimilation and cultural strangulation. Dia!kwain (1875, in Bleek and Lloyd 1911: 236–7) comments on this process:

> People were those who
> Broke for me the string.
> Therefore,
> The place became like this to me,
> On account of it,
> Because the string that which broke for me.
> Therefore,
> The place does not feel to me,
> As the place used to feel to me,
> On account of it.
> For, The place feels as if it stood open for me,
> Because the string has broken for me.
> Therefore,
> The place does not feel pleasant to me,
> On account of it.

In the midst of this volatile process of dispossession and alienation, a time during which 'ringing sound in the sky' (*ibid.*) ceased to resonate, Bushfolk seemed to focus more than ever on that which was undeniable and constant – the rock and rock-art. Over the last millennium or so Bushfolk rock-art seems to have been used more forcefully than before to maintain and intensify connection to places. In fact, new rock-art traditions with a dominant concern with the political and apocalyptic seem to have arisen, though they retained strong shamanistic tones (e.g. Campbell 1986; Dowson 1994; Ouzman and Loubser 2000).

This change in focus is unlikely to be just a modern product; Bushfolk rock-art undoubtedly went through many shifts in emphases and expression during its 30,000 year or more span. Apart from shamanism, a common thread uniting Bushfolk rock-art is its concern with landscape, in particular with the inner spirit world.

Rock-painting and the inner world

Most southern African rock-art research has focused on Bushfolk rock-paintings for many reasons – their visual clarity, detail and density and their location in areas of traditional, excavation-centred archaeological research. A major breakthrough in rock-art landscape research came with Lewis-Williams and Dowson's (1990) paper in which they pointed out that the rock face, far from being a neutral support for rock-art imagery was, in fact, considered by Bushfolk to be as important as the rock-art it supported. The rock was considered a permeable entity that separated the outer world of ordinary experience from an extra-ordinary inner spirit world. Unlike the 'heaven' and 'hell' of Judaeo-Christian thought which have tended to become abstract deictic devices, the Bushfolk spirit world profoundly affected daily life and was believed to be concrete – populated with real, if extra-ordinary, people and beings, having definable places and *loci*. The principal anthropomorphic inhabitants of this world were the Spirits of the Dead who, like the *Mimi* in northern Australia, were desirous of human company, though they were dangerous and unpleasant (e.g. Barnard 1992: 114–15, 257–60). This desire for contact was shared by living people in the outer world, resulting in an eternal struggle between the living and the dead; the shaman travelled back and forth between worlds as champion of the living. Another inhabitant of the spirit world was a trickster deity whom the /Xam called /Kaggen (e.g. Orpen 1874; Lewis-Williams 1981: 117–26; Barnard 1992: 84–5). Again, /Kaggen shows parallels to Australian Ancestral Beings in that he is a powerful being but he is also mischievous, curious and fallible. He and many other spirit world beings regularly visited the outer world.

The most compelling material evidence of the presence of these beings in the outer world is provided by the many examples of animals, humans, therianthropes and fantastic hallucinatory beasts that, like the Australian 'Simple Figures with Boomerangs', are painted emerging from or entering into cracks, steps, folds and such like in the rock face (e.g. Fig. 2.7). By adding an extra axis of depth to the horizontal and the vertical of the rock-art panel, we are now in a position to make the conceptual shift from 'seeing' the rock-paintings as images painted *on to* the rock to understanding these images as being visions of the spirit world *emergent*. More complexly, in many cases, the image *was* the spirit world being. So Bushfolk rock-paintings are not two-dimensional renderings of three-dimensional objects 'out there'. That which is being seen is not a representation, but constitutes a thing in itself (cf. Lewis-Williams 1998). This situation is analogous to certain northern Australian rock-paintings, which are also sometimes believed to be a painting by an Ancestral Being, rather than being a human-authored representation; often the Being is said to be just inside. The painting's three-dimensionality is present but its 'depth' has yet to emerge from behind the rock face in a taut, tantalizing relationship with inner and outer worlds. Sometimes, the 'depth' does emerge, when the imagery is liberated from the rock by flickering firelight or when seen by people in heightened and altered states of consciousness. Certain symbolic and visual literates, typically shamans, were often able to use 'natural' landscape features to create three-dimensionality (e.g. Ouzman 1998a: 34–7).

Southern African rock-paintings enjoy another obvious connection to the landscape – rock-art pigments. The 'classic' Bushfolk rock-paintings of Lesotho's Maluti mountains and South Africa's Drakensberg mountains appear to have been made with exotic pigment. This pigment – a form of micaceous ochre or haematite – comes from the high basalt layers that overlie the Clarens Formation 'cave sandstone' in which the bulk of the rock-paintings are found. To obtain this micaceous ochre would most often have required a journey or trade that spanned 20–100 km – quite a distance in this archaeologically well-populated region over the last 2000 years. One would have had to negotiate a number of social and trade relations. Obtaining pigment probably represented considerable social ingenuity and manipulation, making the pigment a prestige item worthy of still further special treatment

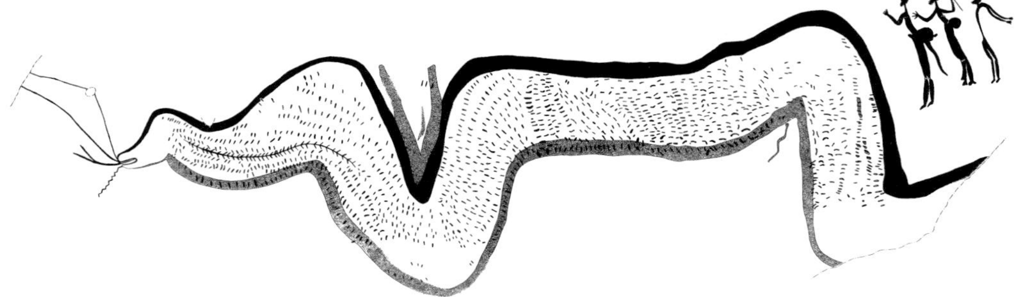

Fig. 2.7. Redrawing of a rock-painting of a fantastic serpent emerging from a step/crack in the rock, central South Africa. Black represents red, stipple represents ochre, dashed lines represent the step/crack in the rock face. Snake measures 1050 mm.

(e.g. How 1970: 35). And we know that the blood and fat of certain potent animals, such as the eland, were used to mix pigment into paint (Lewis-Williams 1986: 11), making the pigment, the paint and the image a powerful entity (see also Lewis-Williams 1998). Part of the power or potency of the image/entity derived from the nexus of social relations and exotic powerful substances that went into its production, each of these constituent parts having a geographic referent.

Rock-engraving and contacting the inner world

Very different geography and rock-art – Bushfolk rock-engravings – tell another story. Unlike rock-paintings, rock-engravings have received relatively little interpretative research attention (Morris 1988; Dowson 1992; Ouzman 1995b; 1996a; 1996b; 2001 are the best examples; see also the monumental quantitative work of Wilman 1968; Scherz 1970; Fock and Fock 1984). Despite the relative lack of interpretative research, it was through a study of rock-engravings that Janette Deacon (1986; 1988) was able to introduce landscape archaeology to southern African archaeology.

Deacon's pioneering work was long overdue: the ethnography that has been used so successfully to inform us of the meaning of Bushfolk rock-paintings was, in fact, gleaned from people who lived in rock-engraving areas and whose relatives had made rock-engravings (Bleek and Lloyd unpublished manuscript L.V. 4. page 5963, reverse; see also Deacon and Dowson 1996). Just as rock-paintings are best considered spirit world visions, even emergent spirit world beings, so rock-engravings inform us of a concern with the inner spirit world beyond the visible rock surface – by virtue of the engraving technique itself. The very act of engraving – removing the dark outer rock cortex to expose the lighter, honey-coloured rock beneath – places the engraved image either directly within the spirit world or in a somewhat ambiguous space, part way into the inner spirit world but still visible and tangible from the outer ordinary world. These engraved images are thus both ambiguous – belonging simultaneously to two worlds – and enabling, in that they show the possibility of permeability and journey between the two worlds. Unlike painting on rock, the act of engraving is very immediate, requiring the engraver to feel each incising, pounding or scraping action, to hear the rock resonate with each blow and to smell the strange rock smell so released. There is abundant evidence in the Bushfolk rock-engraving corpus that cutting, hammering, rubbing and touching engraved

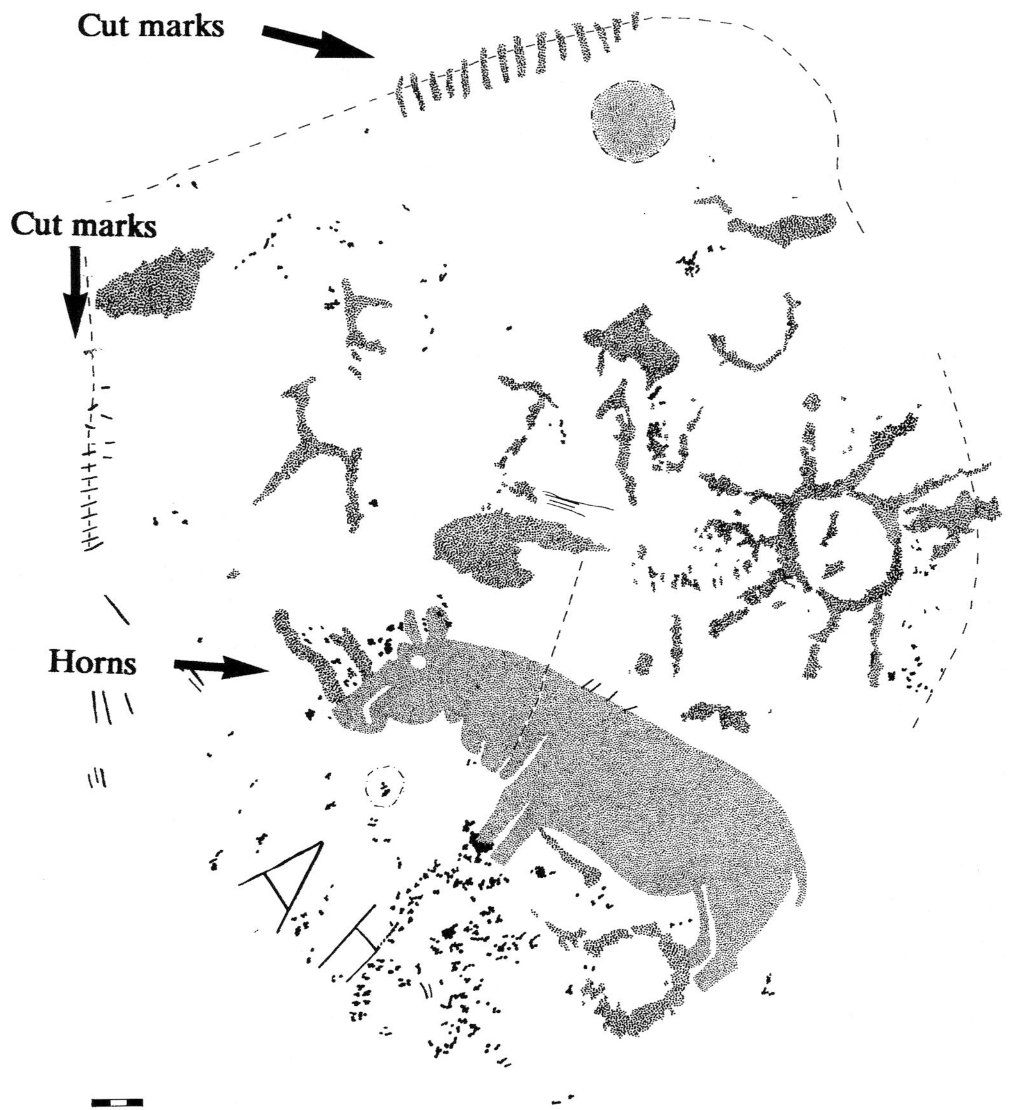

Fig. 2.8. Redrawing of a rubbed and hammered 'rhinopotamus' engraving from Stowlands, central South Africa. Notice also the parallel cut marks on the rock margin. Scale bar is 30 mm.

rocks and images as well as unengraved rocks at engraving sites was an important and widespread practice (Fig. 2.8; Ouzman 1996a; 1996b; see Yates and Manhire 1991 for the rubbing of rock-paintings). Engraved images, as something at least partly of the spirit world, were touched so as to tap into their potency and to connect with another reality (Ouzman 2001).

Rock-engraving techniques offer many possibilities for expressing the belief in inner and outer landscapes. In addition to engraving, cutting, hammering, pounding and so on, one way

Fig. 2.9. Purposefully incompletely engraved images of eland, Wildebeestkuil, central South Africa. Scale bar is 30 mm.

of intensifying the extra-ordinariness of certain rock-engravings that was extensively explored by Bushfolk engravers was not to engrave certain body parts. A limited range of animals – typically eland, rhinoceros, elephant and hallucinatory rain-animals – were purposefully left incomplete. These animals have one or a combination of missing legs, heads, backlines and other body parts. These 'missing' body parts are not a result of taphonomic factors or carelessness: the visible parts are typically carefully and deeply engraved, and finished off where the missing part should be (e.g. Fig. 2.9). Further militating against these images being merely incomplete and mitigating for their being purposeful is the deliberate placement of these incomplete animals within larger rock-engraving arrangements.

Rock-engraving arrangements

In 1998, we visited twenty-three rock-engraving sites to discern and describe better the patterning of these incompletely engraved animals. The reason for this focused exercise was to overturn the tacit assumption that southern African rock-engraving sites lack a discernible internal structure (but see Morris and Mngqolo 1995: 4–5; Ouzman 1996a; 1996b). While the structure of rock-painting sites can be teased out using Harris matrices (e.g. Chippindale and Taçon 1993; Loubser 1993: 352–81) or by considering subject-matter, manner, composition, the placement of imagery and the properties of the rock-painting site (e.g. Ouzman 1997b), rock-engraving sites appear atomistic, 'higgledy-piggledy' and lacking an internal structure. But this is a misleading appearance; by conducting basic archaeology – mapping the sites – it is possible to discern patterns and trends. At some sites discerning these patterns was hindered by the fact that some engravings had been removed by collectors, curators and other vandals during the nineteenth and early to mid-twentieth centuries. However, at three sites we obtained significant results: Wildebeestkuil, Stowlands and Kinderdam.[2] At several other sites we were able to supplement these data. Furthermore, one of us (Ouzman) has documented the patterning of incomplete and hallucinatory creatures at another eighteen rock-engraving sites.

These three sites each consist of a low hill sprinkled with dark volcanic rocks and boulders which have been marked with depictions of animals, humans, fantastic creatures, non-representational marks, and so on. Though these 'hills' are no more than 20–30 m higher than the surrounding topography, they are experienced as 'mountains'. Standing on top of these 'hills', one is often able to see for many kilometres, across the flat, relatively featureless terrain, often through an almost impossibly broad 360° vista; one gains the powerful feeling of being suspended between heaven and earth (see also Bernbaum 1990). This, allied with the visible rock-engravings – themselves suspended between the outer and inner landscapes – would have created a powerful numinous feeling for Bushfolk.

[2] We divulge the names only of managed rock-art sites.

Wildebeestkuil

Wildebeestkuil, now developed by the !Xun and Khwe Bushman communities, is located in the Kimberley District of South Africa's Northern Cape Province (Fig. 2.6); it consists of a low hill 250 m long overlooking a seasonal pan or *kuil*. The hill has three peaks on which over 320 engraved motifs cluster (Morris 1987). One cluster comprises eight engraved animals, five of which are incomplete. The incompleteness of these figures creates the impression that they are moving into or out of the rock surface. These eight animal depictions are found in a 2.6 sq. m area on the highest part of the hill. The animals have been placed on boulders chosen or arranged to form a rectangle that has its sides facing the cardinal directions (Fig. 2.10). The boulders, generally less than 0.5 m high, range in length from 0.5 to 1.1 m and in width from 0.3 to 0.7 m. Examining this arrangement of boulders and images beginning at the north-western tip and moving counter-clockwise along each side of the rectangle we found the following. The western side of the rectangle is formed by boulders 1 m apart, which bear an engraved rain-animal and a headless eland (Fig. 2.10: 1). The southern side of the rectangle consists of boulders 2.5 m apart. The same headless eland on the westernmost boulder is aligned with the easternmost boulder, which has a backless eland engraved on it (Fig. 2.10: 2). This same backless eland begins the eastern side of the rectangle; 1 m north of it is a boulder on which a backless rhino is depicted (Fig. 2.10: 3). The rectangle is completed along its northern end by the same backless rhino that links up with the original rain-animal at which this examination of the rectangle began (Fig. 2.10: 4). Between these incomplete animal engravings there are three

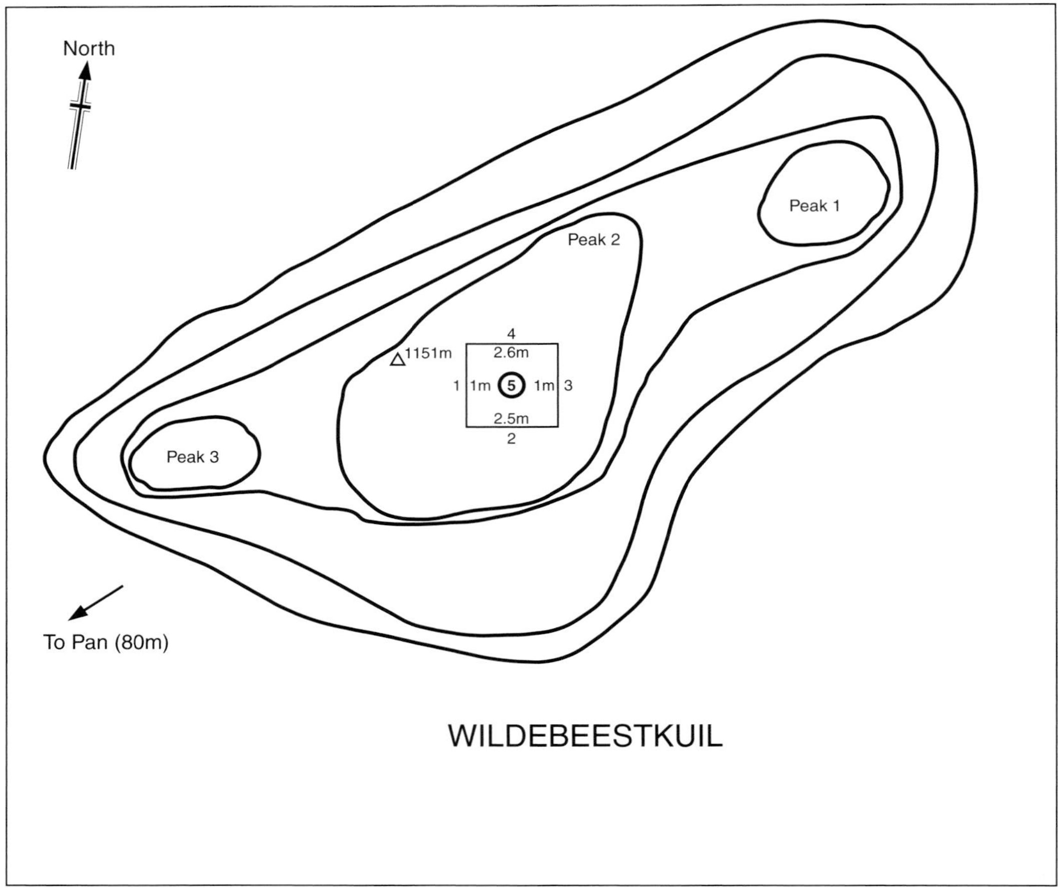

Fig. 2.10. Map of rock-engraving arrangement at Wildebeestkuil, central South Africa. Numbers refer to rocks on/in which incompletely engraved animals have been placed; spatially defining rock-engraving arrangements.

unidentifiable quadrupeds, one of which is incomplete. In the centre of the rectangle there is a stone containing a depiction of another headless eland (Fig. 2.10: 5). This landscape feature very deliberately marks or accentuates the peak of the Wildebeestkuil hill and the cardinal directions (the directions themselves being unimportant but the structure they belie being of prime importance). Through the imagery, the notion of another aspect to the world, below and in the rock, is made manifest. In addition, the imagery combines with the hill, which overlooks a seasonal pan that is for part of the year a water-hole and thus another potential nodal point between inner and outer landscapes.

Stowlands

Stowlands consists of a solid hill overlooking the large Vaal River in the Boshof District of South Africa's Free State Province (Fig. 2.6). It covers an area of over 5000 sq. m with over 342 engraved motifs (Morris and Mngqolo 1995: 4; Ouzman 1998c). Like Wildebeestkuil, Stowlands has an arrangement of three incompletely engraved animals. This cluster is not on the peak of the hill but is located part way down the eastern slope,

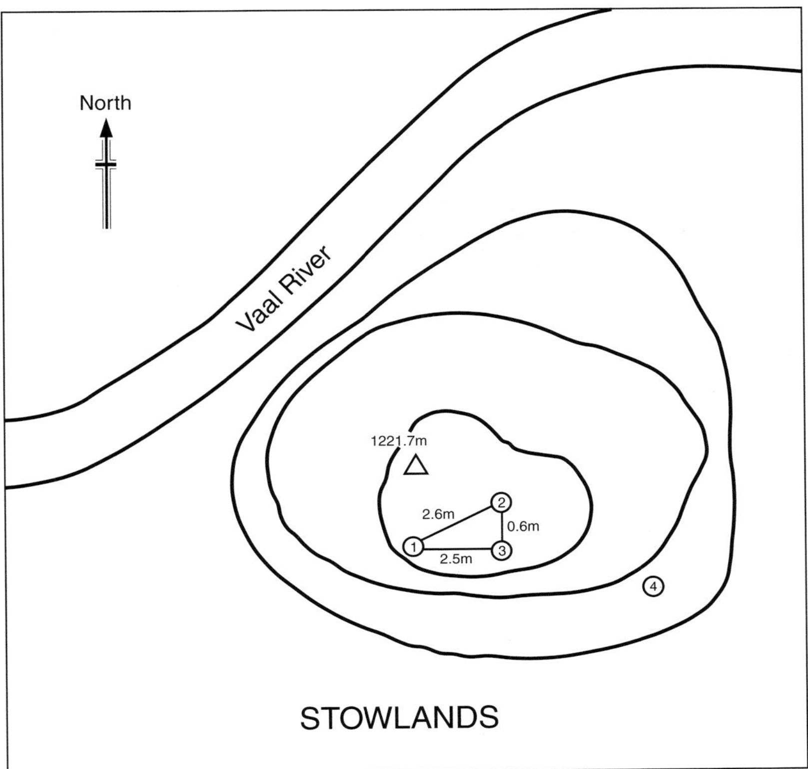

Fig. 2.11. Map of rock-engraving arrangement at Stowlands, central South Africa. Numbers refer to rocks on/in which incompletely engraved animals have been placed; spatially defining rock-engraving arrangements.

less than a quarter of the way to the bottom. This time three boulders form a triangle (Fig. 2.11). Towards the southern end is a boulder bearing a backless eland (Fig. 2.11: 1). To the north-east, at a bearing of 40° and distance of 2.6 m, there is a boulder with the head and neck, but not the body, of a jackal emerging from a crack in the rock (Fig. 2.11: 2). To the north-east of the backless eland, at a bearing of 70° and distance of 2.5 m, is another backless eland 0.6 m from the bodyless jackal (Fig. 2.11: 3). The boulders are comparable in size to those at Wildebeestkuil, if not a bit smaller. Once again, a geometric landscape feature has been formed, and a presumably significant space defined, with images of incomplete animals that appear to move in or out of the rock. There is only one other incomplete animal at the site, a backless gemsbok placed about 55 m to the east and downslope (Fig. 2.11: 4).

Kinderdam

Kinderdam consists of a large, low-lying and boulder-strewn hill in the Vryburg District of South Africa's North-West Province (Fig. 2.6). This is a complex site with over 2400 engraved motifs (Fock and Fock 1984: 73), two rock-gong complexes, and at least three geometric features defined by incomplete and/or supernatural creatures (Fig. 2.12). These three geometric features, in turn, form a huge triangular-shaped space about 20 m by 50 m by 47 m, with one of the hill's two peaks in the centre.

The first cluster of boulders, forming a triangle, bears a backless eland (Fig. 2.12: 1a), a

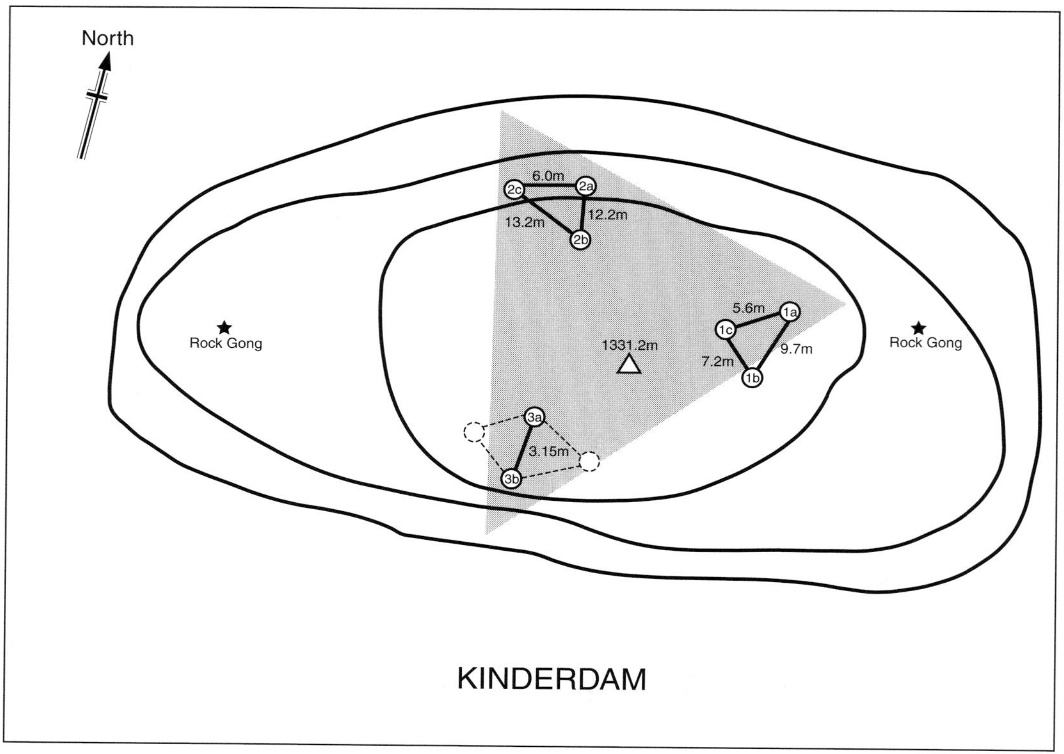

Fig. 2.12. Map of rock-engraving arrangement at Kinderdam, central South Africa. Numbers refer to rocks on/in which incompletely engraved animals have been placed; spatially defining rock-engraving arrangements.

legless eland (Fig. 2.12: 1b) and a fantastic large composite beast (Fig. 2.12: 1c). The composite beast covers much of the largest boulder, measuring 2 m by 1.6 m; composed of elephant, rhino, giraffe, cow and human body parts (Fig. 2.13), it is reminiscent of north Australian composite Rainbow Serpents. The composite beast is surrounded by twenty-three human figures engaged in a medicine dance, situating the panel within an inner shamanic mindscape. The boulder with the legless eland also has an engraved human figure while that with the backless eland has two human figures. One side of the triangle, formed by the backless and legless elands, 9.7 m apart, is perfectly aligned north–south.

The second feature also forms a triangle: boulders contain depictions of a bird-headed figure (Fig. 2.12: 2a), a backless eland (Fig. 2.12: 2b) and a second backless eland (Fig. 2.12: 2c). One of the elands and the bird-headed figure form a side of this triangle that is again aligned north–south. The boulders on which they are found are 12.2 m apart, measuring 2 m by 0.9 m by 0.3 m and 0.6 m by 0.3 m by 0.1 m respectively. The smaller boulder may have been purposefully positioned to form the alignment.

The final feature consists of two boulders, one with an eland head *sans* body (Fig. 2.12: 3a) and the other with a legless eland (Fig. 2.12: 3b). They are 3.15 m apart, on an angle of 20°. A search of the surrounding area failed to turn up a third element – possibly a result of the intensive collecting that took place at this site – but to the immediate east and west there are engraved eland with very faint, almost non-existent heads on otherwise strongly incised bodies (Fig. 2.12). Perhaps they are a variation of the emerging/disappearing animal theme.

Fig. 2.13. Fantastic composite creature, Kinderdam, central South Africa. Stipple represents pecked engraving. Overall length of creature is 100 cm.

As noted above, together the three features form a much larger 'sacred' space around the hill's eastern peak. There are literally thousands of other engraved boulders at Kinderdam but they contain depictions of complete figures: the incomplete/supernatural subjects, clustered to form specific features, are not randomly distributed. Together they define three small, focused landscape features which, in turn, map the largest purposeful feature we have recorded. Cardinal/purposeful directions and hill peaks are emphasized, as well as the inner world to which the creatures depicted appear more appropriately to belong.

These rock-art arrangements of incomplete animals at Wildebeestkuil, Stowlands and Kinderdam were not built up randomly or by chance: they are the product of a structured mind at work. Perhaps, like the Inuit ivory and soapstone carvers who merely release what is already inside the ivory and soapstone, so the Bushfolk engraver chose certain of the many rocks present at engraving sites, to make manifest or apparent the structure that already existed there, in the inner spirit-world just beyond the rock surface. This is not to say the unengraved rocks are not important: they provide a general texture and – like the pauses between musical notes (e.g. Lewis-Williams 1998) – they are an essential, if partly invisible constituent of rock-engraving arrangements.

Cupules as evidence of the earliest landscapes

Cupules, technically a form of rock-engraving or 'petroglyph', are more accurately categorized as a distinct category of rock and place marking that is intimately associated with inner and outer landscapes (Taçon *et al.* 1997). In several regions in southern Africa there are panels and clusters of cupule-covered boulders and shelter walls that are remarkably similar to those encountered in northern Australia. As in northern Australia, the southern African cupules appear to be the oldest surviving form of rock-art – they are often covered with thick silica skins, and they are always underneath other forms of rock-engraving and rock-painting. There is also very little ethnographic evidence relating to cupules (but see Campbell *et al.* 1994), suggesting that they belong to a time beyond the ken of ethnographic memory. Though still very much at a nascent stage, southern African cupule research has already revealed significant clusters of cupule-bearing sites. There are, for example, at least twelve complex cupule sites at Tsodilo Hills in Botswana (see Robbins and Campbell 1989; Robbins 1990; Robbins *et al.* 1996; Ouzman and Taçon's field-notes 1998), and there are more than twenty cupule sites in the Limpopo–Shashi confluence area of northern South Africa and southern Zimbabwe (Cnoops and Eastwood 1995; Ouzman and Taçon's field-notes 1998; Eastwood pers. comm.).

Southern African cupules are not, however, arranged to emphasize smallish natural holes/tunnels as they are in northern Australia. Rather, cupules are often found on long horizontal walls of rock, following natural cracks and contours (Fig. 2.14). Cupule panels can also lead either towards large, thin cracks at the ends of shelters that contain small tunnels or towards long and narrow passageways a person could walk through. Cupules were also used to mark large, prominent boulders, sometimes a series of boulders, in order to highlight shelter entrances, exits, passageways and chimneys. Importantly, many cupule sites – up to 30 per cent – are found in hidden locations (e.g. Campbell *et al.* 1994; Robbins *et al.* 1996), emphasizing the importance of a local, embedded knowledge of the local landscape and connectedness with it. Cupules in these sites, which are small and preclude large gatherings of people, do not have an open and public aspect. Rather, these sites appear to have a more specific inward focus: perhaps the act of making a cupule was something intense and private that allowed the maker, already within a cave-like space, to commune with an inner world and its inhabitants, rather than the cupule being a genuflection to and mimicking of the outer landscape. In that case,

Fig. 2.14. Cupules from Zimbabwe following natural 'panels' defined by cracks and folds in the rock.

the cupule itself was, in some ways, an accidental by-product of the act of communicating with an inner landscape, albeit it in the idiom of that landscape (cf. Taussig 1993).

Cupules and their association with tunnels, cracks and passageways through the rock are purposeful; as in Australia, they hint at a very ancient concern with an inner world that was accessible at certain rocky locales.

Rock-art and the antiquity of inner and outer landscapes

Both northern Australian and southern African hunter-gatherers held strong beliefs in an inner world within stone and an outer world of human experience. Moreover, these beliefs appear to extend back many thousands of years in each case.

Cupules – as a form of rock-marking or, better still, a way humans could genuflect to and communicate with a landscape by mimicking natural rock and topographic features within it – provide strong or 'thick' support to the hypothesis of an ancient concern with inner rock-worlds. These cupules, the oldest surviving rock-marking in both northern Australia and southern Africa, then seem to have attracted subsequent marks in the form of rock-engravings and rock-paintings as well as less tangible attention such as ceremonies, conversations, songs, the touching of rock and image, and so on. These rock-engravings and paintings, with their more easily definable content or subject-matter, represented an important shift in landscape perception, focusing attention more dominantly on the image. This is not to say, however, that focus was ever shifted away from the landscape. Rock-paintings, for example, tended to encourage a more inward-looking mien, with the rock face and the imagery on/in it forcing a more focused contemplation of a limited set of images, their connections with each other and with the rock support or, more accurately, with the world within this rock. Rock-engravings, on the other hand, were themselves of the world within the rock, though they could be seen and touched by people from the outer world. The openness of most rock-engraving sites meant that the distinction between image, rock and landscape was only ever weakly present. We are still in a position where we are seldom certain of the reasons why hunter-gatherers chose to mark certain places with rock-art. Was every rock a potential connection to the inner world? Perhaps rock-art was a way of 'helping' those locales at which the spirit world was somehow less manifest? Some sites no doubt had unusual physical properties (e.g. Ouzman 1997b) or were places at which unusual natural phenomena regularly occurred (see Taçon 1999). For example, the iron-rich rock-engraving sites of southern Africa regularly attract spectacular lightning strikes. Maybe rock-art sites were opportunistically and practically decided upon. Whatever the reasons for their selection, all rock-art sites share a sense of permanence that derives from the rock of which they are made and the promise of an inner world this rock offers.

Did the ideas relating to worlds within stone develop during the symbolic explosion that shook the human world about 50,000 years ago? Or are they much older, perhaps originating with the dawn of anatomically modern humans well over 100,000 years ago? Could they be even older still, a product of humans being mammals, with an instinctive need to demarcate, defend and mark a territory? More prosaically, most hunting-and-gathering societies, especially those that are shamanistic, tend to have a common concept that they are 'people of the land', land that has had many lives and that exists on many planes, being both of the present and of the eternal. This form of social organization sets up the necessary conditions for belief in multiple landscapes; but are the *conditions* of this form of social organization also sufficient? A significant hindrance to answering this question is the relative intractability of rock-art to chronometric dating. In any event, rock-art is almost certainly the most visible manifestation of a basic human practice of marking and socializing places, a practice that began with a human presence, then through our minds and sometimes by means of the visible marks made to objects and places. Although rock-art is by no means the oldest way of socializing spaces, it is perhaps the most theoretically informed means by which to approach these ancient concerns. For example, time – not just dating – remains relatively undertheorized in landscape studies (but see Fabian 1983; Gell 1992; Gosden 1994; Taçon 1994: 126) and may be the next substantive contribution rock-art landscape studies can make to archaeology.

The sheer number of surviving rock-art sites in northern Australia and southern Africa – several hundred thousand sites spread over millions of square kilometres – attests to an enduring and deeply held preoccupation with maintaining connection with the spirit world by producing marks and images on rock. At certain special places, this concern was so strongly felt and articulated that it has endured across time and cross-culturally. Examples in Australia include some of the larger and more accessible geological and rock-art sites, such as Uluru in central Australia or Ubirr in the Top End of the Northern Territory, which have become tourist 'meccas' (Taçon 1990: 31).

In southern Africa, one of the most incredible sites where there is a both current and enduring belief in an inner rock-world is the 'creation' site of Matsieng, in the Kgatleng District of southern Botswana (Fig. 2.6; Wilman 1918; 1919; Molyneux 1921; Walker 1997; see also Ouzman 1995b). This Bushfolk rock-art site comprises 117 engravings, mostly of human and

Fig. 2.15. Engraved footprints around a natural sandstone sump, Matsieng creation site, southern Botswana.

feline footprints clustered around three natural rock-holes or sumps in a sandstone plate (Fig. 2.15; Walker 1997). Many of the prints face the three rock-holes, suggesting a movement from the outer world to an inner world beyond the water-hole. This movement has, however, been reversed by the current-day Tswana who have appropriated this Bushfolk site as their premier creation site at some point in the last 2000 years. It was here that Matsieng, the first or archetypal Tswana, emerged from the inner stone-world into the outer world, leaving his footprints and those of the animals he brought with him on the then soft rock of the still-new world. Past and present merge via an appropriated iconography and shared belief in inner and outer landscapes.

Now the soft rock of the new world has hardened and our need to produce rock-art has largely been replaced by our need, not to genuflect to and respect the landscape, but violently to control it, to make it ours and bend it to our will. A built environment and vague notions of worlds in outer space have replaced the belief in inner worlds. The inner worlds are still immanent, but they are now seldom manifest. Possibly it is the archaeologist's role to remind people of our history, of the inner place whence we have come, we, all the people of this land (*vide* Haar 1993):

> We have ears because we can listen
> Attentively, and thanks to this we may
> Hear the song of the Earth, its trembling
> And quivering that remains undisturbed by
> The huge tumult that man has, for the time
> Being, organised on its exhausted surface

Exhausted surfaces increasingly crumble into the future, for today most rock-art sites are not renewed, repainted or retouched; indeed contemporary western ideas about 'conservation' forbid such things and Indigenous Peoples' ways of life have forcibly changed over the past few centuries. However, the ancient messages left to us, like so many notes in bottles floating across great oceans of time and space, should not be forgotten. In terms of those explored in this study, one of the most important is that the world is not always what it seems. Our everyday experience is literally at the surface of reality; a much larger universe lies beneath if we are willing and able to enter into it.

Acknowledgements

We thank the Australian Museum, the National Museum, South Africa, and the South African Archaeological Society Kent Bequest for funding this research. The financial assistance of the National Research Foundation (South Africa): Social Sciences and Humanities towards this research is also acknowledged. Opinions expressed in this chapter, and conclusions arrived at, are those of the authors and are not necessarily to be attributed to the National Research Foundation. We thank Ed Eastwood for generously sharing unpublished information on South African and Zimbabwean cupule sites. He, Sally Brockwell, Paddy Carlton, Richard Fullagar, Leslie Head, Andrew McWilliam, Ken Mulvaney, Oscar Motsumi, Andrew Reid, Karim Sadr, Alinah Segobye, Biddy Simon, Nick Walker and others are thanked for their help and hospitality in the field. We thank the editors and anonymous referees for commenting on a draft of this manuscript. All photographs and drawings are by the authors except for Fig. 2.3 drawn by Fiona Roberts and Fig. 2.13, which was redrawn by Gabriel Tlhapi.

References

Barnard, A. 1992. *Hunters and herders of southern Africa: a comparative ethnography of the Khoisan peoples*. Cambridge: Cambridge University Press.

Bernbaum, E. 1990. *Sacred mountains of the world*. San Francisco, CA: Sierra Club Books.

Bernstein, R. J. 1983. *Beyond objectivism and relativism: science, hermeneutics, and praxis*. Oxford: Blackwell.

Bleek, W. H. I. 1874. Remarks on J. M. Orpen's 'A glimpse into the mythology of the Maluti Bushmen', *Cape Monthly Magazine* (NS) 9: 10–13.

Bleek, W. H. I. and L. C. Lloyd, 1911. *Specimens of Bushmen folklore*. London: George Allen.

Unpublished notebooks. University of Cape Town, Jagger Library.

Boas, F. 1966. *Kwakiutl ethnography*. Chicago, IL: University of Chicago Press.

Bord, J. and C. Bord. 1988. *A guide to the ancient sites in Britain*. London: Paladin Grafton Books.

Brady, J. E. and W. Ashmore. 1999. Mountains, caves, water: ideational landscapes of the ancient Maya, in W. Ashmore and A. B. Knapp (eds.), *Archaeologies of landscape: contemporary perspectives*: 124–45. Oxford: Blackwell Publishers.

Brody, A. 1984. *Kunwinjku bim: western Arnhem Land paintings from the collection of the Aboriginal Arts Board*. Melbourne: National Gallery of Victoria.

Campbell, A. C., L. H. Robbins and M. L. Murphy. 1994. Oral traditions and archaeology of the Tsodilo Hills Male Cave, *Botswana Notes and Records* 26: 37–54.

Campbell, C. 1986. Images of war: a problem in San rock art research, *World Archaeology* 18: 255–65.

Carpenter, E. 1961. Comment on H. Haselberger's 'Method of studying ethnographic art', *Current Anthropology* 2: 361–3.

Carroll, P. J. 1977. Mimi from western Arnhem Land, in P. Ucko (ed.), *Form in indigenous art: schematisation in the art of Aboriginal Australia and prehistoric Europe*: 119–30. Canberra: Australian Institute of Aboriginal Studies.

Chaloupka, G. 1984. *Rock art of the Arnhem Land Plateau: the paintings of the Dynamic Figure style*. Darwin: Northern Territory Museum of Arts and Sciences.

1993. *Journey in time: the world's longest continuing art tradition*. Chatswood, NSW: Reed Books.

Chippindale, C. and P. S. C. Taçon. 1993. Two old painted panels from Kakadu: variation and sequence in Arnhem Land rock art, in J. Steinbring, A. Watchman, P. Faulstich and P. S. C. Taçon (eds.), *Time and space: dating and spatial considerations in rock art research*: 32–56. Melbourne: AURA. Occasional Publication 8.

1998. The many ways of dating Arnhem Land rock art, north Australia, in C. Chippindale and P. S. C. Tacon (eds.), *The archaeology of rock art*: 90–111. Cambridge: Cambridge University Press.

Chippindale, C., B. Smith and P. S. C. Taçon. 2000. Visions of Dynamic power: archaic rock-paintings, altered states of consciousness and 'clever men' in western Arnhem Land (NT), Australia, *Cambridge Archaeological Journal* 10(1): 63–101.

Clottes, J. 1995. Perspectives and traditions in Palaeolithic rock art research in France, in K. Helskog and B. Olsen (eds.), *Perceiving rock art: social and political perspectives*: 35–64. Oslo: Instituttet for Sammenlignende Kulturforskning.

Clottes, J. and J. D. Lewis-Williams. 1998. *The shamans of prehistory: trance and magic in the painted caves*. New York: Harry N. Abrams.

Cnoops, C. and E. Eastwood. 1995. Stone Age and Iron Age rock engravings, *Die Rooi Olifant* 11: 1–4.

David, B., I. McNiven, V. Attenbrow, J. Flood and J. Collins. 1994. Of Lightning Brothers and White Cockatoos: dating the antiquity of signifying systems in the Northern Territory, Australia, *Antiquity* 68: 241–51.

Deacon, J. 1986. 'My place is the Bitterpits': the home territory of Bleek and Lloyd's /Xam San informants, *African Studies* 45: 135–55.

1988. The power of place in understanding southern San rock engravings, *World Archaeology* 20: 129–39.

1997. My heart stands in the hill: rock engravings in the Northern Cape, *Kronos* 24: 18–29.

Deacon, J. and T. A. Dowson (eds.) 1996. *Voices from the past: /Xam Bushmen and the Bleek and Lloyd collection*. Cape Town: Witwatersrand University Press.

Dowson, T. A. 1992. *The rock engravings of southern Africa*. Johannesburg: Witwatersrand University Press.

1994. Reading art, writing history: rock art and social change in southern Africa, *World Archaeology* 25: 332–45.

Dyer, C. (ed.) 1994. *Kunwinjku art from Injalak 1991–1992: the John Kluge Commission*. North Adelaide, SA: Museum Art International.

Edwards, R. 1979. *Australian Aboriginal art: the art of the Alligator Rivers region, Northern Territory*. Canberra: Australian Institute of Aboriginal Studies.

Eliade, M. 1974. *Shamanism: archaic techniques of ecstasy*. Princeton, NJ: Princeton University Press.

1975. *Rites and symbols of initiation: the mysteries of birth and rebirth*. New York: Harper and Row.

1996. *Patterns in comparative religion*. Lincoln, NE: University of Nebraska Press.

Fabian, J. 1983. *Time and the other: how anthropology makes its subject*. New York: Columbia University Press.

Fagg, M. C. 1997. *Rock music*. Oxford: Pitt-Rivers Museum. Occasional Paper in Technology 14.

Flood, J. 1997. *Rock art of the Dreamtime: images of ancient Australia*. Pymble: Angus and Robertson.

Fock, G. J. and D. M. L. Fock. 1984. *Felsbilder in Südafrika 2: Die Gravierungen auf Kinderdam und Kalahari*. Cologne: Böhlau Verlag.

Gell, A. 1992. *The anthropology of time: cultural constructions of temporal maps and images*. Oxford: Berg.

Gosden, C. 1994. *Social being and time*. Oxford: Blackwell.

Grinsell, L. V. 1976. *Folklore of prehistoric sites in Britain*. Newton Abbot: David and Charles.

Haar, M. 1993. *The song of the earth: Heidegger and the grounds of the history of being*. Bloomington, IN: Indiana University Press.

Heidegger, M. 1962. *Being and time*. Oxford: Blackwell.

How, M. W. 1970. *The mountain Bushmen of Basutoland*. Pretoria: van Schaik.

Jacobs, H. 1975. A Seneca legend: the origin of stories, in A. Chapman (ed.), *Literature of the American Indians*: 25–9. New York: Meridian.

Jolly, P. 1998. Modelling change in the contact art of south-eastern San, southern Africa, in C. Chippindale and P. S. C. Taçon (eds.), *The archaeology of rock-art*: 247–67. Cambridge: Cambridge University Press.

Lewis, D. 1988. *The rock paintings of Arnhem Land: social, ecological, and material culture change in the post-glacial period*. Oxford: British Archaeological Reports. International Series 415.

Lewis, D. and D. Rose. 1988. *The shape of the Dreaming: the cultural significance of Victoria River rock art*. Canberra: Aboriginal Studies Press.

Lewis-Williams, J. D. 1981. *Believing and seeing: symbolic meanings in southern San rock paintings*. London: Academic Press.

1986. The last testament of the southern San, *South African Archaeological Bulletin* 41: 10–11.

1991. Wrestling with analogy: a methodological dilemma in Upper Palaeolithic art research, *Proceedings of the Prehistoric Society* 57: 149–62.

1998. Quanto?: the issue of many meanings in southern African rock art research, *South African Archaeological Bulletin* 53: 86–97.

Lewis-Williams, J. D. and T. A. Dowson. 1990. Through the veil: San rock paintings and the rock face, *South African Archaeological Bulletin* 45: 5–16.

Loubser, J. H. N. 1993. A guide to the rock paintings of Tandjesberg, *Navorsinge van die Nasionale Museum* 9: 345–83.

Maggs, T. M. O'C. 1971. Some observations on the size of human groups during the Late Stone Age, *South African Journal of Science* Special Issue 2: 49–53.

Molyneux, A. J. C. 1921. Note on rock engravings at Metsang, Bechuanaland Protectorate, *South African Journal of Science* 17: 206.

Morris, D. 1987. *Excursion to Wildebeestkuil, Klipfontein, Driekopseiland and Vaalpan, 4th Rock Art Colloquium*. Kimberley: McGregor Museum.

1988. Engraved in place and time: a review of variability in the rock art of the Northern Cape and Karoo, *South African Archaeological Bulletin* 43: 109–21.

Morris, D. and S. Mngqolo. 1995. Survey of the rock engraving site of Stowlands. Unpublished report. Kimberley: McGregor Museum and National Monuments Council.

Mountford, C. P. 1956. *Records of the American–Australian expedition to Arnhem Land* 1: *Art, myth and symbolism*. Melbourne: Melbourne University Press.

1978. The Rainbow-Serpent myths of Australia, in I. R. Buchler and K. Maddock (eds.), *The Rainbow Serpent: a chromatic piece*: 23–97. The Hague: Mouton.

1981. *Aboriginal conception beliefs*. Melbourne: Hyland House.

Mulvaney, K. 1996. What to do on a rainy day: reminiscences of Mirriuwung and Gadjerong artists, *Rock Art Research* 13(1): 3–20.

O'Connor, S. 1995. Carpenter's Gap Rockshelter 1: 40,000 years of Aboriginal occupation in the Napier Ranges, Kimberley, WA, *Australian Archaeology* 40: 58–9.

Orpen, J. M. 1874. A glimpse into the mythology of the Maluti Bushmen, *Cape Monthly Magazine* (NS) 9: 1–13.

Ouzman, S. 1995a. The fish, the shaman and the peregrination: San rock paintings of mormyrid fish as religious and social metaphors, *Southern African Field Archaeology* 4: 3–17.

1995b. Spiritual and political uses of a rock engraving site and its imagery by San and Tswana-speakers, *South African Archaeological Bulletin* 50: 55–67.

1996a. Thaba Sione: place of rhinoceroses and rain-making, *African Studies* 55: 31–59.

1996b. An engraved touchstone from the Free State, *The Digging Stick* 13: 1–3.

1997a. Between margin and centre: the archaeology of southern African bored stones, in L. Wadley (ed.), *Our gendered past: archaeological studies of gender in southern Africa*: 71–106. Johannesburg: Witwatersrand University Press.

1997b. Hidden in the common gaze: collective and idiosyncratic rock paintings at Rose Cottage Cave, South Africa, *Navorsinge van die Nasionale Museum, Bloemfontein* 13: 225–56.

1998a. Toward a mindscape of landscape: rock art as expression of world-understanding, in C. Chippindale and P. S. C. Taçon (eds.), *The archaeology of rock art*: 30–41. Cambridge: Cambridge University Press.

1998b. Mindscape, in P. Bouissac (ed.), *Encyclopedia of semiotics*: 419–21. New York: Oxford University Press.

1998c. Public rock art sites of the Free State: Stowlands, *Culna* 53: 5–6.

Ouzman, S. and J. Loubser. 2000. Art of the apocalypse: Southern Africa's Bushmen left the agony of their end time on rock walls, *Discovering Archaeology* 2(5): 38–45.

2001. Seeing is deceiving: rock-art and the non-visual, *World Archaeology* 33(2): 237–56.

Ouzman, S. and L. Wadley. 1997. A history in paint and stone from Rose Cottage Cave, South Africa, *Antiquity* 71: 386–404.

Prins, F. E. and H. Lewis. 1992. Bushmen as mediators in Nguni cosmology, *Ethnology* 30: 133–47.

Robbins, L. H. 1990. The Depression Site: a Stone Age sequence in the northwest Kalahari Desert, Botswana, *National Geographic Research* 6: 329–38.

Robbins, L. H. and A. C. Campbell. 1989. The Depression Rock Shelter site, Tsodilo Hills, *Botswana Notes and Records* 20: 1–3.

Robbins, L. H., M. L. Murphy, A. Campbell and G. A. Brook. 1996. Excavations at the Tsodilo Hills Rhino Cave, *Botswana Notes and Records* 28: 23–45.

Roberts, R., R. Jones and M. A. Smith. 1990. Thermoluminescence dating of a 50,000-year old human occupation site in northern Australia, *Nature* 345(6271): 153–6.

1993. Optical dating at Deaf Adder Gorge, Northern Territory, indicates human occupation between 53,000 and 60,000 years ago, *Australian Archaeology* 37: 58.

Roberts, R., G. Walsh, A. Murray, J. Olley, R. Jones, M. Morwood, C. Tuniz, E. Lawson, M. Macphail, D. Bowdery and I. Naumann. 1997. Luminescence dating of rock art and past environments using mud-wasp nests in northern Australia, *Nature* 387: 696–9.

Scherz, E. R. 1970. *Die Felsbilder in Südwest-Afrika* 1: *Die Gravierungen in Südwest-Afrika ohne den Nordwesten des Landes*. Cologne: Böhlau Verlag.

Skotnes, P. 1994. The visual as a site of meaning: San parietal painting and the experience of modern art, in T. A. Dowson and J. D. Lewis-Williams (eds.), *Contested images: diversity in southern African rock art research*: 315–30. Johannesburg: Witwatersrand University Press.

Smith, B. W. and S. Ouzman. In press. Introducing the Khoe herder rock art of southern Africa, *Current Anthropology*.

Solomon, A. 1992. Gender, representation and power in San ethnography and rock art, *Journal of Anthropological Archaeology* 11: 291–329.

1997. Landscape, form and process: some implications for San rock art research, *Natal Museum Journal of Humanities* 9: 57–73.

Stevenson, J. 1995. Man – the – shaman: is it the whole story? A feminist perspective on the San rock art of Southern Africa. Unpublished MA dissertation. Johannesburg, University of the Witwatersrand.

Stewart, H. 1982. *Looking at Indian art of the Northwest Coast*. Vancouver, BC: Douglas and McIntyre.

Taçon, P. S. C. 1989. From Rainbow Serpents to 'x-ray' fish: the nature of the recent rock painting tradition of western Arnhem Land, Australia. Unpublished PhD thesis. Canberra, Australian National University.

1990. The power of place: cross-cultural responses to natural and cultural landscapes of stone and earth, in J. Vastokas (ed.), *Perspectives of Canadian landscape: Native traditions*: 11–43. North York: Robarts Centre for Canadian Studies/York University.

1991. The power of stone: symbolic aspects of stone use and tool development in western Arnhem Land, Australia, *Antiquity* 65: 192–207.

1992. 'If you miss all this story, well bad luck': rock art and the validity of ethnographic interpretation in western Arnhem Land, Australia, in M. J. Morwood and D. R. Hobbs (eds.), *Rock art and ethnography*: 11–18. Melbourne: Archaeological Publications. Occasional AURA Publication 5.

1993. An assessment of rock art in the Mann River region, Arnhem Land, N. T. Unpublished report to the Bawinanga Aboriginal Corporation and the Djomi Museum.

1994. Socialising landscapes: the long-term implications of signs, symbols and marks on the land, *Archaeology in Oceania* 29(3): 117–29.

1999. Identifying ancient landscapes in Australia: from physical to social, in W. Ashmore and A. B. Knapp (eds.), *Archaeologies of landscapes: contemporary perspectives*: 33–57. Oxford: Blackwell.

Taçon, P. S. C. and S. Brockwell. 1995. Arnhem Land prehistory in landscape, stone and paint, *Antiquity* 69: 676–95.

Taçon, P. S. C. and C. Chippindale. 1994. Australia's ancient warriors: changing depictions of fighting in the rock art of Arnhem Land, N.T., *Cambridge Archaeological Journal* 4: 211–48.

1998. An archaeology of rock-art through informed methods and formal methods, in C. Chippindale and P. S. C. Taçon (eds.), *The archaeology of rock-art*: 1–10. Cambridge: Cambridge University Press.

2001. Transformation and depictions of the First People: animal-headed beings of Arnhem Land, N.T., Australia, in K. Helskog (ed.), *Theoretical perspectives in rock-art research: Alta II conference proceedings*: 171–210. Oslo: Novus.

Taçon, P. S. C., R. Fullagar, S. Ouzman and K. Mulvaney. 1997. Cupule engravings from Jinmium-Granilpi (northern Australia) and beyond: exploration of a widespread and enigmatic class of rock markings, *Antiquity* 71: 942–65.

Taçon, P. S. C. and M. Garde. 1995. Kun-wardde bim, rock art from central and western Arnhem Land, in M. West (ed.), *Rainbow, Sugarbag and Moon: two artists of the stone country: Bardayal Nadjamerrek and Mick Kubarkku*: 30–6. Darwin: Museum and Art Gallery of the Northern Territory.

Taçon, P. S. C., M. Wilson and C. Chippindale. 1996. Birth of the Rainbow Serpent in Arnhem Land rock art and oral history, *Archaeology in Oceania* 31: 103–24.

Taussig, M. 1993. *Mimesis and alterity: a particular history of the senses*. London: Routledge.

Taylor, L. 1987. 'The same but different': social reproduction and innovation in the art of the Kunwinjku of western Arnhem Land. Unpublished PhD thesis. Canberra, Australian National University.

1990. The Rainbow Serpent as visual metaphor in western Arnhem Land, *Oceania* 60: 329–44.

Taylor, T. 1997. *The prehistory of sex: four million years of human sexual culture*. London: Fourth Estate.

Tilley, C. 1994. *A phenomenology of landscape: places, paths and monuments*. Oxford: Berg.

Vastokas, J. and R. Vastokas. 1973. *Sacred art of the Algonkians: a study of the Peterborough petroglyphs*. Peterborough, Ont.: Mansard Press.

Vinnicombe, P. 1976. *People of the eland: rock paintings of the Drakensberg Bushmen as a reflection of their life and thought*. Pietermaritzburg: University of Natal Press.

Walker, N. 1996. *The painted hills: rock art of the Matopos*. Gweru: Mambo Press.

1997. In the footsteps of the Ancestors: the Matsieng creation site in Botswana, *South African Archaeological Bulletin* 52: 95–104.

West, M. (ed.). 1995. *Rainbow, Sugarbag and Moon: two artists of the stone country: Bardayal Najamerrek and Mick Kubarkku*. Darwin: Museum and Art Gallery of the Northern Territory.

Wilman, M. 1918. The engraved rock of Loe, Bechuanaland protectorate, *South African Journal of Science* 15: 631–3.

1919. The engraved rock of Kopong and Loe, Bechuanaland protectorate, *South African Journal of Science* 16: 443–6.

1968. *The rock engravings of Griqualand West and Bechuanaland, South Africa*. Cape Town: Balkema.

Yates, R. and A. Manhire. 1991. Shamanism and rock paintings: aspects of the use of rock art in the south-western Cape, South Africa, *South African Archaeological Bulletin* 46: 3–11.

3

Rock-art, landscape, sacred places: attitudes in contemporary archaeological theory

Daniel Arsenault

The dominant concerns of archaeology through the 1980s were with the entities that could be measured, things as 'real and measurable' as settlement patterns and ecological constructs, as Brian Molyneaux remarked in the quotation with which this chapter begins. But the Algonkian case to which Daniel Arsenault then moves makes a key point of the 1990s, a point that could be made equally from other regions such as Aboriginal Australia (as in the preceding chapter). Austere and elegant at their best, those 'objective' models do not capture the world as the Native Peoples of Canada see and experience it. So useful theory will have to deal with rock-art and landscape as much more than the results of things 'real and measurable'. How much that has been a concern of the 1990s, and will be a concern of the 2000s, is shown by the references for this chapter, nearly all from that newer decade. Even the pioneers, like Molyneaux, are from the late 1980s; the older literature does not seem to recognize the need for that approach to be through actual human experience and at the same time to offer some practical research means to attain it. Hence the need is for an actual archaeology of the sacred, as that is expressed in sacred images, sacred places, sacred landscapes.

> [T]here is a need in archaeology for a systematic approach to sites in which the veneer of symbolic significance and use of the landscape is treated as a relevant category in the cultural use of space, as real and measurable as settlement patterns or ecological construct.
>
> Molyneaux 1987: 25

Sacred landscape as symbolic construct

The Canadian Shield is just one region of the world where archaeologists seek to understand indigenous cultures with a complex spiritual and symbolic life, looking for significant 'trees' so as to reconstruct the ancient 'forest of symbols' (Turner 1967). But our models and methods are often thin and mechanistic; they deal with hypothetical people whose experience is driven by controlling ecological pressures and whose response is a hyper-rational one of calculated economic efficiency. When they are elegant, these models may have some kind of austere attraction; but they seem scarcely effective to capture how the Native Peoples of Canada see, know and value the world. For the studies of some archaeological materials – lithics or animal bones – those models at least have the merit of dealing with archaeological traces one can record and study with some confidence as simple objects, as things alone: these bones show that those animals were killed and butchered, these stones show that rock was taken from that place or produced and used in this way. Physical materials are involved in the rock-art – the Canadian Shield painted sites are made with red ochre – but the central points of the rock-art, why the figures were made, why they were made at that place, what meanings they held, are not easily to be approached through a focus on the material objects alone.

In this chapter I consider some conceptual tools and a methodology that can be used to articulate these aspects of aboriginal ideology difficult to grasp in the archaeological record but – as Denton (1993: vii–viii) points out – 'existing' none the less as the 'invisible landscape' (see Burch 1971; Bender 1995a: 1), part of the Native cultural landscape in Canada. Arguing about profound reconsiderations and transformations of analytical categories used today in archaeological research, my point is to include novel yet solid research directions and analytical approaches for the archaeology of Native cultural landscape so as to understand better the complexity of the symbolic and material aspects of hunter/fisher/gatherer relationships with their environment in the past and how it could be revealed in the archaeological record.

This chapter explores theoretical aspects to this central point in rock-art research. Their application to the Canadian boreal forest sites is reported in a complementary chapter in the present volume: Daniel Arsenault, 'From natural settings to spiritual places in the Algonkian sacred landscape: an archaeological, ethnohistorical and ethnographic analysis of Canadian Shield rock-art sites' (pp. 289–317).

Initially, pertinent questions regarding this aspect of Native life-ways were articulated in order to develop an explanatory model. For example, what vestiges and archaeological traces are associated with sacred sites and landscapes? What kind of information can be obtained about ideological and socio-political aspects of Native life-ways from the analysis of the material evidence, using models other than 'adaptive strategies' used traditionally by archaeologists working in the Canadian Shield? Also, is it realistic to discuss, from an archaeological point of view, the symbolic aspects of the topographic elements (anomalies and extremes), otherwise often associated with functionalist explanations, and to include at the same time in our analysis information obtained from Native people? In short, can prehistorians reconstruct Native sacred sites and explain their complexity, intricacies, transformations and changing character in long-term history? I have attempted to examine rock-art sites with these questions in mind, formulating new selection criteria to investigate different sectors of a site's natural landscape, my principal aim being the identification of sites which would have been considered adequate or preferred 'sacred sites' by Native Peoples in the past. This renewed concern regarding both the process of site identification and the methodology required to carry it out, however, requires a critical look at how 'wilderness' has been perceived in previous archaeological studies in its untamed and sometimes hostile state (see Kulchyski 1998: 21–2; McCormack 1998: 26), based obviously on our modern Occidental criteria of comfort. This would enable us to place the sites examined in my study in their proper analytical contexts. First and foremost, however, I must define what I mean by the archaeology of landscape.

What is an archaeology of landscape?

There are several ways of studying landscape in archaeology and, more generally, in anthropology. In their introduction to a group of texts on recent archaeological theory, Robert Preucel and Ian Hodder (1996: 32–3) list four different approaches to studying historical landscapes, which may be placed in a conceptual continuum leading from Nature to Culture.

Four approaches: between nature and culture in landscape

The first approach is interested in the theme of the environmental conditions that existed historically in a given physical milieu. It seeks to identify and evaluate what natural resources – animal, vegetal, mineral or water – were available in a region before trying to understand the ways in which they might have been exploited by humans at specific moments in history, or over long periods of time. Working principally from palaeo-environmental reconstructions (see Rapp and Hill 1998; Evans and O'Connor 1999) and palaeo-economic models (e.g. Butzer 1982), this essentially functionalist approach defines landscape above all in terms of ecological niches and their particular resources. In such a context, archaeological interpretation is limited to a normative depiction of human activities; human beings appear as anonymous and anodyne, their actions most often oriented towards basic needs – food, lodging, reproduction. It is impossible with this approach to bring out the cultural attitudes, for example, that might have been held by different social actors with respect to the resources they were exploiting.

A second approach uses elements of systemic models taken from the field of cybernetics; it is typical of processual thought in archaeology. Here the landscape is seen as a dynamic system (the natural environment) within which another (cultural) system that includes human society is integrated in an open and interdependent manner. In this approach, human presence is marked by the ways in which it modifies the landscape, particularly by occupying certain sites and exploiting local resources; that triggers a series of modifications and internal readjustments to the system destined to bring it back into equilibrium. From an archaeological perspective, this systemic approach is interested in the physical variables that bring about evolution within a cultural system, that is, the culture's continuous evolution within its natural landscape. As well, this approach seeks to situate sites related to occupation or exploitation within a structured context, highlighting the economic and technological activities that took place at these sites and in the surrounding region (e.g. Binford 1981; 1989). The approach thus seeks to explain different socio-cultural processes at work in these societies – subsistence modes, power and exchange networks, occupation strategies, changes in social structure, etc. – on the basis of archaeological remains, site distribution and other natural and human factors that may have led to the observed changes (e.g. Cameron and Tomka 1996). Although this approach places a greater emphasis on human society, it still has the disadvantage, as does the first approach, of leaving aside the cosmology, myths and symbolism that give meaning to the natural landscape. The systemic approach seems not to see any point in wondering what individuals and societies might have *thought* about the natural environment with which they were in continuous relationship; as a result, it lacks appropriate methods for recording the physical remains of symbolic phenomena (Bradley 1994: 95; Tilley 1994: 22).

These two approaches to studying landscape are often complementary. Explicitly or not, they have often been applied in the archaeological study of hunters–fishers–gatherers, and especially so in Québec (e.g. Chapdelaine 1989; 1995;

Plourde 1993; Plumet *et al.* 1993; Chalifoux and Burke 1995; Langevin *et al.* 1995; Moreau 1996).

The two other approaches are more recent, and interested in landscape's socio-cultural dimension. In their analyses, they include aspects of what E. S. Burch (1971) called the 'non-empirical environment'. They see the landscape not only as a reservoir of material resources to be exploited, but also as a social phenomenon that is the object of symbolic practices and representations. From this point of view, the natural landscape may be compared to an artefact in material-culture studies: it is an object that, within a given time and space, may be culturally appropriated by social agents during the course of their actions and interactions. Using principles taken from the 'post-processual' paradigm in archaeology (e.g. Shanks and Tilley 1987a; 1987b; Hodder 1991; Preucel 1991), these approaches place humans at the heart of archaeological thought.

The first of these newer approaches sees the natural landscape as a place where power is manifested, as a field *of*, and *for*, social action whose size varies according to the scale of the analysis and within which different power relations (dominance, resistance, etc.) are exercised among groups and individuals (see Bender 1995a: 11; Thomas 1995: 29–30; Tilley 1996: 162, 173; Zedeño 1997: 86; also Bender 1995b; Helskog and Olsen 1995). Landscape also appears as a mediator within the matrix of social relations, in that it is an integral part of the dynamic of social relations among individuals and groups. Case-studies using this approach reveal that archaeological and anthropological indicators of power within the landscape are highly varied and take any number of physical forms. For example, a relationship between power and landscape may be seen in a closely controlled access to resources which are considered to be precious. These resources may be material (Zedeño 1997) or they may have a symbolic character (see Bradley 1997) as in the case of sacred sites where access is controlled by built elements that direct individuals along specific paths (Moore 1992). Power relations can also be seen in examples of contested territorial jurisdiction between groups – which may lead one group to vandalize the sacred sites of the other (Franklin and Bunte 1994). This approach can also shed light on conflict situations where power is divided between rival factions within a group, as reported in Humphrey's (1995) recent study on chiefs and shamans in Mongol communities. A latent tension was detected in the dualistic representation of landscape as constructed by contemporary Mongol society, in which each element was invested by a specific power: the landscape associated with the chiefs' power on the one hand, and the landscape characterized by the shamans' power on the other.

Finally, an approach which remains relatively unused in archaeology defines landscape as the locus, in a very broad sense, of individual and collective experiences. A natural environment is not only seen as such by the people who live there, but is also charged with complex meanings; it is a crucible for symbolic and material expression by the individuals and groups that are in its presence (Ucko 1994: xviii; Thomas 1995: 28–9). Tilley (1994) has called this the phenomenological approach to landscape archaeology. During a lifetime of experiences with their attendant perceptions, sentiments, emotions, ideas and memories, social actors enter into a relationship with the places they frequent and, as a result, give meaning to these places. It is in this context that actors construct their own identities, both individually and collectively (Tilley 1994: 14–15; see also Theodoratus and LaPeña 1994: 22). Seen this way, cultural landscapes are constructed by designating and forging places through human experience. A 'contextual' analysis – in Hodder's (1987; 1991) term – of how sites are created and re-created, of their distribution within a given territory, of the routes that link them and, finally, of the 'cultural topography' formed by all these interrelated elements, can help reconstruct the cosmology of the people who produced the landscape. All these elements reveal how humans experience a natural landscape which thus becomes a cultural landscape.

Natural and cultural in a social landscape

As can be seen in these two approaches, any 'natural' landscape or environment may be revealed as being 'cultural' in the eyes of its social actors. The landscape varies according to the position that each actor occupies and the activities they carry out, according to the sum of all the relationships they maintain with the landscape and among themselves within this landscape (Zedeño 1997: 86; Cummins and Whiteduck 1998: 6–7; Little Bear 1998: 18–19), which can be expressed through a wide variety of systems of material and symbolic representations. The new approaches have given archaeologists better conceptual tools for studying material remains with a view to understanding the symbolic aspects and significant values that were attached to the natural landscape in the past by the people who lived there. Only recently have these approaches begun to be applied in Canadian archaeology (cf. Nicholas and Andrews 1997; Smith and Mitchell 1998; also see Wright 1995; 1999).

With these four approaches and their contributions in mind, we may define the archaeology of landscape as an approach which includes the examination of the rock-art sites *per se* as well as both the natural and socio-cultural environments, that is, the totality of the physical and symbolic resources found within a specific region seemingly associated with sacred sites. In my study of the Algonkian-speaking groups (among whom are the Cree, Ojibway, Algonquin, Innu and Attikamekw), the analysis of the natural features, the Native's perception of the environment and the archaeology of sites taken together should lead to an understanding of the manner in which specific sites were selected (pp. 292–307). In other words, how did the natural landscape acquire its cultural significance within one culture or another? How is a natural landscape transformed into a cultural or a sacred landscape? How do sacred sites retain their significance through time? Answers to these questions are of prime importance in our treatment of the rock-art sites located in the Canadian Shield, sites through which we can determine how the Algonkian sacred landscape is defined. The larger Algonkian territory constitutes an ideal, natural and cultural 'laboratory' in which it becomes important to discover the basis for sacred sites selection and visit, and therefore open a window into the larger sacred world (cosmology) of the Native people who inhabited it.

It is important to note, however, that this type of analysis does not exclude archaeological interpretations of 'political', 'economic' and 'aesthetic' Algonkian landscapes. While each of these landscapes can be attributed to specific locales or sites, they constitute parts of a larger cultural landscape, and are subsumed by it: all those landscapes represent an integral part of a whole and are not mutually exclusive. In fact, they overlap one another, contribute to each other, combine with others or oppose one another, existing together and changing through time, forming in this fashion a renewed, global cultural landscape of a society which transforms itself through time. However, the purpose of this study is to explore specific aspects of the cultural landscape, pursuing our hermeneutic approach to articulate different components of ancient cultural landscapes, and putting forward the possibilities and the limits of an archaeology of landscape in the Canadian Shield. Research circumstances there, and this central issue of understanding the landscape as it was perceived by the social actor, have much in common with those facing rock-art researchers in many a region of the world (e.g. Finnestad 1986; Hood 1988; Layton 1992; Sognnes 1994; Ouzman 1998; Whitley 1998).

'Sacred landscape' and its topography

A 'sacred landscape' can be defined as the totality of topographic elements and sectors modified by social actors in an otherwise natural landscape. However, symbolic values are attached to these transformations, specifically in regard to the religious cosmology of a society (see Hubert 1994; Tilley 1994: 33–4). This type of cultural landscape is comprised of elements which can be as varied as natural rock formations, woods, water sources, caves, natural terraces overlooking valleys, temples, buildings or any other architectural structures associated with religious ceremonies, even entire towns or geographic regions – representing the 'sacred land', a notion still encountered to this day in Native traditions – in essence the totality of sites and regions associated with religious practices and representations. Also, this landscape should be inclusive of the trails and waterways used to reach 'sacred' regions or sites, these access routes sometimes representing veritable pilgrimage roads to and from religious sites. Furthermore, hidden elements and non-physical elements which attract people to sites and regions and constitute part of the sacred landscape must be considered an integral part of it. In other words, a sacred landscape is the sum of physical and symbolic elements associated with the 'sacred geography' of a specific religious tradition.

To become a sacred landscape, a selected locale must be transformed by a cultural group to respond to its particular spiritual needs, creating 'specific contexts' (Humphrey 1995: 151). These transformations can include, under one umbrella, sites where spiritual knowledge is taught and rituals performed, sites commemorating significant actions or events accomplished by the 'ancestors', sites where manifestations of spiritual beings or natural forces have been noted in the past, or even sites where icons designate symbols associated with a cult or a religion, and refer for instance to its practices and social positions of its members. In this fashion, a sacred landscape represents a symbolic universe, defined by the interrelations of the individuals who identify themselves with a specific religion, and their relationship to sacred objects and sites which are needed for enacting and performing rituals, therefore expressing the religious values they share in the context of their social practices and obligations (Tilley 1994: 17).

From a material point of view, this type of landscape can reveal a 'topology' – some scholars would say a 'mental map' (Warhus 1997: 8; Lewis 1998: 53; Woodward and Lewis 1998: 3–4) – specific to itself, with its boundaries, its centre (or centres) and periphery, with specific sanctuaries, roads, trails and routes leading to and from sacred sites or locales, where material and symbolic goods and services are made available, transmitted and exchanged (see Molyneaux 1983: 5; Werbner 1989); in this context, religious ideas and other non-material symbols can be widely spread, becoming an intrinsic part of specific exchange networks. From an historical point of view, this landscape might have been modelled by the practice of one or many traditions which were at the foundations of its topology, consequently helping to maintain, reproduce or transform it in the long term. It could have been the site of generations of social actors, individuals or groups, expounding and promoting interests seemingly vital to the group, some interests either converging or diverging from the accepted norm, and that within particular contexts of religious practices. How are we as archaeologists to reconstruct ancient sacred landscapes with their symbolic elements, including sites and regions which were at the very basis of their foundations in ancient times, so as to understand their history and their religious geography and topology, and, by extension, the cosmology from which these physical and symbolic manifestations took their roots?

Formal attempts to define this sacred landscape have resulted from the efforts of a small group of archaeologists (Garwood *et al.* 1991; Carmichael *et al.* 1994). A few years ago, John Chapman (1991) suggested that the topology of the sacred landscape should include dwellings and public buildings, burial sites and specific natural sites, locales where religious rituals and activities could manifest themselves or where religious activities might find their expression. Recently, Maria Nieves Zedeño (1997: 95–6) suggested that other elements of analysis should be added to Chapman's list, including many other types of dated or undated archaeological sites and traces: cairns, quarries and mines, rock-art sites, known portage trails and the like, faunal and floral remains whether included or not in the realm of food-ways, along with analysed archaeological collections, as these data can shed light on the modes of procurement, opening a window on the appropriation, exploitation and transformation of specific locales and regions. This all-encompassing type of analysis could lead to a better understanding of how environments gained religious significance and how sites were selected for religious practices. While the variety of data used in the analysis is of importance in this type of analysis, it is even more significant to proceed into such an exercise with a rigorous contextualization of the analytical elements from the pool of archaeological information, particularly with regards to the natural and cultural environments, each being specific to the site from which it has been drawn (Bender 1995a: 2). These informations are the sole direct source of data which can lead us to an understanding of past social and religious realities (Thomas 1995: 20).

It is evident that the archaeological identification of a sacred landscape may be difficult to articulate if we are limited by the pool of data at hand. When dealing with a large region occupied by small bands of hunter–fisher–gatherers who did not alter or modify their environment substantially, this reality becomes even more striking (Figs. 3.1 and 3.2). However, there are ways to overcome these difficulties by adding to the archaeological information other data taken from contemporary oral history, including studies of

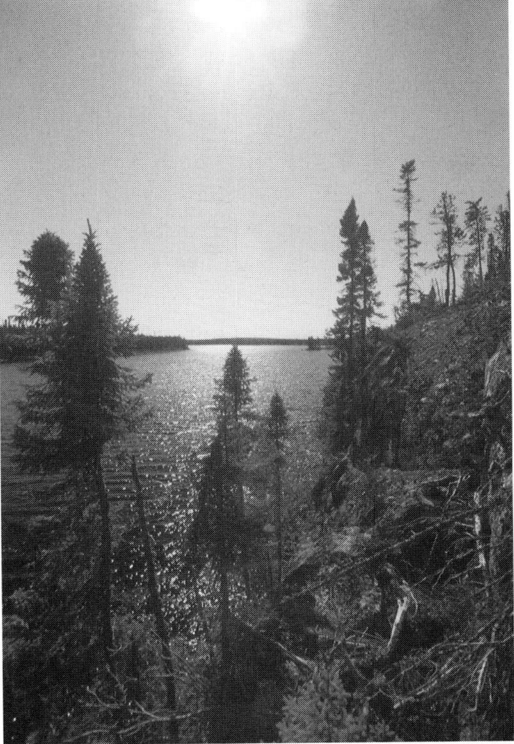

Fig. 3.1. A natural setting could hide a sacred site!

View of a small bay in the north-western part of Lake Nemiskau, traditionally occupied by small bands of Algonkian hunter-fisher-gatherers. This photograph, taken from the summit of a rock formation just above the Kaapehpeshapischinikanuuch site (EiGf-2), offers a good example of how subtle a sacred space and a sacred place can be within the natural landscape when there is no architectural feature to be seen around.

Photograph by Daniel Arsenault, courtesy of PETRARQ.

Fig. 3.2. A Dreaming place.

Distinctive features of the Aboriginal landscapes of Australia are the 'Dreaming places', locales associated with a particular animal, plant or other element in the cultural landscape.

These vertically split rocks in the Arnhem Land escarpment, a great cliff which runs many kilometres through a landscape full of rock-art, are Lightning Dreaming. They make a landmark visible from far away across the woodland below the escarpment.

Photograph by Christopher Chippindale.

aboriginal mythology – information which has survived, albeit modified, sometimes through to this day (see Denton 1997). When archaeological, ethnohistorical and ethnographic information are combined in a contextual study of Algonkian rock-art sites – important cultural traces and symbolic phenomena clearly visible in the archaeology of ancient sacred landscapes (Bradley 1994: 100) – researchers can better grasp material traces in the archaeological data; this will lead eventually to the development of an archaeology of sacred landscape in the Canadian Shield.

Key concepts around which our discussion is articulated are those of the *sacred space*, the *sacred place* and the *sacred landscape*.

The concepts of sacred space and sacred place

Of the concepts of *sacred space* and *sacred place*, no doubt the former is the more abstract. According to Tilley (1994: 10), for example, a space is not simply a neutral container for the social practices that are carried out here, but represents a medium that participates in the actions which 'take place' here. As a social construct, a space becomes intelligible from the moment it becomes an intrinsic element of the events that occur *here* and of the specific forms of social relationships that are manifested *here*. It follows thus that 'the meanings of space always involve a subjective dimension

Fig. 3.3. Visual symbols related to a magic or religious context, some of the few clues still visible on an ancient sacred site.

One of the rock outcrops partly covered with engraved faces on the Qajartalik site (JhEv-1), Hudson Strait, eastern Canadian Arctic. These petroglyphs were made more than 1000 years ago by Dorset people who also reproduced similar human-like faces on their mobiliary art. This type of visual symbol was closely related to the shamanic universe of the Palaeo-Esquimaux and their presence on natural grounds reveals the sacredness of the place even today for some Inuit groups.

Photograph by Daniel Arsenault, courtesy of the Cultural Institute AVATAQ, an Inuit-owned institution in the Nunavik (Arctic Québec).

and cannot be understood apart from the symbolically constructed lifeworlds of social actors' (Tilley 1994: 11). That is to say, from the moment social actors concretely and symbolically appropriate a given physical space, they create a human and social space with lasting significance, even if this significance varies over time as a function of the nature of the actions carried out here, the intentions and interests of the actors present, and the reigning material and symbolic conditions.

As to the example we are concerned with, in order for a physical space to be made sacred, it must acquire a spiritual dimension during the course of religious practices carried out here by social actors, in contexts that are at once socially determined and determinant. A common method of making a space sacred is in the deployment of material and visual symbols expressing the values of this religion (Fig. 3.3). In this context, the cosmology of a given society influences the process through which a space is made sacred, in that it leads social actors to perceive the world they live in and understand it as being linked in precise ways to the religious universe. In other words, this cosmology helps to order and categorize the space itself, in terms of religious practices (see Carmichael *et al.* 1994: 4–5; Price 1994: 260–1; Tilley 1994: 24, 31–3; Richards 1996: 206; Bradley 1997: 6; also Vastokas and Vastokas 1973; Tanner 1979; Sundstrom 1996; Bobiwash 1998). In discussing sacred spaces, many studies in religious anthropology (among others, van Gennep 1969 [1909]: 276; Douglas 1978: 130; Heusch 1986; Werbner 1989; Oakes *et al.* 1998) have shown that different kinds of places, some unusual (e.g. a cave), others quite bare (see Hirsch 1995: 4), may be used for large or small gatherings and for socio-cultural practices with a ritual character. Thus, religious motives may predicate the appropriation of a given space or, at least, influence its one-time symbolic selection for specific individual or collective actions, giving the space a sacred character which it may or may not retain afterwards.

This is especially true for natural sites. In fact, any natural site that is deemed adequate – a beach, a cave (Leroi-Gourhan 1983; Clottes and Lewis-William 1996), a water's edge, a rock outcrop (Vastokas and Vastokas 1973; Rajnovich 1994) or a mountain-top (Reinhard 1992) – may be temporarily transformed into a sacred space for the time needed to carry out the required ritual; then, as soon as the ritual actions are completed, the site loses its sacred condition and returns to its natural state without any real alteration to the site. For the archaeologist, it is clear that such a passing ritual initiation of a site would not leave enough physical traces to allow its past sacred character and associated religious actions to be recognized, or even to allow an evaluation of the extent of the space that was occupied at the time the rituals were carried out (Carmichael 1994: 89). Fortunately, other spaces reserved for the repeated enactment of rituals contain enough material evidence to allow for an archaeological interpretation of their sacredness.

As we can see, a sacred space may be defined as much by the visible and the tangible, as by the invisible and the extrasensory. Precisely because of its abstract nature, the concept of sacred space must be paired with a second notion: the sacred place. A sacred place is defined by the presence of real evidence – material, natural or artefactual – that bears an association with a sacred, symbolic space. In other words, a sacred place is a specific form that is tangibly, materially and socially constructed, to which the sacred space proper is related, regardless of the space's geographic extent. Sacred places, as physical sites that are socially designated and created with the express purpose of marking the presence of religious phenomena, serve to concentrate the spirituality attributed to the surrounding sacred space, that is, they highlight specific religious values or beliefs. What is more, over time these places help to maintain a religious tradition and, by becoming a place of memory and commemoration, to play a role in transmitting the knowledge of historical events and myths that are part of this tradition (see Connerton 1989). A place's symbolic character, much as that of a space, is born of a specific form of relation (here, it is religious) that is established between social actors and their material and spiritual universe; the link with the historical or mythical past that is created in certain places ensures the continuity and reinvention of the religious values attached to those places (Fig. 3.4).

Fig. 3.4. A ceremony performed on a rock-art site.

A ceremony was held on the Nisula site (DeEh-1) by Innu (Montagnais) spiritualists just before my team and I started the analysis of this rock-art site. This kind of ritual was performed for the first time on this site after the local Native people had learned that a very old site had been discovered. For this community this 2000-year-old site, forgotten for so long, is now highly valued and has become again a sacred place for traditional religious activities.

Photograph by Daniel Arsenault, courtesy of PETRARQ.

Archaeology and the sacred

With these notions in mind, it is easier to understand why the periodic return to sacred places scattered over a given territory allows individuals and groups to add meaning to their rituals, to develop their individual and collective experiences as a function of the spiritual instruction they receive and, thus, to construct a memory and a personal and cultural identity during the course of carrying out religious practices in these places (Tilley 1994: 18, 27; 1996: 162). This is all the more so when a sacred place possesses a 'liminary' dimension[1] that is associated with a religious practice, such as symbolic iconography proper to that practice, and allows individuals or groups to experience the 'extraordinary' – that is, those experiences which are outside the normal constraints of everyday life (see Turner 1977: 67–8). This extraordinary experience has the capacity to transform them.

It must be recognized however that, from an archaeological point of view, the sacredness of a site may vary depending on the activities or events which took place here (Zedeño 1997), on the temporary or permanent facilities which were added to it (Bradley 1993; 1997: 12), or on the unique material or symbolic properties that were once attributed to it (Bradley 1993: 17; Carmichael 1994; Cummins and Whiteduck 1998: 5). These fluctuations in sacredness may be due to factors such as a change in the number of people who conducted rituals here (Humphrey 1995: 137), a divergence or convergence of the social actors' interests with respect to the place (Hubert 1994: 16, 18), or the appropriation of the place by new cultural groups during the course of its history (Ucko 1994: xix; Sundstrom 1996). Archaeology allows us to evaluate these variations in sacredness over time, especially for sites that were frequented by different cultural groups (see Garwood *et al.* 1991; Carmichael *et al.* 1994). As Sundstrom illustrates in her study of sacred sites in the Black Hills (1996), when Amerindian groups occupied new territories in Wyoming, Montana and South Dakota, not only did they recognize the existence of sacred sites that were traditionally visited by previous, culturally different groups, but they incorporated the myths and astronomic references of these sites into their own cosmology. We see that the repeated use of sacred places can reveal cultural continuities or discontinuities which leave traces such as monuments with a ritual function as well as residual, more fugitive traces of the activities that were formerly carried out here.

Fig. 3.5. Mont Bego: a prehistoric sacred landscape of ancient Europe inferred archaeologically.

The high and rocky valleys of Mont Bego, in the French Maritime Alps, are filled with later prehistoric rock-engravings, in which a handful of motifs are repeated time after time in closely similar forms. Although there are varied interpretations of its meaning – Lumley *et al.* (1995) see the mountain as a sanctuary of a god of thunder and lightning, whilst Barfield and Chippindale (1997) see its meaning as connected with the masculine role in society – researchers have for a century (Bicknell 1913) been agreed that Mont Bego was a special place, a sacred landscape in prehistoric times.

Photograph by Christopher Chippindale.

While it is true that religious practices such as initiation rites may determine the vocation of some monuments and arranged spaces, it is also true that the appropriation of a place for religious purposes is not necessarily accompanied by the erection of monuments or other kinds of stone formations (Bradley 1991a; Harding 1991). As we have pointed out, the physical integrity of certain sites may be carefully preserved and the nature of the activities which took place

[1] Research done by van Gennep (1969) and Turner's later work (1969) have demonstrated that a ritual space is characterized by a symbolic dimension which may be called 'liminarity'. Liminarity is a condition, or even a state, that expresses the extraordinary aspect of ritual practices, since the latter generally have the effect of placing the participants outside the margins of everyday life, which is shown in concrete ways or through symbolic devices. In the performance of a ritual act, a ritual actor, whether represented by an individual or a group, encounters liminarity either at a particular position in a given space (whether closed or open) and, more specifically, in his relation to a certain place (whether laid out for this purpose or not).

here may be indicated only through the remains of ephemeral artifices, by a simple decoration with visual symbols (Fig. 3.5), or by the mere presence of the faithful during the time of the ritual. Such sites are veritable 'natural monuments' with religious functions (Bradley 1991a: 136–9). In order even to hope to identify them archaeologically, we must learn to recognize any vestiges that might have been part of a religious symbolism in the society in question; in short, a prior knowledge of symbolism is required.

Archaeology of sacred landscapes

For now, the few examples presented in the accompanying Algonkian study (pp. 289–317) demonstrate clearly the pertinence of a procedure that includes the spiritual dimension to be found in oral traditions when it comes to analysing and interpreting ancient cultural landscapes. Rather than an approach to the study of a general ecosystem of ritual practices, what is offered is rather an identification of the conceptual tools and methodologies required to analyse the symbolic and contextual aspects of an ancient Algonkian sacred landscape through the study of its rock-art sites. With a view to systematizing this procedure within an approach to the archaeology of sacred landscapes, I propose a tentative list of material and spiritual criteria for determining whether other types of archaeological sites also represent sacred places and environments. Any programme focused on the study of a sacred landscape should include aspects that deal with the following aims:

1 Theoretical:
   (a) to give serious consideration to the way aboriginal groups think about and designate (through words, objects and images) their natural landscape;
   (b) to question the notion that human behaviour is explicable in terms of simple adaptation and to integrate other aspects related to the context of social practices and the cognitive domain, in particular, the social actors' intentions, interests and capacity for symbolization.
2 Methodological and practical:
   (a) to take a second look at already surveyed zones, especially if they contain sectors with potentially interesting rock formations;
   (b) to develop new tools for investigation, making better use of the information provided by aboriginal religious traditions;
   (c) to standardize the field methods used and find suitable ways of making these methods more explicit in order that the models applied can be scientifically discussed and criticized;
   (d) to encourage collaboration between specialists on the one hand and between specialists and representatives of the Native communities on the other, with the aim of promoting fruitful exchange and establishing data banks that would be accessible to all.

These aims form the main lines of an approach that might be applied not only to the analysis of an archaeological site, with its internal spaces and immediate physical surroundings, but also to the study of regions and sub-regions, particular facts serving to elucidate the general landscape of the culture being studied and vice versa, as they enter the hermeneutic circle (see Shanks and Tilley 1987a: 104–8).

According to Molyneaux (1983), it might be possible to identify places with a potential for sacredness on the basis of their atypical nature alone; this approach would be particularly useful when looking for prehistoric sites that do not reveal any rock-drawings or other unambiguous signs of ritual behaviour (Molyneaux 1983: 5). This view is contradicted by the argument defended by my work in the Canadian Shield and by elements of the procedure outlined above; both emphasize the necessity of contextualizing the available data by looking at various other evidence, in particular historical and ethnographic documentary sources. The only way it will become possible to interpret the sacred character of a given natural landscape in the history of aboriginal groups in Québec and elsewhere in the Shield is through gathering pertinent complementary data, using productive conceptual and methodological tools, and undertaking a procedure that contextualizes and correlates these data – an approach very similar to those advanced by Bender (1995: 2–3), Bradley (1991b) and Zedeño (1997: 95–6). It is only in this way that it will be possible to reconstitute the nature of a sacred landscape and reveal its history in any significant manner, so as to reach some understanding of how it was defined and used by the groups that created and occupied it. In doing this, we may attain a better understanding of the values attributed to such sites and the attitudes adopted towards them over time, as well as the material effects of these values and attitudes.

As argued by Molyneaux (1983: 7) – quoted as an epigraph to this text – archaeologists would be better able to identify new sacred places within a given territory, at the same time enriching archaeological understanding of the religious universe in which aboriginal groups lived, if they applied the concept of sacred landscape. Even if in the next few years landscape archaeology were to become popular among prehistoric researchers as a promising approach, as a result of budget cuts and limits imposed on university programmes, as well as decreasing government interest in research projects on Native heritage, it may be the 'landscape of professional archaeology' that is threatened with the loss of its most active players. But that is part of quite another story, which none the less should be followed.

Acknowledgements

Several aspects treated in this chapter have been published in French in *Recherches amérindiennes au Québec* (see Arsenault 1998). I am very grateful to Marc Lavoie and Brad Loewen who have been very kind in translating this text from French to English.

References

Arsenault, D. 1998. Esquisse du paysage sacré algonquien: une étude contextuelle des sites rupestres du Bouclier canadien, *Recherches Amérindiennes au Québec* 28(2): 19–39.

Barfield, L. and C. Chippindale. 1997. Meaning in the later prehistoric rock-engravings of Mont Bego, Alpes-Maritimes, France, *Proceedings of the Prehistoric Society* 63: 103–28.

Bender, B. 1995a. Introduction: landscape – meaning and action, in B. Bender (ed.), *Landscape: politics and perspective*: 1–18. Oxford: Berg.

Bender, B., (ed.). 1995b. *Landscape: politics and perspective*. Oxford: Berg.

Bicknell, C. 1913. *A guide to the prehistoric rock-engravings in the Italian Maritime Alps*. Bordighera: Giuseppe Bessone.

Binford, L. R. 1981. *Bones: ancient men and modern myths*. New York: Academic Press.

1989. *Debating archaeology*. New York: Academic Press.

Bobiwash, R. 1998. The sacred and the profane: indigenous lands and State policy, in J. Oakes *et al.* (eds.), *Sacred Lands: aboriginal world views, claims, and conflicts*: 203–13. Edmonton: Canadian Circumpolar Institute, University of Alberta.

Bradley, R. 1991a. Monuments and places, in P. Garwood *et al.* (eds.), *Sacred and profane: proceedings of a conference on archaeology, ritual and religion, Oxford 1989*: 135–40. Oxford: Oxford University Committee for Archaeology. Monograph 32.

1991b. Rock art and the perception of landscape, *Cambridge Archaeological Journal* 1: 77–101.

1993. *Altering the earth: the origins of monuments in Britain and continental Europe*. Edinburgh: Society of Antiquaries of Scotland. Monograph Series 8.

1994. Symbols and signposts – understanding the prehistoric petroglyphs of the British Isles, in C. Renfrew and E. B. W. Zubrow (eds.), *The ancient mind: elements of cognitive archaeology*: 95–106. Cambridge: Cambridge University Press.

1997. *Signing the land: rock art and the prehistory of Atlantic Europe*. London: Routledge.

Burch, E. S. 1971. The non-empirical environment of the Arctic Alaskan Eskimos, *Southwestern Journal of Anthropology* 27: 148–65.

Butzer, K. 1982. *Archaeology as human ecology*. Cambridge: Cambridge University Press.

Cameron, C. M. and S. A. Tomka (eds.). 1996. *Abandonment of settlements and regions: ethnoarchaeological and archaeological approaches*. Cambridge: Cambridge University Press.

Carmichael, D. L. 1994. Places of power: Mescalero Apache sacred sites and sensitive areas, in D. L. Carmichael *et al.* (eds.), *Sacred sites, sacred places*: 89–98. London: Routledge.

Carmichael, D. L., J. Hubert and B. Reeves. 1994. Introduction, in D. L. Carmichael *et al.* (eds.), *Sacred sites, sacred places*: 1–8. London: Routledge.

Carmichael, D. L., J. Hubert, B. Reeves and A. Schanche (eds.). 1994. *Sacred sites, sacred places*. London: Routledge.

Chalifoux, E. and A. L. Burke. 1995. L'occupation préhistorique du Témiscouata (est du Québec), un lieu de portage entre deux voies de circulation, in A.-M. Balac *et al.* (eds.), *Archéologies québécoises*: 237–70. Montréal: Recherches Amérindiennes au Québec. Paléo-Québec 23.

Chapdelaine, C. 1989. *Le site Mandeville à Tracy: variabilité culturelle des Iroquoiens du Saint-Laurent*. Montréal: Recherches Amérindiennes au Québec.

1995. Les Iroquoiens de l'est de la vallée du Saint-Laurent, in A.-M. Balac *et al.* (eds.), *Archéologies québécoises*: 161–84. Montreal: Recherches Amérindiennes au Québec. Paléo-Québec 23.

Chapman, J. 1991. The creation of social arenas in the Neolithic and Copper Age of south-east Europe, in P. Garwood *et al.* (eds.), *Sacred and profane: proceedings of a conference on archaeology, ritual and religion, Oxford 1989*: 152–71. Oxford: Oxford University Committee for Archaeology. Monograph 32.

Clottes, J. and J. D. Lewis-Williams. 1996. *Les Chamanes de la préhistoire: transe et magie dans les grottes ornées*. Paris: Seuil.

Connerton, P. 1989. *How societies remember*. Cambridge: Cambridge University Press.

Cummins, B. and K. Whiteduck. 1998: Towards a model for the identification and recognition of sacred sites, in J. Oakes *et al.* (eds.), *Sacred Lands: aboriginal world views, claims, and conflicts*: 3–14. Edmonton: Canadian Circumpolar Institute, University of Alberta.

Denton, D. 1993. Introduction, in *Aspects du patrimoine des Cris de Mistassini: histoire archéologique et documentaire et les parcs proposés [sic] du lac Albanel – rivière Témiscamie et des monts Otish*. Final report of the Cree Regional Administration, Québec: Ministère des Loisirs, Chasse et Pêche du Québec.

1997. Frenchman's Island and the Natuwaau bones: archaeology and Cree tales of culture contact, in G. P. Nicholas and T. D. Andrews (eds.), *At a crossroads: archaeology and First Peoples in Canada*: 105–24. Burnaby, BC: Archaeology Press and Simon Fraser University.

Douglas, M. 1978. *Natural symbols*. Harmondsworth: Penguin Books.

Evans, J. and T. O'Connor. 1999. *Environmental archaeology: principles and methods*. Stroud: Sutton Publishing.

Finnestad, R. B. 1986. The part and the whole: reflections on theory and methods applied to the interpretation of Scandinavian rock carvings, in G. Steinsland (ed.), *Words and objects: towards a dialogue between archaeology and history of religion*: 21–31. Oslo: Norwegian University Press and the Institute for Comparative Research in Human Culture.

Franklin, R. and P. Bunte. 1994. When sacred land is sacred to three tribes: San Juan Paiute sacred sites and the Hopi–Navajo–Paiute suit to partition the Arizona Navajo Reservation, in D. L. Carmichael *et al.* (eds.), *Sacred sites, sacred places*: 245–58. London: Routledge.

Garwood, P., D. Jennings, R. Skeates and J. Toms (eds.). 1991. *Sacred and profane: proceedings of a conference on archaeology, ritual and religion, Oxford 1989*. Oxford: Oxford University Committee for Archaeology. Monograph 32.

Harding, J. 1991. Using the unique as the typical: monuments and the ritual landscape, in P. Garwood *et al.* (eds.), *Sacred and profane: proceedings of a conference on archaeology, ritual and religion, Oxford 1989*: 141–51. Oxford: Oxford University Committee for Archaeology. Monograph 32.

Helskog, K. and B. Olsen (eds.). 1995. *Perceiving rock art: social and political perspectives*. Oslo: Novus Press and the Institute for Comparative Research in Human Culture.

Heusch, L. de. 1986. *Le Sacrifice dans les religions*

africaines. Paris: Gallimard.

Hirsch, E. 1995. Introduction: landscape: between space and place, in E. Hirsch and M. O'Hanlon (eds.), *The anthropology of landscape: perspectives on place and space*: 1–30. Oxford: Clarendon Press.

Hodder, I. 1987. The contextual analysis of symbolic meanings, in I. Hodder (ed.), *The archaeology of contextual meanings*: 1–10. Cambridge: Cambridge University Press.

1991. *Reading the past*. Cambridge: Cambridge University Press.

Hood, B. 1988. Sacred pictures, sacred rocks: ideological and social space in the north Norwegian Stone Age. *Norwegian Archaeological Review* 21: 152–72.

Hubert, J. 1994. Sacred beliefs and beliefs of sacredness, in D. L. Carmichael *et al.* (eds.), *Sacred sites, sacred places*: 9–19. London: Routledge.

Humphrey, C. 1995. Chiefly and shamanist landscapes in Mongolia, in E. Hirsch and M. O'Hanlon (eds.), *The anthropology of landscape: perspectives on place and space*: 135–62. Oxford: Clarendon Press.

Kulchyski, P. 1998. Bush/lands: some problems with defining the sacred, in J. Oakes *et al.* (eds.), *Sacred Lands: aboriginal world views, claims, and conflicts*: 21–4. Edmonton: Canadian Circumpolar Institute, University of Alberta.

Langevin, E., M. T. McCaffrey, J.-F. Moreau and R. G. V. Hancock. 1995. Le cuivre natif dans le Nord-Est québécois: contribution d'un site du lac Saint-Jean (Québec central), in A.-M. Balac *et al.* (eds.), *Archéologies québécoises*: 307–20. Montreal: Recherches Amérindiennes au Québec. Paléo-Québec 23.

Layton, R. 1992. *Australian rock art: a new synthesis*. Cambridge: Cambridge University Press.

Leroi-Gourhan, A. 1983. *Les Religions de la préhistoire*. Paris: Presses Universitaires de France.

Lewis, G. M. 1998. Maps, mapmaking, and map use by Native North Americans, in D. Woodward and G. M. Lewis (eds.), *History of cartography* 2(3): *Cartography in the traditional African, American, Arctic, Australian, and Pacific societies*: 51–182. Chicago, IL: University of Chicago Press.

Little Bear, L. 1998. Aboriginal relationships to the land and resources, in J. Oakes *et al.* (eds.), *Sacred Lands: aboriginal world views, claims, and conflicts*: 15–20. Edmonton: Canadian Circumpolar Institute, University of Alberta.

Lumley, Henry de, *et al.* 1995. *Le Grandiose et le sacré: gravures rupestres protohistoriques et historiques de la région du Mont Bego*. Aix-en-Provence: Edisud.

McCormack, P. 1998. Native homelands as cultural landscapes: decentering the wilderness paradigm, in J. Oakes *et al.* (eds.), *Sacred Lands: aboriginal world views, claims, and conflicts*: 25–32. Edmonton: Canadian Circumpolar Institute, University of Alberta.

Molyneaux, B. 1983. The study of prehistoric sacred places: evidence from Lower Manitou Lake, *Archaeology Paper* 2: 1–7. Toronto: Royal Ontario Museum.

1987. The Lake of the Painted-Cave, *Archaeology* 40(4): 18–25.

Moore, J. 1992. Pattern and meaning in prehistoric architecture: the architecture of social control in Chimu state, *Latin American Antiquity* 3(2): 95–113.

Moreau, J.-F. 1996. Indices archéologiques de transferts culturels par la voie du Québec central, in L. Turgeon *et al.* (eds.), *Transferts culturels et métissages Amérique/Europe XVIe–XXe siècle*: 209–42. Québec: Les Presses de l'Université Laval.

Nicholas, G. P. and T. D. Andrews (eds.). 1997. *At a crossroads: archaeology and First Peoples in Canada*. Burnaby, BC: Archaeology Press and Simon Fraser University.

Oakes, J., R. Riewe, K. Kinew and E. Maloney (eds.). 1998. *Sacred Lands: aboriginal world views, claims, and conflicts*. Edmonton: Canadian Circumpolar Institute, University of Alberta.

Ouzman, S. 1998. Towards a mindscape of landscape: rock-art as expression of world-understanding, in C. Chippindale and P. S. C. Taçon (eds.), *The archaeology of rock-art*: 30–41. Cambridge: Cambridge University Press.

Plourde, M. 1993. *D'Escanimes à Pletipishtuk: perspectives sur la préhistoire amérindienne de la Haute-Côte-Nord du Saint-Laurent*. Québec: Ministère de la Culture et des Communications. Collection Patrimoines, Dossier 80.

Plumet, P., J.-F. Moreau, H. Gauvin, M.-F. Archambault and V. Elliot. 1993. *Le Site Lavoie (DbEj-11): l'Archaïque aux Grandes-Bergeronnes, Haute-Côte-Nord du Saint-Laurent, Québec*. Montréal: Recherches Amérindiennes au Québec. Paléo-Québec 20.

Preucel, R. W. (ed.). 1991. *Processual and post-processual archaeologies: multiple ways of knowing the past.* Carbondale, IL: Southern Illinois University Center for Archaeological Investigations. Occasional Paper 10.

Preucel, R. W. and I. Hodder. 1996. Nature and culture, in R. W. Preucel and I. Hodder (eds.), *Contemporary archaeology in theory: a reader*: 23–38. Oxford: Blackwell.

Price, N. 1994. Tourism and the Bighorn Medicine Wheel: how multiple use does not work for sacred land sites, in D. L. Carmichael *et al.* (eds.), *Sacred sites, sacred places*: 259–64. London: Routledge.

Rajnovich, G. 1994. *Reading rock art: interpreting the Indian rock paintings of the Canadian Shield.* Toronto: Natural Heritage/Natural History.

Rapp, G., Jr and C. L. Hill. 1998. *Geoarchaeology: the earth-science approach to archaeological interpretation.* New Haven, CT: Yale University Press.

Reinhard, J. 1992. Sacred peaks of the Andes, *National Geographic* 181(3): 84–111.

Richards, C. 1996. Monuments as landscape: creating the centre of the World in late Neolithic Orkney, *World Archaeology* 28(2): 190–208.

Shanks, M. and C. Tilley. 1987a. *Re-constructing archaeology: theory and practice.* Cambridge: Cambridge University Press.

1987b. *Social theory and archaeology.* Oxford: Polity Press.

Smith, P. J. and D. Mitchell (eds.). 1998. *Bringing back the past: historical perspectives on Canadian archaeology.* Hull: Canadian Museum of Civilizations. Mercury Series, Archaeological Paper 158.

Sognnes, K. 1994. Ritual landscapes: towards a reinterpretation of Stone Age rock art in Trøndelag, Norway, *Norwegian Archaeological Review* 27(1): 29–50.

Sundstrom, L. 1996. Mirror of heaven: cross-cultural transference of the sacred geography of the Black Hills, *World Archaeology* 28(2): 177–89.

Tanner, A. 1979. *Bringing home animals: religious ideology and mode of production of the Mistassini Cree hunters.* New York: St Martin's Press.

Theodoratus, D. J. and F. Lapena. 1994. *Wintu* sacred geography of northern California, in D. L. Carmichael *et al.* (eds.), *Sacred sites, sacred places*: 20–31. London: Routledge.

Thomas, J. 1995. The politics of vision and the archaeologies of landscape, in B. Bender (ed.), *Landscape: politics and perspective*: 19–48. Oxford: Berg.

Tilley, C. 1994. *A phenomenology of landscape: places, paths and monuments.* Oxford: Berg.

1996. The power of rocks: topography and monument construction on Bodmin Moor, *World Archaeology* 28(2): 161–76.

Turner, V. 1967. *The forest of symbols: aspects of Ndembu ritual.* Ithaca, NY: Cornell University Press.

1969. *The ritual process: structure and anti-structure.* Ithaca, NY: Cornell University Press.

1977. Process, system, and symbol: a new anthropological synthesis, *Daedalus* 106(3): 61–80.

Ucko, P. J. 1994. Foreword, in D. L. Carmichael *et al.* (eds.), *Sacred sites, sacred places*: xiii–xxii. London: Routledge.

van Gennep, A. 1969. *Les Rites de passage.* (Original edition 1909.) New York and Paris: Mouton Publishing and Maison des Sciences de l'Homme.

Vastokas, J. and R. Vastokas, 1973. *Sacred art of the Algonquins.* Peterborough: Mansard Press.

Warhus, M. 1997. *Another America: Native American maps and the history of our land.* New York: St Martin's Griffin.

Werbner, R. P. 1989. *Ritual passage, sacred journey: the process and organization of religious movement.* Washington, DC: Smithsonian Institution Press.

Whitley, D. S. 1998. Finding rain in the desert: landscape, gender and far western North American rock-art, in C. Chippindale and P. S. C. Taçon (eds.), *The archaeology of rock-art*: 11–29. Cambridge: Cambridge University Press.

Woodward, D. and G. M. Lewis. 1998. Introduction, in D. Woodward and G. M. Lewis (eds.), *History of cartography* 2(3): *Cartography in the traditional African, American, Arctic, Australian, and Pacific societies*: 1–10. Chicago, IL: University of Chicago Press.

Wright, J. V. 1995. *A history of the native people of Canada* 1 (*10,000–1,000 BC*). Hull: Canadian Museum of Civilization. Mercury Series. Archaeological Survey of Canada Paper 152.

1999. *A history of the native people of Canada* 2 (*1,000 BC–500 AD*). Hull: Canadian Museum of Civilization. Mercury Series. Archaeological Survey of Canada Paper 152.

Zedeño, M. N. 1997. Landscapes, land uses and the history of territory formation: an example from the Puebloan Southwest, *Journal of Archaeological Method and Theory* 4(1): 67–99.

4

Locational analysis in rock-art studies

William D. Hyder

The two preceding chapters have stressed the need to address landscapes, not as they are commonly measured by the conventions of topographers, but through the ways human beings actually experienced them. Nevertheless, the established methods of locational analysis will have a place. They will be the basis of any systematic knowledge, certainly, when the materials do not exist for an approach through informed methods. An ambition is that already sketched by Arsenault (previous chapter) as a practical programme, in which we reach a sufficient understanding – a 'systematics of the sacred' – that we can recognize the sacred in the landscape by formal methods alone. Always, the perennial issues of definition – what is a motif? a group? a composition? a panel? a site? a zone? a region? – will continue to be important. The scale of analysis will remain key, since any analysis carried through at a scale too large or too small will miss the true variable. And so will a sensitivity to the varied variables involved, in which patterns may arise from a corresponding variety of causes, some more human than others.

Rock-art and rock-art location

Rock-art research generally recognizes location or archaeological context as an important interpretative element in rock-art studies. As Chippindale and Nash (above, pp. 7–11) notice, since rock-art does not move about as portable artefacts do, its location in the landscape will often be among the most secure evidence it offers. Few studies, however, systematically treat location as an interpretative variable, scholars preferring instead to accept location as a phenomenological attribute (e.g. Steinbring 1992; Whitley 1998): sites in high places are religious sites; vulva-shaped sites are female gendered; visible sites are public sites; hidden sites are private. I am not suggesting that these phenomenological interpretations of location are necessarily wrong, rather they are too often assumed to be correct without careful analysis. The use of location or spatial analysis in archaeology has been developed as a formal methodology. The analysis of location in the landscape is also recognized as a formal method in rock-art analysis (Taçon and Chippindale 1998: 8), though not enough has been done to develop fitting methods.

Marquardt and Crumley (1987: 6) identify landscape as 'the spatial manifestation of relations between human groups and their environment'. How people interact with the environment is, in part, a projection of their culture. Patterns in the location of human activities can be interpreted as evidence of cultural behaviours and beliefs. A formal methodology will link locational variables such as points in the landscape, topographic features, linear features, or complex relationships between any combination of two or more points, topographic features or linear features with expected human behaviours. It is the interaction between these variables and human behaviours that defines landscape. The locations of rock-art sites, for example, have been interpreted as evidence of hunting magic (Heizer and Baumhoff 1962) and seasonal activities related to hunting and gathering (Weaver and Rosenberg 1978). The association of higher elevations with religious expression is culturally familiar to us – we expect our clerics to go up high mountains to experience religious revelation – and, therefore, likely to go unquestioned or untested. Researchers at the Spatial Archaeology Research Unit in Cape Town have used distribution patterns of rock-art sites and motifs to study the seasonal aggregation of hunter-gatherer groups in competition with pastoralists (Manhire *et al.* 1983).

An issue here will be how far the perceptions of the modern researcher match ancient experiences – whether modern researchers depend on their own, necessarily cultural expectations ('the site is below an impressive cliff with a view out over the valley to the distant mountains') or on formal measures of variables like elevation, slope, or distance from permanent water. Waddington (1998: 35), for example, reasons that the sandstone escarpments of the Milfield Basin would have been woodland in the Neolithic, and open clearings would have occurred most frequently near rock outcrops. He argues that these clearings would have attracted grazing cattle, pigs and other forest ungulates; therefore Neolithic communities would have attached specific importance to them, and the cups and rings that appear on these outcrops express a symbolic dialogue between people and the 'life-giving' ground. Hartley and Vawser (1997), on the other hand, develop formal measures of visibility or viewshed, slope or least-cost path, and redundancy or information content of a rock-art panel to test functional hypotheses developed to explain observed patterns of rock-art site locations. They argue that rock-art with high redundancy indicates ownership, and that it will be found at storage sites visible from the least-cost path to the site in times of competition for resources. When there is a low risk of pilferage, rock-art will not be found within the viewshed of the storage site. Waddington infers a conclusion about symbolic dialogue from careful reasoning about why a pattern might have occurred. Hartley and Vawser deduce the defensive function of some rock-art from principles derived from information theory and geography.

Location may be explored through a variety of specific locational attributes. In a study of Southwestern rock-art at Bandelier National Monument in New Mexico, Rohn (1989) observes that rock-art occurs in a variety of contexts – inside dwellings, outside dwellings, in ceremonial settings (kivas and retreats), at shrines, and adjacent to agricultural tracts of land. He proposes that rock-art in and around room clusters signals kinship identity because the elements vary from cluster to cluster. The idea that areal patterns of stylistic continuities correlate with ethnic identities is common to many, even most studies of rock-art. Here, rock-art study faces the same concerns as archaeological studies related to ethnicity do more generally (Jones 1997): will the archaeologically defined entities match or equate to other units manifest in different kinds of evidence, especially language groups, biologically defined human populations or ethnic entities of whatever size (Blench and Spriggs 1998)? Schaafsma (1980: 8), for example, proposes that rock-art styles are common across extensive geographic regions and are restricted to culturally defined time-spans. These represent people who shared numerous cultural traits and a common ideology.

Each of these examples argues different kinds of interpretation, ranging from the economics of hunting and gathering societies, to kinship, to ethnic identity. Differing interpretations stem from the assumptions underlying each project, but they are equally a product of the scale of the analysis. The identification of element variability within a site is probable evidence of kinship grouping. The identification of stylistic variability across regions could suggest evidence of ethnicity. There is no reason why different ethnic groups could not co-exist within a site or kinship system be distributed across regions, but we do not expect to find different ethnic groups locally or to recognize kin dispersed across regions. Therefore, the interpretation that seems familiar at one scale of analysis will likely not be detected at another scale of analysis. The definition of a formal methodology for locational or spatial analysis in rock-art must acknowledge the interpretative limitations set by any given scale.

Archaeologists typically recognize three scales or levels of analysis. Butzer (1982: 38) defines these as micro-, meso- and macro-environments. They are respectively the local site environment, the topographic environment and the regional environment. Further, Adler (1996: 4–6) defines these scales as the intrasite, the local community and the region. Scale by Adler's definition ranges from indicators of social integration and ideology, to social identity and defence, to social and economic relationships and systems. Marquardt and Crumley (1987: 7) note that a particular scale is chosen during one moment of analysis because patterns can be comprehended at that effective scale. Because it is tied to our ability to recognize patterns, the scale of analysis can limit as well as enable the range of possible interpretations. The following sections examine a few examples of rock-art interpretations made at different scales of analysis.

The site

Limiting one's analysis to a single site presents a number of difficulties. If rock-art is the only site feature – if there is no other archaeological context – one might look for patterns among the elements themselves to establish chronology, style or themes (e.g. Welté 1989). One might look for patterns that relate the elements to topographic features of the rock surface such as hollows, bulges or cracks (see Ewing 1997). Or, one might concentrate on the mechanics of production or the composition of pigments (see Clottes 1997). Otherwise, analyses of a single site usually rely on comparisons with data drawn from meso- or macro-levels of analysis, for example from ethnographic data, or from ethnographic analogies. I now wish to discuss a few examples that illustrate the strengths and weaknesses of studying a single site.

Lewis-Williams (1992) analysed a single panel from a San site located in South Africa's Orange Free State. His analysis focuses on a panel (defined as a discrete area of rock-art separated from other areas of art); the visual episodes present in the panel (defined as temporal superimpositions); and the identifiable set (defined by shared action, linking action, similar paint, similar style or similar subject-matter). His carefully crafted analysis using 'formal methods' establishes the sequence of superimpositions; identifies discrete episodes; and defines recognizable sets or patterns within the panel design sequence. He interprets the panel, however, using informed methods (also expressed by Taçon and Chippindale 1998: 6–7) or San ethnographic references to shamanism. He applies the shamanistic interpretation to each episode and set, demonstrating how later episodes were constructed

Fig. 4.1. An extract from Hudson and Conti's (1984) recording of the Indian Creek panel showing zoomorphs or mythical creatures in black and geometric or star elements in lighter grey. The section of panel reproduced here is about 2.4 m across.

on earlier themes. Lewis-Williams (1992: 26) concludes:

> We can now see why the rock face became a repository for the accumulated insights of generations, why episode piled up upon episode: the superimposed images on the rock echoed and, in a very real sense, *were* the crowded, kaleidoscopic images that constituted the spirit world. The effect created by superpositioning came out of the shaman-artists' own religious experience; it duplicated the tumult of the spirit world.

Another example of a single-site analysis is Hudson and Conti's (1984) study of the Indian Creek site in California (Fig. 4.1) which follows much the same process. The panel was easily defined since it fills the ceiling of a low shelter. Pigments and the methods of application defined episodes, with the third episode of painting interpreted as a representation of the winter Milky Way at about the time of the Winter Solstice. The elements of this episode are primarily constructed of geometrics, including many circular and star-like elements. Astronomer Katherine Bracher (1984) identified specific constellations in the patterns of these elements and specific stars by assuming the relative size of an element was representative of the brightness of the star. The fourth episode of painting includes zoomorphs superimposed over many of the geometric elements of the previous episode. Zoomorphs are interpreted as representations of mythical creatures associated with the sky, and the act of painting them as the retouching and reinterpreting of perceptual symbols into conceptual ones (Hudson and Conti 1984: 84).

In this study, also an informed analysis, Hudson's assumption that much of Chumash art was created by ritual specialists with a focus on astronomy guided his interpretation of Indian Creek. His earlier work on Chumash astronomy (Hudson and Underhay 1978) identified shaman-priests as enlightened astronomers who administered to the community and to the individual through ritual and rock-art. Hudson and Bracher collaborated on another project to identify the rock-art record of a solar eclipse, again by

Fig. 4.2. A large fish motif located at the entrance to the Cave of the Whales on San Nicolas Island. Ocean waves break on to the rocks where the people are sitting.

identifying geometric elements as specific stars based on image size and star brightness (Bracher 1982; Hudson 1982). As Marquardt and Crumley (1987) note, 'we select our scales of analysis because patterns can be comprehended'.

A final example is drawn from a recently completed study of the Cave of the Whales (Fig. 4.2) on San Nicolas Island off the coast of California (Conti *et al.* 1999). Here, we were forced to adopt the site level of analysis since there is only one known site on the island, and even the ethnicity of the island's inhabitants is open to question. We approached the interpretation of the rock-art by applying Renfrew's (1994) tests for recognizing the location of religious activity. The island is the most distant of California's Channel Islands; canoe trips to it over 60 km (42 miles) of open ocean could be seen as a victory over the threat of death. Two of three canoes, for example, were said to have been lost on one San Nicolas voyage (Hudson *et al.* 1978: 150). In other words, San Nicolas Island lay at what Renfrew and Bahn (1991: 359–60) identify as a boundary between this world and the next, between the earth and the sea. Locations such as these are typically incorporated into religious ritual. The site itself, a sea cave, lies on the boundary between land and ocean. The cave environment serves to focus one's attention with the rhythmic pounding of the waves; a cacophony of sounds of the barking and shrieking seals, sea lions and birds; and the play of reflected sunlight over the rock-art images. It appears to be 'alive'. When space, light and sound combine, one could imagine oneself being inside the belly of a whale.

To shorten a long analysis, the repeated imagery of the caves (Fig. 4.3) – images of fish, dolphins or whales – would have to be linked with known ritual imagery. It so happens that San Nicolas Island is the source of so-called magic stones and stone effigies, which are found in abundance on the island and in ritual settings on mainland archaeological sites. Many of these effigies are of fish and a triangular design similar to the many fin-like elements found in the cave. One can surmise from the imagery of effigies found within ritual settings that the repeated imagery of the cave on the source island is likely to be religious imagery. Note, however, that even though the study cited here is of a single site, its interpretation relied on informed methods (ethnographic references to the island and magic stones) and regional archaeological patterns (the archaeological context of effigies) to arrive at a cogent interpretation.

Lewis-Williams's (1992) paper demonstrates one weakness inherent in the analysis of single sites. Except for internal comparisons that might relate to the chronology of element placement or an exceptional location, there are few within-site comparisons on which one can base an interpretation. Thus, one looks to the rock-art imagery itself in attempting to understand what an unknown artist may have intended. The analysis may be as simplistic as assuming that images of animals are petitions for success in hunting (e.g. Grant *et al.* 1968: 32). Alternatively, it may involve a more complex ethnographic or informed analysis such as that of Lewis-Williams cited here or Whitley's (1998) ethnographic description

Fig. 4.3. K. Conti's drawing of the main panel of petroglyphs that led to the name, Cave of the Whales (adapted from Conti *et al.* 1999).

The petroglyph panel fell from the cave wall in two separate episodes. One slab (the lower portion) is now on display in a mainland museum, and the upper portion is in storage in the same museum. The drawing is approximately 1 m across.

of California rock-art locations. However one approaches this task, the general process closely mirrors one or more methodologies outlined in Twiss and Conser's (1992) survey of the phenomenology of religion.

Phenomenology can be a useful method to break free from one's preconceptions and consider what Husserl termed *pre-predicative* evidence or direct experience (Hammond *et al.* 1991: 23). It can also lead to an assumption that western notions of art or ways of seeing are different from non-western prehistoric artists' (see Lewis-Williams 1992) or to statements that modern researchers think differently because 'unlike Euro-American culture, Native Americans made no separation between sacred and profane' (Whitley *et al.* 1999: 16). The phenomenological approach can fall into the trap of assuming that the western or scientific perspective is somehow an abstraction from the 'real' world unlike alternative non-western modes of thought (cf. Hammond *et al.* 1991: 3). Assumed differences between western and non-western thought are used to lend weight to informed methods by suggesting a *priori* that formal methods are invalid for rock-art interpretation.

The tenets of phenomenology are reflected also in the emic versus etic debate in anthropology (see Harris 1968: 568–604) wherein some conclude that ethnography must be an emic enterprise. Phenomenological observations pervade rock-art studies and prove fruitful in developing insightful interpretations. However, a more careful consideration of phenomenological methods is warranted when evaluating site analyses such as those cited here, as it is easy to fall inadvertently into a normative trap (Twiss and Conser 1992: 16, 38).

The topographic environment

I prefer the term 'topographic environment' to 'local community' when referring to the meso-level of analysis. Adler's definition of the local community refers to time-bounded habitation sites, while Butzer's meso-environment is more appropriate to environmental sciences. The area studied as a community is closely related to a residential site, but it can also be defined as a contiguous geographic area where people interact socially and economically (Wills and Leonard 1994). Community typically invokes an image of a village or town. Topographic environment, as I use the term here, implies some form of boundary defined by natural features for the purposes of a formal as opposed to informed analysis. As noted previously, studies conducted at the meso-level of analysis typically address questions of social identity and collective security. The topographic focus might reveal patterns in the relationships of specific landscape features to habitation and limited-activity sites, to differential distributions in subject matter, or to styles (e.g. Rohn 1989). Further, Hartley and Vawser (1997: 68), using Geographic Information Systems (GIS) in rock-art studies, conclude that 'it is worthwhile to investigate the positioning of rock-art on the landscape as a function of the processes of change in demographics, resource structure, and economic decision-making'. When considered in concert with chronological variations, changing patterns at the community level might reveal something of changing cultural practices.

Kalle Sognnes has conducted a number of studies of Norwegian rock-art that make effective use of locational variables (1998). There, Sognnes compares the distribution of Northern Tradition or hunter rock-art with the distribution of Southern Tradition or farmer rock-art. Hunter rock-art is typically found near the base of prominent topographic features alongside probable transportation routes and is visible from a distance. Sognnes proposes that the Northern Tradition art communicates information between groups that are frequently on the move. Farming rock-art, in contrast, is not easily visible until one is actually upon it. Panels are located away from trails and nearer settlement areas. Farming societies on the whole mark their territory, but with burial cairns placed atop prominent ridges and similar topographic features. While the study cited here is localized to one community, elsewhere Sognnes (1996) notes the wider distribution of Northern Tradition and Southern Tradition rock-art is more varied when one considers the totality of studies conducted in Norway. He summarizes hunter art as humanizing the landscape and farmer art as defining ritual centres for local communities (Sognnes 1996: 22). Where hunters placed rock-art at locations defined by the topography, farmers used rock-art to create special places.

Wallace and Holmlund (1986) conducted an archaeological study of rock-art in Arizona's Picacho Mountains as part of a Bureau of Reclamation aqueduct project. While their multi-faceted study includes routine analyses such as the creation of a stylistic chronology, it is their locational analysis that is of interest here. The analysis revealed patterns in the location of specific elements with distinctive landscape features. For example, petroglyphs are associated with rock-shelters in North Pass and Shelter Gap, but Wallace and Holmlund (1986: 136) detected differences in the diversity measures of the elements at the two sites. Shelter Gap sites exhibit no difference in the diversity of petroglyphs inside shelters and outside shelters; the petroglyphs of North Pass shelter sites are more diverse. They speculate that the North Pass sites were used to avoid rain and heat while travelling along the natural pass. Shelter Gap, however, is off the main trail and the shelters are too small and awkward to provide real shelter. Wallace and Holmlund (1986: 138) conclude that the Shelter Gap sites are private, personal sacred spaces used by a restricted social group, and the North Pass sites are possible shrines related to activities of the larger society (multiple social groups), perhaps serving as trail shrines.

Intrasite analyses identified further non-random associations between petroglyph elements and archaeological features. Petroglyphs were found associated with quarries, and a high diversity of elements was interpreted as indicating their use by multiple social groups. Had diversity been lower than expected, Wallace and Holmlund (1986: 139) would have interpreted the petroglyphs as ownership marks reflecting limited access as they did for Shelter Gap. In addition to associations between rock-art and the two natural travel routes, Picacho and North Passes, a few smaller, recognizable trails also have petroglyphs in association. Although they observed a somewhat higher diversity for petroglyphs associated with the recognizable trails, Wallace and Holmlund (1986: 141) noted that 'if glyph symbolism placed along trails relates to activities performed at the trail's destination, a confused picture could be obtained when the trail glyphs are taken out of context'. Hedges and Hamann (1992) examined two other sites in the southern Arizona region and found similar associations between rock-art and 'summit paths' as observed by Wallace and Holmlund.

Hyder's (1989) study of rock-art and archaeology in the immediate vicinity of Santa Barbara, California, tested an obvious locational pattern (Fig. 4.4) that proved to be less significant than previously thought. Here, Grant (1965: 75) identified Chumash rock-art as 'hidden from the sight of the Spanish in the remote and rugged mountains'. Grant (1965: 89) argued that the mountain location indicated shrines to which people made pilgrimages or perhaps the work of small bands of mountain Chumash. His conception of the mountains as somehow removed from the traditional humanized landscape is a modern cultural construct (see Faulstich 1994 for a discussion of the concept of wilderness). Hyder demonstrated that the Santa Barbara sites are confined to a stratum of Coldwater sandstone, a stone particularly well suited to the survival of the art. Shelters with archaeological deposits in sandstone strata below the Coldwater erode more rapidly. Several centimetres of sterile sand typically cover archaeological deposits in the lower caves. Had paintings been present, they would have eroded long ago. The mountain location may be a simple taphonomic product of what chances to survive.

Lee (1981; 1997) demonstrated that all types of art, not just rock-art, formed part of everyday life in Chumash villages. The lack of rock outcrops along the coastal plain where most villages are located explains the mountain location for rock-art sites just as well as Grant's phenomenological observation. One must be careful in distinguishing between cultural patterns and taphonomic patterns on the landscape.

The ability to compare sites affords greater analytic power than is enjoyed in the analysis of a single site. Where the analysis of a single site is limited primarily to descriptive or informed methods, the analysis of multiple sites within a topographically defined area allows for formal methods such as testing for consistency or patterns in observations across sites or the examination of correlations between landscape features, archaeological features and rock-art. I do not mean to imply that community-level questions are qualitatively better for they also can exhibit methodological weaknesses. While topographic features may suggest appropriate boundaries, the

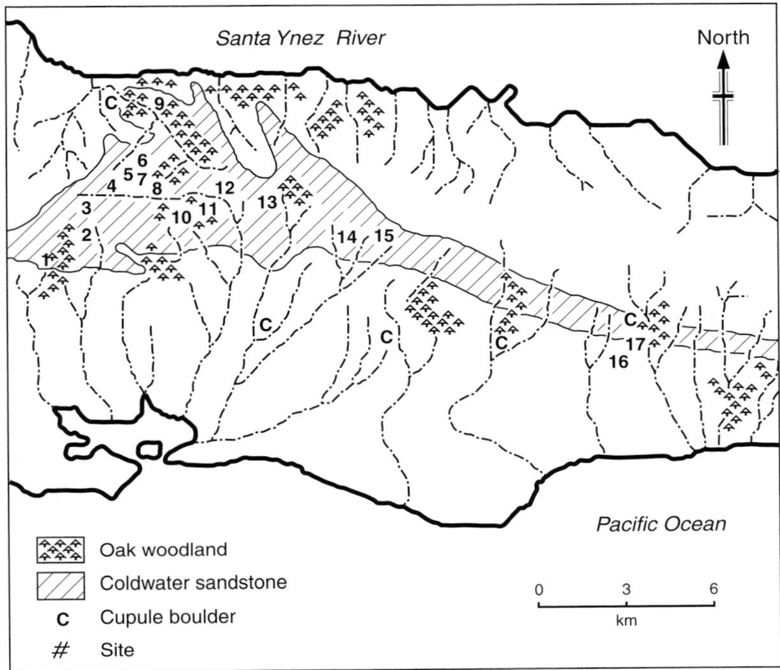

Fig. 4.4. The distribution of rock-art sites in the San Marcos Pass region of Chumash territory in California is restricted to outcrops of Coldwater sandstone (after Hyder 1989).

Each number on the map represents a rock-art site. Archaeological sites are found in shelters in the foothills, but the sandstone walls are extremely friable and eroded. If rock art had been present, it would not have survived.

definition of a topographic environment as used here may not coincide with culturally defined boundaries. Should defined boundaries be inappropriate and cross true community boundaries, non-existent patterns could be seen or real patterns missed (see Hodder and Orton 1976: 41–3 for a discussion of boundary problems in nearest-neighbour analysis).

In the Chumash example cited here, a ridgeline and the coastline define Hyder's (1989) northern and southern boundaries for the Santa Barbara coast study area. The east and west boundaries were somewhat arbitrary, having been defined by obvious breaks in the known distribution of rock-art sites, as well as ethnographic data that suggest the selected boundaries were actual community boundaries at the time of Spanish contact. If the northern boundary is extended into the interior mountains, the strong correlation between rock-art and Coldwater sandstone disappears and is replaced by the dominant pattern of rock-art sites and mountains. The taphonomic patterns are present when the distribution of sites is examined in detail, but they are masked by the dominant regional pattern of site distribution.

Increased analytic power does not prevent one's preferences for familiar patterns from skewing or colouring observations. For example, Sognnes (1998) is interested in differences between the distributions of hunter and farmer site locations. The interactions between hunters and farmers (or even the lack thereof) might have been addressed by considering superimpositions of the two styles at sites. While the presence of superimpositions is briefly discussed, it is within the context of establishing a chronology for the two styles and not as evidence of interaction or cultural transitions.

These examples all involve formal analysis, while researchers such as Wallace and Holmlund (1986) make judicious use of ethnographic data. Some of these studies could just as easily have been conducted using informed methods. Conway (1992) reports that three of four types of historic Ojibwa shamans made rock-art; the kind which each made might be considered a separate style. Without ethnographic data as to a possible functional source for differences in imagery and location, a topographic analysis of site distributions could just as likely lead to the conclusion that different time-periods or cultures were represented in the observed data as to the conclusion that different functional sites were present.

The region

Analysis at a regional level might examine economic or social relationships, intercultural conflict and co-operation, different environmental adaptations, information exchange and other systems questions. Usually, rock-art studies with a regional emphasis define ethnic boundaries based on stylistic continuities and discontinuities (e.g. Schaafsma 1980). Regional studies of the distribution of styles are locational only in the sense that they consider areal distributions of sites. There are few good regional studies to cite that deal with more than the definition of stylistic boundaries. In the absence of professional archaeological interest, rock-art studies have been left to avocationalists in most parts of the world (Hyder and Loendorf 1998), and these archaeological goals have not been central to avocational research interests.

Bradley (1997: 7), for example, criticizes rock-art studies for an overemphasis on discovery and documentation and a lack of attention to archaeological questions central to the study of prehistory. With a few exceptions, the field has developed formal descriptive and comparative methods. However, regional explanatory methods have been slower to develop in the absence of a strong academic interest and influence. One notable exception was published more than a decade before Bradley's critique. Bahn (1983) surveyed the economic catchment areas of a series of Palaeolithic sites across the northern slope of the Pyrenees. Decorated caves are his anchor points, and Bahn's study is one of only a few to place decorated caves into a regional archaeological context. Perhaps most importantly, Bahn's study makes a unique contribution to the study of Palaeolithic art without making the art the primary focus of attention.

Bradley's (1997) archaeological study of Atlantic European rock-art is another of the few regional rock-art studies partially devoted to the landscape. He examines the question of whether rock-art is more closely associated with the hunter-gatherer landscape and less closely associated with the landscape use of farmers. He makes explicit use of at least two levels of analysis, the community and the region. Bradley (1997: 214) demonstrates that rock-art was 'closely' related to paths and significant places along paths. Focusing on Galicia, Spain, his study of its distribution suggests that rock-art was associated with a mobile pattern of resource exploitation. Many rock-carvings are located 'at vantage points that overlook areas of grazing land, trails, springs and waterholes'. While the location of sites shows little variation across the study region, the local distribution of simple sites versus complex sites varies from one extreme of the region to the other.

Lee and Hyder (1991) concentrated on stylistic similarities among rock-art sites at ethnographic ethnic boundaries (Fig. 4.5). The sites were chosen because they were highly visible, located near major villages, and situated along well-travelled trails. Lee and Hyder note that the similarity among these boundary sites is often greater than that between the individual sites and the smaller sites from each general culture area. Their study, one of several papers prepared for a symposium addressing archaeological evidence of tribal interactions in southern California, made the point that rock-art is located at fixed points on the landscape. Unlike most other artefactual components of the archaeological record, it cannot be traded or otherwise moved beyond the range of its creators. Its unique tie to the landscape makes rock-art an important artefact for archaeological analysis.

Discussion: scale of the study, levels of analysis, rigour

According to Bradley, rock-art studies must be conducted in concert with broader archaeological and anthropological questions. Informed and formal methods of archaeology and anthropology are being defined, refined and more fully developed (Layton 1992; Taçon and Chippindale 1998). One popular formal method – locational or landscape analysis – has been in vogue for quite some time, but it remains poorly developed as an analytic methodology for rock-art studies (Schaafsma (1985: 258, 261–3) cites seven examples in her review of rock-art method and theory). In particular, the level of analysis used in locational studies and its influence on explanation and interpretation is not well documented. The first point of this chapter is that the researcher must be aware of the scale of the system to be studied and ensure that there is an appropriate fit between the questions asked and the data to be collected (Adler 1996: 4).

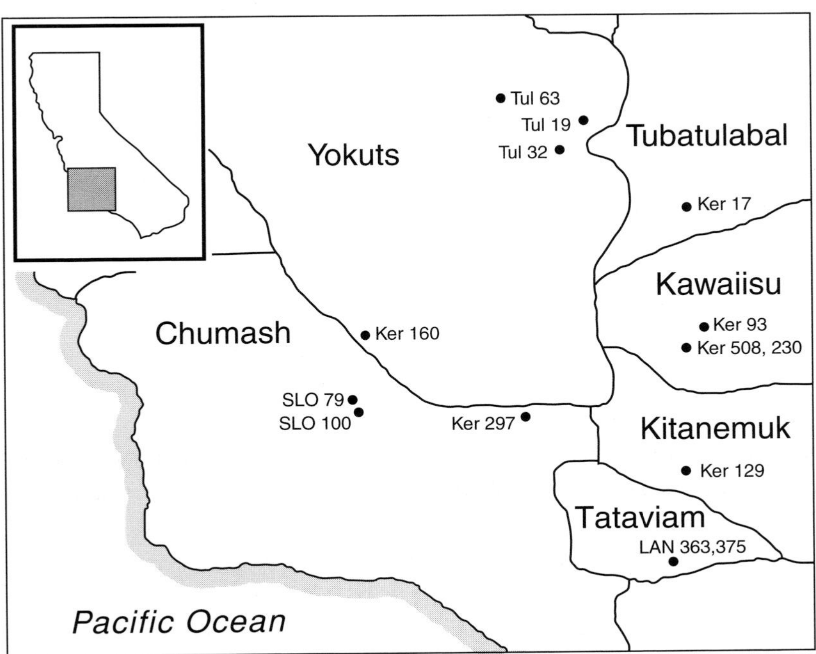

Fig. 4.5. Lee and Hyder (1991) analysed stylistic similarities among rock-art sites falling near ethnographically defined historic boundaries as an indicator of cultural interaction. The map reproduced here shows the location of the sites in relation to the cultural boundaries at the time of Spanish contact.

One example of the dangers of incorrectly defining locational variables can be extracted from the literature. Mandt's (1978) earlier evaluation of the role of location in the interpretation of Norwegian rock-art reached a conclusion opposite to that of a later study by Sognnes (1998). Although Mandt defined two levels of locational variables, micro and macro, they are not comparable to the locational variables defined by Sognnes. Instead, Mandt's micro-location is the type of terrain (shoreline, flat, hilly), and the macro-location is the geographical distribution (coastal zone, farm zone, mountain zone). The micro and macro variables are highly correlated by definition. Mandt expressed her hypothesis as a negative: i.e. location in farmland is not an integrated element of agrarian carvings. The question of the social behaviour of farmers cannot be tested using these locational variables since agrarian activities occurred in all three geographic zones, not just the 'farm zone'. In addition, she defined cup-marks as agrarian carvings, but she then defined farmland as being restricted to the 'farm zone'; therefore, the analysis by definition could not produce a clear association between farming rock-art and 'farm zone'. Mandt (1978: 182) rejects one study that relates cupules to mountain pasturing locations because of uncertainties in dating cupules and pasturing. The macro-location variable defined any cup-marks or agrarian carvings found outside the 'farm zone' as not in association with agrarian activities and determined the results of the analysis before any data were analysed.

Sognnes's analysis provides a better fit between the questions asked and the data collected. Again, proper fit is the result of addressing broader archaeological issues such as differences in the definition of and use of the landscape between hunter-gatherers and farmers. Micro-locational variables included site visibility and relationship to paths, meso variables included the relationship of sites to the patterns of sedentary habitation in the community, and the macro variable compared the consistency of these patterns across multiple communities.

The Sognnes study illustrates a second important point: locational studies may shift focus across analytic levels. The power of each of the levels of analysis can be illustrated in an example drawn from studies being conducted in Utah's Grand Gulch. A well-known site, the Big Panel (Castleton 1987: 255–7), contains many paired anthropomorphs with their right arms raised (Fig. 4.6). When considered as a site, the right-arm-raised convention is interesting as it continues across a variety of painted and pecked Basketmaker and Pueblo styles at the site. This continuity suggests some particular meaning or ideology that transcended many generations. When viewed in the context of the community as defined by Grand Gulch itself, the paired figures can be interpreted as evidence of Basketmaker marking of identity or of lineage territory, given their distinctive raised arm and pairings (cf. Hyder 1997). On the regional level, raised-left-arm anthropomorphs are encountered at a site on Cannonball Mesa in south-western Colorado (Cole 1990: 122; Olsen 1985: 101). Shared imagery from these two distant sites potentially becomes significant when considered in the context of imagery at the Procession Panel located in a saddle at the top of Comb Ridge, a great hogback that neatly divides the two regions.

The Procession Panel (Figs. 4.7 and 4.8) may represent regional ceremonial activities that periodically brought distant clans together (Joe Pachak, pers. com. 1999). Manning (1992: 21–4) describes the panel in some detail, and suggests that it may record an intercommunity ceremony. Approximately 200 anthropomorphic images approach a large central circle from either side. While the figures are small and not well detailed, some clearly have upraised right arms, others

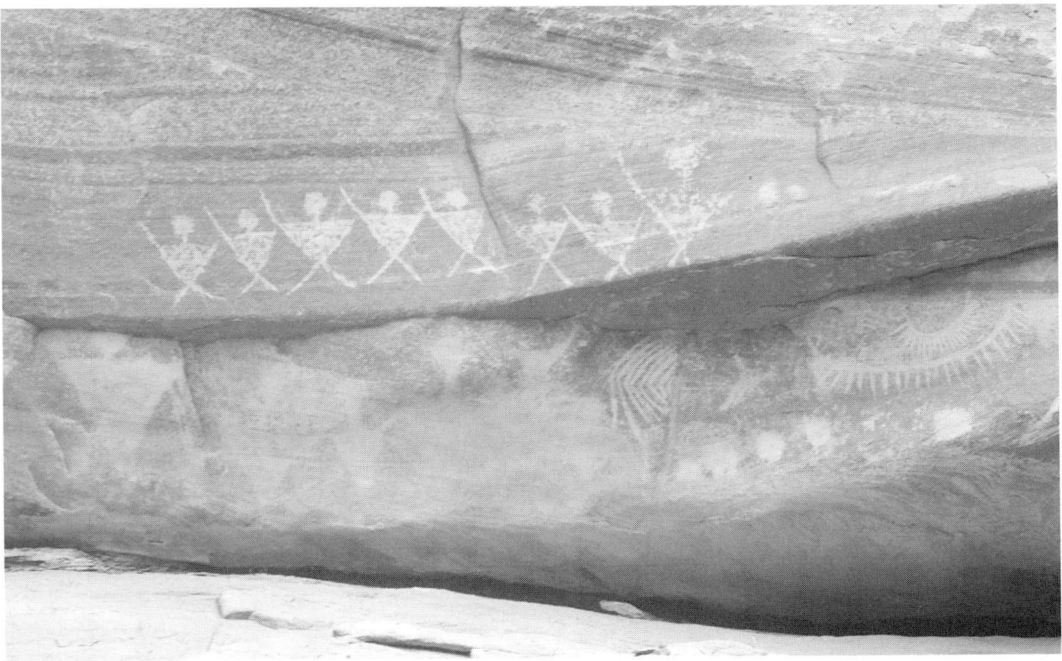

Fig. 4.6. A row of Basketmaker III anthropomorphs with their right arms raised illustrates the distinctive right-arm-raised convention of the Big Panel in Grand Gulch, Utah.

carry staffs, a few have bird heads, others have burden baskets or humps on their backs. One figure carries two lobed circles, and two more lobed circles are present inside the large circle. Manning (1992: 31–2) notes the correspondence between the apparent narrative imagery of the Procession Panel and archaeological artefacts and features of Broken Flute Cave, located some 130 km (80 miles) to the south-east. There, Earl Morris excavated a 12 m diameter, slab-lined circular floor that he identified as a Basketmaker III great kiva (Morris 1980). In this same ruin, Morris found two wooden lobed circles. If the archaeology of Broken Flute Cave can be interpreted as evidence of Basketmaker III ceremonial activities, then the Procession Panel may be a pictorial record of similar ceremonies.

The location of the Procession Panel atop a sandstone monocline further suggests a ceremonial theme of a gathering. From the west, hand-and-toe holds ascend the near-vertical face of Comb Ridge. Access is easier from the east, yet even here steps are pecked into near-horizontal sandstone as if to mark the route. Rock-art and symbolic trails of this sort may be literal forerunners of the ritual roads, great kivas and great houses of the later Chacoan phase of the San Juan region (see Hurst *et al.* 1990; Hurst *et al.* 1993 for a discussion of road segments in this region). More research on the distribution of the specific elements discussed here is needed to evaluate fully the significance of the panel, but exploratory studies of the distribution of decorative headdresses in Basketmaker rock-art suggest that one can detect the existence of macro-social regional affiliations (Robins 1999).

A third, unstated assumption of this review is that rock-art methods, whether informed or formal, should be rigorous in their application (cf. Spaulding 1988). When properly applied,

Fig. 4.7. The right half of the Procession Panel located on Comb Ridge, Utah.

Five figures with their right arms raised are visible to the left of the two large deer. The anthropomorphic figures are approximately 5 cm tall. Details of other distinctive figures are shown in Fig. 4.8.

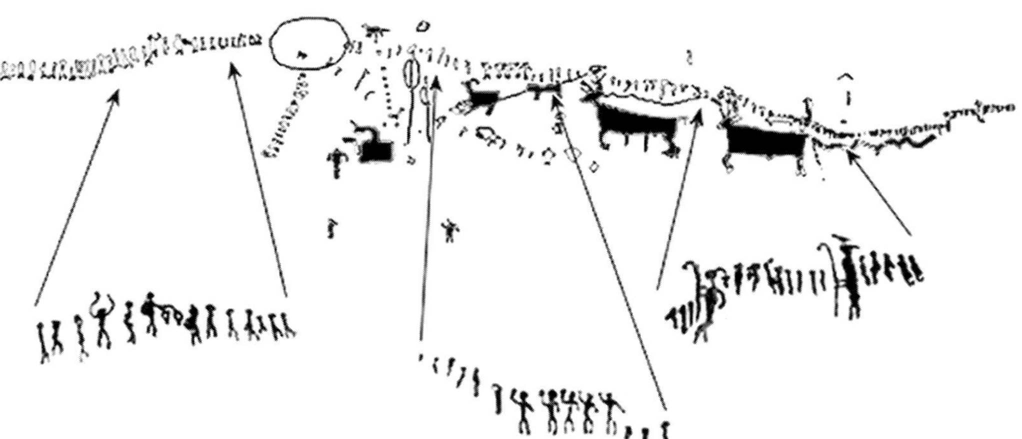

Fig. 4.8. A rendering of the entire Procession Panel on Comb Ridge showing details at various points.

Most of the anthropomorphs in the procession are pecked into the sandstone as lines 3 or 4 cm high, with few details. Some figures have fine, incised fingers and toes. On the left side of the panel, a detail is exploded out here to show an anthropomorph carrying two lobed circles in its hands. Lobed circles are thought to be ceremonial items. Another detail exploded out from the centre of the panel shows the five anthropomorphs with right arms raised. Further to the right, an exploded detail shows two figures carrying staffs and wearing head-dresses.

locational analysis can be a powerful tool in the explanation and interpretation of rock-art data. In turn, rock-art can be a rich data source for furthering our understanding of the cultural behaviours and beliefs that define landscape, since it is tied to fixed points in that landscape. Nevertheless, as we define formal methods for interpreting rock-art and understanding cultural behaviours, we must be mindful of the limitations imposed by our scale of analysis. Interpretations may seem to be confirmed at one level of analysis because supporting patterns are easily recognized while alternative scales of analysis and their corresponding interpretations may be dismissed or go untested. The development of locational analysis as a formal method in rock-art research must identify appropriate questions and appropriate data for testing hypotheses at varying levels of analysis. In turn, researchers must be aware of the interpretative limitations imposed by their choice of scale and not accept or dismiss interpretations for which their data are inappropriate.

References

Adler, M. A. 1996. 'The Great Period': the Pueblo world during the Pueblo III Period, AD 1150 to 1350, in M. A. Adler (ed.), *The prehistoric Pueblo world AD 1150–1350*: 1–10. Tucson, AZ: University of Arizona Press.

Bahn, P. 1983. *Pyrenean prehistory: a palaeoeconomic survey of French sites*. Warminster: Aris and Phillips.

Blench, R. and M. Spriggs (eds.). 1998. *Archaeology and language 2: Correlating archaeological and linguistic hypotheses*. London: Routledge.

Bracher, K. 1982. Painted Cave: a Chumash Indian eclipse record?, *Griffith Observer* 46(5): 2–6.

1984. Appendix B: Comments on celestial representations in rock art at Indian Creek, in *Papers on Chumash rock art*: 91–102. San Luis Obispo, CA: San Luis Obispo County Archaeological Society. Occasional Paper 12.

Bradley, R. 1997. *Rock art and the prehistory of Atlantic Europe: signing the land*. London: Routledge.

Butzer, K. W. 1982. *Archaeology as human ecology: method and theory for a contextual approach*. Cambridge: Cambridge University Press.

Castleton, K. B. 1987. *Petroglyphs and pictographs of Utah 2: The south, central, west and northwest*. Salt Lake City, UT: Utah Museum of Natural History.

Clottes, J. 1997. New laboratory techniques and their impact on Paleolithic cave art, in M. W. Conkey *et al.* (eds.), *Beyond art: Pleistocene image and symbol*: 37–52. San Francisco, CA: California Academy of Sciences. Memoir 23.

Cole, S. J. 1990. *Legacy on stone*. Boulder (CO): Johnson Books.

Conti, K., W. D. Hyder and A. Padgett. 1999. *Rock art of San Nicolas Island: SNI-144 (Cave of the Whales)*. Report prepared for Statistical Research, Tucson, AZ, under contract to the Naval Air Weapons Station, Point Mugu.

Conway, T. 1992. Ojibwa oral history relating to 19th century rock art, in K. K. Sanger (ed.), *American Indian Rock Art* 15: 11–26. San Miguel, CA: American Rock Art Research Association.

Ewing, E. 1997. Preliminary report on crack feature incorporation from the Franco-Cantabrian regions of France and Spain, in S. M. Freers (ed.), *American Indian Rock Art* 23: 147–60. San Miguel, CA: American Rock Art Research Association.

Faulstich, P. 1994. The cultured wild and the limits of wilderness, in D. C. Burks (ed.), *Place of the wild: a wildlands anthology*: 161–74. Washington, DC: Island Press.

Grant, C. 1965. *The rock paintings of the Chumash*. Berkeley, CA: University of California Press.

Grant, C., J. W. Baird and J. K. Pringle. 1968. *Rock drawings of the Coso Range, Inyo County, California*. China Lake, CA: Maturango Museum.

Hammond, M., J. Howarth and R. Keat. 1991. *Understanding phenomenology*. Oxford: Basil Blackwell.

Harris, M. 1968. *The rise of anthropological theory*. New York: Thomas Y. Crowell.

Hartley, R. J. and A. M. W. Vawser. 1997. Wayfinding in the desert: evaluating the role of rock art through GIS, in P. Faulstich (ed.), *Rock art as visual ecology*: 55–76. Tucson, AZ: American Rock Art Research Association. IRAC Proceedings 1.

Hedges, K. and D. Hamann. 1992. Look to the mountaintop: rock art at Texas Hill, Arizona, in D. E. Weaver (ed.), *American Indian Rock Art* 17:

44–55. El Toro, CA: American Rock Art Research Association.

Heizer, R. F. and M. A. Baumhoff. 1962. *Prehistoric rock art of Nevada and eastern California*. Berkeley, CA: University of California Press.

Hodder, I. and C. Orton. 1976. *Spatial analysis in archaeology*. Cambridge: Cambridge University Press.

Hudson, T. 1982. *Guide to Painted Cave*. Santa Barbara, CA: McNally and Loftin.

Hudson, T. and K. Conti. 1984. The rock art of Indian Creek: ritual sanctuary of the gifted Chumash, in *Papers on Chumash rock art*: 47–90. San Luis Obispo, CA: San Luis Obispo County Archaeological Society. Occasional Paper 12.

Hudson, T., J. Timbrook and M. Rempe (eds.). 1978. *Tomol: Chumash watercraft as described in the ethnographic notes of John P. Harrington*. Socorro, NM: Ballena Press; and Santa Barbara, CA: Santa Barbara Museum of Natural History. Ballena Press Anthropological Papers 9.

Hudson, T. and E. Underhay. 1978. *Crystals in the sky: an intellectual odyssey involving Chumash astronomy, cosmology and rock art*. Socorro, NM: Ballena Press; and Santa Barbara, CA: Santa Barbara Museum of Natural History. Ballena Press Anthropological Papers 10.

Hurst, W., D. Davidson and O. Severance. 1990. Anasazi roads in southeastern Utah, *Canyon Legacy* 7: 12–15.

Hurst, W., O. Severance and D. Davidson. 1993. Uncle Albert's ancient roads. *Blue Mountain Shadows* 12: 2–9.

Hyder, W. D. 1989. *Rock art and archaeology in Santa Barbara County, California*. San Luis Obispo, CA: San Luis Obispo County Archaeological Society. Occasional Paper 13.

1997. Basketmaker spatial identity: rock art as culture and praxis, in P. Faulstich (ed.), *Rock art as visual ecology*: 31–42. Tucson, AZ: American Rock Art Research Association. IRAC Proceedings 1.

Hyder, W. D. and L. Loendorf. 1998. The role of avocational archaeologists in rock art research. Paper presented at the 63rd annual meeting of the Society for American Archaeology, 26 March, Seattle, WA.

Jones, S. (ed.). 1997. *The archaeology of ethnicity: constructing identities in the past and present*. London: Routledge.

Layton, R. 1992. *Australian rock art: a new synthesis*. Cambridge: Cambridge University Press.

Lee, G. 1981. *The portable cosmos: effigies, ornaments, and incised stone from the Chumash area*. Socorro, NM: Ballena Press. Ballena Press Anthropological Papers 21.

1997. *The Chumash cosmos*. Arroyo Grande, CA: Bear Flag Books.

Lee, G. and W. D. Hyder. 1991. Prehistoric rock art as an indicator of cultural interaction and tribal boundaries in south-central California, *Journal of California and Great Basin Anthropology* 13: 15–28.

Lewis-Williams, J. D. 1992. *Vision, power and dance: the genesis of a southern African rock art panel*. Amsterdam: Nederlands Museum voor Anthropologie en Praehistorie.

Mandt, G. 1978. Is the location of rock pictures an interpretative element? in S. Marstrander (ed.), *Acts of the International Symposium on Rock Art*: 170–84. Oslo: Universitetsforlaget.

Manhire, A., J. E. Parkington and W. V. Rijssen. 1983. A distributional approach to the interpretation of rock art in the south-western Cape, *South African Archaeological Society Goodwin Series* 4: 29–33.

Manning, S. J. 1992. The lobed-circle image in the Basketmaker petroglyphs of southeastern Utah, *Utah Archaeology 1992* 5: 1–38.

Marquardt, W. H. and C. L. Crumley. 1987. Theoretical issues in the analysis of spatial patterning, in C. L. Crumley and W. H. Marquardt (ed.), *Regional dynamics: Burgundian landscapes in historical perspective*: 1–18. San Diego, CA: Academic Press.

Morris, E. A. 1980. *Basketmaker caves in the Prayer Rock District, northeastern Arizona*. Tucson, AZ: University of Arizona Press. Anthropological Papers 35.

Olsen, N. H. 1985. *Hovenweep rock art: an Anasazi visual communication system*. Los Angeles, CA: Institute of Archaeology, University of California. Occasional Paper 14.

Renfrew, C. 1994. The archaeology of religion, in C. Renfrew and E. B. W. Zubrow (ed.), *The ancient mind: elements of cognitive archaeology*: 47–54. Cambridge: Cambridge University Press.

Renfrew, C. and P. Bahn. 1991. *Archaeology: theories, methods, and practice*. London: Thames and Hudson.

Robins, M. R. 1999. San Juan Basketmakers: rock art, food production, and social relations in a mixed farming and foraging economy. Paper presented at the 12th International Rock Art Conference, 23 May, Ripon, WI.

Rohn, A. H. 1989. *Rock art of Bandelier National Monument.* Albuquerque, NM: University of New Mexico Press.

Schaafsma, P. 1980. *Indian rock art of the Southwest.* Santa Fe, NM: School of American Research; and Albuquerque, NM: University of New Mexico Press.

1985. Form, content, and function: theory and method in North American rock art studies, in M. B. Schiffer (ed.), *Advances in archaeological method and theory* 8: 237–77. Orlando, FL: Academic Press.

Sognnes, K. 1996. Recent rock art research in northern Europe, in P. G. Bahn and A. Fossati (eds.), *Rock art studies: news of the world* 1: 15–28. Oxford: Oxbow Books. Oxbow Monograph 72.

1998. Symbols in a changing world: rock-art and the transition from hunting to farming in mid Norway, in C. Chippindale and P. S. C. Taçon (eds.), *The archaeology of rock-art*: 146–62. Cambridge: Cambridge University Press.

Spaulding, A. C. 1988. Distinguished lecture: archaeology and anthropology, *American Anthropologist* 90: 263–71.

Steinbring, J. 1992. Phenomenal attributes: site selection factors in rock art, in D. E. Weaver (ed.), *American Indian Rock Art* 17: 102–13. El Toro, CA: American Rock Art Research Association.

Taçon, P. S. C. and C. Chippindale. 1998. An archaeology of rock-art through informed methods and formal methods, in C. Chippindale and P. S. C. Taçon (eds.), *The archaeology of rock-art*: 1–10. Cambridge: Cambridge University Press.

Twiss, S. B. and W. H. Conser, Jr (eds.) 1992. *Experience of the sacred: readings in the phenomenology of religion.* Hanover, NH: Brown University Press.

Waddington, C. 1998. Cup and ring marks in context, *Cambridge Archaeological Journal* 8: 29–54.

Wallace, H. D. and J. P. Holmlund. 1986. *Petroglyphs of the Picacho Mountains South Central, Arizona.* Tucson, AZ: Institute for American Research. Anthropological Papers 6.

Weaver, D. E., Jr and B. H. Rosenberg. 1978. Petroglyphs of the southern Sierra Estrella, a locational interpretation, in E. Snyder *et al.* (eds.), *American Indian Rock Art* 4: 108–23. El Toro, CA: American Rock Art Research Association.

Welté, A.-C. 1989. An approach to the theme of confronted animals in French Palaeolithic art, in H. Morphy (ed.), *Animals into art*: 215–35. London: Unwin Hyman.

Whitley, D. S. 1998. Finding rain in the desert: landscape, gender and far western North American rock-art, in C. Chippindale and P. S. C. Taçon (eds.), *The archaeology of rock-art*: 11–29. Cambridge: Cambridge University Press.

Whitley, D. S., J. M. Simon and R. I. Dorn. 1999. The vision quest in the Coso Range, in S. M. Freers (ed.), *American Indian Rock Art* 25: 1–31. Tucson, AZ: American Rock Art Research Association.

Wills, W. H. and R. D. Leonard. 1994. Preface, in W. H. Wills and R. D. Leonard (eds.), *The ancient southwestern community: models and methods for the study of prehistoric social organization*: xiii–xvi. Albuquerque, NM: University of New Mexico Press.

5

From millimetre up to kilometre: a framework of space and of scale for reporting and studying rock-art in its landscape

Christopher Chippindale

Rock-art, so varied in its nature and scale, is accordingly reported in varied ways. One element in that variety concerns the physical scales concerned, from the nuances in a single peck-mark smaller in size than a little fingernail up to patterns of distribution across a continent. Understandable as arising study by study, or region by region, that variety of approaches makes comparison harder than it could be within and between regions. Can a flexible framework be devised that gives some useful unity? Can it deal also with the scales of observation? A set of frames is devised which may do this.

Scales of field observation and inference on Mont Bego

Andrea Arcà's chapter in the present volume (below, chapter 15) addresses the distinctive 'topographic figures', the later prehistoric engravings of the Alpine region which he identifies as maps or pictures of actual ancient landscapes. His study in large part depends on field observations at Mont Bego, the French rock-engraving site where topographic figures are especially numerous and striking.

Those observations concern various physical scales of study.

The smallest scale is of the individual pecked lines that make up the figures, even the individual peck-marks that make up the individual pecked lines: this is one way of detecting sequence, by physical superposition.

An order of magnitude larger is the shape of the figures themselves, as these are constructed as accumulations of individual pecked lines and areas. It is the systematics of those shapes and their repeated modules which is the clue to what the 'topographic' elements represent.

A next larger order of magnitude is the relation of figures to each other and their placing on the engraved surface: this also gives clues as to sequence and to the subject-matter.

Yet larger as a scale of study is the position of the engraved surfaces in the landscape, in the case of the Bego figures, the landscape of a whole Alpine peak and its network of descending valleys.

Henry de Lumley's synthesis of the Bego rock-engravings, *Le Grandiose et le sacré* (Lumley *et al.* 1995), has different research concerns, and takes a different approach in viewing the figures, and in their interpretation. Based on a repeated examination of every single figure of the 30,000 and more on the mountain, it also reports features observed across that same range of scales, from the smallest to the largest. The smallest is the distinct types of pecking (*piquetage*) in the figures; in his field programme over many years thirteen different aspects to the technique of engraving have been systematically recorded (1995: 53–7). Then there is the variety of forms in individual figures, and the recognition of what each recognized class depicts (1995: 60–287). Next is the placing of figures in relation to each other, and as grouped in surfaces or separated as isolated images (1995: 289–97). Finally, for the grand scale of location, more than twenty different zones are defined across the mountain (1995: 39–52).

At a scale still larger, in both Arcà's and de Lumley's work, is the relating of the Bego figures to the wider pattern of prehistoric cultures in the Alps and beyond, as far afield as the eastern Mediterranean (1995: 340–67) and even Pakistan (Arcà, below, pp. 318–49).

Diversity and consistency in units of record

Nearly all the studies in the present volume – or any collection of rock-art papers! – deal with field evidence at these varied physical scales of size. Nearly all move between the scales, as pertinent information is to be found in the largest and in the smallest and in those between.

Nevertheless, the methods used – even in the first step of recording and reporting from the field – and the names for elements are very variable in rock-art studies. That variety and inconsistency has its drawbacks: it makes it hard to compare and contrast bodies of rock-art recorded and reported by different researchers or research conventions. One does not know if a body of rock-art which has 'thirty sites' actually involves more locales than another with 'twenty sites', since the difference may be in the definition of a 'site'. A research convention which tends to 'split' groups into individual sites ends up enumerating many more sites than does one which prefers to 'lump' rocks and panels together under a single site. In consequence, other measures vary: a convention of splitting tends to lead to a small number of figures per site, whilst a convention of lumping tends to large numbers. So a body of rock-art reported as having an average 'eighty figures per site' may in fact have the art *less* concentrated in individual spots than does one reported as an average of 'forty figures per site'. Different judgements as to what constitutes one 'figure' will have been combined with different judgements as to what constitutes one 'site'. And so on.

These issues, ubiquitous in archaeology, have prompted some common or even fixed conventions in other sub-fields of the discipline. The animal-bone reports (Reitz and Wing 1999) often use the MNI, the Minimum Number of Individual animals which must have contributed to a given animal bone assemblage: that measure depends on the certain base of knowing just how many bones of just what form an animal of a given species has. Some ceramic studies have used an analogous measure, the Minimum Number of Individual pots (Gibson 1981) which must have contributed to a given potsherd assemblage. That approach is necessarily less secure than for the animal bones because pots are more free in their variability, and more varied in how they collapse into fragments (Orton 1993). Lithic analysis, the longest-established of the analytical techniques specific to archaeology, has many established conventions (Andrefsky 1998), such as the distinction between a core and a flake, and the distinction between a flake (length less than twice width) and a blade (length more than twice width). These conventions, in ubiquitous use, make for rather exact characterization of lithic assemblages and facilitate a range of comparative studies in which the researcher does not need to record personally each industry in order to ensure a consistency.

A consistency of record and report is not enough in itself. In Australia, for instance, it has repeatedly been found that description of a lithic industry in the conventional terms – the proportions of cores, flakes and blades; the occurrence of burins, end-scrapers, side-scrapers, and other standard recognized types – fails to give a useful account (Mulvaney and Kamminga 1999). The logic of Australian stone tools does not follow the structures that are implicit in measuring and counting those aspects in preference to others; accordingly, Australian researchers are making other kinds of studies which give results meaningful in other ways (see e.g. Hiscock 1986; 1994). Even in Australia, the consistency has been a help, all the same, in identifying how it is that the Australian industries decline to 'behave' as they should. More consistency in approach for rock-art should identify methods and define approaches which are indeed useful, or show why they are variable or of less value.

Recognizing variability in rock-art

Rock-art is enormously variable in its characteristics. Unusual techniques have their own variables. So a key field observation for the unusual beeswax figures of north Australia is the colour and the degree of surface cracking in the beeswax (Nelson *et al.* 1995; 2000) – elements which have no equivalent when it comes to the more common media of painting and engraving. Even in the commonplace paintings and engravings, the aspects which are usefully recorded vary so much according to the original techniques, according to the circumstances of preservation, and according to the research concerns of the study.

Animal bones, a more tractable kind of archaeological relic, conveniently offer distinct units clearly separate each from another – each fragment derives from a bone which was once a distinct single object, and each bone is one of a defined number in the skeleton. Immediately, we have unambiguous elements at two physical scales: the individual bone, and the single skeleton. But equivalent rock-art 'units' at all scales of study can be divided only by the exercise of some judgement – a judgement which can always be disputed. If one defines a 'panel' as a distinct area of rock making a *continuous* surface within a site (however 'site' is defined), then what constitutes 'continuous'? What if an otherwise continuous area is split partly in two by a crack? How completely split must it be before it becomes two panels?

The essentials of how Mont Bego is seen by its field researchers are reported below: a single extensive *site*, running over many square kilometres, is divided into *sectors* and those into *zones*, within which the figures are recorded in *groups* on the surfaces of individual *rocks*. Another of the major European rock-engraving locales is Vingen, on the western Norwegian coast. It shares some broad similarities with Mont Bego, as another place where later prehistoric engravings were cut into the glacially smoothed surfaces of metamorphic rocks in the open air. By analogy with Bego, Vingen should be called a single site. But it is variously referred to in the literature as a single unit and as a group of more or less distinct sites. The name 'Vingen' refers to the main carving area, the south shore of the small Vingepollen bay, where rock-engravings are found in multiple settings, separated by a little expanse of water from a further concentration of rock-engravings at Vingeneset to the north. This entire area is no more than 1 km wide from east to west (Bøe 1932: 13). Bøe seems to regard this area as an entity, but structures his description of 778 engravings by reference to eleven differently named geographical areas. A portable stone with the engraving of an animal found in a field at Hennøya, 5 km west of Vingen, is treated separately. Hallström at much the same time presented the 'huge rock carving complex' at Vingen by way of nine geographical 'groups' (1938: 416ff.), including Vingeneset and Hennøya. Rock-engravings were later recorded at the neighbouring Vingelven farm and at Fura, westwards from Vingen towards Hennøya (Fett 1941). The total number of known figures at the main Vingen site itself more than doubled in the 1960s and 1970s, through Egil Bakka's largely unpublished research; he found the engravings to be distributed over 'a number of localities' along the shore (Bakka 1973: 184). Current fieldwork is recognizing different units into which the group is divided. So references to the rock-art of the Vingen area range from mention of a single 'site' to a 'site-cluster' or 'rock-carving area' (Walderhaug 1998: 286). Without a rather detailed study of what the varied units of record are, it is not possible to make even a straightforward comparison of how rock-art is distributed across the landscape at, say, Vingen and at Mont Bego.

Variation of terminology and scale of this kind has been quite widespread within Scandinavia, the picture being further confused through variability of internal divisions of the overall level of site. The terms *felt* or *lokalitet* are commonly used to describe Norwegian sites and zones within sites; yet this use has not been historically consistent. Both terms have been applied both to smaller and to larger units of scale. Current research approaches to the rock-art in the Vingen area hold different views on the overall and internal divisions of the rock-art material, greatly influencing the total number of spatial and scalar units applied.

Defining units on Mont Bego

To take this exploration forward, let us look again at Mont Bego for how these issues are conventionally treated. This body of engraved rock-art has perhaps been examined more thoroughly and minutely than any corpus of corresponding size in Europe or anywhere. First Carlo Conti attempted a full record (a fragment only published as Conti 1972); then the Lumley team completed one. The Mont Bego figures are mostly on surfaces of schist and sandstone which are not physically hard but are chemically durable: they are comparatively easy to mark, and the marks made are long-lasting. By my estimate (Chippindale in press), that thirty-year campaign recently completed to make a comprehensive record of them has involved a labour input many times greater in the recording than was expended in their making. One body of rock-art in which an even larger number of figures has been recorded is in the major sites of Wardaman country, in Aboriginal north Australia, by the Lightning Brothers project, in the 1980s/1990s (David *et al.* 1990). But the Wardaman figures are more repetitive in form, and they have been recorded in a much more summary fashion.

One useful approach to these definitions, at any physical scale, is in terms of relative separation. When there are several instances rather close together, then a rather large gap before the next, a distinct entity has defined itself by that combination of closeness and separation. Applying that rule, let us begin at the largest scale, the definition of Mont Bego as a distinct region within the Alpine rock-art group.[1]

The Bego figures, inventoried as numbering 32,382 figures, extend over an area of some 12 by 5 km around Mont Bego.[2] All but 94 figures – 99.7 per cent of the total – are in a core area within

[1] One could go a further step up in scale and define the Alpine group by the same means as distinct amongst later prehistoric rock-art traditions in Europe. Extending not many hundred kilometres north–south from central Switzerland to near the Mediterranean coast of France, and east–west from the western Alps of France across to Austria, it is separated by more hundreds of kilometres from the more extensive Scandinavian zone of Denmark, Sweden, Norway, Finland and Karelia.

[2] As known in 1995. A new outlying group is now reported to the west, above the Vallée de la Gordalasque. When recorded, it will make a new sector (because in a new and separate area), a 24th Zone, and extend the overall spread of the Bego group.

4 km of the Bego summit. There are no bodies of rock-engraving of any size within many tens of kilometres. The Valcamonica–Valtellina region of northern Italy, the only Alpine rock-art group larger than Bego in the number of its figures, is at a distance of a few hundred kilometres.

Within the Bego group, there are seven distinct sectors of engravings (Fig. 5.1). They are 'distinct' because each sector holds a number of figured surfaces more-or-less close together, with a more-or-less large space without engravings before the next group. That separating space is decidedly greater than the typical distance between engraved surfaces within any one sector. Those seven sectors are: Lac du Vei del Bouc; Col du Sabion; Lac Sainte Marie; Fontanalba; Valmasque; Valaurette; Merveilles–Arpette.[3] One can call these units 'self-defining'.

Bego researchers have recognized Zones of the rock-engravings, since Conti (1939) defined them in his fieldwork beginning in 1927.[4] Five of these Zones equate to a self-defining sector: Lac du Vei del Bouc is Zone XXII; Col du Sabion is XX; Lac Sainte Marie is XXI; Valmasque is XIV; Valaurette is XIII. The other two areas are internally divided. The single sector of Fontanalba is divided between five Zones, XV to XIX (Fig. 5.2). The single sector of the Merveilles–Arpette is divided between thirteen Zones, 0 to XII. The lines dividing the zones make some topographic sense, in that each follows some break-line or topographic marker in

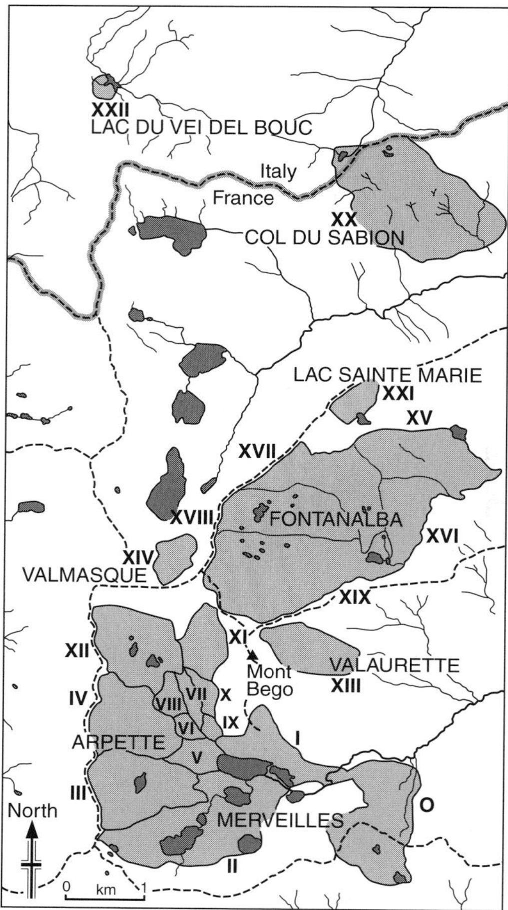

Fig. 5.1. Areas and zones of Mont Bego rock-art, as recognized in 1995.

Dashed lines indicate the main crests of the ridges which divide the valleys. The more solid line is the modern border between France (where all but one of the Bego zones lies) and Italy.

The main areas of figures are in the two large valleys adjacent to the Mont Bego summit: to the south and west the extensive Merveilles area, zones 0–XII (of which the western part is also called the Arpette); to the north-east the Fontanalba area, zones XV–XIX, with the adjacent Lac Sainte Marie area, zone XXI.

Also close to Mont Bego are two smaller areas in separate valleys: to the east Valaurette, zone XIII; to the north Valmasque, zone XIII.

Further removed are two areas to the north: Col du Sabion, zone XX: Lac du Vei del Bouc, zone XXII.

[3] Some of these, close together as seen on a conventional map, are separated by cliff- and ridge-lines in this rugged landscape. Assessing the 'separating space' needs to be in terms of human access experienced on the ground rather than abstracted distances reported on the map. Valaurette and Fontanalba are separated by impassable cliffs; Valmasque and Merveilles, and Valmasque and Fontanalba by steep slopes and a watershed. Only Lac Sainte Marie and Fontanalba lie close together within the same drainage and could be made into a single combined Fontanalba–Lac Sainte Marie area.

[4] Conti originally defined twenty Zones, numbered I to XX. With new discoveries three more were added so there are now twenty-three, numbered 0 to XXII.

Fig. 5.2. An area within the Mont Bego rock-engraving landscape.

The great central slab of the upper Val Fontanalba, Mont Bego. A great sloping mass of rock some 4 sq. km in extent, across and around which are scattered some 15,000 figures.

How many sites are there here? Part only of a single site, the Mont Bego rock-engravings as a whole? A single site itself? One of several sites which together make Mont Bego as a whole? Or 1645 sites, since there are that many distinct rocks or panels enumerated in its survey?

the landscape; but they are placed by an arbitrating judgement rather than being self-defining as the sectors are.

There is good research cause to subdivide the Bego *ensemble* into the Zones. Without them, area studies within the group have an unhappy division. There are only two large self-defining entities, the Fontanalba sector and the Merveilles–Arpette sector. Of the total, some 46.2 per cent of figures are in Fontanalba, 52.4 per cent in Merveilles–Arpette, and only 1.4 per cent in the other five sectors combined. Even collectively as the combined outliers, the other five sectors are too small in the number of figures to be analytically comparable; taken as five separate sectors, they are even less comparable in size. The consequent difficulty is in the fair placing of lines to divide each of the two large and continuous sectors of figured rocks into the Zones.

The Zones are internally divided into Groups; again these are, and must be, distinguished by judged and arbitrary rather than self-defining lines.

The engraved landscape of Bego is for the most part Alpine pasture, above the tree-line. There is much bare rock and some lakes; otherwise the land is covered by grass with herbs, from which innumerable boulders protrude, large and small, some of which bear engravings. Each of these rocks is again self-defining, in that a more-or-less-continuous area of rock is distinctly separated from its neighbours by grass where the rocks are covered over; usually each rock seems to have a distinct edge, and it is separated from its neighbours by a more-or-less large space, so it is reasonable to think that rock surfaces which in that way appear distinct are indeed separate entities. But in some areas, the rock surface is continuous: not a scatter of detached boulders but an extended area of exposed bed-rock. This may make a cliff face; or a swelling hogsback ridge of rock running up to some hundred metres (in Italian a *ciappe*; in French a *roche moutonnée*); or a length of rock which disappears briefly under grass and reappears as evidently part of the same and continuous surface. Dividing those rocky areas into distinct 'Rocks' is an arbitrary matter rather than self-defining. The rule can again apply, that sets of figures define a 'Rock' when they are rather close together and rather separated from the next figures. Many arbitrating judgements will again be needed.

'La Voie Sacrée' (The Sacred Way), one of the larger Fontanalba surfaces, with 284 recorded figures bears an unusually large number of engravings. Geologically, it is a single slab of rock, all on the same plane and running steeply up and down the central Fontanalba hillside. Although some 50 m long, La Voie Sacrée is quite narrow, 2–3 m and sloping transversely as well as with the angle of the mountain side. It appears to me as decidedly a single surface; yet transverse cracks divide it into as many as seventeen areas which one could choose instead to define as seventeen distinct panels or rocks.

On these rock surfaces or panels – however they are distinguished and divided one from another – are individual figures, given individual numbers by the Bego survey. In this way, the Mont Bego group is exceptionally well documented, with every individual figure uniquely specified by Zone, Group, Rock, Figure number as, e.g., 'Z[one]. VIII. G[roup]. II. R[ock]. 8. no. 52'.

Many figures are self-defining, in the terms of this chapter. A figure is generally a continuous area of pecking separate and distinct from any other areas of marking on the rock. Some are not defined that way (Fig. 5.3). Either one can discern distinct shapes or distinctly different kinds of pecking within a continuous area, so the area can by that observation be divided into more than one figure. Or one can recognize that areas of discontinuous marking belong together as part of a single figure. Instances would be the distinct dots within boundaries that are common in the 'topographic' figures. Another would be the group of an ox-team, an ard and a ploughman with detached other human figures which together make a ploughing scene. Besides, varying states of preservation and survival add uncertainties. When a line disappears into an eroded area, and another line emerges from the same eroded area, is one to treat these as two distinct lines? Or to suppose – reasonably and without certainty – they once were one?

A most common Bego figure is the *cornu* (Fig. 5.4), a schematic way of imaging an ox – by means of conspicuous horns with the animal's head and body summarily depicted; one *cornu* is clearly one figure. Frequent, but less common, is the plough-team (Fig. 5.4), in which two *cornus* are joined by the yoke, and linked to the shaft, ard-blade and other components. If the plough-team is a single figure, then it contains within itself two *cornus*. A single complex and composite figure contains smaller and simpler elements which, when occurring on their own, are themselves treated as single figures.

In sum, it is not possible to lay out firm defining rules as to what constitutes a site, an area, a Zone, a Group, a Rock, a surface, a Figure in the collected entity that is Bego rock-art: all these distinctions and definitions depend on an exercise

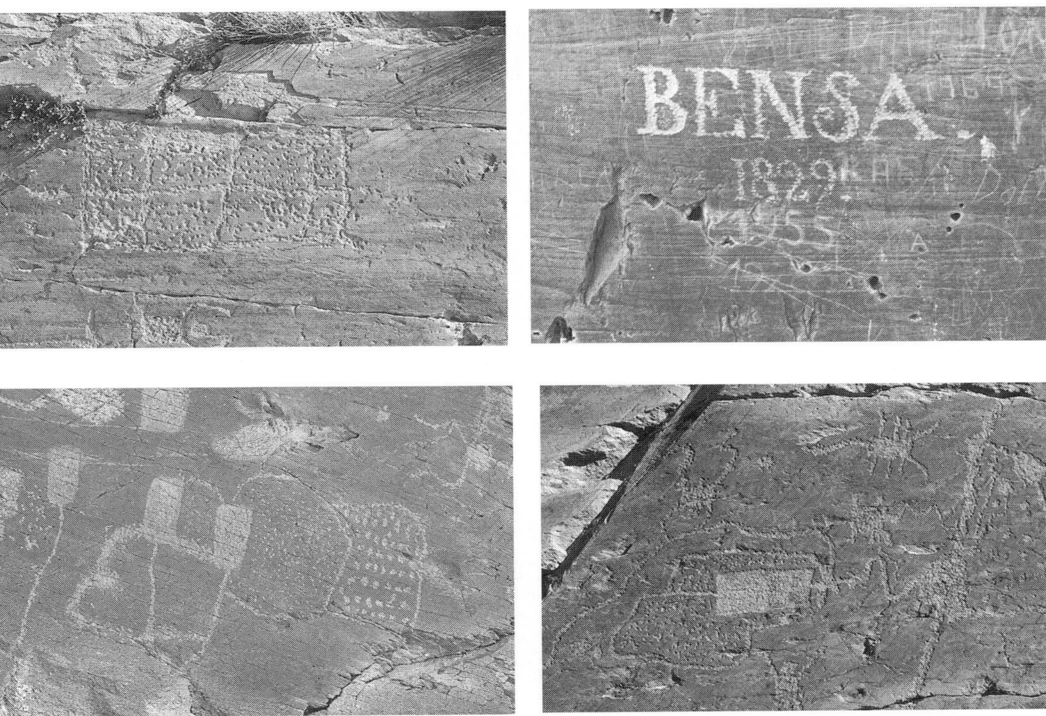

Fig. 5.3. Examples of individual Mont Bego figures which are not self-defining at the centimetre level.

(*above left*) Geometric figure. The many dots within (and some outside) the framing rectangle are treated as part of a single figure, although each dot is a discontinuous small patch of engraving.

(*above right*) Historic inscription. The letters making up BENSA are treated as making a single figure, though again each is a discontinuous area of engraving.

(*below left*) Topographic figure. The complex of solid pecked rectangles, curving and defining lines and arrays of dots are treated altogether as a single figure, rather than a composition of distinct elements.

(*below right*) Eroded figures on crowded surfaces require uncertain judgements in deciding what makes one figure, and what distinguishes one figure from another into which it runs.

Photographs by Christopher Chippindale.

of some judgement in what is divided and what is treated together. The 'self-defining' aspects will be an important guide, but they are not enough. In this respect the Bego rock-engravings are typical of rock-art. I know of not a single rock-art group in which the units that one needs to distinguish for record, study and analysis are fully 'self-defining' or can be recognized without some considered, necessarily arbitrary judgement as to what is separated, what is treated together as a single unit.

That fact should warn us against some standard approach to defining spatial units in rock-art. The handbooks to rock-art recording and study (e.g. Anati 1976; Loendorf *et al.* 1999; Whitley 2001; soon also, Dowson in press) do not effectively do so. The precedent of lithic studies also shows that the common entities which the analysts find they can recognize through technical definitions may not equate to a meaningful class when it comes to inferring from the artefacts to prehistoric human beings. The recognized class of 'scraper' does not correspond to the set of stone tools used in ancient times for scraping.

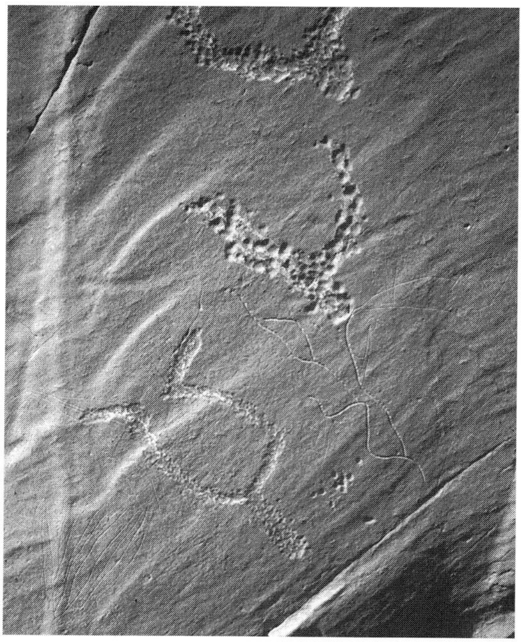

Physical scale from millimetre to kilometre: a uniting factor in rock-art studies

Yet it is also evident that *some* common factors exist across most rock-art groups. And it is useful for recording and analysis to emphasize common factors, as it is their generality which makes possible comparative study. A uniting factor in studies on Mont Bego – those by the Lumley team (e.g. Lumley *et al.* 1995; many reported in Lumley 1991; also e.g. Lumley *et al.* 1994–95; 1997; Serres 1996–97), Arcà's (this volume, pages 318–49; previously Arcà 1998; 1999), the present author's in his PhD thesis (Chippindale 1988), those by other recent researchers of varied approach and persuasion (e.g. Hirigoyen 1978; Dufrenne 1985; Masson 1993; Barfield and Chippindale 1997), by their many predecessors (e.g. Barocelli 1928; Conti 1939), back to Bicknell's fundamental explorations of a century ago (e.g. Bicknell 1899; 1902) and the pioneer reports before him (e.g. Fodéré 1821; Rivière 1878) – is that they deal with spatial patterns *simultaneously* at a *variety* of physical scales. That same uniting factor applies to integrated rock-art studies everywhere.

The millimetre scale: the dimension of technique

A good starting-point for study of *any* archaeological material will begin with the physical stuff itself: just how was it created? At Mont Bego,

Fig. 5.4. Figures existing both as individual engravings, and as elements in composite engravings.

(*above*) The characteristic Bego figure is a simple *cornu*, representative of an ox. On this surface are three *cornus* of varying forms close together.

(*below*) A Bego plough-team incorporates two *cornus*.

The opportunity for studying the variation in pecking, the millimetre scale at which technique is studied, is evident in these examples. The possibility of regularities in their placing on the surface, the metre scale of study, are also evident.

where the prehistoric figures are nearly all made with the pecking technique (*piquetage*), the physical act is to hammer a stone – likely a piece of quartzite[5] – so as to make peck-marks on the rock surface. The individual peck-marks vary in depth and in size. They are generally round in shape, more-or-less, as seen both from above and in cross-section. They are generally a few millimetres in size. So the first scale of study at Mont Bego, and a proper starting-point, is at the *millimetre* level of physical dimensions. This primarily addresses technique, the way the individual marks on the rock are made. There are some ancient and many modern figures made by another technique, scratching the thinnest of lines (*linéaires*); and there are figures dating to recent periods which are made with a thicker and grosser line, evidently chiselled out using a metal tool. All these techniques of engraving are to be measured in millimetres, for the marks they make in the rock. The fainter, shallower and thinner lines of the *linéaires* are the smallest in size, with width and depth of a millimetre or so; the largest peck-marks approach perhaps 10 mm in size. Lumley *et al.* (1995: 53–9) enumerate the thirteen aspects to variability they discern in techniques of pecking alone.

So the *millimetre* level is the right first scale of study at Bego and at rock-engraving sites generally, where the same techniques of pecking, scratching and cutting a line are the common ones.

The millimetre scale applies also to rock-painting since all but the broadest means of applying pigment permit the drawing of elements of a size to be measured in millimetres. Some finer-line rock-painting techniques – such as those of the celebrated 'Dynamic Figures' in Arnhem Land, north Australia (Chaloupka 1988–89; 1993; Chippindale *et al.* 2000), the Bradshaw figures of north-west Australia (Walsh 1994) and the smaller figures in San rock-art, South Africa (Lewis-Williams 1983; Lewis-Williams and Blundell 1998) – are so delicately painted that lines on the rock are but a millimetre or three thick. Contemporary north Australian painters, continuing the rock-painting tradition with the same earth pigments on other surfaces, achieve the finest line in cross-hatching (*rarrk*) with brushes made of a single hair. Although most rock-painting does not use so fine a line, it is reasonable to think of painting technique as operating at the millimetre scale.

The centimetre scale: the dimension of the figure and motif

The minimal prehistoric Bego rock-engraving, which I have observed in the field, will be the single and solitary peck-mark (though it is hard to be certain that a single mark is not a natural mark arising through other causes). The common engraving is an array of tens or hundreds or even thousands of individual peck-marks together making a distinct area. This is the figure or motif. At Bego it is generally to be measured in centimetres, with the typical figure being a few tens of centimetres in size, and the largest some hundreds of centimetres. There are difficulties in defining what is a motif in principle (p. 108 above), and in recognizing just where one figure ends and another begins when a surface is covered by figures which overlap or cut across each other. Here, observable distinction in technique (the millimetre scale) will be pertinent, and so will the experienced fieldworker's knowledge of the repertoire of distinctive forms, which hints at what is likely to be seen at a newly scrutinized surface.

[5] The deposits at the foot of some Bego surfaces were explored at an early stage of study, when it was realized that some figures were buried underground, without much being found of the engravers' tools (Bicknell 1913). Quartzite and quartz outcrop commonly in the Bego area. Small pebbles, excavated at the foot of Valcamonica surfaces and confidently identified as the hammer-stones used to peck figures, are often of quartzite.

Again, Mont Bego presents typical research conditions: those dimensions are typical of rock-engraving traditions generally, and so are the issues in discerning and separating out individual motifs from a palimpsest on a crowded surface.

So this same *centimetre* level is the right second scale of study at Bego and at rock-engraving sites generally, where the researcher isolates and defines the individual figures on each surface.

Rock-paintings, broadly speaking, tend to a larger size of figure than do rock-engravings. In Australia, there are several regional rock-painting traditions in which figures several hundred centimetres in size are not unusual, from the *wandjina* of the north-west (Crawford 1968), through the earlier 'Large Naturalistic' and the later 'X-ray' figures of Arnhem Land (Chaloupka 1993) on the central northern coast, to the *quinkan* figures of Queensland in the north-east (Trezise 1971). By contrast, individual figures in the widespread and early Panaramitee rock-engravings are mostly to be measured in tens of centimetres (Flood 1997).[6] For north America one thinks of the immense paintings of the Pecos River (Kirkland and Newcomb 1967) or of Baja California (Hyland in press), not matched in common size by any regional style of engraving. Even then, one can think of many exceptions to the broad pattern that rock-paintings will often be larger than rock-engravings: the large engraved animals of the Sydney sandstone, south-east Australia (Stanbury *et al.* 1990), and the near-life-size engraved deer of some 'Hunter's rock-art' in Scandinavia (Bøe 1932); the tiny figures that accompany the large motifs in the rock-painting of Arnhem Land or of southern Africa. That range admitted, a scale of centimetres is fitting for rock-painting as it is for engraving.

[6] That example of scale may arise from the subject-matter. The characteristic Panaramitee motif is a same-size representation of a human footprint or animal track – a natural-world object whose size is to be measured at a few tens of centimetres or smaller.

The metre scale: systematics of the surface or panel bearing the figure and motif

The surfaces which carry the Bego figures vary much in size. L'Autel ('The Altar'), very large, bears 1339 figures recorded. The single surface bearing most motifs, it measures 73 m by 43 m, with the engravings distributed patchily in distinct regions within its overall area. Many surfaces are to be measured as a metre or three in one or other dimension; some are smaller. So a scale of metres is a fitting one for the systematics of how figures are placed together on the Bego surfaces. This aspect has sometimes been called 'composition', an unhappy term because composition – the placing of figures together as a considered group in some planned pattern – is only one aspect of the regularities which present themselves, and an exceptionally hard one to identify with any confidence. There are many others at Mont Bego, some less uncertain to deal with: the relation of the human marks to the natural shape and features of the surface; the orientation of figures, where strong patterns are evident as to which direction is 'right way up'; a kind of 'similarity principle' by which figures of a certain class, such as plough-teams or halberds, tend to be grouped together on surfaces, rather than scattered evenly across disparate surfaces; another 'similarity principle' by which figures of the same class on the same surface tend to be similar in shape; the evidence of sequence which may be inferred (with difficulty) from the layout of figures in relation to each other (Arcà, this volume, pp. 334–8); a noticed preference for placing figures towards the base of a surface, by the soil level (Lumley *et al.* 1995: 294); and another by which (especially in the Vallée des Merveilles zones) engravings are placed on a surface such that a central motif or motifs are set on a vertical axis (Lumley *et al.* 1995: 294);

a number of individual surfaces where the placing of a set of figures has the appearance of a single planned grouping – a composition in the strict sense; and the broad issue as to whether figures, which sometimes overlap and sometimes leave gaps of unmarked rock between them, are placed at hazard on the surface, or are placed so as rather to touch and cover each other, or are placed so as rather to avoid each other (Chippindale 1986).

As for the previous and smaller scales, these kinds of issues at Bego are typical both of rock-art study and in the metrical scale at which the pertinent field evidence exists.

In this aspect, rock-engravings and rock-paintings present much the same issues at much the same scale.

The kilometre scale: place of the surface or panel in a broader landscape

As noted above, the Bego figures are patchily distributed across a landscape, a mountain environment full of abrupt slopes and with great differences of elevation within a small distance. As is always the case for rock-art, the pattern of distribution reflects the availability of rock. Some of the empty areas on the map of where the engravings are found (Fig. 5.1, p. 106 above) do correspond to areas where there is little or no exposure of the smoothed surfaces of schist and fine-grained sandstone on which the figures occur. But occurrence of rock is not the whole story. The uppermost areas of the Fontanalba, those to the west near the pass over to the Valmasque valley (the Baisse de Valmasque), have much inviting rock, smooth and strongly coloured, but not many figures. The area of dense concentrations of figures immediately below and to the west of the Mont Bego summit, the Vallée des Merveilles proper in the narrow sense, has much good rock. But there is not so much and so specially inviting rock in this defile as itself to explain both the very high number of figures and the recognized special importance of a small number of singular or unique figures in that little patch – the 'Chief of the Tribes', the 'Sorcerer', the 'False Sorcerer', 'The Anthropomorph with Zigzag Arms', etc.

As in the other scales, the Bego figures show a distribution in the landscape which reflects both the occurrence of suitable rock and a considered choice in which surfaces receive many figures, which receive few or none. As for the other scales, this is typical of rock-art, both engraved and painted. Many of us, with some years of field experience in a given region, have come to a good understanding of where the art will be found. But which of us has not also – and often – been surprised? Going into an 'obvious' shelter, one finds nothing. Looking in an 'unpromising' corner, one finds a figure or panel. The key Arnhem Land figure for a recent interpretation (Chippindale *et al.* 2000) has been one of those surprises. Hard to see on an ill-protected surface, it is on the back and rough side of a boulder which has paintings in a more obvious and inviting shelter in the front. This will be why it was not noticed until Ben Smith spotted it with the present writer in 1996, although it is within a dense concentration of painted panels close to a water-hole which has on several occasions been visited and studied by experienced archaeologists and art researchers.

The value of a systematics of scale

Introducing the present chapter, I referred to the units of record, study and classification which have proved useful in systematically exploring other classes of archaeological material. The ones mentioned there – animal and human bones, potsherds and whole pots, flaked-stone implements – are more amenable to the imposition of standard categories. Bones are each distinct, and bones derive from whole individual

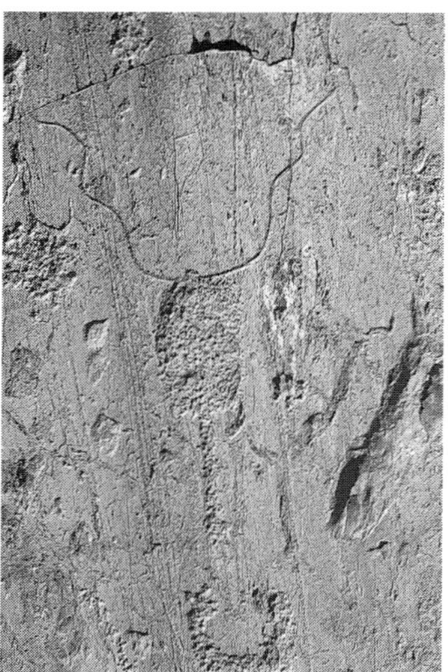

Fig. 5.5. Field observations at Mont Bego at four physical scales.

(*top left*) Millimetre scale: technique. Individual peck-marks and scratched lines are discerned.

(*top right*) Centimetre scale: form of individual figures and of motifs considered as single entities. The systematics of motif shape addresses the overall shape of this Bego *cornu* (horned figure representing an ox). The distinct difference between the fine and shallow pecking of its horns and the deep and coarse pecking of its oval body are a matter of technique to be studied at the millimetre scale.

(*bottom left*) Metre scale: placing of figures across the surface. The shapes of the fifty or so individual figures are a matter to be studied at the centimetre scale.

(*bottom right*) Kilometre scale: location of figured surfaces in the larger landscape. The placing of individual figures on the figured surface, the smooth rock in the foreground, is a matter to be studied at the metre scale.

animals, one skeleton at a time. Pots echo this more weakly, with individual potsherds deriving from single and individual whole pots. Flaked stone is more varied in the forms it takes, but some categories in its analysis have proved robust. The staged nature of stone-working helps, for each step in stone-working generally consists of a single blow or group of blows, and each can make a link in the *chaîne opératoire* which transforms and reduces the starting block into the finished implement.

No such neat and standard order will be possible in studying rock-art (Fig. 5.5) – on Mont Bego or anywhere else. Each defined scale above elides

Table 5.1 *The four physical scales of rock-art study summarized*

Scale	Name	Aspect addressed
thousandths of a metre	millimetre	technique
hundredths of a metre	centimetre	figure and motif
metre	metres	surface or panel
thousands of metres	kilometre	place in a broader landscape

and slides into the next. The single peck-mark (millimetre scale) can itself be a motif (centimetre scale). The individual figure (centimetre) is uncertainly distinguished from the *ensemble* on the surface (metre scale). Recognizing the individual surface or panel (metre) again involves judgement as to when a single surface becomes more than one surface in some spatial relationship to others in the landscape (kilometre scale).[7]

[7] The defining and recognition of four scales itself requires judgement. One could recognize a smaller scale below the millimetre where one could usefully explore the physical impact of rock-engraving on the matrix and structure of the rock surface; this could be at a scale one order of physical magnitude below the millimetre, at the level of one ten-thousandth of a metre – a unit for which the metric system has no commonly used name.

One could also recognize more scales at the large end of the range. The kilometre scale could be subdivided at least once. A scale dealing with distances of the order of hundreds of metres would be fitting for describing and explaining the distribution of figured areas around Mont Bego. If the metric system recognized the unit, this would be at a 'hectometre' scale. For the larger pattern, that of the distribution of rock-engravings across the Alpine arc, one is dealing with tens and hundreds of kilometres, so scales by the 10,000 metre or the 100,000 metre would be fitting. Again these are units for which the metric system has no commonly used name.

The usual benefits and costs of 'lumping' and of splitting apply. My judgement is that the advocated four scales of magnitude will be a good balance, chosen from a potential ten each defined by a tenfold increase within the metric system:

ten-thousandths of a metre – not used
thousandths of a metre – *millimetre* – preferred
hundredths of a metre – *centimetre* – preferred
tenths of a metre – decimetre – not used
metre – preferred
tens of metres – decametre – not used
hundreds of metres – not used
thousands of metres – *kilometre* – preferred
tens of thousands of metres – not used
hundreds of thousands of metres – not used

Table 5.1 summarizes the scales of study, their nesting relationship and the aspects of study each addresses.

An evident weakness in rock-art studies is the limited development of fitting methods by which to approach both the recording of art and the comparative study of what has been recorded. As a special field within archaeology, it benefits from methods which deal with the unique circumstances of that field of study, whilst also benefiting from cognate methods in archaeology and anthropology. A case in point is the distinction between 'formal methods' and 'informed methods' in respect of another aspect to rock-art studies, the availability or absence of pertinent ethnohistoric information by which to glimpse some kind of an 'inside view' of the meaning of a given body of rock-art (above, p. 14). The framework of spatial scale and order sketched here may also be found of use.

Acknowledgements

I thank my PhD supervisor John Coles with whom I studied when this frame of working was devised; Professor H. de Lumley and his Bego team; the friends, acquaintances and strangers who assisted in my fieldwork on Mont Bego; the colleagues who study Alpine and other rock-art for guidance when this frame of working was developed; colleagues and audiences with whom I have since talked about it; Andy Dorse, Emma Jane Read and Eva Walderhaug for advice.

References

Anati, E. 1976. *Metodi di rilevamento e di analisi dell'arte rupestre*. Capo di Ponte: Edizioni del Centro.

Andrefsky, W., Jr. 1998. *Lithics*. Cambridge: Cambridge University Press. Cambridge Manuals in Archaeology.

Arcà, A. 1998. Settlements in topographic engravings of Copper Age in Valcamonica and Mt Bego rock art, in *Proceedings of the XIII International Congress of Prehistoric and Protohistoric Sciences – Forlì 1996* 4: 9–16. Forlì.

1999. Fields and settlements in topographic engravings of the Copper Age in Valcamonica and Mt Bego rock art, in Philippe Della Casa (ed.), *Prehistoric Alpine environment, society and economy: papers of the international colloquium PAESE '97 in Zurich*: 71–9. Bonn. Universitätforschungen zur Prähistorischen Archäologie 55.

Bakka, E. 1973. Om alderen på veideristningane, *Viking* 37: 151–87.

Barfield, L. and C. Chippindale. 1997. Meaning in the later prehistoric rock-engravings of Mont Bego, Alpes-Maritimes, France, *Proceedings of the Prehistoric Society* 63: 103–28.

Barocelli, P. 1928. Le incisioni rupestri delle Alpi Marittime (appunti paletnologiche), *Historia* 2(1): 19–49.

Bicknell, C. 1899. Osservazione ulteriori sulle incisioni rupestri in Val Fontanalba, *Atti della Società Ligustica di Scienze Naturali* 10: 45–52.

1902. *The prehistoric rock engravings in the Italian Maritime Alps*. Bordighera: Pietro Gibelli.

1913. *A guide to the prehistoric rock-engravings in the Italian Maritime Alps*. Bordighera: Giuseppe Bessone.

Bøe, J. 1932. *Felszeichnungen im westlichen Norwegen 1: Vingen und Henøya*. Bergen: Bergen Museum. Bergen Museums Skrifter 15.

Chaloupka, George. 1988–89. Rock paintings of the Dynamic Figures Style, Arnhem Land plateau region, Northern Territory, Australia, *Ars Praehistorica* 7–8: 329–37.

1993. *Journey in time: the world's longest continuing art tradition*. Chatswood, NSW: Reed.

Chippindale, C. 1986. A microcomputer simulation of variable forms in prehistoric rock art, in A. Voorrips and S. Loving (eds.), *'To pattern the past': proceedings of Amsterdam conference on mathematical methods in archaeology*. Brussels: PACT.

1988. The later prehistoric rock-engravings of Val Fontanalbe, Mont Bego, Tende, Alpes-Maritimes, France. Unpublished PhD thesis, University of Cambridge.

In press. Small marks on rocks, large marks with rocks: labour input to rock-art and to a megalithic construction of later prehistoric Europe, in John Steinberg (ed.), *Systematics of chiefdom societies*.

Chippindale, C., B. Smith and P. S. C. Taçon. 2000. Visions of Dynamic power: archaic rock-paintings, Altered States of Consciousness and 'clever men' in western Arnhem Land (NT), Australia, *Cambridge Archaeological Journal* 10(1): 63–101.

Conti, C. 1939. Undici anni di esplorazioni alle 'Meraviglie' di M. Bego, *Rivista Ingauna e Intemelia* 5: 11–30.

1972. *Corpus delle incisioni rupestri di Monte Bego 1: Zona 1*. Bordighera: Istituto Internazionale di Studi Liguri.

Crawford, I. M. 1968. *The art of the Wandjina*. Melbourne, Vic.: Oxford University Press.

David, B., I. McNiven, J. Flood, V. Attenbrow and R. Frost. 1990. The Lightning Brothers Project: the 1988 and 1989 field seasons, *Australian Archaeology* 31: 86–91.

Dowson, T. In press. *Rock art*. Cambridge: Cambridge University Press. Cambridge Manuals in Archaeology.

Dufrenne, R. 1985. Interprétation des gravures rupestres de la Vallée des Merveilles à la lumière de la tradition védique, *Bolletino del Centro Camuno di Studi Preistorici* 22: 110–16.

Fett, P. 1941. Nye ristningar i Nordfjord: Vingelva og Fura. Bergen, *Bergens Museums årbok 1941. Historisk-antikvarisk rekke* 6.

Flood, J. 1997. *Rock art of the Dreamtime: images of ancient Australia*. Sydney: Angus and Robertson.

Fodéré, F.-E. 1821. *Voyage aux Alpes-Maritimes ou Histoire naturelle, agraire, civile et médicale du comté de Nice et des pays limitrophes; enrichi de notes de comparaison avec d'autres contrées*. Paris.

Gibson, A. 1981. *Introduction to prehistoric pottery*. Leicester: Leicester University Press.

Hallström, G. 1938. *Monumental art of northern Europe from the Stone Age 1: The Norwegian localities*. Stockholm: Almqvist and Wiksell.

Hirigoyen, R. 1978. *La Pierre et la pensée: la Vallée des Merveilles – les gravures rupestres du Mont Bego*. Paris: Librairie Orientaliste Paul Genthner.

Hiscock, P. 1986. Technological change in the Hunter Valley and its implications for the interpretation of Late Holocene change in Australia, *Archaeology in Oceania* 21(1): 40–50.

1994. Technological responses to risk in Holocene Australia, *World Prehistory* 8(3): 267–92.

Hyland, J. In press. Talking with the dead: the peninsular ceremonial complex and the great mural tradition of Baja California, in David S. Whitley (ed.), *Ethnography and western North*

American rock art. Albuquerque, NM: University of New Mexico Press.

Kirkland, F. and W. W. Newcomb, Jr. 1967. *The rock art of the Texas Indians*. Austin, TX: University of Texas Press.

Lewis-Williams, J. D. 1983. *The rock art of southern Africa*. Cambridge: Cambridge University Press.

Lewis-Williams, D. and G. Blundell. 1998. *Fragile heritage: a rock art fieldguide*. Johannesburg: Witwatersrand University Press.

Loendorf, L., L. A. Olson, S. Conner and J. C. Dean. 1999. *A manual for rock art documentation*. Privately published.

Lumley, H. de (ed.). 1991. *Le Mont Bego: une montagne sacrée de l'Age du Bronze: sa place dans le contexte des religions protohistoriques du bassin méditerranéen: Colloque International, Tende, Alpes-Maritimes, vendredi 5 au jeudi 11 juillet 1991*. Paris: Laboratoire de Préhistoire du Musée Nationale d'Histoire Naturelle.

Lumley, H. de, A. Echassoux and T. Serres. 1994–95. Signification des gravures corniformes du Chalcolithique et de l'Age du Bronze ancien de la région du Mont Bego, *Bulletin d'Etudes Préhistoriques et Archéologiques Alpines* 5–6 (numéro spécial consacré aux Actes du VIIe Colloque sur les Alpes dans l'Antiquité, Châtillon, Vallée d'Aoste, 11–12–13 mars 1994): 81–141.

1997. Contribution à la lecture des gravures symboliques du Mont Bego, Tende (Alpes-Maritimes): les petits personnages associés à un zigzag, *Gallia Préhistoire* 39: 255–85.

Lumley, H. de, *et al.* 1995. *Le Grandiose et le sacré: gravures rupestres protohistoriques et historiques de la région du Mont Bego*. Aix-en-Provence: Edisud.

Masson, E. 1993. *Vallée des Merveilles: un berceau de la pensée religieuse européenne*. Dijon: Editions Faton.

Mulvaney, J. and J. Kamminga. 1999. *Prehistory of Australia*. Washington, DC: Smithsonian Institution Press.

Nelson, D. E., G. Chaloupka, C. Chippindale, M. S. Alderson and J. Southon. 1995. Radiocarbon dates for beeswax figures in the prehistoric rock art of northern Australia, *Archaeometry* 37(1): 151–6.

Nelson, E., C. Chippindale, P. S. C. Taçon, G. Chaloupka and J. Southon 2000. *The beeswax rock-art of Arnhem Land, Northern Territory, Australia: field records, archaeology, anthropology, dating, chronology and interpretation*. CD-ROM publication. Burnaby, BC: Simon Fraser University, Department of Archaeology.

Orton, C. 1993. How many pots make five? – an historical review of pottery quantification, *Archaeometry* 35(2): 169–84.

Reitz, E. J. and E. S. Wing. 1999. *Zooarchaeology*. Cambridge: Cambridge University Press. Cambridge Manuals in Archaeology.

Rivière, E. 1878. Gravures sur roches des Lacs des Merveilles au Val d'Enfer, in *Association Française pour l'Avancement des Sciences, Congrès de Paris, 1878*: 783–93. Paris.

Serres, T. 1996–97. Vers la comprehension d'un langage symbolique, étude des gravures protohistoriques de la région du Mont Bego, Tende, AM, *Bulletin d'Etudes Préhistoriques et Archéologiques Alpines* 7–8: 83–95.

Stanbury, P., J. Clegg and D. Campbell. 1990. *A field guide to Aboriginal rock engravings, with special reference to those around Sydney*. South Melbourne: Sydney University Press.

Trezise, P. 1971. *Rock art of southeast Cape York*. Canberra, ACT: Australian Institute of Aboriginal Studies.

Walderhaug, E. M. 1998. Changing art in a changing society: the hunters' rock-art of western Norway, in Christopher Chippindale and Paul S. C. Taçon (eds.), *The archaeology of rock-art*: 285–301. Cambridge: Cambridge University Press.

Walsh, G. L. 1994. *Bradshaws: ancient rock paintings of north-west Australia*. Carouge-Geneva: Edition Limitée.

Whitley, D. S. (ed.). 2001. *Handbook of rock art studies*. Beverly Hills, CA: Sage.

6

The canvas as the art: landscape analysis of the rock-art panel

James D. Keyser and George Poetschat

A century of rock-art recording – whether by drawing, tracing or photography – has explored ever-better means to disentangle the rock-art image of interest from the distracting irrelevance of the rock panel which supports it. The ideal is to recover the image as a set of well-defined shapes on the neutral ground of a smooth white sheet of drawing paper. Disconcertingly, and perhaps first in South Africa, researchers have become aware of how much of the art is contained in the support; rock surfaces are not neutral canvases, but themselves shapes of form and meaning. Rock-art does not – at the large scale – exist at simple points on the surface of a uniform earth, points which would be equivalent each with another; rather it is at complex points, each one distinctive on the surface of a varied earth where varied human lives are lived. So that same principle of response to landscape exists at the small scale, that of the individual panel on which the individual motif is placed. Examples from western North America are here reported, and these are related to a strikingly similar interplay of image and rock surface in the art of the European Upper Palaeolithic.

Images and natural features

Throughout the history of rock-art, from the earliest Palaeolithic cave paintings to historic-period images in western North America, artists have incorporated unique natural features of the rock canvas into their pictograph or petroglyph compositions. Frequently it appears that the undecorated surface actually inspired an image in the mind of the artist who then applied paint or pecking to enhance the natural feature and thus to communicate part of the message. Although such utilized natural features occur quite frequently in the rock-art of some areas (e.g. Beltrán 1998: 94, 101–2; Clottes and Lewis-Williams 1998: 86–91), many archaeologists often still miss the relationship between the images and the natural features because they fail to recognize the panel as a landscape in miniature. Our recent research in the Columbia Plateau region of north-western North America illustrates the value of recognizing these micro-landscape features for understanding and interpreting the rock-art images.

Scholars of the European Palaeolithic have long recognized the interplay between landscape features of the rock-art panel and the art painted or scratched thereon (Breuil 1952; Levy 1963: 21–2; Bahn and Vertut 1988: 89–90). This early recognition, and subsequent focus on the

Fig. 6.1. A Palaeolithic artist used a natural rock ledge to form the rear back and rump of this bull at Lascaux.

topic, seems due to a constellation of several factors.

First, much Palaeolithic art (Figs. 6.1 and 6.2) is very realistic and naturalistic in form, which often allows the modern observer to 'know' what the image should show and thus be especially receptive to seeing how natural features were incorporated as parts of the images. A perfect example is the ledge that forms the back and rump of one of the large bulls in Lascaux. Seeing the front quarters of a very realistic bull, the viewer expects the line of the back to extend where the ledge is; the mind accepts the obvious relationship as a logical one without requiring further analysis or understanding. Of course, interpreting the function of this structure requires further analysis and comparison with other examples, but the identification step is obvious, even to an untrained observer. In fact, the senior author's experience leading groups of lay people to sites in several different areas has repeatedly demonstrated the great ease with which non-specialists identify the use of natural features in Palaeolithic cave-art.

Second, much of the art is hidden away in dark caves where artificial light is necessary to view images drawn on undulating walls or among fantastically shaped stalactites, stalagmites and calcite draperies. Often this light magnifies the relationship between the panel and the art; some cave-art images are essentially unrecognizable without the effect of light and shadow (Clottes 1995: 164–5). Were such images painted or carved at open-air sites their recognition would often depend on fortuitous natural lighting restricted to certain times of the day or even certain days of the year. Finally, Palaeolithic rock-art scholars have always had a limited number of often well-preserved sites on which they have had the luxury of investing detailed scrutiny. Such is usually not the case on other continents where thousands of sites – often much less well preserved (and frequently badly defaced with modern graffiti) – showing all manner of stylized and abstract images are found in open-air settings where the effects of lighting are far less easily controlled. Frequently these uncounted thousands of sites vie for such meagre research funding that many still have yet to be

Fig. 6.2. The horse panel in Pech Merle shows a horse's head and front leg profile in the natural rock formation. Clearly, this panel's 'horse landscape' caused the Palaeolithic artist to decorate it with the two painted horse images.

recorded in anything more than location. Only the rarest of sites has been recorded to the extent of someone looking at landscapes on either the macro or micro level.

Given this, and taking cues from rock-art research in Europe and elsewhere, North American scholars have recently begun to notice cases of natural features being used as part of the rock-art image, and examples are cropping up in many regions of North America (Vastokas and Vastokas 1973: 50–2; Loendorf 1994; Whitley 1996). Much still remains to be done; even cursory examination of sites or preliminary site records often yields instances where the incorporation of natural features into the art has not yet been fully recognized (Poetschat and Keyser 1999; see also Tilley 1991 for such an approach at Nämforsen, Sweden).

The panel as landscape in Columbia Plateau rock-art

Although a few examples were previously known where natural features had been incorporated into rock-art on the Columbia Plateau (Woodward 1982: 81; Bettis 1986: 14), recent research into this region's rock-art shows this is significantly more common than previously thought (Keyser *et al.* 1998: 57–8). In the John Day River drainage of north-central Oregon, intensive recording of two sites resulted in the recognition of five different forms of interplay between rock canvas and the art. Some of these are relatively straightforward and simple, such as a rayed arc painted to emphasize a natural 'wrinkle' or a bulge in the basalt. Others show images framed by cracks, spalls or the edges of projecting blocks, and still others use natural rock edges enhanced with pigment to form part of a figure. Some images are painted in, or emerging from, cracks in the rock.

Ethnographic evidence indicates that the great majority of Columbia Plateau art was made as part of the vision-quest trance experience (Keyser 1992; Keyser *et al.* 1998; Hann *et al.* 2003; Keyser and Whitley 2000) undertaken by both shamans and lay persons. Thus, the focus on incorporating the cracks and naturally projecting rock edges into the images suggests strongly that the artist viewed the rock surface (and probably the entire cliff) not as a static canvas but as an interacting part of the trance experience. In other areas of western North America, scholars have noted the relationship between rock-art and cracks in the rock (Loendorf 1994; Whitley 1996). Some ethnographies report that such cracks, holes, caves and other surface irregularities served as portals between the secular and spirit worlds (Whitley 1992). Though the Columbia Plateau ethnographies are nearly silent on this particular aspect, it seems likely that the extensive use of cracks and surface irregularities as part of the images also metaphorically expresses a transition between two worlds for these prehistoric artists. There are limited references to such mechanisms playing a role in Columbia Plateau culture. Among the Wishram, caves figure prominently in the acquisition and use of shamanic power (Spier and Sapir 1930: 240). Likewise, the Klamath/Modoc identify several rock-art caves as types of spirit portals. One cave, decorated with red paint and petroglyphs, was the home of the supreme deity, *Gmok'am'c* (Hann *et al.* 2000). Other lava tube caves with pictographs were said to result from sexual intercourse between *Gmok'am'c* and the earth (Curtin n.d.).

During the vision quest, we suggest, some supplicants focused on the rock surface with such intensity that during the trance itself the 'canvas' came 'alive' and a particular natural feature actually became some part of the spirit world (e.g. an entry portal) or even a spirit being. Then the painted or pecked design was made to enhance or complement the feature, creating the image which served to commemorate the vision. Other artists may have sought natural features not because they were actually part of the specific vision experience, but instead to use them as 'quasi-narrative' devices to enhance the mnemonic function of the image – making it easier to remember and use the component parts of the vision on which the image was based. Although not true narratives in the sense of Plains Biographic Art or Mide scrolls from the northeastern Woodlands (whose symbolism was known to a broad range of culture participants), many vision images painted as Plains shield designs had narrative aspects that assisted the 'owner' of the vision in remembering and describing the experience. Some rock-art on both the Plains and the Columbia Plateau has very similar conventions, suggesting that these images also served a personalized quasi-narrative function.

The above model is formulated using evidence from within the Columbia Plateau: rock-art as a product of the vision-quest trance experience; limited evidence as to importance of natural features; the symbolic meaning of specific motifs (see Keyser and Knight 1976; Keyser 1992; Hann *et al.* 2003). It also derives from analogy with behaviours and beliefs – trance behaviour, quasi-narrative vision imagery and generalized beliefs concerning spirit world portals – from adjacent areas of California, the Great Basin and the Northwestern Plains where rock-art was produced for similar reasons (e.g. Whitley 1992; 1994; Loendorf 1994; Keyser and Klassen 2001). If the model has validity we should regularly be able to find instances where natural features were used in complex ways to create figures that reflect the ethnographic beliefs of Columbia Plateau (and related) cultures. We have selected four examples from three sites in the lower Columbia River region of the Columbia Plateau where it appears that the image uses its interplay with the rock canvas to create a whole greater than could be expressed just by the image alone.

All four images are spirit figures – so classified in Columbia Plateau rock-art because they portray clear anthropomorphic or zoomorphic forms but equally do not represent real people or real animals (Keyser 1992; Keyser *et al.* 1998). All four are part of the Long Narrows (or Columbia River Conventionalized) rock-art style common in the lower Columbia River region and dating to the late Archaic period between AD 500 and AD 1850 (McClure 1984; Keyser 1992).[1] Although each of these motifs was previously recorded and published (some more than once!), it is important to note that the interplay between image and rock surface had never been explicitly recognized.[2] The microcosmic 'landscape' – at the *panel* level – had gone unrecognized, and the images could not really be understood or interpreted.

Rattlesnake Shelter

The first of these spirit figures is at Rattlesnake Shelter (35WH37) in the John Day river drainage of north-central Oregon. At this shelter are two 'horned' rattlesnake spirit figures. The largest, and most obvious, shows horns over human-like eyes and a long, zigzag body with rattles at the bottom (Fig. 6.3). Part human, part animal, this therianthropic figure is more than 170 cm long and visually striking when viewed on site. Just a short distance away is a small flat panel on which an artist painted only the horned eyes, almost identical to those on the larger snake (Fig. 6.4). Almost certainly, this is another snake represented just by the face; this motif was initially recorded as just these eyes. But when the authors took a metaphorical 'step back' and looked at the immediate landscape of this panel, the true form of the image was readily visible. Immediately below the snake face is a segmented basalt column extending to ground surface. Clearly the face was placed so that the naturally occurring basalt segments form the snake's body and/or rattles (Fig. 6.5). In this case, the snake is obviously **of** the rock more than merely *painted* **on** the rock.

Horsethief Butte – the rattlesnake lizard

A second figure, on Horsethief Butte on the north side of the Columbia River just upstream from The Dalles, Oregon (approximately 90 km northwest of Rattlesnake Shelter), displays a similar use of the natural rock shape. This figure is a large, 80 cm long, red-and-white polychrome lizard painted with a clearly segmented rattlesnake rattle on the end of its tail (Figs. 6.6 and 6.7). By itself, the motif is striking, even though the head has been broken off and has long since disappeared. Equally impressive is the positioning of this figure. Head down and curving sharply to the viewer's right, the image is painted on an out-sloping surface of the cliff formed by the intersection of two shallowly pitched rock faces. Probably the result of large-scale fracture mechanics in the massive basalt, the resulting miniature ridgeline forms a shallow backwards C-shape. Extending downwards, this feature gradually rises out of the flat

[1] It seems likely that Long Narrows Style motifs, because of their morphological complexity, lend themselves especially well to the incorporation of natural features. Thus these images may more frequently have been used to create quasi-narrative compositions. Further research should be directed towards testing this hypothesis in Columbia Plateau rock-art.

[2] The four examples described herein were previously recorded or published as follows:

Rattlesnake Shelter (Gannon 1978).

Horsethief Butte – rattlesnake lizard (Woodward 1982: 81, colour plate 37; McClure 1984: 117; Bettis 1987: 17). Woodward comes the closest to recognizing that the panel landscape figures in this image when he says 'the design follow[s] the rock's contours' but he does not elaborate further. Horsethief Butte – a second lizard (Woodward 1982: 82, colour plate 38).

Half and half spirit figure (Strong *et al.* 1930: 132).

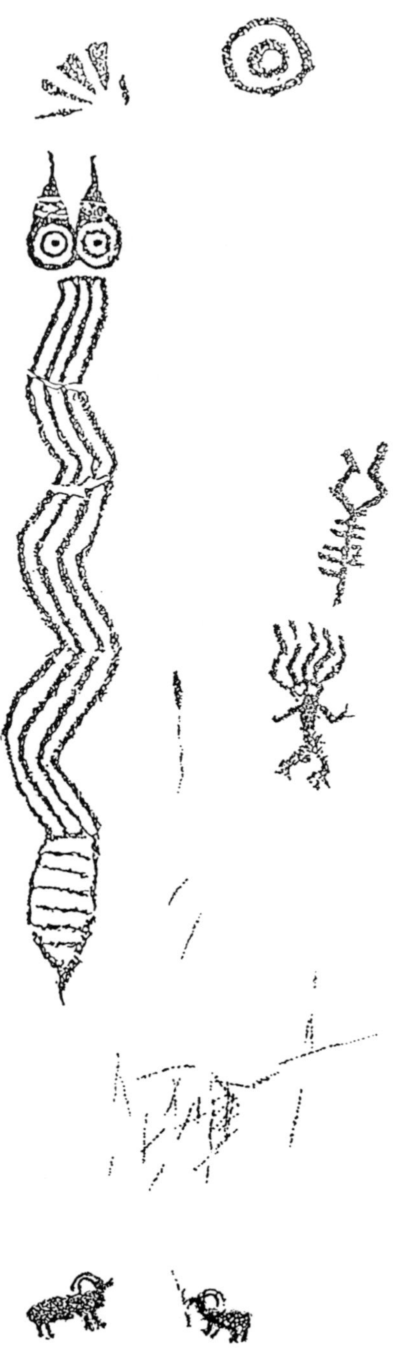

Fig. 6.3. A large zigzag horned snake spirit figure is painted at 35WH37 in north-central Oregon.
Scale bar is 30 cm.

Fig. 6.4. These horned snake eyes are painted at 35WH37 about 5 m from an identical image used as part of a larger horned snake figure (see Fig. 6.3).
This image is digitally enhanced and printed as a negative (so the white image is actually red pigment) to make it clearer.

cliff surface and terminates (now, at the break) as a low-pitched, gable-shaped 'ridge' approximately 18 cm across and standing almost 5 cm higher than the rest of the panel surface. This small ridgeline was used as the backbone of the lizard from its tail to its head (which would originally have been a projecting angular 'knob' on the cliff). Starting at about the midpoint of the rattle, where the ridgeline is nothing more than a slight 'wrinkle' in the cliff surface, it rapidly becomes a more pronounced ridge and continues to rise out of the flat surface to the neck area where the head is broken off. This serves to bring the painted figure into significant relief to an on-site observer. Here, too, the placement of this image could not possibly have been serendipitous – it was carefully positioned to take advantage of the ridge and make it appear that the 'lizard/snake' is curling

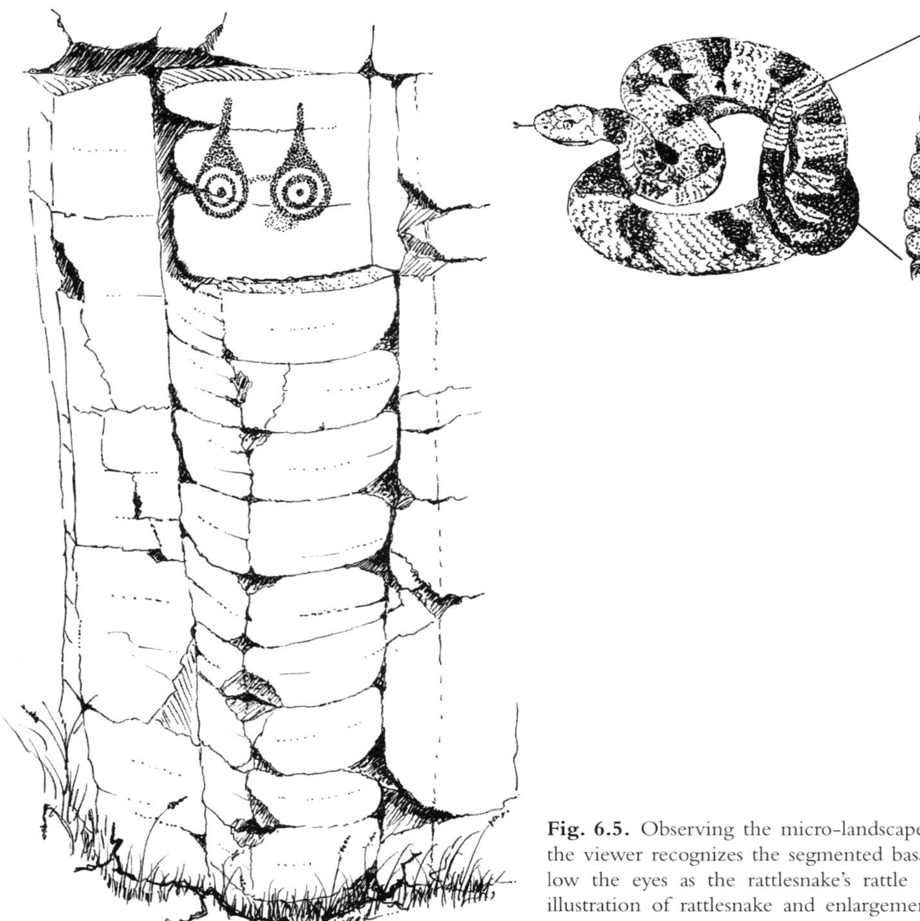

Fig. 6.5. Observing the micro-landscape of this panel, the viewer recognizes the segmented basalt column below the eyes as the rattlesnake's rattle (accompanying illustration of rattlesnake and enlargement of rattle for comparison).

downwards out of the rock towards the viewer. Like the horned snake at Rattlesnake Shelter, this image is also clearly **of** the rock not simply painted on it. In neither case does it take more than a short stretch of imagination to see a prehistoric shaman or vision-seeker experiencing a trance in which the segmented basalt column or the shallow ridge in the cliff became the snake or rattlesnake/lizard. All the vision-seeker did was add some paint to provide the identifying features that bring the cliffs themselves 'alive'.

Is there any ethnographic support for our viewing these images as special spirit beings closely connected to the cliffs on which they were painted? In fact, both of these spirit figures may well illustrate a mythical figure known as the 'Horned Snake' or 'Land Monster' by Sahaptian-speaking and Chinookan-speaking groups from this area. Phillip Cash Cash, a Nez Perce/Cayuse Indian traditionalist,[3] had heard oral traditions from Cayuse and Palouse elders

[3] Phillip has been both a participant on several of our rock-art recording projects and a co-author with us for several research papers (Keyser *et al.* 1998; Keyser and Cash Cash 2002; Hann *et al.* 2003). His expertise in traditional life-ways and contacts with native informants have greatly benefited our research.

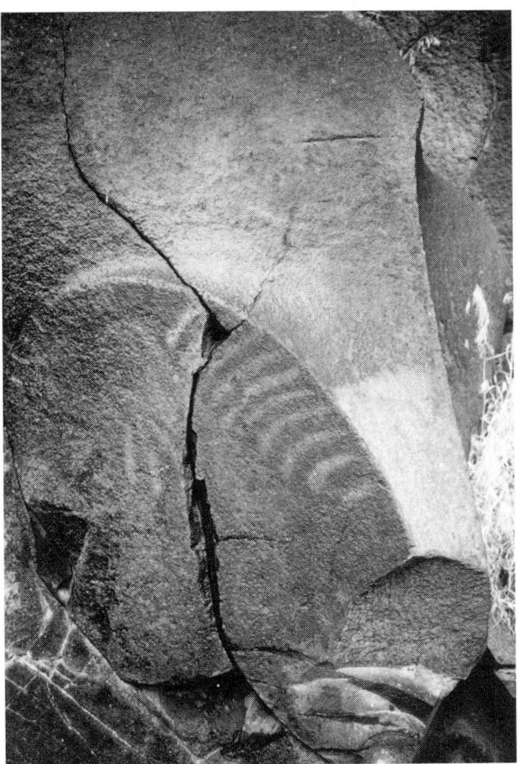

Fig. 6.6. A rattlesnake/lizard at 45KL79 incorporates a natural ridge in the basalt as its backbone. On-site the lizard appears to be crawling out of the rock downward towards the viewer.

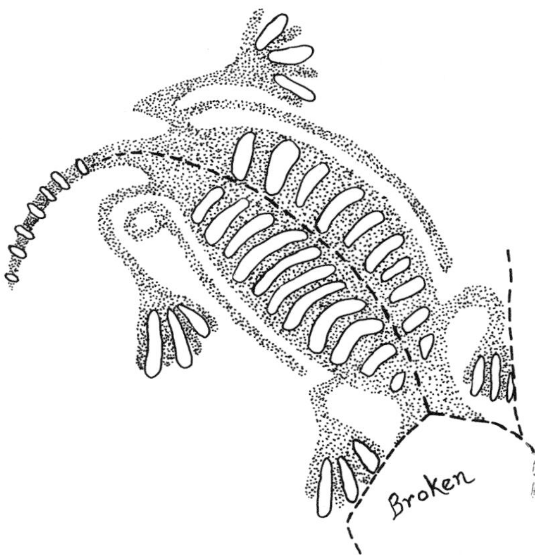

Fig. 6.7. This drawing shows how the lizard/rattlesnake is structured around the natural ridge. Solid lines enclose areas of white pigment, stippling is red paint.

The lizard's dashed midline shows the natural ridgeline, other dashed lines outside the image show broken edges.

(Sahaptian-speakers) about a mythical horned snake who lived in a cliff along the Umatilla river (a first-order tributary to the Columbia not far distant from either of these sites). According to tradition, construction of the railroad in the late nineteenth century killed this being within its rock den. A quite similar story told by the Wishram (Chinookan-speakers) describes the 'Land Monster' – part lizard and part rattlesnake – which left a big track as it crawled about. The Land Monster lived in holes in the cliff on the north bank of the Columbia River; blasting for the highway, it is said, drove it out (Spier and Sapir 1930: 237). These mythical creatures were powerful but dangerous spirit helpers, said to be controlled only by strong shamans. Metaphorically, these two spirit figures at Rattlesnake Shelter and on Horsethief Butte seem a near-perfect fit for the mythical creature known to the Indians in this area – certainly, as they are painted, they do 'live in the rock'.

Horsethief Butte – a second lizard

In addition to the lizard/snake, there are at least four other lizards painted at site 45KL79 on Horsethief Butte, suggesting that this site was particularly noted for spirit power associated with lizards. One of the other lizard figures there (Fig. 6.8) also shows significant interplay between the pictograph and the panel landscape features. Shown crawling down a flat rock surface, the figure has its head lifted up and outwards so that the viewer sees a grinning polychrome face – almost human in appearance. The first thing that strikes the viewer is that the image appears to be

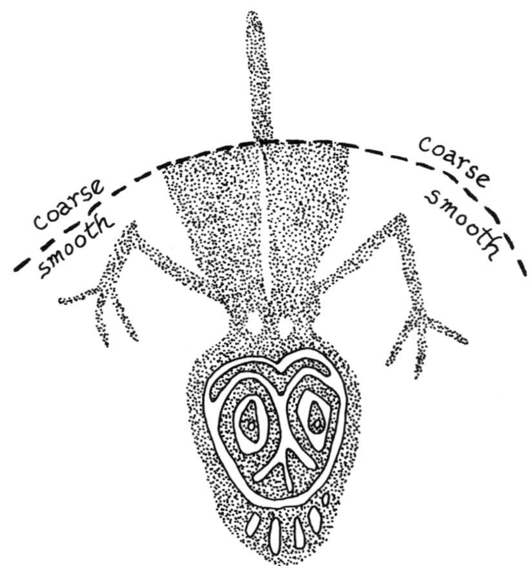

Fig. 6.8. In this composition a lizard is shown entering the rock from above (only its tail is visible) and emerging from the rock below. Solid lines enclose areas of white pigment, stippling is red paint. Two dots and the backbone on the lizard's body are unpainted areas.

only the lizard's front quarters, beginning below a natural 'break' in the cliff surface where a horizontal 'border' divides the lower, much smoother surface from the upper and coarser-textured rock surface. Although it is anatomically impossible for the lizard's face to be turned outwards this far (a full 90 degrees), the posture of the painted image reasonably mimics a real-life lizard partially emerging from a crack in the rock, starting down the cliff surface, and looking outwards and upwards at the observer. However, unless one observes very closely, the 15 cm long tail, painted just above the horizontal 'border' between coarse and smooth panel surfaces would be overlooked. (Previous recorders have missed this tail, and the front legs/feet, because the faded red pigment is difficult to see clearly against the red-brown basalt.) Close examination reveals that there are no hindquarters of this animal painted on the rock.

Once the tail is noted, the upper part of the figure appears to be a lizard retreating into the rock from the top (with only the tail showing above the break to indicate its presence). At the same time, however, the lizard is emerging from the rock below the break (with only its head and front half so far exposed).

This painting – of a lizard with a partial tail and front quarters and with a front-view human-like face – structured around a surface irregularity on the panel, is clearly more than simply a naturalistic depiction of the reptile. What might the artist have been trying to portray with this spirit figure? In many western North American Indian cultures, lizards are shaman's spirit helper 'go-betweens' for contacting the supernatural world precisely because they come and go into and out of the cracks in cliffs – often cliffs on which rock-art is carved or painted. In the lower Columbia River region lizards were thought to have strong power (Spier and Sapir 1930: 236–7) and the Land Monster was one such mythical lizard reputed to live in these very cliffs along the Columbia River. It seems to us that the appearance of this lizard at the same time entering and leaving the rock may well be a visual metaphor for the lizard moving back and forth from this world to the supernatural as a spirit helper to only the most powerful of shamans.

The half and half spirit figure

The last of the four spirit figures we describe is located on a basalt cliff on a large island in the Columbia River. On this panel, rainwater flowing down across part of the cliff face has left a translucent, surface wash of milky-white, mineral precipitate. The result is a swath of whitened surface that contrasts strongly to the normal grey-black basalt. This swath is approximately 12 cm wide. A second, wider swath of the same mineral precipitate (actually formed of several quite narrow streaks that have coalesced) occurs 22 cm to the left of the centrally located narrower one. The

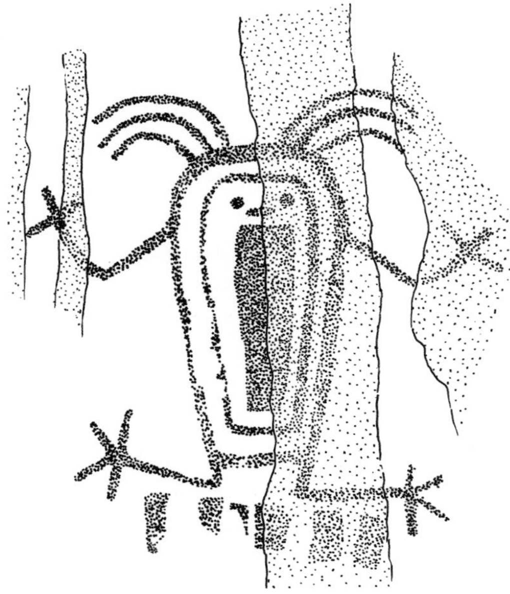

Fig. 6.9. This spirit figure at 45KL62 was carefully composed using areas of white mineral precipitate to create a quasi-narrative image.

edges of these swaths of whitewash are vertical, and the left edge of the wash in the panel's centre is nearly straight. As such it forms a clear, concise, boundary between mineral wash and bare panel. The other edges of both washes are slightly more wavy and ragged.

The straight vertical edge of the precipitate wash in the panel's approximate centre served the prehistoric artist as a midline to structure a composition of an anthropomorphic spirit being (Fig. 6.9). Painted in red pigment, this spirit figure was originally made with half of the body atop the white mineral wash and the other half on the bare rock surface. This naturally occurring vertical midline almost exactly bisects the figure, creating a bilaterally symmetrical image: each side has an eye, half a mouth, half a nose, equal head-dress/antennae elements, and arm and hand, and a flipper-like foot extending straight out from each side of the body. These feet are painted just above and parallel to a horizontally oriented fold in the cliff, giving the figure the appearance of sitting atop this horizontal frame. Just below the spirit figure are six more or less evenly spaced red painted rectangles.

Although the image clearly was originally painted partially over the white mineral precipitate, this wash has continued to accumulate naturally over the right half of the figure, so that this portion is presently slightly less distinct. Close examination, however, shows clearly that the painted figure is 'sandwiched' between layers of precipitate – part of the figure was originally painted on the white wash and natural processes have continued to deposit precipitate over the pigment. Evidence of repainting the obscured parts of the figure indicates that the natural 'opaquing' process was occurring while the figure was still used; the artists maintaining the image attempted to combat its 'fading'.

Lastly, the figure's hand on the viewer's left extends underneath a second swath of mineral precipitate, but it is not as certain that this wash was in place when the figure was originally painted. Close examination shows that removal of a small flake for microscopic examination would be necessary to ascertain if the original wash here also underlies pigment.

Clearly the artist used this natural division of white precipitate and bare surface to structure the painting. This panel was carefully selected from numerous unpainted ones near by, and the seated figure was positioned exactly using the fold in the rock as a bottom and the edge of the white precipitate wash as a midline. More precise bilateralism could have been accomplished only with the aid of modern measuring tapes and graph paper! It stretches credibility to argue that the original placement of this figure with the edge of the mineral wash as a midline was accidental, given the myriad of other available surfaces and what we know from ethnography about how important such spirit figure paintings were and what power they were thought to embody.

So what message might the bilateral symmetry of this figure be trying to communicate? Ethnography shows that Columbia River shamans were very powerful people in that they communicated with and to some extent even controlled the spirit world – by curing, prophecy, making weather, controlling game animals. A common metaphor is that shamans live in two worlds – the everyday one and the supernatural. We can envision no more striking visual metaphor than this figure for portraying a shaman (in the guise of his spirit helper) in two worlds; one clear and natural, the other misty-white and slightly murky where shapes and lines are blurred and indistinct. Carrying this metaphor slightly further, we suggest that it might be more than coincidence that the figure's arm reaches out from the bare rock surface and his hand extends under the second mineral wash.

The rock-art panel as portal to the supernatural

Rock-art sites in several areas of the world, including western North America, are reported ethnographically to be portals or doorways used by shamans in their journeys to and from the supernatural world (Lewis-Williams and Dowson 1990; Whitley 1992). Despite a strong ethnographic record in the Columbia Plateau concerning rock-art (Hann *et al.* 2003; Keyser and Whitley 2000), there is no direct reference to this specific concept of spirit world portal. In the absence of that evidence from the immediate region, we noted the numerous cases where pictographs and petroglyphs show direct interaction with the natural features of the rock surface. Then we constructed a model which could be tested in relation to known ethnographic beliefs which were reflected by specific rock-art imagery and its interplay with the rock canvas. In just a preliminary examination we have discovered four very dramatic instances of such interplay at three sites; and we have noted dozens of other similar panel/image interactions which have yet to be fully documented. While we cannot be certain – in the absence of direct ethnographic verification – that Columbia Plateau groups held this 'rock-art as portal' belief, our finding structures in the rock-art best explained by this or a very similar belief is strong archaeological evidence that such a belief existed. This archaeological evidence runs alongside the ethnographic evidence for vision questing and shamanism, shamans' possession of specific spirit helpers and use of rock-art, the supernatural associations of rock-art sites, and the emphatic supernatural colour symbolism of red and white pictographs (Hann *et al.* 2003).

Our use of Columbia Plateau rock-art as archaeological data in support of part of the shamanic model (in the absence of direct ethnographic evidence) lends credence to a recent proposal that some European Palaeolithic art was created for similar shamanistic purposes (Clottes and Lewis-Williams 1998). Like Columbia Plateau rock-art, much Palaeolithic art uses natural features of the cave walls – cracks, calcite draperies, stalactites, and other aspects of the panel's natural relief – as part of the artistic composition. Of course, we can never know what specific ethnographic beliefs lay behind those artistic creations – since they pre-date history or ethnography by many thousand years; yet the fact that they so frequently express an interplay between the art and the 'canvas' strongly suggests that Palaeolithic artists also saw the rock-art as a portal into their spirit world.

'Canvas' and image

As these examples illustrate, prehistoric artists in many areas of the world selected rock 'canvases' for the presence of natural features that became part of the art. When recording a site or interpreting a particular image, the archaeologist must stand back and visualize the rock surface before the art was applied. One can then ask the question, 'Were natural features of this surface incorporated into the art?' If such features do appear to have been used, then they must be carefully recorded and discussed in interpretation. It may be that the structure of the rock canvas is as important as the image itself. Finally, where available, the ethnographic record and oral traditions must be studied for insights into the meaning of both the motifs and the structure of the images themselves. Often, ethnographic sources contain the cultural metaphors that enable a much deeper understanding and interpretation of these images – painted or carved at the microcosmic level of the rock-art landscape.

Acknowledgements

The authors thank Phillip Cash Cash, whose interest in the traditions of his people, contacts with tribal elders and abilities as a rock-art recorder provided key information for this study. Alex Bourdeau, Greg Bettis, Dan Leen, Lori Watlamet, and a crew of volunteers from the Oregon Archaeological Society and the Archeological Society of Central Oregon provided assistance in recording the sites whose motifs are described herein. Carolynne Merrell provided the enhanced digital image of the snake eyes at Rattlesnake Shelter. Finally, Christopher Chippindale and David Whitley offered encouragement and assistance in the completion of this research.

References

Bahn, P. G. and J. Vertut. 1988. *Images of the Ice Age*. Leicester: Windward.

Beltrán, A. (ed.). 1998. *Altamira*. Paris: Editions du Seuil.

Bettis, G. 1986. *Indian rock art of the lower Deschutes River*. Portland, OR: Rock Art Research Education.

1987. *Indian rock art designs from Oregon, Washington, Arizona, and Utah*. Portland, OR: Rock Art Research Education.

Breuil, H. 1952. *Quatre cents siècles d'art pariétal: les cavernes ornées de l'Age du Renne*. Montignac: Centre d'Etudes et de Documentation Préhistoriques.

Clottes, J. 1995. *Les Cavernes de Niaux*. Paris: Editions du Seuil.

Clottes, J. and D. Lewis-Williams. 1998. *The shamans of prehistory*. New York; Harry N. Abrams.

Curtin, J. n.d. Miscellaneous papers and notes collected by Jeremiah and Alma Curtin from the Klamath and Modoc tribes in 1883–84. Bureau of American Ethnology collections 1299, 1762, 2569, 3538, 3799. Washington, DC: Smithsonian Institution.

Gannon, B. 1978. Field notes and tracings from site 35WH37. On file at Oregon State Museum of Anthropology, Eugene, OR.

Hann, D., J. D. Keyser and P. M. Cash Cash. 2003. Columbia Plateau rock art: a window to the spirit world, in David S. Whitley (ed.), *The ethnography of rock art*. Walnut Creek, CA: Alta Mira Press.

Keyser, J. D. 1992. *Indian rock art of the Columbia Plateau*. Seattle, WA: University of Washington Press.

Keyser, J. D. and P. Cash Cash. 2002. A carved quirt handle from the Warm Springs Reservation: Northern Plains biographic art in the Columbia Plateau, *Plains Anthropologist* 47(180): 51–9.

Keyser, J. D. and M. A. Klassen. 2001. *Plains Indian rock art*. Seattle, WA: University of Washington Press.

Keyser, J. D. and G. C. Knight. 1976. The rock art of western Montana, *Plains Anthropologist* 21(71): 1–12.

Keyser, J. D., G. Poetschat, P. M. Cash Cash, D. Hann, H. Hiczun, R. Malin, C. Pedersen, C. Poetschat and B. Tandberg. 1998. *The Butte Creek sites: Steiwer Ranch and Rattlesnake Shelter*. Portland, OR: Oregon Archaeological Society. Publication 11.

Keyser, J. D. and D. S. Whitley. 2000. A new ethnographic reference for Columbia Plateau rock art: documenting a century of vision quest practices. *INORA: the International Newsletter on Rock Art* 25: 14–20.

Levy, G. R. 1963. *Religious conceptions of the Stone Age*. New York: Harper and Row.

Lewis-Williams, D. and T. A. Dowson. 1990. Through the veil: San rock paintings and the rock face, *South African Archaeological Bulletin* 45: 5–16.

Loendorf, L. L. 1994. Rock art and the Water Ghost Woman on the Wind River, Wyoming. Manuscript on file with the author.

McClure, R. 1984. Rock art of the Dalles-Deschutes region: a chronological perspective. MA thesis, Washington State University, Pullman, WA.

Poetschat, G. and J. D. Keyser. 1999. The canvas as the art: use of natural features in Columbia Plateau rock art. Paper presented at the 64th Annual Meeting of the Society for American Archaeology, Chicago, IL.

Spier, L. and E. Sapir. 1930. Wishram ethnography, *University of Washington Publications in Anthropology* 3(3): 151–300.

Strong, W. D., W. E. Schenck and J. H. Steward. 1930. *Archaeology of the Dalles-Deschutes region*. Berkeley, CA. University of California Publications in American Archaeology and Ethnology 29.

Tilley, C. 1991. *Material culture and text: the art of ambiguity*. London: Routledge.

Vastokas, J. M. and R. K. Vastokas. 1973. *Sacred art of the Algonkians: a study of the Peterborough petroglyphs*. Peterborough, Ont.: Mansard Press.

Whitley, D. S. 1992. Shamanism and rock art in far western North America, *Cambridge Archaeological Journal* 2(1): 89–113.

1994. Shamanism, natural modelling and the rock art of far western North American hunter–gatherers, in Solveig A. Turpin (ed.), *Shamanism and rock art in North America*: 1–43. San Antonio, TX: Rock Art Foundation. Special Publication 1.

1996. *A guide to rock art sites: southern California and southern Nevada*. Missoula, MT: Mountain Press.

Woodward, J. A. 1982. *The ancient painted images of the Columbia Gorge*. Ramona, CA: Acoma Books.

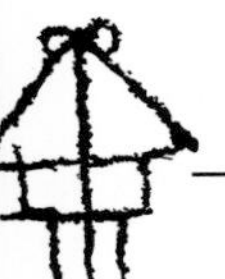

7

The landscape setting of rock-painting sites in the Brandberg (Namibia): infrastructure, *Gestaltung*, use and meaning

Tilman Lenssen-Erz

The Brandberg, the paramount rock-art region of Namibia, presents the usual and the challenging problems of observing and recording rock-art in the field. From its richness is here developed a systematics of landscape which uses the idea of *Gestaltung*, the physical acts which bring about tangible change on a landscape endowed with meaning. It intends to capture the essentials of the series of human decisions which led to the painting of certain motifs at certain places on certain panels at certain locations in the landscape.

The placing of images into a landscape

Rock-art studies in recent years have moved away from the empirical paradigm, bringing about considerable progress – the main impetus given through Lewis-Williams (1981). Interpretation (the hermeneutic circle) has moved to the forefront. Yet the new approaches have to face the dilemma that the first contact and encounter which a researcher or any other visitor has with a rock-art site is empirical by character. First knowledge is won by experience and observation, not by hallucination, dreaming, divination or any other way of perception one might conceive of. Getting to, or often enough struggling your way to, a rock-art site, means experiencing the landscape along the way, sensing the air, smelling plants and animals, hearing the sounds of nature, and eventually feeling the rock and seeing the pictures. The whole sensory system is involved, sending data to the brain. When you come back from a site, you are full of empirical data, gained the 'classical way' through experience and observation.

Of course these data are not meaningful just by themselves. They only become so through theoretical considerations under which they are regarded and processed (Lewis-Williams, e.g. 1984), i.e. through a process of cognition. My aim is to combine empirical data with theoretical considerations – to transform the field notes, as it were, into interpretative patterns. The main transformation is from quantifiable data to a qualifying argument.

Rock-art as a field of study within archaeology is very useful, even gratifying, because it has some advantages over all other archaeological sources of information, especially when analysing it at the juncture with landscape. This is based on the following criteria:

- rock-art is highly visible, and immovable at that;

- its place of production as well as place of consumption is unambiguously determinable;
- rock-art can be recorded comprehensively in a given area, unlike other archaeological resources which are hidden in the ground;
- the proof that phenomena are contemporaneous is dispensable at least for the late phases of a rock-art tradition;
- at one level its function is clearly communicative – it is a means but also a result of communication.

It may sound a commonplace, but is true none the less that rock-art is part of a landscape and also that the landscape makes up part of the meaning of rock-art (e.g. Bradley *et al.* 1994; Schaafsma 1997; Ouzman 1998). Perhaps it is this close link between the two which explains why, however naturalistic it may be, there is no rock-art tradition where landscape features form any part of the motif spectrum worth mentioning.[1] In this respect it is quite different from those art traditions which worked on artificial canvases, be they dynastic Egyptian murals, ancient Roman wall-paintings or mosaics, traditional European oil-paintings, or Chinese watercolour paintings. In all these the landscape had to be expressly brought in, whereas rock-art never comes without landscape since it cannot be moved away from it (or at least, it was not meant to be).

The power of interpreting rock-art in close connection to the landscape lies in the fact that the painters not only interacted with pigment and rocky canvas but also worked with the surroundings. Artists had to walk to the site, they had to negotiate the landscape and, if they stayed at a site, they temporarily had to lead their life there. The space around them, the site as well as the wider landscape, had to be categorized and organized mentally – a mental map had to be designed (Downs and Stea 1982).

While perception and cognition of space is always based on imagination, spatial entities being illusory (Swartz and Hurlbutt 1994), there is an essential base in physical landmarks which seems to be of cross-cultural significance (e.g. Levinson 1991). The continuum of a landscape as a space is structured by phenomena which western cognition expresses through topographical description (Steinbring 1987a; 1987b; 1992): mountains, hills, ridges, narrow gates, passes, rivers, forests, etc. – everything which either brings about discontinuity (see also Ingold 1993: 156; Bradley *et al.* 1994: 380; Schaafsma 1997: 13) or which constitutes unitary continua themselves such as rivers along their flowing direction, plains, lakes or the sea.

This understanding of landscape together with the human impact acting upon it is the starting-point of my analysis and interpretation. The particular landscape I am dealing with is the central western region of Namibia where the coastal Namib Desert turns into a savannah. The Brandberg (Fig. 7.1), as the paramount rock-art region of Namibia, is located as an *inselberg* just in this zone of transformation. Precipitation in this area is only around 100 mm per annum (which is desert climate) but all kinds of large game animals come to the mountain – although unable to climb it – and the vegetation in the upper areas is of a kind that can elsewhere be found in areas with more advantageous climate. Being essentially composed of granite, the mountain can store rainwater in pans, crevices and pot-holes from one rainy season to the other. This may be one reason for the use of the Brandberg by humans since the Middle Stone Age (Breunig 1989: 26ff.).

The mountain covers an area of approximately 570 sq. km, but only the upper areas between the 1800 m and 2200 m contour lines show widespread traces of intensive human occupation, detectable in hundreds of rock-art sites and masses of artefacts from the Later Stone Age onwards

[1] But see the chapters by Arcà and Helskog in this volume, as rare instances where landscape appears depicted.

Fig. 7.1. A landscape in the upper Brandberg. The plain in the foreground is about 100 m wide; in the whole area overlooked here one can find twelve rock-art sites.

(i.e. at least from 6000 BP till the twentieth century). In the bottom area of the mountain only the entrance areas of some of the gorges are furnished with comparable traces of human activities. The slopes all around the mountain – which normally can be negotiated within one day on foot – were occupied only in a spotty manner.

Like almost all rock-painting traditions of southern Africa, the paintings of the Brandberg focus on human figures, with large game animals forming the second-largest group of motifs. A shamanistic tradition has been postulated for the Brandberg paintings (e.g. Kinahan 1991), but this is based on a small spot-check selection of motifs. Rather, social issues (gender relations, social cohesion, etc.), and to some extent ecological issues, seem to be the main concern of the art's meaning (Lenssen-Erz 2001).

The database I am drawing on in the present study embraces exactly 300 sites on the southern flank of the Brandberg which comprise the almost complete inventory of rock-art in an area of 135 sq. km (Lenssen-Erz 2001; ten known sites missing from the records) (Fig. 7.2). This area includes the basal zone, where the Namib Desert encounters the mountain, as well as the inner parts up to the peaks in the centre of the complex. Since this covers all facets of the landscape and comprises almost one-third of the whole body of rock-art on the mountain, the results may certainly be representative of the entire art tradition.

All sites in this study have been recorded in plan and elevation at a scale of 1:100 (Pager 1989; 1993; 1995; 1998; see also Fig. 7.3). In good archaeological spirit, as much attention has been paid to the context of the artefacts as to the artefacts themselves; in some cases documenting the site has consumed more time than the recording of the paintings.

Infrastructure and *Gestaltung*

From the perspective of landscape the Brandberg functions on two levels. On the one hand it is the dominant landmark in the wider central Namibian landscape which constituted the life-world of prehistoric hunter-gatherer painters (Richter 1991); this function of the mountain is dealt with elsewhere (Lenssen-Erz 1997). On the other hand, the Brandberg is a complex landscape of its own – one which is large enough and well enough furnished to be a complete, autarkic life-world in itself. This is what the present chapter deals with.

As one principle of understanding landscape I maintain that landscape has a number of given properties which persist without human interaction or perception. Therefore, I disagree with the standpoint that landscape is merely a construction of human attitudes, wholly decided by the values of human culture (e.g. Ingold 1993). Given elements in the landscape are topography, vegetation and fauna; the landscape is formed by climate and geomorphological processes – all of which exist and develop with or without human interference and independent of human attitude (for elaborate discussions of these issues see Ucko and Layton 1999).

These elements are things which every human being encounters when entering into a landscape. Those parts of the 'Given' which humans can make use or sense of are what I subsume under infrastructure: the natural resources which support mobility, diet, habitation, raw material supply or religious and ritual practice. The human interaction with and action upon them is what I call the *Gestaltung*. This means to give a physical *Gestalt* to something and to endow it with meaning – denoting all acts that bring about some kind of tangible change. This physical change may range from the almost negligible, such as applying a figure on a rock surface, to a change of the whole character of a landscape by

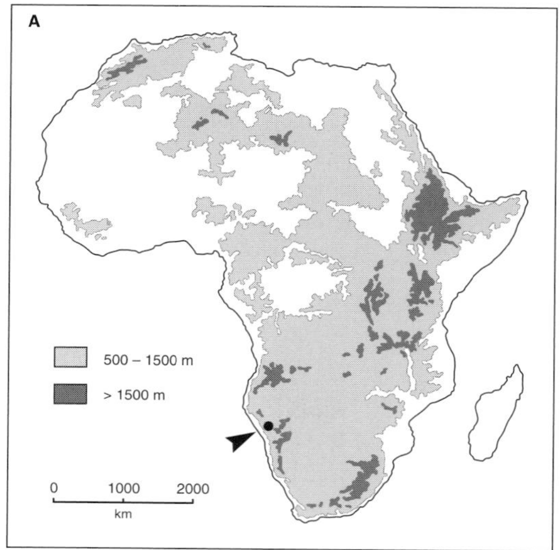

Fig. 7.2. (A) Location of the Brandberg in Africa, and (B) topographical map of the Brandberg. Rock-art sites are marked with dots. The present study deals with the sites marked in the southern part of the mountain. Scale 1: 230,000.

B

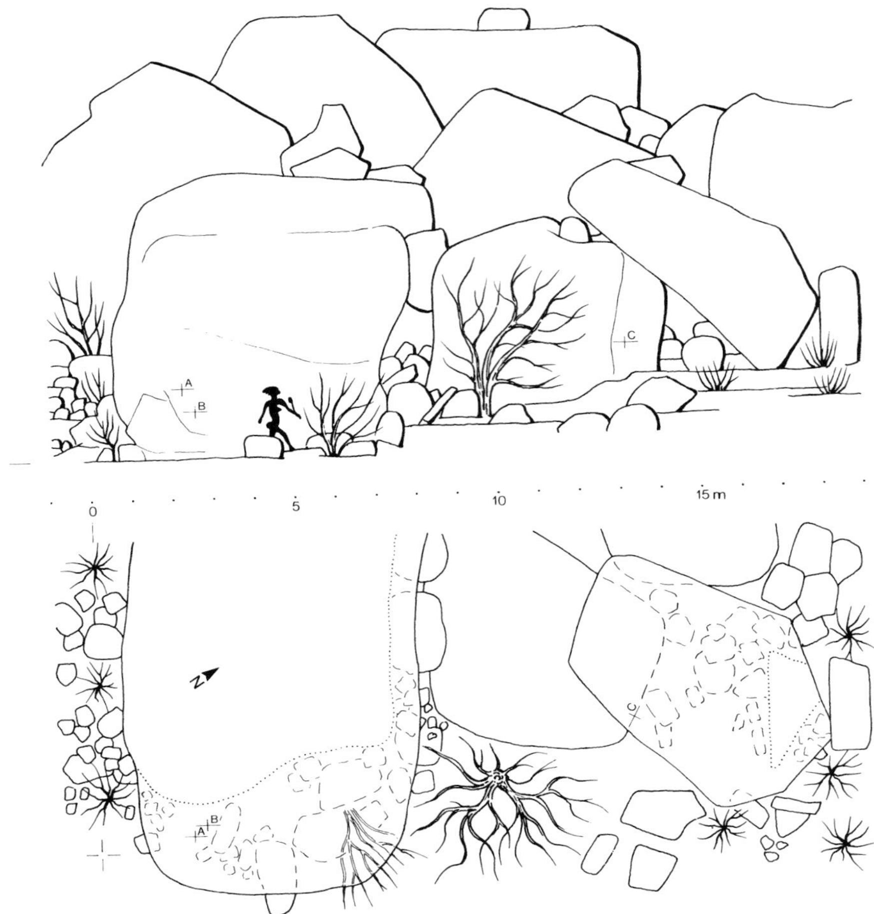

Fig. 7.3. One out of over 800 rock-art sites recorded at scale in the Brandberg in elevation (*top*) and plan (*bottom*). Alphabetical marks help to locate specific panels on the rock since on the reproductions these spots are also marked.

chopping down a forest. Bednarik (1999: 6) defines a *Gestalt* as 'unified symbolic configuration having properties that cannot be derived from its parts'. What we perceive are the physical parts of the *Gestaltung*, while there is also a metaphysical part which, by its nature, is not perceptible to us (thus being analogous to the understanding of the term *Gestalt* in psychology).

In south-western Africa the elements of infrastructure remained practically unchanged from prehistoric times until today – unlike, for example, the changing landscapes of the Sahara – owing to the relative stability of climate (e.g. Van Zinderen Bakker 1980; Deacon and Lancaster 1988). Therefore, today we have access to the same infrastructure as it was for the prehistoric painters. The features of infrastructure which are relevant to hunter-gatherers in view of their mobility, food and water requirements, need for shelter and access to raw materials are expressed in Table 7.1.

Some of these features are relevant to habita-

Table 7.2 *Places of topographical salience (accents of landscape) at which rock-art sites are found.*

	Place of topographical salience	Description
1	pass	e.g. connecting two gorges or valleys
2	waymark	a conspicuous rock located along a natural travel route
3	water-formed feature	a peculiarity of a dry region like the Brandberg where water is not always available but the surface of rocks shows marks of water-power
4	vantage point	a place allowing wide stretches of the landscape to be overlooked
5	focus of landscape	e.g. centre of a basin, outlet of a valley, hilltop, saddle
6	terrace	especially relevant in some parts of the Brandberg
7	cave	(in the Brandberg) often not real caves but deep shelters, closed on all sides except entrance
8	halfway house	isolated rock-art sites more or less in the middle of a long ascent route

Table 7.1 *Infrastructural features of a landscape or a site and the method of gaining empirical data on them.*

Feature of infrastructure	Measurement
open field	distance from site
water supply	distance from site
place (for dwelling)	space
topographic salience (accent of landscape)	diverse features (see Table 7.2)
cardinal points (of site opening)	cardinal points

tion of the landscape (open field, place) or they are relevant to diet (water supply). The 'topographic salience' (or 'accent of landscape') in this list is a collective category by which to grasp various locations in a landscape which are either points of discontinuity or important for mobility or habitation (Table 7.2; for comparable lists see Steinbring 1987a; 1987b; Bradley *et al.* 1994: 380ff.).

Some of the places of topographical salience in Table 7.2 are especially listed because of their relevance in the Brandberg; they might be dispensable in less mountainous areas.

Recognition of the *Gestaltung* of the sites is focused mainly on rock-art as this is the most reliable and permanent indicator of human activities (Table 7.3).

The items of *Gestaltung* as listed in Table 7.3 need some further explanation:

Relative location is assessed in relation to surrounding rock-art sites, linking them to the landscape; therefore, it is broader in scope than other items on this list which only pertain to the site proper.

The analysis of *artefacts* in a study encompassing such a vast number of sites can only take regard of the surface finds. In the Brandberg modern interference by people is negligible, and the microlithic Later Stone Age (which represents the time of the painters: Breunig 1989; Richter 1991) is generally to be found on the surface (as well as in the deposits); so this is a fairly reliable indicator of human activities for the time when paintings were made. The number of artefacts is classified in five categories ranging from single pieces to densely strewn scatters.

The *painting location* is categorized according to twelve positions in a schematized rock-art site

Table 7.3 *Different kinds of* Gestaltung *which a rock-art site experiences; only the artefacts are of a kind which will not inevitably be detectable since there may be no surface finds at the site. All other items will exist as soon as there is rock-art.*

Item of *Gestaltung*	Measurement
relative location	central – marginal – isolated
artefacts	number
painting location	placement categories 1–12
visibility (optical range)	maximum distance
number of paintings	number, classified in six groups
complexity of action depicted	action index 1–16

Table 7.4 *Definitions for the painting locations as drawn schematically in Fig. 7.4.*

Painting location	Definition
1	on a perpendicular wall without overhang
2	at the back of a boulder where painting location 1 is already occupied
3	on the perpendicular 'forehead' of a rock above a shelter or a cave
4	at the lip above a shelter or cave, where the perpendicular 'forehead' edges back towards the ceiling
5	on the ceiling of a shelter or a cave; also slanting ceilings down to about 60 cm above ground
6	close to the ground on the rear wall or the lowest section of a slanting ceiling in a shelter, less than 60 cm above ground
7	outside a shelter or cave, 'around the corner', the shelter being not visible from this spot
8	outside a shelter or cave on the flanking walls left or right; pictures here are visible on entering the shelter/cave, but they are related to the area in front of it, not to the shelter
9	on the left side of the entrance to the covered space, being the left 'door-post', as it were
10	on the side walls inside the shelter/cave (if side- and rear walls can be distinguished), clearly inside, no relation to the outside
11	on the right side of the entrance to the covered space; the right 'door-post', as it were
12	on several boulders scattered over the site area

(Fig. 7.4; Table 7.4), taking into account the fact that many sites do not provide any shelter at all but exhibit simply a perpendicular rock face (Lenssen-Erz 1989; cf. Kechagia 1995).

Visibility expresses the optical range of the pictures at a site by the maximum distance at which they are still perceivable. It is categorized in four classes: up to 1 m; up to 3 m; up to 15 m; and greater than 15 m.

There is a wide range in the *number of paintings* one encounters at a site; it goes from just one to more than 1000 figures (of the latter, there are three sites in the Brandberg, but only one lies in the study area; for the other two see Pager 1998). The numbers of figures have been classified in six ranks (listed in Table 7.5), in which also the weight of each rank for the whole body of art becomes visible.

The last item assessed from the viewpoint of *Gestaltung* is the *complexity of action depicted* (Fig. 7.5). This part of the analysis takes the contents of the art into consideration, its denotational meaning. This complex system can only be outlined here in a very foreshortened manner (Table 7.6; for basic notions see Lenssen-Erz 1994, more detailed in Lenssen-Erz 2001).

The action index, ranging from 1 to 16, allows one to categorize and encode every conceivable physical action by a numeral. '1' indicates a being (human or animal) which is resting (standing, sitting, squatting, lying) without any further activity. As action becomes more complex by moving and/or by operating the arms, the index rises. It rises in steps until its peak at '16', a human who is moving while displaying some supplementary

Table 7.5 *Ranking of rock-art sites according to number of figures. Among the 327 sites which are part of this analysis, twenty-seven are not among those sites which form the database for the study presented in this chapter.*

Rank covering	*n* figures	Number of sites	% of all sites	Sum of figures figures	% of total of figures
i	> 400	5	1.5	3090	17.9
ii	196–400	15	4.6	4131	23.9
iii	60–195	55	16.8	5750	33.3
iv	19–59	89	27.2	2965	17.1
v	5–18	112	34.3	1199	6.9
vi	1–4	51	15.6	149	0.9
total		327	100	17,284	100

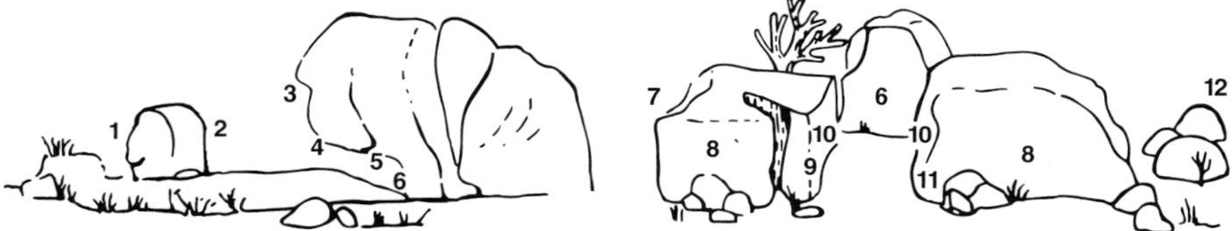

Fig. 7.4. Brandberg painting locations. (After Lenssen-Erz 1989; for definitions see Table 7.4.)

body posture (such as bending over) and using an implement directed towards a goal (such as launching an arrow at a target).

Through this measure, it is possible to arrive at average indices for special selections of motifs (e.g. men as opposed to women), or for sites in a comparative perspective. This average can be calculated irrespective of the number of paintings at a site (by dividing the sum of indices by the total number of respective figures); accordingly a site with many paintings has no 'advantage' over another site with only a few paintings as regards the complexity of action depicted at the site as a whole. A very low average action index at a site goes with there being many animals among the paintings, since animals always have a very low action index. A high action index for a site, on the other hand, represents the dominance of humans who are interacting; this more often than not can be some kind of harmonic action which several persons perform simultaneously.

The items of *Gestaltung* listed above constitute the empirical base of my analysis. They provide quantitative data through the respective measurements which, however, remain meaningless if they are not translated into a qualitative statement.

As an example I demonstrate how the elements of *Gestaltung* 'painting location' and 'visibility' can be schematized into a general 'mode of presentation' (Fig. 7.6).

The twelve painting locations are grouped together with the four classes of the optical range of a picture, which grasps the maximum distance from which a painting can still be discerned. The qualitative leap here is that measures of distance and location on the rock are expressed in terms of the praxis of living people; eventually quantitative data are structured into the two distinctive categories 'private' versus 'public' which bear relevance for every social body (e.g. Hartley and Wolley Vawser 1997: 188; for the same conceptual dichotomy among present-day Kalahari San see e.g. Whitelaw 1994: 224).

The painting locations analysed by these twelve positions were also classified by Kechagia (1995; 1996) who chose the term 'stage' for those modes of presentation which are termed 'private' here. She contextualizes experiencing such pictures with concepts such as security, shelter and family (Kechagia 1995: 112).

As one can see from Fig. 7.6, the range of visibility starts at a maximum distance of less than 1 m – that is classified 'very private' here. This means that depictions of this class were placed in such hidden places on the rock that only one person at one time can view the image or stay in its presence (see Vaccaro 1994: 29 for this phenomenon in the rock-art of the Drakensberg). The contrary is the case with those depictions deliberately placed in locations where they must have been seen by those nearing the site. These pictures have the character of a signal since they can be perceived from a considerable distance. Obviously the private and the public mode of presentation had to do with the addressees of the art; that is, the participants in production as well as consumption of the art were controlled by means of placing it in specific locations (Hartley and Wolley Vawser 1997: 188).

Gestaltung and human behaviour

While the measures given above are concerned with a practical question, issues which are not accessible to measuring and counting should also be dealt with. Therefore, at a more general level the roles should be assessed which infrastructure and *Gestaltung* played for the decisions people made in their praxis of living. In order to understand these people's behaviour some considerations should be made concerning the motivation which led these people to go to the Brandberg and paint there. An activity so clearly structured in its expressions and so clearly aimed at a certain goal must have been based on essential ways of thinking and perceiving in the social group. Certainly the art is not based on arbitrary decisions of individuals who act *ad hoc* – which would be the case if the paintings were made as 'art for art's sake'. The impulse to paint as well as the selection of the motifs and the location were the results of a decision process guided by a consensual system of values – although decisions are eventually made by individuals (Hartley and Wolley Vawser 1997: 189). It should be possible to detect those basic motivations which were the driving force behind the behaviour of whole groups following a certain rationale.

For a fundamental structure of motivations why prehistoric people went to the Brandberg and painted there, two generalizing and competing hypotheses can be put forward (Fig. 7.7).

According to the materialistic hypothesis, a rock-art site came into being after a decision guided by the search of a group of individuals for a prototypical, suitable infrastructure that satisfied those people's needs for shelter, food and water as well as mobility. The function of the site was subordinate to the general infrastructure; the people utilized the place according to their mundane requirements, wherein the number of previous visitors to the site was irrelevant to them. As a model for such a behaviour one may take the seasonal movements of Kalahari foragers, whose mobility patterns are determined by the availability of the infrastructural elements water, as the most important, and plant food, as the second most important (Tanaka 1980: 79; Silberbauer 1981: 202).

When the prehistoric painter people were staying at a place chosen with a materialistic motivation they were apparently prepared and equipped for painting. It was such a common activity that the necessary implements, and pigments in particular, were always at hand. The

Fig. 7.5. A rock-painting in the Brandberg showing people inside houses with bags fixed to the ceilings. Colour red; width of left group 22 cm.

opportunities to paint seem to have occurred in various contexts, either secular or religious, but apparently developing out of a given situation and not having been planned carefully in advance. Consequently, more or less every able adult may potentially have been a painter. The composition of the group followed the 'ordinary' configuration of a hunter-gatherer band; it was not put together by selecting the members according to their specializing in ritual (of which painting would have been a part). In the context of the materialistic hypothesis, painting was more or less a by-product or a consequence of being on the Brandberg, i.e. a reaction to circumstances arising during the stay. Only if a fair number of paintings had accumulated at a site might this kind of *Gestaltung* have influenced the further utilization of the site.

Fig. 7.6. The modes of presentation of rock-art assessed by painting position and optical range of the pictures.

Table 7.6 *Features of the sixteen action indices (left column). Each mode of action (top line) has a static and a dynamic expression. The modes comprise: basic configuration = different kinds of rest or movement; supplementary body posture = e.g. bending over, twisting around; arms action; object involved = handling, carrying, holding material goods; goal of action = living being at which activities are directed.*

	Basic configuration	Supplementary body posture	Arms action	Object involved	Goal of action
1 static	+				
2 dynamic	+				
3 static	+	+			
4 dynamic	+	+			
5 static	+				
6 dynamic	+				
7 static	+	+	+		
8 dynamic	+	+	+		
9 static	+		+		
10 dynamic	+		+		
11 static	+	+	+	+	
12 dynamic	+	+	+	+	
13 static	+		+	+	
14 dynamic	+		+	+	
15 static	+	+	+	+	+
16 dynamic	+	+	+	+	+

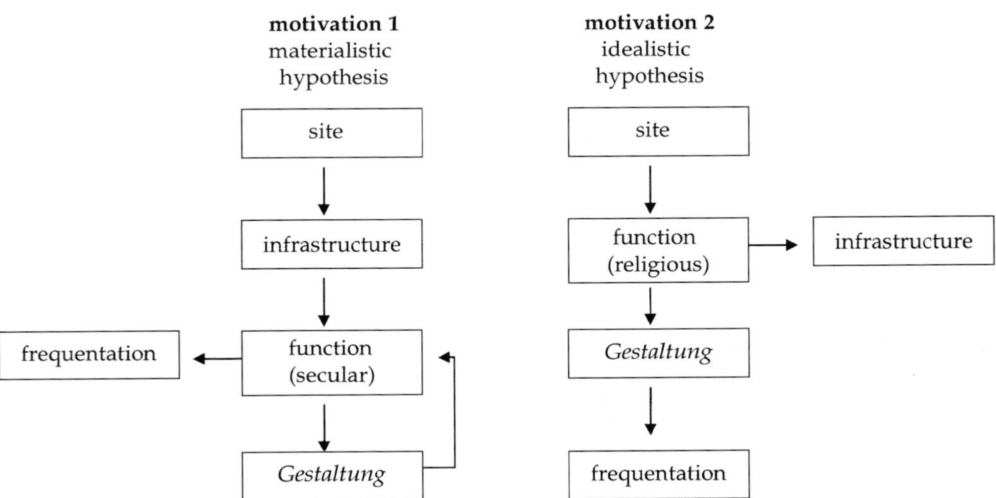

Fig. 7.7. Two competing hypotheses regarding the selection of rock-art sites by prehistoric painters. The term religious in the function of motivation 2 stands for a wide range of metaphysical issues.

If the landscape of the Brandberg was utilized under an idealistic motivation, then a rock-art site was chosen with regard to its specific ritual and religious significance and power. The *Gestaltung* such a place experienced was a direct and planned result of its previously defined function: it did not develop this function through pictures coming into being more or less coincidentally there. In other words, these rocks were meant to be painted because they were particularly powerful or located in a significant location. The ritual and religious power accumulating at a site through the *Gestaltung* with paintings in consequence was the reason which induced further, equally motivated visits. In all this context the infrastructure did not play a substantial role in guiding the choice of the place. One scenario for such a behaviour could be a group of initiates who were guided by some elders to a retreat at which the appropriate rites for initiation would have been carried out.

Structuring rock-art sites – signifying the landscape

After having briefly set out the 'mode of presentation' and 'basic motivation', I introduce another three categorizations which can be structured as dichotomous relations. Together all five cover basic domains of a human society, the domain of praxis and the domain of ideology (Table 7.7). All these relations can be understood as influencing the utilization of landscape and rock-art sites.

Table 7.7 *Five dichotomic relations structuring the utilization patterns of rock-art sites.*

presentation	private vs. public	domain of praxis
frequentation	minimum vs. maximum	
ritual activity	minimum vs. maximum	
basic motivation	materialistic vs. idealistic	domain of ideology
basic function	secular vs. religious	

In order to establish a basic frame for this structure I use the terms praxis (= practice) and ideology. The former refers to 'meaningful actions of knowledgeable agents . . . actions which are mundane, conventional and repeated, produced through practical knowledge or knowhow'. 'Ideology' refers to 'a set of ideas held by a group of people' (Hodder *et al.* 1995: 238, 243), which may include a lot of issues pertaining to social structure, power relations, general world-views and religion.

Of the relations listed in Table 7.7, the frequentation can be assessed comparatively easily; a secure indicator for the presence of people at a site can be seen in the artefacts and remains of habitation which they left behind. Of course visits to a site which are rare, short and/or made with few people leave a different pattern of remains than do visits which are intensive, of greater duration and/or iterative. A site with less than the rough average of artefacts lying on the surface can be classed as towards minimum frequentation, while an above-average number of artefacts indicates maximum frequentation.

More intricate is the assessment of ritual activity. As paintings are seen as an important part of such activities, a high number of paintings at a site would seem to be an indicator of relatively frequent ritual activities. Moreover, it is assumed, ritual activity generally is a communal act; whether it involves the whole group or only a part of it, it has certain minimum requirements of space in which people would be able to move about, e.g. in a dance.

A more or less combined assessment of these two relations is expressed in the 'basic function' – either mainly secular or mainly religious. Here, the relationship between the number of material artefacts and traces of use (such as fireplaces, concentrations of artefacts) to that of paintings is rated; if the ritual artefacts paintings dominate above average while the secular

Table 7.8 *Matrix for the schematic-structural classification of rock-art sites.*

	Function + Presentation: secular–private	Function + Presentation: secular–public	Function + Presentation: religious–private	Function + Presentation: religious–public
Frequentation minimum	*class B* short-term living site M1 R	*class A* landmark site M1 R	*class G* sanctuary, hermitage M2 RR	*class E* casual ritual site M1 RR
Frequentation maximum	*class C* long-term living site M1 R	*class D* aggregation camp M2 RR	*class F* deliberate ritual site M2 RR	*class F/D* M2 RR

M1 = Motivation 1: materialistic hypothesis
R = minimum ritual activity
M2 = Motivation 2: idealistic hypothesis
RR = maximum ritual activity

indicators remain below average, the site can be classified as primarily of religious function. A basic assumption here is that secular life has a certain logic which is dictated by basic needs and in part even by physical laws, while the spiritual/transcendent life-world is essentially non-rational (Seymour Smith 1986: 248ff.). A predominance of those remains at a site which matches the mundane logic consequently points to a secular basic function for the place.

The five dichotomous relations presented in Fig. 7.7 are certainly an excessive simplification; they fulfil the purpose of structuring the mass and variety of features and data which we face in a landscape and relating them to human agency. They can be converted into a matrix (Table 7.8) which permits us to proceed from theoretical considerations to models of practical implementation. The joint assessment of all five relations gives rise to seven functional categories of sites indicating the primary use. The determination of the classes in Table 7.8 is also informed by the elaborate ethnography on southern African hunter-gatherers, helping to reduce the vast number of possible combinations to a reasonable selection of likely functions. Places where foragers live temporarily can be distinguished as to a primary function which the respective place served (e.g. Bartram *et al.* 1991; O'Connell *et al.* 1991). Among the possible functions there are some which it is useless to look for on the Brandberg. For example a large kill site will hardly be found there, since no large game animals can get into higher reaches of the mountain.

Methodologically this deducto-hypothetical approach – defining certain classes of sites in advance and projecting that scheme on to an existing landscape with sites – has been established as the 'settlement pattern concept' of archaeology (Roper 1979: 133).

This matrix of structural classification provides a schema which works essentially with a distinction between secular and religious life. This clear distinction can of course be doubted since both fields form a continuum (e.g. Seymour-Smith 1986: 248); but it serves to give a structural order to activities such as foraging, production of artefacts, communication and mobility (all of which can be but are not necessarily contextualized in a religious/sacred manner) as opposed to rituals, ceremonies or contemplation which are not likely to satisfy basic materialistic needs.

In short these classes have the following characteristics (cf. Lenssen-Erz 2001):

Class A *Landmark site*. These are sites apparently established in order to mark a conspicuous spot in the landscape, often in connection with natural travel routes. An expression of the spatial conceptualization of the painters, they are frequently located in bordering places between larger landscape features (e.g. on a pass or saddle, at the foot of a hill). They could perhaps play a role in territorial concepts.

Class B *Short-term living site*. These are places which cannot have served as camp site for any considerable time owing to lack of space and poor infrastructure. Likely functions are as a resting place on long journeys or as an over-night station for hunters on a long hunting trip.

Class C *Long-term living site*. These provide better infrastructure and more space than class B sites; here a band of 20–40 people could easily camp for a while. There are relatively few paintings but ample traces of secular activities.

Class D *Aggregation camp*. These are places for large gatherings and accordingly they are similar to class C sites; in contrast to the latter, here the traces of ritual activities (i.e. mainly painting) clearly dominate.

Class E *Casual ritual site*. Sites of this class are in some respects similar to those of class B, i.e. infrastructure and available space would suggest groups of twelve to fifteen people staying for one to four days. They did not visit these sites for ritual purposes or for recurrent ceremonies (*rites de passage*); a stay was part of the usual patterns of mobility, but the focus on ritual is evidenced by traces of rather intense painting activity.

Class F *Deliberate ritual site*. Such sites were visited for ritual activity but not as living places. The infrastructure is not particularly advantageous, and the number of paintings stands in a dominant relation to the amount of artefacts and other traces of occupation.

Class G *Sanctuary, hermitage*. These two terms are meant to provide associations rather than being ultimately defined concepts; sites of this class are usually isolated and without any infrastructure worth mentioning, but sometimes they are at a vantage point. Occasionally these are cave-like configurations suggesting contemplative activities and even isolation of those who stayed there; the few but frequently extraordinary depictions relate to the interior of the site, not to the area around as is generally so in other sites.

This classification of sites is comprehensive enough to embrace most aspects of hunter-gatherer life as long as it stands in a context with landscape. Rock-art sites form a meta-space therein, being spatial phenomena that express conceptualizations and cognition of space. Landmarks established through rock-art configure the landscape for the people who use it. The function of the sites, and the weight which certain classes have, stand for the patterned utilization of the whole landscape, indicating whether it was more a resource for material needs or whether its value was mainly a metaphysical one, as a source of power based on ritual/spiritual potency.

In saying all this, it is kept in mind that a distinction under such a functional perspective over-rides the frequent congruence of both fields. However, since we can only have an etic access to archaeological data, it helps us to distinguish fields of activity whose physical logic we can reconstruct and experience; these contrast with those processes having a metaphysical background about which we can only hypothesize – in other words: eating meat only works if killing an animal by force (or by scavenging) while, e.g., healing can take an endless variety of forms.

It also has to be emphasized that the classification is not to establish a mono-dimensional utilization for every site. Each site *can* serve several purposes – yet a small boulder on a steep rocky slope would seem entirely unsuitable for an aggregation camp, to name one example. Generally

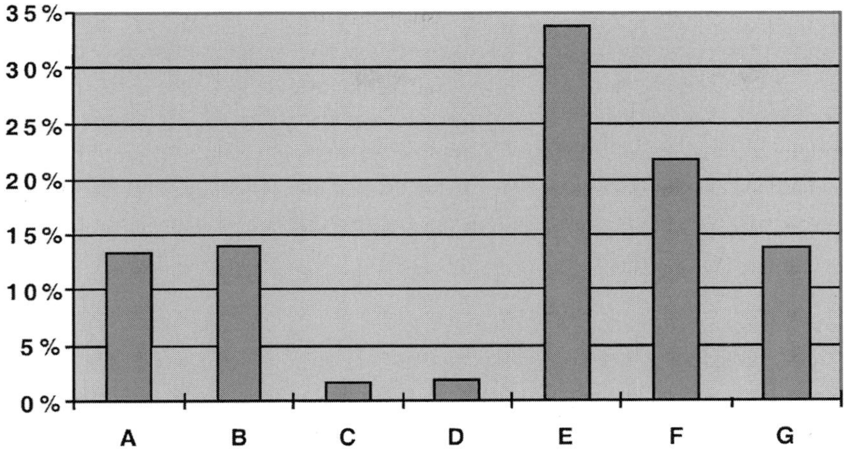

Fig. 7.8. The ratio of classes of sites in the Brandberg. $n = 300$.

the allocation of a class to a site means to point out the tendency of the primary use made of the place, mirroring its connection with and position in the landscape. It is mainly sites of class E which one finds in the Brandberg, while classes C and D are quite rare (Fig. 7.8). Obviously the landscape was not an unstructured continuum for the prehistoric hunter-gatherers, but instead was the matrix on which highly rated values such as mobility, religiousness and social interaction were mapped with rock-art. Reading this map gives us an understanding of the prehistoric utilization and cognition of the landscape, thus reconstructing the painters' mental map.

It is difficult to discern a pattern of the utilization of the landscape simply by weighing quantitatively the classes of rock-art sites. It is more comprehensive in perspective if the structural patterns of the five dichotomous relations (Table 7.7) are rated for all sites within this mountain range. Through them all sites can be synthesized into an 'idealized elementary site' (Fig. 7.9). This archetype of a site, combining all characteristics of the sites in the study area, suggests a pattern of how the landscape was used by the hunter-gatherer painters.

idealized elementary site

domain of ideology	**domain of praxis**
basic motivation	**ritual activity**
materialistic	maximum
basic function of art	**presentation**
religious	public
	frequentation
	minimum

Fig. 7.9. The 'idealized elementary site', the archetype of rock-art site in the Brandberg, comprises the structural features most often found in the mountain.

The structure of the idealized elementary site can be interpreted in view of the consequences this pattern has for the use of the landscape by the painters. Despite a superficial dialectic, expressed in a materialistic basic motivation as opposed to a religious basic function, this pattern suggests a consistent scenario.

The painters went to the Brandberg in order to satisfy their basic needs (food, water, shelter, raw material = materialistic motivation).

They went infrequently and/or in small groups and/or for short-term durations (= minimum frequentation). Once they were at a spot, the place was used for ritual activities (= religious basic function and maximum ritual activity), although the choice of the place had been made according to its infrastructure (= materialistic motivation). It appears there was usually a strong inclination for ritual activities which were expressed in pictorial art. This points to critical circumstances felt by people, since ritual activity increases in frequency if a group is facing more than ordinary problems (Guenther 1975/76). Finally, the rituals were performed as an act for the whole group (= public presentation of the art); this suggests also that the cause for the ritual afflicted the whole group.

It appears, therefore, that the painters mainly went to the Brandberg because of its advantageous ecosystem; but they often seem to have been in a state of crisis (e.g. in times of drought). Strategies chosen against the crises were high mobility, small group sizes and frequent performance of rituals, presumably to cope with the critical circumstances and to stabilize the social system.

This very general pattern is superimposed over other patterns which find their expression in sites deviating considerably from the pattern of the idealized elementary site. One example for such a deviation is class G, sites subsumed under 'sanctuary, hermitage'. These are places that are distracted from the landscape which usually formed the life-world of the painter people. When staying at a 'sanctuary' they were not in need of a specific infrastructure or neighbourhood. Particularly in class G the very shape of the rock with an enclosed configuration seems to have been important, thus emphasizing the quasi self-referential character of these sites. The place itself and its specific power were the characteristics the painters were looking for, perhaps in search of a place providing the ambience for isolation, contemplation or meditation. The landscape did not matter because of specific features, but it mattered only as a whole, as the background to the things happening at the site. It was not a resource for the satisfaction of materialistic needs but rather a source of power in a co-operative spirit. The mere presence of the landscape 'out there' was sufficient back-up for the site.

This stands in contrast to the general pattern of the use of the landscape, in which the Brandberg was primarily seen as a resource for materialistic needs. But in this context, landscape was seen not like a giving mother but rather as a thin-skinned diva who demands constant attendance and steady maintenance by ritual means and *Gestaltung*. There was no unanimous co-operation, but rather frequent small fights in which the goodwill of 'mother nature' had to be won always anew ritually. The landscape was not taken as it is (despite numerous unchangeable properties) but it had to be influenced in interactive processes in order to maintain it as a functioning organism.

Acknowledgements

Research into and publication of the rock-art of the Brandberg has generously been funded by the German Science Foundation (DFG). Invaluable prerequisites for the results of research as presented here are the unequalled documentation of Harald Pager and the lasting support of Rudolph Kuper. I should like to thank A. Zimmermann, C. Chippindale and G. Nash for commenting on earlier versions of this chapter.

References

Bartram, L. E., E. M. Kroll and H. T. Bunn. 1991. Variability in camp structure and bone food refuse patterning at a Kua-San hunter-gatherer camp, in E. M. Kroll and T. Douglas Price (eds.), *The interpretation of archaeological spatial patterning*: 77–148. New York: Plenum Press.

Bednarik, R. 1999. Proposed glossary for rock art research, *AURA Newsletter* 16(1): 3–10.

Bradley, R., F. Criado Boado and R. Fábregas Valcarce. 1994. Rock-art research as landscape archaeology:

a pilot study in Galicia, north-west Spain, *World Archaeology* 25(3): 374–90.

Breunig, P. 1989. Archaeological investigations into the settlement history of the Brandberg, in H. Pager, *The rock paintings of the Upper Brandberg* 1: *Amis Gorge*: 17–45. Cologne: Heinrich-Barth-Institut.

Deacon, J. and N. Lancaster. 1988. *Late Quaternary palaeoenvironments of southern Africa*. Oxford: Clarendon Press.

Downs, R. M. and D. Stea. 1982. *Maps in mind*. New York: Harper and Row.

Guenther, M. G. 1975/76. The San trance dance: ritual and revitalization among the Farm Bushmen of the Ghanzi District, Republic of Botswana, *Journal of the South West Africa Scientific Society* 30: 45–53.

Hartley, R. and A. M. Wolley Vawser. 1997. Spatial behaviour and learning in the prehistoric environment of the Colorado River drainage (south-eastern Utah), western North America, in P. Faulstich (ed.), *Rock-art as visual ecology*: 185–211. Tucson, AZ: American Rock Art Research Association.

Hodder, I. *et al.* 1995. *Interpreting archaeology: finding meaning in the past*. London: Routledge.

Ingold, T. 1993. The temporality of the landscape, *World Archaeology* 25(2): 152–74.

Kechagia, H. 1995. The row and the circle: semiotic perspective on visual thinking, *Rock Art Research* 12(2): 109–16.

1996. Sémiotique visuelle et art rupestre: application sur un corpus de Namibië. Unpublished PhD thesis, Université de Toulouse, Toulouse.

Kinahan, V. J. 1991. *Pastoral nomads of the Central Namib Desert*. Windbook: New Namibia Books.

Lenssen-Erz, T. 1989. The catalogue, in H. Pager, *The rock paintings of the Upper Brandberg* 1: *Amis Gorge*: 343–502. Cologne: Heinrich-Barth-Institut.

1994. Facts or fantasy? The rock paintings of the Brandberg, Namibia, and a concept of textualization for purposes of data processing, *Semiotica* 100(2/4): 169–200.

1997. Metaphors of intactness of environment in Namibian rock paintings, in P. Faulstich (ed.), *Rock-art as visual ecology*: 43–54. Tucson, AZ: American Rock Art Research Association.

2001. *Gemeinschaft – Gleichheit – Mobilität: Felsbilder im Brandberg, Namibia, und ihre Bedeutung. Grundlagen einer textuellen Felsbildarchäologie*. Cologne: Heinrich-Barth-Institut.

Levinson, S. C. 1991. *Primer for the field investigation of spatial description and conception*. Nijmegen: Cognitive Anthropology Research Group. Working Paper 5.

Lewis-Williams, D. 1981. *Believing and seeing: symbolic meanings in southern San rock paintings*. London: Academic Press.

1984. The empiricist impasse in southern African rock-art studies, *South African Archaeological Bulletin* 39: 58–66.

O'Connell, J. F., K. Hawks and N. Blurton Jones. 1991. Distribution of refuse-producing activities in Hadza residential base camps, in E. M. Kroll and T. D. Price (eds.), *The interpretation of archaeological spatial patterning*: 61–76. New York: Plenum Press.

Ouzman, S. 1998. Towards a mindscape of landscape: rock-art as expression of world-understanding, in C. Chippindale and P. S. C. Taçon (eds.), *The archaeology of rock-art*: 30–41. Cambridge: Cambridge University Press.

Pager, H. 1989. *The rock paintings of the Upper Brandberg* 1: *Amis Gorge*. Cologne: Heinrich-Barth-Institut.

1993. *The rock paintings of the Upper Brandberg* 2: *Hungorob Gorge*. Cologne: Heinrich-Barth-Institut.

1995. *The rock paintings of the Upper Brandberg* 3: *Southern gorges*. Cologne: Heinrich-Barth-Institut.

1998. *The rock paintings of the Upper Brandberg* 4: *Umuab and Karoab gorges*. Cologne: Heinrich-Barth-Institut.

Richter, J. 1991. *Studien zur Urgeschichte Namibias: Holozäne Stratigraphien im Umkreis des Brandberges*. Cologne: Heinrich-Barth-Institut.

Roper, D. C. 1979. The method and theory of site catchment analysis: a review, in M. B. Schiffer (ed.), *Advances in archaeological method and theory*. New York: Academic Press.

Schaafsma, P. 1997. Rock art, world views, and contemporary issues, in P. Faulstich (ed.), *Rock art as visual ecology*: 7–20. Tucson, AZ: American Rock Art Research Association.

Seymour-Smith, C. 1986. *Macmillan dictionary of anthropology*. London: Macmillan Press.

Silberbauer, G. B. 1981. *Hunter and habitat in the central Kalahari Desert*. Cambridge: Cambridge University Press.

Steinbring, J. 1987a. Rock-art site classification, *La Pintura* 14(1): 8–9.

1987b. Rock-art site classification: part two, *La Pintura* 14(2/3): 9–11.

1992. Phenomenal attributes: site selection factors in rock-art, *American Indian Rock Art* 17: 102–13.

Swartz, B. K. and T. S. Hurlbutt. 1994. Space, place and territory in rock art interpretation, *Rock Art Research* 11(1): 13–22.

Tanaka, J. 1980. *The San hunter-gatherers of the Kalahari*. Tokyo: University of Tokyo Press.

Ucko, P. J. and R. Layton (eds.). 1999. *The archaeology and anthropology of landscape: shaping your landscape*. London: Routledge.

Vaccaro, V. L. S. 1994. *Southern San rock paintings: meaning and function*. Johannesburg: SARARA. Occasional Publications 2.

Van Zinderen Bakker, E. M. 1980. Comparison of Late-Quaternary climatic evolution in the Sahara and the Namib-Kalahari region, *Palecology of Africa* 12: 381–94.

Whitelaw, T. M. 1994. Order without architecture: functional, social and symbolic dimensions in hunter-gatherer settlement organization, in M. P. Pearson and C. Richards (eds.), *Architecture and order: approaches to social space*: 217–43. London: Routledge.

Part Two

Informed methods: opportunities and applications

The studies in this second part concern informed methods, those used when there is some sound basis for insight into meaning acquired from a direct cultural record.

8

Rock-art and the experienced landscape: the emergence of late Holocene symbolism in north-east Australia

Bruno David

Landscapes are very much constructed within our minds; what we see in landscape becomes experience. Certain spaces within landscape are identified and become places, places with names and importance. In south-east Cape York, north-east Australia, place has become arguably a series of experiences. This is reflected not only in the rock-art present but also in the siting of rock-art within the landscape. Hunter-gatherers within this region would have applied the many components of landscape to the art, establishing a strong sense of place which would have inextricably linked to symbolism and the subjectivity of the art, in this case the painting of certain animals.

Experienced landscapes and created landscapes

In his book, *About this life*, Barry Lopez writes that modern-day Americans have forgotten their own homelands. This, he suggests, is more true than we would care to admit. Lopez (1998: 131) was specifically talking of a landscape 'of rivers, mountains, and towns', of a world 'out there' – an American landscape increasingly bespoilt by people in a modern world. He laments the great cost of this lack of awareness; the destruction of one's lived environment and of the experience of life itself.

Landscapes, however, are not just around us, for our experiences of the world are created by participation *in* place. They are much a part of us, and to give our known landscapes their proper nuance we need first to consider their *construction* in the social and cultural world. It is the histories of such constructions that are reflected in changing relationships between people and land; relationships that express the identity not only of the land but, through participation, of the people who inhabit it.

This chapter considers long-term trends in the way people related to their surroundings in one part of Australia – south-east Cape York – by considering patterns of continuity and change in the way animals are represented in the rock-art through time. Set in archaeological context, rock-art symbolism is treated as a window into worlds created, to attain not meaning, but the emergence of ethnographically documented world-views at definable points in time.

I begin by setting the rock-art in its archaeological context.

South-east Cape York

People have been in north-east Australia for at least 45,000 years, and some would say for as much as 53,000 years (e.g. Roberts *et al.* 1990). During that time, sea-levels have changed, large parts of the continental shelf having been exposed, inundated by rising seas, exposed and inundated again. In tandem with lowering and rising sea-levels, Papua New Guinea, Tasmania and many smaller islands have been linked and again severed from the Australian mainland (see Flood 1995 for general details).

Cape York is located in the north-east corner of the Australian mainland, a peninsula 800 km long that points northward to the island of New Guinea. The south-eastern corner of the peninsula is a varied landscape. In the east is the Pacific coastal zone, flat plains never exceeding a few kilometres in width. Westward, Australia's major mountain range, the Great Divide, rises sharply to a maximum height of 1611 m above sea-level, then gently decreases along its western slopes. In the north, around Laura and the Koolburra Plateau, sandstone ranges dominate, whereas volcanics characterize much of the rest of the study area. A discontinuous band of elevated limestone karst outcrops 10 km wide juts out of the landscape from just north of the Palmer River southward to Ootan. This limestone belt is divided into two sections, the Mitchell–Palmer in the north and Rookwood–Mungana–Chillagoe in the south. In between, the limestone dips below the ground surface over a north–south distance of 60 km which includes the Walsh River (Fig. 8.1).

Palaeo-environments in south-east Cape York are fairly well known, largely owing to the work of Peter Kershaw and his colleagues on pollen cores in the eastern rainforests and offshore (e.g. Kershaw 1986; 1994). The major long-term trends of the period of human occupation include the last glacial maximum (22,000–17,000 BP), when arid conditions prevailed until 14,000–13,000 BP. During this time, sea-levels were low, and effective rainfall levels about one-third of today's. Both rainfall levels and temperatures then rose rapidly after 10,000 BP, so that by 6500–5900 BP rainfall levels were nearly five times what they had been during the terminal Pleistocene. They then decreased slightly after 3000 BP, without again reaching the low levels of 22,000–13,000 BP. We do not know whether these were year-round or seasonal fluctuations; today this tropical region is highly seasonal, as would have been the case throughout the Quaternary period. Today's mean annual rainfall of 800–1100 mm falls almost entirely (90 per cent) during the wet season months of November to April. Standing water, rare during the dry season, is usually restricted to a few widely spaced creeks and water-holes. During ethnographic times, these circumstances constricted human seasonal schedules and systems of land use throughout the region (e.g. Roth 1897; 1910; Richards 1926; McConnel 1939–40; Sharp 1939; Tindale 1974; Anderson 1984; Anderson and Robins 1988; Strang 1997).

The human past

Our knowledge of the human history of south-east Cape York relies largely on excavations at thirty-one caves and rock-shelters. All but three are inland sites, and all of the latter possess rock-art. Together, the excavated sites present a useful archaeological context for the rock-art.

Archaeologically, one major long-term trend overwhelms all others: the quantitative and qualitative changes of the mid to late Holocene. That broad-scale cultural changes took place during the last *c.* 5000 years has long been known to Australian archaeologists, but it is only in the last years of the twentieth century that the nature of these changes has begun to take concrete shape. At a broad regional scale, we know that they involved massive increases in scales of regional occupation. This can be seen by the various tests undertaken by different researchers. 'Rick's Method' (Rick 1987) quantifies trends in the incidence of radiocarbon dates within and between regions, anticipating that these trends will

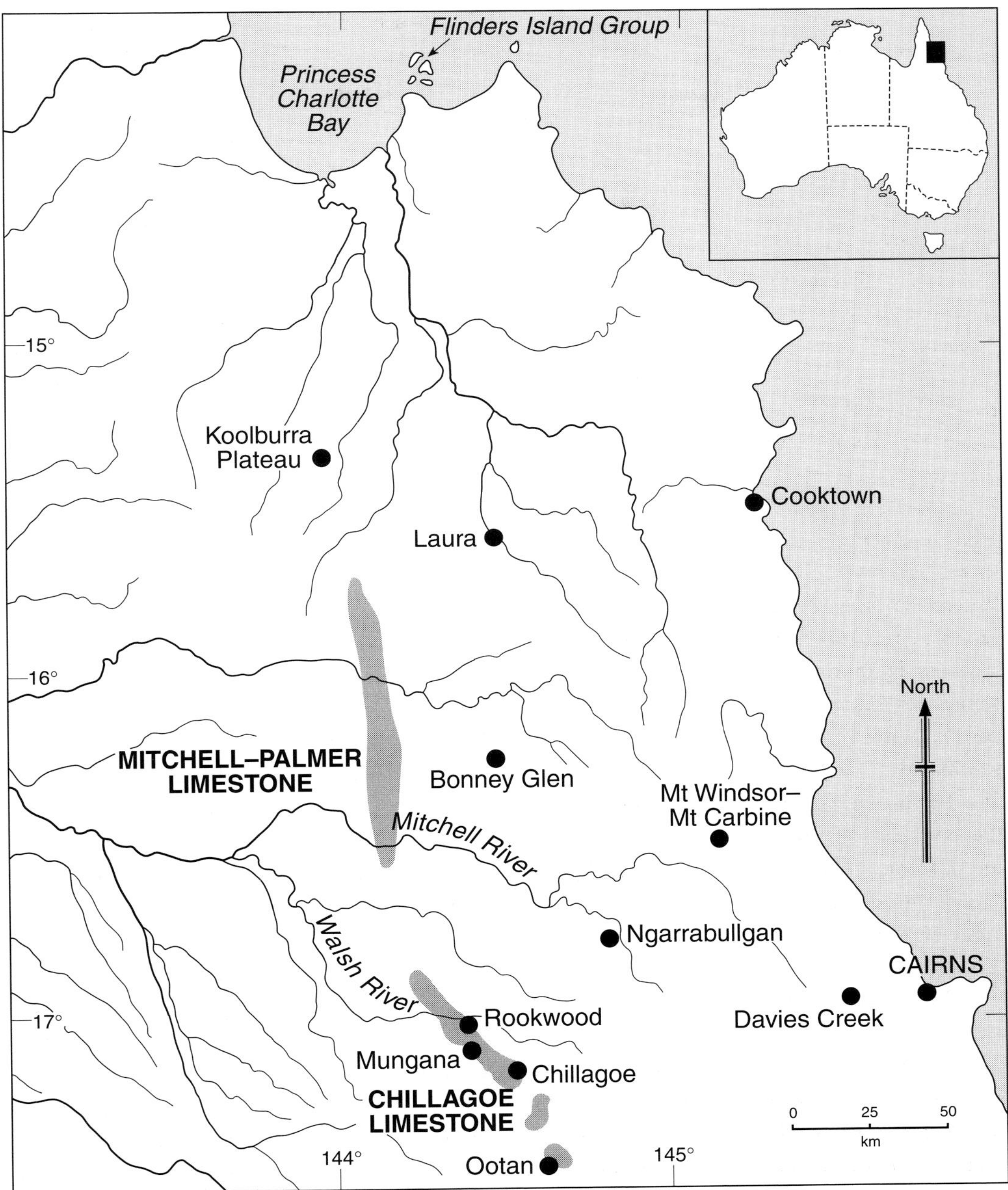

Fig. 8.1. South-east Cape York, showing locations of regions mentioned in text.

roughly represent occupational trends. Of course, the position of samples used for radiocarbon dating down a stratigraphic sequence is *selected* by archaeologists; taphonomic processes will have affected different parts of a deposit in different ways, resulting in the differential survival of charcoal available for radiocarbon dating; and processing procedures will have skewed the availability of

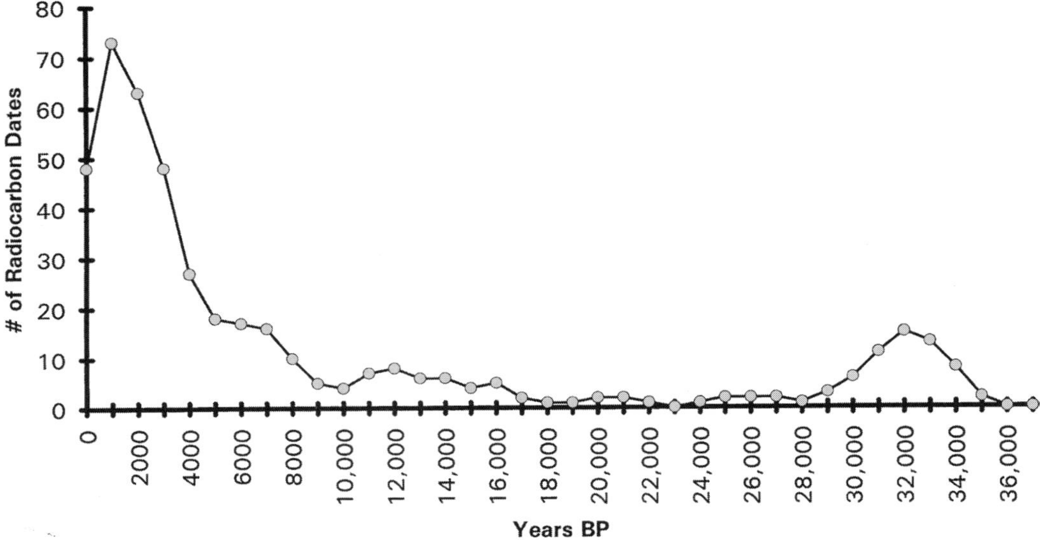

Fig. 8.2. Distribution of rock-shelter radiocarbon dates, in sliding 1000-year intervals measured every 500 years. After Rick (1987).

datable organic materials such as charcoal in various ways. But given enough researchers each targeting different research questions, we can then use the incidence of radiocarbon dates to ask why there are more dates during certain periods of time, fewer in others? It may be that the answer is simply taphonomic – a matter of survival – or one of selectivity, of researchers' choice. But if not, do the radiocarbon trends indicate occupational tendencies within or between regions?

A total of 165 radiocarbon dates that relate to cultural activity have been obtained from rock-shelters in south-east Cape York. They come from many different projects, directed by nine different researchers. Harry Lourandos and Bruno David (1998) have applied Rick's Method to this database by plotting all the radiocarbon dates in 1000-year blocks measured in 500-year overlaps. The sliding scales even out minor fluctuations and show the general trends. The clear pattern is a major increase around 4000 BP (Fig. 8.2). Lourandos and David (1998) have taken this as an indication of rising occupational intensities of both sites and regions. As most archaeologists working in south-east Cape York have actively sought *Pleistocene* sequences and focused on the earliest occupational levels of excavated sites, the trends cannot be seen simply as a function of research biases.

Other tests have given similar results. The direct count of known occupied sites shows peak occupation of rock-shelters during the Holocene, with highest levels during the mid to late Holocene. Rates of site *establishment*, as measured by the timing of initial occupation, also show a jump around 5000–3500 BP: 45 per cent of excavated sites were first occupied sometime after 4700 BP. Following Lourandos's (1983) lead, David and Lourandos (in press) have suggested an intensification of regional systems of land use, and likely also absolute population increases.

Evidence for changing levels of land use have also been obtained by quantifying changing rates of sedimentation and deposition of cultural materials within sites. Sedimentation rates usually largely reflect either changing degrees of firing behaviour within rock-shelters – with more fires comes more ash and the like, and increased rates of exfoliation of rock walls – or changing degrees of landscape instability or clearance, again largely through increased burning of the vegetation resulting in higher rates of slope erosion.

The evidence from south-east Cape York shows that in all sites where sedimentation rates vary noticeably, they increase during the mid to late Holocene. This is particularly noticeable after 3700 BP, where 70 per cent of sites show evidence of significant increases. Similarly, stone artefact deposition rates increase markedly after 4500 BP in 75 per cent of rock-shelters. There is no evidence for changes in lithic reduction systems, raw material types or other technological explanations for this trend, although more work is needed adequately to address this issue. In a similar vein, 94 per cent of the eighteen excavated rock-shelters with buried pieces of ochre have major increases in ochre deposition rates after 5400 BP. In 72 per cent of cases, these increases occur after 3800 BP (David and Lourandos in press).

The above trends are also associated with qualitative changes. The most obvious is the arrival of the dingo from south-east or southern Asia sometime between 4000 and 3500 BP (Gollan 1984). Cultural innovations also include the first appearance of Burren adzes, standardized woodworking implements with working edges around 60–80° located laterally to the striking platform, in an area where formal tool types are rare (David and Chant 1995; but see Morwood and L'Oste-Brown 1995a). The adzes recovered from thirteen excavated sites always occur in stratigraphic contexts dated to the last 4000 years BP; in eleven sites, they date to younger than 3800 BP. Similarly, blades and microblades always date to the last 3800 years BP (but at Early Man Rockshelter, they begin some unknown time between 5500 and 1000 BP; cf. Rosenfeld *et al.* 1981). Both blades and microblades are rare, never implying widespread or specialized blade-making industries. They are occasional finds in late Holocene percussion industries, where finished products are otherwise amorphous in shape (see David and Chant 1995 for a review).

Other qualitative changes include the beginning of systematic seed-grinding sometime after 3800 and before 1900 BP. This has major implications for demographic trends in the region, for seeds are known to have formed *the* major food staple in many parts of arid and semi-arid Australia during ethnographic times. Ethnographically, edible seeds were commonly available in large numbers and gathered for mass consumption (e.g. Smith 1986). They were a dietary prerequisite for many ceremonial events associated with community agglomerations. Without seeds and seed-grinding, other staples would be required – but those have not been forthcoming from any of the pre-3800 BP archaeological deposits excavated in south-east Cape York.

The late appearance of seed-grinding stones in the region implies an increased ability to support large populations, including large, intermittent communal gatherings, after 3800 BP. One other food source ethnographically known to have served a similar function is the toxic plants such as *Cycas media*, common to many parts of south-east Cape York. Again, they first appear in the archaeological record during the late Holocene – around 2000 BP at the Mulgrave 2 site and 1000 BP at Jiyer Cave – along the coastal fringes and rainforests to the immediate south-east of the study region. These toxic plants were staple resources during ethnographic times, thanks to knowledge of technologies to remove their toxins (Horsfall 1987). The implication of the widespread emergence of the abundant grass seeds and toxic plants as food staples – behavioural innovations that arose in tandem during the late Holocene – is an increasing ability to support large populations. New plant staples did not simply replace previous ones that had much the same dietary role. The implications are intensified levels of land use along with increasing human populations.

In the north, John Beaton (1985) found massive shell mounds at Princess Charlotte Bay, at times measuring more than 4 m in height. These first began to form around 1700 BP, although the chenier plains on which they were built have remained relatively stable since at least 4000 BP, and possibly since 6000 BP (Chappell 1982; Chappell *et al.* 1983; Beaton 1985). The mounds are seen as testimony at once to specialized foraging patterns focusing on mangrove systems and *Anadara* shell beds in particular; to high-intensity exploitation of an abundant and focused food resource; to centralized disposal patterns over a period of at least 1200 years; and to the presence of territorially bounded consumption bases, used and reused until high mounds eventually formed (David and Chant 1995). The emergence of mounds along the northern coastline only during the late Holocene implies the emergence of new and intensive settlement, exploitation and consumption systems.

All in all, many cultural practices appear to have changed in south-east Cape York by 3800 BP. Sometimes, these changes emerged from identifiable antecedents; there are the relatively slow increases in the numbers of occupied sites during the early to mid Holocene. At other times, they suddenly commence around 4000–3500 BP; the Burren adzes are new. These changes imply not just alterations in intensities of use of specific sites or even of whole regions; they imply a very reorganization of life itself, a rethinking of one's place in the world, of a scheduling of life, of the relationship between people and the world. An example of this is the emergence of grass seeds and toxic plants as edible resources. During ethnographic times, seed-gathering and seed-grinding were gendered tasks, the exclusive province of women. These time-consuming tasks, crucial to survival in semi-arid zones, were a source of power (as distinct from domination), participating in gendered divisions of society. The absence of systematic seed-grinding during the mid Holocene and earlier times implies a society ordered along different social, economic and gender lines.

Once they are brought into use as a food staple, the status in the world of edible seeds and toxic plants, and their relationship to people, necessarily changed. They became a resource, necessitating a rescheduling of daily and seasonal rounds, and a reconceptualization of relationships between people and between plants and people. We can only imagine how the changing place of such items in the everyday life of people was symbolized and legitimated in belief systems, necessitating not just their incorporation in existing world-views, but a modification of those very (gendered) views. I return to some of these points below.

The rock-art

The rock-art of south-east Cape York can be divided by technique into three major types: engravings, paintings, stencils/prints. The engravings are mostly peckings, created by hammering or pounding, although there are also some rare abraded designs. Some early researchers, such as Lesley Maynard (1976; 1977; 1979), suggested that peckings were created by indirect (hammer and chisel) percussion. This is by no means certain; chisels have never been found archaeologically, and most researchers now think that the Cape York peckings were done by direct hammering.

The 'paintings' include designs undertaken in both wet pigments ('paintings' proper) and dry pigments ('drawings'). I do not distinguish paintings from drawings here, partly because of a lack of consistency between previous researchers, and partly because of the difficulty of ensuring correct identification in some cases.

Stencils – mainly of hands, but sometimes of other anatomical parts or of items of material culture – are common throughout the area, with no obvious chronological patterning. As the rarity of all but hand stencils limits their usefulness for the concerns of this chapter, they are not addressed here.

The peckings

Peckings are found from the Koolburra Plateau in the north to Chillagoe in the south (Flood 1987; David and David 1988). They are particularly abundant in sandstone outcrops, such as commonly found around Laura and the Koolburra Plateau. While present in the limestone karst towers of the Mitchell River, Palmer River, Rookwood, Mungana and Chillagoe, they are by no means as common there as in the sandstones. Peckings are almost never found among the hard volcanic rocks.

When found under overhangs, the peckings are usually either heavily patinated or hardly patinated at all. The cases where patination is intermediate are almost all in the Laura sandstones. The heavily patinated peckings include tridents, pits, curvilinear or rectilinear mazes, circles, rayed designs and rounded enclosures with internal patterns (Fig. 8.3); in some places patinated macropod (kangaroo and wallaby) and bird tracks are also found. They never include figurative designs of people or animals. These are the motifs found across the entire study area, although some of the rarer forms (e.g. rectilinear mazes) have not yet been found in areas where peckings are less abundant (e.g. Rookwood).

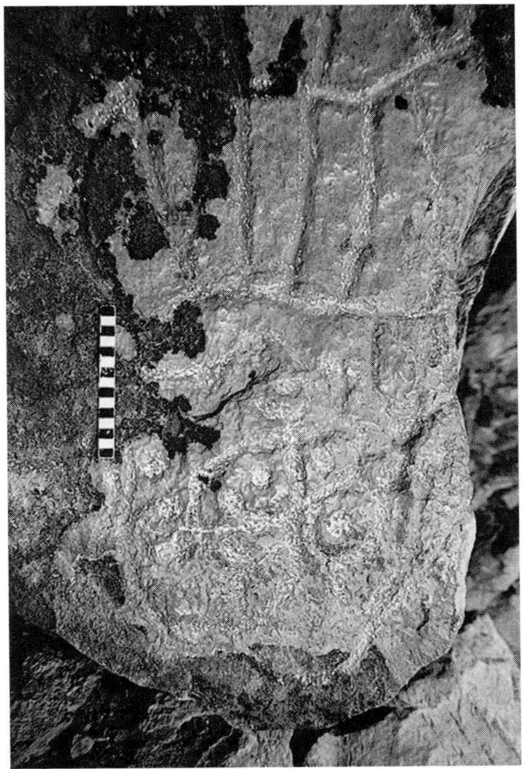

Fig. 8.3. Patinated pecking, Sandy Creek 1. Photograph by Josephine Flood.

The patinated peckings have been argued to date to late Pleistocene and/or early Holocene times by almost all researchers who have worked in the region. In some cases, the discovery of peckings buried beneath dated sediments gives minimum ages for the art: 13,000 BP at the Early Man site (Rosenfeld *et al.* 1981); 12,620±370 BP at Sandy Creek 1 (Morwood *et al.* 1995); 1570±60 BP at Green Ant Shelter (Flood and Horsfall 1986; Flood 1987); 950±50 BP at Yam Camp (Morwood and Dagg 1995). In others, there are associations between dated occupational events and rock-art within excavated sites: between

26,010±410 and *c.* 17,000 BP at Fern Cave (David *et al.* in press); before 15,950±770 BP at Walkunder Arch Cave (Campbell and Mardaga-Campbell 1993).

However, the most direct evidence for the antiquity of peckings has come from the dating of oxalates captured in stratified, laminated cortex found immediately above the pecked surface. These recently obtained results have come both to support and to extend the existing chronological patterns. At Walkunder Arch Cave, Campbell and Mardaga-Campbell (1993: 59) reported a single radiocarbon date of 7085±135 BP for oxalates *over* a patinated set of radiating lines; the pecking must be older than this. At Sandy Creek 1, a minimum date of 2810±150 BP has been obtained over a linear non-figurative design, again offering a minimum age. A minimum age has been reported for the Deighton Lady site (2784±85 BP, Cole *et al.* 1995), although we are warned by the researchers that this pecking was retouched during relatively recent times; the radiocarbon date probably relates to this most recent event. A pecked bird track and a set of radiating lines with unreported degrees of patination have also been dated to >1210±245 BP (Kennedy River site) and >2850±115 BP (Quinkan B6 Rockshelter) respectively (Cole *et al.* 1995).

However, not all peckings are old. At both Laura and the Koolburra Plateau, they continue into more recent times, although they probably ceased to be created during the late Holocene in the Mitchell–Palmer and Rookwood–Mungana–Chillagoe limestone outcrops. The continued creation of peckings at Laura and the Koolburra Plateau until very recent times – probably not ceasing until the arrival of Europeans in the late nineteenth century – is evident in the relatively recent repecking of the Deighton Lady design around 2784±85 BP, and in the presence of unpatinated peckings, which include motifs also found in the dated late Holocene paintings (including dogs) (Cole and Trezise 1992; Cole *et al.* 1995).

Fig. 8.4. Anthropomorph with pendant and rudimentary writing, Laura.

The motifs found among the patinated peckings continue in the more recent, unpatinated designs. In addition, a new set of figures is added, including figurative motifs such as birds, macropods, dogs and items of material culture (Figs. 8.4–8.10). Andrée Rosenfeld (Rosenfeld *et al.* 1981) has suggested that this change from an early, purely non-figurative tradition of the late Pleistocene and early Holocene to a figurative mid- to late-Holocene artistic tradition took place via the addition of animal track designs sometime during the mid Holocene. The mid-stage of this developmental sequence remains uncertain; in some areas – in particular the Koolburra Plateau – macropod and bird tracks predominate among the *most* patinated designs between them accounting for 75 per cent of patinated engravings (Flood 1987: 100).

Pioneer researchers suggested that the change from non-figurative to both non-figurative and figurative designs involved a change in motif forms only (e.g. Maynard 1976; 1979; Rosenfeld *et al.* 1981). Later researchers have emphasized changes in *technique* as much as changes in motif forms (e.g. David and Chant 1995; Morwood and Hobbs 1995). Hence, David and Chant (1995) and David and Lourandos (in press) have recently reviewed all the excavated evidence for the use of ochre in rock-shelters. Of the eighteen sites where ochre was recovered, seventeen have peak deposition rates during the mid to late Holocene. In many sites, ochre pieces occur exclusively during this time. They conclude that while it is clear that pigment art was undertaken well into the late Pleistocene – and as far back as 32,000 BP at Sandy Creek 1 (Morwood *et al.* 1995) – there was a major increase in painting/stencilling activity after *c.* 3500 BP, culminating in the highest levels of the last 2000 years. These conclusions support and refine Flood's (1987: 117) earlier sentiment that a 'flowering of the Koolburra stencil and painting art' had taken place after 2500 BP.

There is now general agreement that painting activity increased markedly throughout south-east Cape York after 3500 BP, an increase associated with the emergence of figurative art in many parts of the region. The original dating of the art relied entirely on indirect evidence: the dating of buried ochre pieces in decorated rock-shelters; patterns of superimposition; the presence of fauna of known antiquity in the art; the presence of paintings in fragile pigments incapable of surviving long periods of time; the depiction of Europeans, of animals introduced from Europe (e.g. horses, pigs), of western items of material culture (e.g. horse-shoes), and even rudimentary writing in traditional methods (Figs. 8.4 and 8.5). Recently, however, more direct evidence for the antiquity of the paintings has emerged, in all cases supporting the original chronology. The first signs came in 1992, when a single radiocarbon date of 2056±81 BP was obtained for a charcoal drawing from the Racecourse Site near Chillagoe (David 1992). Soon after, two more radiocarbon determinations of 725±115 and 730±75 BP were reported on plant fibres (probably brush filaments) caught in the paint matrix of two adjacent anthropomorphs at the Yam Camp site near Laura (Watchman and Cole 1993). More recently, together with Marvin Rowe's team of chemists from Texas A and M University, and Ewan Lawson's radiocarbon-dating team from the Australian Nuclear Science and Technology Organisation, the author has begun a systematic dating project for south-east Cape York rock-art (e.g. Armitage *et al.* 1998; David *et al.* in press). So far, dating has concentrated on charcoal paintings, as the extraction of datable organic binders remains controversial (e.g. Loy *et al.* 1990; Nelson 1993; Gillespie 1997).

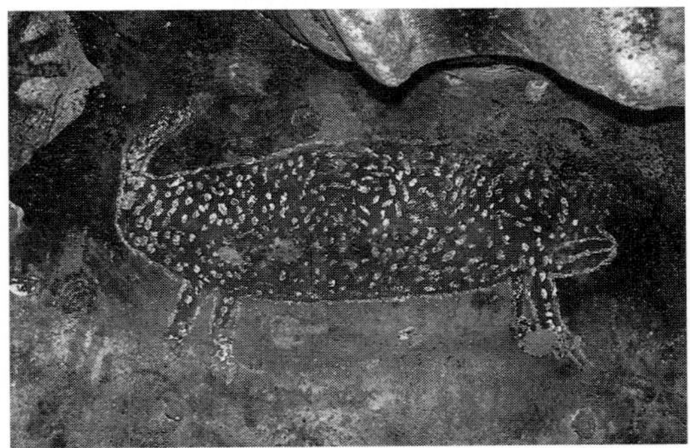

Fig. 8.5. Painting of a pig, Mitchell River.

Seventeen new AMS radiocarbon determinations have been obtained from the Rookwood, Mungana and Chillagoe regions. All are less than

3350±350 BP (David *et al.* in press). A further ten dates have been obtained on Mitchell and Palmer rivers paintings, all later than 2420±130 BP (OZC–849). They include both figurative and non-figurative paintings, sampling both faded and unfaded designs. Some of the dated paintings are under others, so the dates also represent maximum ages for those superimposed designs. The dating programme has so far strengthened the original chronological model.

Another line of evidence has tested and refined the chronological model. Geochemist Alan Watchman has laser-ablated carbon-bearing compounds closely associated with pigment art as revealed in cross-sections of cave-wall cortex (e.g. Watchman *et al.* 1993; Watchman *et al.* in press). The method involves the manual removal of rock cortex over an area of a few square centimetres at the most, and its microscopic examination in the laboratory. Laminated rock cortex often possesses fine oxalate layers from which the carbon can be released with a laser for AMS radiocarbon dating. When such layers are near layers of pigment, minimum or maximum ages can be calculated, depending on whether the art layer is below or above the oxalate.

A number of archaeological sites from the Laura and Chillagoe regions have been investigated in this way. At Yam Camp, Sandy Creek 1 and the Quinkan B6 Shelter, traces of pigment art occur immediately above dates of 2850 to 725 BP (Cole *et al.* 1995: 155). Much older pigment art has been revealed in rock cortex cross-sections at Sandy Creek 2 and Walkunder Arch Cave, where a number of Pleistocene laminae have been identified. Since the method reveals pigment buried within the surface deposits only over the very small area taken by the sample, we do not know whether the art was painting or stencil, or what motifs it followed – only that there was pigment applied at that stage in the evolving stratigraphy of the rock surface.

Late Holocene regionalization

During the last 3500 years, it was common practice to paint – and at Laura and the Koolburra Plateau also to engrave – figurative and non-figurative motifs in the caves and rock-shelters of south-east Cape York. However, unlike the widespread non-figurative conventions of earlier times – when motif shapes were of a limited range – there emerged at this time a series of highly regionalized artistic traditions. In the north is a bounded region, delimited by Princess Charlotte Bay and the Flinders Island group, where marine themes are common. In each of the five sections of this coastal zone examined, marine animals and items of material culture (e.g. ships) form a significant component of the painted art. In each case also, moths/butterflies and zoomorphs with crescent heads predominate, never accounting for less than 43 per cent of paintings. Those motifs are never found elsewhere (David and Chant 1995; David and Lourandos 1998).

Eighty kilometres to the south is the Koolburra Plateau; there marine themes disappear altogether, but terrestrial fauna and anthropomorphs become common. Here an unusual figure is commonly found, an echidna–human therianthrope (Fig. 8.6). Never occurring amongst the earlier peckings, these are almost entirely restricted to this area; the only other examples known are in one of the Kennedy River shelters, at Boomerang Shelter and possibly in a shelter near the Quinkan Galleries in the Laura region a few kilometres to the south-east (Rosenfeld 1987: 122; pers. comm. 1999). These endemic figures account for more than a quarter – 28 per cent – of the Koolburra Plateau paintings (Flood 1987).

In the Laura region to the immediate east and south-east, a broad range of motif forms can be found. What gives this region its unique character is not a specific motif type, but the mode of

Fig. 8.6. Echidna–human therianthropes, Koolburra Plateau Photograph by Josephine Flood.

painting. Both anthropomorphs and zoomorphs are common, many in bicolour and some in polychrome (Fig. 8.7). Unlike surrounding regions, internally decorated designs abound, including both anthropomorphs and zoomorphs with sets of sub-parallel lines, dots or multiple crossing lines on their bodies. Pendants are sometimes depicted on the anthropomorphs (Fig. 8.4). These decorative conventions almost never occur in surrounding regions (David and Lourandos 1998).

To the south of the Palmer River is the area ethnographically identified with the Kuku Yalanji language group. It includes the Palmer and Mitchell rivers, Bonney Glen Station and Mt Windsor/Mt Carbine. In each area, anthropomorphs account for more than 62 per cent of paintings. They are almost always portrayed in front-view monochrome infill (Fig. 8.8), and in many cases – but never in the majority – they are depicted upside-down (David and Chant 1995).

At Bare Hill, 70 km to the south-east, anthropomorphs again predominate; here zoomorphs are also common. Unlike their northerly neighbours, the anthropomorphs are depicted in an endemic pose, with up-raised arms and down-curved legs (Clegg 1981; David and Chant 1995).

To the south, west and south-west of these regions are the major waterways of the Mitchell and Walsh rivers. On the other side of the rivers, painted motif forms change dramatically. This was not the case for the earlier peckings, whose range of motifs was homogeneous and widespread. In all regions – Ngarrabullgan, Rookwood, Mungana, Chillagoe and Ootan – the paintings are overwhelmingly non-figurative; figurative motifs never account for more than 10 per cent of the art. Everywhere simple geometric

Fig. 8.7. Late Holocene paintings, Laura
Photograph by Josephine Flood.

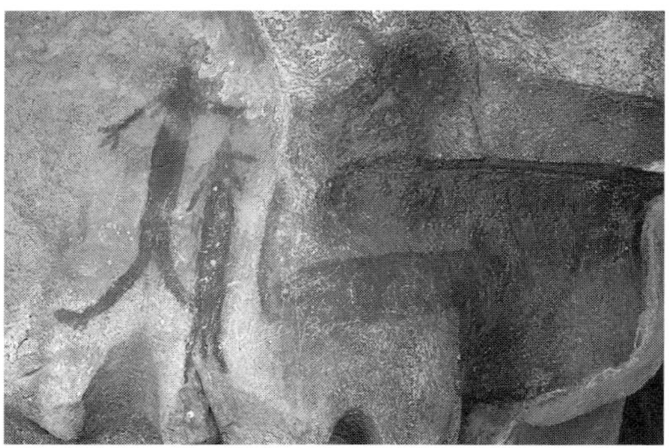

Fig. 8.8. Dog and generalized anthropomorphs, Mitchell-Palmer limestone belt.

motifs – radiating lines, circles and circle variants, single and sets of parallel lines – grids and extended linear designs can be found, as well as animal tracks. The changeover from the northern figurative traditions is sudden, occurring at the Mitchell and the Walsh rivers. There is no gradual increase in percentage of non-figurative motifs as one approaches from the north.

The late Holocene paintings of south-east Cape York are therefore highly regionalized in motif forms; David and Chant (1995) have also documented overlapping regionalism in colours used and in the linearity of depictions and frequency of internal decorations. These spatially bounded artistic traditions emerged from widespread, homogeneous beginnings around 3500 BP; they were thriving by 2000 BP. Coupled with the archaeological evidence for increased rates of ochre deposition within the excavated sites, the rise of regional artistic networks, we can say, was coincident in time with an absolute increase in painting activity. It is this combination of features that David and Lourandos (1998) see as evidence for a restructuring of socio-demographic systems during the late Holocene, with the emergence of an increasingly localized marking of the land, implying increasing localization of access to and control of places.

Social, political and demographic implications

Together, the rock-art and its associated cultural trends as understood from the archaeology speak of increase, of geographical fragmentation and of innovation. I have elsewhere sought to explain these changes by reference to absolute population increases and increases in the scale of regional interaction, and by the increasing formalization of regional integration (David 1991; David and Chant 1995; David and Lourandos 1998). The model proposed involves rising populations from the early to mid Holocene, resulting in heightened levels of social and political tension by 3500 BP. McNiven (in press) has reviewed the Australian ethnographic literature for regionalization as a process, noting the political fragmentation of interacting populations once group numbers reach a critical size, typically around 500 individuals. Based on both archaeological and ethnographic materials, David (1991) suggested that regional Aboriginal residential groups were growing in size throughout south-east Cape York; the result was that groups with access to land fragmented by 3500 BP into geographically circumscribed, formally recognized social and political units. These increasingly localized and increasingly formalized land-controlling groups, with their emergent system of difference in rock-art styles marking the land, eventually led to the ethnographically documented territorial networks of the nineteenth century (e.g. Tindale 1974; Sutton 1995).

The regionalization process is explained by reference to increasing levels of conflict caused by increasing absolute population sizes – the original cause(s) of which remains unknown. Existing sets of people fragmented into manageable sizes, probably forming more localized groups. These were landed, territorial units, the locations of

Fig. 8.9. Generalized anthropomorphs with slanted heads/head-dresses, Palmer River, site PM 32.

territories and boundaries being broadly recognized. The nature of land-marking behaviour and the accessibility of land to artists may be able to be investigated by reference to the distribution of idiosyncratic unusual artistic conventions; I would like eventually to construct a more explicit, testable model for this. If groups with access to land involved closely related and interacting individuals, who after 3500 BP required increasingly formal authority to cross short-spaced territorial boundaries, we would expect individual artists to retain the right to paint or engrave only within their own territories. A marking of landscape outside their own places would be beyond their territorial rights. Before 3500 BP, when territorial units and social interaction were broader ranged, I suggest that individual artists decorated shelter walls spread over relatively broad distances. This is consistent with the restricted spread of specific late Holocene painted motifs across the landscape. There are eleven thin, monochrome infilled anthropomorphs with slanted heads/head-dresses (Fig. 8.9); all occur in a single cave in the Palmer River limestones. There are three generalized anthropomorphs with rayed heads/head-dresses (Fig. 8.10); they occur within 2.3 km of each other, towards the northern end of the Palmer

Fig. 8.10. Anthropomorph with rayed head/head-dress, Palmer River.

River area. There are three anthropomorphs with knobbed head-dresses; they are found in two sites found 4.5 km apart, again in the Palmer River area, and immediately to the south of where the rayed head-dresses are found. There is no overlap between these two areas. Yet a single, generalized anthropomorphic tradition is common throughout the Palmer and Mitchell rivers areas. While the Palmer and Mitchell rivers areas constitute a single, bounded stylistic region distinct from Laura to the north, and Ngarrabullgan and Rookwood to the south-east and south, within it more individual (spatially restricted) artistic conventions can be found. The systematic mapping of these individuated motifs within and between regions would be worthwhile; their distribution is consistent with the work and behaviour of individuals or members of individual groups painting within their own territories. The absence of spread of such non-generalized motifs across a broad geographical expanse – unlike the earlier peckings – supports the above contentions: that individuals' access to land, and to mark the land, became more geographically restricted after around 3500 BP.

From 3500 BP, I suggest that interaction between land-using groups necessitated more formal arrangements as the crossings of physical and conceptual territorial boundaries were negotiated. This led to the emergence of relatively distinctive cultural conventions, including those affecting rock-art. The major, twofold division between the late Holocene paintings found to the north and south of the Walsh and Mitchell rivers – a northern figurative and a southern non-figurative tradition – expresses these social and political conditions, the formation of two broad political blocs and interaction spheres. In a review of the ethnographic literature, David and Cole (1990) showed that during the nineteenth century these two artistic zones coincided with the geographical position of two relatively distinct Aboriginal social, political and economic blocs. In the north, interaction tended towards short distances and was based on individual trade partnerships; in the south, long-distance interaction was based on infrequent but large-scale ceremonial gatherings.

Late Holocene artistic regionalism within each of these two areas – and in particular in the north – matches these ethnographic details, and is highlighted by the well-bounded nature of distinct stylistic conventions, as evidenced in the restriction of moth/butterfly motifs in Princess Charlotte Bay and the Flinders Island group; of echidna–human therianthropes in the Koolburra Plateau; of internally decorated anthropomorphs and zoomorphs at Laura; of generalized anthropomorphs in what is today Kuku Yalanji country; and of a predominance of anthropomorphs with up-raised arms and down-curved legs at Bare Hill.

The social construction of rock-art

While archaeological evidence for the emergence of regionalism in artistic behaviour after 3500 BP is evident – coincident in time with independent archaeological evidence for peak populations, peak levels of site use and peak levels of regional land use – the symbolic nature of this artistic behaviour remains unexplored. It is this point I now explore by reference to animal representations in the art, and their relationship to animals in the landscape and animals as sources of food.

Animals in nature

The vertebrate fauna of south-east Cape York is poorly known, owing largely to the area's remoteness, the broad range of microhabitats found and the relatively small number of zoologists who have ventured into its wilds. Some observations can nevertheless be made.

By world standards Australia in general lacks any forms of large terrestrial mammals. This has not always been so. The pre-glacial maximum period saw a number of megafaunal species – such as *Diprotodon*, *Macropus titan* and *Zygomaturus* – which became extinct likely before 40,000 BP, and possibly earlier (but see Horton 1980); the dating of megafaunal extinctions is still very much a matter for debate (e.g. Flannery 1990).

The largest terrestrial animals in the study region are the macropodoids (more commonly, but erroneously when including the bettongs, called macropods) – kangaroos, wallabies and bettongs – and the flightless emu (up to 2 m tall) and cassowary (up to 1.8 m tall). The macropodoids are very common throughout the mainland, although their abundance varies considerably by environmental zone, by local conditions during particular years and by season. The few surveys that have been done in the region indicate that macropod densities of sixteen per sq. km are not uncommon (David 1983). The only species present are: eastern grey kangaroo, *Macropus giganteus* (4–66 kg body weight); common wallaroo, *Macropus robustus* (25–47 kg); antilopine wallaroo, *Macropus antilopinus* (16–49 kg); swamp wallaby, *Wallabia bicolor* (13–17 kg); agile wallaby, *Macropus agilis* (9–27 kg); northern nailtail wallaby, *Onychogalea unguifera* (6–8 kg); spotted-tailed quoll, *Dasyurus maculatus* (4–7 kg); rock wallabies, *Petrogale godmani* and *P. mareeba* (4–5 kg); pademelon, *Thylogale stigmatica* (4–5 kg); spectacled hare-wallaby, *Lagorchestes conspicillatus* (2–5 kg); and northern brown bandicoot, *Isoodon macrourus* (1–3 kg). Smaller marsupials are: common brushtail possum, *Trichosurus vulpecula* (1–5 kg); rufous bettong, *Aepyprymnus rufescens* (3–4 kg); northern bettong, *Bettongia tropica* (1 kg); common ringtail possum, *Pseudocheirus peregrinus* (1 kg); northern quoll, *Dasyurus hallucatus* (1 kg); the monotreme short-beaked echidna, *Tachyglossus aculeatus*, also known as the spiny anteater (2–7 kg); and the sub-kilogram striped possum, *Dactylopsila trivirgata*; sugar glider, *Petaurus breviceps*; feathertail glider, *Acrobates pygmaeus*; long-tailed pygmy possum, *Cercartetus caudatus*; red-cheeked dunnart, *Sminthopsis virginiae*; kultarr, *Antechinomys laniger*; common planigale, *Planigale maculata*; and fourteen species of rodents (rats and mice), all weighing less than 1 kg except for the large water-rat (*Hydromys chrysogaster*, up to 1 kg). There is also a wide range of bats and flying foxes, all weighing less than 1 kg (see entries in Strahan 1995).

Three other mammals have come or gone during the late Holocene in south-east Cape York: the dingo – Australian dog, *Canis lupus dingo* – (9–24 kg); the once-widespread dog-like marsupial thylacine, *Thylacinus cynocephalus* (15–35 kg); and the Tasmanian devil, *Sarcophilus harrisii* (7–9 kg) (Strahan 1995). It is thought that both the thylacine and the Tasmanian devil became extinct as a result of competitive pressures from the dingo after its arrival in mainland Australia sometime between 4000 and 3500 BP (Horton 1980).

Other widespread and common vertebrates include many species of snakes, some of which are highly venomous; lizards, including goannas (*Varanus gouldii*, *V. panoptes*, *V. semiremex*, *V. mertensi*, *V. timorensis*, *V. tristis*, *V. varius*) which can measure up to 2 m in length; turtles; fish (most but not all species weighing less than 1 kg); and well over 150 species of birds. Along the coastal fringes and northern and eastern waterways, saltwater crocodiles are found, as is the freshwater crocodile throughout rivers of the study region (Cogger 1996).

With respect to body shapes, as recognizable in generalized figurative artistic traditions, we can divide the above fauna into seven groups:

1 macropodoids, characterized by their long legs/feet and very small arms/hands;
2 mammalian quadrupeds other than macropodoids, with the four limbs of roughly equal length;
3 bipedal birds;
4 lizards and crocodiles, with long tails and relatively short limbs;
5 echidna and turtles, with their protruding heads and opposing short tails, and short lateral extensions for arms and legs;
6 snakes;
7 fish.

While every species is not found in all parts of the study region, representatives of each category commonly are. In some cases, individual species or sets within each of these broad types can be further differentiated by general body shape, such as dogs (including dingos) with up-turned and possums with down-turned tails. The interested reader is directed to Andrée Rosenfeld's (1982; 1984) detailed discussions on identifying mammalian species from the rock-art of Laura.

Animals as food: archaeological evidence

Not all animals were eaten. For one reason or another – be it palatability, catchability or the presence of cultural restrictions – some animals find their way to the dinner table while others do not. We must be careful to avoid overgeneralization here: some animals may be eaten by one group of people, or by certain individuals, during certain seasons or following certain culturally recognized times of the year only. And cultural habits change. We need to identify, for each area and for each period of time, which animals were eaten and which were not. This is difficult, for archaeological data, by definition, is biased towards faunal remains that have survived within the particular sites investigated. Where data from various sites have accumulated – such as in south-east Cape York – we can nevertheless proceed with caution. When diet breadths are repeated between sites, and when the relative proportions of species are consistently represented, we may say that archaeologically and culturally meaningful patterns have been identified.

Identifiable faunal remains have been recovered from rock-shelters and caves from five broad regions: Princess Charlotte Bay and the Flinders Island group (three sites), Laura (seven sites), Mitchell and Palmer rivers (one site), Ngarrabullgan (one site), and Rookwood–Mungana–Chillagoe (three sites). Of these, some faunal remains are attributable to cultural activity, others are not. I have excluded from the following discussions the bone remains identified as non-cultural by the original excavators and all remains of cave-dwelling bats, rodents, skinks and geckoes, none of which has been reported to show any trace of human origin (such as burning or cut-marks). I have also eliminated the domestic dog – the few remains of which show no evidence of burning or cut-marks – and European-introduced pig remains. What we are left with are those bones that can reliably be treated as food remains. I deal only with vertebrates; remains of other kinds such as crustaceans – rare among the remains – egg-shell, and saltwater, freshwater and land snail-shells are omitted.

Princess Charlotte Bay and the Flinders Island group is the only coastal region considered in

Table 8.1 *Bone record from the archaeological sites (Minimum Numbers of Individuals, vertebrates): Princess Charlotte Bay and the Flinders Island group.*

Taxa	Endaen Shelter	Walaemini Rockshelter	Alkaline Hill	Total	Per cent
macropodoid	2–3	1	1	4–5	44–50
fish	1	1		2	20–22
turtle	1			1	10–11
bird		1		1	10–11
dugong	1			1	10–11
Total	5–6	3	1	9–10	

this study. Excavations by John Beaton (1985) at Endaen Shelter, Walaemini Rockshelter and Alkaline Hill – all of which date to the late Holocene – revealed a predominance of shellfish, both gastropods and bivalves. The remains of the marine dugong, saltwater turtle and fish were recovered in low numbers from Endaen Shelter, along with those of two to three wallabies (species not identified). Some fragments of macropod, bird and fish were recovered from Walaemini Rockshelter, but these were rare, with shellfish again predominant. Sporadic macropod bones were found at Alkaline Hill, again amidst abundant shellfish remains (Table 8.1). Although Beaton (1981; 1985; n.d.) does not attempt to quantify the faunal remains from these sites by their stratigraphic position, a predominance of shellfish and the occasional but repeated presence of macropods are apparent. A single, even small macropod offers more meat weight than thousands of shellfish, a point previously noted by Betty Meehan (1977) who argued that shellfish offered gathering and hunting peoples reliable rather than rich returns, while the less predictable terrestrial vertebrates may well have supplied greater albeit more sporadic returns.

No identifiable bone remains were recovered from the two excavations to have been undertaken in the Koolburra Plateau to the south of Princess Charlotte Bay (Flood and Horsfall 1986). While more sites have been excavated in the Laura sandstone belt than in any other part of south-east Cape York, faunal remains are not abundant in their acid soils. Fortunately, the Laura bone remains are relatively intact for the period addressed in this chapter, the last 3500 years.

Table 8.2 presents the Minimum Numbers of Individuals recovered from the late Holocene levels at the Laura sites (raw data obtained from Morwood and L'Oste-Brown 1995b; papers in Rosenfeld *et al.* 1981; Morwood and Hobbs 1995). Some common features are apparent: the small macropod *Petrogale* predominates in every site, in total accounting for twenty-eight of the hundred individual animals represented (28 per cent). The smaller quadruped mammals – possums, bandicoots, *Petaurus* – occur occasionally but repeatedly, especially the bandicoots and possums. Together these represent the larger herbivorous mammals of the region. Snakes, a recurring and at times important food source, never predominate. Goannas, flying foxes, echidnas and birds are present in low numbers.

Noticeable is the absence of fish and crocodiles, both common in the landscape. Both also are found in riverine environments, with most of the excavated sites occurring near waterways abundant in both fish and freshwater crocodiles. I will return to these points below.

To the south are the Palmer River and Mitchell River limestones, where faunal remains excavated

Table 8.2 *Bone record from the archaeological sites (Minimum Numbers of Individuals, vertebrates): Laura.*

Taxa	Early Man (Levels 1–6)	Sandy Creek 2	Magnificent Gallery	Yam Camp	Red Horse	Red Bluff 1	Hann River 1	Total	Per cent
macropodoid	7	3	2	22	10	6	2	52	52
possum	2	1	1	6		1		11	11
snake	1			5	5			11	11
bandicoot			1	4	2	1		8	8
goanna	3		1	1				5	5
Petaurus	3			1				4	4
flying fox			1	3				4	4
bird	2		1	1				4	4
echidna				1				1	1
Total	18	4	7	44	17	8	2	100	

Table 8.3 *Bone record from the archaeological sites (Minimum Numbers of Individuals, vertebrates): Palmer and Mitchell rivers limestone zone.*

Taxa	Mordor Cave	Per cent
macropodoid	21	55
possum	5	13
bandicoot	5	13
snake	4	11
goanna	1	3
dasyurid	1	3
bird	1	3
Total	38	

from one cave have been identified: Mordor Cave (David and Dagg 1993; David and Chant 1995) (Table 8.3). This is a late Holocene site, occupation beginning about 1500 BP.

As was the case at Laura, *Petrogale* predominates, accounting for twelve of the thirty-eight individual animals represented (31 per cent). As at Laura also, possums, bandicoots and snakes form a secondary but recurrent presence. A small range of other taxa make their occasional presence, never in high numbers. Fish and crocodile remains are again totally absent.

At Ngarrabullgan Cave to the south, bone remains are uncommon, with only three individuals present: two 'large' mammals (almost certainly macropodoids) and one possible bird. Macropodoids appear to dominate this tiny sample (David 1994: 85).

Further to the south, three caves have been excavated – Echidna's Rest, Walkunder Arch Cave and Fern Cave (Campbell 1982; David 1984; 1990; David and Chant 1995). The Fern Cave cultural remains, almost certainly entirely Pleistocene in age, are not discussed here. Walkunder Arch Cave contains near-continuous sediments dating back to over 15,000 BP; I am only concerned here with the bones from the last 3700. Similarly, I am only concerned with the bone from Stratigraphic Units 1 and 2 of Echidna's Rest, which date to the last 3000 years (Table 8.4).

As in the north, *Petrogale* is again the most common species in both sites, accounting for 61 out of a total of 111 individual animals (55 per cent). Bandicoots, snakes and possums are again important although not numerically dominant.

In all regions, the range and order of predominance of eaten fauna are similar: *Petrogale* predominates, followed by other macropodoids, bandicoots, possums and snakes. Macropodoids account for about half the Minimum Number of Individuals recovered from every region. I return to these widespread patterns below when

Table 8.4 *Bone record from the archaeological sites (Minimum Numbers of Individuals, vertebrates): Mungana and Chillagoe limestone outcrops.*

Taxa	Walkunder Arch Cave (Layers 1–7)	Echidna's Rest (Stratigraphic Units 1–2)	Total	Per cent
macropodoid	54	16	70	63
bandicoot	16	4	20	18
snake	10	2	12	11
possum	1	3	4	4
goanna	2		2	2
bird		2	2	2
echidna	1		1	1
Total	84	27	111	

considering their relationship to faunal representations in the art.

Animals in the art

The world around us is not just 'out there'; by ordering and giving it meaning, we structure the very way we live and view existence. Order helps us form our world as experienced, and in the process construct our identity as social beings. This is achieved through symbols as much as through language, both helping to construct particular relationships between people and relationships between people and the material world. The position of animals in our experience of the world is no exception. While they may at times form an important source of subsistence, even food needs to be ordered and given meaning in society and culture. Animals are not just good to eat, but good to think with (Lévi-Strauss 1962).

Relationships between animals and people express how we order the world, and through this, aspects and contexts of worldviews. These relationships are operationalized through both communication and everyday action. Communication is itself accessed archaeologically through symbols; action through the material results of everyday activity. In this section, I discuss the range and frequency of animals people chose to depict in the rock-art of various parts of south-east Cape York. My aim is to explore spatial patterning in symbolic behaviour, a further exploration of the late Holocene regionalism already identified in the rock-art (see above).

I consider below only figurative motifs. Nonfigurative images may also represent animals or other material things, but I am interested in *form* here, in how people used shapes from the surrounding world to decorate and express their life (and death) spaces. The choice of form is culturally mediated, and it is this choice – habitual, but also involving conscious choice – that I am targeting to access spatio-temporal trends in artistic/symbolic behaviour.

The rock-art of nineteen regions of southeast Cape York has been systematically quantified and reported (see David and Chant 1995 for a detailed presentation of recording methods and multivariate statistics). In the north, the five regions that together comprise Princess Charlotte Bay and the Flinders Island group – Clack Island, Cliff Island, Flinders Islands, Bathurst Head, Jane Table Hill – contain 1246 paintings of animals (Grahame Walsh, pers. comm. 1996); 223 (18 per cent) are of marine fauna. Many are invertebrates – squid, octopus and crustacean. Curiously, another 74 per cent are of moths and butterflies or zoomorphs with

Table 8.5 *Painted record from the rock-art (vertebrates): Princess Charlotte Bay and the Flinders Island group.*

Fauna	Number	Per cent
sea turtle	123	41
dugong/shark	47	16
crocodile/lizard	34	11
bird	32	11
stingray	25	8
snake	15	5
dog	14	5
fish/eel	13	4
Total	303	

Table 8.6 *Painted record from the rock-art (vertebrates): Koolburra Plateau.*

Fauna	Number	Per cent
crocodile	21	38
turtle	13	23
lizard	12	21
fish	8	14
snake	2	4
Total	56	

crescent heads that closely resemble moths and butterflies.

In archaeological contexts, few of these would be recoverable food items if eaten. We cannot, therefore, compare and contrast them to diet breadths as identified from the excavations. Of the vertebrates, 303 stingrays, dugongs/sharks, fish/eels, turtles, birds, crocodiles/lizards, snakes and dogs are represented in the art. Table 8.5 presents their absolute and relative frequencies.

Marine items predominate. Sea turtles and dugongs/sharks are the most common, together accounting for 57 per cent of vertebrate fauna in the art. Recall that turtles and dugongs were also recovered among the excavated food remains. Macropodoids are totally absent from the art; yet they appear in *every* excavation, and they predominate as vertebrate food items in all sites. While the animals commonly found in the marine environment are represented in the art, the terrestrial fauna are not. Nor does the art accurately reflect diet breadths.

In the Koolburra Plateau to the south, the range of painted fauna is extremely small (Flood 1987) (Table 8.6) – only fifty-six paintings of animals in total, excluding the echidna–human therianthropes. Of these, crocodiles are the most common, followed by turtles, lizards, fish and snakes. A total absence of mammals implies that it is unlikely that the painted animals are subsistence-related.

If we include the echidna–human therianthropes, the pattern becomes more curious, for now 126 of 182 animal paintings (69 per cent) relate to echidnas (monotreme mammals). In the Koolburra Plateau too, we do not see the macropodoids that are among the largest and most readily visible animals in the landscape, as well as the most common vertebrate food items everywhere across south-east Cape York.

At Laura to the south there are 730 animal paintings, excluding the rare introduced animals such as horses and thirteen sets of invertebrates (bees) (Maynard 1976; David and Cole 1990; Cole 1992; Cole and David 1992; David and Chant 1995; see David and Lourandos 1998 for a compilation of data) (Table 8.7). The most common animals are flying foxes and fish, followed by birds and macropodoids. Flying foxes and birds contributed only 4 per cent of the excavated (eaten) fauna; fish were totally absent. Macropodoids were numerically important, accounting for 52 per cent of food items. Other marsupials – possums, bandicoots and *Petaurus* – together accounted for 23 per cent of food items. They account for <1 per cent of the art. There is a clear difference between the faunal range as represented in the food remains and those represented in the paintings.

Table 8.7 *Painted record from the rock-art (vertebrates): Laura.*

Fauna	Number	Per cent
flying fox	193	26
fish	137	19
bird	91	12
macropodoid	83	11
snake	63	9
dog	44	6
eel/fish	38	5
turtle	33	5
echidna	21	3
crocodile	14	2
crocodile or lizard	8	1
other mammal	3	<1
stingray	1	<1
lizard	1	<1
Total	730	

In the Palmer and Mitchell rivers to the south, the seventy-five paintings again include a relatively broad range of animal taxa (a painting of the introduced pig is excluded) (Table 8.8). As was the case at Laura to the immediate north, flying foxes predominate, with 44 per cent of the art. Dogs are also numerically important (31 per cent), with birds, eel/fish and turtles coming next. No marsupials of any kind are represented, including macropodoids, despite their predominance as a meat food (David and Chant 1995).

To the south are the Mitchell and Walsh rivers, on the other side of which the art is almost entirely non-figurative. The number of identifiable animal representations is therefore very low. At Ngarrabullgan, two animals – a crocodile and a snake – occur. In the Rookwood–Mungana–Chillagoe region to the south, five animals are found, two snakes, two echidnas and one turtle. Again, the marsupials fail to be depicted, including the ubiquitous food item, *Petrogale*.

So what is happening? What is the position of animals in the lived and experienced world of the people we are dealing with? What is

Table 8.8 *Painted record from the rock-art (vertebrates): Palmer and Mitchell rivers.*

Fauna	Number	Per cent
flying fox	33	44
dog	23	31
bird	7	9
eel/fish	5	7
turtle	4	5
lizard	1	1
crocodile	1	1
echidna	1	1
Total	75	

the relationship between people and animals as a whole as well as specific species? Let us get closer to the symbolic content of the animals represented in both the art and in the diet by considering the ethnographic record – the end-product of the rock-art changes that began around 3500 BP.

Animals expressing world-views: ethnography

To understand people's relationships with the world in Aboriginal Australia during ethnographic times we must begin with the Dreaming.

The Dreaming, or Dreamtime, is a pan-Australian cultural trait, although its specific expression in stories, songs and the like is different in different places. The Dreaming is not a religious belief, nor is it a method of interpretation. It 'corresponds to absolute or whole reality, that which comprehends everything and is adequate to everything. It is the total referent of which anything else is a *relatum*' (Stanner 1960: 246). It is a world-view, an ontological framework through which people position themselves in the world and the world in themselves. It is, so to speak, a positioning of existence, an ordering of being. Let me offer some specific examples.

Unlike Christian thought, the Dreaming is based on a view of the world as a single, interrelated network without subjects or objects. People are not separate from the 'out there'. They are, rather, linked to the world in such a way that it is not possible to take any item as an isolated essence. The Dreaming relates to the creation of the world, to a timeless past when 'people' and 'animals' were of the one, neither having yet attained their defining features, and when the present world emerged from the unformed.

The Dreaming is not of the past, for Dreamtime is motionless (while at the same time imbued with change, and paradoxically therefore with movement). It is also of the present, operationalized in life itself. An individual whose Dreaming is kangaroo is imbued with kangarooness. A hill that may have been created in the Dreaming when the kangaroo lay there and was transformed into that hill is part and parcel of that person. There is a mutual relationship here – even to say that the essence is not in the kangaroo, but in the mutuality – each element helping to define the other. Francesca Merlan (1989: 4–9) captures this point well when discussing relationships between people and between people and land in Wardaman country in Australia's Northern Territory:

> The Wardaman use the word *laglan* 'country, place, site' (also camp) to refer to tracts of country and places within them to which they claim attachment, as in the phrase *nganinggin laglan* 'my country'. Each such country is composed of many different sites, at least some principal ones of which are associated with estate-linked *buwarraja*, that is, creator figures or 'dreamings' which are saliently or exclusively identified with that particular country. An example is the association of *girribug* 'pheasant coucal' with a particular country . . . of which the Willeroo homestead and some neighbouring places are focal sites. In addition to these estate-linked and bounded dreamings, through each country there pass at least some mythological paths of other, long-range dreamings, many of which . . . happen to come from the west and northwest . . . Thus each country, or 'estate' (see Maddock 1982) is defined by a particular constellation of far-travelled and more local dreamings and sites.

But the Dreaming relates to more than lore and the attachments of people to the world; it can equally be translated as tradition and Law, the rules of life itself. It involves every aspect of life; to cite the words of Paddy Japaljarri Stewart (1994: 305):

> This is the story about jukurrpa (Dreaming) in the old ways what they used to do and used to learn from their old grandfathers, grandmothers and grandparents and in the Dreamtime this is what they used to learn.
>
> . . . When my father was alive this is what he taught me. He had taught me traditional ways like traditional designs in body or head of kangaroo Dreaming . . . and eagle Dreaming. He taught me how to sing song for the big ceremonies. People who are related to us in a close family they have to have the same sort of jukurrpa Dreaming, and to sing songs in the same way as we do our actions like dancing, and paintings and our body or shields or things, and this is what my father taught me. My Dreaming is the kangaroo Dreaming, the eagle Dreaming and budgerigar Dreaming so I have three kinds of Dreamings in my jukurrpa and I have to hang on to it. This is what my father taught me, and this is what I have to teach my sons, and my son has to teach his sons the same way my father taught me, and that's the way it will go on from grandparents to sons, and follow that jukurrpa.

Anderson (1984: 80) has said of Kuku Yalanji country in south-east Cape York:

> The environment for Kuku-Yalanji was not, in a sense, an objective entity, fixed in nature and external to human life. Environment was 'culturized', humanized landscape termed *bubu*, or 'country'. It was often described in human terms; changes in it were interpreted as changes in the human and social world. In turn it *re*-acted by providing goods and resources or by withholding them and bringing hardship or climatic catastrophe upon humans . . . The landscape was socialised by the projection of a human persona onto it. Minute changes in the environment were read immediately and wholly in social terms . . . Major changes, too, such as floods, fire, drought, seasonal resources not appearing on time or not being of the right quality,

were perceived as being brought about by action in the social world . . . relations among people and among groups were seen also as relations among territories or countries.

In Djungan country near-by (Ngarrabullgan), Sharp (1939: 439–49) similarly noted that people were organized around named patrilineal moieties 'associated with strongly developed totemic patterns . . . and by clearly defined local patrilineal clans responsible for the practice of a totemic ancestor cult'. The moieties were *Raku* and *Walar*, *Mirki* and *Muranggan*, each of which was further divided into two sections, *Kupandji*, *Worpu*, *Djilandji* and *Karpandji*. According to Sharp (1939), the *Kupandji* and *Karpandji* sections were of the *Raku/Walar* moiety, and *Worpu* and *Djilandji* were of the *Mirki/Muranggan* moiety. This organizational system was common throughout much of south-east Cape York at the end of the nineteenth century (see David 1998 and David and Wilson in press for more detailed discussions).

In south-east Cape York, during ethnographic times each person therefore belonged to a specific, named section, which recognized descent through strict lines according to indigenous Law as given in the Dreaming. In their turn each of these sections belonged to one of two named moieties. Sharp (1939: 443) noted that 'each of the moieties has its own peculiar totems and . . . there is a strict tabu against any person killing, eating, or in any way harming the chief of these moiety totems'. The moiety name *Raku* refers to a local, small, nocturnal bird which Sharp could not identify, but which he noted was 'characterised by its regular metallic call' (Sharp 1939: 269). As he also noted, *Mirki* referred to 'the night owl or mopoke. These birds and their eggs, although not good eating anyway, are tabu . . . where they are the moiety totems.' *Walar*, a small yellow bee, is a supplementary totem, as is *Muranggan*, a larger black bee. However, 'there are no totemic tabus on the use of the honeys produced by these bees' (Sharp 1939: 443).

Sharp (1939: 443) noted that each year,

or at less frequent intervals . . . a member of one moiety kills the bird totem of the opposite moiety and publicly desecrates and exposes the body. There then follows a ceremonial mock combat between the males of each moiety, in which harmless reed spears are ordinarily used. Occasionally, however, the sacrilege may be considered more seriously; recently among the Wakura [a group neighbouring Djungan, and which also recognized similar moieties] a *Raku* man who had killed *mirki* was speared through the leg by *Mirki* men.

According to a myth . . . the two moiety birds, as anthropomorphic mythical ancestors, were the original inhabitants of the country. Eventually, when other ancestors had come into the land, *Mirki* was attacked, surrounded by grass fires, and even though he took refuge in a hollow tree, as *mirki* does not, he had to change into a bird to escape. This action led all the other ancestors to change into the various bird, animal, and other forms they have now, and thus brought to a close the mythical ancestral period at the beginning of time.

. . . The patrilineal totemic clan is an important element in the social structure . . . The clans normally have multiple totems. The local term for dream [*nguyar*] is generally used to designate clan and sometimes moiety totems, and dreams are interpreted totemically.

. . . The land is divided up into unnamed clan domains which include a number of individual named countries. The several countries constituting a clan domain need not be contiguous . . . Each individual member of the clan is associated with a few of these countries, which become the person's 'homeland' . . . and which may provide him with a personal name.

Each moiety had a number of secondary totems, many of which were animals (see also Anderson 1984 for similar observations among the Kuku Yalanji). People, animals, land and so forth were intimately interconnected, land rights articulating the nature of these relations. In this way, the human order was not isolated from the rest of existence. Social identification was closely tied to the world order. The conception of an ordered 'natural' world could through a Dreaming world-view be substituted for an ordered 'cultural' world and territorial mosaic, the distinctions between each being redundant.

In short, through the Dreaming, Law, people, land and every aspect of one's life was positioned in relation to everything else. Animals were an important part of one's being – of one's identity – and were themselves defined by their own relationships not simply with but *in* the world. This has important implications for our consideration of the rock-art, which can be understood not just by reference to *meaning*, but by reference to the very ordering of the world and the position of animals in the world-view, in south-east Cape York based in the Dreaming during ethnographic times.

Animals as symbols: emergent social formations of the late Holocene

In this chapter I have followed archaeological changes that speak of increases in site and regional land use from deep in antiquity to the more recent past. These changes did not coincide with the major environmental changes, which took place between 22,000 and 13,000 BP – peak aridity, which included the last glacial maximum – and during the early Holocene (peak wetness). Along with the major archaeological changes of the mid to late Holocene came a regionalization of artistic behaviour and the emergence of a new symbolic order. Animals played an important role in this new order, representing more than things 'out there' and more than mere food items. For the first time, around 3500 BP there emerged a new relationship between people and animals that saw certain taxa as subjects appropriate for a marking of the land. These included crocodiles, flying foxes, echidnas and moths/butterflies, with geographical discontinuity in the predominance of specific taxa across the landscape. The new iconography expressed the changing place of animals in the constructed, social and cultural landscape, in the way that the world itself was perceived and ordered.

Let us now trace back the implications of this change by beginning with its end-product, the ethnographic present. Animals, like all things, are essentially linked in the Dreaming. In their identification with a landscape that is ordered in the Dreaming, they are metaphors for the human world. People and fauna are, literally, of kindred spirit. Through the Dreaming, every person and group of people has specific relationships with the animals in the land. During ethnographic times, these relationships were depicted in the art (and in some places continue to be so), not just on rocks, but on bark, on bodies, on weapons (e.g. Caruana 1993; Morphy 1998). What we fail to find in the rock-art of pre-3500 BP times, I suggest, is not a change in meaning or social action, but something much grander – the very world-views through which the two operated, the way people identified in the world. There was a changing geography of being.

In Princess Charlotte Bay and the Flinders Island group, the moth/butterfly paintings were called *motjala* – moth/butterfly – by local Aboriginal people in the recent past, and occur in the general area of the *motjala* patriclan (Hale and Tindale 1933–34). Both the art and the clan system relate to social and cultural relations with animals (amongst other things), articulating their ontological position in the world.

I would further suggest – although this is not the place to explore this in detail – that the changes observed during the mid to late Holocene were not restricted to south-east Cape York. Elsewhere in Australia, major rock-art discontinuities also took place around this time, such as in western and central Arnhem Land with the cessation of 'yam figures' and beginnings of X-ray art (see Chippindale and Taçon 1998 for a review). These changes were accompanied during the mid Holocene by the emergence in the rock-art of depictions of structured group activity – what Paul Taçon and Christopher Chippindale (1994) have interpreted as organized group warfare, and David Welch (1996; 1997) as ritual performance: perhaps signs of increasing populations and increasing socio-demographic (structural) complexity. By considering the linguistic evidence, Nicholas Evans and Rhys Jones (1997) have even suggested that the now-widespread Pama-Nyungan languages began to expand in Australia around this time (5000–3000 BP). An exploration of faunal representations in Arnhem Land, along the lines of the present chapter, would be warranted; I would predict that the types and frequencies of animals known from ethnographic details only emerged in the art during the mid to late Holocene, most notably around 3500 BP.

An implication of the above is that the ethnographically documented world order, as expressed in the Dreaming, has a limited antiquity probably not going beyond 3500 BP, and possibly originally associated with an incoming proto-Pama-Nyungan language. (It is possible that a slightly earlier point of origin may be identified somewhere.) Before then, the cultural system is unrecognizable. While the earlier cultural system and world-view(s) need logically to be considered as antecedent to the modern, I would argue that any interpretation of the older rock-art by analogy with modern cultural details should proceed with extreme caution, and perhaps should be avoided altogether.

Barry Lopez has noted that present-day Americans have forgotten their worlds (1998). I would suggest that this is the stuff of change. It is not the 'rivers, mountains, and towns' that have gone amiss in social life; rather, for better or for worse, relationships have moved on with the changing times. This is not something just of the modern world. Rather, in looking back we are merely exploring ourselves (the present) in the past, a nostalgia that could find its soulmate in the bigger picture, as evidenced by similar processes of change elsewhere in the world, as always has been, as always will be.

Acknowledgements

I thank the Department of Geography and Environmental Science, Monash University, under whose auspices this work was undertaken; Monash University for a Logan Fellowship; the Australian Institute of Nuclear Science and Engineering for a series of grants to AMS radiocarbon date rock-art, and Ewan Lawson and his team from the Australian Nuclear Science and Technology Organisation for doing the dating; Sammy Wason and his family, the Grainers, Archers, Neals and the Kuku Djungan Aboriginal Corporation for permission for the Ngarrabullgan work; Rita Maddigan, William Johnston, Daphne Brumby and Johnny Fred for permission to work at Chillagoe; Lana Little for assistance at Chillagoe; members of the Grogan, Brady, Mitchell, Rosendale, Lee Cheu and Colless families for permission to work in Kuku Yalanji country; Christopher Chippindale, George Nash, Nicolas Peterson and Meredith Wilson for comments on aspects of this chapter; Gary Swinton for drafting Fig. 8.1.

References

Anderson, J. C. 1984. The political and economic basis of Kuku-Yalanji social history. PhD thesis, University of Queensland, St Lucia.

Anderson, J. C. and R. Robins. 1988. Dismissed due to lack of evidence? Kuku-Yalanji sites and the archaeological record, in B. Meehan and R. Jones (eds.), *Archaeology with ethnography: an Australian perspective*: 182–205. Canberra: Department of Prehistory, Research School of Pacific Studies, Australian National University.

Armitage, R. A., B. David, M. Hyman, M. W. Rowe, C. Tuniz, E. Lawson, G. Jacobsen and Q. Hua. 1998. Radiocarbon determinations on Chillagoe rock paintings: small sample Accelerator Mass Spectrometry, *Records of the Australian Museum* 50(3): 285–92.

Beaton, J. 1981. Princess Charlotte Bay archaeological report: second interim report. Unpublished report to the Australian Institute of Aboriginal Studies, Canberra.

1985. Evidence for a coastal occupation time-lag at Princess Charlotte Bay (North Queensland) and implications for coastal colonisation and population growth theories for Aboriginal Australia, *Archaeology in Oceania* 20: 1–20.

n. d. Report on archaeological fieldwork in the Flinders Island/Bathurst Heads/Princess Charlotte Bay area, north Queensland, 1979. Unpublished report to the Australian Institute of Aboriginal Studies, Canberra.

Campbell, J. B. 1982. New radiocarbon results for north Queensland prehistory, *Australian Archaeology* 14: 62–6.

Campbell, J. B. and M. Mardaga-Campbell. 1993. From micro- to nano-stratigraphy: linking vertical and horizontal dating of archaeological deposits with the direct dating of rock art at 'The Walkunders', Chillagoe (north Queensland, Australia), in J. Steinbring, A. Watchman, P. Faulstich and P. S. C. Taçon (eds.), *Time and space: dating and spatial considerations in rock art research*: 57–63. Melbourne: Australian Rock Art Research Association. Occasional AURA Publication 8.

Caruana, W. 1993. *Aboriginal art*. London: Thames and Hudson.

Chappell, J. 1982. Sea levels and sediments: some features of the context of coastal archaeological sites in the tropics, *Archaeology in Oceania* 17: 69–78.

Chappell, J., A. Chivas, E. Wallensky, H. Polach and P. Aharon. 1983. Holocene palaeoenvironmental changes, central to north Great Barrier Reef inner zone, *Bureau of Mineral Resources Journal of Geology and Geophysics* 8: 223–35.

Chippindale, C. and P. S. C. Taçon. 1998. The many ways of dating Arnhem Land rock-art, north Australia, in C. Chippindale and P. S. C. Taçon (eds.), *The archaeology of rock-art*: 90–111. Cambridge: Cambridge University Press.

Clegg, J. 1981. *Mathesis words, mathesis pictures*. Sydney: Clegg Calendars.

Cogger, H. G. 1996. *Reptiles and amphibians of Australia*. Port Melbourne: Reed Books.

Cole, N. 1992. 'Human' motifs in the rock paintings of Jowalbinna, Laura, in J. McDonald and I. Haskovec (eds.), *State of the art: regional rock art studies in Australia and Melanesia*: 164–173. Melbourne: Australian Rock Art Research Association.

Cole, N. and B. David. 1992. 'Curious Drawings' at Cape York: a summary of rock art investigation in the Cape York Peninsula region since the 1820s and a comparison of some regional traditions, *Rock Art Research* 9(1): 3–26.

Cole, N. and P. Trezise. 1992. Laura engravings: a preliminary report on the Amphitheatre site, in J. McDonald and I. Haskovec (eds.), *State of the art: regional rock art studies in Australia and Melanesia*: 83–8.

Cole, N., A. Watchman and M. Morwood. 1995. Chronology of Laura rock art, in M. Morwood and D. R. Hobbs (eds.), *Quinkan prehistory: the archaeology of Aboriginal art in SE Cape York Peninsula, Australia*: 147–160. St Lucia: Anthropology Museum, University of Queensland. Tempus 3.

David, B. 1983. To pick a bone. BA thesis, Australian National University, Canberra.

1984. Walkunder Arch Cave: a faunal report, *Australian Archaeology* 18(1): 40–54.

1990. Echidna's Rest, Chillagoe: a site report, *Queensland Archaeological Research* 7: 73–94.

1991. Fern Cave, rock art and social formations: rock art regionalisation and demographic changes in southeastern Cape York Peninsula, *Archaeology in Oceania* 26: 41–57.

1992. An AMS date for north Queensland rock art, *Rock Art Research* 9(2): 139–41.

1994. A space–time odyssey: rock art and regionalisation in north Queensland prehistory. PhD thesis, University of Queensland, St Lucia.

1998. Introduction: 'a mountain once seen never to be forgotten', in B. David (ed.), *Ngarrabullgan: geographical investigations in Djungan country, Cape York Peninsula*: 1–26. Melbourne: Monash University. Monash Publications in Geography and Environmental Science 51.

David, B. and D. Chant. 1995. *Rock art and regionalisation in north Queensland prehistory*. South Brisbane: Queensland Museum. Memoirs of the Queensland Museum 37(2).

David, B. and N. Cole. 1990. Rock art and interregional interaction in northeastern Australian prehistory, *Antiquity* 64: 788–806.

David, B. and L. Dagg. 1993. Two caves, *Memoirs of the Queensland Museum* 33(1): 143–62.

David, B. and M. David. 1988. Rock pictures of the Chillagoe-Mungana limestone belt, north Queensland, *Rock Art Research* 5(2): 147–56.

David, B. and H. Lourandos. 1998. Rock art and socio-demography in northeastern Australian prehistory, *World Archaeology* 30(2): 193–219.

In press. Landscape as mind: land use, cultural space and change in north Queensland prehistory, *Quaternary International*.

David, B., M. Rowe, R. A. Armitage and E. Lawson. In press. Time and space in north Queensland prehistory: modelling change in the structure of cultural behaviour in NE Australia through rock art, *Archaeology in Oceania*.

David, B. and M. Wilson. In press. Re-reading the landscape: place and identity in northeastern Australia during the late Holocene, *Cambridge Archaeological Journal*.

Evans, N. and R. Jones. 1997. The cradle of the Pama-Nyungans: archaeological and linguistic speculations, in P. McConvell and N. Evans (eds.), *Archaeology and linguistics: Aboriginal Australia in global perspective*: 385–417. Oxford; Oxford University Press.

Flannery, T. 1990. Pleistocene faunal loss: implications of the aftershock for Australia's past, *Archaeology in Oceania* 25(1): 45–67.

Flood, J. 1987. Rock art of the Koolburra Plateau, north Queensland, *Rock Art Research* 4(2): 91–126.

1995. *Archaeology of the Dreamtime: the story of prehistoric Australia and its people*. Sydney: Angus and Robertson.

Flood, J. and N. Horsfall. 1986. Excavation of Green Ant and Echidna shelters, Cape York Peninsula, *Queensland Archaeological Research* 3: 4–64.

Gillespie, R. 1997. On human blood, rock art and calcium oxalate: further studies on organic carbon content and radiocarbon age of materials relating to Australian rock art, *Antiquity* 71: 430–7.

Gollan, K. 1984. Prehistoric dingo. PhD thesis, Australian National University, Canberra.

Hale, H. M. and N. B. Tindale. 1933–34. Aborigines of Princess Charlotte Bay, *Records of the Australian Museum* 5(1): 64–116; 5(2): 117–72.

Horsfall, N. 1987. Living in rainforest: the prehistoric occupation of north Queensland's humid tropics. PhD thesis, James Cook University, Townsville.

Horton, D. 1980. A review of the extinction question: man, climate and megafauna, *Archaeology and Physical Anthropology in Oceania* 15: 86–97.

Japaljarri Stewart, P. 1994. Dreamings, in D. Horton (ed.), *The encyclopaedia of Aboriginal Australia*: 305–6. Canberra: Australian Institute of Aboriginal and Torres Strait Islander Studies.

Kershaw, A. P. 1986. Climatic change and Aboriginal burning in north-east Australia during the last two glacial/interglacial cycles, *Nature* 322: 47–9.

1994. Pleistocene vegetation of the humid tropics of northeastern Queensland, Australia, *Palaeogeography, Palaeoclimatology, Palaeoecology* 109: 399–412.

Lévi-Strauss, C. 1962. *La Pensée sauvage*. Paris: Plon.

Lopez, B. 1998. *About this life: journeys on the threshold of memory*. London: Harvill Press.

Lourandos, H. 1983. Intensification: a late Pleistocene–Holocene archaeological sequence from south-western Victoria, *Archaeology in Oceania* 18: 81–94.

Lourandos, H. and B. David. 1998. Comparing long-term archaeological and environmental trends: north Queensland, arid and semiarid Australia, *The Artefact* 21: 105–14.

Loy, T., R. Jones, D. E. Nelson, B. Meehan, J. Vogel, J. Southon and R. Cosgrove. 1990. Accelerator radiocarbon dating of human blood proteins in pigments from late Pleistocene art sites in Australia, *Antiquity* 64: 110–16.

McConnel, U. 1939–40. Social organisation of the tribes of Cape York Peninsula, *Oceania* 10(1): 54–72; 10(4): 434–55.

McDonald, J. and I. Haskovec (eds.). 1992. *State of the art: regional rock art studies in Australia and Melanesia*. Melbourne: Australian Rock Art Research Association.

McNiven, I. In press. Fissioning and regionalisation: the social dimensions of changes in Aboriginal use of the Great Sandy Region, South East Queensland, in J. Hall and I. McNiven (eds.), *Australian coastal archaeology*. Canberra: Research School of Pacific and Asian Studies, Australian National University.

Maddock, K. 1982. *The Australian Aborigines: a portrait of their society*. Ringwood: Penguin.

Maynard, L. 1976. An archaeological approach to the study of Australian rock art. MA thesis, University of Sydney, Sydney.

1977. Classification and terminology of Australian rock art, in P. Ucko (ed.), *Form in indigenous art: schematisation in the art of Aboriginal Australia and prehistoric Europe*: 387–402. Canberra: Australian Institute of Aboriginal Studies.

1979. The archaeology of Australian Aboriginal art, in S. M. Mead (ed.), *Exploring the visual arts of Oceania*: 83–100. Honolulu, HI: Hawaii University Press.

Meehan, B. 1977. Man does not live by calories alone: the role of shellfish in a coastal cuisine, in J. Allen, J. Golson and R. Jones (eds.), *Sunda and Sahul: prehistoric studies in Southeast Asia, Melanesia and Australia*: 493–531. London: Academic Press.

Merlan, F. 1989. The interpretive framework of Wardaman rock art: a preliminary report, *Australian Aboriginal Studies* 1989(2): 14–24.

Morphy, H. 1998. *Aboriginal art.* London: Phaidon Press.

Morwood, M. and L. Dagg. 1995. Excavations at Yam Camp, in M. Morwood and D. R. Hobbs (eds.), *Quinkan prehistory: the archaeology of Aboriginal art in SE Cape York Peninsula, Australia*: 107–115. St Lucia: Anthropology Museum, University of Queensland. Tempus 3.

Morwood, M. and D. R. Hobbs (eds.). 1995. *Quinkan prehistory: the archaeology of Aboriginal art in SE Cape York Peninsula, Australia.* St Lucia: Anthropology Museum, University of Queensland. Tempus 3.

Morwood, M., D. R. Hobbs and D. M. Price. 1995. Excavations at Sandy Creek 1 and 2, in M. Morwood and D. R. Hobbs (eds.), *Quinkan prehistory: the archaeology of Aboriginal art in SE Cape York Peninsula, Australia*: 71–91. St Lucia: Anthropology Museum, University of Queensland. Tempus 3.

Morwood, M. and S. L'Oste-Brown. 1995a. Chronological changes in stone artefact technology, in M. Morwood and D. R. Hobbs (eds.), *Quinkan prehistory: the archaeology of Aboriginal art in SE Cape York Peninsula, Australia*: 161–177. St Lucia: Anthropology Museum, University of Queensland. Tempus 3.

1995b. Excavations at Hann River 1, central Cape York Peninsula, *Australian Archaeology* 40: 21–8.

Nelson, D. E. 1993. Second thoughts on a rock art date, *Antiquity* 67: 893–5.

Richards, F. 1926. Customs and language of the western Hodgkinson Aboriginals, *Memoirs of the Queensland Museum* 8(3): 249–65.

Rick, J. W. 1987. Dates as data: an examination of the Peruvian Preceramic radiocarbon record, *American Antiquity* 52: 55–73.

Roberts, R. G., R. Jones and M. Smith. 1990. Thermoluminescence dating of a 50,000-year-old human occupation site in northern Australia, *Nature* 345: 153–6.

Rosenfeld, A. 1982. Style and meaning in Laura art: a case study in the formal analysis of style in prehistoric art, *Mankind* 13: 199–217.

1984. The identification of animal representations in the art of the Laura region, north Queensland (Australia), in H.-G. Bandi (ed.), *La Contribution de la zoologie et de l'éthologie à l'interpretation de l'art des peuples chasseurs préhistoriques*: 399–422. Fribourg: Editions Universitaires.

1987. Comment, *Rock Art Research* 4(2): 122–3.

Rosenfeld, A., D. Horton and J. Winter. 1981. *Early man in north Queensland.* Canberra: Department of Prehistory, Research School of Pacific Studies, Australian National University. Terra Australis 6.

Roth, W. E. 1897. *Ethnological studies among the north-west-central Queensland Aborigines.* Brisbane: Government Printer.

1910. North Queensland ethnography 18: social and individual nomenclature, *Records of the Australian Museum* 8(1): 79–106.

Sharp, R. L. 1939. Tribes and totemism in north-east Australia, *Oceania* 9: 254–75, 439–61.

Smith, M. 1986. The antiquity of seed grinding in central Australia, *Archaeology in Oceania* 21: 29–39.

Stanner, W. E. H. 1960. On aboriginal religion 2: sacramentalism, rite and myth, *Oceania* 30(4): 245–78.

Strahan, R. (ed.). 1995. *The mammals of Australia.* Chatswood: Reed Books.

Strang, V. 1997. *Uncommon ground: cultural landscapes and environmental values.* Oxford: Berg.

Sutton, P. 1995. *Country: Aboriginal boundaries and land ownership in Australia.* Canberra: Aboriginal History. Aboriginal History Monograph 3.

Taçon, P. S. C. and C. Chippindale. 1994. Australia's ancient warriors: changing depictions of fighting in the rock art of Arnhem Land, NT, *Cambridge Archaeological Journal* 4(2): 211–48.

Tindale, N. 1974. *Aboriginal tribes of Australia*. Berkeley, CA: University of California.

Watchman, A. and N. Cole. 1993. Accelerator radiocarbon dating of plant-fibre binders in rock paintings from northeastern Australia, *Antiquity* 67: 355–8.

Watchman, A., B. David, I. J. McNiven and J. Flood. In press. Micro-archaeology of cortex from engraved and painted rock surfaces at Yiwarlarlay, Northern Territory, Australia, *Journal of Archaeological Science*.

Watchman, A., J. Sirois and N. Cole. 1993. Mineralogical examination of rock paintings pigments near Laura, north Queensland, Australia, in B. Fankhauser and R. Bird (eds.), *Archaeometry: current Australasian research*: 141–50. Canberra: Department of Prehistory, Research School of Pacific Studies, Australian National University.

Welch, D. M. 1996. Material culture in Kimberley rock art, Australia, *Rock Art Research* 13(2): 104–23.

1997. Fight or dance? Ceremony and the spearthrower in northern Australian rock art, *Rock Art Research* 14(2): 88–112.

9

Linkage between rock-art and landscape in Aboriginal Australia

Josephine Flood

A distinctive aspect of Australian Aboriginal social knowledge is the special place of 'country', through the close relation between person and place which structures Aboriginal society. To (over-)summarize in a sentence, it is less a case that people own land, more a case that land shapes and defines people. One element is the idea of the 'Dreaming', that time when the land was created, and people were placed in their ordered places in it. Another is the set of pathways, the 'Dreaming Tracks' which Ancestral Beings took in travelling across the landscape, tracks which now direct and structure the landscape which people walk across. Rock-art makes images on the land everywhere, but the placing of images has extra meaning, even an extra dimension, when the relation between people and landscape has the character it does in Aboriginal Australia where rock-art serves to explain and map the country.

Rock-art, landscape, religion: a trinity of Aboriginal Australia

Rock-art in Australia (Flood 1997b) strongly reflects Aboriginal emphasis on spiritual and social relationships to the land. Indeed, rock-art, landscape and religion in Aboriginal Australia are so inextricably intertwined that it is necessary first to outline the nature of Aboriginal religion before considering linkages between rock-art and landscape. The essence of Aboriginal religious belief is that the entire landscape was created by Ancestral Beings, who existed before there was any human life on earth and who, during their epic journeys, created the landscape and all living creatures as they are today. These spiritual beings are still present in the land and exert a continuing influence on their world. The original era of creation is known as the Dreamtime or Dreaming, a translation made by Baldwin Spencer and Gillen (1899) of the Central Australian Arrernte (Aranda) people's term *Altyerrenge* (*Alcheringa*) for the ancestral past.

This complex religious concept has been well explained by anthropologist Howard Morphy in his recent book, *Aboriginal art* (1998: 68, 84, 100). Morphy, treating the terms Dreaming and Dreamtime as synonyms, notes that they should not be understood in their ordinary English sense but as simply a name for a unique Aboriginal cosmology:

> The Dreaming is as much a dimension of reality as a period of time. It gains its sense of time because it was there in the beginning, underlies the present and is a determinant of the future; it is time in the sense that once there was only Dreamtime . . .

> The Dreamtime is as concerned with space as with time – it refers to origins and powers that are located in places and things. In most if not all Aboriginal belief systems there was a time of world creation before humans existed on earth. Often it is said that in the beginning the earth was a flat featureless plain. Ancestral beings emerged from within the earth and began to give shape to the world . . .
>
> . . . The places where they emerged from the earth became water-holes or the entrances to caves; where they walked, watercourses flowed; and trees grew where they stuck their digging sticks in the ground . . . The landscape was not only formed as a by-product of ancestral action; it was also a result of the transformation of ancestral beings' bodies or bodily substances. Sources of ochre throughout Arnhem Land are formed from the blood or fat of ancestral beings . . .
>
> The most direct manifestations of the ancestral beings are the features of the landscape, and as people walk through that landscape they are reminded at every stage of the ancestral actions that created it. But the ancestral beings also left behind more explicit representations of themselves and their actions in the form of art . . . They were concerned that the humans who succeeded them on the earth would continue in their footsteps, would follow the rules of conduct that they had instituted and would commemorate their lives. As the ancestral beings journeyed across the earth they therefore made a record of their actions not only in the form of the landscape, but also in the songs, dances, paintings, ceremonies and sacred objects that they created on the way . . . selecting as they went along certain interesting or characteristic features and recording them in word or design . . .
>
> . . . Through painting their own bodies and the rocks, and through making ground sculptures and ceremonial grounds, the Aboriginal people establish direct contact with the ancestral powers and thus can harness manifestations of these powers for human purposes. By keeping alive the presence of the ancestral beings, people ensure the regeneration of the landscape, the fertility of the land and the source of conception spirits.

In Australia, rock-art researchers have the great advantage that Aboriginal art is a living tradition. Whilst most of this art is now expressed not on rock but in other mediums, in remote northern Australia rock-art is still alive. Not only can some elderly Aboriginal people still explain meanings of rock-art, but retouching of rock-paintings is still practised in some areas. And in September 1999, in a rock-shelter in the eastern Victoria River region in the Northern Territory, Christopher Chippindale and I had the memorable experience of coming across a fresh petroglyph, so newly made that the rock dust was still in its grooves.

Traditional Aboriginal art takes many forms; rock-art is the only one which leaves a long-term, immovable record in the landscape. The rest of this chapter will therefore be devoted to explanations of the location of rock-art in Australia both across vast expanses of country and on the small, inter- and intrasite scale (Fig. 9.1). I make no apologies for a heavy reliance on ethnography, both written accounts by anthropologists in the nineteenth and early twentieth centuries and more recent work in parts of northern Australia where the role and rationale for rock-art is still partially understood. Whilst I am well aware of the dangers of far-flung ethnographic analogy, many insights may be gained from living people where there is direct historical and geographical continuity from past to present.

Rock-art as 'maps' in the broad landscape of central Australia

Aboriginal Australia is criss-crossed by Dreaming Tracks, 'Songlines', the routes taken across the landscape by Ancestral Beings in the Dreamtime as they gave the landscape its present form. Dreaming Tracks are marked by a series of sites, and their associated songs and stories. Those Dreaming sites are places imbued with the creative force of the Ancestral Being who created that element of the landscape. Also known as sacred, story, living, mythological, traditional or ethnographic sites, they are of particular religious significance to contemporary Aborigines. Dreaming sites may or may not have rock-art or other traces of past human activity; their significance comes

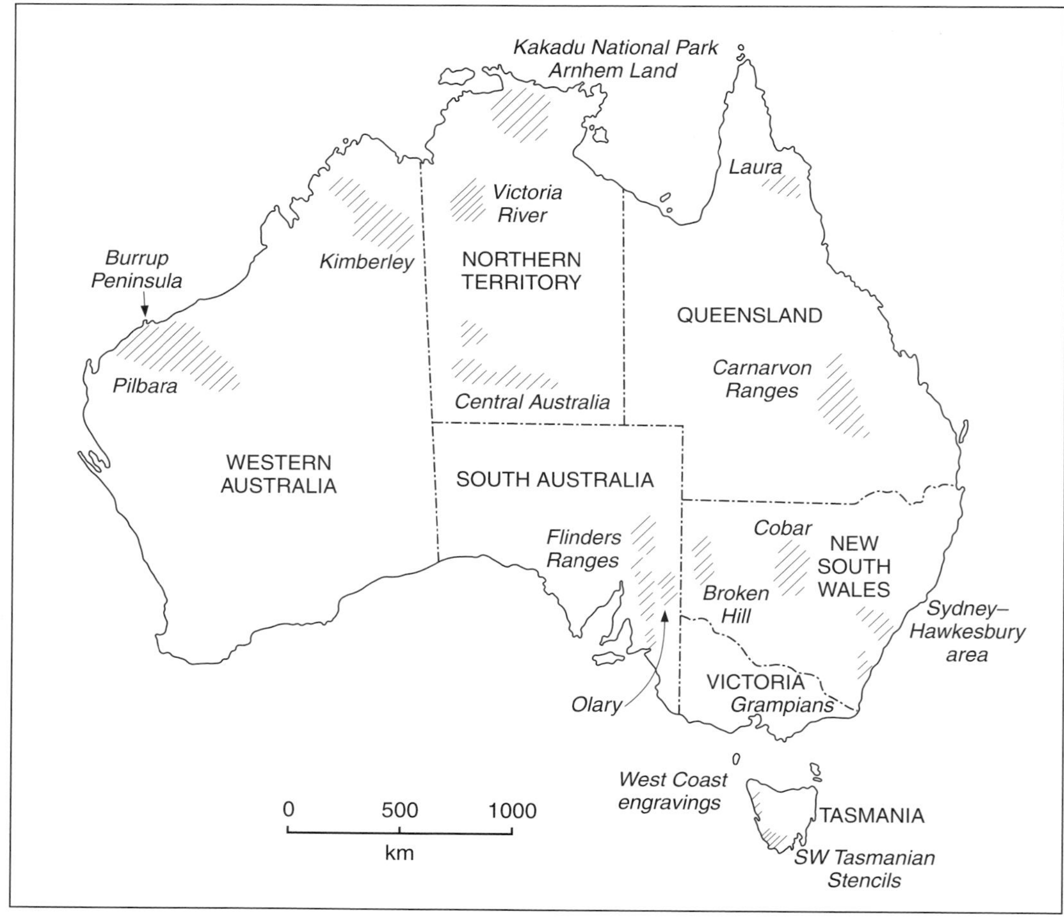

Fig. 9.1. Major rock-art regions in Australia (shown by cross-hatching). Map by J. Flood.

from the oral traditions associated with them rather than any associated material evidence.

In the arid environment of Central Australia, the Dreaming sites serve to link people across vast distances and act as an *aide mémoire* to the location of resources such as ochre, particular food supplies and permanent water. The graphic system of the desert country is geometric, particularly circle-line designs, O–O, which Nancy Munn in her classic study of Walbiri iconography termed the 'site path' motif (Munn 1973). Many Aboriginal people in central Australia now earn their living by painting designs on to canvas in the dot style, usually maps of the landscape in which the named sites created by ancestral beings are represented by circles and the journeys that connect them by straight lines. The various geometric elements such as concentric circles, arcs and dots together with animal tracks are combined to represent the mythological landscape as seen from a plan or bird's eye (or worm's eye?) view (cf. Flood 1997b: 174–6).

These paintings are the modern equivalent of the traditional large ground-paintings done at

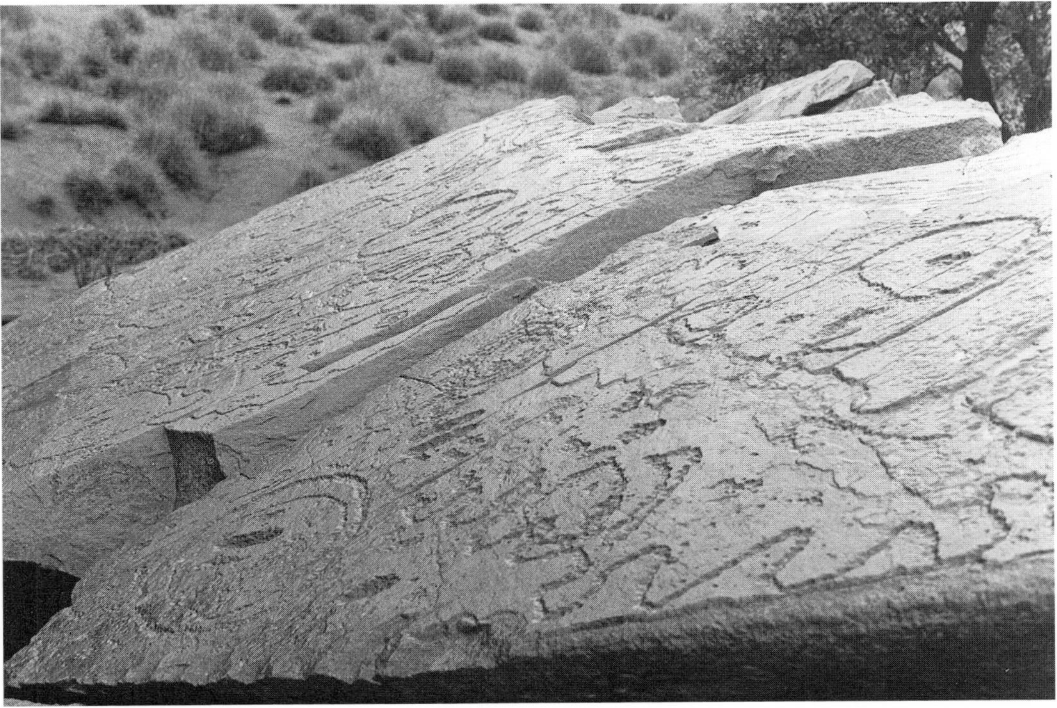

Fig. 9.2. Petroglyphs in the Panaramitee style at Ewaninga near Alice Springs, Northern Territory. Photograph by J. Flood.

the time of ceremonies in the desert; there are also rock-paintingswhich map the totemic geography of the landscape (Figs. 9.2, 9.3 and 9.4). Aboriginal explanations for some of these rock-paintings are on record, from which it is clear that they record the travels of creative Ancestral Beings across the landscape. There is a close resemblance between the contemporary art of Central Australia and the petroglyphs and rock-paintings of the prehistoric Panaramitee tradition, named after the 'type site' of Panaramitee in the Olary region of South Australia (Flood 1997b: chapters 5, 6 and 7). The Panaramitee style is characterized by thousands of small petroglyphs, most less than 10 cm long, pecked out either in outline or as a solid, intagliated form. The range of motifs is extremely limited; circles and tracks strongly predominate. Among the tracks, macropod, bird and human are very common; they sometimes occur in 'trails' as if the surface had been walked across. Frequent geometric motifs consist of simple or complex circles, 'pits' or 'dots' (small pecked concavities) and lines, either simple, paired, complex, crescent, radiating or meandering. Occasional figurative motifs such as lizards also occur.

The antiquity of the Panaramitee tradition is Pleistocene, but the startlingly old dates previously put forward by Dorn have now all been withdrawn and must be discounted (Dorn 1997). Likewise the claims of great antiquity for occupation and cupules at Jinmium have been disproved (Roberts *et al.* 1998). Whilst there is little direct ethnographic evidence on the meaning of Panaramitee petroglyphs, their close resemblance to recent ground-paintings and the clear

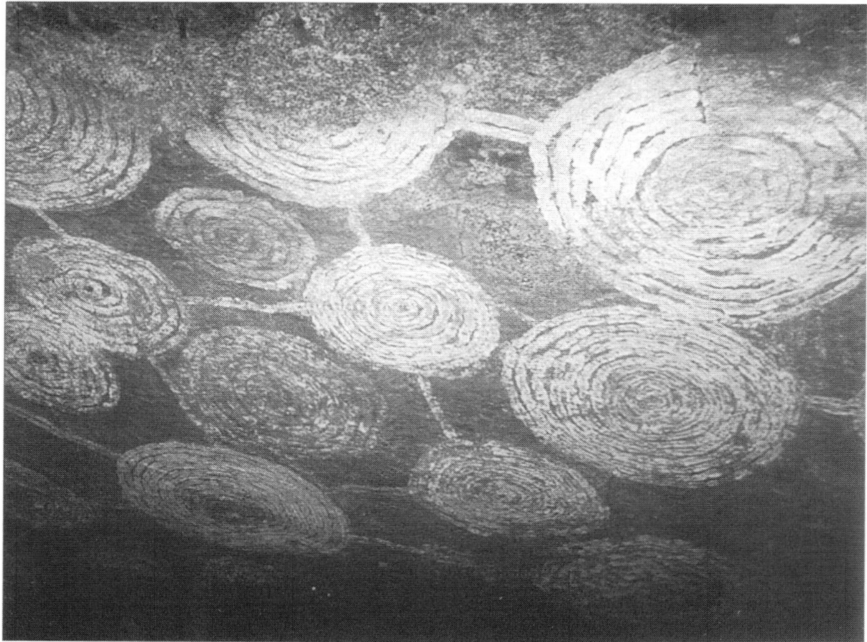

Fig. 9.3. Paintings displaying linked concentric circles at Gunadjari, Central Australia, Northern Territory.
Photograph by R. Edwards.

continuity and stability of artistic traditions in arid Australia support the view that the ancient rock-art of Central Australia probably functioned in a similar way to its modern counterpart; that is, to map and explain the landscape.

Dreaming Tracks in northern Australia

I now wish to turn to the Wardaman group of the eastern Victoria River district west of the town of Katherine in the Northern Territory (Fig. 9.5). This country contains outcrops of soft sandstone with many rock-shelters. These have thousands of paintings and petroglyphs on their walls; there are also a number of open-air petroglyph sites on rock slabs or pavements. I carried out five major seasons of fieldwork in Wardaman country between 1988 and 1992 (funded by Earthwatch) and further work in September 1999 with Christopher Chippindale (funded by the Australian Institute of Aboriginal and Torres Strait Islander Studies). Here, rock-art still plays a meaningful role for this contemporary group whose parents or grandparents were hunter-gatherers, and who sixty years ago camped in the rock-shelters whose walls they or their ancestors decorated.

In the region which we have been studying, the present territory of the Wardaman, we have recorded more than 200 rock-art sites containing some 50,000 individual marks. This ongoing project involves recording mythology and oral traditions as well as more traditional rock-art recording, archaeological excavation and relative and absolute dating of petroglyphs, in which several archaeological colleagues have been involved, notably Bruno David and more recently Christopher Chippindale and Alan Watchman. As this work has been published elsewhere or is

Fig. 9.4. Contemporary desert art at Papunya, Northern Territory.
Papunya is one of the Western Desert communities where Walbiri and Pintupi render their traditional sand-paintings in synthetic acrylic paints on hardboard and canvas. In this painting, propped up outside the home of the painter, the characteristic linked circles are prominent.
Photograph by J. Flood, 1980.

in press (David *et al.* 1990; 1994; 1995; Flood *et al.* 1992; 1994; 2000; Attenbrow *et al.* 1995; Clarkson and David 1995), here I focus only on a generalized argument about the landscape of rock-art in Australia.

There are many Dreaming Tracks in northern Australia, which serve to explain phenomena such as river meanders, water-holes or deep-cut gorges. Dreaming Tracks of snakes are particularly common: for example, the black-headed python (Fig. 9.6) travelled from the Kimberley and created the gorge of the Victoria River before finally going to ground in a cave in Wardaman country – the site of Giyeyn which was refound by a traditional owner in the company of Chippindale in 1998 after its location had been almost forgotten. Most widespread of all is the myth of the Rainbow Serpent, a supernatural being which combines the features of many different animals, including humans, on the body of a large python. But why Rainbow? Dramatic phenomena – rainbows, thunder, lightning, sparkling water, the red glow of rock such as Uluru at sunset – needed explanation and were interpreted as signs of the powers of Ancestral Beings. Rainbows are of special significance because they appear not only in the sky but also on land in places such as waterfalls. Their multi-coloured surface appears both to shine and to create the appearance of movement; indeed as one walks towards the foot of a rainbow uncannily it keeps moving away.

This quality of brilliance, shininess and vibrant shimmering is of great significance in Aboriginal religion and art (Taçon 1991); it is seen in the

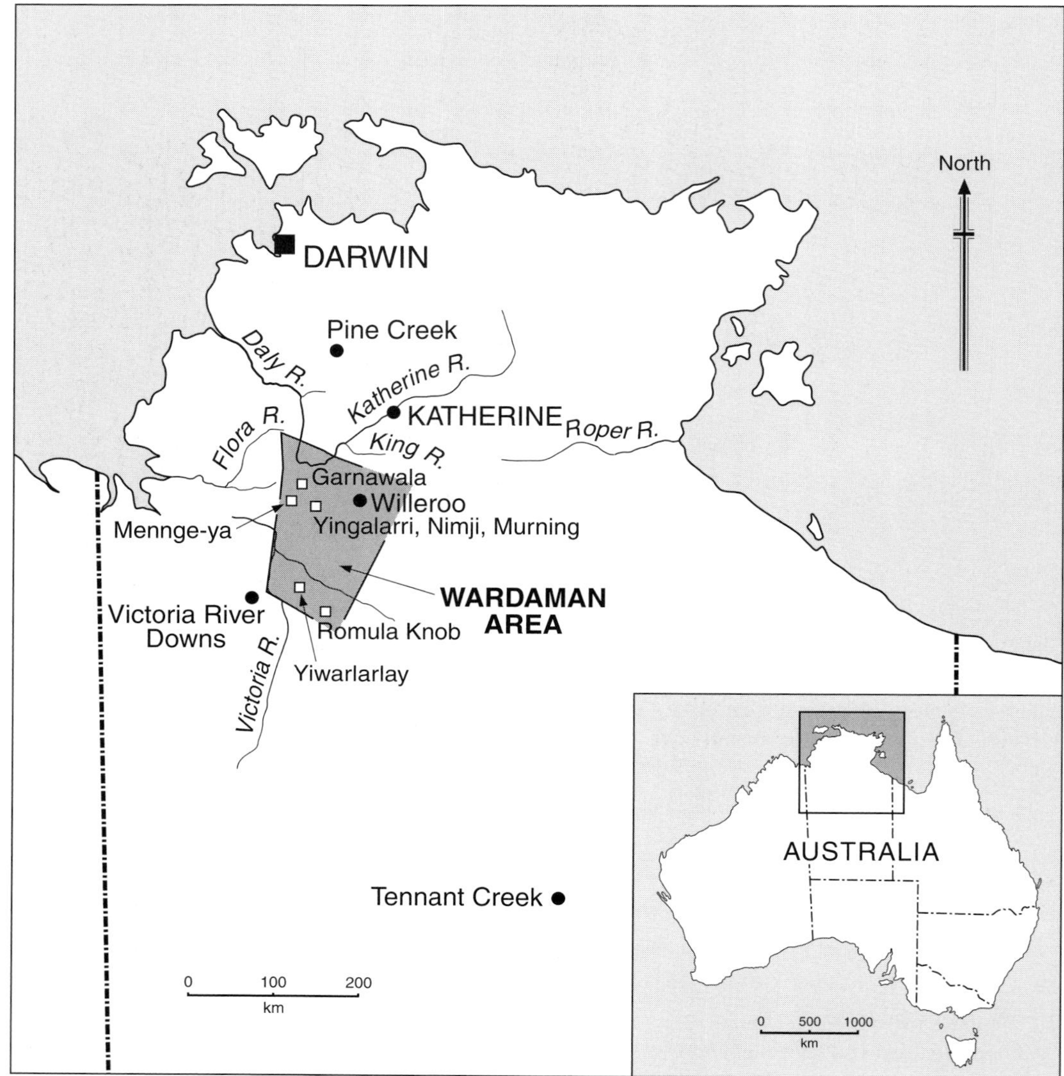

Fig. 9.5. Wardaman country and its wider region
Map by Gary Swinton, reproduced by courtesy of Bruno David/Monash University School of Geography and Environmental Science.

engraved pearl shells from the Kimberley, used in sacred ceremonies and widely traded across the continent (Akerman and Stanton 1994). Pearl shells were used in ceremonies in rock-shelters on the Dreaming Track of the Rainbow Snake, *Gorrondolmi*, in Wardaman country. *Gorrondolmi* created a series of springs and water-holes on his way from Port Keats on the coast to Garnawala and Yingalarri (Ingaladdi) (Flood and David 1994). At Garnawala in the north of Wardaman country, many natural features and rock-paintings were explained in terms of the Rainbow Serpent story. The rock 'window' above the main site was made by 'Rainbow', as was the hole in the roof of

Fig. 9.6. The black-headed python, *Gurrbijinman*, painted in red with a white outline in a rock-shelter near Johnstone Water-hole, Wardaman country, Northern Territory.
Photograph by J. Flood.

a small cave on the opposite side of the outcrop, which has a painting of a snake immediately below it.

The story of the Rainbow Serpent's travels (Flood and David 1994; Merlan 1994) recounts how he came from the coast with two women, whom he had apparently taken away from other men in the Port Keats area. He was followed by the bat, who was planning to take the women from him. Rainbow also had his own wife with him. Pregnant, she laid eggs visible as small rounded stones at a site called Jarrug-ja, along the top of the cliff at the south-western end of Yingalarri water-hole. At Yingalarri water-hole the bat – a really good dancer – began to dance for Rainbow, while bat's ally, diver duck, played the didgeridoo for him. Bat danced and Rainbow watched, but not very closely, for he did not notice when occasionally bat would stamp and gesture to the women with a turn of his head to follow him off into the bush. After dancing for a while, bat said he had to go off into the bush to relieve himself. But he was lying. He actually went and got a spear, dragged it close between his toes, and speared Rainbow. Rainbow rolled around on the ground in anguish and bat and diver duck ran off with one woman each, back to the coast. Rainbow stood himself up as the big bottle tree at Yingalarri water-hole, went into the water there and went on to the rock-shelter of Wirlin.gunyang. Meanwhile his wife went into a cave on the south face of Garnyiwarnyirr, a high, steep rock outcrop north of the bottle tree, and blasted her way up to the top, making an enormous hole inside the outcrop (Fig. 9.7). She then decided that the place was 'bad', and travelled on to Wirlin.gunyang, where she remained.

Fig. 9.7. The outcrop of Garnyiwarnyirr towers as a high cliff over the woodland. This is where Rainbow's wife burst up through the rock, leaving the centre of this outcrop as a mass of collapsed rock.
Photograph by Christopher Chippindale.

There are very few paintings of any of these creatures in rock-shelters along the Dreaming Track, until its end at Wirlin.gunyang, where paintings of two huge snakes with forked tongues stretch across the rock-shelter's 20 m wide back wall (Fig. 9.8). It was not till 1991 that we found and recorded the elusive site of Wirlin.gunyang.

Fig. 9.8. The rock-shelter of Wirlin.gunyang, where the Rainbow Serpent (on the left) and his wife painted themselves on to the wall at the end of their Dreaming Track.
Photograph by J. Flood.

The senior traditional owner, Ngamunugarri, remembered its approximate location and had asked us to find it. He had not been there for sixty years and could not walk far. When we finally got a four-wheel-drive vehicle within half a kilometre of the site and helped him over the rocky ground, tears came into his eyes when he entered the rock-shelter and saw the huge horizontal figures with forked tongues, one larger than the other, of *Gorrondolmi* and his wife. Ngamunugarri explained that at the end of their travels they had painted themselves on to the walls of this beautiful, shady shelter, above a permanent water-hole rich in bush food such as goannas and water-lily tubers. The paintings, not made by humans, are the images or shadows of the ancestral beings themselves in their final resting place. 'To make them look good' the paintings need retouching from time to time, and this was done when people came to camp in the rock-shelter. There are no prohibitions on access to the site, but the paintings themselves must not be touched except by a 'proper painter'. Some of the site's significance derives from the presence near by of a red ochre deposit said to be the 'fat' of peewee Dreaming Beings (*gulirrida*) represented at art sites such as Nimji and Murning near Yingalarri water-hole.

In summary, myths explain unusual features of the Wardaman landscape: 'windows' in the rock, rounded boulders, water-holes, a very large baobab tree (extremely rare in this region), a tall outcrop with a deep 'crater' in its middle, a deposit of red ochre. Rock-art is used as an *aide mémoire* to illustrate and commemorate the doings of those creative Ancestral Beings and to reinforce the moral lessons to be learnt from the stories by generation after generation.

Rock-art as a by-product of ritual

Some rock-art sites came into being through the apparently supernatural characteristics of certain features in the landscape. Classic examples are sites with an echo and ringing rocks such as that on the beach at Trial Harbour in south-west Tasmania (Fig. 9.9). Here, nineteen circular rings, including some with central pits, have been engraved on top of a single, massive granite boulder which rings when struck on top (Flood 1997b: 237, 239; Cosgrove 1983). Whilst no ethnography is available for this site, Tindale (1963) recorded the great significance of ringing rocks to Aboriginal people in the Western Desert, who regarded them as the voice of the ancestors.

Fig. 9.9. Petroglyphs on Ringing Rock, Trial Harbour, Tasmania.
Photograph by P. Sims.

Other unusual features in the landscape such as rocks with a phallic, anthropomorphic or zoomorphic form will give rise to a mythological explanation. Such rocks are sometimes modified by human markings, but in some cases the symbolic, non-utilitarian marks which we term 'rock-art' may in fact be the by-product of ceremonies rather than the end-product of deliberate marking behaviour.

Cupules, which tend to be called pits or dots in Australia, are non-utilitarian symbolic marks and should be treated as 'rock-art' (Taçon *et al.* 1997). In the past the term 'cupule' has been used very loosely; Breck Parkman in his recent study of cupule petroglyph occurrences in the American West (1995) has defined a cupule as 'a cup-shaped depression which has been ground or pounded into a rock surface'. They occur on a vertical surface, 'or, if found on a horizontal surface, those depressions having a diameter of 10 cm or less and a depth of 4 cm or less'. In other words, their position, form and/or small size distinguishes them from bedrock mortars or grinding hollows, those utilitarian by-products of grinding up foodstuffs, ochre or other commodities.

In Central Australia during the 1940s Mountford recorded and photographed the production of such pounded hollows at an increase site in the Musgrave Ranges (1976: 213 and plate 206). The site is a curiously eroded large boulder, which is believed to be the totemic body of the pink cockatoo woman, *Tukalili*, who was killed in this creation story. The cavities in the side of the boulder symbolize the wounds in her body. During the rituals held for the increase of pink cockatoos (*Kakatoe leadbeateri*) and their eggs (an important food source) 'the Aborigines pound the floor of the cavity' in the boulder – totemic body of *Tukalili* – 'with a small stone'. Mountford continues: 'This causes the release of the *kuranita* [life essence] of cockatoos with which the boulder is impregnated. This *kuranita*, rising into the air in the form of dust, fertilizes the living female cockatoos, causing them to lay more eggs. The small pot-holes [cupules] in the totemic body of *Tukalili* are caused by the abrasion of the rock during these rituals.'

Mountford (1976: 213) commented: 'Although these pot-holes [cupules] are well known at other totemic places in central and northern Australia, and possibly elsewhere, this is the first time the writer has been able to find out definitely their function and their means of production.' Mountford (1976: plates 68, 87, 265, 266, 287, 319, 326, 333, 708, etc.) has also put on record numerous instances of rubbing of rock surfaces to release their life essence in the course of ceremonies to maintain and increase natural resources such as the supply of mistletoe berries, mulga seed or edible tree gum, but in those cases the rubbed surface would not usually be regarded even as gestural 'rock-art'.

The usual caveats must of course be added when considering this ethnographer's account; cupules may have different derivations and meanings in different contexts in time and space, and therefore one cannot simply extrapolate from the desert centre to the rest of Australia or to the rest of the world. Nevertheless, this ethnographic evidence adds a new consideration to the analysis of petroglyphs: the concept that the rock dust arising from the abrasion, incision or pounding of the rock may have been far more significant than the end-product of the process left as an enduring mark on the rock.

The belief that rock dust arising from pounding a rock surface contains the life essence of the Totemic Being who has been metamorphosed into that formation could explain the battering of the rims of ledges in rock-shelters and caves. It would also account for the hundreds of cupules found on vertical walls in some rock-shelters without any other forms of petroglyphs present, as they are known in the Kimberley (Fig. 9.10 and cf. Flood 1997b: 145) and in Arnhem Land (cf. Edwards 1979: plate 40). In these instances, cupules are a form of gestural rock-art, where it was the *action* involved that was important and the mark left behind was just the incidental by-product. In other cases, the same type of small cup-shaped hollow is a referential type of petroglyph, for example, one of a clutch of eggs in an emu's nest (cf. Flood 2000: plate 20).

Fig. 9.10. Cupules and abraded grooves on the wall of Drysdale River 3 rock-shelter, Kimberley, Western Australia.
Photograph by D. Welch.

Factors affecting the distribution of decorated rock-shelters

When I commenced work in the eastern Victoria River region in 1988, very little research had been done and few sites were known. It is relatively flat and featureless country covered with savannah woodland with little permanent water; at first we predicted where sites would be found from examining aerial photographs for dark patches where taller trees grew – signs there was likely to be more water. This approach was reasonably successful but sometimes we walked across country – it is mostly too well-treed to land helicopters and there were at that time almost no roads or even tracks – only to find water but no rock-shelters and thus no rock-art. There is almost no rock-art in the open spaces of this region. Only a handful of open-air petroglyph sites on rock pavements or boulders are known. Paintings were always done in rock-shelters, we were told, so 'that they will last'. In other words, to find rock-art you have to find rock-shelters.

In the tropical, monsoon lands of northern Australia the primary use of rock-shelters was for habitation and shelter from rain and from the fierce sun in the summer wet season. The climate in Wardaman tribal territory is dry monsoonal, with year-round high temperatures, no frost and markedly seasonal rainfall. Annual average rainfall is between 500 and 600 mm, almost all of which falls between November and April. The slightly cooler months of May to September are virtually rain-free. Annual evaporation significantly exceeds rainfall, and by the end of the dry season all but permanent water sources such as springs and large water-holes have dried up.

In the dry season, occupation focused on permanent water-holes such as Yingalarri and their rich aquatic food resources. People tended to camp in the sandy river beds or on the banks where large paperbark trees provided shade. The main use of rock-shelters, as we were often told, was in the wet season, to provide shelter from tropical downpours and shade from the hot summer sun. In areas which lack rock and therefore rock-shelters, bark huts were built. In wetter regions such as Arnhem Land the bark huts were raised to form platforms above the ground; there, the inside of the large sheets of bark forming the walls and roof were painted (cf. Morphy 1998: plate 24). This is the origin of the tradition of painting on bark which is still alive today (Morphy 1998), although rock-painting has now virtually ceased all over Australia.

In regions where rock-shelters are available – such as most of Wardaman country – the shelters were intensively used, and decorated, in the wet season when rain falls daily, often as heavy downpours. Flooding and the boggy mud of the black-soil plains make travel difficult. In the two wettest months, January and February, people tended to stay in one locality, where large shady rock-shelters were available and food such as fruits and yams was plentiful. Water, available everywhere in the 'wet', was not an important factor in the choice of sites for occupation at that time of year.

The need to camp in rock-shelters for at least part of the year explains the presence of both occupation and rock-art in the vast majority of rock-shelters in Wardaman country, but by no means every rock-shelter contains rock-art. Small rock-shelters high on escarpments have been seldom either occupied or decorated. Gradually over the course of five seasons of fieldwork, I came to realize that the occurrence of decorated shelters could be predicted from the geological map (Sweet 1972). Whilst the whole region is sandstone, there is one particular variety of sandstone which produces capacious rock-shelters and large, smooth walls ideal for rock-art. Rock-shelters with some art do occur in other types of sandstone and on conglomerate; but the major site complexes (groups of sites) are on cross-bedded quartz sandstone of the Antrim Plateau Volcanics. This lies in beds up to 150 m thick tending from north-west to south-east in a series of 'mesas' or massive outcrops containing dozens of rock-shelters.

Examples of this type of rock formation are the site complexes of Garnawala with some fifty rock-art sites and Yingalarri with more than eighty. This cross-bedded sandstone also produces spectacular land-forms such as high pillars,

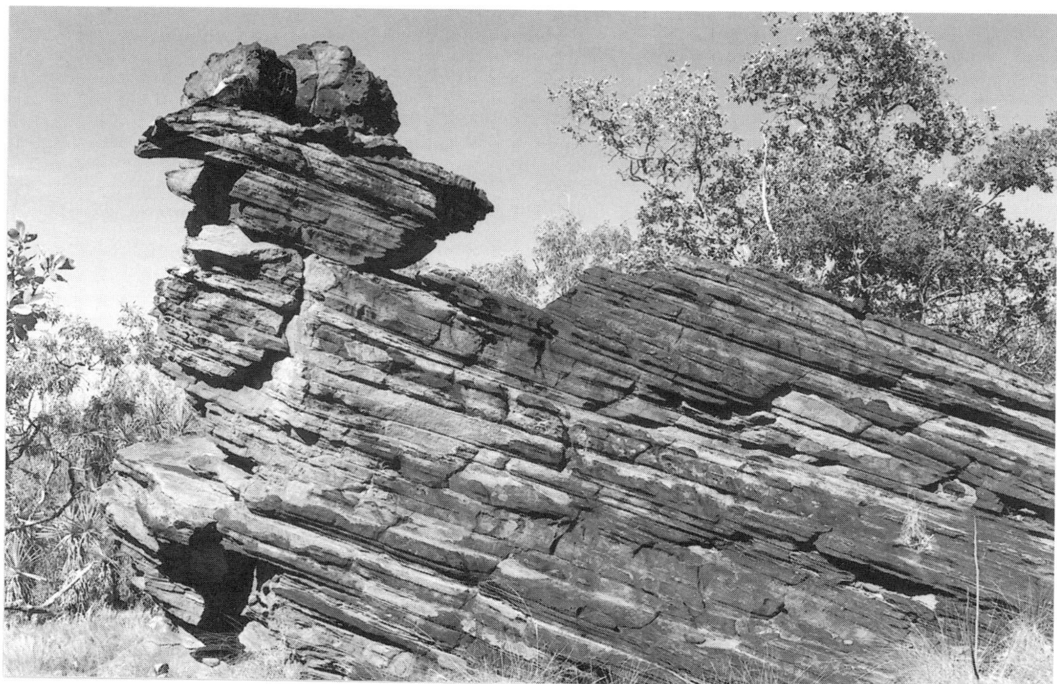

Fig. 9.11. White Sulphur-Crested Cockatoo Dreaming rock near a rock-shelter with paintings of Ancestral White Cockatoo Beings. Winybarr (Wynbarra) rock-hole, Innesvale, Wardaman country, Northern Territory. Photograph by J. Flood.

mushroom-shaped balancing rocks, and the like. All these are named, story places. Some have little or no rock-art because of their form and lack of rock-shelters; a high pillar or 'stack' at Garnawala which has no art is a sacred phallic symbol to Wardaman women, as we discovered when with much giggling they asked to have their photographs taken beside it.

Criteria for choice of sites

Striking anthropomorphic or zoomorphic rock formations sometimes lead to the decorating of near-by rock-shelters which otherwise might well not have been selected for use because of their uncomfortable, rocky floors or lack of room. Near Winybarr (Wynbarra) rock-hole some irregular-shaped stone columns of dark orange-red conglomerate give the impression of discs piled unevenly one on top of the other. On some of these stacks the topmost disk is the largest, resembling the comb on a cockatoo's head (Fig. 9.11). These columns are said to be *menngen*, sulphur-crested white cockatoos transformed into rock. Rock-shelters in the vicinity are small with generally rocky floors, but all bear paintings and engravings relating to the White Cockatoo Dreaming (Merlan 1989). On the back wall of the shelter opposite the cockatoo pillars is a large reclining painted figure said to be old man white cockatoo. Two long, thin, red, leaf-like structures overlapping this figure were identified as *galijba* (kapok or wild cassava, *Cochlospermum fraseri*), a locally abundant plant

Fig. 9.12. Balancing rock at Jigaigarn, Innesvale, Wardaman country, Northern Territory.
Photograph by J. Flood.

with bright yellow flowers supposedly gathered by white cockatoo's two wives as they foraged about the country (Raymond *et al.* 1999: 33). Another White Cockatoo Dreaming site lies a few hundred metres downstream. It is a large painting site in a small, very low rock-shelter. The main figures are five very tall, vertically striped beings with head-dresses distinctive for their tall feathered appearance. Other cockatoo-like stone columns lie very close to this site. On the rock wall are also three painted circular forms connected to each other, identified as bush potatoes. On a near-by low boulder are rare cupules pecked on a near-vertical surface, which informants said were bush foods provided for the Ancestral Beings to eat. (The dominance of food animals in much Aboriginal art may also be explained in this way rather than as 'hunting magic'.)

Another group of twenty-seven art sites in an outcrop named Jigaigarn relates to a spectacular rock on the skyline balancing on a tiny base (Fig. 9.12). This is a Grasshopper Dreaming. A large but boulder-strewn rock-shelter below this is a major rock-art and occupation site dominated by a huge striped figure – an ancestral grasshopper. The floor of part of this shelter (known as Gordol-ya) was excavated in 1991, and charcoal from 11 cm above the base of the occupational deposit gave a determination of 10,060±110 bp (uncalibrated; Beta-68163) (David *et al.* 1995).

Sacred and secular rock-art

Most major Aboriginal decorated rock-shelters are both sacred and secular, in that they may have pictures of sacred Ancestral Beings on the walls but are also used as family camping places. Aboriginal people used to move around their tribal territory in 'bands', typically of about twenty-five people, often an extended family group. They would camp in the same rock-shelter; often the teenage boys would be sent a little distance away, for example round the corner from the main rock-shelter at Nimji to a much smaller and less comfortable shelter (see Flood 1997a for the Aboriginal use of rock-shelters).

Access to the vast majority of Wardaman sites is unrestricted, although some restrictions may apply; one may be told not to touch or to look too long at the paintings. Likewise, there are very few 'men only 'or 'women only' art sites; but in a women's site a man may say that he was meant to cover his eyes and not look at the paintings. Certain rock-shelters were used as women's birthing places, but they were not reserved exclusively for that purpose.

In Wardaman tribal territory one remote rock-shelter situated high above the valley floor at the foot of a high escarpment was a sacred, 'men only' site (Film Australia 1987). This one was probably selected for its inaccessible position and high, smooth back wall – an ideal 'canvas' on which to paint huge, more than human-life-size images of two sacred Ancestral Beings on the wall. (A major Dreaming story in Wardaman country concerns the doings of the two Lightning Brothers; and here there are two beings rather than the single dominating figure more customary.) Ceremonies such as initiation were held in these remote sites, from which women and children were strictly barred. Women also had their own sacred sites, which might or might not contain rock-art; men were barred from one of these because any visitor to it was guaranteed to become pregnant!

Inter-site and intra-site relationships

Within each group of sites there is usually one major site. As one would expect, it is the largest, shadiest rock-shelter with a soft earth floor that contains the most occupational debris and the greatest quantity of rock-art. Such shelters also appear to contain the oldest occupation and the oldest art, the preliminary finding of fieldwork in September 1999 devoted to looking closely at a relative and absolute chronology for Wardaman rock-art (Flood *et al.* 2000).

In a typical Wardaman site complex all the art sites have the same name, for example Garnawala. The art in the major site is distinguished by a centrally placed figure or pair of figures which are Ancestral Beings, larger than human-life-size, finely painted with elaborate internal polychrome decoration and with certain supernatural characteristics (Figs. 9.13 and 9.14). The fifty art sites at Garnawala are located on two adjacent outcrops stretching over a kilometre but they are all considered as one entity. At Yingalarri, the eighty art sites are in separate outcrops with a kilometre or more between them; these outcrop groups have different names – Nimji, Murning and Garnyi-warnyirr – and there is a different major site in each complex.

Rock-art sites containing Dreaming Beings also usually have many secular or non-Dreaming pictures (David *et al.* 1990; 1994; Flood *et al.* 1992; Frost *et al.* 1992). The Dreaming figures generally dominate the site by their large size.

Fig. 9.13. Larger than life-size figures of Ancestral Beings centrally placed in the main rock-shelter at Murning near Yingalarri water-hole, Wardaman country, Northern Territory.
These figures are visible from some distance away.
Photograph by J. Flood.

Often they are surrounded by many pictures of animals, humans and other motifs – some secular and some 'made in the Dreamtime'. Secular sites contain paintings that appear to be more casual. They were usually painted for fun, decoration, love magic, sorcery; to record a visit to a site, or illustrate a story. Our Wardaman colleagues tend to be rather offhand and derogatory about them, and attribute many of the rougher, small drawings to children. These, which tend to be low on shelter walls, are generally drawn with charcoal or painted in a thick white pigment. Favourite subjects are small macropods, dingoes and stick-like humans. A few are above high rock ledges, only reachable by the agile. Some small white figures of this type are exposed to water run-off; as the white pigment does not endure and these are exposed to the weather, they are probably very recent.

With regard to placement of figures within a site, not only are the main Dreaming figure or figures centrally placed, but they are also sometimes located so as to be visible from a considerable distance away. At the site of Nawurla-ya the huge,

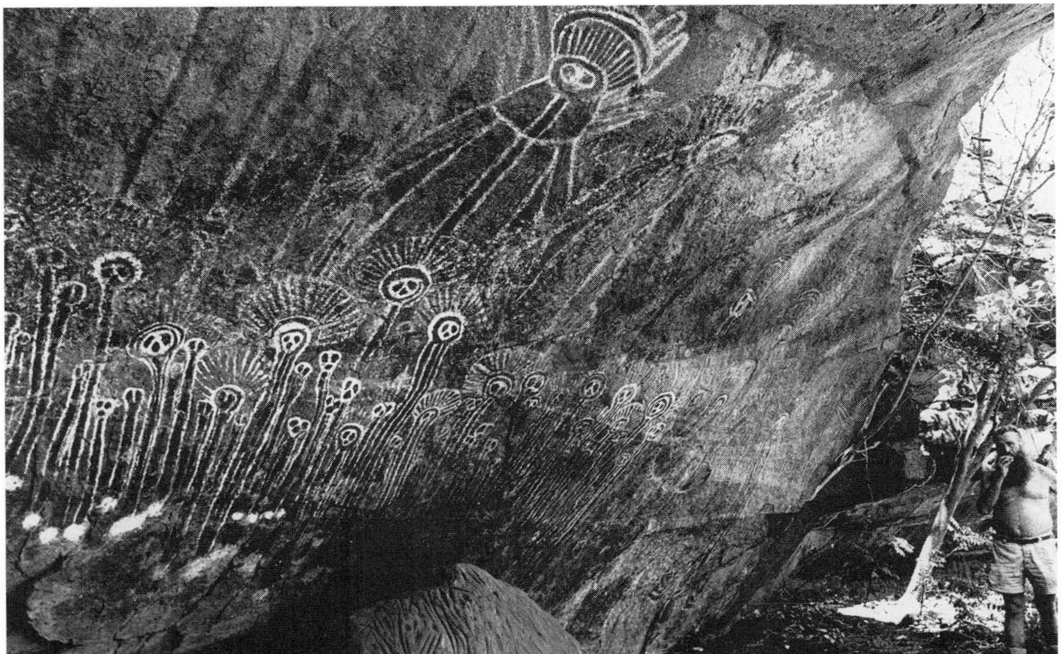

Fig. 9.14. The central panel of figures in the main rock-shelter of Garnawala, Innesvale, Northern Territory. Photograph by G. Chaloupka.

striking figure of *Nawurla* is visible over the top of a large boulder to anyone walking up that valley (Fig. 9.15). *Nawurla* was a woman who was severely punished for breaking tribal law; her image on the wall serves as a warning to others of the dire consequences of such transgression.

Conclusions: landscapes past and landscapes future

Australian Aboriginal rock-art serves to explain and map the landscape. 'It both tells the story and evokes it; it is the text and visual aid; it is the map, the code and the very terrain under which lies buried a world of meaning . . . fully accessible only to the initiated' (Brennan 1998: 164). Rock-art is a tangible expression of the continuing presence of Ancestral Beings who moulded and humanized the landscape.

On the large scale in the arid heart of Australia, geometric pictures are diagrammatic maps of Dreaming Tracks of ancestral creative beings as they journeyed across the land, linking people across vast distances. They explain unusual natural features and teach initiates the whereabouts of vital food and water resources, of springs and permanent water-holes. The landscape is full of significant and named sites; some of them are subject to symbolic marking behaviour. This may take the form of pounding the rock to make the life-essence of the ancestral being rise as rock dust, or of engraving circles round pits pounded to sound the voice of an ancestor on a ringing rock. In these cases what we call rock-art is a by-product of actions that arouse the ancestral powers which are everywhere in the landscape.

So close is the link between Aboriginal religion and everyday life, at least in Wardaman

Fig. 9.15. The rock-shelter of Nawurla-ya near Yingalarri water-hole, Wardaman country, Northern Territory.
The figure of *Nawurla* (the now-faded striped female figure in the centre of the close-up photograph) is centrally placed high on the wall to be visible to anyone walking up this valley, past the rock-shelter.
Photographs by J. Flood and Christopher Chippindale.

country, that there is little or no distinction between sacred and secular sites. The major occupation rock-shelters are also often major galleries of rock-art. Where rock-shelters occur in groups on an outcrop or along a cliff-line, the largest habitable rock-shelter is usually both the major camping place and the main Dreaming site.

Within rock-shelters the main figure or figures are generally located in the central dominant position. They are often over human-life-size, stretching from top to bottom of high rock panels or stretching from end to end of wide walls. In other words, they fill the principal available space. And the Dreaming figures are placed in the shelter of overhangs so that they will last for ever, with the help of regular retouching. Wardaman people know that the paintings have always been there since the Dreaming beings painted themselves on the wall after they had created the landscape and all living creatures within it.

Rock-art and the whole landscape came into being in the Dreamtime. They are still of just as great significance in the present and the future. It was the pre-eminent importance of the land to all Australian Aboriginal people that gave rise to the land-rights movement, which is going from strength to strength even as rock-art is replaced by other, more practical expressions of Aboriginal art in modern media. At least in Australia, art is a living tradition which helps us to understand prehistoric rock-art in a way which is not possible in other parts of the world.

Acknowledgements

The information on which much of this chapter is based comes from Wardaman traditional owners and custodians, to whom I owe a great debt of gratitude for introducing me to their culture, rock-art and traditional life-ways. The Wardaman Aboriginal Corporation and Mick Peirce have facilitated this on-going project and the main Aboriginal participants have been the late Ruby Alison, Riley Birdum, the late July Blutcher, Daisy Gimin, Lily Gin.gina, Billy Harney, Queenie Ngabijiji, Ngamunugarri, the late Elsie Raymond, and Oliver, Barbara, Michael, Lindsay, Tilley and Jason Raymond. I would also like to thank the owners and managers of Scott Creek, Willeroo, Delamere and Innesvale stations for occasional access to their land. My thanks go to Earthwatch for funding fieldwork in 1988, 1989, 1990, 1991 and 1992, to the Australian Institute of Aboriginal and Torres Strait Islander Studies for funding the 1999 field season, and to Max Bourke, Sharon Sullivan, Robert Bruce, Denise Robin and others at the Australian Heritage Commission for their moral support over a long period.

In the field, Earthcorps volunteers carried out most of the archaeological work and rock-art recording and I am grateful to them and to my fellow researchers, Val Attenbrow, Bryce Barker, Christopher Chippindale, Jackie Collins, Bruno David, Robert Gunn, Susi Juarez, Ian McNiven and Alan Watchman, and to Charlie McCracken, Margaret Opie, Graham Parker, Nigel Peacock and Bryn Williams for their invaluable practical skills. Useful, relevant discussions with other researchers over the years are acknowledged, notably Robert Bednarik, Hugh Cairns, George Chaloupka, John Clegg, Ian Dunlop, Natalie Franklin, Robin Gregory, Ken Hedges, Peter Hiscock, Dick Kimber, Vincent Megaw, Francesca Merlan, Mike Morwood, Margaret Nobbs, Ken Mulvaney, Sue O'Connor, Kelvin Officer, Norma Richardson, Andrée Rosenfeld, Claire Smith, Paul Taçon, Grahame Walsh and David Welch. Finally I am particularly grateful to Francesca Merlan for her help and advice on Wardaman linguistics and anthropology; her orthography has been adopted here.

References

Akerman, K. with J. Stanton. 1994. *Riji and Jakuli: Kimberley pearl shell in Aboriginal Australia*. Darwin, NT: Northern Territory Museum of Arts and Sciences. Monograph Series 4.

Attenbrow, V., B. David and J. Flood. 1995. Mennge-ya and the origin of points: new insights into the appearance of points in the semi-arid zone of the Northern Territory, *Archaeology in Oceania* 30: 105–20.

Baldwin S., W. and F. J. Gillen. 1899. *The native tribes of central Australia*. London: Macmillan.

Breck Parkman, E. 1995. California dreamin': cupule petroglyph occurrences in the American West, in J. Steinbring (ed.), *Rock art studies in the Americas*: 1–12. Oxford: Oxbow Books.

Brennan, F. 1998. Land rights – the religious factor, in M. Charlesworth (ed.), *Religious business*: 142–75. Cambridge: Cambridge University Press.

Clarkson, C. and B. David. 1995. The antiquity of blades and points revisited: investigating the emergence of systematic blade production south-west of Arnhem Land, northern Australia, *The Artefact* 18: 22–44.

Cosgrove, R. 1983. *Tasmanian west coast Aboriginal rock art survey*. Hobart: Tasmanian National Parks and Wildlife Service. Occasional Paper 5.

David, B., J. Collins, B. Barker, J. Flood and B. Gunn. 1995. Archaeological research in Wardaman country, Northern Territory: the Lightning Brothers Project 1990–91 field seasons, *Australian Archaeology* 41: 1–8.

David, B., M. David, J. Flood and R. Frost. 1990. Rock paintings of the Yingalarri region: preliminary results and implications for an archaeology of inter-regional relations in northern Australia, *Memoirs of the Queensland Museum* 28(2): 443–62.

David, B., I. McNiven, V. Attenbrow, J. Flood and J. Collins. 1994. Of Lightning Brothers and White Cockatoos: dating the antiquity of signifying systems in the Northern Territory, Australia, *Antiquity* 68: 241–51.

Dorn, R. 1997. Uncertainties in the ^{14}C ages for petroglyphs from the Olary province, South Australia, *Archaeology in Oceania* 32(3): 214–15.

Edwards, R. 1979. *Australian Aboriginal art: the art of the Alligator Rivers region, Northern Territory*. Canberra: Australian Institute of Aboriginal Studies.

Film Australia. 1987. *Land of the Lightning Brothers*. Sydney. Video (27 minutes.)

Flood, J. 1997a. Australian Aboriginal use of caves, in C. Bonsall and C. Tolan-Smith (eds.), *The human use of caves*: 193–200. Oxford: British Archaeological Reports. International Series S667.

1997b. *Rock art of the Dreamtime: images of ancient Australia*. Sydney: Angus and Robertson (an imprint of HarperCollins Publishers).

2000. *Archaeology of the Dreamtime: the story of prehistoric Australia and its people*. New edition. Sydney: Angus and Robertson (an imprint of HarperCollins Publishers).

Flood, J., C. Chippindale and A. Watchman. 2000. Chronology of Wardaman rock-art. Paper presented at AURA Congress, Alice Springs, July.

Flood, J. and B. David. 1994. Traditional systems of encoding meaning in Wardaman rock art, *The Artefact* 17: 6–22.

Flood, J., B. David and R. Frost. 1992. Dreaming into art: Aboriginal interpretations of rock engravings: Yingalarri, Northern Territory (Australia), in M. J. Morwood and D. R. Hobbs (eds.), *Rock art and ethnography*: 33–8. Melbourne: Australian Rock Art Research Association. Occasional Publication 5.

Frost, R., B. David and J. Flood. 1992. Rock art in transition: discussing the interaction of visual forms and symbolic contents in Wardaman rock pictures, in M. J. Morwood and D. R. Hobbs (eds.), *Rock art and ethnography*: 27–32. Melbourne: Australian Rock Art Research Association. Occasional Publication 5.

Merlan, F. 1989. The interpretive framework of Wardaman rock art: a preliminary report, *Australian Aboriginal Studies* 1989(2): 14–24.

1994. *A grammar of Wardaman: a language of the Northern Territory of Australia*. Berlin: Mouton de Gruyter.

Morphy, H. 1998. *Aboriginal art*. London: Phaidon.

Mountford, C. P. 1976. *Nomads of the Australian desert*. Adelaide: Rigby.

Munn, N. 1973. *Walbiri iconography*. Ithaca, NY: Cornell University Press.

Raymond, Mrs E., J. Blutja, L. Gin.gina, M. Raymond, O. Raymond, L. Raymond, J. Brown, Q. Morgan, D. Jackson, N. Smith and G. Wightman. 1999. *Wardaman ethnobiology: Aboriginal plant and animal knowledge from the Flora River and south-west Katherine region, north Australia*. Darwin: Northern Territory University Centre for Indigenous Natural and Cultural Resource Management/Parks and Wildlife Commission of the Northern Territory. Centre for Indigenous Natural and Cultural Resource Management Occasional Paper 2. Northern Territory Botanical Bulletin 25.

Roberts, R. G., M. Bird, J. Olley, R. Galbraith, E. Lawson, G. Laslett, H. Yoshida, R. Jones, R. Fullagar, G. Jacobsen and Q. Hua. 1998. Jinmium rock shelter in northern Australia, *Nature* 393(6683): 358–62.

Sweet, L. P. 1972. *Delamere Northern Territory: 1:250 000 Geological Series – explanatory notes*. Canberra: Australian Government Publishing Service.

Taçon, Paul S. C. 1991. The power of stone: symbolic aspects of stone use and tool development in western Arnhem Land, Australia, *Antiquity* 65: 192–207.

Taçon, P. S. C., R. Fullagar, S. Ouzman and K. Mulvaney. 1997. Cupule engravings from northern Australia: new insights from the world's oldest known network of symbolic sites, *Antiquity* 71: 942–65.

Tindale, N. B. 1963. Totemic beliefs in the Western Desert of Australia, Part II, *Records of the South Australian Museum* 14(3): 499–514.

10

Places of power: the placement of Dinwoody petroglyphs across the Wyoming landscape

Lawrence Loendorf

A fundamental of landscape is height, and as an elevation it makes a component which is easily measured in numerical terms. The Dinwoody rock-engravings, in the high mountain country of Wyoming, show a striking pattern in the elevations where they occur, and in what is depicted at different heights. Their social meaning provides an explanation.

Petroglyphs and pictographs in central Wyoming

The large and elaborate petroglyphs of central Wyoming, known as the Dinwoody Tradition, were first described more than a century ago (Mallery 1886) and they continue to fascinate researchers to the present (Francis and Loendorf 2002).[1] Gebhard and Cahn (1950) initially assigned the petroglyphs to a style designation, and Gebhard (1951; 1969) discussed and modified it through the years. Dinwoody petroglyphs display many distinct characteristics. They are nearly all made as pecked outline forms and dominated by large frontal views of human-like forms. The bodies are frequently rectangular in outline with rounded corners. Torsos are filled with designs. Some contain rows of parallel vertical lines lengthwise down the torso and others have undulating, zigzagging, or groups of dots and loops filling their bodies. Heads may be an extension of the body or set atop a short neck. Facial features are purposefully left off many figures while others have very detailed eyes, nose and mouth. Head ornaments include horns or other forms. One figure has another small human standing on its head.

Many figures display upper body limbs that resemble wings and the appellation human-like is misleading for viewers who see birds more readily than humans. An important characteristic on some figures is the addition of large hands and feet, some with five digits and others with three digits, that are sometimes on normal arms and legs and other times at the ends of short stubby limbs. Frequently there are extra lines near the humans; sometimes they encase the human forms while other times they are added to the scene as wavy lines. These lines can connect to smaller figures or zigzag like lightning across the rock face. Smaller human forms are also found in the style, sometimes displaying much the same form as the larger figures and other times more realistic

[1] These petroglyphs are also referred to as the Interior-line Style. The name Dinwoody comes from a large site near Dinwoody Lake on the Wind River Shoshone-Arapahoe Reservation. This site is recognized as a traditional cultural property or sacred site with restricted use. The Wind River Reservation cultural commission controls access to it. Although the Dinwoody site has been extensively photographed (Sowers 1939; 1941; Wellmann 1979), the cultural commission does not approve photography of the site nor does it recommend use of photographs for calendars, other publications or presentations. No images from the main Dinwoody panels are used in this document.

representations of humans. Long linear pecked bodies tend to be used to represent the smaller anthropomorphs at some sites.

Quadrupedal animals are usually solid pecked and shown in profile, and although they may be connected to the scenes by a pecked line they do not display the extra embellishment of the anthropomorphic forms. One group of the animals most closely resembles dogs and other recognizable forms include bison. One form may be a bison and human conflation. Large bears are rare but the ones that are recorded have the same sort of interior body decoration as the human forms. Bear tracks are found at a select group of sites.

Well-made bows with arrows are found with one group of the figures. In one region the figures also have arrow points attached to their limbs or as a pendant around their necks. Rattle-like objects are held in the hands of several of the figures. Shields, so common at petroglyph sites to the east and north, are seldom found with Dinwoody petroglyphs.

The distribution of Dinwoody Tradition petroglyphs

One of the important aspects of Dinwoody petroglyphs is the small geographic region in which they are found in central Wyoming[2] (Fig. 10.1). This region is drained by the Wind River, a stream that flows east from the Wind River Mountains before it turns north through a narrow canyon in the Owl Creek Mountains and continues along the western flank of the Bighorn Mountains to its junction with the Yellowstone River in south-central Montana. Like so many western rivers, its name changes – to the Bighorn River after it passes through the Owl Creek Mountains. The upper reaches of the Wind River are at elevations of some 10,000 feet (3078 m) but the large petroglyph sites are about 7000 feet (2154 m). The middle course of the Wind River, before it passes through the Owl Creek Mountains, ranges at elevations of 6000 to 5500 feet (1846 to 1692 m). Sites are found at several locations along the river in this region. The lower Wind River and its tributaries are at elevations of 5000 to 4000 feet (1538 to 1231 m). Sites are numerous in this region, especially to the west of the Bighorn River in the vicinity of Thermopolis, Wyoming. The elevation changes in the locations of Dinwoody Tradition sites is important to understanding their 'landscape pattern', but before discussing the pattern I shall present information on the rock or the substrate selected for Dinwoody Tradition petroglyphs.

The vast majority of Dinwoody petroglyphs are found on Tensleep or Frontier sandstones. Tensleep is a windblown sandstone that formed during Pennsylvanian times, and Frontier is a water-laid sandstone that developed during Cretaceous times. Although they formed in different ways and more than 100 million years apart, the two substrates are remarkably similar. Both are light tan to buff in colour, and they tend to develop thick dark-coloured varnishes. Pecking through this varnish offers a good contrast for the rock-art and this was probably an important factor in their selection for petroglyph palettes. Cavities and holes are common in Frontier Sandstone where layers of less resistant materials have eroded away leaving an uneven surface. Tensleep is also cross-bedded and subject to differential weathering, with areas of less resistant material interlayered with harder materials. This apparently did not affect the selection of these sandstones for making petroglyphs and there is evidence that it may have been better suited

[2] Sally Cole (1990: 96–108) extends the distribution of Dinwoody Tradition petroglyphs to Colorado and Utah. While there are similar petroglyphs in these areas, I cannot agree that they are directly related to Dinwoody. A single panel, at Manila, Utah along the Green River, immediately south of Wyoming may be related. This was traditional Shoshone territory.

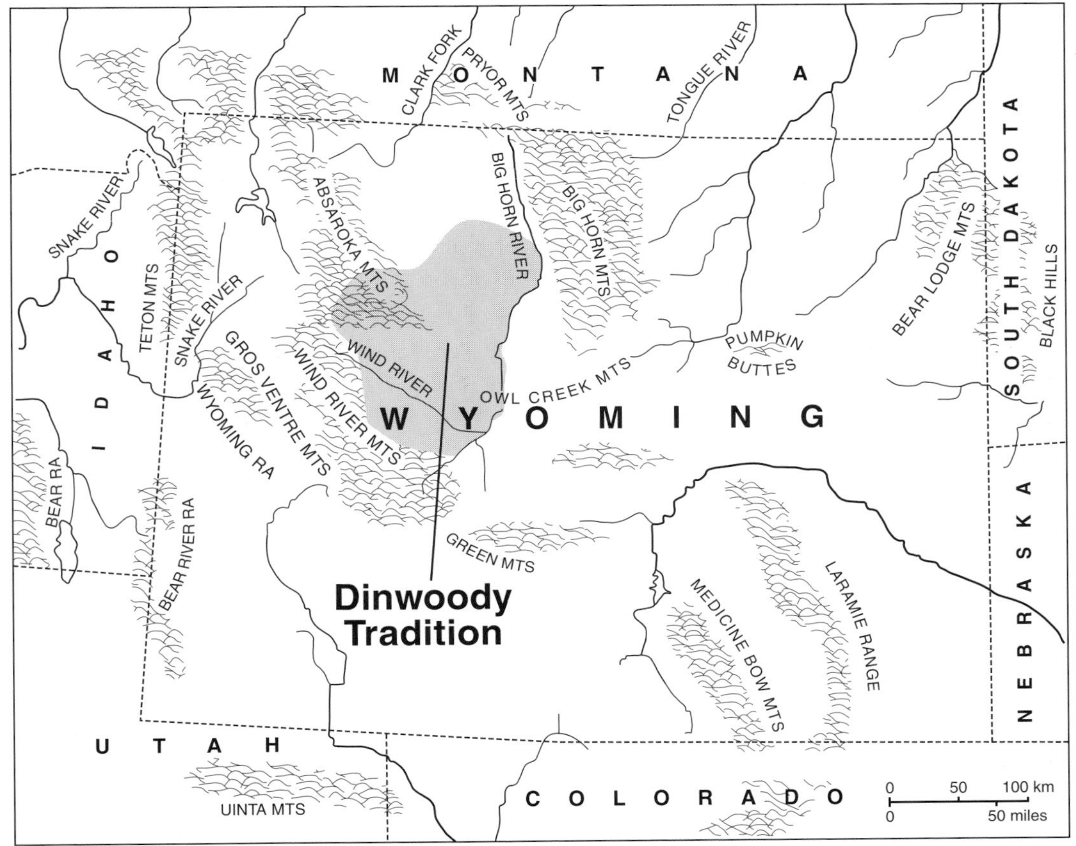

Fig. 10.1. Map showing the location of Dinwoody Tradition petroglyphs in Wyoming. The Wind River flows east before turning north into the Bighorn Basin where its name changes to the Bighorn River.

for the petroglyphs than other smoother surfaces. North of Thermopolis, in particular, petroglyphs are found on Frontier Sandstone with uneven and eroded surfaces in settings where there are good smooth sandstone surfaces in the immediate vicinity. At first glance the surfaces appear to have eroded since the petroglyphs were placed there, but on closer examination it is clear that the pecked marks go into the cavities, meaning the eroded surfaces pre-date the manufacture of the petroglyphs. This suggests the petroglyph manufacturers, at least in this location, were selecting the eroded surfaces over smooth ones. It is also important to note that Tensleep and Frontier sandstones are found across a wide area of Wyoming below 7500 feet (2038 m) but most Dinwoody petroglyphs occur in a relatively small part of this area along the Wind River and its tributaries.

A large number of factors appear to affect the location of Dinwoody petroglyph sites. In addition to elevation, they are located with regularity near lakes and springs (in particular hot springs) and drainages that feed to these features. It is also common to find sites near highly eroded rocks or spherical shaped rocks, some of which have human-like forms and are often called hoodoo rocks. The hoodoo rocks can be in the same sandstone formations as those selected for petroglyphs, but they can also be other rock outcrops in the vicinity of the petroglyph sites.

Dinwoody petroglyphs tend to face the lakes, the river or stream or the valley in which they are found but they are not always oriented towards the water. Apparently most of the petroglyphs face the water because that is the orientation of the cliff faces. In the Torrey Valley area, for example, the greatest numbers of panels face east and west, which is the orientation of the exposed sandstone outcrops flanking the valley. Thus, many panels face the lakes in the bottom of the valley, but about a third of the petroglyphs face south or north where they are not oriented towards water. This suggests that no single direction for orienting a Dinwoody petroglyph was preferred over another, and the orientation of the exposed surfaces of the rock outcrops is the main factor in the direction they face.

Cultural affiliation for Dinwoody Tradition petroglyphs

Dinwoody petroglyphs are associated with the Mountain Shoshone, who are also known as the Tukudika or Sheep Eaters. They occupied the Wind River and the Absaroka Mountains, where they are known as the primary Indians to occupy the region surrounding Yellowstone National Park (Hultkrantz 1957; 1961b; Dominick 1964). The Mountain Shoshone practised seasonal transhumance, following herds of bighorn sheep as they grazed in the high mountain meadows and then moving down slope to winter pastures. Elaborate sheep traps, remnants of the Mountain Shoshone hunters, are found in the same area as the Dinwoody Tradition petroglyphs. The traps are made of deadfall timber fences aligned in v-shaped drive lines and corral-like catch pens where the hunters dispatched the sheep. The Mountain Shoshone were known for their large wolf-like dogs that they used to drive the bighorns into the traps (Nabokov and Loendorf 2002). These dogs were also packed to carry Mountain Shoshone belongings in their seasonal movements.

There is debate as to the length of time the Mountain Shoshone have lived in Wyoming. One popular hypothesis suggests they separated from Great Basin Shoshone and migrated to Wyoming within the past 1000 years, although this is subject to considerable debate (see Madsen and Rhode 1994 for various aspects of this debate). Others have maintained that the Shoshone lived in the north for 8000 to 9000 years (Swanson 1958; Husted and Edgar 2002), and more recently Richard Holmer (1994) has excavated archaeological sites which demonstrate the Shoshone have lived in Idaho for at least 3000 years. Increasingly Wyoming archaeologists have recognized evidence of the Shoshone. House pits, coiled baskets, small animal snares, fragments of netting, net weights, compound arrows with partial cane shafts and Rose Springs projectile points are found in Wyoming sites and attributed to an association with the Great Basin. These artefacts which range from 2000 to 6000 years in age are found in the same region as Dinwoody Tradition petroglyphs. It is important to recognize that Dinwoody petroglyphs are also dated by AMS ^{14}C dating, cation ratio dating and combined with relative age estimates to establish the age of the Dinwoody Tradition from the historic period and 6000 years BP (Francis *et al.* 1993). Standard radiocarbon dates from cultural levels overlying a Dinwoody petroglyph establish its age at 2000 years BP, so even if researchers do not trust the new dating methods, there is solid evidence to support at least two millennia of antiquity for the tradition (Francis 1989).

A large body of ethnographic material associates Dinwoody petroglyphs with the Shoshone (Hultkrantz 1961a: 35ff.; 1987: 52ff.; Shimkin

1986: 325; Vander 1997: 228). Hultkrantz (1987: 52–3) describes the Shoshone experience of obtaining visions at rock-art sites in a ritual called *puhawilo*, or sleeping at the medicine-rocks. The visions were most commonly sought by young men who went to the petroglyph sites, bathed in a near-by stream or lake, and then sat, facing the panel, while they waited for several days for a visit from a supernatural power. When the vision came, according to Hultkrantz, the pattern went as follows (Hultkrantz n.d. II: 51):

> There is the frightening trial, the manifestation of the spirits who tends to change forms – now a man, now an animal – the imparting of supernatural power, the conditions for the ownership of this power, and the regulations concerning ritual paraphernalia.

This description makes the conflation between humans and animals apparent. Any depiction of such a creature, as a petroglyph, would have characteristics of both humans and animals. Power also came from recognizable animals like eagles, rattlesnakes and bears, or from forces of nature like lightning, and from seemingly inanimate objects like strangely shaped rocks. Petroglyph depictions of recognizable power animals might be expected to resemble more closely those animals, while depictions of something like a strangely shaped rock might be difficult to identify.

It is from this fantastic array of creatures, real and surreal, that the great majority of rock-art images had their origin. To reduce these possibilities, I have followed Vander (1997: 154), who categorized the creatures into the Shoshone taxonomy for the animal kingdom as the sky people, the ground people and the water people. Identifying them as people is important because the Shoshone anthropomorphized animals, giving them the ability to talk and interact with humans. The animals include the mysterious ogres and water-ghosts that were also sought for power, although according to Hultkrantz (1981: 22) they were not as commonly identified as spirit helpers as the large power animals (Table 10.1).

While categorizing animals into three groups sounds simple, it is in fact difficult because so many creatures can travel from one element to another. Water birds, for example, can fly, walk on the land and dive beneath the water, and it is difficult to identify the realm with which they are most closely associated. It is sometimes possible to find ethnography to clarify the realm of various creatures, as with ducks and geese which are recognized as water people even though they can fly (Vander 1997: 195). I have added lightning spirits and rattlesnakes to the list, as both are reported as power sources for Shoshone visionaries.

Petroglyphs at Dinwoody Tradition sites

Petroglyphs at the highest mountain sites include a mixture of human-like figures and flying figures, with very few quadrupeds. The Torrey Valley site serves as a good example. Torrey Valley is located in the Wind River Mountains above Dubois, Wyoming, at an elevation of about 7000 feet (2154 m). The valley contains three deep lakes, remnants of former glaciers, and exposures of Tensleep Sandstone along the valley sides. Petroglyphs are found at various positions on the exposures and on blocks of the sandstone which have rolled down the side slopes.

Birds or flying figures dominate Torrey Valley petroglyphs. Some of the flying figures can be recognized as power birds by the Shoshone. For example, one small bird form with propeller-like wings and a long beak is believed to represent a hummingbird (Fig. 10.2). Other flying figures that are larger, with outstretched wings, are more likely eagles (Fig. 10.3). The Mountain Shoshone equate both hummingbirds and eagles with the thunderbird. A shaman told Hultkrantz (1987: 46) that the thunderbird is *tongwoyaget* (crying clouds), a sharp-nosed bird as small as a thumb

Table 10.1 *Attributes used for classification. Only animal forms (mammals, birds, reptiles and amphibians) are classified. Plants, objects like bows and arrows or non-realistic figures like circles and dots are not included in the study although all of these things (and many more) can be found in Dinwoody Tradition petroglyphs. The attributes are polythetic inasmuch as no figure has to possess all of them to be placed in the class. In other words, a horned figure may have horns but only one leg and still be classed as a horned figure. At the same time, if a figure has horns, it is classed as a horned figure regardless of the number of digits on its hands or feet.*

Attributes	Types
outstretched wings with pendant lines	pendant-wing bird
vertical body and large concentric eyes	owl
vertical body, propeller wings and long beak	hummingbird
biped with a horned head	horned figure
biped with three-digit hands or feet	three-digit anthropomorph
biped with more than three digits	four- or five-digit anthropomorph
biped with large hands or feet, encased in wavy lines	water-ghost
attributes of above but with breasts or vulva	female water-ghost
horizontal body with four legs	undifferentiated quadruped
quadruped with straight tail, often connected to anthropomorphs	dog
Classed on resemblance	
lightning	
bison	
bighorns	
bears	
horse/rider	
turtles	
frogs	
snakes	
butterflies	

that looks like a hummingbird but moves faster. In the hierarchy of spirit powers the Shoshone place lightning at the top, with the thunderbird, represented by hummingbirds and eagles, immediately below it (Hultkrantz 1981: 34). Zigzag lines around these flying figures represent lightning (Hultkrantz 1981: 33).

Owls represent another group of powerful spirit birds to the Shoshone. One notable spirit bird is the cannibal owl *wokaimumbic*. This giant flying creature talks and behaves like a human being, but resembles and looks like an enormous dragonfly. When it flies the earth shakes, and there is noise like thunder (Nabokov and Loendorf 2002: 158). The monster grabs hold of children, flies away with them and eats them. It is apparently an elaboration of the hooting owl, *mumbic*, and is perhaps identical with the evil spirit of the night, *toxabit narukumb*, whose sounds tchi-tchi-tchi-tchi may be heard at night. These shrieks frighten people out of their wits because they believe the owls are predicting evil (Fig. 10.4).

Steward (1943: 390) records that a Shoshone man who had owl power told about being in a hunting camp when an owl flew into a tree, spoke to him, and warned him that an enemy war party was approaching. This account suggests the primary power obtained from *wokaimumbic* was

Fig. 10.2. A sky person, the hummingbird is recognizable by its propeller-type wings.

Fig. 10.3. A pendant-wing petroglyph, perhaps representing an eagle. Sky people petroglyphs are associated with the thunderbird by the Shoshone. They are frequently associated with zigzag lines representing lightning.

Fig. 10.4. A sky person, the owl with concentric eyes and three-digit feet.

prophecy or the ability to see into the future. Individuals who have this sort of power are also capable of travelling into the past to find lost objects or to learn the facts about a past event (Hultkrantz 1981: 32).

Magpies, sage hens, blackbirds and other small birds were also important to the Shoshone, especially during the Ghost Dance (Vander 1997: 228–37). These birds might also be depicted in the petroglyphs, but if so their images are not as easily recognized. What is clear, however, is that birds are the most common petroglyph image in the mountains. One hundred and sixteen animals in the Torrey Valley, not covered by lichens or badly eroded, are classed into types (Table 10.2). Flying figures or birds dominate the petroglyphs, constituting 40.5 per cent, while anthropomorphs with three-digit hands or feet represent another 32 per cent of the animal petroglyphs. Quadrupeds account for only 9.5 per cent while water-ghosts are represented by even fewer figures. When we consider the possibility that the three-digit anthropomorphs may also be representations of humans with bird-like talons, the entire assemblage is nearly three-quarters bird images or bird-like images. Even without these human/bird conflations the number of bird images is significant.

Dinwoody Tradition petroglyphs at middle elevations along the Wind River between Burris and Shoshoni, Wyoming, have not been studied in the same detail as those in the Torrey Valley. Eleven sites on Bureau of Reclamation controlled lands along Boysen Reservoir were studied in the

Table 10.2 *Attributes of Dinwoody Tradition petroglyphs at middle elevations along the Wind River.*

Animal types	Torrey Valley		Middle sites		Lower sites	
Birds	number	%	number	%	number	%
pendant wings	29	25	4	5.3	1	1.5
propeller wings	8	6.9	0	0	0	0
owls	10	8.6	0	0	0	0
sub-total	**47**	**40.5**	**4**	**5.3**	**1**	**1.5**
Anthropomorphs	number	%	number	%	number	%
three digits	37	31.9	4	5.3	1	1.5
four or five digits	3	2.6	26	34.6	14	21.2
horned	7	6	9	12	2	3
stick	5	4.3	6	8	6	9.1
sub-total	**52**	**44.8**	**45**	**59.9**	**23**	**34.8**
Quadrupeds	number	%	number	%	number	%
dogs	1	0.8	5	6.7	8	12.1
bison	0	0	1	1.3	3	4.5
bighorns	3	2.6	0	0	0	0
bears	0	0	3	4	0	0
bear tracks	0	0	2	2.7	0	0
horse/rider	0	0	1	1.3	0	0
undifferentiated	7	6	13	17.3	5	7.8
sub-total	**11**	**9.5**	**25**	**33.3**	**16**	**24.4**
Water-ghosts	number	%	number	%	number	%
no sex depicted	4	3.4	2	2.7	14	21.2
female	1	0.8	0	0	3	4.5
sub-total	**5**	**4.2**	**2**	**2.7**	**17**	**25.7**
Other animals	number	%	number	%	number	%
turtles	0	0	0	0	2	3
frogs	0	0	0	0	2	3
snakes	0	0	0	0	3	4.5
butterflies	0	0	0	0	1	1.5
sub-total	**0**	**0**	**0**	**0**	**8**	**12**
total	**116**	**100**	**75**	**100**	**66**	**100**

greatest detail (Tipps and Schroedel 1985) while five sites were photographed in the 1930s (Sowers 1941). The sites are smaller than the Torrey Valley site but in many ways they are similar. Petroglyphs are found on exposures of Frontier Sandstone along the Wind River or tributary streams to the Wind River. One spectacular site is situated on the south flanks of the Muddy Creek valley where it was originally on a large sandstone monolith. One panel about 4 m in length by 2.5 m in height was found facing south-west about 2.5 m above the ground surface. Since Tipps and Schroedel recorded the site, this large panel has detached and rolled to the valley floor, some 30 m below, to end up with the panel facing upright. Using the illustrations of these middle elevation sites I am able to identify seventy-five animal figures and classify them using the same criteria as for the Torrey Valley figures (Table 10.2).

Anthropomorphs with three-digit hands and feet decrease from 35 per cent to 4.3 per cent but this is contrasted with a significant increase,

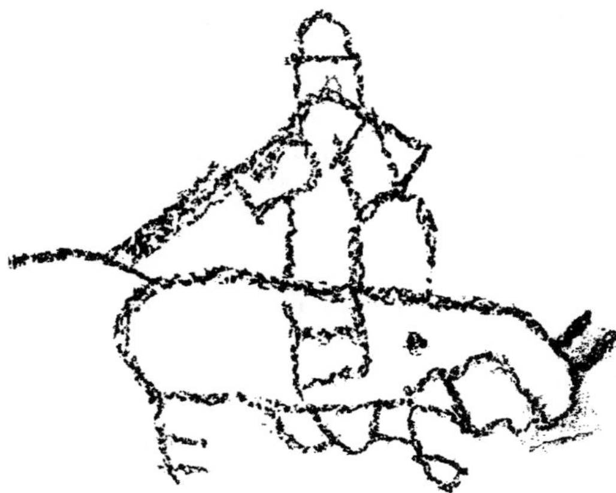

Fig. 10.5. A horse or mule and its rider. Although rare, such images are occasionally found at middle-elevation Dinwoody sites.

from 2.6 per cent to 34.6 per cent, in the anthropomorphs with four- or five-digit hands and feet (Table 10.2). Birds decrease from 40.5 per cent to 5.3 per cent. These are significant differences. Birds and humans with bird-like hands or feet are definitely more popular at higher elevations. At the same time, horned figures increase in the middle elevations, and quadrupeds increase dramatically from 9.5 per cent to 33.3 per cent. The quadrupeds include many that cannot be identified with confidence but five appear to be dogs, three bears, two bear tracks, one a well-made bison, and one a horse and rider (Fig. 10.5). Several long, low quadrupeds may be depictions of weasels and at least one animal with a long linear body, feet with claws and a long tail may be a lion.

Hultkrantz (1981: 34) identifies bears, beavers and weasels as important ground people spirits, followed by buffalo, otter and antelope in importance to the Shoshone (Fig. 10.6). Wolves and coyotes were also important (Hultkrantz 1981: 41). These were animals one was likely to encounter out on the plains, and spirit bears, for example, were said to resemble actual bears except that they appear only briefly (Hultkrantz 1981: 151). One Shoshone medicine man described how he once saw bears dancing the Sun Dance near Sweetwater Gap, out on the flats below the mountains (Hultkrantz 1981: 149).

Bison are also spirit animals. In particular the water buffalo (*Pa gwic*) is a spirit animal that lives beneath the waters of lakes or streams, but its habitual abode is Bull Lake on the west side of the Wind River Mountains. One explanation for this beast is that it is the progeny of a Ute hunter who turned into *Pa gwic* after eating the meat of the water buffalo. This association with a human suggests the animal might be depicted as a human and bison conflation. The few mentions of the beast in the literature suggest it is a male but there are few other descriptive attributes. Hultkrantz (1981: 155) believes this creature is unique to the Wind River Shoshone and there is little evidence as to whether it is classed as a ground person or a water person.

The actual bison that was common on the plains is obviously a ground person and an important animal in Shoshone ceremonies like the Sun Dance where the eagle and the bison represent the sky people and the ground people, respectively (Hultkrantz 1987: 71). This association notwithstanding, bison are not common spirit helpers to Shoshone shamans. They are only mentioned in one Shoshone Ghost Dance song. Vander (1997: 225) believes this is because bison were nearly extinct at the time of the Ghost Dance. In post-horse times the Plains Shoshone were active bison hunters but in pre-horse times they were apparently more dependent on other game like antelope in the basins and bighorn sheep in the mountains.

The horned anthropomorphs may represent the spirit water buffalo (Fig. 10.7). Sowers (1939: plate 49) identifies the figure as the bison medicine man but it is not clear where he learned that identification. None the less the figure looks like a combination of a human and a buffalo and

Fig. 10.6. A Dinwoody Tradition petroglyph representing a bear. Bears were important ground people for the Shoshone.

quite possibly it is intended to represent a buffalo spirit of some sort.

The increase in quadrupedal animals and the decrease in birds suggest that the power found in the mountains and that found on the plains is represented differently in the petroglyphs. Examining the petroglyphs in the region around Thermopolis strengthens this reasoning.

Large hot springs are found in the region surrounding Thermopolis, Wyoming, where more than a dozen petroglyph sites are also found. The petroglyphs at these sites are presently being recorded in detail. Before describing the figures I should make several points regarding the process by which I developed the sample. I did not return to the field but selected photographs and sketches of the petroglyphs from eight sites. I simply classed the figures until I had a respectable sample. I did not try to include all of the figures at every site. I recognize that this sample was not developed through a scientific process but I make no claims to that effect. In this respect the findings should be considered preliminary, as there will likely be some minor differences in the results when the site recording is finished. None the less the overall results will remain relatively close to those reported in this chapter. Finally, I did not include any petroglyphs from the large Legend Rock site, which has a mixture of figures with some that may predate the development of the Dinwoody Tradition

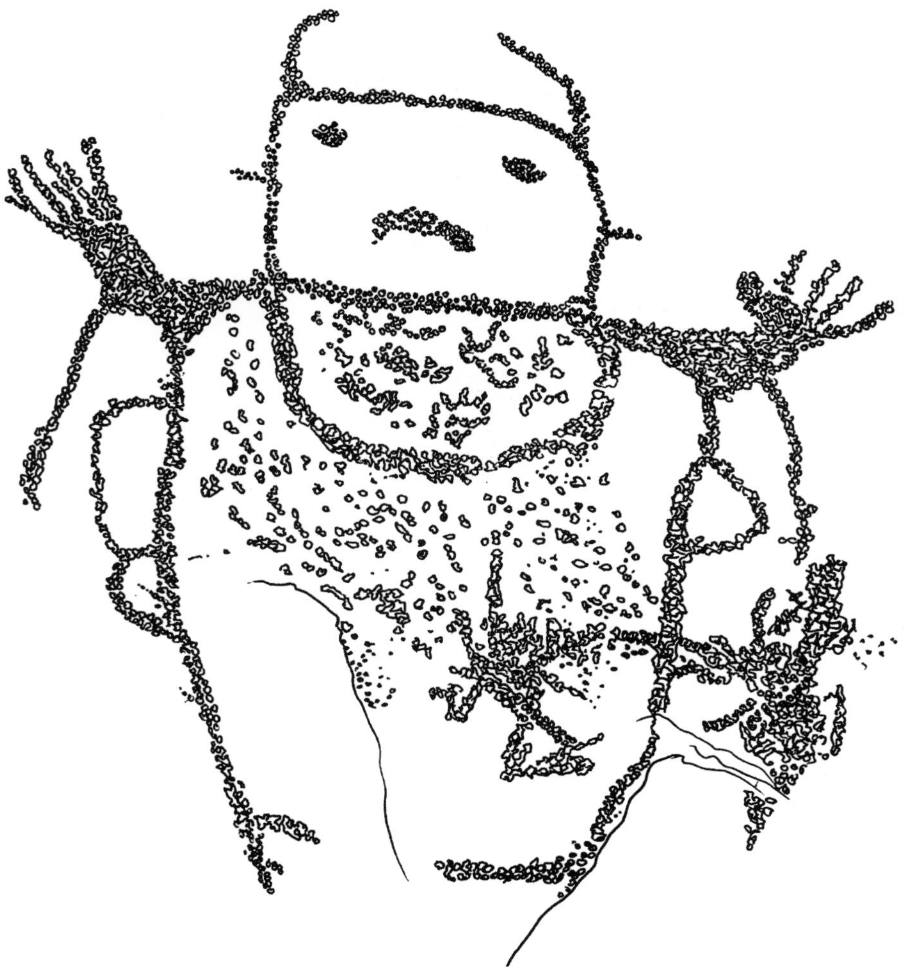

Fig. 10.7. A horned figure that may represent a bison and human conflation. These figures are most abundant in middle elevations.

and others that apparently represent cultures that were not related to the makers of the Dinwoody petroglyphs.

The water-ghosts were among the power animals encountered in visions or dreams. During earlier research at the sites in the Thermopolis region I identified a class of water-ghost petroglyphs (Loendorf 1993). These figures are recognizable because they are encased in or under wavy lines that represent water. They also frequently have large hands and feet, with the hands protruding out from beneath the water (Fig. 10.8). Water-related spirits or water people among the Shoshone included the *pa: unha*, evil 'children of the water', or 'water babies', who lived in creeks, rivers and lakes. These creatures were usually small, with long hair, and said to make the hot water in geysers and springs (Hultkrantz 1986: 633). Water babies 'sound like babies and look like small human beings. They are one and one half feet tall but so heavy that one cannot move them' (Hultkrantz 1987: 49).

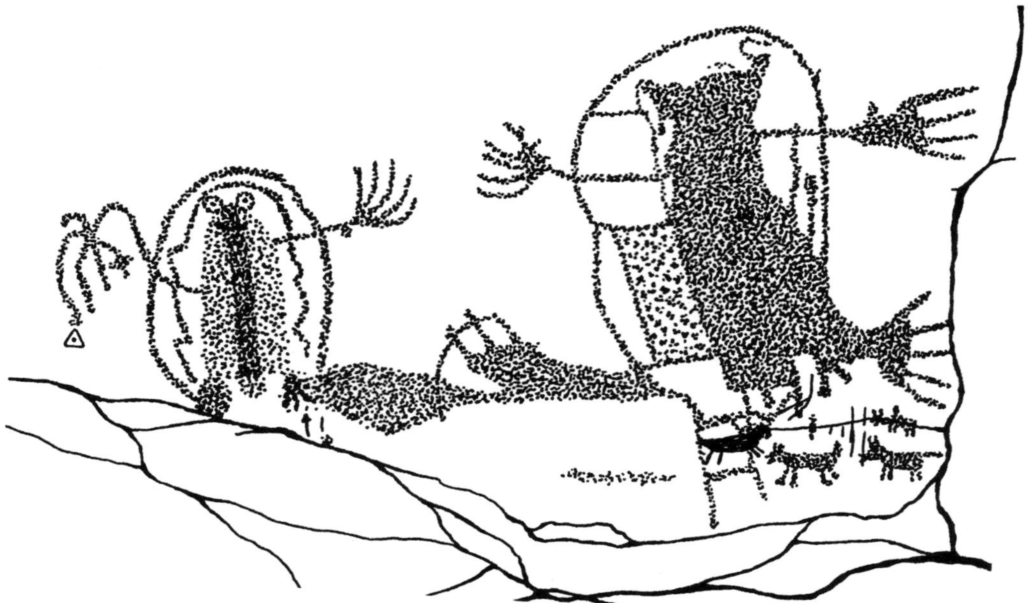

Fig. 10.8. Dinwoody Tradition petroglyphs that represent the water-ghost beings. They have large hands and feet that protrude out from the encasing lines thought to represent water. Water-ghost beings are dominant in sites at the lowest elevations.

A second class of water spirits includes the *pandzoavits*. These creatures were large, tough-skinned 'water-ghosts', or ogres, who occupied lakes and drowned people so as to eat them. Lowie (1909: 234) relates: 'Pa'-n-dzo'avits is a giant with enormous hands and feet, who lives in the water. He sleeps on rocks in the water, holding his hands before his face.' A special class of these water-ghosts is female. Known as *pa: waip*, these spirits preyed on men; enticing them into the water through the pretence of a sexual encounter, the female water-ghosts would then drown their victims.

About a quarter of the petroglyphs in the Thermopolis region represent water-ghosts (Table 10.2). Petroglyphs of frogs and turtles in the region also convey the water-related theme (Fig. 10.9). I believe this increase is related to the presence of the hot springs where the Shoshone went to seek the power of these water spirits. Some of the most powerful medicine people among the Mountain Shoshone obtained their power at hot springs. For example Togwotee, a Tukudika leader and shaman, had power from *pandzoavits* or water-ghosts (Nabokov and Loendorf 2002: 235).

Flying figures and three-digit anthropomorphs decrease significantly in the Thermopolis region. This is understandable because power from these spirits was found in the mountains. The increase in the number of dogs is more difficult to understand. The dogs may have an association with the four- and five-digit anthropomorphs, which would explain why they are both found in the same sites. Ethnographic information to explain the nature of this association is not readily apparent, however.

Finally it is important to note that the only petroglyphs of snakes in the entire region are found at the lowest elevation. Snake power, in particular that of rattlesnakes, was important among

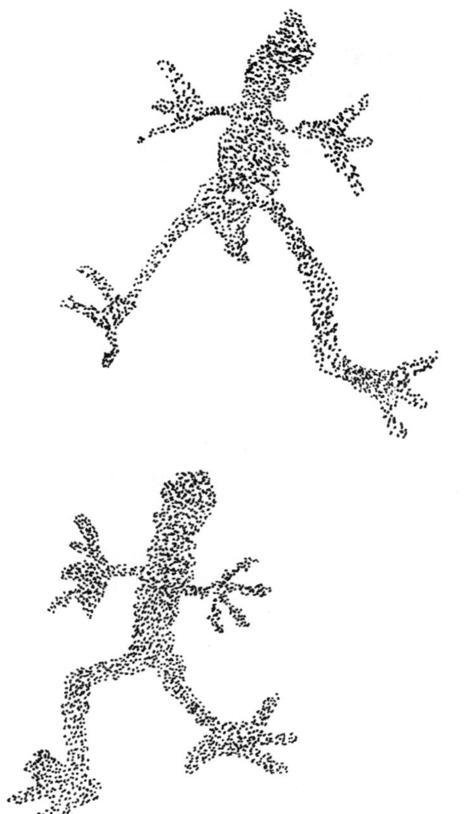

Fig. 10.9. Dinwoody petroglyphs that represent frogs. They are found near the water-ghost beings.

the Shoshone shamans, who used it to cure snake bites. Shamans with rattlesnake power could also bring the rains to cool the heat of the day (Hultkrantz 1981: 32). Rattlesnakes are found in the vicinity of all the Dinwoody sites. They are uncommon in the Torrey Valley and abundant in the Thermopolis region.

Conclusions: the Dinwoody Tradition, landscape and world-view

Dinwoody Tradition petroglyphs are definitely distributed in a 'landscape pattern'. Birds and three-digit anthropomorphs are abundant in the mountains, quadrupeds increase at middle-elevation sites, and water-related figures are most common at the lowest sites. Part of this pattern is related to the relative abundance of the *puha* or power that traditionally inhabited a particular landscape. Vision-seekers who sought a particular power would fast in the place where that power was the most abundant. In this explanation a person who wanted the power of the sky people would go to the mountains to find it and a person who wanted the power of the water people sought it in the places near their traditional abodes.

Petroglyphs of the animals or creatures that possessed the *puha* are the most common in the appropriate landscape. These petroglyphs reinforced the pattern. This is particularly true of the flying figures in the Torrey Valley where more than 40 per cent of the images represent actual birds, and if the three-digit petroglyphs are also bird related nearly three-quarters of the petroglyphs represent flying or 'sky people'. A person who wanted the power of the 'sky people' went to the landscape where their power was abundant. Furthermore their images were all over the rocks to validate their presence. A small number of 'water people' petroglyphs in the mountains should not be surprising because there are lakes with water creatures in the area, as well. However, a supplicant seeking the power of the 'water people' would not choose the mountain lakes to fast and pray because the traditional place to get power from the water spirits was in the Thermopolis region.

Another part of the explanation appears to be related to the Shoshone world-view. James Goss (1972: 128) presents a model for Numic-speaking peoples where elevations are associated with different animals and colours along a sacred mountain. Eagles are at the zenith in the sky, rattlesnakes are at the nadir or bottom of the mountain, and the four-legged creatures are found in the middle

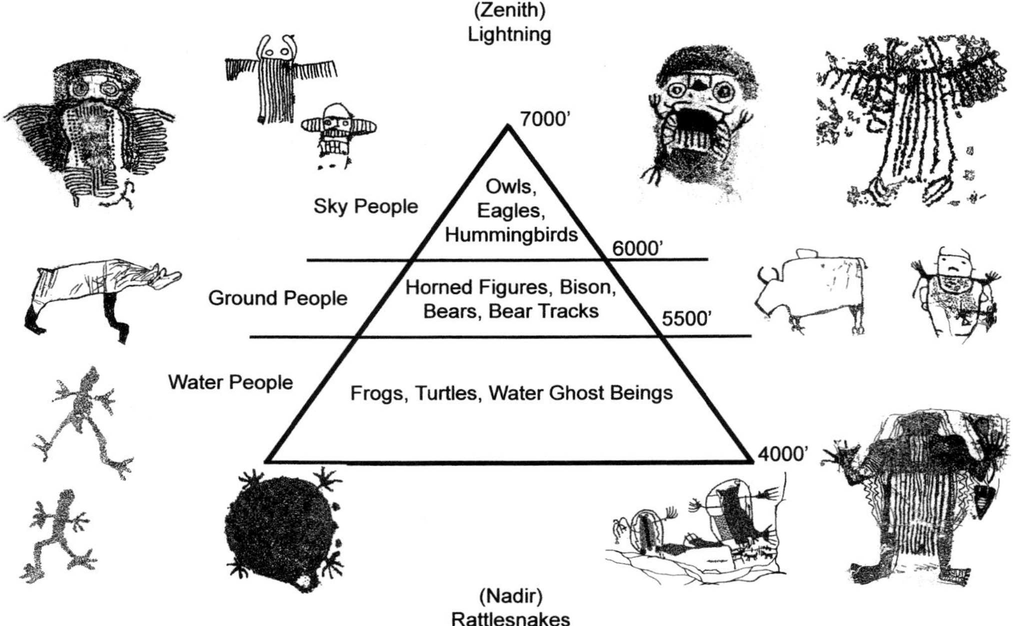

Fig. 10.10. Dinwoody Tradition petroglyphs arranged according to their elevations in the Wyoming landscape. The placement of the petroglyphs reflects the Shoshone world-view with sky people at the top, ground people in the middle and water people at the bottom. Relative scale between individual images is not accurate.

elevations. Much of the information in the model is derived from the Ute Indians but Goss (1999) indicates that all Numic groups have essentially the same ecological world-view. Judith Vander (1997: 226) discovered a very similar world-view model for the Wyoming Shoshone in her study of Ghost Dance songs.

Dinwoody Tradition petroglyphs display this same world-view but they do it as a component of the landscape, and in this regard there is a valuable lesson for archaeologists who are interested in the ideological or religious aspects of former life-ways (Fig. 10.10). The use of Shoshone ethnography was extremely helpful in understanding the meaning of the distribution of Dinwoody petroglyphs. I was also helped by the homogeneous nature of the Dinwoody petroglyphs and the relatively constricted boundaries in which they are found. At the same time, and this is an important point, it would have been possible to postulate such a world-view by studying only the distribution and elevation of the flying figures, the four-legged figures and the water figures. In other words, any archaeologist could examine the relationship between petroglyph images and their setting in the landscape and arrive at the same conclusion.

Finally it is important to note that time is not the most important variable in developing the Dinwoody model. The distribution of the petroglyphs and their formal attributes are more important variables than the age of the petroglyphs for deriving the world-view model. The horse and rider image indicates that Dinwoody petroglyphs were still made in the historic period, and this lends credibility to the use of modern ethnography for understanding the meaning of the petroglyphs. At the same time, it is but one of the four-legged creatures in the middle-elevation sites, and even if we did not recognize it as a horse and rider, it would be in its proper position with regard to the world-view model.

Based on this model, I suspect that the relative positions of winged petroglyphs versus terrestrial or aquatic images will fit patterns elsewhere in the world. The model will likely work best in regions where former hunters and gatherers practised transhumance by moving up and down mountain slopes according to resource availability. It may also work in areas where lacustrine or marine resources were exploited part of the year and dry land or inland resources another part of the year. Archaeologists interested in the ideologies of former cultures would do well to study the distribution of the rock-art.

References

Cole, S. J. 1990. *Legacy on stone: rock art of the Colorado Plateau and Four Corners region*. Boulder, CO: Johnson Books.

Dominick, D. 1964. The Sheepeaters, *Annals of Wyoming* 36(2): 131–68. Also published in W. A. Allen, *The Sheep Eaters*: 79–116. Fairfield, WA: Ye Galleon Press, 1989.

Francis, J. E. 1989. Rock art at Legend Rock, in Danny N. Walker and Julie E. Francis (eds.), *Legend Rock Petroglyph Site (48HO4), Wyoming: 1988 archaeological investigation*: 151–208. Laramie, WY: Office of the Wyoming State Archaeologist. Submitted to the Wyoming Recreation Commission, Cheyenne, WY.

Francis, J. E. and L. L. Loendorf. 2002. *Ancient visions: petroglyphs and pictographs of the Wind River and Bighorn Country, Wyoming and Montana*. Salt Lake City: University of Utah Press.

Francis, J. E., L. L. Loendorf and R. I. Dorn. 1993. AMS radiocarbon and cation-ratio dating of rock art in the Bighorn Basin of Wyoming and Montana, *American Antiquity* 58: 711–37.

Gebhard, D. S. 1951. The petroglyphs of Wyoming: a preliminary paper, *El Palacio* 58: 67–81.

1969. *The rock art of Dinwoody, Wyoming*. Santa Barbara, CA: The Art Galleries, University of California, Santa Barbara.

Gebhard, D. S. and H. A. Cahn. 1950. The petroglyphs of Dinwoody, Wyoming, *American Antiquity* 15: 219–28.

Goss, J. A. 1972. A Basin–Plateau Shoshonean ecological model, *Desert Research Institute Publications in the Social Sciences* 8: 123–8.

1999. Rocky Mountain high culture: look, the Utes aren't marginal anymore! Plenary paper presented at the 4th Rocky Mountain Anthropological Conference, Glenwood Springs, CO.

Holmer, R. 1994. In search of the ancestral Northern Shoshone, in David Madsen and David Rhode (eds.), *Across the West: human population movement and the expansion of the Numa*: 179–87. Salt Lake City, UT: University of Utah Press.

Hultkrantz, A. n.d. The Sheepeaters of Wyoming: culture history and religion among some Shoshoni mountain Indians. Handwritten manuscript in 2 volumes. In Hultkrantz's possession.

1957. The Indians in Yellowstone Park, *Annals of Wyoming* 29(2): 125–49. Originally published 1954, *Ymer* (Sweden) 2: 112–40. Also published 1974, in *Shoshone Indians*, translated by Astrid Liljeblad: 215–56. New York, NY: Garland.

1961a. The masters of the animals among the Wind River Shoshone, *Ethnos* (Stockholm, Sweden) 26(4): 198–218.

1961b. The Shoshones in the Rocky Mountain area, *Annals of Wyoming* 33(1): 19–41.

1981. *Belief and worship in Native America*. (Edited by Christopher Vecsey.) New York: Syracuse University Press.

1986. Mythology and religious concepts, in Warren L. D'Azevedo (ed.), *Handbook of North American Indians* 11: *Great Basin*: 630–40. Washington, DC: Smithsonian Institution.

1987. *Native religions of North America: the power of visions and fertility*. San Francisco, CA: Harper and Row.

Husted, W. M. and R. Edgar. 2002 *The archaeology of Mummy Cave, Wyoming: an introduction to Shoshonean prehistory*. Midwest Archeological Center, special report 4; Southeast Archeological Center technical report series 9; US Department of the Interior, National Park Service.

Loendorf, L. 1993. The Water Ghost Woman along the Wind River, Wyoming. Paper presented at 'Shamanism and rock art: interpretations from around the world'. Trinity University and the Witte Museum, San Antonio, TX.

Lowie, R. 1909. The Northern Shoshone, *Anthropological Papers of the American Museum of Natural History* 2(2): 165–306.

Madsen, D. and D. Rhode (eds.). 1994. *Across the West: human population movement and the expansion of the Numa*. Salt Lake City, UT: University of Utah Press.

Mallery, G. 1886. Pictographs of the North American Indians: a preliminary paper, in *Fourth Annual Report of the Bureau of American Ethnology*: 3–256. Washington, DC: Smithsonian Institution.

Nabokov, P. and L. Loendorf. 2002. *American Indians and Yellowstone National Park: a documentary overview*. National Park Service, Yellowstone Center for Resources, Yellowstone National Park, Wyoming.

Shimkin, D. 1986. Eastern Shoshone, in Warren L. D'Azevedo (ed.), *Handbook of North American Indians* 11: *Great Basin*: 308–35. Washington, DC: Smithsonian Institution.

Sowers, T. C. 1939. Petroglyphs and pictographs of Dinwoody. Federal Works Progress Administration, Archaeological Project Report, Casper, WY. Original copy on file at the Coe Library, University of Wyoming, Laramie, WY.

1941. The Wyoming Archaeological Survey: A Report. Federal Works Progress Administration, Archaeological Project Report, Casper, Wyoming. Original copy on file at the Coe Library, University of Wyoming, Laramie, WY.

Steward, J. 1943. Culture element distributions, XXIII: Northern and Gosiute Shoshoni. *University of California Anthropological Records* 8(3): 263–392.

Swanson, E. H., Jr. 1958. Problems in Shoshone chronology, *Idaho Yesterdays* 1(4): 21.

Tipps, B. L. and A. R. Schroedl. 1985. *The Riverton rock art study, Fremont County, Wyoming*. P-III Associates, Inc., Salt Lake City, UT. Submitted to the US Bureau of Reclamation, Great Plains Region Office, Billings, MT.

Vander, J. 1997. *Shoshone Ghost Dance religion: poetry songs and Great Basin context*. Urbana, IL: University of Illinois Press.

Wellmann, K. F. 1979. *A survey of North American Indian rock art*. Graz: Akademische Druck-u. Verlagsanstalt.

11

Friends in low places: rock-art and landscape on the Modoc Plateau

David S. Whitley, Johannes H. N. Loubser and Don Hann

On the Modoc Plateau, in far western North America, rock-art is to be found at low altitudes but not on the heights. The largest rock-art site of the region is at the foot of the Modoc Indians' creation mountain. The pattern of other kinds of sites is strikingly different – and there is a key exception existing as one rock-art site. Why the pattern? Why the exception? A model for landscape symbolism recognizes functional, locational and metaphysical aspects – and it is the last which may be the most important. Insight from regional indigenous knowledge gives the clues to the rationale, in which symbolic meaning is indeed central.

> The contrast between Christianity and its interpretation of history – the temporal dimension – and the American Indian tribal religions – basically spatially located – is clearly illustrated when we understand the nature of sacred mountains, sacred hills, sacred rivers, and other geographical features sacred to Indian tribes. The Navajo, for example, have sacred mountains where they believe they arose from the underworld. Now there is no doubt in any Navajo's mind that these particular mountains are the exact mountains where it all took place. There is no beating around the bush on that. No one can say *when* the creation story of the Navajo happened, but everyone is fairly certain *where* the emergence took place.
>
> Vine Deloria, Jr 1973: 138; emphasis added

Landscape: a physical place, socially constituted

Landscape is a physical place: mountains and valleys and streams. But landscape is culturally and socially constituted, which is to say that it is as much symbolic and conceptual as it is geomorphological. For Native Americans, a central quality of the landscape is its numinous character (Walker 1991) – the fact that it is more or less everywhere inhabited by spirits and shades. This means that any activity on the landscape has the potential to result in a religious experience and to be charged with symbolic meaning. Contrary to Durkheim, the distinction between sacred and profane for the Native American is thus one of time, not simply of space (Walker 1996).[1] Landscape moreover also serves as a 'topographic mnemonic' (Nabokov 1996: 22) which reflects cosmogony and structures ritual acts. In a reflexive sense, landscape is therefore both the product of and the justification for religious belief. Equally importantly, landscape constitutes a strong force in the *prescriptive* aspects of cultural performance and the interpretation of meanings (see Sahlins 1985). This is to say that, because it does not move and because its symbolic meanings are widely shared, landscape is a key conservative element in the transmission of cultural beliefs. Contributing to this prescriptive conservatism is the fact that the ritual acts conducted on the landscape are often still evident, making landscape studies particularly well suited to research on the archaeology of religion.

[1] Thus, the bumper sticker for the California Indian Council reads: 'Everything is Sacred.'

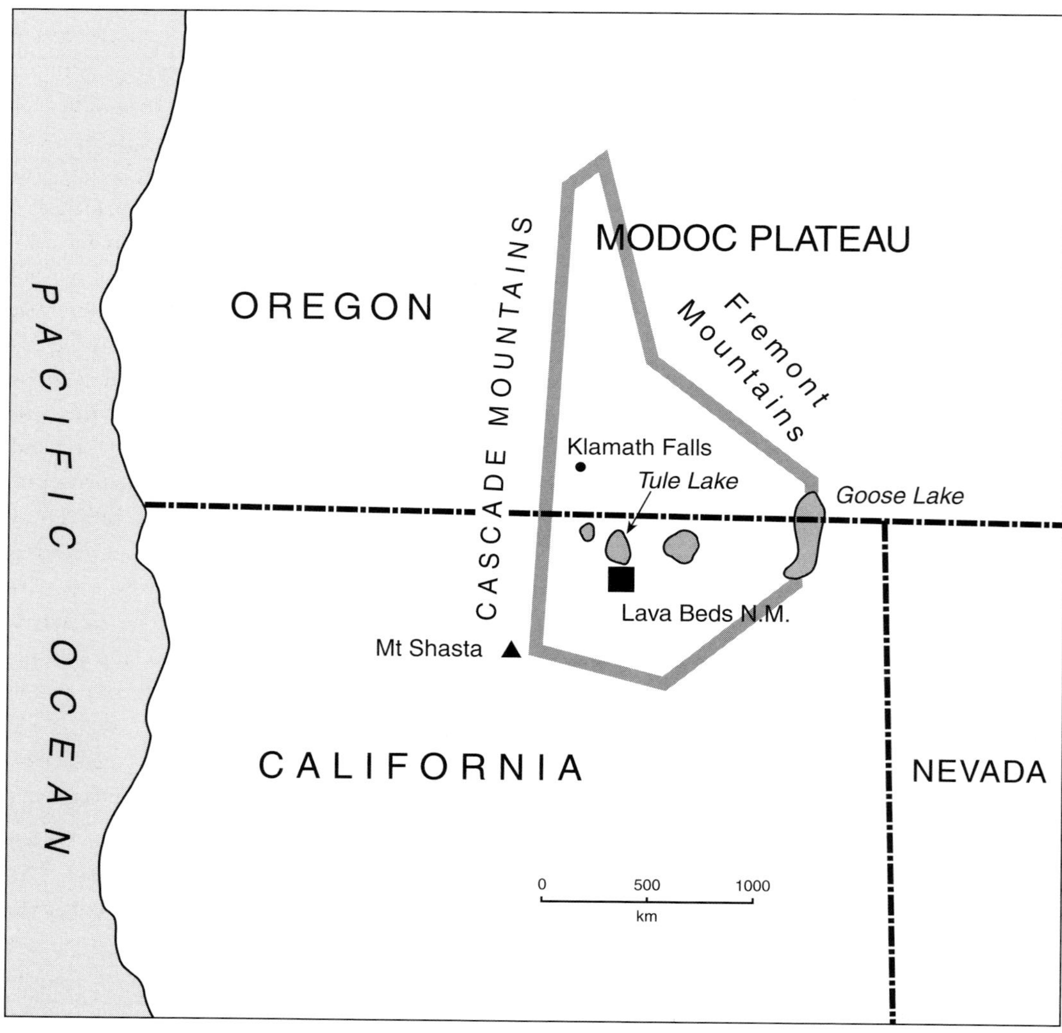

Fig. 11.1. Location of the Modoc Plateau, far western North America.

This is especially true for rock-art, which has in fact been defined along this precise line as *landscape art* (Whitley 1998a: 11; 2000a: 1). In this chapter we consider rock-art sites as an expression of landscape symbolism in a specific region of Native America: the Modoc Plateau (or Klamath Basin), which straddles the California/Oregon border in the western USA (Fig. 11.1). Although rich in paintings and engravings, this area is all but unstudied by rock-art researchers. It provides a valuable opportunity to explore and expand our existing model for Native American landscape symbolism with respect to rock-art sites (Whitley 1998a), as well as to consider some wider issues concerning the nature of shamanistic rock-art.

Rock-art of the Modoc Plateau

The Modoc Plateau is a remote upland region bounded to the west by the Cascade Mountains and to the north, south and east by the Great Basin. Largely volcanic in origin, it is dominated by the internally draining Klamath Basin as its core. Unlike the adjacent but xeric Great Basin, however, the Klamath Basin still contains a series of large bodies of water fed by snow melt from the near-by Cascades, creating an unusually rich and marshy environment.

The Modoc Plateau was occupied historically by the closely related Klamath and Modoc peoples, semi-sedentary hunter-gatherer-fishers who maintained a relatively unique adaptation to their marsh and lake-shore environment. The cultural position of these peoples, even concerning their linguistic affiliation, has been a point of some controversy among anthropologists. Current opinion identifies them as a southern extension of the Columbia Plateau culture area and lists their language as part of the Plateau branch of the Penutian stock (Stern 1998). What is perhaps more important for our purposes is the fact that great time-depth has been documented archaeologically for the adaptations and cultural traditions of these peoples. Sampson (1985) suggests that they may have been in place for as long as 6000 years, a period generally supported by the relative linguistic isolation of the Klamath/Modoc tongue.

The region contains distinctive rock-paintings and engravings in sufficient quantities to justify its identification as one of the rock-art 'style areas' of the far west (e.g. Wellman 1979). A recent regional classification (Whitley 2000b) defines this rock-art as the Modoc Variant of the larger Plateau Rock-Art Tradition, as previously outlined by Keyser (1992).[2] Based on this reclassification, Keyser (in Hann *et al.* in press) has suggested the term 'Klamath Basin Style' as an alternative appellative for this corpus, defined as a regional style dominated by zigzag and circle motifs.

Regardless of name, the engravings are commonly found at open-air sites on relatively soft volcanic tuff and, perhaps for this reason, include a substantial quantity of scratched and abraded motifs along with pecked designs. Paintings are often found in caves, especially basalt lava tubes that are a common geomorphological feature of this region.[3] Pecked, scratched and abraded designs also occur in the tubes, but are far less frequent than paintings. In a few instances scratched and abraded images occur on top of painted black images (Fig. 11.2). Time and/or culture differences cannot be inferred from this superpositioning, however, since no stylistic or preservational differences separate the two besides manufacturing technique. More specifically, the paintings, abradings and scratchings share a common motif repertoire that is dominated by zigzags, circle designs, herringbones, dot patterns, concentrics, sets of parallel lines, hachures/gridirons and

[2] Other descriptions and classifications of this art are provided by Swartz (1978), Gates (1980), Crotty (1981), Lee *et al.* (1988), Hyder and Lee (1990) and Ritter (1999).

[3] The Modoc Plateau has one of the largest concentrations of lava tubes in North America, if not the world, a fact reflected in the existence of Modoc Lava Beds National Monument where many of these are located, and where many of the rock-art sites are found, including the Schonchin Butte site complex, discussed below.

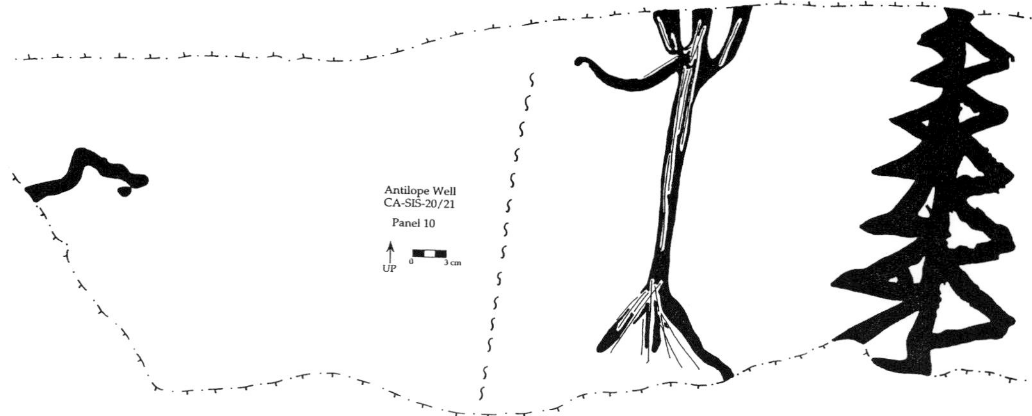

Fig. 11.2. Some of the Modoc Plateau rock-art panels combine both paintings and engravings, although no clear pattern in their possible temporal or stylistic differences has yet been identified. This example is from Antilope Well, one of the Schonchin Butte sites. It combines paintings in black with over-scratching and a pecked motif (vertical broken sinuous line in centre is a salt drip).

simple stick-figure humans (Fig. 11.3); that is, motifs that primarily consist of what we, as Euro-Americans, *identify* as 'geometric patterns'. In the paintings, finger dot compositions are especially common (Fig. 11.4). Of a total of 517 painted motifs recorded in the tubes, black is the dominant colour ($n = 472$, or 91 per cent), followed by red ($n = 27$, or 5 per cent), and white ($n = 18$, or 3 per cent). Most motifs are monochrome but about 10 per cent are bichrome and, more rarely, polychrome. The pigment used was predominantly applied in a liquid medium ('wet paint'), but approximately 16 per cent of the motifs were in fact applied in a dry state ('drawings'), most likely with charred sticks (Loubser and Whitley 1999).

As in many regions in the world, the chronology of Modoc Plateau rock-art is based on disparate lines of often equivocal evidence. Still, a few firm facts matched by some conjectures give us some indication of age. First, there are clear even if rare ethnographic references to the making of the art, demonstrating that it continued to be produced into the historical period – the latter half of the nineteenth century in this region (Hann 1998; Hann *et al.* in press; Keyser and Whitley 2000; Whitley 2000b). In one case, a painted site can be plausibly inferred to date specifically to AD 1872–73, the so-called Modoc Indian War (Loubser and Whitley 1999), supporting ethnographic evidence with respect to age. Another painted site has been AMS radiocarbon dated, yielding chronometric ages for three motifs that range from AD 1020 to post-1440 (Armitage *et al.* 1997). Late prehistoric, protohistoric and historical production of at least some Modoc rock-art seems fairly certain.

Second, on the Columbia Plateau more widely, an engraved panel and a painted roof spall have been found that are stratigraphically buried by Mt Mazama ash (Randolph and Dahlstrom 1977; Cannon and Ricks 1986), indicating in both cases an age greater than 6700 BP and demonstrating rock-art production in this portion of the far west during the early Holocene. Although as yet unconfirmed, geomorphological conditions at Petroglyph Point, a major engraved site on the Modoc Plateau (discussed below), suggest to us that this site may have been in use for more than 5000 years (cf. Lee *et al.* 1988). As yet, however, no indication of significant change over time has been identified

Fig. 11.3. The majority of the painted and engraved motifs on the Modoc Plateau are geometric in shape. This example is one of the more elaborate painted panels from Symbol Bridge, one of the Schonchin Butte sites. All motifs on this panel are painted in black; dotting indicates lighter black pigment.

in the regional corpus, perhaps matching other identified examples of great time-depth and continuity in far western North American rock-art (e.g. Whitley *et al.* 1999a).

Modelling Native American landscape symbolism

The existing model of landscape symbolism for far western North American rock-art was developed with reference to south-central California, the Great Basin and the Colorado River areas (Whitley 1998a). In brief, it has three components. The first concerns the *functional* aspects of rock-art landscape symbolism: sites were thought to be numinous and to serve as portals between this and the supernatural world. In both cases, these functional qualities were tied to the belief that sites maintained unusual quantities of supernatural power or, more precisely, that sites

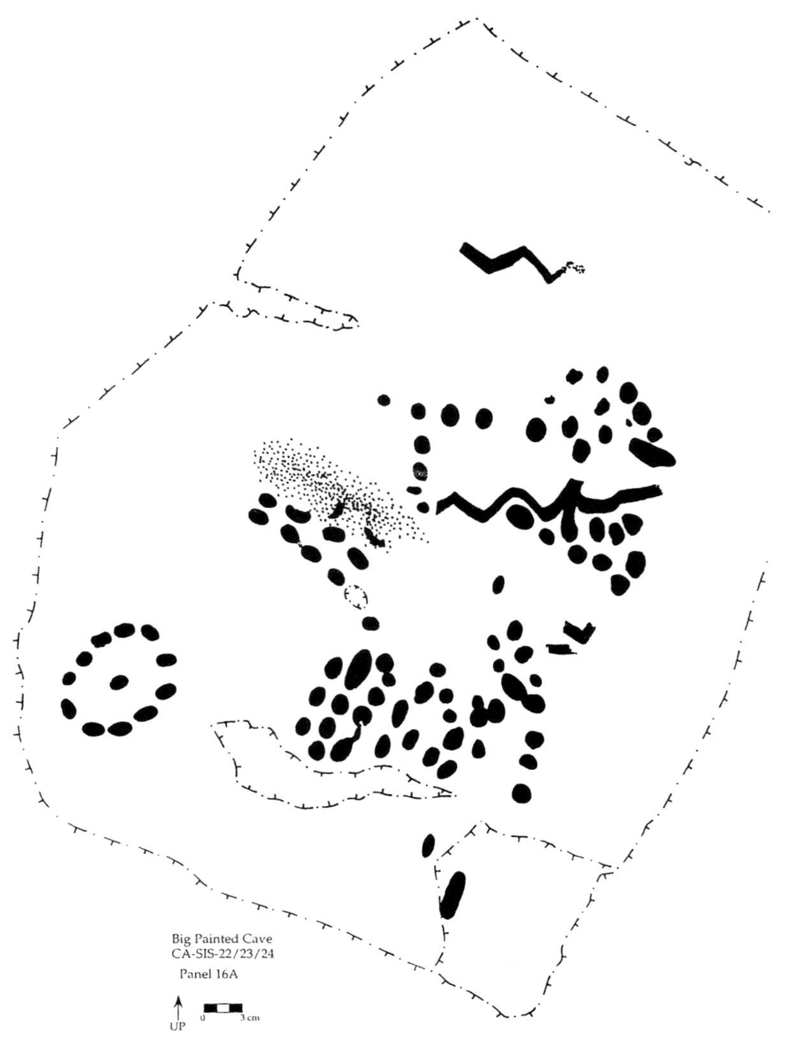

Fig. 11.4. Finger dots, made by dipping a finger in wet pigment and then pressing it against the panel face, are common at certain Modoc sites. In many cases the finger dots are arrayed in distinctive patterns, as shown in this example by the left-most motif. This panel is from Big Painted Cave, one of the Schonchin Butte sites. The dots and lines are all black pigment. A faint area of red pigment, shown by light dotting, is also present on this panel.

were places where this potency came closest to the earth's surface. Rock-art was produced at these locations during vision quests, broadly defined, during which the supplicant entered the supernatural realm to acquire and/or manipulate its power.

The second aspect of the model is *locational.* Rock-art site location was predicated on the distribution of particular kinds of potency, and these have more-or-less predictable distributions. As a general rule, sites occur at relatively low places on the landscape (e.g. at the foot as opposed to on top of a mountain). In a more specific example, the Coso Mountains contain a massive concentration of engravings resulting from the acquisition and manipulation of shamans' rain-making power. In both cases the conceptual logic of these locational patterns was based on a symbolic inversion, with the supernatural thought the inverse of the natural world. Because shamans were predominantly male, and because they sought masculine kinds of power in the sacred, they then used feminine-gendered – low – places on the landscape, which led them to masculine aspects of the supernatural. This also caused them to avoid high peaks as rock-art sites, even though such locations were recognized as potent, because of their masculine associations in the natural world. In a similar fashion, shamans went to the Cosos ('fire' in the Numic languages), effectively the hottest and driest place on the natural landscape, to access its inverse, the wet and verdant aspect of the supernatural, from whence they could best obtain rain-making power.

The third aspect of this model involves its *metaphysical* underpinnings, which are culture-specific. Although this might seem the most esoteric aspect of the model, in fact it may be the most important in terms of relating rock-art sites specifically to more general cultural models of landscape symbolism. In south-central California and the Great Basin, religion maintained a distinction between the supernatural realm of the shaman and the mythic world. The landscape was symbolically structured by both, but the two essentially formed non-intersecting sets. This reflected the belief that mythic time-space, which involved a period prior to human origins, was distinct from supernatural time-space, which parallels the 'modern' natural world. Hence rock-art sites are not at locations of mythic events, nor did shamans generally see mythic actors in the supernatural, and the 'mythic landscape' was therefore distinct from the 'shamanistic landscape'. In contrast, the supernatural was entirely conflated with mythic time-space for Yuman-speakers along the Colorado River, with shamans acquiring their supernatural power precisely by re-experiencing the mythic creation of the world during their vision quest. One result is the location of the largest rock-art and vision quest site in this region, Grapevine Canyon, at the foot of the creation point, *Avikwaame* or Spirit Mountain. In this case mythic and shamanistic landscapes were one and the same.

As is immediately apparent, our existing model for rock-art landscape symbolism identifies widespread commonalties as well as cultural differences in the way that the landscape was conceptualized and ritually used, despite the fact that, in all cases, shamanistic rock-art was involved. As we shall see, the landscape symbolism of Modoc Plateau rock-art further illustrates the variability that exists in shamanistic rock-art.

Ethnography and Modoc Plateau rock-art

One of the main justifications for identifying Modoc Plateau rock-art as a variant of the larger Columbia Plateau Tradition is the fact that its ethnographic production and use are more similar to the pattern seen in this region to the north, rather than to those in the adjacent Great Basin or California Traditions (Whitley 2000b). Modoc rock-art then provides us with a useful comparative case relative to the previously examined regional patterns in landscape symbolism derived from south-central California, the Great Basin and the Colorado River region.

As in other portions of hunter-gatherer North America, Columbia Plateau ethnography ties rock-art to shamanism, and links the motifs to the visionary imagery of trance. Hann *et al.* (in press) have provided the most detailed synthesis of this ethnography (see also Boreson 1975; Benson and Buckskin 1985; Benson and Sehgal 1987; Keyser 1992; York *et al.* 1993; Hann 1998; Keyser and Whitley 2000; Whitley 2000b). According to their synthesis, Columbia Plateau rock-art was made with, used in or maintained symbolic associations with five contexts: (i) shamanic vision questing; (ii) non-shamanic (or *shamanistic*) vision questing;[4] (iii) mythic events, actors and places; (iv) hunting magic; and (v) mortuary complexes. The first three of these are pertinent to the Modoc Plateau (Loubser and Whitley 1999).[5] We discuss the ethnography of shamanic and shamanistic vision questing before turning, in the next section, to the larger issue of mythic associations.

Shamanic vision questing

Following the general Columbia Plateau pattern, a number of ethnographic accounts link Modoc Plateau rock-art with shamanic vision questing; that is, the vision quest conducted by the shaman *per se*. In a letter written in 1878, for example, Dennison claimed that rock-art was still being created at that time and was considered sacred. He described circular rock-paintings near Klamath Lake as 'made by doctors and . . . inspire fear of the doctor's supernatural power' (see also Rau 1882: 65); others he attributed to the creator being or culture hero, *Gmok'am'c*. Riddle, writing in 1890, described a rock-art-filled cave, east of Tule Lake, as a 'medicine man's cave'. Gatschet (n.d.), also writing in the late nineteenth century, referred to a near-by rock-art site with circular motifs as 'conjurer's drawings', likewise meaning those of a shaman. Spier (1930: 142), slightly later, provided the following comment: '[The Klamath] refer to [rock-paintings] as shamans' *mu'lwas*, paraphernalia, or better, objects pertaining to a shaman. They are repainted from time to time by old men, 'who work for a shaman', by which my informant may have meant shamans' interpreters.' Spier (1930: 21) also noted that weather shamans drilled holes in the rock – apparently a reference to cupules or cup-marks – to control the direction of the wind. And like Dennison much earlier, Spier (1930: 142) and Stern (1998: 459) indicated that the rock-paintings were made by the culture hero *Gmok'am'c*. Benson (1998), working with modern consultants, has recorded the making of rock-art by shamans, to portray their visions.

Two points in these comments are most salient. First, that the rock-art is at once said to have been made by shamans yet also by a specific supernatural being parallels other examples in western North America (Whitley 1992; 1998c) and Australia (see Layton 1992: 13). On the Columbia River, for example (Ranck 1926, quoted in Hann *et al.* in press):

> One night a medicine man of the Wishram mixed some paint made from roots. Then an unseen power guided his hand and his brush across the stone . . . The man could not see what he was painting. He worked hard, so that his work would be done before morning came . . . Later he was found, in a trance, at the foot of a rock. A ghostly eye was looking down at him and on the people who came to him. All knew that *Tahmahnawis* [powers, spirits] had painted it.

Among the Modoc specifically, in fact, an individual experiencing a vision was the tool or servant of the visionary spirit, 'doing their will and entirely lacking in personal volition' (Ray 1963: 32). Art created by a spirit was simply a metaphoric attribution to its creation by a shaman.

Second, that the rock-art was described as shamans' *mu'lwas*, paraphernalia, further ties the

[4] Following Taçon (1983), we distinguish *shamanic* from *shamanistic*, with the first meaning 'of or by the shaman, *per se*', whereas the second implicates those acts or practices – or rock-art – of non-shamans which are based on shamanic beliefs and principles.

[5] The specific ethnographic record for the Modoc *per se*, it needs be noted, is relatively limited as a result of the previously mentioned Modoc Indian War (see Riddle 1914; Murray 1959; Dillon 1973). This resulted in the forced removal of the Modocs to a reservation in Oklahoma, where many of them remain today. Most of what exists, perforce, has been collected from the Klamath (see Dennison 1878; Gatschet 1890; n.d.; Curtin 1912; n.d.; Spier 1930; Nash 1937; Ray 1963; Stern 1966; 1998).

motifs to the visionary imagery of the shaman's trance. As was true elsewhere in western North America (Whitley 1998c), this is because all of the shaman's ritual objects were said to be made by the spirits seen during trance (Curtin n.d., myth-127.0). Supporting this contention, Stern (1998: 460) defines *mu'lwas* – the term that Spier (1930) recorded as a name for rock-art motifs – as the objects that represent the shaman's tutelary power.

There is thus a relational implication to these statements, which is important for reasons discussed below. Over a century of ethnographic commentary documents the fact that shamans painted or engraved the spirit helpers of their trances on the rocks. And *Gmok'am'c*, the culture hero, was one of the specific helpers sometimes associated with these shamans.

Modoc Plateau ethnography contains a number of descriptions of the shamans' vision quests, including the procedures followed and the visionary imagery experienced. According to Ray (1963: 33), a prospective shaman spent five nights alone visiting places associated with spirits, while fasting and praying. The most important of these places were deceased shamans' abandoned housepits, and pits and depressions containing snakes and other 'mythological' beings, which is to say low places on the landscape. On the fifth (and most important) night, 'As he stepped into the pit, the seeker fell "dead", that is, unconscious. A fleeting glimpse of a half-human form was had, a figure that resembled vaguely a skeleton' (Ray 1963: 34). Commonly, shamans were described as bleeding copiously from the mouth or nose while in their trance (Spier 1930: 93; Voegelin 1942: 240; Stern 1998: 459). According to Curtin (n.d., myth-127.0):

> Then they would dream. And whatever they dreamed of, grizzly bear, black bear or wolf, coyote, skunk and all kinds of birds, whatever they dreamed of became their medicine [i.e., supernatural helper] and they doctored with it. And snakes, fishes, everything became their medicine.

While the visionary spirits were identified as particular animal species, it is important to note that their 'true' identity and their visionary form were often distinct. Ray (1963: 34) notes that: 'The spirits are butterflies and yet they are human. Their bodies are small, somewhat larger than butterflies. They have small waists and are crystal clear. You can look right through them.' Ray (1963: 31) also states that 'Many spirits appear in kaleidoscopic transition', elsewhere noting that they look like 'sparks' (1942: 237), while they have also been described as 'flashes of fire' (Spier and Sapir 1930: 24). Moreover, a number of ethnographers recorded the appearance of human/animal conflations (Teit 1918: 2; 1930: 194; Ray 1932: 183; Cline 1938: 139; Turney-High 1937: 27; 1941: 170). According to Ray (1963: 33) again: 'all of the spirits of the universe appeared to him but they did not speak. Most of these appeared in animal form, but some looked more like men, women, or children, often of miniature size – "not larger than one's finger".'

The Modoc Plateau ethnography, then, associates shamanic vision questing with low places on the landscape, and relates the creation of this art to the visionary imagery seen during the quest. It also suggests that the form of the visionary image perceived by a shaman differed from its identification or interpretation. Many visionary spirits in fact had the appearance of geometric patterns (sparks, flashes or transparent butterflies), suggesting that the art itself should primarily take such forms. This is apparently a reference to the entoptic light images that are a common component of the mental imagery of trance (see Lewis-Williams and Dowson 1988).

Shamanistic vision questing

In addition to the production of rock-art by shamans to portray the trance imagery of their vision quests, non-shamans also appear to have made rock-art in two related contexts. The first occurred during puberty initiations.[6] These were individual rituals, conducted in isolation and with fasting, that were performed by all people. Typically, these quests did not occur in one location but instead involved the intentional visitation and use of a number of locales on the landscape. These included mountain tops and ridges, which is to say high places on the landscape, lakes and ponds, as well as 'traditional' locales with supernatural associations (Ray 1963: 80). The making of rock structures (cairns and alignments) was particularly common during the puberty quest, especially at high elevations. Indeed, cairns are often the most common kind of archaeological remains at high spots, both here and elsewhere on the Columbia Plateau (e.g. Winthrop *et al.* 1995).

In contrast to the creation of the rock structures, rock-art was apparently never created at high locations but instead was placed lower on the landscape.[7] Included here in at least some cases are shamanic rock-art sites; hence there is not always a distinction between sites made by shamans and by non-shamans. The rock cairns commonly then are not *locationally* associated with the rock-art, even though they are functionally, temporally and ritually linked to it. In this instance the locational distinction between these different types of archaeological features reflects a kind of ritual path across the landscape, involving an intentional movement from high to low places on the terrain.

Like puberty initiations throughout western North America, the primary purpose of the quest was to acquire a spirit helper (Driver 1941). Assuming that the general Columbia Plateau pattern holds for the Modoc region, as all evidence suggests, the art portrays the visionary images of these dream helpers (e.g. Teit 1906: 282; 1909: 590; 1918: 1–2; 1930: 194, 203; Spinden 1908: 231–2; Cline 1938: 136–8; Lerman 1954: 99; York *et al.* 1993: 6; Kennedy and Bouchard 1998a: 184; 1998b: 249).

The second kind of shamanistic vision questing involving rock-art occurred at times of life crisis, such as the birth of a child, marriage, the death of a spouse and so on, sometimes including a downturn in gambling luck (Driver 1941: 31; Ray 1963). These involved adults and in form and substance were essentially identical to puberty quests. Their objectives may have differed in minor detail, but they revolved around three themes: good luck, good health and long life, the attainment of which necessitated spiritual assistance.

The ethnographic record makes two points that are worth noting. (1) Rock-art motifs created during these types of quests were repeated until the power they embodied 'worked' (Gates 1998). Thus occasional repeated motifs on panels may represent multiple visits to a site, engendered in an effort to coax the received power to perform satisfactorily. (2) Some geographical specialization in the kinds of powers obtained at specific places appears to have existed (Ray 1963: 80). This apparently parallels the case in the nearby Great Basin (Whitley 1998a; Whitley *et al.*

[6] It is important to note that Modoc Plateau ethnography is ambiguous with respect to puberty initiation rock-art. No ethnographer directly recorded the making of art during the initiation, nor however was it denied, and it was a very common and widespread practice on the Plateau as a whole (see Hann *et al.* n.d.). Logically, it follows that it did occur in this region, although this is a point that requires verification. On the other hand, life-crisis rock-art was directly documented by Driver (1941: 31). The existence of this practice makes the creation of puberty rock-art all the more likely, if not effectively certain.

[7] The one exception to this pattern that we have been able to identify is discussed below. Although our argument is inferential, there is strong justification for concluding that 'the House of the Rising Sun' was the result of shamanic, not shamanistic, vision questing.

1999b), where specific spirit helpers were more commonly attained at specific locations although, in theory, any kind of power could be obtained at any given vision quest spot.

Rock-art and mythology

A third attribute of ethnographic Columbia Plateau rock-art is the apparent association of certain sites with mythological events, locations and/or actors (Hann *et al.* in press). In fact, determining the significance and implications of such associations is often difficult because many early ethnographers failed to distinguish between mythology, *sensu strictu*, as a kind of pre-human past, and shamanistic tales, which may involve supernatural beings and events and may even be allegorical, yet which occur after the creation of humankind and which putatively include at least one 'real' (i.e. historical) human being (Blackburn 1975). Still, careful attention to a mythic corpus as a whole allows the disentanglement of these different elements.

As noted above, a strict distinction between mythic time-space and the supernatural was maintained in some parts of the far west, with the shamanistic supernatural world carefully separated from the mythic. In other areas the two were entirely conflated, with the shaman's visionary experiences involving re-experiences of past mythic events. On the Columbia Plateau, the distinction between myth and supernatural was instead somewhat fluid. And on the Modoc Plateau specifically, the locations of shamanistic events (including vision quest locales) were often places where mythic events were said to have occurred. Three site examples illustrate this kind of intermediate pattern, which triangulates rock-art site location and landscape symbolism between mythic and supernatural time-space and place.

Schonchin Butte rock-art rites

Schonchin Butte is a locally prominent (1616 m elevation) volcanic cone located within the very rugged *malpais* of the Lava Beds National Monument, California. Its southern and eastern sides are bordered by an extensive system of lava tubes and collapses. These west–east aligned tubes contain a number of rock-art sites and loci, including four sites with six loci, running from east to west, known as Antilope (Antelope) Well, Big and Little Painted Caves, and Symbol Bridge (Fig. 11.5). This complex is located immediately south of the butte, below 1450 m elevation, and represents the biggest concentration of rock-paintings on the Modoc Plateau. Detailed documentation at this complex resulted in the recording of 181 panels containing 449 individual motifs. Over 96 per cent of these are painted; the remainder are scratched or abraded. Dots, straight lines, circles, zigzags and stick-figure anthropomorphs are the most common motifs, with black the most common colour (about 95 per cent of total), followed much less commonly by red and white (Loubser and Whitley 1999).

During our documentation of this Schonchin Butte rock-art for the National Park Service in 1998, some interesting patterns became apparent, notably in terms of placement of the panels. Most immediately apparent is that only a small number of tubes and associated collapse sinks contain rock-art, even though a profusion of 'sterile' tubes and sinks contain protected surfaces perfectly suitable for paintings and engravings. The occurrence of rock-art at only a few locations should accordingly be viewed as the result of deliberate choice. Furthermore, within the selected tubes, rock-art panels tend to occur in certain locations. Most panels are near and/or immediately inside the entrances to the tubes, and no rock-art has been located within the dark zones

Fig. 11.5. The Schonchin Butte site complex, Lava Beds National Monument, consists of a series of lava tubes containing primarily painted images, located at the foot of the locally prominent butte. The entrance to the Antilope Well site is shown here in centre shadow, with the butte in the background.

of the deeper tubes. More specifically, most of the rock-art panels occur at the eastern entrances to the tubes (Table 11.1), all of which face Schonchin Butte. Second, the number of rock-art panels increases from east to west, with Symbol Bridge, the tube closest to Schonchin Butte, having the most panels (Table 11.1).

A notable characteristic of certain panels at these sites is the location of the motifs in near-inaccessible and/or barely visible spots. In some cases this included paintings that are inside very narrow cracks; in others, motifs found under very small and low boulder overhangs (e.g. < 30 cm high). Both circumstances made motif tracing (let alone their original painting) physically difficult. When combined with the fact that the large majority of the images are black pigment on black basalt surfaces, it is apparent that the process of making the art was more a concern than its subsequent visibility. This conclusion is further supported by the relative remoteness of these sites from major villages.

The relationship of these sites to mythological events is demonstrated in two texts, both collected by Jeremiah and Alma Curtin (n.d.) in the 1880s. The first is a myth titled 'Old Man Who Turned into a Screw' (Curtin n.d.: myth-019) which describes the origin of the lava tubes themselves as places on the landscape. The story concerns the treatment of Old Man by his daughter-in-law. Old Man was known as *Lulus-dewieas,* from *lulus*, 'medicine,' implying shamanic power. Following poor treatment by his in-law, Old Man

Table 11.1 *Placement of rock-art panels within the Schonchin lava tubes.*

Lava tube site name	Eastern entrance	Western entrance	Total
Antilope Well	32 panels	0 panels	32 panels
Painted Cave	46 panels	19 panels	65 panels
Symbol Bridge	68 panels	16 panels	84 panels

crept outdoors and sat at the south of the house by the door . . . And as he sat there his thing (*Kak* [penis]) swelled up very big, great big thing, and he took black paint and painted his thing with black stripes, and pretty soon he (it) began to turn and turn and throw up the dirt, and his hair began to be red as flannel, and as the hole got big, and he began to sink in it. There was a great hole . . . And the old man went on boring, and as he went he burst and broke up the dirt. And once in awhile he would raise himself up a little and at such places you might think it was level for a little but the next instant the ground sinks down in a great hole. And he went on every little way bursting and throwing up great piles of dirt, wide openings in the earth . . . And all along the lava beds, he went under (the ground) clear to the other side of Shasta Mountain.

This myth is typical of much Native American symbolism in that it encodes different levels of symbolic meaning. At a superficial level it associates the origin of the lava tubes – the locations of these rock-art sites – with a supernatural event; thus, the sites are not mundane places but instead are ones only created by special powers and circumstances. By this logic they should only be used for special, probably supernatural, purposes. Second, the creation of these tubes is related to painting with black pigment, the most common paint colour at the sites. Painting and black pigment were thus actively implicated in the origin of these sites. Third, this myth also encodes prevailing sexual symbolism. In this case it is apparent that the lava tubes were created by a kind of metaphoric sexual intercourse and thus that they are, specifically, metaphoric vaginas or wombs or, more generally, feminine-gendered places. This fits the far western-wide pattern in the sexual symbolism of rock-art sites that has been discussed above and in detail elsewhere (Whitley 1996; 1998a; 2000b).

Concordance with general sexual/landscape symbolism is further emphasized in this case by three additional facts. The first is the location of this site concentration essentially at the foot of Schonchin Butte, thereby matching the *high:masculine/low:feminine* oppositions seen elsewhere. Confirmation of the local relevance of this symbolic opposition, second, is demonstrated by another Modoc myth (Curtin n.d., myth-001). This specifically locates a woman's 'medicine cave', used for girls' puberty initiations, on the top of a mountain, thus implying the symbolic opposition seen elsewhere. Third, and more generally, sexual intercourse was a widely used metaphor for supernatural trance (Whitley 1994a; 1996; 2000b). That Old Man created the caves by a kind of (metaphoric) sexual intercourse, and that this specifically involved painting, thereby further links these rock-art site locations to trance.

A more direct connection between the *malpais* of the lava beds, presumably therefore the area containing the sites, and vision questing in general is provided in a second myth, 'The Blue *Latkakawas*' (Curtin n.d., myth-107). In this text the culture hero, *Gmok'am'c*, specifically instructed his son *A'isis* to go to the lava beds 'to pile up rocks'; that is, to conduct a puberty quest. The area of the sites is specifically identified by mythic reference as an appropriate location for vision questing.

The relationship between the mythological landscape and the Schonchin Butte rock-art sites is then straightforward. Their existence as supernatural places is a function of certain mythic events. Their use for vision questing and thus rock-art creation, moreover, is also given warrant by myth. Yet there is no direct indication that the supernatural world accessed from these sites was in any way connected with the mythic past. Equally importantly, their location in symbolic terms fits perfectly the general pattern for landscape-gender symbolism seen in other parts of the far west.

Petroglyph Point

A second example of the relationship of rock-art to the mythic landscape is provided by Petroglyph Point (Fig. 11.6), the largest rock-art site in the region (Swartz 1978; Crotty 1981; Lee *et al.* 1988; Hyder and Lee 1990). The rock-art here primarily consists of engravings on a large outcrop of volcanic tuff that, prior to recent alterations in lake levels, extended as a peninsula out into Tule Lake. (Hence the scouring of different lake levels has been used to infer the ages of certain rock-engravings.) According to tabulations by Crotty (1981), the motifs present are almost entirely 'geometric', with circles/ovals, single and parallel lines, zigzags, and dot or punctate patterns predominating. Modoc Plateau engravings then differ from paintings primarily by technique although, in this case, there is a further distinction in that this is a large open site on cliff faces, contrasting with the sheltered and remote nature of the Schonchin Butte sites, which are primarily painted.

Fig. 11.6. Petroglyph Point is the largest rock-art site on the Modoc Plateau. Most of the motifs here are engraved into the relatively soft volcanic tuff which once extended as a peninsula into Tule Lake. The lower portions of the cliff face have been worn smooth by wave action. This site is recorded in Modoc myth as the creation point.

The connection between this large site and mythology stems from the identification of this location as the origin point, where the culture hero *Gmok'am'c* created the physical world, and which constituted the centre of the Modoc realm (Ray 1963: 18; Hann 1998).[8] Mythology then provides the justification for the existence of this sacred place. Again, however, there is no indication that supernatural time-space was otherwise connected to mythic time-space based on this fact: vision questers came to Petroglyph Point because of the power implied by its mythological significance but, once there, seemingly had no direct involvement with the mythic past.

[8] Importantly, cosmogony in far western North America commonly involved two distinct mythic events. These are frequently confused. The first is the creation of the *world*, meaning the physical landscape.

Still, that Petroglyph Point is the largest (and potentially oldest) rock-art site in the region logically follows, for what would be more sacred than the origin point? Like the Schonchin Butte sites, Petroglyph Point furthermore reflects the gendered symbolism of sacred places on the landscapes, sitting at a relatively low rather than high elevation. Indeed, given that the site periodically has been partly inundated by Tule Lake, it is literally *the lowest* possible place on the regional landscape. Strength of supernatural potency and importance, as suggested by the size and age of the site and the nature of its mythic association, may then be partly signalled by its elevational placement at the lowest spot in the Klamath Basin.

The most common theme for world creation is called the 'Earth-Diver Motif' (e.g. Dundes 1962). This involved the actions of (typically) a bird who brought mud up from a primeval sea-bottom to create the land. In the Modoc/Klamath case, *Gmok'am'c* was the responsible party. Mythic events then commonly ensued on the newly created landscape involving the entire repertoire of mythic actors. Almost invariably, the highest mountain in any given group's region was considered the point at which world creation occurred, a mountain that was often inhabited by a female spirit, reflecting the gender inversion that was common in landscape symbolism (see Whitley 1998a).

The second cosmogonic phenomenon involved the creation of *humans*, which occurred after the mythic events and effectively terminated mythic time. This is commonly recounted in terms of a theme referred to as 'The Council of the Elders' (Whitley 1994b) or 'The Transformation of the Animals' (Gayton and Newman 1940; Applegate 1978). In this myth, the so-called 'first people' congregated to decide on their form and fate in the approaching human-cycle of time, and to establish the nature of humanity. In a number of cases, this event constituted the mythic warrant for the appearance of spirit helpers and thus was appropriately associated with some rock-art sites (Malouf and White 1953; Applegate 1978; Whitley 1994b).

In so far as we have been able to establish, the Modoc/Klamath are unusual in citing a relatively low place on the landscape, Petroglyph Point, as the world creation spot, instead of a high mountain, which is the common pattern in the far west (Whitley 1998a). Relatively speaking, Petroglyph Point, however, is the effective centre of Modoc territory, so at least there is a general locational logic to its selection in this sense. This circumstance may reflect the fact that the Modoc Plateau is a large basin ringed by high mountains, none of which was really in Modoc/Klamath territory; hence there is no prominent central mountain which could serve as the creation point. Moreover, *Gmok'am'c*, a male spirit, is said to inhabit the site. Inasmuch as a female spirit, Dwarf Old Woman, is recognized as the inhabitant of at least one nearby high peak, Mt McLaughlin (aka Mt Pitt; see Spier 1930: 119), *Gmok'am'c*'s association with Petroglyph Point otherwise appears to follow the high:low oppositional logic seen elsewhere.

Gmok'am'c's House

The third rock-art site is *Gmok'am'c*'s House, or 'House of the Rising Sun' (Hann 1998). This is a small cave on a high butte east of Tule Lake. The cave measures about 3.5 m wide by 2 m deep, and 1–2 m in height, with an oval entrance about 1 by 1.7 m in size. A notable characteristic of the cave is a second natural opening or 'window', about 50 cm in diameter, in the southern wall. The cave's exterior and interior walls along with the surrounding reddish-orange volcanic tuff cliff face are covered with deeply incised and abraded rock-engravings. In a fashion similar to the Petroglyph Point and Schonchin Butte sites, the primary motifs present are curvilinear meanders, zigzags, V-shaped designs, circles and concentric circles, with the last two elements particularly common. In contrast to these other sites, however, *Gmok'am'c*'s House is located towards the top of the butte, effectively at the highest possible place on the local landscape.

The ethnographic record contains a variety of kinds of information about this site. The first is a manuscript map, drawn by Modoc consultant Jeff Riddle, who sent it to Albert Gatschet at the Bureau of American Ethnology (Riddle 1890). This locates the site on the butte and describes it as a 'ghost cave, medicine man's cave'. The implication of this statement is clear: Riddle identified the site specifically as a shamans' cave, which is to say one used by shamans but not by non-shaman vision questers, and suggested that it was inhabited by spirits ('ghost cave').

A second reference is found in the mythic corpus in a series of accounts of *Gmok'am'c* and his son *A'isis*. These record the existence of mythic events that occurred at '*Gmok'am'c*'s House', one of which involved *Gmok'am'c* instructing and sending his son off on a vision quest (Curtin n.d., myth-107), discussed above. That is, vision questing was given its mythic warrant at this location.

The mythic cycle also describes the site in question and states in part the following (Curtin 1912: 7, 10):

> They went to the top of a high mountain and built a house among the rocks. The house was red and nice to look at. *Gmok'am'c* thought that people around Tule Lake would see his house, but couldn't climb up to it. *Gmok'am'c* had the north side, *A'isis* the south side of the house; the door opened towards the east . . . The house in which *Gmok'am'c* reared his son is seen half way up the mountain. One sees the crimson interior of the dwelling through the openings (windows) above the house.

A series of previous events in the myth, at named spots, make the locational identification of this particular site as *Gmok'am'c*'s House reasonably certain. Reference to the 'openings (windows)' of the house is apparently to the natural aperture or window in the south wall; the red or crimson interior is the cast of the natural reddish-orange volcanic tuff.

Additional ethnographic facts and comments clarify the significance of this location and its rock-art (Hann 1998). First, *Gmok'am'c* was symbolically associated with the Sun and the Morning Star, and his emblem and source of power was a circular disk which he wore on his back. We believe that the circular motifs at the site may be a specific reference to *Gmok'am'c*'s power image; regardless, circular motifs were ethnographically identified as shamans' marks (Gatschet n.d.). Second, although some ethnographers claimed that *Gmok'am'c* was not a shaman's spirit helper, it is well documented that he was the teacher of shamanic knowledge (Ray 1963: 19), which implies if not requires just this role. Likewise, his role as the putative creator of the motifs, recorded in a number of different cases (e.g. Spier 1930: 142; Denison 1878; Curtin n.d., myth-111), further supports this conclusion, as does the association between this site and its rock-art. Third, additional '*Gmok'am'c*'s Houses' have been identified ethnographically, within Klamath rather than Modoc territory (Spier 1930: 143; Curtin n.d., myth-142). This reflects the fact that local variation existed in specific details of the mythic landscape. We thus suspect that the association between *Gmok'am'c* and shamans may be more widespread than the ethnography currently suggests;[9] still, the ambiguity in the ethnographic record on this point suggests that this association was unusual or relatively uncommon.

Gmok'am'c's House then conforms to certain aspects of the general far western North American model for landscape symbolism, but varies on others. As a rock-art site, there is direct evidence tying it to shamans, as is generally the case. Some of the specific motifs at the site have also been independently identified as shamans' marks. And, following the pattern specific to the Modoc Plateau, the site is linked with mythic events and actors, including a spirit that appears to have served as a particularly potent dream tutelary (Hann *et al.* in press).

But what is perhaps more interesting is the manner in which this site varies from the general model; specifically, the symbolic opposition that results in rock-art sites at low landscape positions. As should be clear, *Gmok'am'c*'s House is high, not low on the landscape, thus contrasting with the Schonchin Butte and Petroglyph Point sites and many other localities in the far west. Indeed, in so far as we have been able to determine, the high-elevational placement of *Gmok'am'c*'s House is essentially unique within the Modoc Plateau.

Why this divergence occurs is unclear and it may result from any of a number of circumstances. The primary of these is the possibility that its unique placement reflects some kind of specialized function within the larger context of

9 The ethnographic descriptions of the locations of these additional sites are too ambiguous to allow more than very general placement on the landscape. For this reason, we have not been able to check whether they also contain rock-art.

shamanic vision questing and rock-art production. This possibility is supported by evidence that certain vision quest locales may have yielded specialized kinds of potency (Ray 1963: 80); logically, in this case this implies some kind of unusual power stemming from *Gmok'am'c*, the creator spirit, as a dream tutelary. But only additional ethnographic research will fully resolve this issue.

The making and meaning of shamanistic landscapes

A comparison of the landscape symbolism of Modoc Plateau rock-art with the general landscape model for far western North America raises some important issues concerning the nature of traditional cultures and our ability to interpret the symbolism of even the recent archaeological past. For some archaeologists, seemingly any attempt to employ a general interpretative model, as we have done here, smacks of *essentialism*. By this is meant a monolithic, ahistorical explanation which asserts the existence of invariable and fixed properties, the 'true essences of things'. Commonly, it is contrasted with *difference* which, among others, promotes personal variability, individual agency and change. While essentialism has deep intellectual roots, extending back to the rationalist arguments of Plato and Socrates, it has recently suffered substantial criticism, particularly in feminist and post-colonialist studies. To be sure, the essentialist argument partly reflects larger post-modernist debates over scientific method and knowledge, and the importance of the particular over the general.

The post-modernist debate over science is one we do not wish to enter here beyond noting that both sides engage it using the same tools – computers and telecommunications – developed by the scientific method which one side claims is all wrong. Instead, some general points are in order concerning the implications of the empirical evidence we have developed in the foregoing. First, it is important to emphasize that, in Native America, a tension existed between widely shared belief and symbolic systems, and regional and even personal variations thereof. While far western North American hunter-gatherer religions were fundamentally and inextricably shamanistic, for example, in no way does this somehow negate variability or difference, or imply complete uniformity. Indeed, as Park (1938: 2) stated long ago, 'A merely superficial examination of North American shamanism reveals quite striking differences in content, in meaning, and in the way practices and beliefs are combined with other customs.' This reflects the fact that shamanism is a religious *system*, not a unique *religion, per se*.

Landscape symbolism, ritual and rock-art sites on the Modoc Plateau, then, both fit with but also contrast against the patterns exhibited by neighbouring hunter-gatherer groups, depending upon the scale at which the problem is viewed. All groups at some level distinguished between the sacred and the natural realms, but how they conceptualized the sacred itself varied substantially: Yuman-speaking groups entirely conflated mythic time-space with the supernatural realm of the shaman; the Numic and various south-central California groups made a hard distinction between the two; whereas for the Modoc and Klamath the distinction was quite fluid and, perhaps, not really of concern to them. Yet each of these differing conceptualizations influenced if not determined the form and complexity of their sacred landscapes. Likewise the Modoc/Klamath case shows a general correspondence to widespread patterns in the landscape gender symbolism of rock-art sites. But, in at least one important case, there is also complete (probably intentional) variance from the gender landscape model, for reasons that we do not yet understand. When these facts are combined with the distinctions we have identified concerning the different age and social groups who were responsible for making visionary rock-art in the far west (e.g. Whitley 1998b: 24), arguments that the shamanistic interpretation is monolithic (e.g. Matheny *et al.*1997; Bury 1999; Quinlan 2000; Woody and Quinlan 1999) can then only be understood as the projection of these critics' own essentialist attitudes about shamanism onto the interpretation they are criticizing. As is clear, the model is just a conceptual framework for understanding similar patterns of belief and behaviour, not a prescriptive and invariant structure which implies one single form.

Moreover, as the long history of research on one of the most intensively studied topics in Native American shamanism – the Ghost Dance – has shown (e.g. Mooney 1896 [1996]; Nash 1937; Kehoe 1989; Stoffle *et al.* 2000), nowhere does the shamanistic interpretation deny the possibility of change over time. Yet this fact too must be recognized as playing to another tension that existed in traditional cultures, between continuity and change, especially in light of recent arguments for long-term continuity in shamanistic beliefs in parts of the far west (Whitley *et al.* 1999a; 1999b). Critics of shamanistic interpretations maintain that almost any argument for long-term cultural continuity is 'ahistorical', which thereby denies that prehistoric actors had self-will and personal agency. From this view culture change is then the norm and research should instead address the 'lived experiences' of prehistoric peoples which, presumably, were characterized by variability and difference, not sameness.

Yet it is a well-established fact that traditional cultures and religions are intrinsically conservative (e.g. Steward 1955; Bloch 1974) and thus that continuity, not change, was the norm. In part this results, as Lévi-Strauss has noted, because traditional societies (Lévi-Strauss and Eribon 1991: 125): 'view themselves as primitive, for their ideal would be to remain in the state in which the gods or ancestors created them at the origin of time. Of course this is an illusion, and they can no more escape history than other societies.' Partly explaining this conclusion, Horton (1982) has shown that the cognitive and symbolic systems of traditional, small-scale societies are commonly 'open', meaning that, when confronted with alternatives, they attempt to accommodate new ideas, beliefs, gods and rituals into a pre-existing structure, rather than to replace one system with another. They are accretionary and syncretic, thus contrasting with the kind of 'closed' cognitive system characteristic of the modern west, where different theories, beliefs and religions are always in competition, and where only one is accepted at the expense of the others. Cultures are then differentially prone to change, while certain aspects of cultures are more likely to change than others (e.g. stone tool technology as opposed to religious beliefs) and may not change in tandem (Sahlins 1985).

The point of general models, such as the one that we have explored here, is then not to promote narrowly essentialist views of the past. Rather it is to situate the investigation of the past partly in empirical evidence, and partly in anthropological models that are directly relevant to small-scale traditional cultures, instead of entirely in post-modernist rhetoric and sloganeering, as too often seems now to be the case. With respect to landscape symbolism, this requires acknowledging both that traditional cultures were commonly conservative, and that the landscape itself was a contributing factor in cultural continuity. This of course does not mean that regional variability never existed or that change never occurred. But culture change ultimately is an empirical problem in the archaeological record (Huffman 1986). Where change has occurred in ideological and belief systems, it should be archaeologically discernible in rock-art (e.g. Whitley 1994c) and, as David and Wilson (1999) have shown, in the landscape symbolism of a given region. In the specific case of the rock-art sites of the Modoc Plateau, both widespread similarities with and regional variations from the rest of far western North America existed. This reflects the fact that Native American shamanism itself was a widespread but intrinsically variable phenomenon.

Acknowledgements

The authors would like to thank Gordon Bettles and Mary Gentry, of the Klamath Tribe, and Anne Schneider, for their assistance in the organization and transcription of the Curtin notes; Arlene Benson, who was the first to note the correlation between 'The House of the Rising Sun' site and the myth about *Gmok'am'c*'s House; Tony Greiner, Joe Simon and Dan Leen for their extraordinary efforts during our fieldwork at Lava Beds National Monument; Anne King Smith, Craig Dorman, Chuck Barat, Kelly Fuhrmann and Barney Stoffel, at the Monument, for their aid in numerous ways; Jim Keyser for his participation, commentary and insight into Columbia Plateau rock-art; and the editors of this volume for the opportunity to contribute, along with the help that they have provided us.

References

Applegate, R. B. 1978. *Atishwin: the dream-helper in south-central California*. Socorro, NM: Ballena Press.

Armitage, R. A., M. Hyman, J. Southon, C. Barat and M .W. Rowe. 1997. Rock art image in Fern Cave Lava Beds National Monument, California: not the AD 1054 (Crab Nebula) supernova, *Antiquity* 71: 715–19.

Benson, A. 1998. Interview in film *Eyes in stone: rock art in Modoc*. USDA Forest Service.

Benson, A. and F. Buckskin. 1985. Modoc-75, in Ken Hedges (ed.), *Rock art papers* 2: 133–42. San Diego, CA: San Diego Museum of Man. Museum Papers 18.

Benson, A. and L. Sehgal. 1987. The light at the end of the tunnel, in Ken Hedges (ed.), *Rock art papers* 5: 1–17. San Diego, CA: San Diego Museum of Man. Museum Papers 23.

Blackburn, T. C. 1975. *December's child: a book of Chumash oral narratives*. Berkeley, CA: University of California.

Bloch, M. 1974. Symbols, song, dance and features of articulation: is religion an extreme form of traditional authority? *Archives, European Journal of Sociology* 15: 55–81.

Boreson, K. 1975. Rock art of the Pacific Northwest. MA thesis, University of Idaho, Pocatello, ID.

Bury, R. 1999. Too many shamans: ethics and politics of rock art interpretation, *American Indian Rock Art* 25: 149–54.

Cannon, W. and M. Ricks. 1986. *The Lake County, Oregon, rock art inventory: implications for prehistoric settlement and land use patterns*. Portland, OH: Association of Oregon Archaeologists. Contributions to the Archaeology of Oregon 3.

Cline, W. 1938. Religion and world view, in L. Spier (ed.), *The Sinkaietk or southern Okanagan of Washington*: 133–82. Menasha, WI: Laboratory of Anthropology. General Series in Anthropology 6, Contributions from the Laboratory of Anthropology 2.

Crotty, H. 1981. Petroglyph Point revisited: a Modoc County site, in C. W. Meighan (ed.), *Messages from the past: studies in California rock art*: 141–68. Los Angeles, CA: Institute of Archaeology, UCLA. Monograph 20.

Curtin, J. 1912. *Myths of the Modocs*. Boston, MA: Little, Brown.

n.d. Unpublished ethnographic notes on the Modoc and Klamath. National Anthropological Archives.

David, B. and M. Wilson. 1999. Re-reading the landscape: place and identity in NE Australia during the late Holocene, *Cambridge Archaeological Journal* 9: 163–88.

Deloria, V., Jr. 1973. *God is red*. New York: Grosset and Dunlap.

Denison, J. S. 1878. Letter to Samuel Gatschet. Bureau of American Ethnology document 315. Washington, DC: Smithsonian Institution.

Dillon, R. 1973. *Burnt-out fires: California's Modoc Indian war*. Englewood Cliffs, NJ: Prentice-Hall.

Driver, H. E. 1941. *Cultural element distributions, XVI: Girls' puberty ceremonies in North America*. Berkeley, CA: University of California. Anthropological Records 6(2).

Dundes, A. 1962. Earth-diver creation of the

mythopoeic male, *American Anthropologist* 64: 1032–51.

Gates, G. R. 1980. A preliminary report on the prehistoric rock art of the Modoc National Forest, *Journal of the Modoc County Historical Society* 2: 79–104.

1998. Interview in film *Eyes in stone: rock art in Modoc.* USDA Forest Service.

Gatschet, A. S. 1890. *The Klamath Indians of southwestern Oregon.* Washington (DC): US Geographical and Geological Survey of the Rocky Mountain Region. Contributions to North American Ethnology 2 Part 1.

n.d. Miscellaneous papers and notes collected from the Klamath and Modoc tribes. Bureau of American Ethnology documents 610, 1995, 2019, 2849, 2975, 3686, 3990. Washington (DC): Smithsonian Institution.

Gayton. A. H. and S. S. Newman. 1940. *Yokuts and western Mono myths.* Berkeley, CA: University of California Press. Anthropological Records 5(1).

Hann, D. 1998. House of the Rising Sun: using the ethnographic record to illuminate aspects of Klamath Basin rock art. Paper presented at the 63rd Annual Meeting of the Society for American Archaeology, Seattle, WA.

Hann, D., J. D. Keyser and P. M. Cash Cash. In press. Columbia Plateau rock art: a window to the spirit world, in David S. Whitley (ed.), *Ethnography and western North American rock art.* Walnut Creek, CA: Altamira Press.

Horton, R. 1982. Tradition and modernity revisited, in M. Hollis and S. Lukes (eds.), *Rationality and relativism*: 201–60. Cambridge, MA: The MIT Press.

Huffman, T. N. 1986. Cognitive studies of the Iron Age in Africa, *World Archaeology* 18: 84–95.

Hyder, W. and G. Lee. 1990. Modoc rock art: a reevaluation, *American Indian Rock Art* 16: 237–52.

Kehoe, A. 1989. *The Ghost Dance: ethnohistory and revitalization.* New York: Holt, Rinehart and Winston.

Kennedy, D. and R. Bouchard. 1998a. Lillooet, in D. Walker, Jr. (ed.), *Handbook of North American Indians* 12: *Plateau*: 174–90. Washington, DC: Smithsonian Institution.

1998b. Northern Oakanagan, Lakes and Colville, in D. Walker, Jr. (ed.), *Handbook of North American Indians* 12: *Plateau*: 238–52. Washington, DC: Smithsonian Institution.

Keyser, J. D. 1992. *Indian rock art of the Columbia Plateau.* Seattle, WA: University of Washington Press.

Keyser, J. D. and D. S. Whitley. 2000. A new ethnographic reference for Columbia Plateau rock art: documenting a century of vision quest practices, *INORA: International Newsletter of Rock Art* 25: 14–20.

Layton, R. 1992. *Australian rock art: a new synthesis.* Cambridge: Cambridge University Press.

Lee, G., W. Hyder and A. Benson. 1988. The rock art of Petroglyph Point and Fern Cave, Lava Beds National Monument. Report on file, Lava Beds National Monument, Tulelake, CA.

Lerman, N. H. 1954. Okanogan (Salish) ethnology. Field notes and manuscript. Melville Jacobs Collection, University of Washington Library Archives, Seattle, WA.

Lévi-Strauss, C. and D. Eribon. 1991. *Conversations with Claude Lévi-Strauss.* Chicago, IL: University of Chicago Press.

Lewis-Williams, J. D. and T. A. Dowson. 1988. The signs of all times: entoptic phenomena in Upper Paleolithic art, *Current Anthropology* 29: 201–45.

Loubser, J. H. N. and D. S. Whitley. 1999. Recording eight places with rock imagery: Lava Beds National Monument, Northern California. Report on file, Lava Beds National Monument, Tulelake, CA.

Malouf, C. I. and T. White. 1953. The origin of pictographs, *Montana State University Anthropology and Sociology Papers* 15: 30–1.

Matheny, R. T., T. S. Smith and D. G. Matheny. 1997. Animal ethology reflected in the rock art of Nine Mile Canyon, Utah, *Journal of California and Great Basin Anthropology* 19: 70–103.

Mooney, J. 1896. The Ghost-Dance religion and the Sioux outbreak of 1890, *Fourteenth Annual Report of the Bureau of Ethnology* part 2: 645–1136. Washington, DC: Government Printing Office. (Facsimile reprint. North Dighton: JG Press, 1996.)

Murray, K. A. 1959. *The Modocs and their war.* Norman, OK: University of Oklahoma Press.

Nabokov, P. 1996. Native views of history, in B. G. Trigger and W. E. Washburn (eds.), *The Cambridge history of the native peoples of the Americas* 1: *North America* Part 1: 1–59. Cambridge: Cambridge University Press.

Nash, P. 1937. The place of religious revivalism in the formation of the intercultural community on Klamath Reservation, in F. Eggan (ed.), *Social anthropology of North American tribes*: 377–442. Chicago, IL: University of Chicago Press.

Park, W. Z. 1938. *Shamanism in western North America: a study in cultural relationships*. Evanston, IL: Northwestern University Press. Northwestern University Studies in the Social Sciences 2.

Quinlan, A. 2000. The Ventriloguists dummy: a critical review of shamanism and rock art in far western North America. *Journal of California and Great Basin Anthropology* 22: 92–108.

Ranck, G. 1926. Tribal lore of Wishram Indians rich in traditions of Columbia, *Sunday Oregonian* (Portland, OR), 7 February.

Randolph, J. and M. Dahlstrom. 1977. *Archaeological test excavations at Bernard Creek Rockshelter*. Moscow, ID: University of Idaho. Anthropological Research Manuscript Series 42.

Rau, C. 1882. *Observations on cup-shaped and other lapidarian sculptures in the Old World and in America*. Washington, DC: Bureau of American Ethnology. Contributions to North American Ethnology 5.

Ray, V. 1932. *The Sanpoil and Nespelem: Salishan peoples of northeastern Washington*. Seattle, WA: University of Washington Press.

1942. *Cultural Element Distributions, XXII. Plateau*. Berkeley, CA: University of California. Anthropological Records 8(2).

1963. *Primitive pragmatists: the Modoc Indians of northern California*. Seattle, WA: University of Washington Press.

Riddle, J. C. 1890. Letter to Albert Gatschet. Bureau of American Ethnology document 3743.

1914. *The Indian history of the Modoc War*. Reprinted, San Jose, CA: Urion Press, 1974.

Ritter, E. W. 1999. Boundary, style and function: extrapolations from the Keno, Oregon, pictographs, *American Indian Rock Art* 25: 81–101.

Sahlins, M. 1985. *Islands of history*. Chicago, IL: University of Chicago Press.

Sampson, C. G. 1985. *Nightfire Island: later Holocene lakemarsh adaptation on the western edge of the Great Basin*. Eugene, OR: University of Oregon. Anthropological Papers 33.

Spier, L. 1930. Klamath ethnography, *University of California Publications in American Archaeology and Ethnology* 30(1): 1–338.

Spier, L. and E. Sapir. 1930. Wishram ethnography, *University of Washington Publications in Anthropology* 3(3): 151–300.

Spinden, H. J. 1908. *The Nez Percé*. Washington, DC: American Anthropological Association. Memoirs 2(3).

Stern, T. 1966. *The Klamath Tribe: a people and their reservation*. Vancouver: University of Washington Press.

1998. Klamath and Modoc, in D. Walker, Jr. (ed.), *Handbook of North American Indians* 12: *Plateau*: 446–66. Washington, DC: Smithsonian Institution.

Steward, J. H. 1955. *Theory of culture change: the methodology of multilinear evolution*. Chicago, IL: University of Chicago Press.

Stoffle, R. W., L. Loendorf, D. E. Austin, D. B. Halmo and A. Bulletts. 2000. Ghost Dancing the Grand Canyon: Southern Paiute rock art, ceremony and cultural landscapes, *Current Anthropology* 41(1): 11–38.

Swartz, B. K., Jr. 1978. *Klamath Basin petroglyphs*. Socorro, NM: Ballena Press.

Taçon, P. S. C. 1983. An analysis of Dorset Art in relation to prehistoric culture stress, *Inuit Studies* 7(1): 41–65.

Teit, J. 1896. A rock painting of the Thompson River Indians, *American Museum of Natural History Bulletin* 8: 227–30.

1906. The Lillooet Indians, *Memoirs of the American Museum of Natural History* 2(5): 193–300.

1909. The Shushwap, *Memoirs of the American Museum of Natural History* 2(8).

1918. Notes on rock painting in general, 1918. Unpublished manuscript, Glenbow Alberta Institute Archives.

1930. The Salishan tribes of the Western Plateau, in *Bureau of American Ethnology 45th Annual Report*: 23–396. Washington, DC: Smithsonian Institution.

Turney-High, H. H. 1937. *The Flathead Indians of Montana*. Washington, DC: American Anthropological Association. Memoirs 48.

1941. *Ethnography of the Kutenai*. Washington, DC: American Anthropological Association. Memoirs 56.

Voegelin, E. W. 1942. Culture element distributions: XX, Northeast California, *University of California Anthropological Records* 7(2): 47–252.

Walker, D. E., Jr. 1991. Protection of American Indian sacred geography, in C. Vecsey (ed.), *Handbook of American Indian religious freedom*: 100–15. New York: Crossroad Publishing.

1996. Durkheim, Eliade and sacred geography in northwestern North America, in D. Dumond (ed.), *Chin Hills to Chiloquin: papers honoring the versatile career of Theodore Stern*: 63–8. Eugene, OR: University of Oregon Press.

Wellmann, K. F. 1979. *A survey of North American Indian rock art*. Graz: Akademische Druck-u. Verlagsanstalt.

Whitley, D. S. 1992. Shamanism and rock art in far western North America, *Cambridge Archaeological Journal* 2: 89–113.

1994a. Shamanism, natural modeling and the rock art of far western North American hunter–gatherers, in Solveig A. Turpin (ed.), *Shamanism and rock art in North America*: 1–43. San Antonio, TX: Rock Art Foundation. Special Publication 1.

1994b. Ethnohistory and south-central California rock art. Paper presented at 1994 IRAC, Flagstaff, AZ. (In press, IRAC proceedings, edited by K. Hedges.)

1994c. By the hunter, for the gatherer: art, social relations and subsistence change in the prehistoric Great Basin, *World Archaeology* 25: 356–73.

1996. *A guide to rock art sites: southern California and southern Nevada*. Missoula, MT: Mountain Press.

1998a. Finding rain in the desert: landscape, gender and far western North American rock-art, in C. Chippindale and P. S. C. Taçon (eds.), *The archaeology of rock-art*: 11–29. Cambridge: Cambridge University Press.

1998b. Cognitive neuroscience, shamanism and the rock art of native California, *Anthropology of Consciousness* 9: 22–37.

1998c. Meaning and metaphor in the Coso petroglyphs: understanding Great Basin rock art, in E. Younkin (ed.), *New perspectives on the Coso petroglyphs*: 109–74. Ridgecrest, CA: Maturango Museum.

2000a. Rock art and rock art research in a worldwide perspective: an introduction, in David S. Whitley (ed.) *Handbook of rock art research*: 7–54. Walnut Creek, CA: Altamira Press.

2000b. *The art of the shaman: Native American rock art of California*. Salt Lake City, UT: University of Utah Press.

Whitley, D. S., R. I. Dorn, J. M. Simon, R. Rechtman and T. K. Whitley. 1999a. Sally's Rockshelter and the archaeology of the vision quest, *Cambridge Archaeological Journal* 9: 221–47.

Whitley, D. S., J. M. Simon and R. I. Dorn. 1999b. The vision quest in the Coso Range, *American Indian Rock Art* 25: 1–31.

Winthrop, R. H., K. R. Winthrop and D. J. Gray. 1995. Rock feature sites on the Mt Hood national forest: an inventory and evaluation. Unpublished report on file, Mt Hood National Forest, Gresham, OR.

Woody, A. and A. Quinlan. 1999. Marks of distinction – rock art and ethnic identification in the Great Basin. Paper presented at the biennial Great Basin Anthropological Conference, Bend, OR.

York, A., R. Daly and C. Arnett. 1993. *They write their dreams on rocks forever: rock writings of the Stein River Valley of British Columbia*. Vancouver, BC: Talonbooks.

12

Dangerous ground: a critique of landscape in rock-art studies

Benjamin W. Smith and Geoffrey Blundell

Recent decades have seen a flourishing new approach to southern African rock-art that draws on Khoi-San ethnohistory. It is instructive to see the perceptions of landscape that lie behind both the earlier work and the current studies. And the routine approaches to landscape of the archaeologists, it turns out, lead to negligible insights – because San knowledge turns out to have different concerns, different parameters. Fortunately, we have sufficient informed knowledge to gain some actual insight into the pattern of San rock-art, and of the images also made in the landscape by farming and by herding peoples, each with their own experience of landscape, each with their distinctive attitude to landscape.

Finding one's place

The northern part of South Africa (Fig. 12.1) is a rich area for landscape studies because, unusually for the whole subcontinent, it has rock-arts made by both Bantu-speaking farmer and Khoe-speaking herder peoples alongside, and amongst, the better-known art of San hunter-gatherers (Hall and Smith 2000). Ethnographic and ethnohistorical records for these three peoples provide some indications as to how each group perceived and used the landscape (Eastwood and Blundell 1999; Hall and Smith 2000; Smith and Van Schalkwyk 2002). We therefore chose this region to ask crucial methodological questions about the varied approaches advocated by 'landscape archaeology'. How might a chapter on northern South African rock-art have looked had we no relevant ethnography but only theoretical underpinnings? The best way to find an answer to this question is to construct an interpretation of northern South African rock-art and its place in the landscape without recourse to ethnography. Indeed, the region provides an unusually useful 'laboratory' for 'testing' key aspects of landscape methodology as it is widely practised today. The results of our evaluation proved more valuable than we had anticipated – and alarming.

We begin with a critique of some early approaches to the relationship between rock-art and landscape. From this we move on to a history of inappropriate Eurocentric assumptions that implicitly underpin – and vitiate – many landscape studies. Finally, we turn to our study area and, drawing on ethnography, discuss these methodological issues in relation to the three rock-art traditions. Our findings show that certain rock-art/landscape studies are in fact seriously flawed.

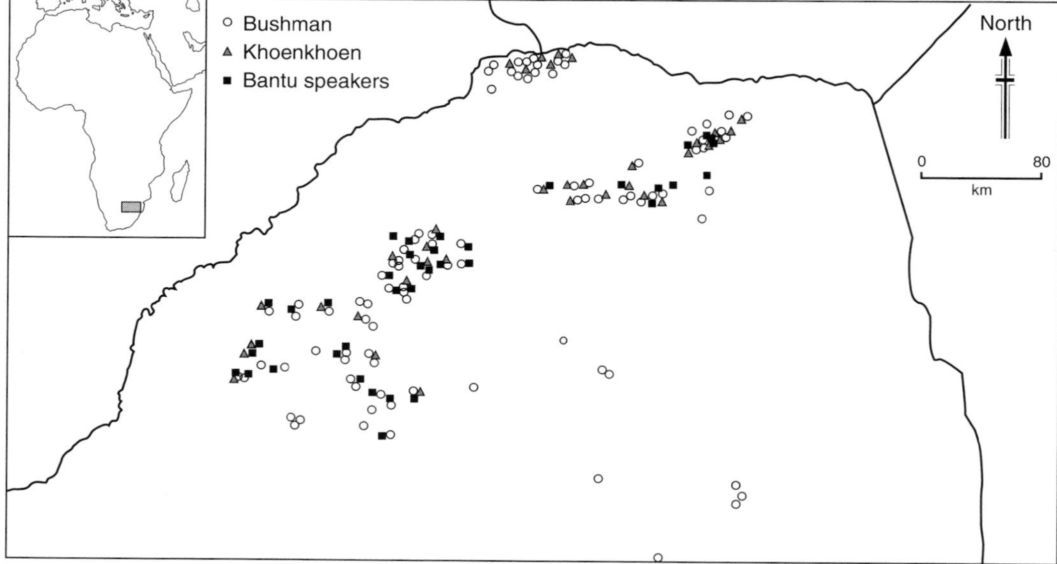

Fig. 12.1. Map of southern Africa showing the northern part of South Africa that forms the study area, with rock-art sites.

A naïve approach to landscape

A consideration of landscape in southern African rock-art research is not new. Prior to the 1970s, writers tended to start with an account of the landscape. For example, Alex Willcox, writing in 1963, began (Willcox 1963: 4):

> The rationale of the distribution of the rock-art becomes clear only if considered in relation to the geomorphology of the country. Other problems involve consideration of climate, petrology and general archaeology. This chapter aims to review the elementary facts of the subjects – as far as relevant to South Africa and our theme – for the benefit of the newcomer to such studies.

Six years later, Cran Cooke wrote (Cooke 1969: 27–8):

> In Rhodesia [now Zimbabwe] the paintings occur, almost without exception, in the granite areas. These areas consist primarily of bare hills and deep gorges which have been eroded along the natural joint fractures in the rock. The country amongst these hills is very broken and the granite sands below them not very suitable for agriculture . . . In these granite hills after normal rainy seasons, natural foods are abundant . . . The region teems with animal life.

Both these studies were products of their time; they followed old perceptions that southern African painters, as primal ecologists, were deeply influenced, and perhaps conditioned, by the landscape in which they lived. It therefore seemed natural that to understand the art one had to understand the landscape, though the ways in which the art was moulded by landscape were seldom made clear: assertion was sufficient. Willcox (1984: 1) was one who did try to be more specific. He began his later visitors' guide to Drakensberg rock-art:

> If you go hunting yourself for painting sites you might find a few under any overhang, but remember that the inhabited caves sizeable 'galleries' usually face north or east – the Bushmen liked sun, especially in the mornings – and have a fair amount of level floor, not too steep an approach and water hard by.

This idyllic picture seemed reasonable enough to those who believed the San had some sort of mystical relationship with preternatural 'Nature'. In fact, this distribution is a function of the geology and geomorphology. It is a feature of the geomorphology of the Drakensberg that virtually all habitable shelters face north or east. Where the geology allows there are south-facing shelters with paintings. The pattern of sites on the landscape is therefore not a conscious plan of the artists.

Looking at these descriptions, one can see that they go hand-in-hand with beliefs not only about the San but also about their art. In particular, the belief that the images were done as a pleasing backdrop to everyday life infected all aspects of research. The art was portrayed as embellishing, or marking, parts of a landscape that conditioned the daily lives of the painters. Researchers therefore emphasized the closeness of paintings to material sustenance – food sources, water, shelter and so on.

We dub this the 'Heizer and Baumhoff approach' after its original US advocates. In their remarkably detailed study, Robert Heizer and Martin Baumhoff (1962) examined the placement of every motif in their Nevada and eastern California study area. When they came to explain the patterns of distribution, their perception of Native American rock-art as a product of sympathetic magic that was intimately associated with material life led them to hypothesize a link between the images and food procurement. They found that the patterns discovered correlated strongly with places of the 'hunting of large game' and weakly with places of 'seed collecting, rabbit hunting or fishing' (1962: 239). They therefore claimed to have 'proved' a link between the art and large-game hunting.

The 'Heizer and Baumhoff approach' encouraged a generation of archaeologists to plot the positions of sites in the landscape and then to juxtapose the distribution pattern that they found with natural features, like game trails and narrow defiles. As archaeological theorists moved from processual to post-processual perspectives, this kind of spatial analysis largely fell away. The shift happened at a time when researchers began to emphasize that, although landscape may appear to be a given, all perceptions of it are culturally mediated. This means that archaeologists may not perceive factors that may have been crucial in determining the placement of a set of sites. In Heizer and Baumhoff's case, we ask how many other patterns, such as places where important vision quests had been experienced (Loendorf 1994; Whitley *et al.* 1999), or where great healing events had occurred, would have shown a stronger correlation with the pattern of Nevada and eastern California images than the pattern of sites suited to game hunting? As we shall see, these are not idle or mischievous questions.

A phenomenological approach to landscape

As a reaction to such naïve approaches, there developed what have been called phenomenological approaches to landscape. Such approaches owe much to the phenomenological philosophy of Martin Heidegger and Maurice Merleau-Ponty (see, for example, Bender 1993; Tilley 1994; David and Wilson 1999). These perspectives 'at best . . . promise . . . guidance towards a new perspective and experience of archaeology, a new exploration of the past' (David and Wilson 1999: 295). This is a large claim. How justified is it? Phenomenological approaches consider the ways in which landscape was symbolically experienced by the peoples in the archaeological record. Landscape, so these approaches contend, is about 'identity', about 'being-in-the world'. Phenomenological studies seek to go beyond researchers' subjectivity and to embrace 'other' and 'individual' perceptions of landscape and examine how these 'informed' past behaviour.

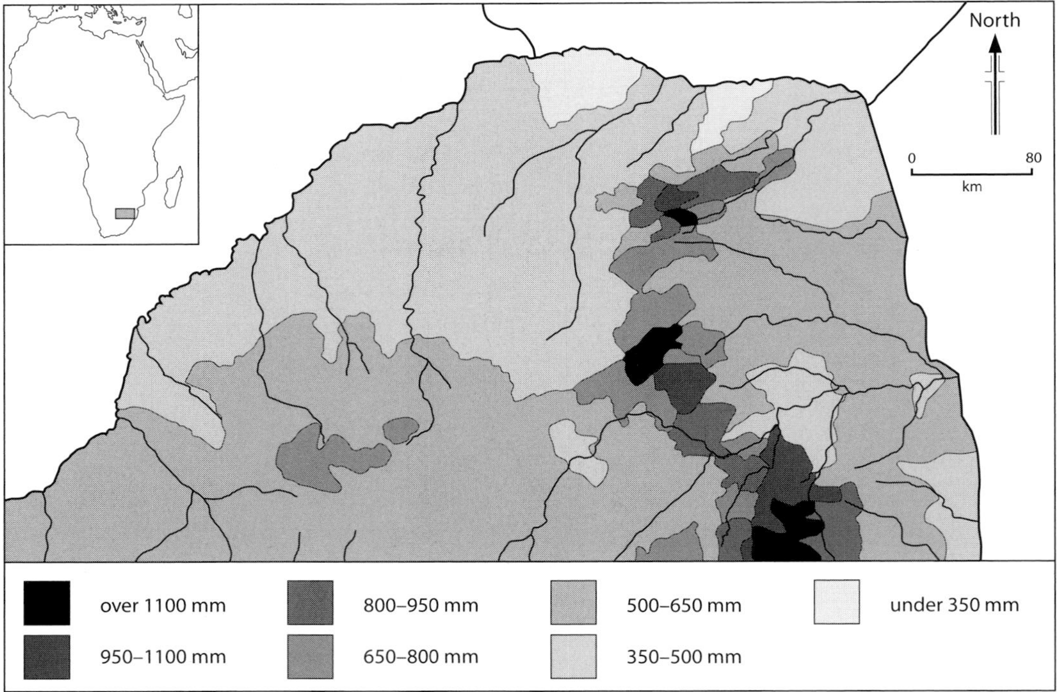

Fig. 12.2A. Rainfall figures for the northern part of South Africa. After Low and Rebelo (1996: 405).

In choosing an approach for our northern South African landscape study, we felt strongly inclined towards this kind of phenomenological approach. So far as we could determine from the literature, the methodology of phenomenology required us to 'immerse' ourselves in the landscape; we would have to try to *experience* the landscape as the makers of the art did. We did not see this as a problem. With a great deal of field experience in this place, and much experience in similar landscapes, between us we did indeed feel, at least partly, 'immersed'. Long stints of camping in the varied terrain have left us with no doubt of the perils and harshness of the area, and our experience seemed to encourage our confidence in the phenomenological approach. One can get little sense of this feeling of place from studying maps of northern South Africa. These show a land dominated by flat sand and gravel plains, with rainfall varying from 250 mm to 2000 mm (Fig. 12.2A). The maps do not suggest a sense of the overwhelming dryness, barrenness, dustiness and inhospitable nature of the plains. It is regularly too hot, dry and difficult for us to live and work comfortably.

Low and Rebelo, the compilers of the South African vegetation maps, explain that northern South Africa falls into their 'savanna biome' vegetation area (Fig. 12.2B). They characterize the area 'as a grassy ground layer with a distinct upper layer of woody plants' (Low and Rebelo 1996: 19) and then list many plant names to emphasize an unusually rich botanical diversity. Again, our perceptions are different from those of Low and Rebelo. For us, the grassy ground layer is notable for its ability to support a generous quantity of

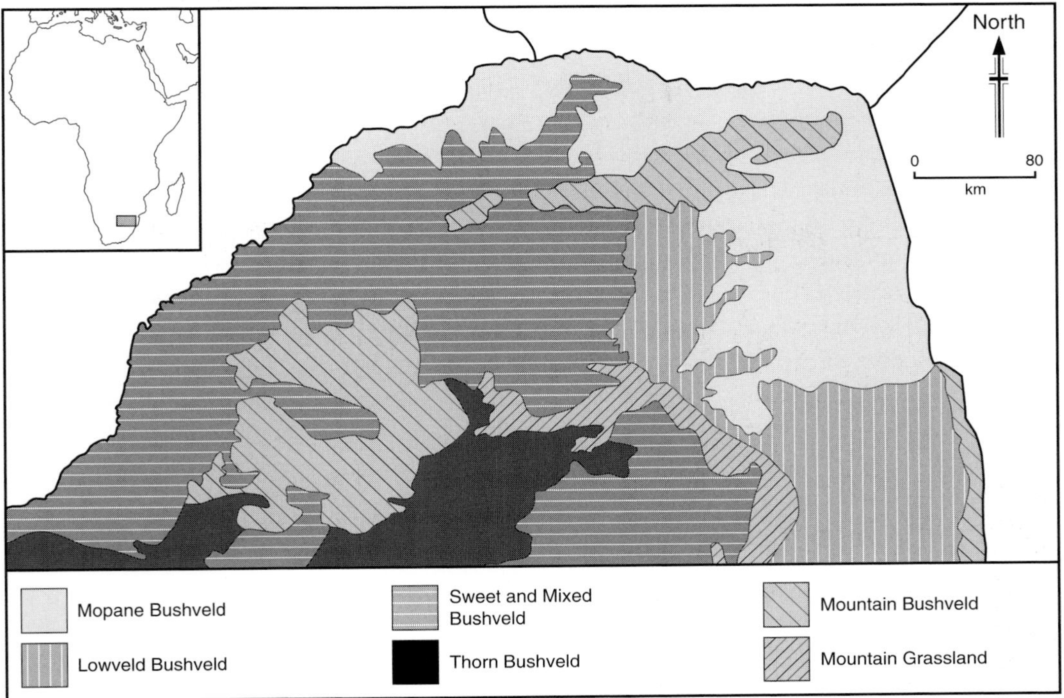

Fig. 12.2B. Vegetation zones for the northern part of South Africa. After Low and Rebelo (1996: 405).

game and domestic stock. It is observably fragile, quickly and seriously damaged if overgrazed. The upper woody layer is more notable to us for its occasional shade than for its distinctive or diverse characteristics that are foregrounded by Low and Rebelo. The trees become particularly meritworthy in autumn when their *marula* fruits allow the production of bountiful local beer. The vegetation as a whole falls between the Low and Rebelo categories of Shrubveld and Woodland. It is known locally as Bushveld. The Bushveld of the plains is somewhat stunted and annoyingly dense in thorn trees and spiky plants. In the past, the area was rich in wildlife, and therefore a fine home for those hunters brave enough to face all of Africa's most dangerous larger mammals. We are constantly reminded that some of these dangerous creatures still lurk in the surrounding bush as we record the images of them that feature in the art.

Rivers run across the plains seasonally, all ultimately discharging into the crocodile-filled Limpopo River, which forms the South Africa–Zimbabwe border and the northern boundary of the study area. This pattern of plains and seasonal rivers is broken occasionally by what geologists describe as hill ranges of 'quartzitic sandstone with inclusions'. These are known locally as *bergs*. Some are impressive, towering nearly 1000 m above the surrounding plains. One can read from the rain and temperature maps that these areas are cooler and better watered, but the maps do not represent the degree to which the hills seem more shaded, sheltered and tolerable. Moreover, it is impossible to see from the maps that these hills harbour some fine rock-shelters. The hills are comforting and tranquil, at least in those places where one is able to gain access between the many impenetrable thickets of vegetation. Despite the vegetation, we strongly prefer working in the hills, though we seldom feel completely relaxed as these areas are home to an array of poisonous snakes, spiders and scorpions. Our experience of the art is often interrupted by the sudden appearance of these creatures.

From our phenomenological 'immersion' we have no doubt that the strongest influence upon our perceptions of this landscape, and thus on our research, are these and other personal field experiences. We recognize these experiences as perceptions of the landscape, ones that are different from those offered by maps. At the same time, we conclude that the painters would have had an even more different perception because they were even further removed in cultural background from the cartographers. Our perception of place focused on land-forms, flora, fauna, soils, temperature, comfort levels and water availability. We recognize this perception as European in origin; inevitably we look through cultural filters. The painters would have had different filters. They probably focused on many other things that they considered of greater importance, such as colours, textures, the nature of the night skies, smells, access to stimulants, spirits, sickness places, auras, and so on. In sum, our experimental 'immersion' taught us a key problem in phenomenological approaches: the considerable extent of cultural variation in people's landscape experiences and perceptions. It has not provided us with the 'other's' perceptions of landscape that we hoped would, in turn, provide insight into the rock-art.

Conceptual filters

Still, it has given us a strong sense of the cultural filters that define our perceptions when in the field. We recognize four such filters. First, our view is filtered by the selection of the places in which we make observations. Second, it is filtered through a received western emphasis on macro-topographical features. Third, it is filtered through various levels of imposed boundedness. Fourth, the way we relate the images to landscape is filtered by assumptions implicit in our reading of the images themselves. These assumptions do not seem to be confined to our own study. On the contrary, they underpin a great many landscape studies of rock-art and other archaeological materials. We now examine the history of these assumptions and consider the problems they pose. As we shall see, once the development of the assumptions is exposed their debilitating effect becomes clear.

Selected observation of place

The first point may be dealt with more briefly than the others because it derives from the personal experiences that we have described. Our introspection led us to try to uncover the implicit reasons for our choice of study area. We concluded that we had chosen the area because it was within a day's drive of the Rock Art Research Institute, and it was underresearched yet rich in rock-art. Northern South Africa is not, however, the only area to fit these requirements. More importantly, the choice of area for research was defined by our wish to work in a place that felt more 'African' than the well-watered grasslands of the Drakensberg Mountains. We were fascinated by the otherness of the big-game-filled, baobab-strewn wilds of northern South Africa (Fig. 12.3). Ironically, but as for most landscape studies, it was preconceptions of the landscape itself that underpinned our choice of study area and defined our field of study. We now recognize that, when we enter a landscape in which we seek to immerse ourselves, we are not open to absorbing whatever

Fig. 12.3. The 'African-ness' of the landscape of northern South Africa is typified by striking baobab trees.

is around us; rather, it is at this initial point that we start to impose a tacit framework, that has long been held in mind, upon the topography, the bounds of which have *already* been defined by personal experience and cultural inheritance.

Macro-topographical features

Commenting on a collection of papers dealing with rock-art and landscape, Paul Taçon and Paul Faulstich (1993: 81) make the following statement: 'rock-art sites are invariably clustered around or associated with spectacular and prominent geographic features, often commanding stunning vistas and situated near permanent water'. Observations such as this are common; landscape studies often consider the placement of sites in relation to major topographical features, such as mountains and rivers, or some other prominent feature. A focus on impressive topographical features is, however, not an inevitable given; it comes from a deeply entrenched western perception of landscape that may be traced at least as far back as the Renaissance. It is important to appreciate the significance of this history for landscape studies of rock-art.

At the time of the Renaissance, western painting was most concerned with the human subject; landscape was primarily seen as *parergon* – a by-work to the main human subject (Andrews 1999: 7ff). The first inkling that the subsidiary role of landscape in painting was to change came from Joachim Patinir (*c.* 1485–1524). For him, the human subject was still primary and in the foreground of the painting, yet he used the landscape to include historical events in the subject's life (1999: 44 ff). In his pictures, the subjects are necessarily smaller than previous Renaissance works to allow for important scenes of the subject's life (Fig. 12.4). Importantly, for Patinir, 'landscape appears to be shaped by a painstaking attempt to give illusion of a single view across a great tract of countryside at a particular moment'.

By 1612, the process that Patinir had partly founded emerged into a tradition in which landscape was painted and drawn for itself and was no longer a subsidiary to the human subject. From Patinir up until the Romantic and post-Romantic periods the history of landscape art was 'predominantly the record of surfaces only' (1999: 180). From the early nineteenth century onwards this changed owing to advances made in the natural sciences, such as geology, zoology and botany. Emphasis came to be placed on the *authenticity* of landscape: every rock, tree and animal had to be accurately depicted (1999: 182). In order to create such authentic works, artists 'immersed' themselves in the landscape; they left their studios and went into the country to paint.

Detail thus assumed prime importance. Some of John Constable's (1776–1837) realistic works are examples (Fig. 12.5). Yet, even though detail was accurately portrayed in many landscape paintings, it seldom overshadowed the wider 'view'. Rarely were paintings made in which the viewer was immersed in the detail of the landscape; looking at the paintings from this period, one never 'misses the forest for the trees'. In the rare instances in which artists painted smaller areas of detail, these were depicted always with

Fig. 12.4. Joachim Patinir, *Landscape with St Jerome*, *c.* 1515–19. St Jerome, the main subject of the painting, is smaller than he appears in other Renaissance works with the same subject.
Reproduced by permission of Bridgeman Picture Library.

the intention of elucidating the broader, usually hidden patterns, that they believed structured 'Nature'. Romantic landscape art was still about the view; the view was now just more realistically and accurately portrayed.

In the nineteenth century, the invention of photography took over from painting the mantle of 'the chief instrument of pictorial naturalism' (1999: 197). Photography, too, was concerned with the view across space. One need only compare the spectacular black-and-white landscape photographs of Ansel Adams (1902–84) with the paintings of Constable to see that the camera conformed to the brush and canvas (Fig. 12.6): the way landscape was painted during the early nineteenth century was the way it came to be photographed.

Today, the camera is archaeology's primary tool of representation. So often, the photographs taken by archaeologists reproduce the 'western gaze' across landscape. Take Christopher Tilley's influential, *A phenomenology of landscape: places, paths and monuments* (1994) as an example. Many of the photographs in this book have captions that begin, 'View from . . . ' or 'Looking towards . . . '; indeed, of the forty-nine landscape photographs

Fig. 12.5. John Constable, *The Cornfield*, 1826.
Reproduced by permission of The National Gallery, London.

in the book, one is an aerial image, nine are relatively close-up images and as many as thirty-nine are of western gaze views. A similar situation obtains in rock-art books. Frequently, publishers admonish researchers in this field for taking too many photographs of the rock-art itself and not enough with the rock-art in its natural setting. Owing partly to pressure from publishers, partly to the influence of photographers such as David Muench, who produces impressive calendars of rock-art imagery (Fig. 12.7), popular books on rock-art now have far more 'rock-art in the landscape' images than a decade ago.

We argue, then, that the way rock-art is perceived as 'commanding stunning vistas' (Taçon and Faulstich 1993: 81) says more about an inherited western perception of landscape than it does about the artists' experience of that landscape. The difficulty with the inherited emphasis on impressive topographical features is that

Fig. 12.6. Ansel Adams, *Cathedral Peak and Lake Yosemite National Park, California*, 1963.
Reproduced by permission of Ansel Adams Publishing Rights Trust.

ethnography often shows that hunter-gatherers place a different kind of emphasis on the landscape.

The !Kung San (Ju/'hoansi) of the Kalahari, for example, show a marked interest in the smaller features of their territory, features less impressive to the western eye. Elizabeth Marshall-Thomas (1959: 10) notes of the !Kung:

> Each group also knows its own territory very well; although it may be several hundred square miles in area, the people who live there know every bush and stone, every convolution of the ground, and have usually named every place in it where a certain kind of veld food may grow, even if that place is only a few yards in diameter, or where there is only a patch of tall arrow grass or a bee tree, and in this way each group of people knows many hundred places by name.

Clearly, the features of a territory that are important to the San are often small. It is especially the areas where food resources grow that are important and are therefore named.

Hunter-gatherers in other parts of the world show a similar interest in the micro-features of their areas. The Huichol of northern Mexico, for example, make an annual pilgrimage to Wirikuta, their spiritual homeland, in the Sierra Madre Occident in order to collect the hallucinogenic cactus, peyote. The journey is marked by a series of strict taboos and ritual inversions of daily social life. The place of Wirikuta is filled with numerous important symbolic landmarks, including two sacred mountains. Yet, most of the important features of Wirikuta are as Barbara Myerhoff (1974: 139) points out, 'inconspicuous and even invisible to an untrained observer – heaps of pebbles, tiny water holes, tree stumps, small caves, hillocks, and little clumps of rocks'.

The examples of the San and the Huichol show that landscape for hunter-gatherers is sometimes more like an archaeologist's close-up photograph of a dense lithic scatter than it is like 'the single view across a great tract of countryside'. So often for foragers themselves, landscape resides in the small and minute detail and not in the prominent and spectacular topographical features we choose for our views. While hunter-gatherers certainly do not miss the forest for the trees, they do seem frequently to be far more interested in the trees than in the forest; indeed, it is often bits of decayed wood that are important to them. Archaeologists, however, tend to miss the trees because they seldom consider minutiae such as pebbles, holes and so forth; instead, they concentrate on the prominent macro-features of the landscape. The small but crucial things are those least likely to survive in the archaeological record. Yet, if phenomenological approaches are to live up to their promise of 'a new perspective', it is precisely these elements that we need to consider if we are to avoid simply imposing the western gaze on the archaeological record.

Landscape as boundary

Apart from the ethnographic challenge to landscape archaeology, the emphasis on macro-topographical features is disconcerting because of the connotations so many writers

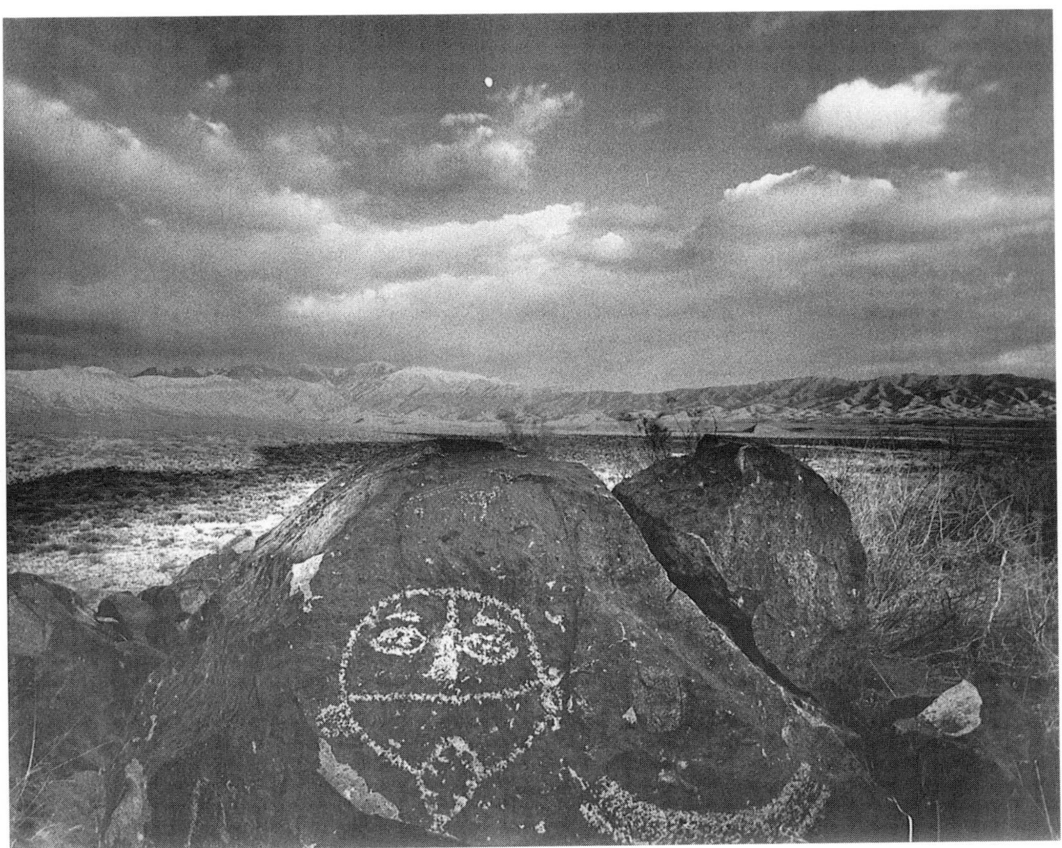

Fig. 12.7. David Muench, 1993, *Images in stone: southwest rock-art*, 1994 Calendar (May). Reproduced by permission of David Muench Photographers.

unquestioningly attach to them. These connotations are easily transmuted into interpretation. Gro Mandt, for example, comments on the Vingen rock-engraving sites in Norway (1995: 278; our emphasis): 'The tiny fjord, surrounded by steep and *seemingly impassable* mountains, with its large number of rock pictures *gives the impression* of a very special – even a sacred – place. The *view* from Vingen towards a characteristic mountain formation called Hornelen adds to this impression.' Note, first, that her notion of 'impassable mountains' implies a boundary and, second, that it is her purely subjective response to 'the view' that gives her an 'impression' of a 'sacred place'. Such is the upshot of uncritical 'immersion'.

Mandt is not alone. Macro-topographical features are frequently associated with the idea of a sacred landscape in western thought (e.g. Mt Sinai). Indeed, the received idea of sacred landscape has a number of connotations that are important in understanding the sort of assumptions that undermine many landscape studies.

To illustrate these connotations, we begin with Mark Twain's comments on Alfred Bierstadt's (1830–1902) celebrated nineteenth-century painting *The Domes of Yosemite* (1867).

Fig. 12.8. Albert Bierstadt, *Among the Sierra Nevada Mountains, California*, 1868. Reproduced by permission of Bridgeman Picture Library.

Twain, looking at the painting (Fig. 12.8), commented (quoted in Anderson 1992: 12–13):

> those snow-peaks are correct – they look natural; the valley is correct and natural; the pine trees clinging to the bluff on the right, and the grove on the left, and the boulders, are all like nature . . . But when I got around to the atmosphere, I was obliged to say 'this man imported this atmosphere from some foreign country, because nothing like it was ever seen in California' . . . It is more the atmosphere of Kingdom-Come than of California.

Twain's comments point to the near-religious connotations that Bierstadt's images held for many viewers. The sheer size of his paintings, with their exaggerated mountains that dwarf the animals or people in the foreground, and the unearthly light that illuminates the scenes, combine to convey the impression of a sacred place. Bierstadt was just one of many nineteenth-century artists who responded to a call in the American art world for an art that was 'based on distinctly American subject matter' (Anderson 1992: 18). But the majority of these artists, including Bierstadt, had studied and travelled, if not been brought up, in Europe. There they had been exposed to the Romantic and post-Romantic works of Turner and others. Yet, when they returned home and painted they 'ignored European sources and influences. To acknowledge such sources would diminish the much-desired national character of the works' (Anderson 1992: 24). Instead, Bierstadt and others found their subject-matter in the landscapes and inhabitants of the American West.

In choosing the West, they sought to illustrate the unique essence of the frontier and the ideology of manifest destiny. In so doing, they expressed the ideas on which American national identity would be forged. The West for these artists was about identity – an identity, moreover, that was grounded in a vision of landscape as a mystical, near-religious experience. The celebrated western gaze or view that emerged in Renaissance landscape painting acquired the connotations of identity. 'Boundedness' and identity thus came to be closely associated. This is an association that we need to explore in order to understand the notion of identity in landscape studies of rock-art.

American landscape art was by no means the only art to be tied into the production of identity. The South African artist Jacob Hendrik Pierneef (1886–1957), like Bierstadt and other American landscape artists, travelled to Europe to explore European art. In the mid 1920s he met Willem Adriaan Van Konijnenburg, the Dutch landscape painter. Van Konijnenburg clearly had a marked effect on Pierneef's ideas, yet Pierneef denied his influence because he wished to achieve fame in South Africa as a pioneer of an indigenous Afrikaner art that was closely associated with Afrikaner identity.

Pierneef's landscapes, while lacking the epic grandeur of a Bierstadt, are none the less impressive. His views often include large mountains; behind these, clouds tower up into the sky. Yet, his landscapes are devoid of people. Even when he paints villages or farmhouses, there is a marked absence of humanity (Fig. 12.9). Of course, the land itself was not empty; numerous indigenous people occupied the spaces that Pierneef painted. The reasons for this lack of people lie in the circumstances of Afrikaner life in the 1920s and the 1930s.

Throughout those two decades, Afrikaans farmers increasingly left their farmlands to find employment in cities. The Great Depression gave even more impetus to this migration. Once in the cities, they faced stiff competition from black urbanites in the labour market. Unskilled and alienated, many of these city-dwellers looked back to the rural areas with fondness. It was in this context that Pierneef thrived. A popular idea began to emerge (Coetzee 1992: 23; our translation):

> landscape painting is somehow special to, and revealing of, the Afrikaner. This does not mean that other nations cannot appreciate or practise it. It is rather intended to convey the Afrikaner's sense of being mystically linked to the land. Afrikaners derive their historical being and identity from this relationship; they are products of the land *natuurmense* (nature people) – or, at the very least, *plaasmense* (farm people).

Pierneef's art was, then, a conscious effort to construct an Afrikaner nationalism that had its foundations in the land. By excluding people from his landscapes, he invited the white viewers of his art to take ownership of the land because it was empty and therefore did not belong to anyone (Coetzee 1992: 25). Nevertheless, in creating a vision of identity as situated in the land, Pierneef's paintings masked a truly formative component of Afrikaner nationalism. Increasingly through the 1920s, 1930s and 1940s Afrikaner nationalism was created in opposition to a black 'other'. It was partly on these grounds that the National Party won the 1948 election, and then implemented *apartheid*, largely on the slogan *Die Swart Gevaar* (The Black Menace). By not painting black people, Pierneef denied their inextricable role in Afrikaner national-identity formation.

Both Bierstadt and Pierneef thus sought to situate identity in landscape; in the case of Pierneef, that effort served to mask the real process of identity-formation. Landscape art 'has from early on been implicated in nationalist, imperialist and socio-economic ideologies, and often most potently so when, superficially, least touched by suggestions of any political agenda' (Andrews 1999: 175).

In asserting that landscape is fundamental to the construction of people's identity in the archaeological record, researchers often seem unaware of the historical trajectory that we have outlined. They do not realize that their claims

Fig. 12.9. Jacob Hendrik Pierneef, *Mont-aux-Sources*. Johannesburg Station Panel, *c*. 1925–32. Reproduced by permission of Transnet Heritage Foundation, Library and Documentation Centre collection on loan to the Johannesburg Art Gallery.

about landscape are part of an historically situated western perception of landscape. It cannot be merely assumed, as many archaeologists do, that landscape is a human universal component of identity-formation. Even more dangerous than assuming that landscape and identity are necessarily linked is the conception that some writers display about the nature of identity. They tie identity to a bounded space. As a result they see rock-art as a territorial boundary marker. Such assumptions need to be demonstrated for particular peoples in space and time, and not merely theoretically asserted.

Indeed, hunter-gatherer ethnography points to flaws in assuming that landscape and identity necessarily interdigitate. The way that the !Kung San conceive of their territories is an apt example. Each territory is defined in terms of natural resources and each has an owner. Collections of natural resources are called *n!oresi* (Marshall and Ritchie 1984: 82), and their owners are known as *kxai k'xausi* (Marshall 1976: 184). Each *n!ore* is usually formed around a permanent or semi-permanent water-hole. It is only the water-hole that is really 'owned' in any sense of the word (Smith 1994: 373). Rights to use the *n!ore* are inherited through kinship or established through residence (Barnard 1986), and the !Kung often have rights in many overlapping *n!oresi*. Indeed, to use the resources of a particular *n!ore* one simply joins a camp or one asks permission (Lee 1979: 336). While !Kung *n!oresi* are not clearly defined, some other San groups, the G/wi for example, consider the boundaries more important. Natural landmarks mark these boundaries. Yet, as George Silberbauer (1981: 193) states, 'The boundaries of a territory are roughly defined by landmarks or, more correctly, in terms of areas surrounding these landmarks.' For the G/wi, it is the areas of natural resources between the major landmarks that are more important.

Three important features emerge from this account. First, the boundaries of the territories are natural – no cultural marking, such as rock-art, demarcates them. Second, the territories are conceptualized in terms of utilizable resources, not by any prominent macro-feature of the landscape. Third, the territories overlap and the boundaries between them are in no way fixed like those of a modern country. Importantly, the San of the present-day Kalahari do not make rock-art. These observations carry implications for arguments that stress rock-art as a territorial boundary-marker on the landscape. The !Kung, and many other hunter-gatherers, are capable of identifying territories without having to mark by means of rock-art. Hunter-gatherers are also more flexible in the way that they allow usage of territories than researchers who talk of rock-art markers assume. The usable, but unmarkable, resources of plants and small water-holes determine the permeable boundaries of hunter-gatherer territories more frequently than prominent topographic features.

Of course, the situation is likely to be different amongst different groups world-wide, yet researchers who relate rock-art to the marking of territory seldom draw on ethnographic specifics to support their arguments. Instead, they draw on a model implicit in western thought that, as a result of the history we have outlined, sees identity as inextricably concretized in a bounded landscape. Bland statements that art is part of identity-formation have in turn created a rhetoric that suggests that identity-formation is an end in itself. This rhetoric gives the impression that identity-formation is the ultimate goal of all cultural processes – including the making of rock-art. It is as if the hunter-gatherers of the archaeological record were constantly obsessed with their own ontological well-being and every act they performed was consciously concerned with making a statement about their identity.

Image, assumption and landscape

So far, we have considered two ways in which archaeological studies of landscape are influenced by historically inherited European perceptions of landscape. We now turn our attention to a third, more veiled, way in which archaeological studies of landscape are thus influenced. It is often the hope amongst those studying rock-art that the landscape context of the art will provide some clue to the meanings of the images.

Ralph Hartley and Anne Wolley Vawser (1998), for example, argue a more nuanced case than most for the use of rock-art as territorial marker, but it is founded on assumptions about the images. Using computer-assisted techniques, they plot the distribution of rock-art sites in relation to food storage sites in south-eastern Utah. They argue that the associated rock-art sites were used to communicate an unambiguous '"message" of ownership or affiliation' and 'served as a visual marking of restriction' (Hartley and Wolley Vawser 1998: 194–5).

What guides their interpretation is the imagery of human hands, anthropomorphs and mammals at sites that seem to be closely associated with storage facilities (cf. Hartley 1991). The unwritten and undemonstrated association that handprints were markers of identity, especially, informs their argument. If the images at these sites were only of animals, one wonders whether the same argument would have been put forward.

It is in the hidden logic of movement from image to landscape significance that problems occur. Often, assumptions about the significance of rock-art images are implicitly used to infer the cultural significance of a landscape for past peoples. The cultural significance of the landscape is then used to argue for the placement of the images in particular places. The argument thus becomes a circular, self-fulfilling prophecy about the images. The circularity is hidden, however, because researchers do not realize that their arguments about the past landscape are guided by assumptions about the meaning of specific motifs, which in turn articulate well with their Eurocentric perceptions of the present landscape. Hartley and Wolley Vawser's argument is no more than an assertion of an assumption.

Landscape and the rock-art of the Northern Province

From this examination of key components of the history and rationality of landscape studies it will be clear that the assumptions to which we found ourselves falling prey as we 'immersed' ourselves in the rock-art and landscape of northern South Africa are subversive. Nevertheless, they are pervasive in the literature on landscape and rock-art and undermine many texts.

Our landscape study of northern South Africa clearly faces the kind of dilemmas that bedevil all landscape studies. Whether we use a naïve or a phenomenological framework, can we ever break out of our cultural perceptions of landscape and glimpse the cultural perceptions of the painters without considering ethnography? How can we identify the subtle and perhaps unrecognizable ways in which our perceptions influence our study? We are not convinced that we can. No matter how often we acknowledge that the painters of northern South Africa will have had a different perception of landscape from ours, and no matter how willing we are to look for this other perception, we cannot observe or reconstruct their perceptions from archaeological sources and our own subjective knowledge of the landscape.

At best, all we shall be able to see is a *possible* link between rock-art sites and features of the northern South African landscape *that we perceive*. Without relevant ethnography our work is inherently constrained by our own limited cultural experiences of the landscape. This means that our landscape study can offer insights only if the practice of painting (1) was affected by 'things' the painters perceived in the landscape *and* (2) we have been fortunate enough to perceive these same 'things' in the landscape *and* (3) the pattern of positioning in relation to these 'things' is striking enough that we can demonstrate a link. As we have shown, it is certain that the majority of our perceptions will be misleading.

With our Eurocentric perceptions of the northern South African landscape exposed, and with a definite sense of unease, we now turn to the rock-arts of the region. At least three traditions can be identified. Repeated overlays allow us to determine the sequence of the traditions.

The oldest is executed in fine brushwork, typically in red pigment but occasionally with certain details in white and black; rarely, figures are in white or black only. Humans and animals (Fig. 12.10) dominate the subject matter of this art. In the Limpopo Flats, in the northern part of the study area, depictions of women outnumber those of men (Eastwood and Cnoops 1999; Eastwood and Blundell in press). This pattern is reversed in the hills farther south. There is high species diversity in the animals depicted in the art, with the most common being kudu, giraffe, elephant and (locally) hartebeest. The fine and detailed manner of these images is characteristic of San hunter-gatherer art which is found

Fig. 12.10. San fine-line image of zebra. The stripes are of red pigment while the body is of white.

throughout southern Africa. Local peculiarities in the choice of subject-matter are a well-recorded feature of this art (Maggs 1967; Vinnicombe 1967; Garlake 1995; Walker 1996).

Alongside the San tradition lies an art of geometric designs, applied by finger in a wide variety of pigments from red through orange to white. These designs are strikingly different from the earlier forager art. They are much larger and conform to a different set of conventions, with new and unrecognizable subjects. In the superposition sequences, the geometric tradition motifs most often overlie San art, but it is not uncommon to find the reverse – geometric designs overlain by San figures. The identity of the painters of this tradition is unknown (but see Smith and Ouzman in press).

Finally, to complete the sequence, there is a varied collection of images, daubed in powdery white and off-white pigments that overlie both the other traditions. Subjects depicted include a wide range of quadrupeds, spread-eagled designs, people, locomotives, wagons and guns (Smith and Van Schalkwyk 2002; Van Schalkwyk and Smith in press). This art follows a manner of depiction typical of that used by Bantu-speaking farmer peoples in many parts of eastern, central and southern Africa (Smith 1997; 1998). We now consider the relationship between each of these traditions and the landscape.

San art in the landscape

When we relate the position of San art sites to features that *we perceive* in the landscape, no clear pattern emerges. San art is everywhere. The number of sites we have visited is now in excess of three hundred. Wherever there are sheltered surfaces, no matter how small, one finds San paintings. In a few places, where there are no sheltered surfaces but low flat hard rock, one finds San engravings rather than paintings. At a few sites there are San engravings on sheltered surfaces. Within this general spread there are areas with concentrations of art: on the flats around the Shashi–Limpopo confluence, in the northern part of the Makgabeng hills, in the western half of the Soutpansberg, and in the northern section of the Waterberg hills (Fig. 12.1). We can find no explanation for these concentrations within our knowledge of rock types, soil types, vegetation types, fauna occurrence or rainfall. We therefore assume that the explanation lies in elements of San beliefs, practices or history that do not conform to our perceptions of the landscape.

This is a more promising observation. We notice that there are big and small sites, and we have the same sense that Patricia Vinnicombe (1976: 137–9) had in the South African Drakensberg of there being certain

> sites with a large number of superpositions surrounded by many smaller sites with few or no superpositions . . . [C]learly . . . artists selected specific shelters for repeated visits in order to paint and re-paint particular surfaces over a period of time. Since not all the superimposed shelters show evidence of repeated occupation, it would seem that the shelters were associated with special ritual or ceremonial functions that did not necessarily include regular habitation.

Nick Walker (1995; 1996) describes a similar pattern in the Zimbabwean Matopos, though he explains it within a 12,000-year sequence of changing land rationalization (1995: 239–41).

Like Walker, we have a sense that the choice of subject-matter varies between the large, often-returned-to, public sites and the surrounding, infrequent-use, small sites. And, like him, we struggle as soon as we try to quantify this perception. Part of the problem is the abundance of medium-sized sites that have certain large-site characteristics and certain small-site characteristics and which therefore blur any attempt at categorization. Our perception is probably an illusion.

Another problem is that, in common with Walker's Matopos research, analyses of the many features that seem to us to characterize the art of large sites fall into an awkward statistical trap. Walker suggested that complex 'formlings' were, in the Matopos, a feature particular to the large shelters (1996: 32). Unfortunately, each large shelter usually has just one or two. With a mere handful of large sites, complex formlings are therefore very rare. They are thus only likely to occur at sites with huge numbers of paintings (i.e. the largest sites). Formlings also tend to be big, and so one could argue that their form is naturally best suited to larger sites. To an ethnographically informed David Lewis-Williams (pers. comm.), who contends (1) that our perceived patterns of placement in the rock-art of northern South Africa are meaningless constructs, (2) that large shelters are few and in the nature of things tend to be surrounded by many smaller sites, and (3) that San art bears no meaningful relationship to the landscape features that we perceive, we have no satisfactory reply.

We must accept that insights derived from a landscape analysis of San art, without recourse to ethnography or historical context, are negligible. It is now generally accepted (based on study of ethnography) that San art relates to the power and experiences of San religious specialists in their negotiations with the other world – the realm of god, the spirits and the mythical creatures (Lewis-Williams 1981; 1990; Lewis-Williams and Dowson 1989; Yates *et al.* 1990; Woodhouse 1992; Garlake 1995; Walker 1996; Solomon 1997). Current debates concern which elements of the other world are represented, what was being negotiated and how. It is argued that painting sites were places of negotiation at a number of levels; most importantly, they were places where the things that came to be painted were accessed and experienced (Lewis-Williams and Dowson 1990; Lewis-Williams *et al.* in press).

We could not have derived any part of this understanding from a landscape study, even though issues of placement may have been crucial and formative for individual artists. For instance, the informing micro-level placements within sites that have been reported in the South African Drakensberg, such as animals walking out from cracks in the rock face (Lewis-Williams and Dowson 1990), have not been noted in northern South Africa. There is one case where figures in an unusual tumbling posture are positioned 2 m above a prominent rock recess (Hall and Smith in press); we think it unlikely that the significance of this posture and its micro-placement would have been recognized in the absence of the ethnography.

The San conceptual landscape 'floats above' the topographical material landscape. It was 'projected down' onto the topography where the topography allowed for the making of images. It is not possible to work in reverse and to construct the conceptual San landscape from the places where it happens to have been 'projected down' onto the material world.

Geometric art in the landscape

The geometric art evinces a similar overall distribution to that of San art, although there are far fewer geometric sites than San sites. Geometric sites are found in both plains and hill areas and show no preference for any particular vegetation or rainfall zone (Fig. 12.11). Again, we struggled

Fig. 12.11. Red geometric images found in the Northern Province are often close to water.

to see any recognizable pattern to the choice of sites, although one of us thought there might have been a tendency to choose sites near to running water. This pattern proved impossible to substantiate because surface-water run-off is a short-term seasonal event throughout most of the region. The number of streams that run for any span of time has also been dramatically reduced in recent years by overgrazing which has caused many older water-courses to silt up beyond recognition.

There does, however, appear to be an intriguing relationship between geometric art and San art. Geometric art commonly avoids surfaces with San art, but, where the two are found together, they seem to vie for visual primacy. At these sites one finds geometric art both overlying and underlying San images (see, for example, Hall and Smith in press). These patterns may in future provide insights into geometric art, but, with fewer than thirty sites belonging to this tradition in all of northern South Africa, our sample is too small for us to be confident that the observed patterns of placement have a statistically demonstrable significance.

On the other hand, an analysis of geometric art using ethnographic and historical information is currently in preparation. It is argued that this art belonged to herder groups who passed through the area during the first millennium AD, following the major water-courses (Smith and Ouzman in press). If this migration argument is correct, then a landscape study would have missed a crucial spatial dynamic that would have helped to establish its authorship. Even though our study area is more than 200 km in diameter, it is too small to pick up the landscape patterns critical to discerning the authorship of both San and geometric art.

Farmer art in the landscape

In contrast to San and geometric arts, farmer art occupies a highly selective position in the landscape (Fig. 12.1). It is confined to the western part of the Soutpansberg, the Makgabeng and the Waterberg – all hill areas. No examples of this art have been found on the plains. It is also not found in all hill areas; it does not occur, for example, on hills in the eastern half of the study area. The distribution conforms closely to the area historically occupied by peoples of the Northern Sotho language group. This pattern is key in determining, first, the authorship of the art and, second, which farmer ethnography is relevant. There is plentiful ethnography that allows us to explain many of the painted and positioning features of the art. But first we consider what a landscape study might have concluded had this ethnography not existed.

The limited distribution of the tradition would have been immediately striking and, given that this art consistently overlies all other art, we believe we would have recognized the farmer authorship. A broader archaeological survey would certainly have picked this up, as the art distribution links closely to that of certain ceramic types and decoration. A closer look at the distribution shows that a significant section of the art is placed in shaded valleys near to perennial water sources. The makers of this art chose those places that we consider most pleasant in the landscape; parts of the environment where we most like to work. Given an 'immersion' approach, we may have concluded that the farmer artists chose to live only in the best of places. Unfortunately, the archaeological remains do not support this. The bulk of hill areas, if occupied by farmers at all, have been occupied for only brief periods (van der Ryst 1998; Huffman 1990). We might have noticed this had our rock-art research included a wider archaeological survey (which it rarely does).

Accepting that farmer communities have generally chosen to live around the bases of hills and not upon the hills themselves, we may have used a seemingly crucial piece of knowledge gained from the vegetation maps. Although limited in size, the hill river-valleys are some of the best-watered and richest areas for grazing in the region. During bad droughts, they are among the few good grazing grounds. This would have allowed us to refine our conclusion by arguing that, although the painters were not living in the area, they were choosing to herd their sheep and cattle there because of its grazing value. To support this argument one could point to many paintings of sheep and cattle, the continued use of these areas by cattle-herders today, and the recovery of cattle bones in most excavation sequences. Another important landscape pattern seems to support this explanation. It is unusual for cattle-herders to graze their cattle more than a day's walk from the village because cattle are returned to their kraal at night. (Admittedly we would have been close to using ethnography here, but we may have guessed this from observations made during excavations that cattle kraals held an important central place in all village configurations.) The art follows this pattern exactly; there is a marked fall in the number of farmer painted sites as one moves more than a day's walk into the hill areas.

This association of farmer art with fertile valleys seems to be conclusive; it is self-supporting in a number of ways. Could one hope for any stronger pattern from a landscape perspective? In most areas, but not all, farmer art sites are widely spaced; there are usually one or two in each river valley. This is the pattern that one would expect if the art were a marker to warn away herders from other groups. This inference could also explain why the images are so large and visually striking. In vivid white pigment, paintings can be seen from far away. Further, it could explain the notable differences in art subject-matter between areas. It seems inevitable that in this marginal environment, with only very limited areas of good grazing and regular droughts, access to these prime grazing areas would have been fiercely contested. Even with rock-art carefully placed to mark out the territory, one could expect occasional conflicts over grazing rights. One does not have to look far for evidence of conflict. There are fortifications on top of some of the hills and the rock-art is full of images of aggression, including large scenes in which people fight each other with knobkerries and guns (Fig. 12.12). It seems that the gradual increase in population that we see in the archaeological layers led to conflict. That the conflict came late in the sequence is also supported by the art: paintings of conflict are some of the last images that were painted.

Fig. 12.12. Late White tradition images of human figures with guns; this tradition is full of aggressive imagery.

If we had followed a typical landscape approach to farmer rock-art we would have produced an explanation that drew on a wide range of observations and logical deductions, all of which seem to be borne out by the data, to be internally consistent, and to be mutually supporting. But we would have been wrong to do so.

An examination of Northern Sotho ethnography shows us that the farmer art has nothing to do with herding or internal conflict. We need to consider the social rather than the economic issues surrounding the production of the art.

The oldest images were associated with boys' initiation observances. They were placed within a day's walk from the village to allow the women to bring food to the boys each day. Sites are near to rivers not because of suitable grazing but because they relate to the point in the ceremony when circumcision is carried out and this is, traditionally, conducted beside a river so that the boys can bathe their wounds after the cutting. Sheep and cows are painted not because people herded them there but for important instructive educational purposes that need not concern us here. The images of aggression do not reflect internal conflict but show the upheavals of the nineteenth century, in the time of Mzilikazi's Ndebele and Swazi raiders. Later, conflict with the colonial government caused the same movement of people and forced people, briefly, to flee to the hills for sanctuary. The hilltop forts date to this same time. Although the landscape reading of the data seemed entirely plausible, even persuasive, it was a total fabrication. It seemed plausible because it played neatly into our western history of perceptions of landscape and our subjective expectations of farmer behaviour.

A landscape view of the rock-art of northern South Africa

How, then, would a landscape archaeological study of the rock-art of northern South Africa without recourse to ethnography have fared? The answer is alarming: it would have been embarrassingly far off the mark in all its major contentions. Does this mean, however, that all landscape approaches are doomed? Clearly not; many of the chapters in this volume, and elsewhere (e.g. Whitley 1998; Helskog 1999) make convincing arguments about rock-art and its situation in a symbolic landscape. It is notable that the most convincing arguments are often those that include ethnographic material. Yet, good arguments can still be made without the luxury of ethnography. What is of concern to us here are those arguments that treat landscape as an unproblematic given; statements that are so obviously Eurocentric are often unquestioningly accepted simply because they come under the rubric of landscape. Even more disturbing are those arguments about landscape that come in a complex theoretical framework that merely disguises simplistic 'gaze and guess' type assertions about rock-art and landscape; theory is not the value-free enterprise that so many archaeologists implicitly assume it to be. Most often the theoretical statements derive from philosophers and social theorists who themselves are 'immersed' in a western value system. Outside of the hard-line 'immersion school', few researchers adopt the extreme position we have taken for our experimental study of the rock-art of northern South Africa, that of relying on landscape alone to provide insights into rock-art. Although each approach may be weak, together they become strong (see, e.g. Chippindale, Smith and Taçon 2000). In this chapter we have spotlighted the single strand of landscape, not to lampoon a particular kind of rock-art research, but to question the wisdom of its increasing prominence. We feel it is essential that someone question the premise of this book: that the landscape strand is so good and so important as to have a special or a dominant place over rather than alongside others.

Acknowledgements

We thank David Lewis-Williams, Christopher Chippindale and Eva Walderhaug for reading through drafts of this chapter and making useful comments. Ghilraen Laue typed up various corrections and checked references. Olivia Tuchten prepared certain images, and Owen Tucker drew the maps. The Rock-Art Research Institute is funded by the University of the Witwatersrand and the National Research Foundation. The views expressed in this chapter are solely those of the authors and any errors are their responsibility and not those of the funding agencies, commentators and assistants on this paper.

References

Anderson, N. K. 1992. Curious historical artistic data: art history and western American art, in J. D. Prown (ed.), *Discovered lands, invented pasts: transforming visions of the American West*: 1–35. New Haven, CT: Yale University Press.

Andrews, M. 1999. *Landscape and western art.* Oxford: Oxford University Press.

Barnard, A. 1986. Rethinking Bushman settlement patterns and territoriality, *Sprache und Geschichte in Afrika* 7: 41–60.

Bender, B. 1993. *Landscape: politics and perspectives.* Providence, RI: Berg.

Blundell, G. and E. B. Eastwood. 2002. Identifying Y-shaped images in the rock art of the Limpopo–Shashi confluence area, *South African Journal of Science* 97: 305–308.

Coetzee, N. J. 1992. *Pierneef, land and landscape: the Johannesburg Station Panels in context.* Johannesburg: CBM Publishing.

Cooke, C. K. 1969. *Rock art of southern Africa.* Cape Town: Books of Africa.

David, B. and M. Wilson. 1999. Re-reading the landscape: place and identity in NE Australia during the late Holocene, *Cambridge Archaeological Journal* 9: 163–88.

Eastwood, E. B. and G. Blundell. 1999. Re-discovering the rock art of the Limpopo–Shashi confluence area, southern Africa, *Southern African Field Archaeology* 8: 17–27.

Eastwood, E. B. and C. Cnoops. 1999. Capturing the spoor: towards explaining kudu in San rock art of the Limpopo–Shashi confluence area, *South African Archaeological Bulletin* 54: 107–19.

Garlake, P. S. 1995. *The hunter's vision: the prehistoric art of Zimbabwe.* London: British Museum Press.

Hall, S. and B. W. Smith. In press. *Empowering places: rock shelters and ritual control in farmer–forager interactions in the Northern Province, South Africa.* Cape Town: South African Archaeological Bulletin Goodwin Series.

Hartley, R. J. 1991. Rockshelters and rock-art: an assessment of site use, in A. Hutchinson and J. E. Smith (compilers), *Proceedings of the Anasazi Symposium 1991*: 165–90. Mesa Verde, CO: Mesa Verde National Park.

Hartley, R. J. and A. M. Wolley Vawser. 1998. Spatial behaviour and learning in the prehistoric environment of the Colorado River drainage (south-eastern Utah), western North America, in Christopher Chippindale and Paul S. C. Taçon (eds.), *The archaeology of rock-art*: 185–211. Cambridge: Cambridge University Press.

Heizer, R. F. and M. A. Baumhoff. 1962. *Prehistoric rock art of Nevada and eastern California.* Berkeley, CA: University of California Press.

Helskog, K. 1999. The shore connection: cognitive landscape and communication with rock carvings in northernmost Europe, *Norwegian Archaeological Review* 32: 73–94.

Huffman, T. N. 1990. The Waterberg research of Jan Aukema (obituary), *South African Archaeological Bulletin* 45: 117–19.

Lee, R. B. 1979. *The !Kung San: men, women and work in a foraging society.* Cambridge: Cambridge University Press.

Lewis-Williams, J. D. 1981. *Believing and seeing: symbolic meaning in southern San rock paintings.* London: Academic Press.

1983. *The rock art of southern Africa.* Cambridge: Cambridge University Press.

1990. *Discovering southern African rock art.* Cape Town: David Philip.

Lewis-Williams, J. D., G. Blundell, W. Challis and J. Hampson. 2000. Threads of light: re-examining a motif in southern African San rock art, *South African Archaeological Bulletin* 55: 123–36.

Lewis-Williams, J. D. and T. Dowson. 1989. *Images of power: understanding Bushman rock art.* Johannesburg: Southern Book Publishers.

1990. Through the veil: San rock paintings and the rock face, *South African Archaeological Bulletin* 45: 5–16.

Limerick, P. N. 1987. *The legacy of conquest: the unbroken past of the American West*. New York: W. W. Norton.

Loendorf, L. 1994. Finnegan Cave: a rock art vision quest site in Montana, in Solveig Turpin (ed.), *Shamanism and rock art in North America:* 125–37. San Antonio, TX: Rock Art Foundation. Special Publication 1.

Low, A. B. and A. G. Rebelo (eds.). 1996. *Vegetation of South Africa, Lesotho and Swaziland*. Pretoria: Department of Environmental Affairs and Tourism.

Maggs, T. M. O. 1967. A quantitative analysis of the rock art from a sample area in the western Cape, *South African Journal of Science* 63: 100–4.

Mandt, G. 1995. Alternative analogies in rock art interpretation: the west Norwegian case, in Knut Helskog and Bjorn Olsen (eds.) *Perceiving rock art: social and political perspectives*: 263–91. Oslo: Novus Forlag.

Marshall, J. and C. Ritchie. 1984. *Where are the Ju/wasi of Nyae Nyae?* Cape Town: Centre for African Studies, University of Cape Town.

Marshall, L. 1976. *The !Kung of Nyae Nyae*. Cambridge, MA: Harvard University Press.

Marshall-Thomas, E. 1959. *The harmless people*. London: Secker and Warburg.

Myerhoff, B. G. 1974. *Peyote hunt: the sacred journey of the Huichol Indians*. Ithaca, NY: Cornell University Press.

Nash, G. D. 1990. *Creating the West: historical interpretations 1890–1990*. Albuquerque, NM: University of New Mexico Press.

Silberbauer, G. B. 1981. *Hunter and habitat in the central Kalahari Desert*. Cambridge: Cambridge University Press.

Smith, A. B. 1994. Metaphors of space: rock art and territoriality in southern Africa, in T. A. Dowson and J. D. Lewis-Williams (eds.), *Contested images: diversity in southern African rock art research*: 373–84. Johannesburg: Witwatersrand University Press.

Smith, B. W. 1997. *Zambia's ancient rock art: the paintings of Kasama*. Livingstone: National Heritage Conservation Commission.

1998. The tale of the chameleon and the platypus: limited and likely choices in making pictures, in C. Chippindale and P. S. C. Taçon (eds.), *The archaeology of rock-art*: 212–28. Cambridge: Cambridge University Press.

Smith, B. W. and S. Ouzman. In press. Taking stock: identifying herder rock art in southern Africa, *Current Anthropology*.

Smith, B. W. and J. A. Van Schalkwyk. 2002. The White Camel of the Makgabeng, *Journal of African History* 43(2): 235–54.

Solomon, A. 1997. The myth of ritual origins? Ethnography, mythology and interpretation of San rock art, *South African Archaeological Bulletin* 52: 3–13.

Taçon, P. S. C. and P. Faulstich. 1993. Introduction: expressing relationships to the land by marking special places, in J. Steinbring *et al.* (eds.), *Time and space: dating and spatial considerations in rock art research*: 81–3. Melbourne: Australian Rock Art Research Association. Occasional AURA Publication 8.

Tilley, C. 1994. *A phenomenology of landscape: places, paths and monuments*. Oxford: Berg.

Van Der Ryst, M. M. 1998. *The Waterberg Plateau in the Northern Province, Republic of South Africa, in the Later Stone Age*. Oxford: British Archaeological Reports. International Series S715.

Van Schalkwyk, J. and B. W. Smith. In press. No cannons, no war? Rewriting the history of the Malaboho war of 1894, *South African Archaeological Bulletin*.

Vinnicombe, P. 1967. Rock painting analysis, *South African Archaeological Bulletin* 22: 129–41.

1976. *People of the eland*. Pietermaritzburg: University of Natal Press.

Walker, N. J. 1994. Painting and ceremonial activity in the Later Stone Age of the Matopos, Zimbabwe, in T. A. Dowson and D. Lewis-Williams (eds.), *Contested images: diversity in southern African rock art research*: 119–30. Johannesburg: Witwatersrand University Press.

1995. *Late Pleistocene and Holocene hunter-gatherers of the Matopos*. Uppsala: Societas Archaeologica Upsaliensis.

1996. *The painted hills: rock art of the Matopos*. Gweru: Mambo Press.

Whitley, D. S. 1998. Finding rain in the desert: landscape, gender and far western North American rock-art, in C. Chippindale and Paul S. C Taçon (eds.), *The archaeology of rock-art*: 11–29. Cambridge: Cambridge University Press.

Whitley, D. S., R. I. Dorn, J. M. Simon, R. Rechtman and Tamara K. Whitley. 1999. Sally's Rockshelter and the archaeology of vision quest, *Cambridge Archaeological Journal* 9: 221–47.

Willcox, A. 1963. *The rock art of South Africa*. London: Nelson.

1984. *Rock paintings of the Drakensberg*. Cape Town: Struik.

Woodhouse, H. C. 1992. *The rain and its creatures, as the Bushmen painted them*. Johannesburg: William Waterman Publications.

Yates, R., J. Parkington and A. Manhire. 1990. *Pictures from the past: a history of the interpretation of rock paintings and engravings in southern Africa*. Pietermaritzburg: Centaur.

Part Three

Formal methods: opportunities and applications

The studies in this third part begin with formal methods, those which can be used when there is not insight into meaning acquired from a direct cultural record.

13

Landscapes in rock-art: rock-carving and ritual in the old European North

Knut Helskog

Noticed, recorded, conserved, researched for more decades and with more diligence than nearly all bodies of rock-art, the rock-carvings on the open slabs of Scandinavia have to most scholars seemed beyond informed knowledge. There are striking patterns in the locations of this art, the strongest and the best-known being its placing close by water or the sea-shore; so consistent is its placing that elevation above the modern sea-level has proved the best guide to relative chronology. Motifs occur in tens or hundreds on panels; they have been seen as accumulations of individual images or, at most, structured by groupings of a few figures belonging together. The unusual carvings at Alta, in northernmost Norway, permit a different interpretation. Major panels there can be read as large-scale compositions. The undulations and irregularities of the surface make sense when seen as physical models of the landscape. And time is present alongside place: these spatial compositions also incorporate time, for the events they show belong to certain seasons in this harsh northern climate.

Ritual in the landscape

Rock-carvings are here taken to represent religious beliefs and rituals. The rock-carvings have a part in rituals, here defined as an enactment of religious beliefs by which people communicate with the supernatural. Several elements may be involved: some form of (physical) performance; an oral text/incantation; some form of material religious object. When dealing with prehistoric societies, the evidence for ritual activities lies in representations – objects, structures, depictions – to which religious beliefs may be attached. In this chapter I deal with rock-carvings, some of which actually illustrate ritual performance, one of the other elements in rituals. Besides the meaning(s) intended by the makers, the carvings reflect cultural and natural life at the time. We can recognize bears and boats, but we have no direct knowledge about what they metaphorically symbolize. We might guess, or give non-testable probability statements – reasoned guesswork – based on our understanding of the ethnographic record; these are the starting-points for interpretation. In context with our knowledge of the societies that produced the carvings, it gives us some idea of associated beliefs, as well as how the societies were structured and how inhabitants perceived the world in which they lived. It is towards this perception, specifically about the perception of landscapes, that this chapter is oriented.

Previous discussions of rock-art and landscape have focused on why panels of art are located at particular places in landscapes (e.g. Hood 1988; Mandt 1991; Sognnes and Haug 1998; Whitley 1998; Nordström 1999) and on how landscapes were perceived (e.g. Bradley 1994). This chapter examines landscapes which may be represented *in the panels themselves* in Alta in northern Norway, at Nämforsen in northern Sweden, and on the River Vyg on the south-west coast of the White Sea in northern Karelia, Russia. The individual figures, the compositions of figures and the rock surface may, singly or in combination, signal some type of landscape. Furthermore, the figures and, at least at times, rock surfaces are elements in a story which in itself would signal the landscape in which it was enacted. These stories are, of course, unknown to us. But, when there is a story there is often an essential dimension of time. The dimension of time is represented in some carvings. In essence, the actors, place and time – essential ingredients in any story – are represented in the carvings.

In the ethnographic record of northern populations it is often claimed that the worlds of the spirits were a mirror of or modelled on the world in which the people lived (e.g. Bogoras 1902; 1909; Shirokogoroff 1935; Kannisto *et al.* 1958: 71–2; Anisimov 1963). Assuming that some rock-carvings represent stories with spirits and people, the modelling implies that the landscapes in the stories are informative about the makers' perception of landscape whether in a spirit world or in the world where people live and interact with spirits. This chapter is about recognizing such landscapes.

Stories

In the nineteenth century, it was suggested that Scandinavian rock-art documented and commemorated historic events, such as battles and conquest (Glob 1969: 156–7). This view was soon rejected and replaced by the view that it was all associated with religion and rituals (Almgren 1926). This became the dominant view in Scandinavia, Russia and beyond; the association with rituals, myths and cosmology has for long been a common hypothesis. As Tilley (1991: 145) phrases it in the analysis of Nämforsen: rock-art is a 'visual statement of myths, of cosmic categories and associations held to structure the supernatural world and human existence'. When looking to ethnography to search for clues about the meaning of visual art such as rock-carvings, once an association to beliefs is made, the connection to myths in which spirits, spirit ancestors, spirit masters and spirit helpers, souls, soul masters, giants, 'trolls', humans and animals interact appears plausible. One cannot but be struck by the significance different beings in these mythological stories had for the life of the human populations, and the rituals and cunning (such as with tricks) undertaken to control or defeat these beings, beings considered to be a real part of the world. In a Frazerian (Segal 1998: 5) view, myths serve to explain the world, and rituals are required to communicate with the spirits who control the forces of nature. Specifically, the communication could have been associated with changes in nature: through rites of transition (Durkheim 1915), the gods of nature are revived, imaginary beings and places are reified and made into real 'things' by social actions. To cite Rappaport (1999: 9) 'Each human society develops a unique culture, which is also to say that it constructs a unique world that includes not only a special understanding of trees and rocks and water surrounding it, but of other things, many unseen, as real as those trees and animals and rocks.' Nothing seems more important than to communicate with 'the other things', the life of the supernatural, for human benefit, and those who have the benefit of the spirits have indeed done well. The rock-carvings are part of this communication.

Rules, both implicit and explicit in religious beliefs and practice, would have restricted meaning and form at any time. Given that rituals and beliefs are strongly bound to tradition, meanings may have prevailed over long periods of time. Yet, judging from other changes in the archaeological record and changes in the art itself, forms and meanings also changed. There may have been room for some variation in the stories told by those who conducted rituals, while tradition may have given little room for deviation in the meaning the stories portrayed and were associated with. Drastic changes may have been associated with changing beliefs caused by strong external influences. Both makers and later users of the rock-art had a perception of landscapes, but it is only the actual maker and those closely culturally bound to him/her who are likely to have perceived the signals as they were intended by the maker. Later viewers, such as ourselves, receive signals, but these are processed through other, often multiple contexts related to our desire to interpret. This we will always do. A good example of multiple interpretations of rock-art is Tilley's (1991) challenging analysis of Nämforsen.

In folklore similar stories can be found over large areas and among different peoples. Stories travel. When reading Qvikstads' (1927–29) collections of Sami myth and lore, one recognizes elements in the stories as shared in many cultures, and many elements are culture specific. But, there is not a simple one-to-one correlation between folklore and other aspects of society (Georges and Jones 1995: 160–71). On the other hand, the setting is Sami; the stories are a part of Sami identity. Stories, such as creation stories, are connected to groups of people, ethnic groups, and are told in the appropriate contexts. Notably, in the literature I have come across different creation stories associated with the Sami; it is unclear to me if the differences are group specific or general for the population as a whole. Similar specificity and generality can be claimed for the stories among the Fenno-Ougriennes (Finno-Ugrians) (Kannisto *et al.* 1958) and for songs connected with the hunt and the cult of the bear (Edsmann 1994). In a sense, some stories connect to different peoples or groups of peoples/cultures; some are a part of their rituals and identity. Some of this identity may be reflected in the carvings.

My analysis starts with the suggestion I recently put forward (Helskog 1999) that stories, in which the bear as the central actor embraces the three worlds of the universe, are depicted in the rock-art in Alta. The cosmos was divided into three fundamental sections, the upper and lower worlds where spirits lived, and the middle world on earth where people and spirits lived. Even among the Chuckee (Bogoras 1902: 590; 1909) who once distinguished nine worlds, the three fundamental sections existed. The existence of three cosmic worlds appears to be (close to) a universal phenomenon within systems of beliefs; its wide distribution in space and culture indicates a long antiquity. The observation is often repeated (e.g. Jochelson 1908: 25; Bogoras 1925: 213; Shirokogoff 1935; Kannisto *et al.*: 1958: 71–2; Anisimov 1963; Vasilevich 1963: 56; Alekseev 1990: 96–101) that spirits structure their life according to the world where people live. The same applies to the realm of the dead (Chernetsov 1963: 34). So the structures and the interaction between the rock-art figures may reflect how people organized their life. Therefore similarities between the worlds are to be expected. The problem is where and how to look.

It is possible to examine the elements in the carvings. While deciding which elements (figures) compose stories is definitely problematic, it is not impossible. Where the combination of figures is formally repeated, as it is in the compositions with the bears, one can see the compositions as variations on a story. In the carvings of any one phase and of different phases in Alta, no two compositions or congregations of figures are identical. There are similarities, definitely – figures/elements and details are repeated – but the panels as a whole are always different. Also, if several panels together form a story, the variation becomes more complex.

In the three areas examined here there are small and large panels, from those of a few square metres to those covering 70 sq. m. The size and borders of a panel appear sometimes to be set by the size of the rock surface itself, by cracks and depressions dividing the surface. At other times the panel covers an area considerably smaller than the available surface; or it clearly cuts across cracks and depressions, or even incorporates them in the composition. Perhaps the different panels, as single entities, were in some way connected into large entities where the rock surface in between also had a meaning. Landscapes may be represented by multiple surfaces and panels. My choice as researcher is to treat panels as single entities. When there is more than a couple of metres between groups of figures, or when the rock between closer-spaced panels is useless for carving, I do not treat them together.

Landscapes

The first signal comes from the carvings themselves and their location. There is an interaction between the art and my recognition and interpretation of what I see, as a person far removed in social context from the original maker. I see things which have the same physical shape for me as in prehistory, such as boats, reindeer, halibut and human figures. Where I can identify what the carving imitates, I may recognize one or several elements of landscape in the story.

The problem, of course, is that I see these marks as a twentieth-century male who grew up in a certain cultural environment, a man with an academic education, which is nothing like the life-experience of the prehistoric populations of the arctic.

'Landscape' refers to the way land – mountains, lakes and the ocean, life therein – is perceived and used. The perception, classification and use is connected to, for example, historic tradition, subsistence-settlement patterns, function, rituals, systems of beliefs, age groups and gender (Engelstad 1991; Ingold 1993; 1996; Tilley 1994).

The culture groups who made the rock-art discussed in this chapter were hunter-fisher-gatherers. Judging from the ethnographic evidence, which is partly a relic of prehistoric cultural patterns and beliefs, the groups of people were a part of an environment with spirits and other non-human beings with which they interacted (Ingold 1996). The landscape was alive. Ingold's (1996) elaborate discussion of comprehending the world of which the hunter-gatherers were/are a part distinguishes between society and nature as separate interacting entities in a western constructionist way (a process of mental representation) and as an environment in which all are engaged – humans, other humans, non-human animals, plants and inanimate entities. According to Ingold, in the knowledge of the hunter-gatherers themselves they did not separate nature from culture (Ingold 1996: 128):

> In their account here are not two worlds, of nature and society, saturated with personal powers and embracing humans, the animals and plants on which they depend, and the features of the landscape in which they live and move. Within this one world, humans figure not as composites of body and mind but as undivided beings, 'organism-persons' relating as such both to other humans and non-human agencies end entities in their environment. Between these spheres of involvement there is no *absolute* separation, they are but contextually delimited segments of a single field.

The hunting-fishing-gathering populations of Alta 4200–1800 BC would, according to Ingold (1996), probably have lived in an environment in which everything was interwoven. If aspects of the belief system of prehistoric populations have survived into the ethnographic present, these should be expected to be found among similar populations in geographically connected regions where the animal life is somewhat similar, simply because this animal life was a significant part of the belief system. The fact that the same animals are emphasized in prehistoric rock-art and animal effigies as in the ethnographic stories indicates some similar choices, at least. The ethnographic record is more detailed, and is not a record of prehistoric beliefs and practices; these span approximately 180 generations (2000 years). The ethnographic material is not solely from populations classified as hunter-fisher-gatherers; most would be classified as pastoral nomads for whom hunting was an important activity, all of whom share major elements within their systems of beliefs. It is these common elements which are of particular interest. One such element is that the universe was perceived to consist of different worlds.

Judging from the ethnographic record I see no strong reasons to suggest that the populations of these northern areas separated society and nature rather than being totally integrated with their environment. This does not mean that the environment was not perceived as consisting of different parts in relation to different forms of life, undertakings and beliefs. Indeed people were aware of the diversity of nature and the beliefs associated, and their own actions therein. In this sense, the environment may have been divided into landscapes – the used and perceived part of the environment at any given time. In this sense, the concept of landscape is contextual, but, regrettably, it is a concept and term which we do not know if prehistoric populations ever had.

Understanding landscapes as contextual entities means that any environment in which people lived and/or which they used in different ways could have been perceived as consisting of different landscapes. For example, in historic times coastal Sami in northern Norway hunted, fished and picked berries in the same mountain region through which pastoral Sami drove their reindeer during spring and autumn; the religious beliefs related to the land appear to have been similar in both groups. The same geographic area was associated with different subsistence-economic emphasis while the ritual engagement with it appears to have been similar. The Tungus in Transbaikal and Manchuria, by their knowledge of their environment, distinguished (Shirokogoroff 1933: 46–9) several areas associated with subsistence activities – reindeer-breeding, reindeer-breeding and hunting, hunting, cattle-breeding, agriculture. Associated with these activities were rituals and spirits. The environment changed with the seasons of the year; associated with all were spirits and rituals. There was a great deal of dynamism. Further south, in the central region of northern Nepal different ethnic groups engaged the same geographical area differently with different economies and rituals (Evans 1998).

For the Sami, there is no direct knowledge about how space and time were understood and divided prior to Christian and Scandinavian influences (Rydving 1995: 96), which eventually replaced aboriginal rituals. For example, among the Lule Sami (Rydving 1995) and the Nenets (Samoyeds) (Lethisalo 1924), there were a few sacred places where the entire community and people from other communities met, and rituals were performed. Second, there were many ritual places along the migratory routes, especially where the routes coincided for several families/groups. Third, rituals were associated with individual families, in daily rituals near the tent. Among the Sami the centre of the ritual process was the tent and the place where it stood (Rydving 1995: 99–103). Transition rituals could be performed at more than one type of place, and crisis rituals at any place. The seasonal nomadism indicates that the different sacred places were visited year after year according to a recurrent pattern. In essence, there were areas with special ritual significance which connected the life in the different worlds. The environment was like an irregular lattice with ritual places. The ritual places marked the special places in the environment, and landscapes were the elements in the lattice connecting how the worlds met. Some of the rituals were conducted at specific places, as exemplified by the rock-carvings or the Sami *seide* stones (Manker 1957), while others were conducted at appropriate places where spirits could be contacted. In between was the environment with landscapes, perceived and changing according to context.

In essence, there were spiritual/ritual/cosmic landscapes, farmers/hunters/fishers/group/clan/territorial landscapes and so on. Landscapes such as these could be represented in the rock-art.

Strikingly, there is a distinct focus on outdoor life and activities in the carvings at Alta (K. Helskog 1983), at Zalavruga (Ravdonikas 1936; Savvatejev 1970) and at Nämforsen (Hallström 1960) – animals, boats and associated activities, human figures in hunting and fishing scenes, and human figures in processions. The question to be answered is if any of these can be connected with landscapes.

The likeness of human and animal figures in the rock-carvings to the natural form indicates that spirits were perceived to take abode in or have the form of existing life-forms and natural features – mountains, stones, lakes and rivers – as well as the forest, in trees and in animals, and in objects and structures made by people. But not all depictions may represent spirits. A drawing by an old Evenk illustrates how a shaman and a shamanic spirit move through a complex space – a landscape – to heal a sick person (Anisimov 1963: 106–7). It includes clan territories, settlements, a river with tributaries, sacred vegetation, shaman, people and spirits, and a passage to the underworld – altogether thirty-eight elements all in the world where the people live. So the complex composition informs us not only about aspects of healing but also about a landscape both with spirits and with cultural and natural features; yet the intent of the story was not to inform about the landscape itself.

Judging from ethnographic information, a story can contain spirits, humans, animals, and natural features and phenomena, as are illustrated by the old Evenk, and as also indicated by the compositions at Alta where bears play a central part (Helskog 1999). The world of the people is integral to the cosmology, and the spirits are integral to the human world. At times they are one and the same. This 'mirror effect' – by which the spirit and human worlds are structured alike – means that the human world is represented in whatever worlds on which the depictions may focus. Interestingly enough, the compositions with the bears described at Alta (Helskog 1999) focus on the middle world. The lower world appears to be represented by the rock basin with water through which the bear enters, and by the upside-down figures. The upper world is represented by the sun and the moon symbols and by the inverse figures at the top of the panel (at Kåfjord).

Part of the landscape is provided by the rock surface. The old argument that a rock surface or part thereof – the cracks, depressions and protrusions – may have meaning (Lewis-Williams and Dowson 1990; Ouzman 1998) can have a landscape perspective. The rock-carvings are elements in a landscape which may be represented in the rock-art itself. In this sense some landscapes are really multi-layered. Points/elevations on the rock surface may represent mountains, water-pools may represent lakes, depressions valleys, running water rivers, cracks openings into the lower world, and so on. Different colours in the rock itself may be important. Also, sunlight plays a role, since light from any source at a low angle to the carvings brings out structure in both the rock and the carvings, and gives a three-dimensional effect to the surface, as for example Savvatejev (1984: 170) noted for Zalavruga. And so on.

Time

Time in the carvings is represented, indirectly or directly, by features of climate, geography and differing behaviour among animals and people. Elements of time can be extracted from representations associated with the large-scale seasonal changes in climate, fauna and temperature in northernmost Europe, an area 'constantly' transforming itself within a cyclic pattern. The belief that these changes were controlled by spirits had a profound effect on the ritual world of beliefs and associated activities. Among the Lule Sami (Rydving 1995), there appear to have been four rituals which were repeated every year; of these, the great Autumn Festival held at the slaughter of reindeer at the end of September was the most important. Rituals associated with changing seasons varied, sacrifices varied; owing to the mobility of this society, different seasons meant different places (Lehtisalo 1924; Rydving 1995). Changes in seasons meant that rituals occurred in different places. Thus, a particular place/landscape is associated with differences in season, differences in time.

The sun and the moon are two of the most significant spirits of the cosmic universe among people all over the world. At the Arctic Circle the sun is permanently below the horizon from 21 November to 21 January when it reappears for barely one minute the first day, increasing gradually day by day. Around Christmas there are hardly two/three hours of dim daylight. The sun is constantly above the horizon from 21 May until 21 July, when the days gradually begin to be shorter. The moon has a strong presence during the winter, but is seldom seen during the middle part of summer. So the growing season in northernmost Europe is short; the winter is long (7–8 months) and fairly cold, with some variation between coast and inland, and according to altitude. The vegetation withers away in the autumn; most of the fauna responds by migrating, to reappear in the spring. Some migrations are between biotopes not too far apart, between coast and inland or from barren areas to forests; some animals and birds do not migrate. There is always food in the sea, rivers and lakes. The sea along the Norwegian coast does not freeze during winter and provides basic resources throughout the year.

In the region of the River Vyg, at the southwest corner of the White Sea in Karelia, Russia, the annual cycle of an inland climate is as dramatic as in the coastal area of northernmost Norway. Also, the White Sea freezes for several kilometres off-shore during winter, sometimes totally I have been told. In northern Sweden, where Nämforsen is located on the Ångerman River, the annual changes are similar and equally distinct.

Rituals are associated with major changes in nature, such as the return of spring. Different characteristics of different animal figures reflect differences in time/season. From ethnographic evidence and the state of the animals themselves, the large-scale co-operative reindeer hunt is to be associated with the autumn migration from the coast to inland. Reindeer without antlers indicate late winter/early spring (Nordkvist 1966). Herds of reindeer with large antlers indicate summer, possibly males before the rutting season. An elk (*Alces alces*) depicted without antlers but with a large beard will be an image of a male

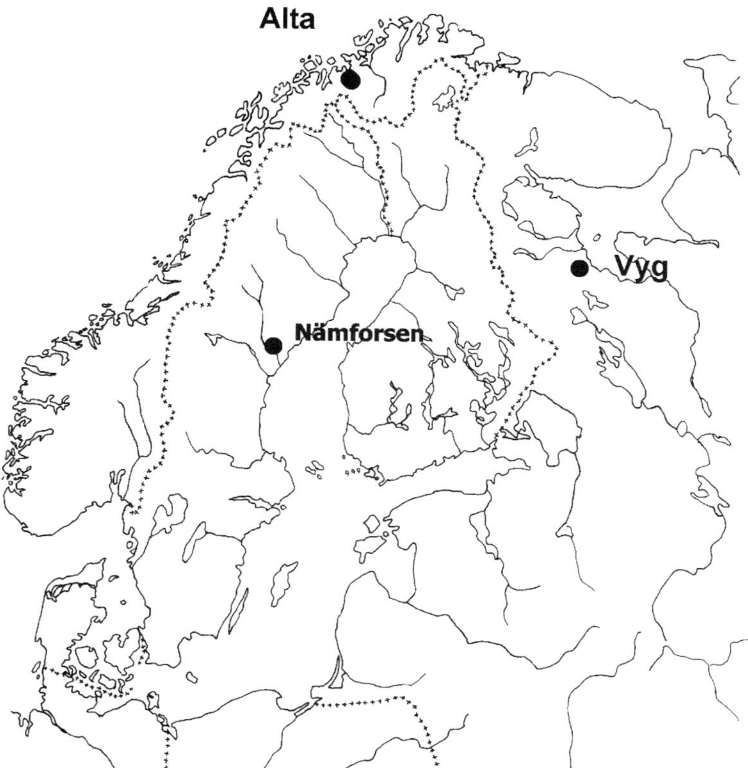

Fig. 13.1. Map of northernmost Europe with site locations mentioned in the text.

elk during midwinter (Lönnberg 1923). Female elk have small beards; depending on beards alone to distinguish male and female is tenuous. Elk without beards and antlers are female at any time of the year, and when in a herd represent winter. Elk with antlers indicate males in the period from late winter/early spring to winter when they lose their antlers. Any obviously pregnant mammal indicates late winter to early spring, the time when the calves are born. Bears suggest spring, summer or autumn because they hibernate during the winter. Most birds depicted indicate spring to autumn. Beluga whales in the White Sea indicate early spring to late autumn (Heptner 1996: 776), especially when hunted from boats. These associations between animals and seasons are an important way of recognizing temporal differences.

The case-studies

The carvings I examine to demonstrate the existence of pictured landscapes are from the two oldest phases of carvings in Alta, north Norway, from Nämforsen in northern Sweden, and from Zalavruga and Besovi Sledki at the mouth of the River Vyg in northern Karelia, Russia (Fig. 13.1). The analysis is qualitative; stories and landscapes are to be recognized not by numbers but by figure orientation and associations. In addition, different frequencies of stories represented may have some bearing upon ritual frequencies, their importance or associated culture groups, questions I do not address at this point.

Chronologically some of the panels in the three regions overlap within the period from the late fifth to the early second millennium BC. The three

Fig. 13.2. The main section of the panel Bergbukten I, Alta, northern Norway.

The panel is smooth, partly glacially striated, undulating, with surfaces of various sizes and orientation. There are pools of rainwater. One set of bear tracks leads from the den to the right and enters the largest and deepest of these pools, one set extends upwards, while the third set extends to the left through a long depression in the rock surface, as if through a valley, and ends in a hunting scene in front of the gate in a large reindeer corral.

It is as if stories are illustrated and narrated, such that features in the rock surface and the pools of water, together with the actual places in the stories, constitute or illustrate the landscape in which they take place. As such the landscapes are constructed within the environment which constitutes the universe.

The carvings are painted to make them visible for visitors.

Drawing: Ernst Høgtun.

areas contain the largest number of panels, figures and compositions in northernmost Europe. They have a common shore location, and all are associated with hunter-fisher-gatherer societies. All three areas have been extensively studied and interpreted (e.g. Ravdonikas 1936; Savvatejev 1970; 1984; Simonsen 1979; E. Helskog 1983; Helskog 1988; Tilley 1991; Olsen 1994; Baudou 1995).

Alta

My examination of the rock-art landscapes in Alta includes panels from phases I and II, dated approximately 4200–3300 and 3300–1800 BC (Helskog 2000), commencing with the compositions with the bears at Bergbukten I, phase I (Fig. 13.2). From the den – the hibernation place – depicted as an open circle on a slightly slanting surface, bear tracks are leading upwards, downwards and horizontally (Helskog 1999: fig. 5). After leaving the den in the spring the bears walked horizontally along the bottom of a long shallow depression in the rock surface to emerge, towards the autumn, on a sloping surface where they are surrounded by armed human figures and attacked. The tracks from the den go downwards into water and connect the bear with the spirits in the lower world, while the tracks upwards lead to higher parts of the terrain such as mountains to contact spirits in the upper world(s). The topography of the rock surface represents the topography of a landscape through which bears walk, a landscape connecting the worlds of the universe.

In a composition at Kåfjord (Fig. 13.3) there are two bears in dens 8 m apart, connected by their tracks. In the den to the left the bear faces the opening as if leaving in the spring, while in the other it is facing the back as if entering in late autumn. Tracks, perhaps from the same bears, from between possible sun and moon symbols higher up on the rock surface connect to the track between the two dens, close to spring, and continue downwards into a basin which today fills with rain- or melt-water. Above the symbols of the sun and the moon there are only two figures,

Fig. 13.3. A section of the panel at Kåfjord in Alta.

The bears appear to move from one den to another, from spring to autumn, into the ground through a fissure (where rainwater collects), and from the sky at a place between the moon and the sun.

It is a story where the bear moves through a landscape which includes the main dimensions of a universe. Other animals – reindeer and elk – and human-like figures are a part of the story or stories, which take place in an environment which combines different landscapes. In this the rock surface and the water also play a part.

a reindeer and an elk, facing each other. They are inverted, as if the two animals are standing in dimensions/worlds which are upside down to each other. At the scene of the hunt of the bears at Bergbukten I there are two human figures in a similar inverted position.

The human figures at Kåfjord, dancing under the sun and the moon, represent an associated ritual, perhaps acting out the return of the bear and of life in spring. The reindeer corral to the right, similar to that at Bergbukten I, suggests autumn. Both scenes point to a story where the bear is moving through time and space (Helskog 1999), where the rock surface signifies at least part of the landscape in the story. In three of the compositions the tracks of the bear enter a basin which fills with water during rain; the basin may represent a lake through which the bear enters or leaves the nether world (Helskog 1999). In the fourth example the tracks leading downwards may have met the high-tide level. The compositions focus on the middle world. Illustrating the bear walking between the three worlds of the universe, the composition also presents a cyclic dimension of time. There appear to be several different routes. The point is that the bear walks through the yearly seasons, through time and space, in a landscape which appears to be partly real and partly cosmic.

The panel Bergbukten IVB (Fig. 13.4) illustrates an equal variety of figures and activities. A

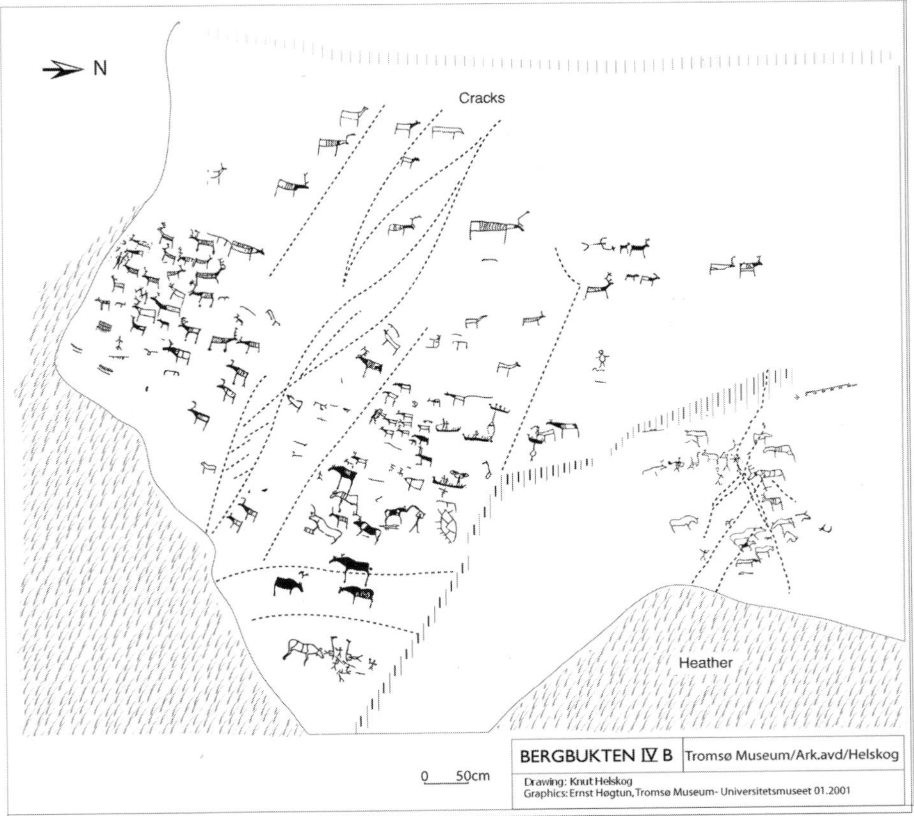

Fig. 13.4. Bergbukten IVB, Alta.

This panel is on a relatively flat surface. Here there appear to be several stories and concentrations of figures. For example, to the left there is a hunting scene with reindeer, while to the right reindeer, bears, boats and halibut, and human figures are intermixed.

Given that the scenes represent stories, the makers of the carvings appear to have mixed animals and cultural phenomena in a way which can be done only in stories and not in real life. Yet, if the stories represent lore connected to beliefs, then what is represented was probably regarded as a real part of the environments in which people, animals, spirits and souls lived.

human figure aims an arrow at a herd of reindeer, a bear and two cubs facing in the same direction. On the other side, to the right, is a boat with two human figures, of which the one in front is aiming at the same reindeer from behind. To the upper right there is a boat and halibut. Higher up on the upper left is a human figure who stands and aims an arrow at a reindeer herd. Further down is a herd of elk. At the bottom, a composition with human figures and elk-headed poles marks the lowest part of the panel. Elk appear to dominate the lower part of the panel, close to the water-level. This fact, the place of water as a route to the underworld, the presence of boats with elk-heads, and the role of boats as a possible vehicle for transporting the deceased to the world of the dead, has made me wonder if elk may be strongly associated with the world of the dead, a representation for a spirit associated with the transition from life to death, as well as the revival of life.

None of the figures overlaps another; they are on the same surface, and if they are in no way related why depict them so close, rather than using

Fig. 13.5. A section of the panel Bergbukten IVB, Alta. The boat with human figures who have caught a halibut may simply represent sympathetic magic. On the other hand, the bear facing the halibut, under water where bears do not belong in nature, clearly indicate that the composition is a story with element of beliefs where such a combination is possible, in a landscape where both halibut and bears, or the spirits they represent, can travel. Together they appear not to be connected with sympathetic magic. Photograph by Knut Helskog/Tromsø Museum.

other parts of the surface? Certainly those who originally related to the carvings must have seen all the figures and, I assume, knew the associated stories. Judging from the elements, whether one or several stories, the landscape(s) was (were) many-sided, but not necessarily excluding any of the cosmic worlds.

Further to the right, at Bergbukten IVB (Fig. 13.5), is a boat with two human figures from which extends a long fishing-line with a halibut on the hook. To the left of the boat is a small reindeer (?) and a symbol with fringes like an amulet or a solar symbol. Again, the maker chose to make the carvings on a separate surface and not on the surface where the majority of the other carvings are. Also, the boat is carved on a fairly horizontal 'ledge', and the fishing-line extends over the 'edge' as if from the top of the sea and down under. A bear faces the halibut and, together with the fishing-line and the boat, stands as a separate entity. There is room enough. The rock surface has become a *part* of the composition, rather than just a blank support for carving. Clearly only a spirit in the shape of a bear belongs in the sea together with a halibut. So, the composition includes a landscape that goes from above water to within the water where halibut and a bear, or spirits in their shapes, met in a landscape only possible in a cosmic context, in a story. If this is part of a story, the story is beyond human experience.

In most panels the recognition of patterns is vastly more difficult. At the small complex panel Ole Pedersen IX (Fig. 13.6), on an almost horizontal surface, there is no shortage of space, yet a small area is for some reason packed with carvings. Perhaps there was some element in the surface itself which made it special, like the lighter and weaker section immediately to the north; and carvings had to be crammed into a small area of the surface. Yet few figures overlap, and I suggest that the panel should be seen as one complex composition. The elements of the stories exclude water and the sky yet include figures which do not

Fig. 13.6. The panel Ole Pedersen IX, Alta. The figures in this small panel, on a flat almost horizontal surface, illustrate several different activities and animals, from rituals with elk-headed poles, to human or human-like figures, some with bows and arrows, to bears, elks, a reindeer and a bird and two hares. The fact that the figures are congregated together on a small part of the rock surface indicates that they may be part of a set of related stories – possibly connected to specific ceremonies – set in different perceived landscapes but within the environment represented by all the carvings and the rock surface. Photograph by Knut Helskog/Tromsø Museum.

Fig. 13.7. The boat figures in the panel Bergbukten IIIA, Alta, point towards a constructed marine landscape and a story where swimming reindeer are connected with human figures and boats (with elk-heads).
Photograph by Knut Helskog/Tromsø Museum.

'naturally' belong together. Their occurring together indicates that, in a world where spirits and all other life are integrated, these might naturally belong together.

Lastly, I take a short look at the younger and small panel Bergbukten IIIA (Fig. 13.7), located on a small and well-defined rock surface. On the for left is a small 'necked' oval figure (a bird?), and to the right of this are two elk figures, one incomplete. Continuing rightwards, there are three reindeer swimming behind a boat with three human figures, two men and one woman, as if hunted or led. Below is an unmanned boat where a line extends upward from the elk head to a small circle in front of a small animal (reindeer calf?) which is facing downwards, an unusual orientation. To the left is another boat with three human figures, this time two women and one man; and to the right of this again are six boats of which four are unmanned and only one is facing to the left. Above this boat is a swimming reindeer also moving towards the left. This composition combines the maritime and the terrestrial, with a focus on the maritime which comprises the right two-thirds of the panel.

Nämforsen

The carvings here are located on two small islands and sections of the river bank below the waterfall named Nämforsen on the Ångerman river in north Sweden (Hallström 1960). At 5700 years ago, with a different sea-level, the panels were located on the shore of the Bay of Bothnia; this sets a maximum date (Tilley 1991; Baudou 1995) for the figures as earlier the rocks were under water. The carvings are dominated by three types of figures – elk, boats and human. Each surface is documented as a separate unit. Unfortunately, the documentation by Hallström (1960) does not show the physical features on and between the carved rock surfaces.

As at Alta, there are compositions, here with elk, boats and human figures, singly or in various combinations, in land- and water-associated activities. Birds and fish are rare. A fairly typical large panel, panel G: 1 in Main Group I (Fig. 13.8), has thirty-six elk, four crewed boats, two human figures, two geese and six sickle-shaped items. Human figures in the boats hold moose-headed poles. Whatever story or stories they represent, the landscapes combine elements from land (dominant), water and sky (least). Other compositions combine elements from two dimensions, while some only represent one. Composition C: 1 in Main Group I consists mainly of elk, some human figures and one fish; Q: 1 in Main Group II is a composition of elk and human figures; while a marine landscape appears to be the main one in, for example, A: 1 and Z: 1 in Main Group I. The drawings of Hallström (1960) show, among inverted figures as symbols of upside-down worlds, only one elk and a few boats (in Main Group I

Fig. 13.8. The maritime landscape which appears to be constructed in the story/stories at panel G (Main group I. Subgroup G: 1) at Nämforsen in northern Sweden include elk, boats, human figures and aquatic birds – a landscape which connects water and land. The marine aspect and the connection of elk with lakes and swampy areas point towards a focus on the marine association.
After Hallström 1960: plate XIII.

D: 5 (elk) and Z: 1, in Main Group IIIB: 1, and in Main Group IID: 5).

The focus at Nämforsen is on the elk. The human figures with elk-headed poles point towards the elk as a representation of a spirit significant in ritual where the elk represents a cosmic being of some sort. The most frequent compositions are groups of elk, often interpreted as small herds. Elk form herds in winter. Winter is indicated by the lack of antlers on males, which are also distinguished by their large beards. Some compositions include only female animals (without antlers and beard), and a female with a small calf would signify spring to autumn. Many of the panels appear as compositions in stories, but the directionality of the story is not obvious, unless it follows the direction in which the figures are facing. In many cases figures face each other as in a meeting, as when a herd of elk is intermixed with human figures with outstretched arms as if redirected by human figures blocking their way. Seen in relation to Alta, the Nämforsen carvings display less variation in elements, compositions and themes. The seasons represented cover the entire year, with a focus on winter rituals (Ramqvist 1990).

The River Vyg

There are three sites to be explored, Old and New Zalavruga and Besovi Sledki, located close to the mouth of the River Vyg which flows into the White Sea (Savvatejev 1984: 125). The adjacent panels at Old and New Zalavruga are located on the shore of an island. The surface of the site named Old Zalavruga and a part of New Zalavruga gently slope towards the river. According to Savvatejev (1977: 82–3; 1984: 184) the earliest carvings were made from the last half of the fourth millennium BC into the earliest half of the second millenium BC. Most of the surface of New Zalavruga is relatively horizontal and water collects in shallow pools between the carvings (Savvatejev 1984: 195). In none of these pools is there any carving, as if purposely avoided. Besovi Sledki is located on what was once a small island in the middle of the stream.

Most if not all of the panels at Zalavruga appear to represent compositions since each has more than one figure, often engaged in some sort of activity (Savvatejev 1970; 1984). There are scenes of hunting elk, reindeer and bears; white whales (beluga) are harpooned from boats; there are herds of animals, particularly reindeer and moose, and a flock of geese. As Savvatejev (1970: 170) suggests, in the carvings at Zalavruga there were representations of social patterns, especially connected with co-operative hunting, and to my mind also possible representations of the landscapes where the hunts were undertaken. Savvatejev (1984: 149) recognizes an element of landscape in the carving: in group XV an undulating line, 3 m long together with boats and three small animals (calves and female elk) in a line, may represent, he suggests, an old topographic sketch of a mythological river.

The scene where elk are hunted by three human figures on skis (Fig. 13.9) is perhaps the best example of where the rock surface plays a part in the landscape of the composition. The short skis can be used both to slide and to walk. The tracks appear on the highest point of the rock surface to the left, first as marks of walking on a horizontal surface, then sliding on a sloping surface, then walking (horizontal), then sliding (slightly sloping), and lastly walking on a horizontal surface. The tracks are from three hunters; two are shooting elk with bows and arrows, while the third sticks a spear in the back of a third elk. It appears that the hunters have followed the elk for some distance, judging from the tracks. The elk walked in a single line through the snow before being separated and killed. The story moves through a hunters' winter landscape. The elk to the far right in the elk hunt is facing a white whale (beluga) which is harpooned from three boats. It is as if two stories or two times, winter to the left and summer to the right, are meeting. Notably, to the right the whole year is represented in several other compositions, as if several stories also constitute a single larger/longer story. Footprints are associated with a human figure walking through a landscape. A bear (Savvatejev 1970: fig. 18), which has run to a tree and climbed to the top, is penetrated with arrows from a male hunter on skis. The skis signify winter and the landscape forested, while hunting of beluga is associated with sea/river and summer.

At another panel at New Zalavruga, group VIII, a beluga whale is harpooned from six boats (Fig. 13.10). The landscape appears first to be that of beluga-hunters in the White Sea. The whale faces three bears, and a human figure aiming an arrow at an elk: there are a duck and a swan, three bears coming in from the lower right, a beluga, two spears/harpoons, and three human figures. The diverse scenes of figures point towards a story with a very complicated landscape, or a story moving through several landscapes. The rock surface, level and horizontal, appears to form no obvious landscape features itself. Again, figures are from the middle world. The story and landscape combine elements which normally do not interact, except in mythology, and as such only in cosmic landscapes.

Hunting seems a main theme at New Zalavruga. For example, fifteen of the sixteen geese in group VI (Savvatejev 1970: fig. 42 and 43) are shot by arrows, apparently from a human figure standing in a boat. Adjacent to the boat there stands a human figure (male) with an elaborate head-dress, holding an L-shaped weapon (?). The landscape is a lake or river.

At Old Zalavruga (Ravdonikas 1936; Savvatejev 1970; 1984) there is a focus on elk, human figures and boats. The panel appears to be divided in two parts, one with the line

Fig. 13.9. Part of a panel at New Zalavruga on the River Vyg in northern Karelia in Russia.
This is another example where the topography of the rock surface was used as a part of the landscape in the story. The skiers came in from the upper left, walked on the flat top surface before sliding down a slope on the rock surface, then walking and then again sliding down a slight slope, before walking on a horizontal surface and catching up with the three elk. To the right are boats, human figures, harpooned belugas and two bears penetrated by arrows and spears. Here are several landscapes, from the land through which the skiers walked to the figures to the right, which combines several different landscapes on land as well as above, on and under the sea. Again the landscapes depicted are constructed to 'fit' the stories (or the stories were in the rock and thereafter visualized). In their individuality the compositions and figures represent nature as known by the natural sciences while together they represent the environment in which prehistoric people believed they lived. In that environment bears belonged together with belugas.
After Savvatejev 1984: 164–5.

of three approximately 2 m long elk on top of six approximately 1 m long boats. In front is a wedge-shaped herd (two herds?) of twenty elk – ten bulls (with antlers) and ten does. The elk are moving through a landscape. The only apparent feature on the rock is that the figures are on the highest part of the rock surface – as if they reach for the top, the upper world? Beluga are absent from this panel, although the maritime dimension is represented by boats in both panels.

Another example from Old Zalavruga is the group of human figures on skis, maximum five in a row, each with a ski-pole (Fig. 13.11). Some skis leave tracks, others not (Savvatejev 1970: fig. 14). The rock surface is flat, as if the skiers are being depicted as moving forwards in a flat landscape. That actually is a fair description of north Karelian topography. In his discussion Savvatejev (1984: 170) asserts that the rock, the colour of the rock, the slope and the orientation of the shore are meaning-giving features. He also states that carvings cover the 'optic' favourable part of the rock, by which he means areas conducive to light and shadow effects. The three-dimensionality of the carvings is especially visible in the low light from the rising and setting sun, a common feature for all carvings. There are few representations of imaginary fable worlds, because the carvings are easily identifiable. They express the most important sides in the collective hunt of sea animals. Therefore, what is seen is not always or only part of

Fig. 13.10. This composition, group VIII, at New Zalavruga represents a landscape of belief, as we know that in the natural world bears do not belong together with a harpooned beluga whale and boats, a human figure with bow and arrow, reindeer and swans, except in stories.

After Savvatejev 1970: fig. 48.

rituals but also complex patterns in the context of the society (Savvatejev 1984: 170).

Clearly the stories take in three landscapes: one, as shown above, is on land; a second is at sea; and the third is in the sky, represented by compositions involving birds.

Besovi Sledki

Besovi Sledki consists of a single panel (Savvatejev 1984: 127–34) with a mixture of beluga whales, elk, reindeer, bears, ducks, swans, boats, a few human figures and some 'geometric' symbols (Fig. 13.12), on the edge of a ledge adjacent to a waterfall. Altogether there may be more than 470 figures divided into three stylistic phases. The panel is divided by the ledge, exfoliations, fissures; some surfaces are distinguished by different colours. Indeed, at first glance the panel looks like a jumble of figures. A closer examination reveals compositions of large swans in the centre lower part, groups of beluga, rows of elk, activities such as the harpooning of beluga from boats, a human figure on skis. Strikingly, across the lower part of the panel, there is a straight row of four large footprints, alternating left and right, from the large human figure – in profile with a large penis – depicted as having walked across the panel from left to right. The footprints and adjacent figures are carefully placed not to overlap each other, as if a part of a large cross-cutting composition, but nevertheless not to interfere with other and smaller

Fig. 13.11. Skiers at Old Zalavruga.

The figures are located on the east slope of a small 'point' profunding into what is now a dry river bed (see Savvatejev 1970: fig. 16). The surface is even and water worn with no obvious 'topographic' features, yet the narrated/embedded stories, where human figures on skis play a central part, must have taken place somewhere. The environment, however complex, is at least partly represented by the surface on which the figures are carved, besides being shaped in the minds of the actors. The adjacent different and considerably larger figures on the top and on the west slope of the point, signal (to me) another part or a different story, and another complex environment. The figures are oriented according to the slopes of the rock surfaces.

After Savvatejev 1970: fig. 14.

compositions. Footmarks like these are depicted at New Zalavruga. It is as if a human-shaped being has walked across the panel. In the words of Almgren (1926: 212–18), these are the footprints of a god. It is as if the prints are uniting or emphasizing the cohesion of the figures in the panel and demonstrating the power of the large human figure, the 'demon' as it has been named by the Russian researchers. Again, the panel represents an accumulation of elements from different sides of nature which normally do not belong together, except when the supernatural is an integrating factor. As such there are both cosmological spiritual landscapes and landscapes defined by hunting activities of summer and winter. But surely there was no such thing as a landscape solely defined by the presence of humans and animals, of natural features and climate. Spirits, other non-human and animal life-forms, were always present. Any landscape, as exemplified by the carvings at Besovi Sledki, is bound to contain both natural features/elements of the land and the spirits, souls, demons, etc. which abide therein.

Carvings in the landscape

In ritual communication, the carvings represent liminal places where spirits and people met to maintain and reinforce relationships (Helskog 1999), to maintain social order, to reinforce and negotiate ties, and to distribute rights to resources, for example between coast and inland populations (Hood 1988).

The three concentrations of rock-art panels discussed here are the largest grouping of panels

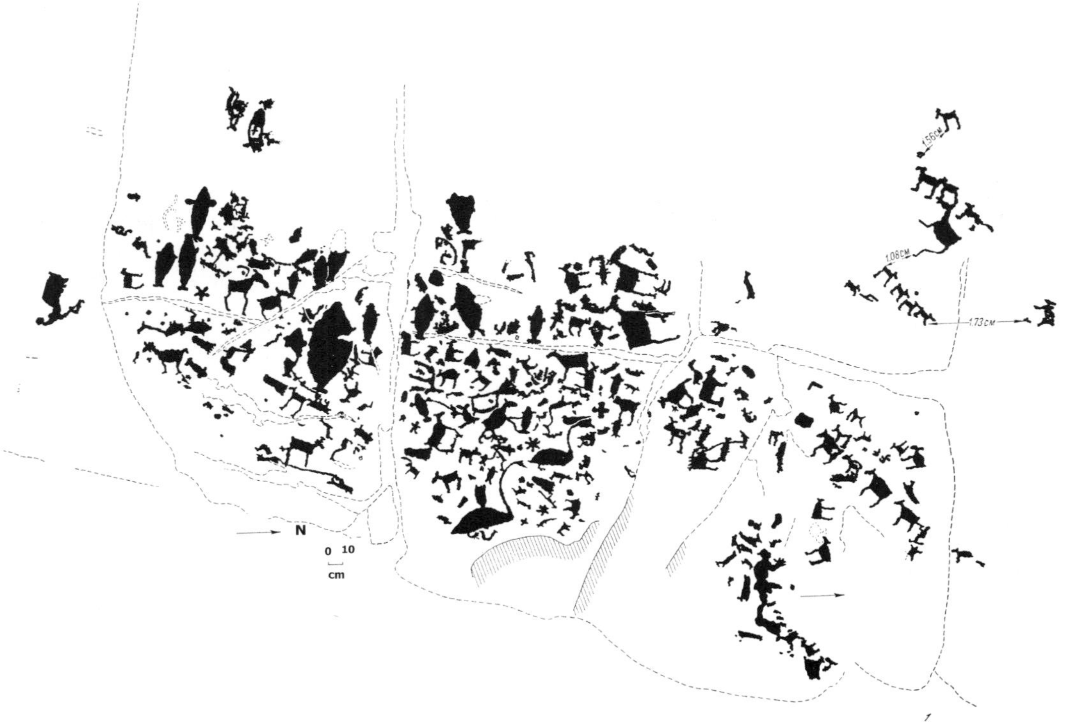

Fig. 13.12. Besovi Sledki, on the River Vyg in Karelia, Russia.

Any story/narrative associated with combinations of marine and maritime fauna combines mutually exclusive habitats, according to present scientific knowledge. On the other hand, in a cosmological scheme with worlds where the activities of natural phenomena, humans, animals, plants and souls of the dead were believed to be decided by the spirits and human influence upon them, the boundaries were probably fluent. In a cosmological sense, the figures at Besovi Sledki can belong together at a place and in an environment chosen by the spirits. In a way, bringing the figures and cosmic landscapes together unites the surrounding environment at this specific place.

After Savvatejev 1970: fig. 6.

in northernmost Norway, Sweden and Karelia; they probably represent three of the most important ritual places in the regions. The fundamentally similar shore-location of these ritual places indicates similar ideas of where the worlds of the cosmos were located and where contacts with life-forms both in the upper and lower worlds of the cosmos were made. The carvings in Alta were always on the coast. The carvings on the lower reaches of the River Vyg and at Nämforsen on the Ångerman were originally located on the coast. As the low-gradient terrain rose with the post-glacial isostatic recovery, they came to be located increasingly farther inland but were still used as ritual meeting places. The shore location on the river, below the waterfall, secured the continued ritual significance of the localities, for several thousand years. As such, the basic understanding/construction of spiritual landscapes where rock–art has a part appears not to have changed significantly.

The land changed with changes in its physical features, from cold to 'warm', from winter to summer, with migration of animals and changing vegetation. In a sense the changing features/elements have a part in defining landscapes.

It is possible that throughout the time that we know as a year, the spiritual and ritual connection to the landscape (and some of its content) would change. Supernatural beings might move and perhaps change abode during different seasons. If the spiritual worlds or the habits of the spirits were a 'mirror' of a 'real world' which is constantly and cyclically transforming and changing, affecting the populations and their choice in subsistence-settlement, then changes in the recognition of landscapes, even of spiritual landscapes are to be expected.

Landscapes with much rock-art may also have been ritually more significant than landscapes with little. The Alta area with its large number of carvings and panels near the head of the fjord contrasts with the ten small panels on boulders 40–100 km further out on the coast. The largest concentration there consists of the five boulders at the site of Slettnes (Hesjedal *et al.* 1996), apparently connected to habitation. Individual panels, or the concentration of a few small panels on boulders, appear to be connected to a village, a single group of people, families or individuals. The large congregation of panels may reflect ritual places where several groups of people met – when moving between coast and inland and/or as a place to which people travelled only for ritual purposes. In northern Sweden and northern Karelia, where the geography is quite different from the Alta region, there is no comparable distribution of rock-art panels. In northern Sweden one small panel is found at a waterfall, Stornorrfors, 150 km north-east of Nämforsen. In Karelia the nearest panels are at Lake Onega, 300 km to the south, with many large panels. In essence, these observations underline how rock-art panels signify permanent places in the landscapes where individuals, and larger or smaller groups of people, address the spirits through rituals for purposes associated with event/time and place. The larger ritual places where people from different groups/clans met at specific times of the year could have been ritually more significant than the smaller areas connected to fewer peoples or a single group/clan or a family. Also, some rituals may have been more important, such as those connected with the major transitions in nature, such as from winter to spring. As the land and as people's subsistence and settlements changed with the seasons, so changed the ritual places and landscapes where people met.

Landscapes in the carvings

Given that the spiritual worlds 'mirror' the human world, the selected elements in the landscapes which are depicted represent real landscapes. Parts of these landscapes may be represented by elements on the rock surface such as water, depressions, fissures, elevations and boulders. There are several examples where this is clearly so. On a larger scale, areas between panels may similarly represent part of the landscape, for example the pools, fissures and ledges between the panels at New Zalavruga or between the panels at Bergbukten. In this way the panels may be connected in large heterogeneous landscapes.

The focus on outdoor stories and figurative carvings is similar in all three areas. In Alta and the River Vyg the variety of animals and activities depicted is much larger than at Nämforsen, and the panels are scattered over a larger area. The more heterogeneous areas at Alta and Vyg may represent a larger variety of rituals and perhaps meanings than Nämforsen, given that variety in form and content reflects variety in stories and associated meanings.

Similarities in beliefs between the three areas with carvings is signalled by the location of the carvings; by the selection of motifs such as the elk-headed poles, the boats with elk-heads on the prow, the bears; by the emphasis on fauna, hunting and fishing; by the figures' likeness to animals in nature; and so on. Surprisingly, I have recognized only one elk-headed pole in the Vyg area (Savvatejev 1970: fig. 78), while at Alta and Nämforsen they are relatively common. Yet artefacts sculpted with elk heads are found in all three regions. Strikingly, the full-bodied human figures at Vyg are depicted in profile (almost 100 per cent), while at both Nämforsen and Alta almost 100 per cent are depicted from the front or the back. This is a fundamentally different perception of how to depict human figures moving in a landscape. So the human figures at Vyg are carved in the same perspective as the animals, while at Alta and Nämforsen they are not.

Terrestrial mammals are dominated by the largest animals, the birds by the larger birds, the fish by halibut (Alta) and salmon (Nåmforsen), and the ocean mammals by whales (Zalavruga, Alta). Beluga whales are recognized only at the sites in the Vyg area; there are other whales in Alta and none at Nämforsen. Reindeer are almost totally absent from Nämforsen, common at Zalavruga and Alta. But the differences are of selection, not absolute presence or absence. White whales appear along the coast of Arctic Norway; the main regions are the White Sea (early spring, late autumn) and the Barents Sea (winter). Swans were found in all three areas, as were reindeer and elk. Some differences are connected with the choices people made of what to depict.

One explanation may simply be that the emphasis on white whales at Vyg on the White Sea reflects that hunting of beluga was a prime occupation there, but not in Alta. Different types of landscapes associated with this activity and the associated beliefs and rituals are represented. This undoubtedly explains some of the differences between the rock-art sites. Others are to be found in the stories told, stories connected with different groups of people, and in the symbols and metaphors used in rituals. The differences do not necessarily mean that the cosmic superstructure was fundamentally different between the three areas of rock-art; they are more probably variations on the same themes.

Conclusions: rock-art, place and story

In this chapter I have seen rock-carving as representing stories, stories which have elements of actors, of place and of time. The focus has been on the element of place recognized as the landscapes in which the stories are enacted. The most important points are as follows.

1 Landscapes are represented in the rock-art. These landscapes consist of supernatural beings, animals, humans, vegetation and topographic features. The landscapes can integrate elements from the sky, land and water, and they can change seasonally. In several instances it appears obvious that the rock surfaces are a part of the representations of landscapes in the stories. Other aspects are represented by the largest animals in the sea, the earth and the air.
2 The element of seasonality represented by animals and activities appears to place the stories themselves in the cycle of the seasons; some stories evolve from one season to another, while others appear specifically oriented towards a single event. Alongside time, place is represented: where animals might be at certain seasons of the year and where human activities might take place. These elements are central to defining the landscapes.
3 The differences in the figures and compositions between northern Norway, north Sweden and northern Karelia partly reflect ecological and

geographic differences. But, certainly, there are also differences in choice of symbols and metaphors, in the stories narrated and in the landscapes constructed. The most fundamental difference appears to be the profile view in which human figures are depicted in the panels at the River Vyg in Karelia versus the frontal (back) perspectives at Nämforsen and Alta.

4 Yet, the general principles of where and how to depict stories and landscapes seem to have been similar in all three regions. These populations had similar ideas of the cosmos and of where to conduct rituals to communicate with the supernatural of all the cosmic worlds. The carvings are located where all cosmic worlds met, and as such, where all landscapes met.

Acknowledgements

Thanks to Ericka Engelstad and Christopher Chippindale, whose comments have been most welcome.

References

Alekseev, N. A. 1990. Shamanism among the Turkic peoples of Siberia, in M.-Mandelstaum Baltzer, *Shamanism: Soviet studies of traditional religion in Siberia and Central Asia*: 49–109. New York: M. E. Sharpe.

Almgren, O. 1926. *Hällristningar och kultbruk: bidrag till belysning av de nordiska bronsaldersristningarnas innebörd*. Stockholm: Kungl. vitterhets historie och antikvitets akademiens handlingar 35.

Anisimov, A. 1963. Cosmological concept of the people in the north, in H. Michael (ed.), *Studies in Siberian shamanism*: 157–229. Toronto: University of Toronto Press.

Baudou, E. 1995. *Norrlands forntid – et historiskt perspektiv*. Bjästa: CEWE-fsrlaget, Kungl. Skytteanska Samfundets Handlingar 45.

Bogoras, V. 1902. The folklore of northeastern Asia, as compared with that of northwestern America. *American Anthropologist* (NS) 4: 577–684.

1909. *The Chuckchee*. Leiden: E. J. Brill. Memoirs of the American Museum of Natural History 11.

1925. Ideas of space and time in the conception of primitive religion, *American Anthropologist* (NS) 22(2): 205–66.

Bradley, R. 1994. Symbols and signposts – understanding the prehistoric petroglyphs of the British Isles, in C. Renfrew and E. B. W. Zubrow (eds.), *The ancient mind: elements of cognitive archaeology*: 95–106. Cambridge: Cambridge University Press.

Chernetsov, V. N. 1963. Concepts of the soul among the Ob Ugrians, in H. Michael (ed.), *Studies in Siberian shamanism*: 3–45. Toronto: University of Toronto Press.

Durkheim, E. 1915. *The elementary forms of the religious life* (translated from the French by Joseph Ward Swain). London: Allen and Unwin.

Edsmann, C.-M. 1994. *Jägaren och makterna: samiska och finska björnceremonier*. Uppsala: Dialekt och folkminnesarkivet i Uppsala, ser. C. 6.

Engelstad, E. 1991. The symbolism of everyday life in prehistory, *Archaeology and Environment* 11: 23–32.

Evans, C. 1998. Cognitive maps and narrative trails: fieldwork with the Tamumai/Gurung of Nepal, in R. Layton and P. Ucko (eds.), *Shaping your landscape: the archaeology and anthropology of landscape*: 439–57. London: Routledge.

Georges, R. A. and M. O. Jones. 1995. *Folkloristics: an introduction*. Bloomington, IN: Indiana University Press.

Glob, P. V. 1969. *Helleristninger i Danmark*. Copenhagen: Gyldendal. Jysk Arkæologisk Selskabs Skrifter 7.

Hallström, G. 1960. *Monumental art of northern Sweden from the Stone Age*. Stockholm: Almqvist and Wicksell.

Helskog (Engelstad), E. 1983. *The Iversfjord locality: a study of behavioral patterning during the late stone age of Finnmark, north Norway*. Tromsø: Tromsø Museums Skrifter 19.

Helskog, K. 1983. Helleristningene i Alta: en presentasjon og en analyse av menneskefigurene, *Viking* 47: 5–42.

1988. *Helleristningene i Alta: spor etter ritualer i Finnmarks forhistorie*. Alta: Knut Helskog.

1999. The shore connection: cognitive landscape and communication with rock-carvings in northernmost Europe, *Norwegian Archaeological Review* 32(2): 73–94.

2000. Changing rock carvings – changing societies?, *Adoranten* 5–16.

Heptner, V. G. (eds.). 1996. *Mammals of the Soviet Union* 2(3): *Pinnipeds and toothed whales*. Washington, DC: Smithsonian Institution Libraries and the National Science Foundation. (Translated from Russian, edited by V. G. Heptner and N. P. Naumov. Russian edition, Moscow: Vyssha Shkola Publishers, 1976.)

Hesjedal, A., A. Damm, B. Olsen and I. Storli. *Arkeologi på Slettnes: dokumentasjon av 11.000 års bosetning*. Tromsø: Tromsø Museums Skrifter 26.

Hood, B. 1988. Sacred pictures, sacred rocks: ideological and social space in the north Norwegian Stone Age, *Norwegian Archaeological Review* 21(2): 65–84.

Ingold, T. 1993. The temporality of the landscape, *World Archaeology* 25(2): 152–74.

1996. 1990 debate: human worlds are culturally constructed, in T. Ingold, *Key debates in anthropology*: 99–146. London: Routledge.

Jochelson, W. 1908. *The Jusup North Pacific Expedition* 6: *The Koryak*. New York: Memoirs of the American Museum of Natural History 6.

Kannisto, A., E. A. Virtanen and M. Liimola. 1958. *Materialen zur Mythologien der Wogulen*. Helsinki: Mémoires de la Société Finno-Ougrienne 113.

Lehtisalo, T. 1924. *Entwurf einer Mythologie der Jurak-Samojeden*. Helsinki: Mémoires de la Société Finno-Ougrienne 53.

Lewis-Williams, J. D. and T. H. Dowson. 1990. Through the veil: San rock paintings and the rock surface, *South African Archaeological Bulletin* 45: 5–16.

Linevski, A. M. 1939. *Petroglifi Kareli* [Rock-engravings of Karelia 1]. Petrozavodsk: Karelian State Publishing House, Karelian Scientific Research, Institute of Culture.

Lönnberg, E. 1923. Sveriges Jaktbara dyr, in P. Hellström (ed.), *Svenska Jordbrukets bok: illusterad handbok för jordbrukets och dess binäringar*. Stockholm: Bonnier.

Mandt, G. 1991. Vestnorske ristninger i tid og rom: kronologiske, korologiske og kontekstuelle studier. PhD dissertation, University of Bergen.

Manker, E. 1957. *Lapparnas heliga ställen: kultplatser och offerkult i belysning av Nordiska Museets och landsantikvariernas fältundersökningar*. Stockholm: Nordiska Museet. Acta Lapponica 13.

Nordkvist, M. 1966. Renkroppens byggnad och funktion, in *Renskstsel*: 30–64. Bor's: Lts Forlag.

Nordström, P. 1999. Ristningarnas rytm: om hällristningar och landskap – eksemplet Boglösa, Uppland, in P. Nordström and M. Swedin, *Aktuell arkeologi* 8: 127–36. Stockholm: Arkeologiska Institutionen, Stockholms Universitet. Stockholm Archaeological Reports 36.

Olsen, B. 1994. *Bosetning og samfunn i Finnmarks forhistorie*. Oslo: Universitetsforlaget.

Ouzman, S. 1998. Toward a mindscape of landscape: rock-art as expression of world-understanding, in Christopher Chippindale and Paul S. C. Taçon (eds.), *The archaeology of rock-art*: 30–41. Cambridge: Cambridge University Press.

Qvikstad, J. 1927–29. *Lappiske eventyr og sagn*. Oslo: Aschehoug. Instituttet for Sammenlignende Kulturforskning Skrifter Serie B 3, 10, 12, 15.

Ramqvist, P. 1990. Hunting and fishing petroglyphs and their use in interpreting contemporary cultural-historical connections, *Åbo landskapsmuseum rapport 11/Finlands Anthropologiska Sällskaps Publikasjoner*: 41–51.

Rappaport, R. A. 1999. *Ritual and religion in the making of humanity*. Cambridge: Cambridge University Press.

Rapoport, A. 1975. Australian aborigines and the definition of place, in Paul Oliver (ed.), *Shelter, sign and symbol*. London: Barrie and Jenkins.

Ravdonikas, V. I. 1936. *Naskal'nye izobrazenija Onezskogo ozera i Belogo morja* (*Les Gravures rupestres des bords du lac Onega et de la mer Blanche*). Moskva: Izdatel'stvo Akademii Nauk SSSR.

Rydving, H. 1995. *The end of drum-time: religious change among the Lule Sami 1670s–1740s*. Uppsala: Acta Universitatis Upsaliensis. Historia Religionum 12.

Savvatejev, J. A. 1970. *Zalavruga: arkheologicheskiye pamyatniki nizovya reki Vyg* 1: *Petroglifi*. Leningrad: Akademia Nauka. Otvetstvennyie redaktor A. M. Linevsky.

1977. Rock pictures of the White Sea, *Bolletino del Centro Camuno di Studi Prehistorici* 16: 67–86.

1984. *Karelische Felsbilder*. Leipzig: Veb. E. A. Seeman Verlag.

Segal, R. A. (ed.). 1998. *The myth and ritual theory*. Oxford: Blackwell.

Shirokogoroff, S. M. 1933. *Social organization of the northern Tungus*. Shanghai: The Commercial Press.

1935. *Psychomental complex of the Tungus*. London: Kegan Paul.

Simonsen, P. 1979. *Veidemenn på Nordkalotten: Yngre Steinalder og overgangen til Metalltid*. Tromsø: Universitetet i Tromsø. Instituttet for Samfunnsvitenskap, Stensilserie B, Historie 17.

Sognnes, K. and A. Haug. 1998. Searching for hidden images: rock art geography in Stjørdal, Trøndelag, Norway, *Rock Art Research* 15(2): 98–108.

Tilley, C. 1991. *Material culture and text: the art of ambiguity*. London: Routledge.

1994. *A phenomenology of landscape*, Oxford: Berg.

Vasilevich, G. M. 1963. Evenk concepts about the Universe, in H. Michael (ed.), *Studies in Siberian shamanism*: 46–83. Toronto: University of Toronto Press.

Whitley, D. S. 1998. Finding rain in the desert: landscape, gender and far western North American rock-art, in Christopher Chippindale and Paul S. C. Taçon (eds.), *The archaeology of rock-art*: 11–29. Cambridge: Cambridge University Press.

14

From natural settings to spiritual places in the Algonkian sacred landscape: an archaeological, ethnohistorical and ethnographic analysis of Canadian Shield rock-art sites

Daniel Arsenault

The Canadian Shield, that great expanse of rock, water and forest, is yet another human landscape marked by rock-art, both painted and engraved. And it is yet another human landscape where western interpretations have too much depended on external suppositions, often of people who lived in a state of simple nature thanks to a balanced and bounteous ecosystem. Attention to Algonkian indigenous knowledge tells a different story, and one which is usefully combined with the field evidence of the archaeology and the rock-art. Once more, there is distinctive patterning in the rock-art – where it is placed, how it is done, what it depicts and what it omits – and once more that distinctive patterning makes every sense in relation to indigenous knowledge. And once more that indigenous knowledge is one of spiritual places within a landscape which is very much a sacred construct.

The Canadian Shield, its people and archaeology

The idea that North American Native Peoples have always lived as one with their environment before the arrival of European settlers has long been generally accepted in western popular imagery. This is particularly true of the Native Peoples living in the Canadian Shield. It is as if these peoples had developed in harmony within balanced ecosystems, drawing the resources necessary to their survival and well-being, without noticeably affecting or changing the make-up of these environments throughout their occupations spanning many thousand of years. The same line of thinking puts forward the idea of plenty, where an ever-renewable bounty awaited, and a great variety of resources was easily accessed by all. This is exemplified by the perception that these same Natives were primitive and essentially lacking socio-political organization (Vincent and Arcand 1979; Delâge 1996; Dickason 1996: 114; Laberge 1997). This picture of the simple life of the 'Noble Savage' emerging from this line of thought has parallels in the equally erroneous perception of a virtually untouched and pristine natural landscape within which Native Peoples spent their lives.

Whether the 'Savages' received positive or negative reviews (see Dickason 1984; Smith 1996; McCormack 1998), they would inevitably be tied to a fixed or unchanging ecosystem, therefore frozen in evolutionary time as a people without history. While some archaeological studies occasionally promoted seasonal variability, as they should, the physical space and the variety found within the environments where Natives 'evolved' were seemingly fixed in time, an unchanged 'terrestrial paradise', in a manner of speaking (Denevan 1992). Invariably, the emphasis placed on Amerindians (and Inuits, further north) and the natural landscape drew a blind on the cultural landscape as perceived by the different Native Peoples throughout their history. To look at the ambient forest, and at some of its trees only, did not open a window on the 'forest of symbols' as Turner (1967) so succinctly remarked, that other world which was hidden by the natural landscape.

During the last quarter of the twentieth century, archaeological studies in the Canadian Shield began to change this antiquated view of Native Peoples, particularly in regard to their relationships with the natural environment and, to a far lesser degree, with the symbolism so important in Native Peoples' lives. We lack a definition, and no well-grounded notion of 'cultural landscape' has been articulated in theoretical archaeology. An explanatory model of cultural landscapes in the archaeology of Native Peoples in the Canadian Shield was essentially non-existent until the beginnings of the 1990s (Moreau 1994; Hanna 1997: 76). Also, this is true for research in Inuit ancestral lands (see Maxwell 1985; McGhee 1996). Approaches for the interpretation of past cultural landscapes have not been developed to date (see Denton 1997; n.d.; Hanna 1997). Physical and cultural landscapes overlap, as well as complement, one another; partial reconstruction, using finite and limited data, from the traces of activities left behind by the individuals and groups occupying sites is a very difficult task in itself. From a material point of view, the natural environment where sites were occupied over time more often presents a 'palimpsest' where inscriptions are forever renewed (Bender 1995: 9; Thomas 1995: 25). Researchers exploring the physical limits of the environment – its varied resources, topographic and architectural elements and activity areas (at times transformed) – in an intellectual exercise, that is to say an archaeological interpretation, will reconstitute a *variety* of cultural landscapes (Zedeño 1997: 95–6).

Archaeological research in the prehistory of Québec, as for other regions of the Canadian Shield, has led to the identification of many and varied ancient aboriginal cultures occupying many regions of this large area of North America over the past 8000 years (see Cinq-Mars and Martijn 1981; Clermont 1982; 1987; 1988; Moreau 1994; Wright 1995; 1999; Martijn 1998). However, from an anthropological perspective, it has remained relatively difficult to this day to explore the diversity of the cultural landscapes inhabited by both the ancestors of the Amerindians and the Inuits, as theoretical models are often verbalized out of context, resulting in simplistic and inadequate interpretations (Dumais 1994: 43). A case in point is the analysis of prehistoric occupations, of the exploitation of natural resources and of symbolic resources (see Chapdelaine 1989; 1995; 1996; Chrétien 1995), which has been oriented solely towards cultural ecology, systematics and the processual paradigm (see Preucel 1991).

Invariably, research designs have been tailored to answer specific questions about subsistence activities of the various prehistoric groups who occupied this large territory. Lithic and ceramic typologies, procurement activities including fishing and hunting strategies, settlement patterns and exchange networks have been examined, emphasizing adaptive strategies of ancient Native Peoples, the utilization of specific ecosystems and procurement methods. In doing so, researchers have not been so much concerned with the manner in which the Native Peoples traditionally perceived and valued the natural landscape in

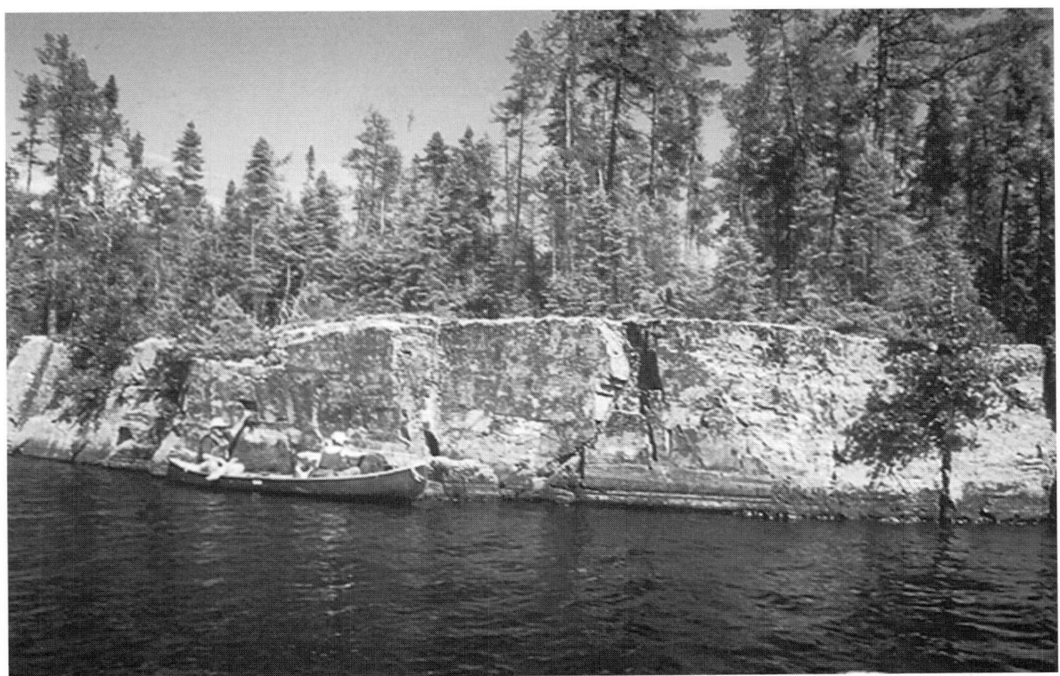

Fig. 14.1. The general setting of finger-painted site DaGu-1, in the Abitibi.
Note that the terrain is very rocky and would not lend itself to human occupation. Those who came here may have had other purposes than that of simply obtaining natural resources, for the presence of a rock-art site suggests that this place was once part of the Algonkian sacred landscape.
Photograph by D. Arsenault, courtesy of PETRARQ.

which they acted (Hanna 1997: 75–6) and how they viewed themselves as social actors, producing and using symbols within a particular environment or another. Theoretical and methodological orientations as well as the limits placed by the choice of analytical categories in the many case-studies in Shield prehistoric research have not promoted an exploration of the relationships between Native Peoples and the various material and symbolic components of the natural landscape with which they dealt – and in some instances, continue to deal nowadays. However, studies by Denton (1993; 1994; 1997) and by Hanna (1997) show some promise in this direction.

Since the mid-1990s, I have conducted research on a number of rock-art sites in varied regions of Québec and north-east Ontario, covering three distinct cultural areas of North America, that is, the north-eastern, sub-Arctic and Arctic areas. Throughout this undertaking I have endeavoured to seek out new ways of examining cultural landscapes associated with varied aboriginal groups in the Canadian Shield (e.g. Arsenault *et al.* 1995; Arsenault 1998a; n.d.; Arsenault *et al.* 1998).

There are many issues involved – a sufficient number that they are surveyed in a separate and complementary chapter in the present volume: Daniel Arsenault, 'Rock-art, landscape, sacred places: attitudes in contemporary archaeological theory' (pp. 69–84). The present chapter seeks to apply that new attitude to the rock-art sites in the Canadian Shield, which are well suited to this type of analysis thanks to their specific physical context (Fig. 14.1).

Rock-art sites in Québec: description and localization

Sixteen rock-art sites have been identified in Québec to date (Fig. 14.2); seven are petroglyph (rock-engraving) sites, and nine are rock-painting (sometimes called pictograph) sites. The seven petroglyph sites are distributed as follows: four along the southern shores of Hudson Strait, in the Inuit territory of Nunavik (Fig. 14.2, sites A to D; Saladin d'Anglure 1962; 1963; 1966; Gendron *et al.* 1996; Arsenault *et al.* 1998); two in the Abitibi region (Fig. 14.2, sites E and F; Arsenault n.d.); one in the Eastern Townships (Fig. 14.2, site G; Levesque 1965; Arsenault 1993; Graillon 1995; 1996; Gagnon and Arsenault 1996). The nine red ochre pictograph sites, all to the north of the St Lawrence valley (Fig. 14.2, sites 1 to 8; Arsenault n.d.), are nestled in the heart of the boreal forest (Tassé and Dewdney 1977; Arsenault n.d.; Lemaître 1994): one in the James Bay region (Arsenault 1998b; 1999); three in the Abitibi (Tassé 1977a; Arsenault and Gagnon 1996a; Arsenault n.d.); one in the Témiscamingue region (Arsenault and Vigneault 1996); two in the Ottawa Valley (Tassé 1977a; 1996; Arsenault n.d.); one in the Mauricie region (Béland 1959; Tassé 1976; 1977b; 1995); and one on the Upper North Shore of the St Lawrence river (Arsenault 1994a; 1994b; Arsenault *et al.* 1995; Arsenault and Gagnon 1996b; 1998a).

These nine latter sites were made only with red ochre, which in general was simply applied with fingers, hence the term 'finger-painted sites', which I use to refer to these sites from here on. In the discussion that follows, I consider solely this type of pictographic site; the approach proposed here could be equally applied to the study of petroglyphs in any given sacred landscape.

If we are to identify clearly the significant features that distinguish these rock-art sites and to determine whether such sites are indeed part of a certain sacred landscape, our first task is to look carefully at the characteristics they present and, in particular, their similarities and differences. The characteristics of rock-art in Québec, with respect to both similarities and differences, are best accounted for by examining three complementary aspects of finger-painted sites. These aspects are: (a) graphic content, (b) rock support and (c) physical setting. It is worth mentioning here that the Québec sites are in many respects comparable, both in form and content, to the some six hundred finger-painted sites scattered throughout the other northern portions of the Canadian Shield, in the provinces of Saskatchewan, Manitoba and Ontario. As will be seen, the value of pursuing this comparison becomes especially evident in consideration of the fact that all these sites were part of the cultural universe of Amerindian groups that were linguistically related, in speaking languages of the vast Algonkian family.

Similarities and differences in graphic content

The finger-painted sites in Québec display works of rock-art of varying complexity, the graphic content always presenting the same basic elements (Fig. 14.3). These elements include the application of a single type of colouring material so as to produce a monochrome painting, similar drawing techniques and a respect for certain rules of composition, such as the predominance of geometric motifs, the orientation of the pictures and the respective size of figures. (For a detailed description of these characteristic elements, see Arsenault and Gagnon 1998b: 216–17.)

Alongside the common elements, there are also notable differences in graphic content. For example, certain Québec rock-art sites reveal less than a dozen motifs, while others display over one hundred. Furthermore, when the contents of these sites are compared to those of sites in other regions of the Canadian Shield, formal differences

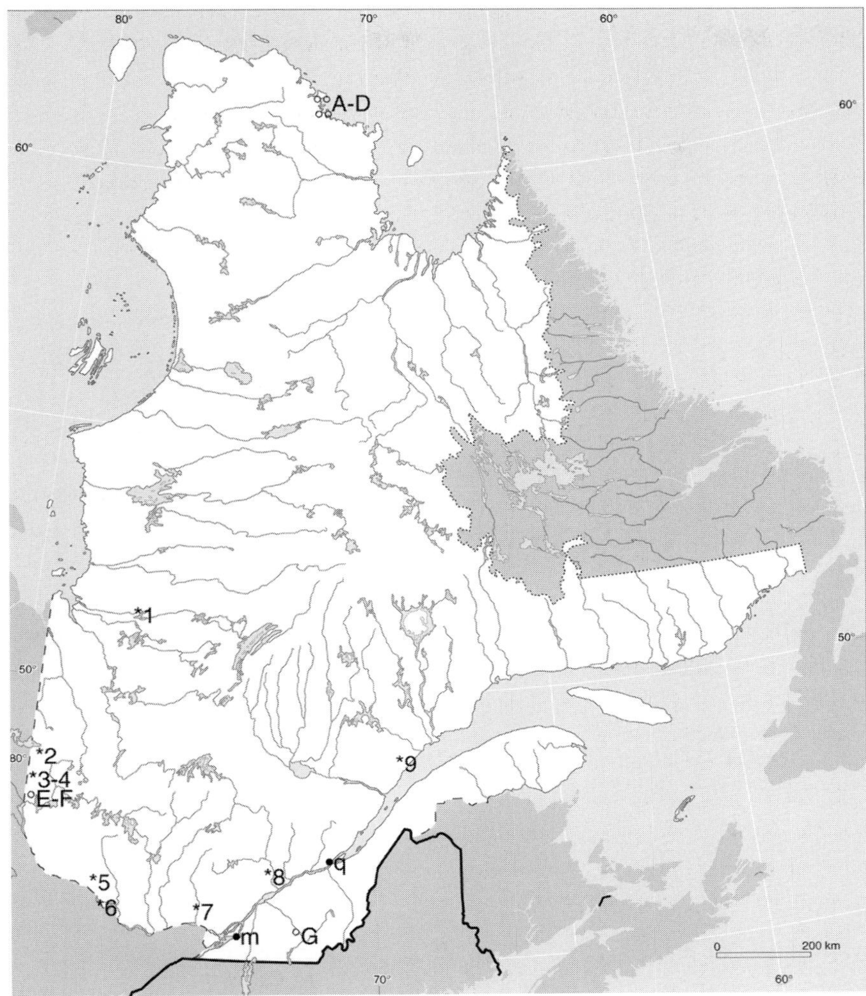

Fig. 14.2. Map of rock-art sites identified in Québec.

Map made by D. Arsenault based on a map collection courtesy of the Laboratoire de traitement des informations géographiques at Université Laval, Québec.

Red ochre finger-painted sites (rock-paintings):

1 The Kaapehpeshapischinikanuuch site (EiGf-2), Lac Nemiskau, James Bay region

2 Site DcGt-41, Lac Duparquet, the Abitibi region

3–4 Sites DaGu-1 (includes engraved motifs) and DaGv-16, Lac Buies, the Abitibi region

5 Site CcGh-18, Rivière Dumoine, the Témiscamingue region

6 The Rocher-à-l'Oiseau site (CaGh-2), Ottawa River, Ottawa Valley

7 The Cap Manitou site (B1Fs-2), Lac Simon, Ottawa Valley

8 Site CdFg-5, Lac Wapizagonke, the Mauricie region

9 The Nisula site (DeEh-1), Lac de la Cassettte, Upper North Shore

Engraved rock sites (petroglyphs):

A–D sites in the Kangirsujuaq region, including Qajartalik site (JhEv-1), on Qikertaaluk Island, in Hudson Strait, Nunavik

E–F Sites DaGt-3 and DaGt-10, Lac Opasatica, the Abitibi region

G The Brompton site (BiEx-19), Eastern Townships

m = Montréal

q = Québec

Fig. 14.3. Detail of one of the decorated panels (Panel II, measuring about 4 sq. m) at the Nisula site (DeEh-1). On it can be seen very pale finger-painted motifs schematically representing human, animal and hybrid forms. Note, in particular, the image of a tall person walking towards the right with outstretched arms.
Photograph by D. Arsenault, courtesy of PETRARQ.

are observable. Such differences may reflect the existence of more than one style of rock-art representation (Steinbring 1998), since certain works are the result of several phases of graphic production, spread out over a number of years, if not decades and even centuries. However, the most important difference – and it is crucial to grasping the difficulty of interpreting the semantic aspect of rock-art images (see Arsenault and Gagnon 1998b) – is no doubt the fact that no two finger-painted sites share exactly the same graphic content, that is, an identical combination of figurative and geometric motifs. This is true not only of such sites in Québec but also of those in the rest of the Canadian Shield. It is as if the people who made the drawings did not have the intention of strictly and faithfully reproducing elements related to a given mythological theme or a particular historic account.

Quite apart from these similarities and differences, the producers of rock-art seem to have called upon the same basic repertory of visual symbols, taken directly from the ideological melting-pot shared throughout the Algonkian-speaking communities of the Canadian Shield. In fact, the presence of several figurative motifs with remarkably similar morphologies – such as the anthropomorphic horned-headed figure, the turtle, and the canoe with canoeists – suggests that the main visual symbols were widely shared and spread over a vast area within the Shield, therefore creating a complex exchange network of visual imagery which appears to have lasted many centuries. Such motifs must have embodied certain major cultural and spiritual values for people living throughout a vast territory, stretching over

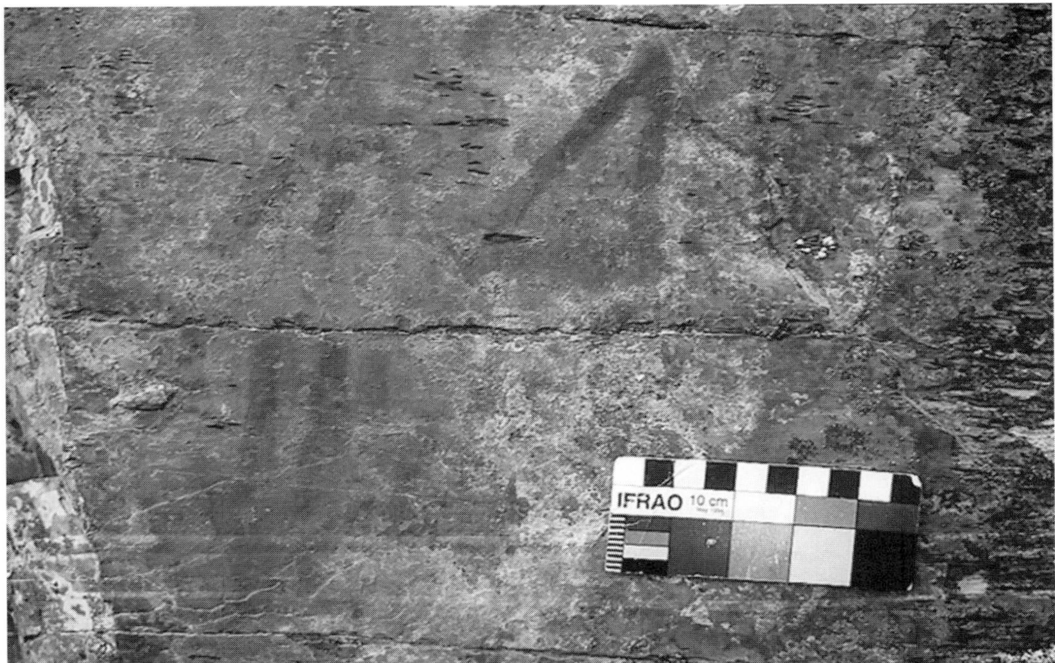

Fig. 14.4. View of one of the decorated walls at the DaGu-1 site, in the Abitibi.

Note the undulating relief and the relatively polished surface of this vertical wall. The people who produced Algonkian rock-art generally preferred to use this type of surface, with little or no roughness or flaking, as a support for their red ochre markings.

Photograph by D. Arsenault, courtesy of PETRARQ.

2000 km from northern Saskatchewan to eastern Québec (see Dewdney and Kidd 1967; Rajnovich 1994; Arsenault *et al.* 1995; Steinbring 1998).

Similarities and differences in rock support

Interesting similarities may be observed among the rock formations whose vertical walls serve as support for the red ochre drawings. All the motifs visible today were traced on vertical or steeply sloping areas of these formations[1] (Fig. 14.4). But the position of the motifs does not appear to have been related simply to a desire to give the rock-art better visibility or to ensure that it was properly protected from the weather. For the motifs were most often drawn near certain formal or topographical features presented by the rock outcrop. On the one hand, on or near the decorated surfaces, the outcrop may display morphological characteristics such as cracks, fractures and splits, overhangs providing rock-shelters, and even caves. On the other hand, finger-painted work seems to be closely associated with certain visible characteristics of the rock's surface: smoothness, marbling, a film of amorphous silica, and quartz inclusions. As will be explained further on, these various characteristics of the rock support may have had important symbolic and spiritual values for the Algonkians who once produced rock-art sites and visited them.

[1] In Ontario and Manitoba, however, there are a few sites where finger-painted motifs can be seen on the ceiling of a rock-shelter or of a shallow cave (see Molyneaux 1980; Conway and Conway 1989; Steinbring 1998).

Fig. 14.5. General view of the cliff with decorated walls (at the far lower left of the cliff) at the Nisula site (DeEh-1). This impressive rock formation displays not only cracks, anfractuosities and overhangs, but also long streaks of siliceous material (appearing in the photograph as the palest vertical lines on the rock's surface). These noticeable natural elements may have been interpreted by the ancient Algonkians as clear signs of the presence of supernatural entities or forces in this place, thus conferring a sacred character on the cliff.
Photograph by D. Arsenault, courtesy of PETRARQ.

There may also be discernible differences in the rock support. Red ochre motifs were traced on a variety of geological types, including granite, migmatite and pelite. As well, there are differences in shape and size of rock formations; the finger-paintings may be done on a low or high cliff, or on a boulder. The decorated walls may present different configurations – either flat, concave or convex surfaces. A certain amount of variation may be observed in the direction faced by walls bearing rock-art; although many are oriented towards the south, south-east or south-west, there are a few that face directly west or north. Moreover, finger-painted surfaces may cover less than a metre or extend vertically for several metres, which, in passing, raises the question of what production techniques were used to apply paint up to such heights. This variation in the surface covered by rock-art in one site as compared to another also suggests how important it must have been in some cases for the graphic content to have been visible, or concealed, to those who passed by the site.

Similarities and differences in the physical setting of rock-art sites

With respect to physical setting, Québec rock-art sites present a number of similarities. To begin with, these sites form an integral part of an open natural environment (Fig. 14.5) rather than a sheltered or enclosed environment (such as a cave). Second, the decorated rock outcrops are almost always situated at the edge of a body of water, on the shores of a lake or river,[2] so that a person wishing to examine a work of rock-art in greater detail is generally obliged to approach the site by boat (or, in winter, on foot across ice). Third, these sites present no signs of architectural structures, nor do they seem to have been located near occupation sites.

The rock-art sites identified in Québec also show differences in their physical setting with respect to their geographic situations. Some of them are found directly along the main waterways that made up the traditional networks of communication (for example the Ottawa River, which was a major highway between the St Lawrence Valley to the south and the James and Hudson bays regions to the north); others are situated on the outskirts of these main waterways, along either secondary or even tertiary routes that seem to have been used less frequently by nomadic groups in prehistoric times. Furthermore, only a few rock-art sites appear to have been established near a portage trail or at a strategic point on an unavoidable route over a body of water (for example, at the entrance to a channel); the others do not seem to have been associated with such elements. In either case, however, it is possible that the rock-art sites served as points of reference along a given waterway.

Considering the importance accorded to the natural setting when it came to displaying visual symbols embodying a certain spiritual value, it seems appropriate to ask what factors influenced the choice of places for establishing Algonkian rock-art sites. This leads us directly to a look at how aboriginal communities in the boreal forest saw the physical environment in which they lived.

[2] During the 1999 survey, I discovered a site (DaGv-16) which was located in the middle of an old portage trail linking two small lakes. This site, as a few others in the Shield (B. Molyneaux, pers. comm. 1999; Steinbring 1998: 112), is only approachable by land.

Sacred landscape and its components in Algonkian oral traditions

In the Native societies of North America, from the prehistoric period to the present, knowledge related to the natural environment and spiritual values has been passed down from one generation to the other mainly through oral language, although visual language (such as gesture, costume and images) may have played a role in certain circumstances (see Burnham 1992; Lewis 1996; 1998: 77, 82). In Native oral traditions, the particularities of a natural landscape and the cultural events that once took place there are described in a narrative through the use of deictic language, that is to say, situational language that refers directly to the characteristics of a given situation or context, evoking the surroundings and the moment as they are experienced in the place being described (Lewis 1996: 367–8). As will be seen further on, deictic references are particularly evident in place-names. The study of aboriginal toponymy shows that Native place-names convey various meanings, which may refer not only to the place described but also to the historical or mythical events related to it. The place-name may mention the individuals who once lived there; it may highlight the presence of natural resources or topographical features; it may evoke mythological situations such as the legendary activities of supernatural beings hundreds or thousands of years ago; or it may recall more recent historical events (see, for example, Denton 1993: viii; 1997; Kritsch *et al.* 1994: 8–9). The oral tradition seeks to preserve the memory both of places and of historic or mythological events. It follows that space and time cannot be dissociated in discourse related to the perception and interpretation of the natural landscape.

Encompassing both metaphor and metonymy, the semantic amalgam that characterizes the construction of geographical meanings in Native oral traditions is also evidence of the degree to which the borderline between the natural and the supernatural is less clearly defined in Amerindian concepts of the world than it is in western thought. Thus, in what may be termed the Algonkian concept of the universe, the natural world and the spiritual world coexist; they cannot be understood independently of one another (see Diamond *et al.* 1994: 38; also Denton 1993: vii–viii; 1997: 120–1; Hultkrantz 1993: 36–48; Spielman 1993: 110; Little Bear 1998). This cosmology is made up of distinct but complementary regions – celestial, terrestrial, underwater and subterranean (Rajnovich 1994: 35). Each of these regions is inhabited by its own entities or forces, which may be either good or evil for human beings and which are sometimes personified (for example, the Windigo, the Attuus or the Mistaapew; see Tanner 1979: 99, 113–15; also Johnston 1995). Since human beings, who inhabit the terrestrial region, do not live separately from the entities in the other regions, they must learn to deal with them by showing them respect and carrying out the rituals stipulated by tradition (Tanner 1979: 96–9; Hultkrantz 1993; Brown 1996: 28–32). Humans may meet entities from the other regions in the course of their daily lives, for example, in the context of hunting, when the lives of hunters intersect with those of certain animals and their spirits (Tanner 1979; Hirschfelder and Molin 1992: 126; Hultkrantz 1995: 46). Meetings may also occur during unusual events (Joly de Lotbinière 1993), in dreams or through trances and visions provoked by fasting (Honigmann 1981: 718–20; Leacock 1981: 195; Rogers and Leacock 1981: 182, 184; Hirschfelder and Molin 1992: 83; Moondance 1994; Hultkrantz 1995: 59–60; Brown 1996: 90). Moreover, it is in nature and through its elements that humans receive a part of their sacred knowledge and learn to live in harmony with their surroundings (Tanner 1979; Diamond *et al.* 1994: 8, 52; Brown 1996: 48–9; Little Bear 1998).

As a result of the aboriginals' intimate relationship with the natural and spiritual properties of the physical environment – a relationship experienced both in bodily movement through space and in the passage of time (Tilley 1996: 162) – this environment became humanized, socialized and endowed with certain religious meanings. This was true to such an extent that the presence of topographical elements in the landscape sometimes came to be explained by attributing a human or supernatural origin to them (also see Denton 1993: viii; 1997; Kritsch *et al.* 1994: 9). Gabriel Sagard, a Recollet missionary who was canoeing – probably on the Ottawa River – on his way back to Québec City after one year (1623–24) spent in the country of the Hurons, wrote: 'After these rapids, within about the range of a harquebus, we found by the water's edge an impressive rock . . . that my Savages believe to have been a mortal man, like us, who metamorphosed and was turned into stone, through the authority and will of God' (1982 [1632]: 171). For, as pointed out by Diamond *et al.* (1994), 'the experience of where people are situated geographically – the expression of that physical experience of the landscape is so central to philosophy, music, culture' [of Native Peoples of North America] (Diamond *et al.* 1994: 19) that it gave rise to a whole series of religious expressions in both practices and symbolization. People maintained their close relation with the dual (natural and spiritual) world. They marked their experience of it in certain spaces or places by performing various rituals that could be carried out by all the members of their community, by offering tobacco (Laure 1959: 42–3; Paper 1988) or through vision quests (Moondance 1994; Hultkrantz 1995). This praxis also found other forms of religious and spiritual expression, notably through the graphic communication of religious experience on rock formations, which led to the establishment of rock-art sites (Molyneaux 1983: 6).

In this same vein, it may be noted that in Québec such ritual actions may sometimes have been performed by individuals or groups when they passed by certain rock formations. Such actions are reported over four centuries. During a canoe trip on the St Lawrence River, Father Sagard's Native companions showed him a mighty rock in the effigy of a man 'to which they pay respect and offer tobacco when passing it in their canoes, not always, but when they are in doubt of a successful issue to their journey' (1939 [1632]: 251–2). On his way to Hudson Bay, Chevalier de Troyes (1918 [1686]: 36–7) noted in his journal that on the Ottawa River there was a great cliff, known to the Algonquins at that time as 'Rocher-à-l'Oiseau' (meaning 'Rock of the Bird' and later becoming 'Weasel Rock' in English), at whose summit the Natives would shoot arrows with a leaf of tobacco attached to them. In the eighteenth century the Jesuit Pierre-Michel Laure mentions that at Lac Mistassini, the Algonkian communities in the region at that time worshipped a great rock, to which they offered 'a little black tobacco, a piece of sea-biscuit, or some beaver or fish bones, which they placed upon the rock' (Laure 1959 [1720–30]: 43). In his memoirs (compiled by Bouchard 1980) covering more than fifty years of evangelization, the Oblat missionary Joseph-Etienne Guinard (Bouchard 1980: 39) reports:

> A few miles after starting along the Abitibi River, a great rock rose up in the middle of the water. If one used some imagination, this rock looked like an old woman. The Indians call it *Kokomis*, or 'grandmother'. Before they were converted, Indians passing in front of Kokomis used to offer the rock gifts so that the stone woman would calm the waves of the great lake [Abitibi]. To amuse themselves, or to have a little rest, our Indians threw tobacco and matches to the rock.

Since these rituals related to passing a rock outcrop continued to be practised throughout the historic period, it is very likely that they also existed in prehistoric times. It seems very probable as well that these rituals, belonging to spiritual traditions going back several hundred years, may have sometimes included the production of rock-art. The presence of sites with decorated rock walls in the boreal forest of Québec, some of which may be extremely ancient (see Arsenault *et al.* 1995), lends strong support to the idea that this spiritual relation with certain topographical elements and, therefore, the ritual actions intended to underline such a relation were part of a conceptual and religious universe that dated back 1000 to 2000 years, if not more (cf. Steinbring 1998). None the less, it remains problematic that only a few rock outcrops were decorated on Québec territory. However, archaeological research as well as field interviews conducted in Ontario (Conway and Conway 1990: 12) and Manitoba (Steinbring 1998) suggest that rock-art sites represented only part of the Algonkian sacred landscape. In Québec as well, archaeologists have begun to document the present diversity of Algonkian sacred places, especially among the Cree (Denton 1993; 1994; 1997; n.d.; Arsenault 1998b; 1999). On Lac Mistassini, Cree informants have identified a cliff along the shore that is said to be inhabited by *Mamakwaasiuch*, but its vertical walls do not seem to have been decorated with finger-painted rock-art (D. Denton, pers. comm. 1997). Similarly, on Lac Kempf, in the upper Mauricie region, there exists an imposing rock wall that is marked in places with large, deep incisions; these are apparently of natural origin (C. A. Martijn, pers. comm. 1994) but form designs considered by the Attikamekw of Manawan to be sacred markings made by their ancestors or the spirits. These two examples, as well as that of the marble cave recorded by Laure

(1959 [1720–30]: 48), are clear evidence that certain natural sites in Québec were considered sacred and deserve to be further investigated. Some of them might even provide archaeological material if excavated, making it possible to document certain aspects of the religious practices associated with these sites in the past. With respect to archaeological research, however, rock-art sites may constitute primary evidence in the reconstitution of the oldest sacred landscapes.

The context of shamanism and the creation of sacred places and areas

According to certain Native traditions, some people, usually men but sometimes women, were more gifted than others in their ability to establish contact with the forces and spiritual entities that lived in nature: these people were shamans. As ritual specialists, they acted as intermediaries between the suprasensible powers and human beings; to communicate with these forces and entities, shamans frequently undertook vision quests (Hoffman 1888; Honigmann 1981: 718–19; Leacock 1981: 194–5; Bragdon 1995; Hultkrantz 1995; Hedden 1996; Moondance 1994). Both ethnohistorical documents and ethnographic investigations concerning the Algonkians generally indicate that when shamans wanted to establish contact with spiritual-beings, they went to certain places: either man-made places, like the sweat-lodge or shaking tent (Savard 1974: 46, note 31; Tanner 1979: 111–17; Honigmann 1981: 719, 735; Rogers and Leacock 1981: 184; Hirschfelder and Molin 1992: 259–60; Carmichael 1994: 93–4; Hultkrantz 1995: 65–8; Brown 1996: 28–9, 31), or places in the natural landscape, in particular rock formations (Conway and Conway 1989; also Hallowell 1936; Tanner 1979: 98; Reeves 1994: 278; Theodoratus and LaPeña 1994: 23). In the eighteenth century in Québec, Father Pierre-Michel Laure (1959 [1720–30]: 48) observed:

> The most remarkable of all the curiosities that may be seen in the forest in the Nemiskau region is a cave of marble . . . Inside it, in a corner, there is a lump of the same material, but somewhat rough, and it sticks out to form a sort of table that serves as an altar; the savages thus think that this is a house of prayer and counsel, where the spirits meet. This is why not everyone takes the liberty of entering there, but only jugglers,[3] who are like their Priests, go there to consult their oracles.

But what significance did the rock formations have for the shamans? According to a number of Amerindian informants, steep rocks have always constituted places filled with power, since they display the raw energy of the earth and shelter known supernatural entities (Tanner 1979: 98; Conway and Conway 1990: 11; Carmichael 1994: 92–3; Mohs 1994: 195, 198; Theodoratus and LaPeña 1994: 24). In 1891, Rev. Peter Jones, an Ojibwa who had converted to Christianity, wrote about the places that formed part of the sacred landscape of his people in the following terms: 'Any remarkable element in the natural setting or in awe-inspiring places becomes an object of fear and superstitious veneration, in the belief that it must be a dwelling place of the gods' (Molyneaux 1983: 4). As well, Algonkian oral traditions provide considerable evidence of the spiritual and religious value attributed to such sites. For example, Diamond *et al.* (1994: 28) report that certain natural places in the Canadian boreal forest, as well as other tangible phenomena of the physical world – such as the strong winds and gushing springs with which these places may be associated – were considered as signifying a manifestation of the forces of nature, which themselves testified to the presence of spirits (also see Tanner 1979: 96). Furthermore, according to this

[3] In the original French, Laure uses the term 'jongleurs' to refer to shamans, since the word 'shaman' did not yet exist at the time. As this passage of the Jesuit's relation makes clear, it was already common practice for shamans to seek a natural place where they could establish contact with the spirits. It seems more than probable that this practice must have existed in the Canadian boreal forest during the prehistoric period as well.

concept, the foot of cliffs, as well as the caves and large cracks that were sometimes seen in them, constituted points where the celestial, terrestrial, subterranean and underwater worlds of the Algonkian cosmological universe intersected (Rajnovich 1994: 35; also Vastokas and Vastokas 1973; Conway and Conway 1989).

Algonkian religious traditions also show that for certain rites of initiation or of passage, a person – who might become a shaman – had to depart from the community for a while and seek visions; isolated in nature, the person would fast and might possibly meet a guardian spirit who would serve as a guide and counsellor for the rest of his life (Hultkrantz 1995: 46). The guardian spirit might present sacred symbols, both visual and material (minerals, plants or any other object imbued with magic power), which would henceforth be associated with the person (see Hoffman 1891; Honigmann 1981: 719; Rajnovich 1994: 125–7; Brown 1996: 114–15). The areas around certain rock outcrops could provide isolated places that would be suitable for a person on a vision quest. In any case, shamans sought those areas since they would make it easier to contact the spiritual entities that could provide new sacred knowledge. In this context, a rock formation could serve as a privileged place for learning; this is why some settings were called 'teaching rocks' for that purpose, such as Peterborough Petroglyph site and Agawa site in Ontario (Johnston 1995: 241–2; Kulchyski 1998: 22). Contact was established by carrying out a series of ritual actions, in which songs, incantatory gestures and offerings figured largely. According to a number of researchers (Hoffman 1888; 1891; Flannery 1931; Dewdney and Kidd 1967; Vastokas and Vastokas 1973; Steinbring 1982; 1998; Whelan 1983; Young 1985; Molyneaux 1987; Conway 1989; Rajnovich 1989; Moondance 1994), it was in the ritual context that the shaman would produce a work of rock-art; the marks he made in red ochre on the surface of rocks were thus intended to illustrate aspects of his vision and, in particular, his present relationship with one or several of the beings in the suprasensible world. It follows that the creation of a rock-art site was related to a ritual act, sometimes of an intensely personal nature, that was specific to the site and that was an integral part of Algonkian shamanism. In other words, when the shaman performed ritual acts beside a rock, he made the place where he stood into the exact physical centre of his experience with the sacred world, thereby linking an attainable and natural place to a distant and invisible space, the world of spirits.

The spirits that the shaman might meet were said to be generally of two types. In almost all the Algonkian religious traditions, it is held that certain rock formations could serve as homes for natural spirits who often took the shape of small, furry creatures – called *Memekueshuat* by the Montagnais, *Memegwe'djo* by the Naskapi, *Mamakwaasiuch* by the Cree, *Maymaygwashi* by the Ojibway and *Memegueshi* by the Algonquins (see on this subject Flannery 1931; Speck 1935: 73; Martijn and Rogers 1969: 196, note 5; Fabvre 1970: 70; Silvy 1974: 145; Tanner 1979: 139; Molyneaux 1980: 10; Bacon and Vincent 1994; Denton 1994; n.d.; Diamond *et al.* 1994: 71; Rajnovich 1994). These entities were not considered malevolent beings; although they liked to play tricks, they could also offer help to people in difficulty (Flannery 1931: 3). In certain traditional tales, they are also seen as the first beings to have made finger-paintings, using their own blood, on the rocks of the Canadian Shield (G. Rajnovich, pers. comm. 1988; see also Martijn and Rogers 1969: 196, note 5). It should be noted that cracks, crevices and cave entrances in cliffs and rocks served as passageways for these spiritual beings; when a shaman wished to communicate with them, he would send his auxiliary spirit into the rock through these openings (Flannery 1931:

160). Those cavities were also where various offerings, especially tobacco (Paper 1988), were placed to signify the respect due to the spirits living there; this solemn act is still practised by certain groups of Algonkians (Steinbring 1998: 8). In 1988, when I had just identified a previously unrecorded finger-painted site in Sabaskong Bay, on Lake of the Woods, Ontario, I observed that the custom of offering tobacco at rock-art sites is still practised by certain Ojibwa communities living in north-west Ontario. Between the time I 'discovered' the site and the next morning, when I went to make a scientific record of it, at least one person had gone there discreetly to place tobacco on two little ledges just below a small cave that had a few finger-painted motifs above its entrance.

The other type of spirit – although somewhat less widespread than the small entities in Algonkian religious imagery, at least in the historic period – was the dominant figure of the thunderbird. This mythical animal, generally depicted as an extraordinary bird of prey with horns on its head, represented a being invested with enormous power (Gile 1995). The thunderbird was one of the rare supernatural beings that could go to all the different regions of the spiritual universe. He was also capable of producing overwhelming power, which could have either beneficial or harmful effects on human beings. It was therefore essential for shamans to maintain contact with this type of being. It might be mentioned, as well, that in Algonkian cosmology, the presence of nests built by ravens and great birds of prey on cliff tops and high ledges was seen as a metaphor for the suprasensible presence of this mythic animal (Conway and Conway 1990: 12).

This brief overview of certain aspects of Algonkian spiritual and religious traditions demonstrates the great symbolic importance accorded to cliffs and other rock formations in the Canadian Shield. These strange or exceptional-looking places in the natural landscape could have represented a very valuable ideological resource with a sacred aspect that certain individuals, particularly shamans, sometimes sought to emphasize by applying motifs to the surface of the rock. This is why individual ritual acts, such as offering tobacco, were sometimes carried out in these places when people passed by them. Furthermore, as Vastokas and Vastokas (1973: 48–54) suggest, boulders and other rock outcrops with unusual features – clefts, holes, crevices, etc. – or dimensions can have been not only a focal point for shamanistic visionary experiences but a meeting place where people could 'commune' with supernatural spirits. It now remains to be seen whether these various pieces of information taken from oral traditions and gathered from the rock-art sites themselves constitute enough data to undertake the archaeological reconstitution of the Algonkian sacred landscape and to test the validity of the analytical tools proposed by the archaeology of landscape.

Rock-art sites and features of the natural landscape

We have seen that Algonkian oral traditions distinguished particular kinds of natural places, especially rock formations, as having spiritual energy to some degree, which gave them a certain sacred value. It may now be asked how this situation arose. It seems that certain myths, certain historic events experienced by Algonkian groups and even certain images that came to shamans in trances and dreams played a decisive role in such places becoming sacred and in some cases being decorated with special visual symbols, or rock-art motifs (see Vastokas and Vastokas 1973; Conway 1989; Conway and Conway 1990; Graham 1998: 25). Furthermore, the intention behind tracing motifs on a rock surface may have been to mark, recall or underline the sacred aspect of the place (Kinew 1998: 34–5). For (Diamond *et al.* 1994: 28),

> importance of place is overt and dramatic with regard to Anishnabe rock-art . . . where the sun's rays, the natural markings, or the environmental sounds may be powerful images in themselves, images which inspire enhancement . . . Design may have been added after the fact to point up the mythic importance of a place or to call beings to a specific site.

In order for an archaeological analysis to be carried out, it is first necessary to identify all the material signs, including the physical criteria for selecting a site, that may have led to this intention and motivated the creation of a work of rock-art on a given rock formation. In other words, if the sacred aspect of the site is to be better understood, it becomes necessary to study not only the different decorated panels of a rock-art site, but also their relation with near-by topographical elements and thus the environment surrounding the decorated rock outcrop. The approach supported here – and part of a growing trend in the study of rock-art sites (see, for example, Schaafsma 1985; Young 1985; Finnestad 1986; Hultkrantz 1986; Simonsen 1986; Llamazares 1989; Bradley 1991; 1994; 1997; Leroi-Gourhan 1992; Sognnes 1994; Clottes and Lewis-Williams 1996; McRanor 1997: 71–2; Steinbring 1998) – consists of investigating the natural setting of these sites and attempting to determine what elements in this setting would have been seen and considered by aboriginal viewers as motivating the choice of this site rather than another as a place where age-old sacred symbols would be left. This archaeology of landscape is based both upon an understanding of the Algonkian religion (drawn from archaeological remains, oral traditions and ethnohistorical and ethnographic documents) and upon an in-depth study of the natural landscape in which this religion was practised. The complementarity of these two aspects of the question is crucial to taking such an analysis further.

As stated above, finger-painted sites are found directly on the surface of rock formations that are usually quite steep and situated along a lake or river. Decorated cliffs generally look out over a wide empty space, corresponding to the expanse of water. It is plausible that such a physical situation meant not only that the sites were open places and therefore visible from a certain distance, but also that they possessed unusual visual and acoustic qualities that might impress people who gathered there. Depending on the time of day when these people met, they could have encountered special material conditions offered by the site's natural setting. I have identified four such material conditions:

- the intrinsic properties of the rock outcrop that supports the rock-art;
- the visual effect of the rock outcrop;
- the acoustic qualities of the site;
- the location of the decorated wall in relation to the other parts of the rock outcrop.

Intrinsic properties of the rock outcrop

Several rock-art site analyses in the Canadian Shield have emphasized how the finger-paintings succeeded, sometimes to an astonishing degree, in exploiting elements of the rock outcrop which could be used to enhance or enrich the content of the work (see Molyneaux 1980; 1983; 1987; Reid 1980; Lambert 1983; 1985; Rajnovich 1989; 1994; Smyk 1991a; 1991b; Rusak 1992; Arsenault *et al.* 1995; Steinbring 1998). Among these elements are the sort of material that characterizes the rock, the quality of the rock support – its texture, colour, polish and patina – and its morphology. The preferred sort of material for supporting rock-art was granite, sometimes with quartz inclusions. According to Conway and Conway (1990: 34), certain Algonkian legends depict veins of quartz as sources of power; they were also supposed to be tangible marks left on stones struck by the lightning of thunderbirds. If this is the case, rocks like those at the Nisula site, on the Upper North Shore (Arsenault *et al.* 1995), and the Kaapehpeshapischinikanuuch site, in the James Bay region (Arsenault 1999), may have been perceived by those who originally visited them as places that testified to the existence of this supernatural being – even though the mythical bird of prey is not represented on them – or as sources of sacred energy because numerous veins of quartz occur directly where the surface is decorated.

With respect to the quality of the rock support, it can be seen that those who made the finger-paintings generally avoided surfaces with granular textures, preferring well-polished surfaces with a patina and showing little sign of flaking or cracks (see Fig. 14.4). At first sight, this choice of smooth sections of the rock support might seem best explained by practical reasons rather than religious motives. However, the conspicuous nature of the decorated surfaces is such a common factor that it remains an important criterion in strategies for discovering rock-art sites. As well, these surfaces are often covered somewhat unevenly with a fairly thick coating of amorphous silica, sometimes referred to as a 'silica film' (Arsenault *et al.* 1995: 25) or 'silica skin' (Watchman 1990), left by run-off water (see Fig. 14.5). The fact that such a coating recurs from one site to another suggests that its presence may have a sacred dimension. Indeed, Native informants met by Thor and Julie Conway in north-east Ontario interpreted these whitish deposits of silica as indirect evidence of the existence of thunderbirds' nests, since the deposits look somewhat like the traces of bird droppings left on rocks (Conway and Conway 1990: 13). In Québec, several finger-painted sites have a similar silica film over the decorated surface or near by; the quantity of the deposit can be quite large, as it is at the CcGh-18 site, in the Témiscamingue region, or at the Rocher-à-l'Oiseau and Cap Manitou sites, in the Ottawa valley. These silica films must have already been in existence when the pictographic motifs were made, since the process by which this material accumulates is very slow (A. Watchman, pers. comm. 1994).

Furthermore, certain sites have smooth vertical, or steeply sloped, portions as well as convex or concave portions, so that the rock as a whole has a somewhat complex and polymorphous profile. These various elements can accentuate aspects of the painting on the rock wall, as if they served to complete or emphasize the characteristics of certain motifs or were meant to delimit the drawing or parts of it. Within a broader context, that morphology may also have been interpreted as being the representation of the petrified form of a human or animal, for which ritual acts, such as offerings of tobacco, were performed, as observed by Sagard and Guinard in the accounts reported above (also see Molyneaux 1980: 10; Steinbring 1998: 8, fig. 4 on p. 5, fig. 48 on p. 66; Tanner 1979: 127). For the moment, the criterion of the decorated rocks' general profile remains to be confirmed through more extensive observation of Québec rock-art sites and through a systematic analysis of traditional Native stories so as to be able to identify such symbolic forms in the Québec territory.

Visual effect

We can now proceed further in the contextual analysis of rock-art sites by looking at the visual effects that may have been originally produced by these sites. The work carried out by various researchers in north-west Ontario (Reid 1980; Lambert 1983; 1985; Rajnovich 1989; 1994;

Smyk 1991a; 1991b; Rusak 1992) shows, for example, that the majority of decorated surfaces in sites in the Canadian Shield have south-east, south or south-west exposures. This is also the case for most of the finger-painted sites identified in Québec (seven out of nine). These surfaces, which often have a patina, are therefore oriented to receive the most light possible, a situation that made it easier both to draw the red-ochre motifs and to view them afterwards. In other words, the painted surfaces face in directions that make the most of the luminosity resulting from the sun's rays. It is quite possible that the play of sunlight on the decorated walls and on the water just below these sites could produce dramatic effects of reflected light: the pictorial motifs might be perceived suddenly to disappear, or, just as suddenly, to reappear, or even can be seen as if some of them were animated. Moreover, in some cases, the graphic content of a site can be reflected in the water below during calm conditions (Steinbring 1998: 92), creating a dual image, a mirror-effect, that could have provoked awe or surprise for those approaching the site during the day. According to Diamond *et al.* (1994: 149, note 27), light and luminosity were important in the aesthetics of Algonkians in the northern forests, the sun representing the ultimate source of light, and light-reflecting materials being considered to indicate the presence of supernatural beings. From this perspective, it seems likely that the capacity for reflection shown by the surfaces of certain rocks was taken as a manifestation of the supernatural; it may have contributed to their being made into sacred places. This quality may have been a factor in deciding to decorate a rock outcrop with motifs and may have motivated the performance of certain rituals when passing near by; it may even have been exploited to make an impression on the uninitiated. The phenomenon is very remarkable at the Nisula site, where the reflective capacity of the decorated walls is further accentuated by their polished surfaces and the presence of a silica film (Fig. 14.6).

Acoustic qualities

The morphology of the decorated walls and the rocky surfaces that surround them may also possess particular acoustic qualities that possibly accentuated the spiritual or sacred nature of the rock-art site (Sognnes 1994: 39; Steinbring 1998: 91–3). It is not rare to find a decorated wall with large vertical or horizontal cracks, a hollow or even a cave or grotto, just above the surface of the water, which could have served as a 'resonance box' (see Lambert 1983: vii–viii; Smyk 1991b: 3–4; Steinbring 1998: 77, 92). Some imposing cliffs also have rocky overhangs sticking out above the decorated wall; these tend to make the site into a natural amphitheatre. This is particularly true of the Rocher-à-l'Oiseau and Nisula sites (see Fig. 14.5). According to certain Algonkian traditions (see Speck 1935; Diamond *et al.* 1994: 39 note 7, and 71), the amplification of natural sounds was a medium through which the spirits made themselves heard.

It is not impossible that those who produced Algonkian rock-art sought natural environments with such rock formations; there the sounds of normal conversation or the music of instruments (drums and rattles) and singing associated with certain rituals (see Diamond *et al.* 1994), would have been considerably modified, thus reinforcing the spiritual dimension of the sacred place. However, it remains to be verified, with appropriate measuring instruments (see Waller 1993), which of the Canadian Shield rock-art sites presenting such formal characteristics could have contributed to the production of acoustic effects, for example an echo or the amplification of the sound made by the human voice, thunder,

Fig. 14.6. Low-angle view of Panel II at the Nisula site (DeEh-1).

Note the strong reflection of the sunlight on the surface of the rock at this place, which can make it momentarily difficult to see the motifs painted in red ochre. It is possible that such visual effects accentuated the unusual nature of the rock-art site by giving it an almost supernatural brilliance. The subjective aspect of how the site's graphic content was perceived, and consequently how its immediate physical setting was perceived as well, is another element to be considered in studying the sacred dimension attributed to certain natural places by the ancient Algonkians.

Photograph by D. Arsenault, courtesy of PETRARQ.

the singing of the wind or even the lapping noise of waves breaking on the rock at the foot of the cliff. In Québec, at least seven finger-painted sites present some impressive resonance, among which the most important is the Rocher-à-l'Oiseau site.

Particular location of the decorated walls in relation to the rest of the rock support

The fourth physical criterion, the position of the rock-art site with respect to the whole rock formation, may also reveal a close association between the natural environment and the spiritual world. As was mentioned previously, a good number of sites are found on cliffs that present crevices and other, larger breaks in the surface (anfractuosities), such as rock-shelters or cave entrances. And, as has been seen, openings like these were used by beings of the underground world when they wished to communicate with the terrestrial world, as well as by shamans seeking knowledge and power. There appears to have been an important relation between the work of rock-art and the proximity of entrances to the underground world. It seems highly unlikely that the situating of certain Québec rock-art sites in environments with such geomorphological features is attributable to mere coincidence. At the Nisula site, there is a large crack near the water-line and just below the decorated wall; 3 m away from a decorated surface at the DcGt-41 site, in the Abitibi, lies a great fault opening, caused by the fall of a huge rectangular block; the Kaapehpeshapischinikanuuch site, in the James Bay region, presents both a rock-shelter and a low grotto in the middle of the decorated walls. In these cases, at least, there seems to be some support for arguing that the choice of a location for a rock-art site was linked to the morphological features of the surroundings. It would follow that these rock-art sites are potentially sacred places. Such a symbolic correspondence is also suggested by rock-art sites in the rest of the Canadian Shield (see Dewdney and Kidd 1967; Pohorecky and Jones 1968; Vastokas and Vastokas 1973; Conway and Conway 1989; Rajnovich 1994; Steinbring 1998).

Finally, in addition to these particular geomorphological features, it is possible that the wind played a role in determining the location of rock-art sites; certain of them – the CdFg-5 site, in the Mauricie National Park (Fig. 14.2 above), the Rocher-à-l'Oiseau site and the Nisula site – rise above an area of water where the wind blows almost continuously. The notion that wind was a factor in choosing a site for pictographic production remains to be tested through a systematic recording of the environmental conditions that prevail at such sites in Québec and elsewhere in the Canadian Shield. Nevertheless, it seems clear that if strong winds blew at certain times when the rock-art was being produced or when the site was visited, it could have been a decisive element in suggesting or recalling the presence of supernatural beings (see Brown 1996: 104–5) in the surroundings of the decorated rock outcrop. Moreover, when one considers how important some prevailing winds could have been traditionally for Algonkian nomadic groups – for example, those winds blowing from one of the four cardinal directions were used to predict storms (Tanner 1979: 94–101) – it is possible that some rock-art sites were used in the past for performing weather control rites. Rock-art sites could have been made or frequented during winter time; winter can be a very harsh season when snow- or ice-storms, or frostbite weather, could be very harmful to people living in the bush. It is possible that the Algonkians performed weather control rites before engaging on a long journey or for the chance of collecting enough food (especially game) during their peregrinations (Fig. 14.7).

As applied to the interpretation of the ritual contexts of rock-art sites, criteria as subjective as the visual, acoustic and even tactile effects of the rock outcrops' location will draw criticism from certain positivist archaeological quarters on the grounds that this risks making the contextual analysis of such religious sites, and consequently that of the sacred landscape, too speculative; the basis for such an analysis could not be reproduced or refuted and would therefore be unscientific. But should these somewhat subjective aspects continue to be ignored in the process of archaeological interpretation when it is clear that the perception of time and space that social actors have in the context of their ritual performances – and that is a crucial element of individual and collective experience in a religious context – is necessarily the product of the senses (see, for example Turner 1986: 23)? Even though, in studying the sacred aspect of the natural landscape, it is difficult and in some cases even impossible to quantify the impact or frequency of perceptual effects, it is best to recognize explicitly that such effects, taken as signs of supernatural manifestations in the Algonquian spiritual universe, may have existed and may have constituted the right, or even necessary, conditions for carrying out certain social acts, in particular the production of rock-art.

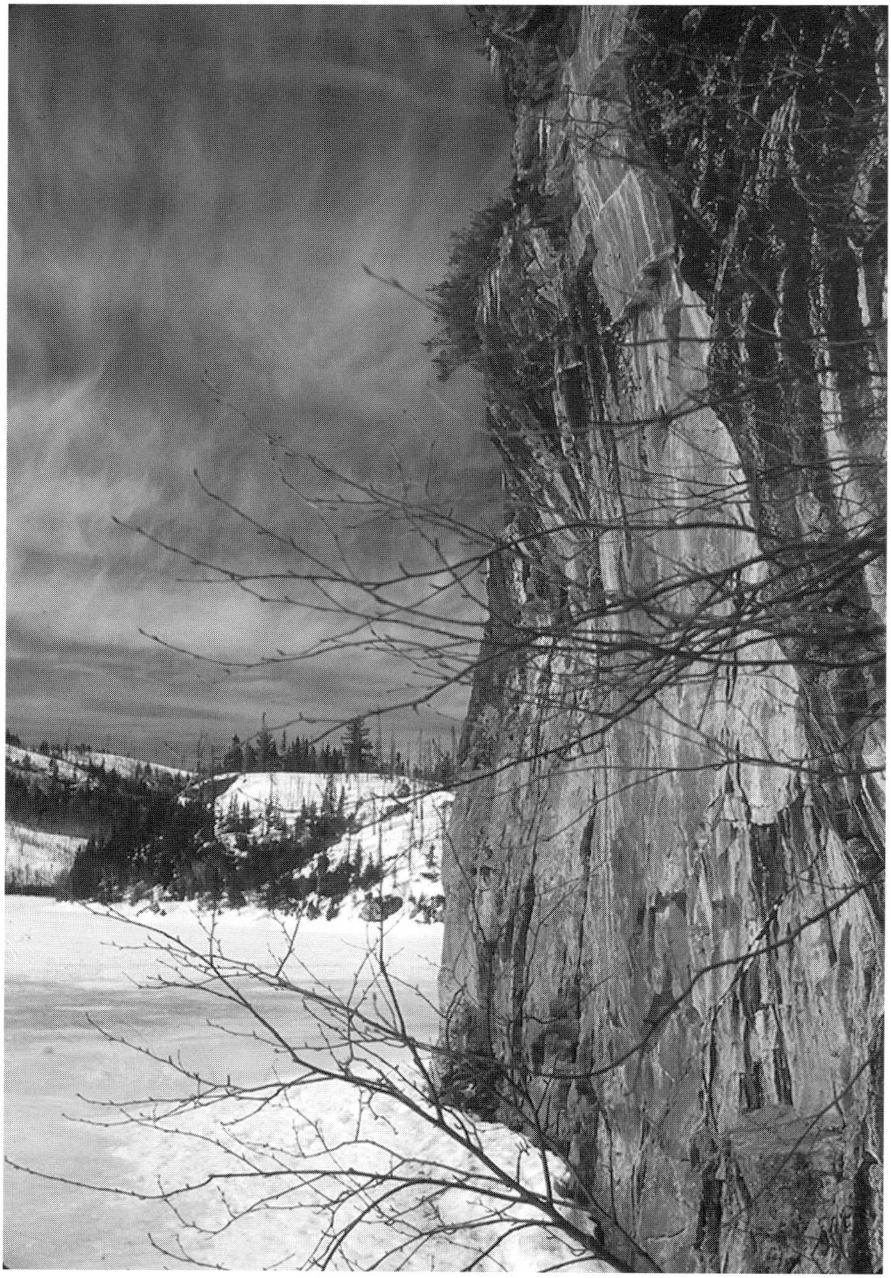

Fig. 14.7. Winter view of the cliff on the Upper North Shore where the Nisula site (DeEh-1) is found.

Note that the lake has frozen over, making it possible to reach the decorated walls on foot across the ice. If rock formations served as special places where Algonkian shamans once met spirits or supernatural beings and if, as is plausible, such meetings could take place in all seasons, the conditions in such places (such as acoustic and visual effects, the texture of the rock's surface, etc.) might vary greatly from one time to another. If this is the case, rock-art may have been produced in winter as well as summer, but in response to different contexts.

Clues provided by the study of place-names

While the data provided by archaeological, ethnohistorical and ethnographical records are of precious value, they are sometimes incomplete and may be profitably complemented by toponymical analysis. In the case of the Canadian Shield, especially in Québec, there exists a place-name database[4] that provides a wealth of information and deserves to be used in full. It contains the place-names given on many old maps (see Laure and Guyot 1732–33; Rousseau 1970; Martijn 1992; 1993), and some of these toponyms were inspired directly from the place-names used by aboriginal people (Denton 1994; n.d.; Lewis 1996). In the regions that have been most fully documented by archaeologists, in particular north-east and north-west Ontario, it can be seen that rock-art sites traditionally had their own names.

Among the rock-art place-names that have remained in the Amerindians' collective memory, the most frequently encountered include words that refer to birds of prey and are thus associated metaphorically with the concept of the thunderbird (Conway and Conway 1990). Other names may make reference to species of animals that were equally important in the Algonkian cosmology, for example the turtle – whose name is one of the designations traditionally given to the lake where the DaGu-1 site is found in the Abitibi (see Tassé 1977a: 44–5). It is therefore worth asking whether this type of place-name may have characterized the designation of rock-art sites and other sacred places in Québec. Answering this question represents an immense task, which remains to be done, but which would no doubt help to direct fieldwork. In addition to looking for the names of animals that were accorded a certain spiritual value, a study of existing aboriginal place-names should also identify those containing the names of supernatural entities (like Manitou, Mamakwaasiuch and Windigo; see Denton n.d.; Poirier 1969) and even references to the material used for decorating objects (for example 'Nominingue', an Algonquin word meaning red ochre or vermilion, or 'Romaine' – a French mis-spelling of an Innu word, *oulaman*, which refers to the ochre used for paintings), as suggested by my colleague Charles A. Martijn (pers. comm. 1994). For example, there is a finger-painted site located in the James Bay area, in the middle of Québec Cree territory, whose name is *Kaapehpeshapischinikanuuch* (EiGf-2). This Cree word refers to the drawings that have been made on the rock surface. When one compares this site name with the name *Pepéchapissinagan*, appearing in a few maps made by a Jesuit, Father Pierre-Michel Laure (Fig. 14.8), in the years 1731–32 and 1733, one becomes puzzled by the strong similarity. On those maps, the name (and its French translation made at that time that can be read as 'one can see on the rock some figures naturally painted') indicates another rock-art site (currently the so-called Nisula site) located on the Upper North shore of the St Lawrence river, within the actual Innu territory. Two hundred and fifty years separate the two references, but it appears that they carry the same concept for two related Algonkian groups in relation specifically to rock-art sites.

Archaeology of the Algonkian sacred landscape

A few key elements in the archaeology of landscape are exemplified in this brief look at the Algonkian sacred landscape, approached through the contextual study of rock-art sites, which

[4] This database would have been even richer if it had not been for a campaign, undertaken between 1912 and 1920, aimed at eliminating the Amerindian names borne by geographical places and replacing them with French or English names (Bouchard 1980: 78, note 2), which often had no relation to the original Native names.

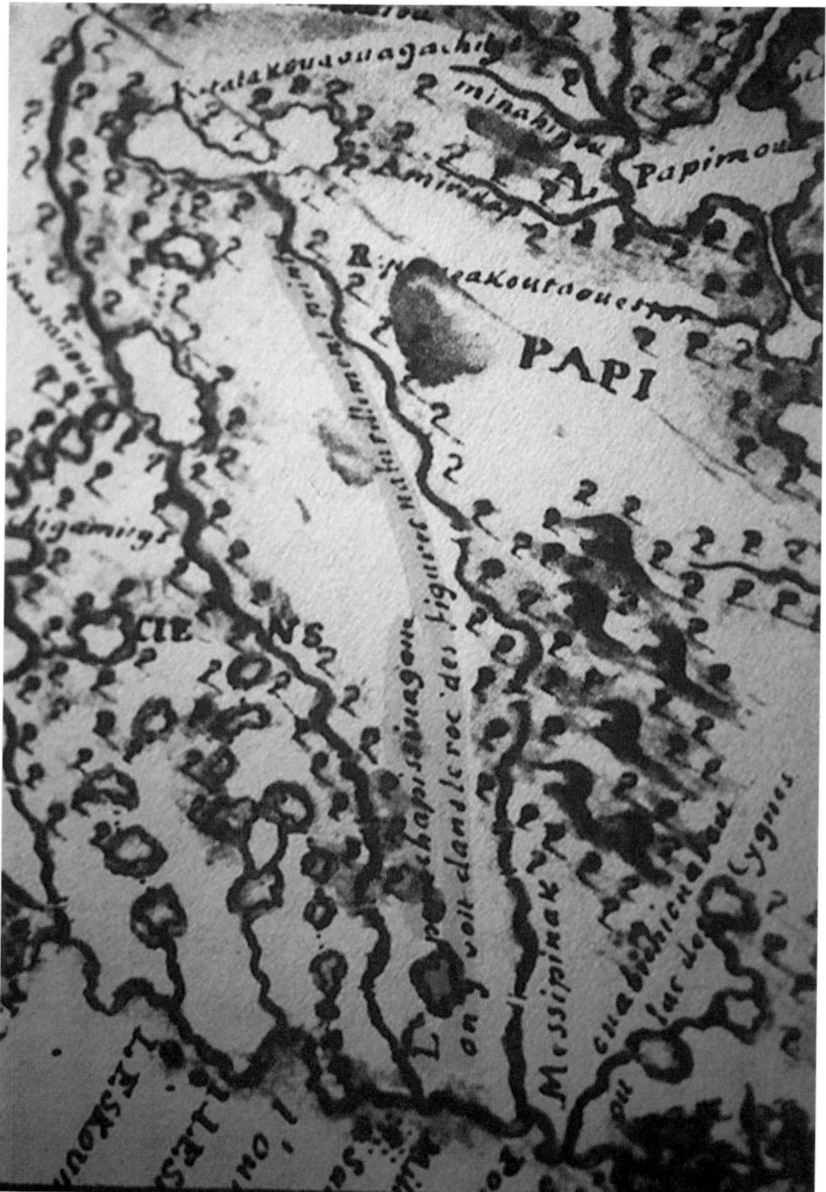

Fig. 14.8. Detail of a map drawn in 1733 by Father Pierre-Michel Laure (Laure and Guyot 1733).

Laure was the first European to report the presence of rock-art sites in Québec, and probably also in Canada. On a series of maps produced by this Jesuit missionary between 1731 and 1733, there is also a reference to another rock-art site called 'Chétaskouachioueou' which has not yet been found (see Martijn 1993; also Bahn 1998: 19). Up the centre of this map of 1733 as well as on three others (out of eight), one can read the words written in French: '*L. Pepéchapissinagan . . . on y voit dans le roc des figures naturellement peintes*' (in English: 'One can see on the rock some figures naturally painted'). As depicted the situation of the lake corresponds exactly to the geographical location of Lac Cassette where the actual Nisula site (DeEh-1) can be seen on the Upper North-Shore of the St Lawrence River; incidently, this pictograph site was only reported to the scientific community in 1985 by a Finnish-born woman, Anne Nisula, during a fishing trip on this lake.

should now be considered as centres of spiritual manifestation and of religious and shamanic experience. Certain aspects of this question remain to be investigated however, in particular the diachronic nature of this sacred landscape. This cannot be accomplished, though, until a sufficient number of rock-art sites have been age-estimated through the AMS-dating method, making it possible to understand how widespread the phenomenon was in prehistoric times, to correlate it with other aspects of the Algonkian religious and shamanic universe and, in particular, to estimate how it might have been spread over time and in space, so as to attain a better understanding of ideological transformations in the long term.

The Algonkian case-study provides an exemplar for a method of broad application to sacred landscapes, as they are made visible in rock-art: that broader programme is presented at the end of chapter 3, the complementary chapter to this, on theoretical approaches to rock-art (pp. 69–84 above).

Acknowledgements

I am the director of the multidisciplinary research programme called PÉTRARQ (Programme d'étude, de traitement et de reconnaissance en archéologie rupestre au Québec). My analysis of rock-art sites in Québec, undertaken in 1995, has been supported by three research grants, two from the Social Sciences and Humanities Research Council of Canada, and one from the Fonds FCAR of the Québec Ministry of Sciences, Research and Technologies.

Some aspects of this chapter have been published in French in *Recherches Amérindiennes au Québec* (see Arsenault 1998a).

I would like to express my hearty thanks to some Québec First Nations communities and institutions (the Innu community of Betsiamites, the Council of the Attikamekw Nation, The Algonquin Band Council of Maniwaki, the Algonquin Corporation Matshitewea, the Cree Band Council of Nemaska, the Inuit commuity of Kangirsujuaq and the Inuit Cultural Institute Avataq), and to some of their representatives, without whom it would not have been possible to carry out this research on rock-art sites in Québec; it was they who permitted me to proceed with an exhaustive analysis of rock-art sites, and who assured me that it would be advantageous to acquire more archaeological information on the subject. Moreover some members of these communities extended a warm and welcome hospitality to my team and myself during our various archaeological fieldworks, which was greatly appreciated.

I am also much obliged to Charles A. Martijn, Louis Gagnon, Daniel Chervrier, Norman Clermont and Florence Piron for their comments on the first drafts of this chapter, as well as to Jane McCauley for the translation of the text from French to English. Finally, I wish to thank Christopher Chippindale for his kind invitation to publish this chapter here.

References

Arsenault, D. 1993. Les pétroglyphes du site Jones de Vale Perkins, Canton de Potton. Evaluation des diverses thèses proposées et discussion à propos des significations à donner aux gravures rupestres de ce site. MS. Sherbrooke, Qc: Direction de l'Estrie, Ministère de la Culture et des Communications du Québec.

1994a. Une énigme venue de la préhistoire: les sites d'art rupestre au Québec, *Cap-aux-Diamants* 37: 62–5.

1994b. Des images dans la préhistoire: un exemple d'art rupestre au Québec, *Eurêka* 2nd edn: 7–8, supplement to *Interface* 5(15) and *Québec-Science*.

1998a. Esquisse du paysage sacré algonquien: une étude contextuelle des sites rupestres du Bouclier canadien, *Recherches Amérindiennes au Québec* 28(2): 19–39.

1998b. Preliminary study of a pictograph site (site EiGf-2), Lake Nemiskau, Cree territory, and proposals for its detailed archaeological analysis. MS. Nemaska, Qc: Band Council of Nemaska, and Québec: Direction Régionale du Nord-Québec, Ministère de la Culture et des Communications du Québec.

1999. The Kaapehpeshapischinikanuuch Project 1998–99: results of the first fieldwork of research on a unique pictograph site (EiFg-2), Cree territory. MS. Nemaska, Qc: Band Council of Nemaska, and Québec: Direction Régionale du

Nord-Québec, Ministère de la Culture et des Communications du Québec.

n.d. Les sites rupestres du Québec. MS with the author.

Arsenault, D. and L. Gagnon. 1996a. Evaluation archéologique de deux sites à pictogrammes de l'Ouest du Québec (site DaGu-1 du lac Buies et site du lac Opasatica, Abitibi). MS. Québec: Ministère de la Culture et des Communications du Québec.

1996b. Le défi de la conservation et de la mise en valeur d'un site à pictogrammes (site Nisula DeEh-1) de la Haute-Côte-Nord du Québec, in C. Mousseau (ed.), *Actes du colloque ICAHM-Montréal 1994: vestiges archéologiques, la conservation* in situ – *archaeological remains,* in situ *preservation*: 123–33. Montréal: Comité International pour la Gestion du Patrimoine Archéologique de l'ICOMOS.

1998a. Etude des conditions hivernales sur le site Nisula. MS. Québec: Ministère de la Culture et des Communications du Québec.

1998b. Pour une approche sémiologique et contextuelle en archéologie rupestre du Bouclier canadien, in R. Tremblay (ed.), *L'Eclaireur et l'Ambassadeur: essais archéologiques et ethnohistoriques en hommage à Charles A. Martijn*: 213–41. Montréal: Recherches Amérindiennes au Québec. Paléo-Québec 27.

Arsenault, D., L. Gagnon and D. Gendron. 1998. Le site à pétroglyphes de Qajartalik, région de Kangirsujuaq (Nunavik): bilan des deux premières campagnes de recherche sur un site rupestre exceptionnel de l'Arctique canadien, *Etudes/Inuit/Studies* 22(2): 77–115.

Arsenault, D., L. Gagnon, C. A. Martijn and A. Watchman. 1995. Le Projet Nisula: recherche pluridisciplinaire autour d'un site à pictogrammes (DeEh-1) en Haute-Côte-Nord, in A.-M. Balac *et al.* (eds.), *Archéologies québécoises*: 17–57. Montréal: Recherches Amérindiennes au Québec. Paléo-Québec 23.

Arsenault, D. and F. Vigneault. 1996. Découverte préhistorique dans l'Outaouais, in *Québec-Science* 35(4): 11.

Bacon, J. and S. Vincent. 1994. Les œuvres rupestres du site Nisula: enquête auprès des Innus de Betsiamites. MS. Montréal: Ministère de la Culture et des Communications du Québec.

Béland, J. 1959. Peinture et outils de pierre indiens au lac Wapizagonke, *Le Naturaliste Canadien* 30 (3): 46–52.

Bender, B. 1995. Introduction: landscape – meaning and action, in B. Bender (ed.), *Landscape: politics and perspective*: 1–18. Oxford: Berg.

Bouchard, S. 1980. *Mémoires d'un simple missionnaire: le père Joseph-Etienne Guinard, o.m.i.* Québec: Ministère des Affaires Culturelles.

Bradley, R. 1991. Rock art and the perception of landscape, *Cambridge Archaeological Journal* 1(1): 77–101.

1994. Symbols and signposts – understanding the prehistoric petroglyphs of the British Isles, in C. Renfrew and E. B. W. Zubrow (eds.), *The ancient mind: elements of cognitive archaeology*: 95–106. Cambridge: Cambridge University Press.

1997. *Signing the land: rock art and the prehistory of Atlantic Europe.* London: Routledge.

Bragdon, S. 1995. The shamanistic 'text' in southern New England, in M. E. D'Agostino *et al.* (eds.), *The written and the wrought: complementary sources in historical anthropology: essays in honor of James Deetz*: 165–75. Berkeley, CA: Kroeber Anthropological Society. Papers 79.

Brown, J. E. 1996. *L'Héritage spirituel des Indiens d'Amérique.* Monaco: Editions du Rocher et Le Mail.

Burnham, D. K. 1992. *To please the caribou: painted caribou-skin coats worn by the Naskapi, Montagnais, and Cree hunters of the Québec-Labrador Peninsula.* Toronto: Royal Ontario Museum.

Carmichael, D. L. 1994. Places of power: Mescalero Apache sacred sites and sensitive areas, in D. L. Carmichael *et al.* (eds.), *Sacred sites, sacred places*: 89–98. London: Routledge.

Chapdelaine, C. 1989. *Le Site Mandeville à Tracy: variabilité culturelle des Iroquoiens du Saint-Laurent.* Montréal: Recherches Amérindiennes au Québec.

1995. Les Iroquoiens de l'est de la vallée du Saint-Laurent, in A.-M. Balac *et al.* (eds.), *Archéologies québécoises*: 161–84. Montréal: Recherches Amérindiennes au Québec. Paléo-Québec 23.

1996. Des 'cornets d'argile' iroquoiens aux 'pipes de plâtre' européennes, in L. Turgeon *et al.* (eds.), *Transferts culturels et métissages Amérique/Europe XVIe–XXe siècle*: 189–208. Québec: Les Presses de l'Université Laval.

Chevalier de Troyes. 1918. *Journal de l'expédition du Chevalier de Troyes à la Baie d'Hudson, en 1686.* (Original 1686.) Edited with comments by the Abbé Ivanhoé Caron. Beauceville, Qc: L'Eclaireur.

Chrétien, Y. 1995. Les lames de cache du site Lambert (CeEu-12) à Saint-Nicolas, in A.-M. Balac *et al.* (eds.), *Archéologies québécoises*: 185–202. Montréal: Recherches Amérindiennes au Québec. Paléo-Québec 23.

Cinq-Mars, J. and C. A. Martijn. 1981. History of archaeological research in the subarctic Shield and Mackenzie Valley, in J. Helm (ed.), *Handbook of North American Indians* 6: *Subarctic*: 30–4. Washington, DC: Smithsonian Institution Press.

Clermont, N. 1982. Quebec prehistory goes marching in, *Canadian Journal of Archaeology* 6: 195–200.

1987. La préhistoire du Québec, *L'Anthropologie* 91(4): 847–58.

1988. Archaeology in Québec, *The Canadian Encyclopedia* 1: 94. Edmonton: Hurtig.

Clottes, J. and J. D. Lewis-Williams. 1996. *Les Chamanes de la préhistoire: transe et magie dans les grottes ornées.* Paris: Seuil.

Conway, J. and T. Conway. 1989. An ethno-archaeological study of Algonkian rock art in northeastern Ontario, *Ontario Archaeology* 49: 34–59.

Conway, T. 1989. Scotia Lake Pictograph Site: shamanic art in northeastern Ontario, *Man in the Northeast* 37: 1–23.

Conway, T. and J. Conway. 1990. *Spirits on stone: the Agawa Pictographs.* San Luis Obispo, CA: Heritage Discoveries.

Delâge, D. 1996. Les premières nations d'Amérique du Nord sont-elles à l'origine des valeurs écologiques et démocratiques contemporaines?, in L. Turgeon *et al.* (eds.), *Transferts culturels et métissages Amérique/Europe XVIe–XXe siècle*: 317–45. Québec: Les Presses de l'Université Laval.

Denevan, W. M. 1992. The pristine myth: the landscape of the Americas in 1492, in W. Butzer (ed.), *The Americas before and after 1492: current geographical research, Annals of the Association of American Geographers* 82(3): 369–85.

Denton, D. 1993. Introduction, in *Aspects du patrimoine des Cris de Mistassini: histoire archéologique et documentaire et les parcs proposés [sic] du lac Albanel – rivière Témiscamie et des monts Otish.* Final report of the Cree Regional Administration, Québec: Ministère des Loisirs, Chasse et Pêche du Québec.

1994. The land as an aspect of Cree history, in G. Ioannou (ed.), *The waters, the land, and the people: an anthology of writings on Hudson and James Bay*: 57–79. Toronto: University of Toronto Press, Sierra Club of Canada.

1997. Frenchman's Island and the Natuwaau bones: archaeology and Cree tales of culture contact, in G. P. Nicholas and T. D. Andrews (eds.), *At a crossroads: archaeology and First Peoples in Canada*: 105–24. Burnaby, BC: Archaeology Press and Simon Fraser University.

n.d. What is in a name? Cree place-names and archaeology in Subarctic Quebec. MS with author.

Dewdney, S. and K. E. Kidd. 1967. *Indian rock paintings of the Great Lakes.* Toronto: University of Toronto Press, Quetico Foundation.

Diamond, B. M., S. Cronk and F. von Rosen. 1994. *Visions of sound: musical instruments of First Nations communities in northeastern America.* Chicago, IL: University of Chicago Press.

Dickason, O. P. 1984. *The myth of the savage (and the beginnings of French colonialism in the Americas).* Edmonton: The University of Alberta Press.

1996. Associer les Amérindiens à l'histoire du Canada, in L. Turgeon *et al.* (eds.), *Transferts culturels et métissages Amérique/Europe XVIe–XXe siècle*: 105–16. Québec: Les Presses de l'Université Laval.

Dumais, P. 1994. Bilan critique de la recherche en archéologie préhistorique, *Archéologiques* 8: 40–4.

Fabvre, B. 1970. *Racines montagnaises compilées à Tadoussac avant 1695 par le père Bonaventure Fabvre, jésuite.* (Original *c.* 1695.) (Transcribed by G. E. McNulty.) Québec: Université Laval, Centre d'Etudes Nordiques. Travaux Divers 29.

Finnestad, R. B. 1986. The part and the whole: reflections on theory and methods applied to the interpretation of Scandinavian rock carvings, in G. Steinsland (ed.), *Words and objects: towards a dialogue between archaeology and history of religion*: 21–31. Oslo: Norwegian University Press and the Institute for Comparative Research in Human Culture.

Flannery, R. 1931. A study of the distribution and development of the Memegwecio concept in Algonquian folklore. MS. Washington, DC: Catholic University of America Libraries.

Gagnon, L. and D. Arsenault. 1996. Evaluation des portions gravées prélevées sur le site à pétroglyphes de Bromptonville et conservées au Musée du Séminaire de Sherbrooke. MS. Sherbrooke: Direction de l'Estrie, Ministère de la Culture et des Communications du Québec.

Gendron, D., D. Arsenault and L. Gagnon. 1996. A propos du projet de sauvetage des pétroglyphes de Qajartalik. Réplique à la lettre de M. Patrick Plumet, *Etudes/Inuit/Studies* 20(2): 117–22.

Gile, M. A. 1995. The thunderbird and underwater panther in the material culture of the Great Lakes Indians: symbols of power. MA thesis, Michigan State University, East Lansing.

Graham, L. R. 1998. *A face in the rock: the tale of a Grand Island Chippewa*. Berkeley and Los Angeles: University of California Press.

Graillon, E. 1995. Dossier sur les pétroglyphes de Bromptonville. MS. Sherbrooke, Qc: Musée du Séminaire.

1996. Localisation et enregistrement du site des pétroglyphes de Bromptonville (BiEx-19). MS. Sherbrooke: Direction de l'Estrie, Ministère de la Culture et des Communications du Québec.

Hallowell, A. I. 1936. The passing of the midewiwin in the Lake Winnipeg region, *American Anthropologist* 38: 32–51.

Hanna, M. 1997. 'We can go a long way together hand-in-hand', in G. P. Nicholas and T. D. Andrews (eds.), *At a crossroads: archaeology and First Peoples in Canada*: 69–84. Burnaby, BC: Archaeology Press and Simon Fraser University.

Hedden, M. 1996. 3,500 years of shamanism in Maine rock art, in C. H. Faulkner (ed.), *Rock art of the Eastern Woodlands*: 7–24. San Miguel, CA: American Rock Art Research.

Hirschfelder, A. and P. Molin. 1992. *The encyclopedia of Native American religions.* New York: Facts on File.

Hoffmann, W. J. 1888. Pictographs and the shamanistic rites of the Ojibway, *American Anthropologist* 1: 209–29.

1891. The Midé'wiwin or 'Grand Medicine Society' of the Ojibwa, in J. W. Powell (ed.), *Seventh annual report of the Bureau of Ethnology to the Secretary of the Smithsonian Institution*: 143–300. Washington, DC: Government Printing Office.

Honigmann, J. J. 1981. Expressive aspects of Subarctic Indian culture, in J. Helm (ed.), *Handbook of North American Indians* 6: *Subarctic*: 718–38. Washington, DC: Smithsonian Institution Press.

Hultkrantz, A. 1986. Rock drawings as evidence of religion: some principal points of view, in G. Steinsland (ed.), *Words and objects: towards a dialogue between archaeology and history of religion*: 42–66. Oslo: Norwegian University Press and the Institute for Comparative Research in Human Culture.

1993. *Religions des Indiens d'Amérique.* Aix-en-Provence: Le Mail.

1995. *Guérison chamanique et médicine traditionnelle des Indiens d'Amérique.* Aix-en-Provence: Le Mail.

Johnston, B. 1995. *The manitous: the supernatural world of the Ojibway*. Toronto: Key Porter Books.

Joly de Lotbinière, P. 1993. Des wampums et des 'Petits Humains': récits historiques sur des wampums algonquins, *Recherches Amérindiennes au Québec* 23(2–3): 53–68.

Kinew, T. 1998. 'Let them burn the sky': overcoming repression of the sacred use of Anishinaabe lands, in J. Oakes *et al.* (eds.), *Sacred Lands: Aboriginal world views, claims, and conflicts*: 33–6. Edmonton: Canadian Circumpolar Institute, University of Alberta.

Kritsch, I., A. Andre and B. Kreps. 1994. *Gwychya Gwich'n* oral history project, in Jean-Luc Pilon (ed.), *Bridges across time: the NOGAP archaeology project*: 5–13. Hull, Qc: Canadian Archaeological Association. Paper 2.

Kulchyski, P. 1998. Bush/lands: some problems with defining the sacred, in J. Oakes *et al.* (eds.), *Sacred Lands: Aboriginal world views, claims, and conflicts*: 21–4. Edmonton: Canadian Circumpolar Institute, University of Alberta.

Laberge, M. 1997. Création d'une nouvelle iconographie sur les Amérindiens du Nord-Est de l'Amérique à partir des données ethnohistoriques datant d'avant 1760. PhD thesis, Department of History. Québec: Université Laval.

Lambert, P. J. 1983. *The Northwestern Ontario rock art project: the 1982 results*. Kenora: Heritage Branch, Ministry of Citizenship and Culture Ontario. Conservation Archaeology Report, Northwestern Region, 2.

1985. *The Northwestern Ontario rock art project: the 1984 results.* Kenora: Heritage Branch, Ministry of

Citizenship and Culture of Ontario. Conservation Archaeology Report, Northwestern Region, 8.

Laure, P.-M. 1959. Relation du Saguenay, 1720 à 1730, in R. G. Thwaites (ed.), *The Jesuit relations and allied documents: travels and explorations of the Jesuit missionaries in New France 1610–1791* 68: 23–119. (Original *c.* 1730.) New York: Pageant.

Laure, P.-M. and le sieur Guyot. 1733. *Carte du Domaine du Roy en Canada dressée par le P Laure miss. J. et dediée en 1731 à Monseigneur le Dauphin augmentée de nouveau revue et corrigée avec grand soin par le même en attendant un exemplaire complet l'automne 1732 Guyot f. 1733.* Carte du Recueil 67 (ancien 4044 B) 9. Paris: Service Hydrographique de la Marine.

Leacock, E. 1981. Seventeenth-century Montagnais social relations and values, in J. Helm (ed.), *Handbook of North American Indians 6: Subarctic*: 190–5. Washington, DC: Smithsonian Institution Press.

Lemaître, S. 1994. Les peintures rupestres amérindiennes du Québec: essai d'étude ethno-archéologique. MA thesis, Faculté de Philosophie et de Lettres, Université Libre de Bruxelles.

Leroi-Gourhan, A. 1992. *L'Art pariétal: langage de la préhistoire*. Paris: Jérôme Millon.

Lévesque, R. 1965. Les pétroglyphes de Brompton. MS. Québec: Centre d'Etudes Nordiques, Université Laval.

Lewis, R. M. 1996. Communiquer l'espace: malentendus dans la transmission d'information cartographique en Amérique du Nord, in L. Turgeon *et al.* (eds.), *Transferts culturels et métissages Amérique/Europe XVIe–XXe siècle*: 357–65. Québec: Les Presses de l'Université Laval.

1998. Maps, mapmaking, and map use by Native North Americans, in D. Woodward and G. M. Lewis (eds.), *Cartography in the traditional African, American, Arctic, Australian, and Pacific societies*: 51–182. Chicago: University of Chicago Press.

Little Bear, L. 1998. Aboriginal relationships to the land and resources, in J. Oakes *et al.* (eds.), *Sacred Lands: Aboriginal world views, claims, and conflicts*: 15–20. Edmonton: Canadian Circumpolar Institute, University of Alberta.

Llamazares, A. M. 1989. A semiotic approach in rock art analysis, in I. Hodder (ed.), *The meanings of things: material culture and symbolic expression*: 242–8. London: Unwin-Hyman.

McCormack, P. 1998. Native homelands as cultural landscapes: decentering the wilderness paradigm, in J. Oakes *et al.* (eds.), *Sacred Lands: Aboriginal world views, claims, and conflicts*: 25–32. Edmonton: Canadian Circumpolar Institute, University of Alberta.

McGhee, R. 1996. *Ancient people of the Arctic*. Vancouver: University of British Columbia Press.

McRanor, S. 1997. Maintaining the reliability of aboriginal oral records and their material manifestations: implications for archival practice, *Archivaria* 43: 64–88.

Martijn, C. A. 1992. Note préliminaire sur une étude comparative des cartes de 1731, 1732 et 1733 du Père Laure: l'art rupestre. MS. Québec: Direction du Nord-Québec, Ministère de la Culture et des Communications du Québec.

1993. Québec rock art references on the 18th-century maps of Father Pierre-Michel Laure. Paper read at the 26th Annual Meeting of the Canadian Archaeological Association held in Montréal.

1998. Bits and pieces, glimpses and glances: a retrospect on prehistoric research in Québec, in P. J. Smith and D. Mitchell (eds.), *Bringing back the past: historical perspectives on Canadian archaeology*: 163–90. Hull, Qc: Canadian Museum of Civilizations. Mercury Series, Archaeological Paper 158.

Martijn, C. A. and E. S. Rogers. 1969. *Mistassini-Albanel: contributions to the prehistory of Québec.* Québec: Centre d'Etudes Nordiques, Université Laval. Travaux Divers 25.

Maxwell, M. S. 1985. *Prehistory of the eastern Arctic.* Orlando, FL: Academic Press.

Mohs, G. 1994. *Sto:lo* sacred ground, in D. L. Carmichael *et al.* (eds.), *Sacred sites, sacred places*: 184–208. London: Routledge.

Molyneaux, B. 1980. Landscape images. Rock paintings in the Canadian Shield, *Rotunda* 13(3): 6–11.

1983. The study of prehistoric sacred places: evidence from Lower Manitou Lake, *Archaeology Paper* 2: 1–7. Toronto: Royal Ontario Museum.

1987. The Lake of the Painted-Cave, *Archaeology* 40(4): 18–25.

Moondance, W. 1994. *Rainbow medicine: a visionary guide to Native American shamanism.* New York: Sterling Publishers.

Moreau, J.-F. 1994. Archéologie amérindienne au Québec: 1979–1994, *Archéologiques* 8: 68–72. Québec: Association des Archéologues du Québec.

Paper, J. 1988. *Offering smoke: the sacred pipe and Native American religion*. Moscow, ID: University of Idaho Press.

Pohorecky, Z. S. and T. E. H. Jones. 1968. Canada's oldest known pictograph?, *Saskatchewan History* 21(1): 30–6.

Poirier, J. 1969. Les êtres surnaturels dans la toponymie amérindienne du Québec, *Revue Internationale de Numismatique* 4: 287–300.

Preucel, R. W. (ed.). 1991. *Processual and post-processual archaeologies: multiple ways of knowing the past*. Carbondale, IL: Southern Illinois University Center for Archaeological Investigations. Occasional Paper 10.

Rajnovich, G. 1989. Visions in quest for medicine: an interpretation of the Indian pictographs of the Canadian Shield, *Midcontinental Journal of Archaeology* 14(2): 179–225.

1994. *Reading rock art: interpreting the Indian rock paintings of the Canadian Shield*. Toronto: Natural Heritage/Natural History.

Reeves, B. 1994. *Ninaistákis* – the *Nitsitapii*'s sacred mountain: traditional native religious activities and land use/tourism conflicts, in D. L. Carmichael *et al.* (eds.), *Sacred sites, sacred places*: 265–95. London: Routledge.

Reid, C. S. 1980. *The archaeology of Northwestern Ontario 2: Indian rock art paintings and carvings*. Kenora: Historical Planning and Research Branch, Ministry of Culture and Recreation Ontario.

Rogers, E. S. and E. Leacock. 1981. Montagnais-Naskapi, in J. Helm (ed.), *Handbook of North American Indians* 6: *Subarctic*: 169–89. Washington, DC: Smithsonian Institution Press.

Rousseau, J. 1970. Les concepts cartographiques du Lac Mistassini avant l'ère de l'arpentage, *Revue de Géographie de Montréal* 24(4): 403–16.

Rusak, J. A. 1992. *The White Otter Lake pictograph project: 1991 results*. Kenora: Ontario Rock Art Conservation Association. Papers in Ontario Rock Art 1.

Sagard, G. 1982 [1632]. *Le Grand Voyage du pays des Hurons*. Montréal: Cahiers du Québec/Hurtubise, HMH.

Saladin d'Anglure, B. 1962. Découverte de pétroglyphes à Qajartalik sur l'île de Qikertaluk, *North/Nord* (November–December): 34–9.

1963. Discovery of petroglyphs near Wakeham Bay, *The Arctic Circular* 15(1): 6–13.

1966. *Rapport succinct sur le travail effectué au cours de l'été 1965 pour le Musée national du Canada*. Ottawa: Musée de l'Homme.

Savard, R. 1974. *Carcajou et le sens du monde: récits montagnais-naskapi*. Québec: Ministère des Affaires Culturelles. Cultures Amérindiennes 3.

Schaafsma, P. 1985. Form, content, and function: theory and method in North American rock art studies, in M. B. Schiffer (ed.), *Advances in archaeological method and theory* 8: 237–77. New York: Academic Press.

Silvy, A. 1974. *Dictionnaire Montagnais-Français*. (Transcribed by L. Angers, D. E. Cooter and G. E. McNulty; original *c.* 1678–84.) Sainte-Foy: Les Presses de l'Université du Québec.

Simonsen, P. 1986. The magic picture: used once or more times?, in G. Steinsland (ed.), *Words and objects: towards a dialogue between archaeology and history of religion*: 197–211. Oslo: Norwegian University Press and the Institute for Comparative Research in Human Culture.

Smith, D. B. 1996. Amerindians in Quebec and Canada, half-a-century ago – and today, in L. Turgeon *et al.* (eds.), *Transferts culturels et métissages Amérique/Europe XVIe-XXe siècle*: 117–37. Québec: Les Presses de l'Université Laval.

Smyk, D. 1991a. On record: the Nippigon Bay pictographs, *Oraca Newsletter*: 20.

1991b. Images on stone: the White Otter Lake Pictograph Project, *Oraca Newsletter*: 3–6.

Sognnes, K. 1994. Ritual landscapes: towards a reinterpretation of Stone Age rock art in Trøndelag, Norway, *Norwegian Archaeological Review* 27(1): 29–50.

Speck, F. G. 1935. *Naskapi: the savage hunters of the Labrador Peninsula*. Norman, OK: University of Oklahoma Press.

Spielman, R. 1993. *Makwa Nibawaanaa*: analyse d'un récit algonquin concernant les rêves sur les ours, *Recherches Amérindiennes au Québec* 23(2–3):109–17.

Steinbring, J. 1982. Shamanistic manipulations and the Algonkian idiom in the archaeology of rock art, *American Indian Rock Art* 7–8: 212–26.

1998. Aboriginal rock painting sites in Manitoba, *Manitoba Archaeological Journal*, 'Archaeology Today' series, 8(1–2).

Tanner, A. 1979. *Bringing home animals: religious ideology and mode of production of the Mistassini Cree hunters*. New York: St Martin's Press.

Tassé, G. 1976. Les peintures rupestres du lac Wapizagonke, Parc national de la Mauricie. MS. Ottawa and Montréal: Parks Canada, Department of Indian and Northern Affairs Montréal, Laboratoire d'Archéologie de l'Université du Québec à Montréal.

1977a. Premières reconnaissances, in G. Tassé and S. Dewdney (eds.), *Relevés et travaux récents sur l'art rupestre amérindien*: 35–69. Montréal: Laboratoire d'Archéologie de l'Université du Québec à Montréal. Paléo-Québec 8.

1977b. Les peintures rupestres du lac Wapizagonke, in G. Tassé and S. Dewdney (eds.), *Relevés et travaux récents sur l'art rupestre amérindien*: 71–112. Montréal: Laboratoire d'Archéologie de l'Université du Québec à Montréal. Paléo-Québec 8.

1995. Etude microscopique et datation des peintures rupestres, in A.-M. Balac *et al.* (eds.), *Archéologies québécoises*: 59–68. Montréal: Recherches Amérindiennes au Québec. Paléo-Québec 23.

1996. Les peintures rupestres du lac Simon. *Recherches Amérindiennes au Québec* 26(1): 65–8.

Tassé, G. and S. Dewdney (eds.). 1977. *Relevés et travaux récents sur l'art rupestre amérindien*. Montréal: Laboratoire d'archéologie de l'Université du Québec à Montréal. Paléo-Québec 8.

Theodoratus, D. J. and F. LaPeña. 1994. *Wintu* sacred geography of northern California, in D. L. Carmichael *et al.* (eds.), *Sacred sites, sacred places*: 20–31. London: Routledge.

Thomas, J. 1995. The politics of vision and the archaeologies of landscape, in B. Bender (ed.), *Landscape: politics and perspective*: 19–48. Oxford: Berg.

Tilley, C. 1996. The power of rocks: topography and monument construction on Bodmin Moor, *World Archaeology* 28(2): 161–76.

Turner, V. 1967. *The forest of symbols: aspects of Ndembu ritual*. Ithaca,: Cornell University Press.

1986. *The anthropology of performance*. New York: Performing Arts Journal Publications.

Vastokas, J. and R. Vastokas. 1973. *Sacred art of the Algonquins*. Peterborough: Mansard Press.

Vincent, S. 1992. Présentation, *Recherches Amérindiennes au Québec* 22(2–3): 3–6.

Vincent, S. and B. Arcand. 1979. *L'Image de l'Amérindien dans les manuels scolaires du Québec*. Montréal: Hurtubise HMH, Cahiers du Québec.

Waller, S. J. 1993. Sound reflection as an explanation for the content and context of rock art, *Rock Art Research* 10(2): 91–101.

Watchman, A. 1990. What are silica skins and how are they important in rock art conservation, *Australian Aboriginal Studies* 1: 21–9.

Whelan, J. P., Jr. 1983. Context and association in Canadian Shield rock art systematics, *Canadian Journal of Archaeology* 7(1): 77–84.

Wright, J. V. 1995. *A history of the native people of Canada* 1: (*10,000–1,000 BC*). Hull: Canadian Museum of Civilization. Mercury Series. Archaeological Survey of Canada Paper 152.

1999. *A history of the native people of Canada* 2: (*1,000 BC–500 AD*). Hull: Canadian Museum of Civilization. Mercury Series. Archaeological Survey of Canada Paper 152.

Young, M. J. 1985. Images of power and the power of images: the significance of rock art for contemporary Zunis, *Journal of American Folklore* 98(387): 3–48.

Zedeño, M. N. 1997. Landscapes, land uses and the history of territory formation: an example from the Puebloan Southwest, *Journal of Archaeological Method and Theory* 4(1): 67–99.

15

The topographic engravings of Alpine rock-art: fields, settlements and agricultural landscapes

Andrea Arcà

Since their discovery a century ago, the later prehistoric rock-engravings of Mont Bego, now in the French Maritime Alps, have made a major grouping. Distinctive in some of its zones are complex geometrical motifs, which have the look of maps; these are the 'topographic' engravings. With benefit of their being discovered elsewhere in the Alps, they can now be set in the regional chronology. Their regularities show that they are maps of a certain kind, and the regularities in what they do and do not represent offer important clues as to social values expressed in these ancient European landscapes.

Images of landscape in Alpine rock-art

Rock-art in the landscape – or landscape in rock-art?[1] As it is important to find the rules that guide the execution of the engraved panel in some particular sites, in the same way it should be interesting to open the chapter of landscape depiction *on* the rock-art surfaces.

It is possible to group these depictions into a class of so-called 'topographic engravings': even if we can try to recognize some details of the surrounding landscape, this does not mean that they were engraved *as* maps, in order to depict real elements or to show the way to reach them. As they were surely executed by local people, there would be no sense in showing ways and paths that they knew well. Probably the only point they have in common with real maps is the (imaginary) perspective view they give, of a landscape as seen from above.

I will deal with the Alpine situation, giving an overview of the most important rock-art, particularly focusing on Valcamonica and Mount Bego, which are by far the most representative, both in number and in quality. Here, it is possible to define a detailed chronology, which is important to achieve a better understanding of the corresponding economy and culture. Relationships among engravings, Alpine territory and mountain culture are considered as mainly relevant; interpretations suggested by contemporary landscapes, exposed by relating topographic tracings to pictures of mountain slopes, are positively stimulating.

While speaking about landscapes, it is important to specify not only *what* is shown, but also *where*. The position of the engraved panels could play an important role, in a passive way – *from* where is it possible to see the engraved rock? – or

[1] This chapter derives from previous publications (Arcà 1998; 1999), while presenting a more detailed analysis of the entire Alpine situation.

in an active one – what is it possible to see *from* the engraved rock? The first case seems to have poor importance: not one of the most important surfaces is situated on a particularly prominent rock outcrop. On the contrary, in many cases there is instead a large view over a surrounding panorama, often positioned below. It means that the surfaces have been chosen in order to see from them (or to dream/remember) and not for the surfaces to be seen from afar.

As we know, prehistoric rock-art is never merely descriptive: each motif, each sign, bears a deep significance, not always immediately intelligible. In the case of the Alpine topographic engravings, we must consider that although it is in many cases possible from the engraved rocks to have a direct look over a wide panorama, and so over the (supposed) depicted landscape, in other cases the engraved patterns seem to pertain to distant areas, lower in altitude. In this sense the meaning should be metaphoric.

The most important point is that the depictions are never related to natural landscapes or panoramas; no mountains, no rivers, no trees are depicted.[2] But they are always inspired by human modifications of the slopes, so by a kind of huge hand-made territorial object (and project). This modification is mostly produced by agricultural settlement, although showing some features related to village elements. This interpretative key allows us to speak about agricultural landscapes, clearly showing an Alpine farmer-shepherd economy starting from the Neolithic.

Valcamonica and Mount Bego, the major regions for the topographic figures, are the two largest zones of Alpine rock-art. Valcamonica, an elongated valley on the south-facing Italian slopes of the main Alpine chain, has many occurrences of rock-engravings, amounting to many tens of thousands of figures; and there are numerous engravings also in the adjacent Val Valtellina. Mount Bego, in the French Maritime western Alps far to its west and south, is a single mountain, its summit nearing 3000 m, with some 30,000 engravings scattered in distinct areas of its high valleys.

[2] With the exception of the Rocio Clapìer rock, examined below, where anyway the depiction of natural landscape elements is conjectural.

Definition: the 'topographic engravings'

In the Alps, topographic engravings refer to repeated geometric modules, regularly delimited and subdivided, which bring to mind the representation of a settlement, in the form of built-on or cultivated adjoining plots of ground (Fig. 15.1, right).

The different modules are commonly found associated on the same surfaces and repeated many times, making plausible their belonging together in the same and unique thematic class of rock-engraving motifs. The same modules are represented in variant forms: either completely pecked or demarcated by a contour-line; they show various shapes, irregular, rectangular or rounded. The most common is a rectangle with a double base-line and one or more vertical lines as inner partitions. Other rectangles are engraved to make subdivided grids. Very common also are 'dot-patterns' or 'macaroni-patterns', in which dots or elongated marks are regularly distributed as if to fill a 'fenced' area. Vast completely pecked rectangular areas are also frequent. The compositions are in some cases 'protected' by a single perimeter line, like a defensive wall.

Another distinctive type of topographic pattern has square modules and an orthogonal distribution of the dots; this other type is dated to the Iron Age, a period decisively later than that of the first type.

To the first important scholar of the Mount Bego rock-art, Clarence Bicknell (Bicknell 1913),

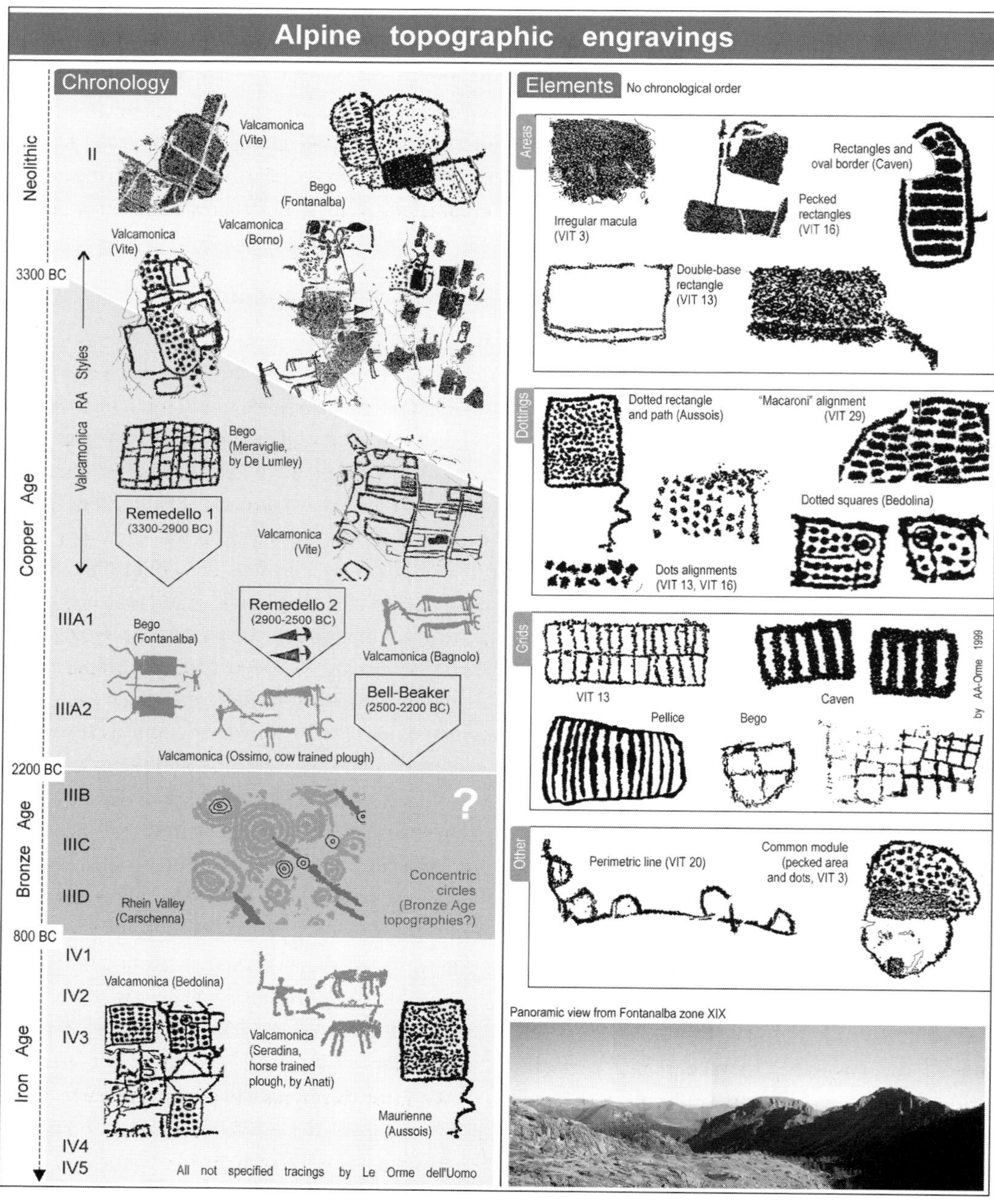

Fig. 15.1. Alpine topographic engravings: overview of chronology and form.

one owes the original hypotheses regarding such engravings. He thought they were depicting 'ploughs with oxen, or probably roofing'. Particularly in one area (the 'XIX zone'[3]) of Fontanalba, Mount Bego, we can find rectangular areas that are totally pecked. These 'nuclei' to a figure are surrounded by curved lines and defined areas. The areas are filled by dots laid out in an orderly arrangement (Fig. 15.2). Even today whoever observes a *gias* from above – *gias*, in the local piedmontese dialect, is the seasonal mountain refuge for cows and sheep, built of stone – would have to agree with Bicknell. Whoever in any Alpine valley observes from the opposite side in spring a newly ploughed field must see the geometric shape which stands out as brown against the green of the surrounding grass.

Also in Valcamonica a topographic interpretation was suggested. Already in 1934, Battaglia (1934) described a rock at Bedolina as a depiction of fields and fences and dated it to the Iron Age. The rock, one of the most famous Valcamonica engravings, is today known as the 'Bedolina map'.

Outside Valcamonica a topographic interpretation was suggested for the cup-marked Rocio Clapìer (Chisone Valley, western Alps, TO, Italy) (Borgna 1980: 226–35), also called the 'lithic map of Rocio Clapìer'. This rock is covered by little cup-marks, often set in lines. It is a clear example of a dominating rock which has been made an art site. The author presents comparisons with the (real) topographic map of the area, and suggests the possibility of recognizing perfectly various natural and human landscape features – springs, ridges, woods, villages – in this rock-art assemblage.

[3] Researchers divide the areas of rock-engravings at Mount Bego into numbered zones. There are two main areas of engravings on the mountain, Val Fontanalba to the east, and the Meraviglie–Arpetto group of valleys to the west and south; each main area is divided between several zones. See Chippindale (pp. 105–10 above) for an account of the distribution of the engraved figures and the definition of these zones around Mount Bego.

Distribution: topographic engravings in the Alpine arc

Mount Bego and Valcamonica, these two most important poles of Alpine rock-art, are also the most important sites for the study of the topographic engravings. They show in the early phases a striking similarity.

Valcamonica

In Valcamonica the distribution of these early topographic engravings is probably larger than is that for the better-known engravings of the immediately subsequent periods, for example Copper Age menhirs and boulders (Remedello and Bell-Beaker) or weapons compositions of the early and middle Bronze Age. We can cite (in alphabetical order) the zones of Bagnolo, Bedolina, Costa Peta, Dos Cuì, Dos dell'Arca, Foppe di Nadro, Luine, Ossimo, Paspardo Dos Sottolajolo, Paspardo town, Pia' d'Ort, Pian Camuno, Pie', Seradina, Sonico, Vite, at various frequencies of occurrence, with between one and thirty topographic compositions in each area. There are consequently hundreds of the 'modules' which comprise the topographic figures. It is possible to find very simple compositions – of only one or few modules – and more complex ones constructed of various geometric modules, ordered dots, perimeter lines. A first phase of irregular completely pecked marks – *maculae* – is also present; this precedes those compiled from the 'modules'.

We must distinguish between the early phase of all these Neolithic–Eneolithic topographics and the later topographics from the Iron Age. The chronology in both cases is well testified by analysis of superimpositions. Although the first class of the topographics to be much noticed in Valcamonica, the Iron Age examples are rare; they are present only at two sites, Bedolina and Pia' d'Ort.

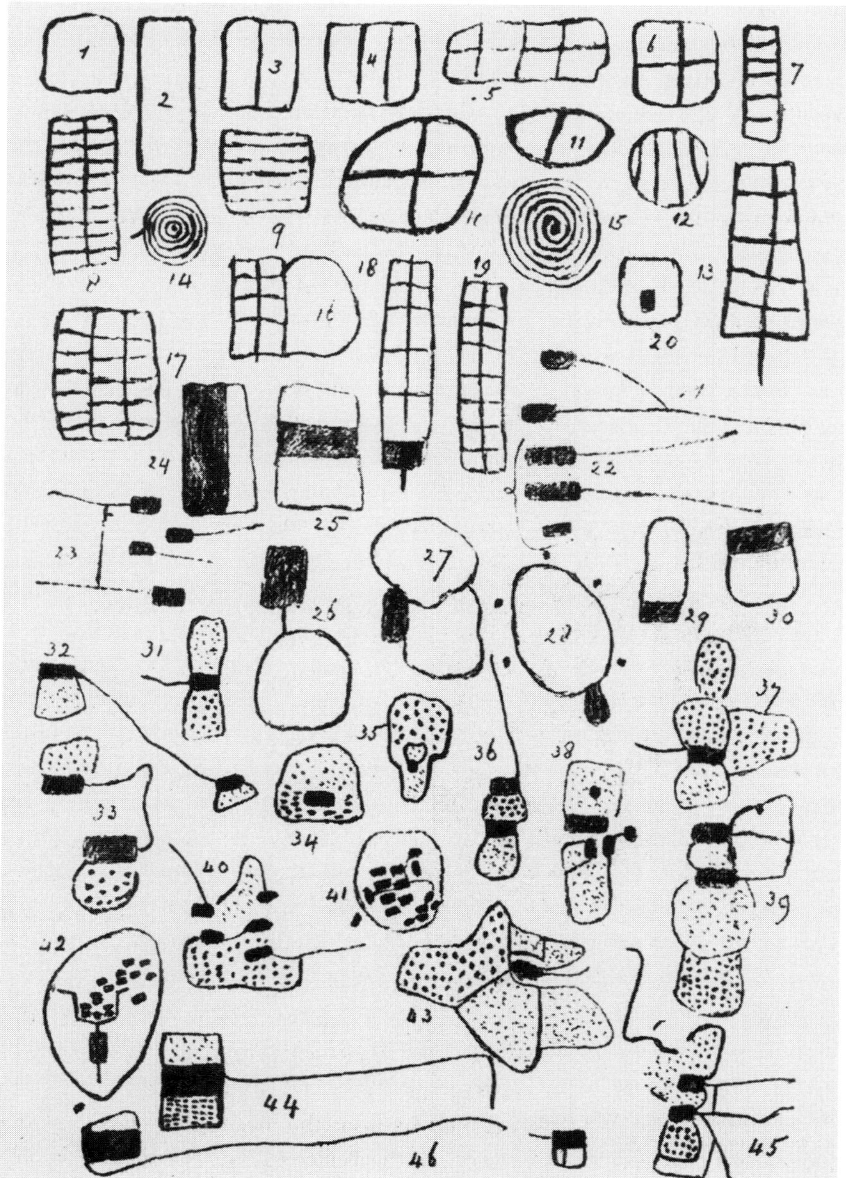

Fig. 15.2. 'Geometric figures, huts and fences', Fontanalba, Mount Bego.
From Bicknell (1913), the early publication which explored the distinctive forms of the topographic engravings.

Mount Bego

In the Mount Bego area the topographic engravings have been put within the class of geometric figures, comprising also concentric circles and spirals. Geometric figures of all types at Mount Bego represent 15.8 per cent of the significant engravings (Lumley *et al.* 1995).

We must distinguish between the two different main areas at Mount Bego: Fontanalba and the Valle delle Meraviglie.[4] Compositions of pecked rectangles accompanied by ordered dots or 'macaroni' in areas protected by curved lines are very common in the Fontanalba, particularly its zone XIX. This characteristic pattern is very similar, if not identical, to that in Valcamonica, so constituting a kind of 'common module'. In the Fontanalba it is often organized in very large compositions. One of these surfaces was named by Bicknell 'The Monte Bego village',[5] here recognizing the depiction of a settlement. This case is quite important: the engraved surface lies in the higher part of the valley, where the surrounding panorama is a completely rocky landscape.[6] Such a village being an impossibility so high on the mountain, this is a depiction of elements not directly to be seen. The Fontanalba topographics constitute the most ancient phase, as testified by various superimpositions on the 'Three Hundred Rock', another of the valley's surfaces.

In the other Bego valley, the Valle delle Meraviglie, that 'common module' is quite absent, while on the contrary simple or complex grids are very frequent. It seems possible to recognize the depiction of stone-terracing on slopes or of stone enclosures for herds, like the ones described by Geist (1995) at Fontan Cime de Causéga, on the southern slope of the Mount Bego massif. These stone enclosures – clearly related to a shepherd economy – accomplish a double job, also freeing the slope from stones and increasing surface of pasture.

Amongst the grids it is also possible to distinguish some superimpositions. On the rock of the 'False Sorcerer' (ZIV GII R11A[7]) a grid is superimposed by three triangular blade daggers and by a horned figure. On the rock of the 'Anthropomorph with Zig-zag Arms'[8] (ZIV GIII R16D), a grid is superimposed by an anthropomorphic figure.

So grids on Mount Bego seem also to belong to the most ancient phases, a chronology corresponding once more with that in Valcamonica. Grids are present in Valcamonica also, mostly at Luine (Anati 1982) and Vite.

Western Alps: Ponte Raut, Val Pellice, Rocher du Château, Sion

Speaking about grids, a striking similarity can be found in the white rock-paintings of Ponte Raut (Pons 1938; Seglie and Ricchiardi 1988; Arcà 1995), Germanasca Valley (western Alps, TO, Italy). Popularly known as *Rocio 'dla Fantino* ('Rock of the Fairy'), they present a complex grid with square and rectangular boxes, a rectangle and a crossed shield (Fig. 15.3). They were made on a vertical surface over a rock-shelter, placed on a steep slope, densely terraced with stone walls.

Two more rock-paintings in the western Alps present some elements which can be interpreted as topographic.

Not far from the area of the 'Rock of the Fairy', in the Pellice valley (TO, Italy) a notable

4 [The present author uses the Italian names, such as 'Valle delle Meraviglie', whereas other contributions to the present book use the French 'Vallée des Merveilles'; the other place-names differ – if at all – only by a letter or two between the languages. For the mountain itself, the present author uses the English 'Mount Bego', whereas others use the French 'Mont Bego'. *Eds.*]

5 Before the systematic numbering of zones, rocks and individual figures in the complete inventory of its rock-art, first organized by C. Conti, charged by the Italian Archaeology Superintendence from 1927 to 1942, many Mount Bego rocks were given informal names, as the 'Three Hundred Rock' for its so numerous figures. These names persist alongside the inventory numbering, and exist in English, Italian and French forms.

6 Fig. 5.2 (p. 107) is taken in the region of 'Mount Bego village' and shows well its rocky settings.

7 In the systematic numbering, the zones are divided into groups, the groups into individual rocks, and individual figures on each rock are individually numbered. 'Z IV G II R 11A' is Zone IV Group II Rock 11A.

One celebrated figure and surface in the Arpetto region is fancifully called 'Le Sorcier' ('The Sorcerer'; Italian 'Il Mago') as it makes the shape of a grotesque human face; so another figure not far away and with some similarity which could be mistaken for the 'Sorcerer' is called the 'Le Faux Sorcier' ('The False Sorcerer').

8 'L'Anthropomorphe aux Bras en Zigzag'.

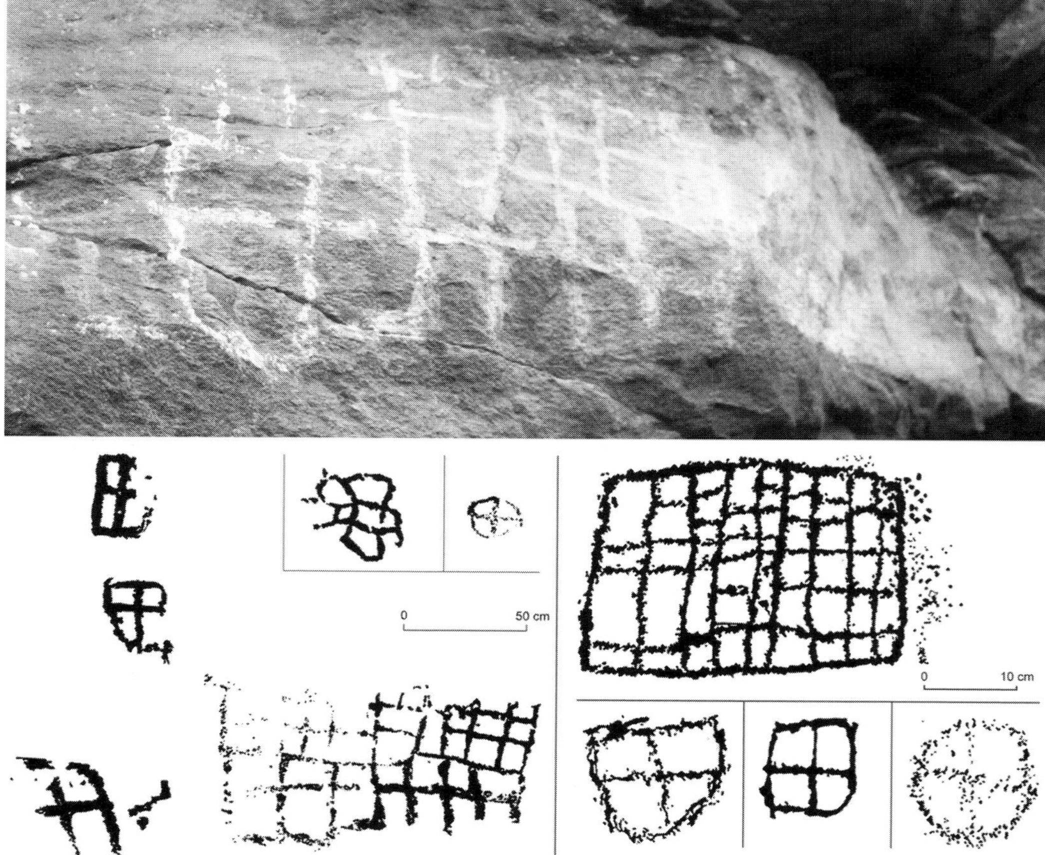

Fig. 15.3. Comparison between Ponte Raut paintings (*above and left*) and Mount Bego net- or grid-like geometrical figures (in French, *reticulés*) (*lower right*).
The Bego figures from Lumley *et al.* (1995).

red-painted surface has been recently discovered (Nisbet 1994). Three rectangular grids with vertical lines are accompanied by schematic anthropomorphic figures, both in rows and isolated,[9] sometimes reversed (Fig. 15.4). The rock-shelter is situated in the lower part of a south-facing slope, dominating the underlying plain of the valley bottom, now showing the shapes of close cultivated fields. An archaeological dig at the base of the shelter could reveal the presence (or the absence) of possibly related material, while an AMS examination of the pigment could deliver interesting dating results. In a comparison with Valcamonica, it is possible to recognize two known elements there: the topographic grids of Vite and the 'shield-shaped' figures of Luine. While these two figures have been interpreted in different ways – the first one in a topographic sense and the second in relation to early and middle Bronze Age weapons, and so like a wooden shield – this is a very particular subject, not yet exhaustively treated. It shows similarities with the topographics of the northern area of Valcamonica and with those of Valtellina. It also means that the

[9] The individual figures have been distinguished through a photo-enhancing digital treatment.

Fig. 15.4. Val Pellice paintings: grids and row of human figures. Digitally enhanced photograph (*left*) and preliminary photographic tracing (*right*).

shield-shaped figures could be put into the class of the topographic engravings – interpreting the relation with the Bronze Age weapons as merely casual – and so belonging to previous phases.[10]

Another important situation is presented at the Rocher du Château, Haute Maurienne, France (Nelh 1989; Fossati 1995). Along the huge vertical panel, where seven deer have been painted, are also open red grids and double-base rectangles painted in white-yellow. The red grids seem to have been painted with fingers, while the white-yellow figures show a thicker pigment.

Both the Val Pellice and the Rocher du Château paintings, like others in the western Alps such as Ubaye and Rocca di Cavour (Gambari 1992), show a clear relationship with Mediterranean elements found in the paintings of Provence, France, such as Abri des Essartènes, Gorges de la Véroncle (Hameau 1989), and of Andalusia, Spain, such as Paloma I–III–IV and Los Penascales shelters).[11]

The case of the Rocio Clapìer has been already cited. If the topographic interpretation is correct, then the alignments of little cup-marks could correspond with the analogous alignments of round dots in the Valcamonica maps, either Copper Age or Iron Age in date.

At Chemin des Collines, Sion (Switzerland), a series of menhirs surrounded a necropolis of slab tombs of the Chamblandes type (middle Neolithic, Cortaillod period, 3900–3200 BC). On one of these menhirs is a completely irregular pecked area (Blain 1975), analogous to the *maculae* of Valcamonica. Not far away, at the Crête des Barmes site (St Léonard: Courboud 1986) a cup-marked flat surface shows a few rectangular filled areas, possibly interpretable as topographic elements.

Valtellina

One of the most important areas for the topographics is the Valtellina (central Alps, SO, Italy). Five sites can be cited: Tresivio; Dosso Giroldo,

[10] This fact is also testified by a superimposition on Luine rock 35, where a shield-shaped figure is covered by an axe.

[11] This is the famous, and not yet clear, case of 'schematic art', stylistically dated by Iberian scholars in a long time-range from the Final Neolithic until the Iron Age (Breuil and Burkitt 1929; Acosta 1968; Beltrán Martínez 1983). A Bronze Age date is preferred, hypothesizing a starting point for the art tradition in coincidence with the arrival from the east of metal-working peoples. The identification of some topographic elements could bring a new element of interest into the schematic art.

Fig. 15.5. Dosso Giroldo: topographic engravings.

near the Rupe Magna (Grosio); Val di Tej near Grosotto; Caven near Teglio; San Giovanni near Teglio. All the sites are situated on south-east-facing slopes, with surfaces polished by the glaciers and with a large panoramic view over the plane bottom of the valley.

At Tresivio 1 sector E (Sansoni *et al.* 1999), rectangular pecked areas seem to be very faint and superimposed by early and middle Bronze Age axes.[12]

At Dosso Giroldo (Fig. 15.5) the engraved rocks were discovered and partially recorded by D. Pace in the 1970s (Pace 1972). At least three rocks show topographics. The most important, the 'Rock of the Warriors', shows a series of completely pecked rectangles and outlined rectangles with a central dot. A unique figure is composed of five elongated rectangles, which seem to depict the shape of strip fields, fields of a type still existing today on the flat valley floor below. Topographics are clearly superimposed by standing warriors of the First Iron Age.

On the Val di Tej rocks, recently recorded,[13] is a rectangle with an oval-shaped upper part filled by aligned and completely pecked inner rectangles.

[12] S. Gavaldo proposes an early to middle Bronze Age date for the topographics of Tresivio, pointing to the uniformity of all the figures. The pecked topographic elements are anyway present only in one sector, and probably (I have not seen the rock, only the tracing) superimposed by the axes.

[13] Footsteps of Man (Orme dell'Uomo) 1997, unpublished.

That same kind of design, clearer and better executed, is present at Teglio,[14] where there are some thirty modules. One can find rectangles with the upper part oval-shaped (and with three to seven inner rectangles), squares, in some cases concentric, filled squares and grids (Fig. 15.6). The engraved surface is not far from the discovery site of the famous Copper Age stelae of Teglio. A similar pattern occurs on rock 1B of S. Giovanni di Teglio (Gavaldo 1999). Some of these modules curiously make one think of certain symbols of the shield-escutcheon (*idole-écusson*) type on the Breton megalithic structures, e.g. at Mane-er-Hroeck, Locmariaquer (Briard 1990) or of the stelae of Collado de Sejos, Spain (Bueno Ramirez *et al.* 1985), which hypothetically could have a topographic value. The same pattern occurs in the upper part of the Valcamonica, at Sonico, not far from Valtellina. The same rectangle with an oval-shaped upper part also pertains to the shield-shaped figures of Luine (above, pp. 324–5) which are superimposed by Bronze Age axes, and to the figures of sector AL of the Rupe Magna (Arcà *et al.* 1995). These last are dated to the Copper Age.

Iron Age topographics: Aussois

Topographics of later, Iron Age phases show different modules, although once more with contoured rectangles and alignments of dots. The rectangles are indeed squares (rather than being decidedly wider than high), the dots are differently distributed, and some zigzag or meandering lines join like paths the separated units. The main site is surely Aussois (Fig. 15.7), in the French Haute Maurienne Valley (Ballet and Raffaelli 1991; 1993; 1996). Its Iron Age date is testified by comparison with analogous Valcamonica engravings and by superimpositions. A similar

[14] Discovered in 1975 by Mr and Mrs De Piazzi, recorded by Footsteps of Man (Orme dell'Uomo) 1997, partially published (Pace *et al.* 1985; Arcà *et al.* 1999).

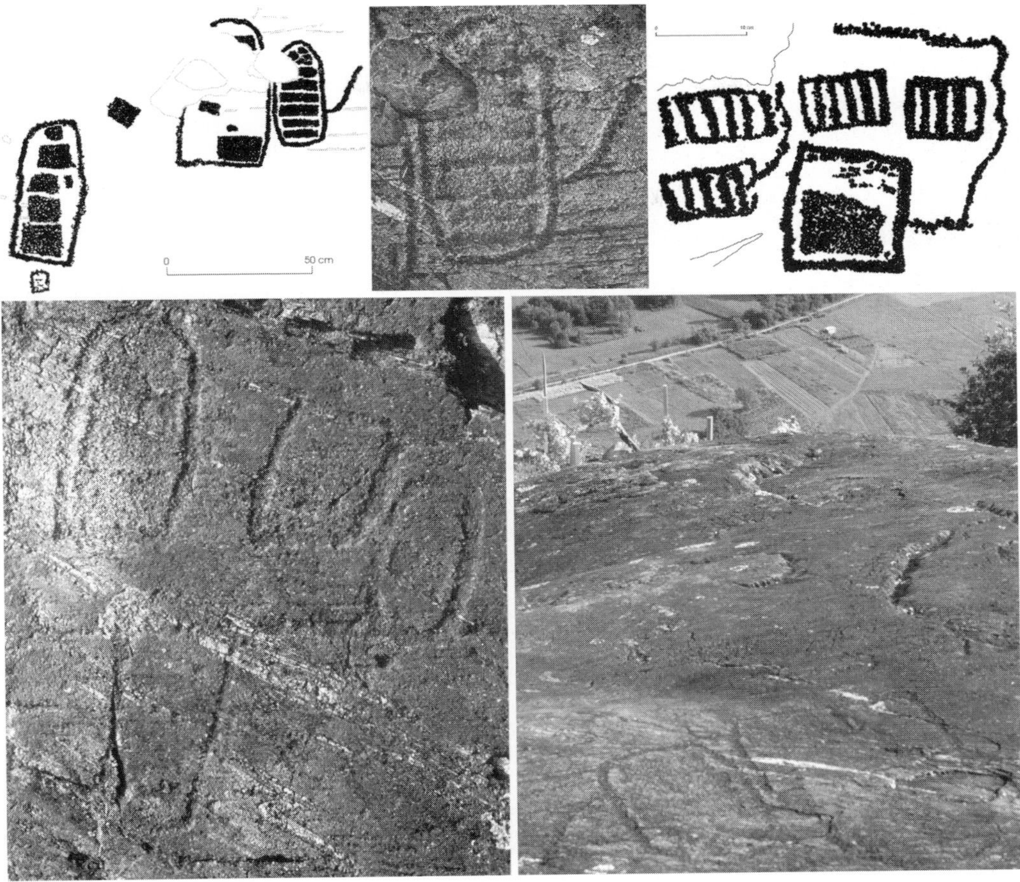

Fig. 15.6. Caven: topographic engravings. Tracings and photographs, with (*lower right*) panoramic view from the engraved surface over the valley bottom.

engraving is present on one rock of the recently discovered site of the high Valcenischia in the western Alps (TO), Italy: Arcà *et al.* 1996; in press).

Tuva Republic: a remote coincidence

A very curious comparison must be added.[15] The same Valcamonica and Fontanalba 'common module' (Fig. 15.8) is present at a very distant site, located in the Ulug-Khema valley (the valley of the big river) at Mugur-Sargol (Devlet 1976), in the Upper Yenisei–Tuva Republic between Mongolia and Siberia (Fig. 15.8c). In that region vast areas are devoted to the cultivation of cereals and to stock-raising. A merely casual coincidence is statistically most improbable, as the resemblance is so close. Are similar motifs present in many other (and less distant) areas?

Chronology

In trying to set a chronological frame, it is possible to define two distinct and distant phases. The first is related to a Neolithic to early Copper Age

15 Thanks to a recent suggestion of Prof. Burchard Brentjes.

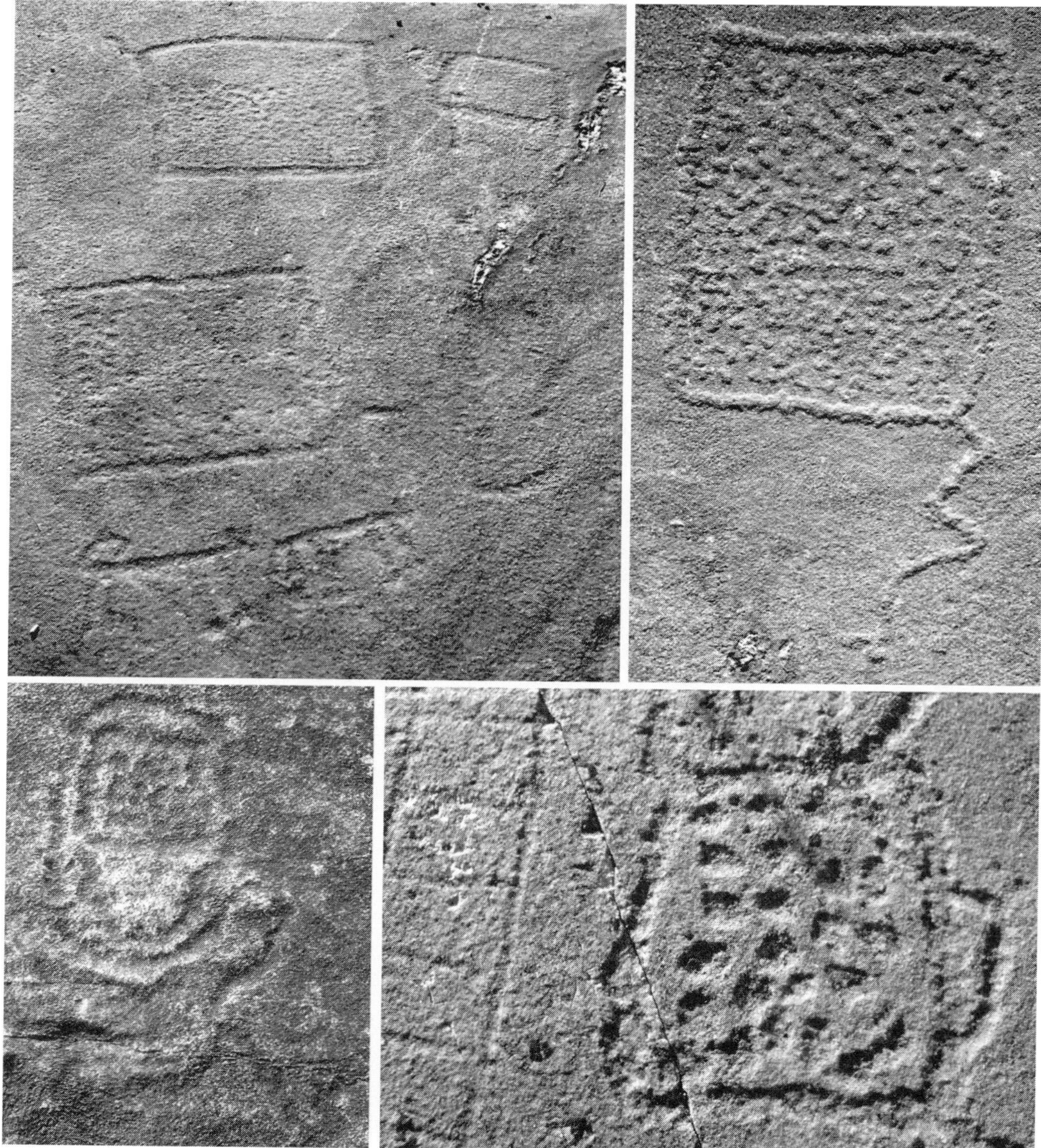

Fig. 15.7. Aussois: dotted rectangles and outgoing 'paths' (zone 9,11). These are now protected underground.

range (Valcamonica and Mount Bego), and the second to the Iron Age (Valcamonica and Haute Maurienne). All the phases are well testified by superimpositions, demonstrating a good parallelism between the western Alps and the central Alps (Arcà 1995). This coincidence should be related – if not to the pertinence to the same culture – at least to a derivation from the same roots, and to the presence of analogous agricultural practices and of commercial contacts.

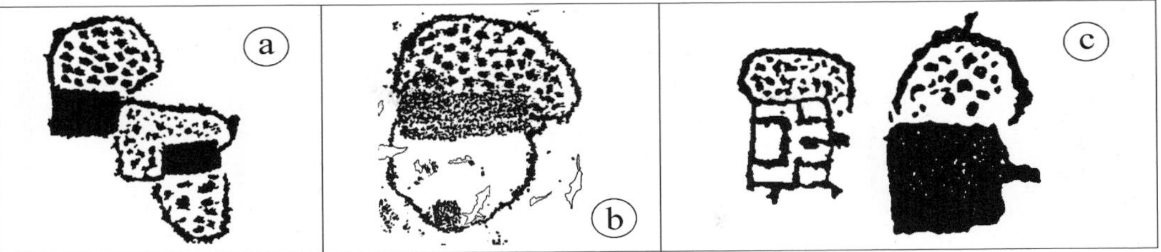

Fig. 15.8. The 'common module' in and beyond the Alps.
(a) Mount Bego: Fontanalba zone XIX.
(b) Valcamonica: Vite rock 3.
(c) Tuva republic (Russia), Mugur Sargol.

Neolithic–Copper Age topographics: Valcamonica

Studying the superimpositions makes it evident that the topographics of Valcamonica are covered by Copper Age figures: they are older. As no other type of figure is so stratified, they must constitute the most ancient phase of Valcamonica post-Palaeolithic rock-art.[16] There are three main cases (Fossati 1994a): on the Borno I boulder face B[17] (Frontini 1994), where filled rectangles with double base, *maculae* and alignments of dots are superimposed by Remedello daggers and ploughing scenes (Fig. 15.9), at Bagnolo 2, where a double-base rectangle is covered by a sun figure, and at Ossimo 8, where a series of orderly arranged dots are superimposed by a ploughing scene. In the first and in the second case, the topographics are under a figure of phase IIIA1, the Remedello,[18] in the second under a figure of phase IIIA2, Bell-Beaker. Topographics are also superimposed by Bronze Age rayed circles at Luine rock 44 (Anati 1989: 260) and by First Iron Age warriors at Vite rock 13 (Arcà 1992). So topographical engravings have been executed starting from a more ancient period than the IIIA1 phase (Remedello 2 period), i.e. before 2900 BC; they should correspond to a Remedello 1 period.[19] We can find figures that superimpose topographics, but we cannot find figures superimposed *by* topographics,[20] except the *maculae*; we have a *terminus ante quem* but not a *post quem*. We can say that topographics belong to a first Copper Age phase, but we cannot exclude a more ancient, Neolithic date-range.

The same fact is also demonstrated by comparisons: the 'village-maps' of Vite present 'eyelets' (semicircles divided by vertical *intaglio*, Fig. 15.10c) in the perimeter lines very similar to those of the Camunian and Valtellina Chalcolithic stelae (Vangione 1 and 2, Valgella 3, Borno 1 face D, Borno 6, Ossimo 3). The same eyelets can be compared with, and interpreted as, the bastions of

16 The figures of humans in a distinctive posture said to be one of adoration or prayer – *orants* in French, *oranti* in Italian, *prayers* in English – are ascribed to the Neolithic in the Anati chronology (Anati 1976). A revised view (Ferrario 1992; 1994; Fossati 1994) now shifts them to the Bronze Age (Arcà in press). No figure of a *prayer* is covered by Copper Age engravings.

The rare figures of large animals are ascribed to an Epi-Palaeolithic in the Anati chronology (1976).

17 The Borno I boulder is one of the many movable stones, rather than areas of fixed bedrock, which are a major element in the Alpine rock-art traditions. These statue-stelae are identified and numbered by their locality: so Borno I is the first of the series in the Borno locality; Borno I boulder face A is the first of the engraved surfaces on it.

18 I.e. to the first phase of III style, full Copper Age, as described by De Marinis (1994a), and dated to 2900–2500 BC (De Marinis 1997), corresponding to the Remedello 2 archaeological period.

19 First Copper Age, 3300–2900 BC (De Marinis 1997).

20 Citing a superimposition on rock 23 of Foppe di Nadro, S. Gavaldo (Sansoni *et al.* 1999: 124) individuates some dots of a topographic composition covering a Bronze Age dagger. The dagger is indeed very similar to the daggers of Vite rock 36, where maps are also present, and shows a different handle but the same triangular blade of the Remedellian-style daggers, to which it is more probably related (A. Fossati, pers. com.).

Fig. 15.9. Borno I boulder face B, Valcamonica.
Ploughing scene, animals, Remedello daggers and foliated flint halberd of IIIA1 style (Remedello 2 Copper Age), drawn in black, are superimposed on topographic engravings, drawn in grey.

the external stone walls in some early Copper Age settlements (and fortresses or monuments) like Castelo Velho do Freixo da Numão or Leceia,[21] Portugal (Cardoso 1997; Fig. 15.10a), Los Millares,[22] Spain (Fig. 15.10b) and Chalandriani, Greece. The grids recall strongly some cell-plan structures (Brentjes 1998) of the Anatolian and Indus Valley early Neolithic (Fig. 15.11a, b), with a seventh to fourth millennium BC range.

As regards archaeological finds, a greenstone axe associated with fragments of coarse ceramics was excavated in 1993 at Vite (Arcà *et al.* 1996); it can be dated to the middle Neolithic or to the early phases of the Chalcolithic. The axe was found near an engraved rock (VIT36) with topographic figures; it appears to have been left there intentionally.

For the map-related engravings, the Vite[23] area (*commune* of Paspardo) seems one of the most interesting. A new research zone (Arcà 1995), it has been studied by 'Footsteps of Man' for eight recent summer seasons. It lies on the left slope of Valcamonica, facing west, in a 700–800 m range of elevation. From many places, some with topographic engravings, it is possible to have a

21 After a final Neolithic settlement, at Leceia during the First Copper Age (2870–2400 BC) there is the planning and the building of the defensive stone wall with bastions.

22 Drawing of the outside wall in Renfrew (1973).

23 'Vite' means grape-vine, cultivated in the area till a few decades ago.

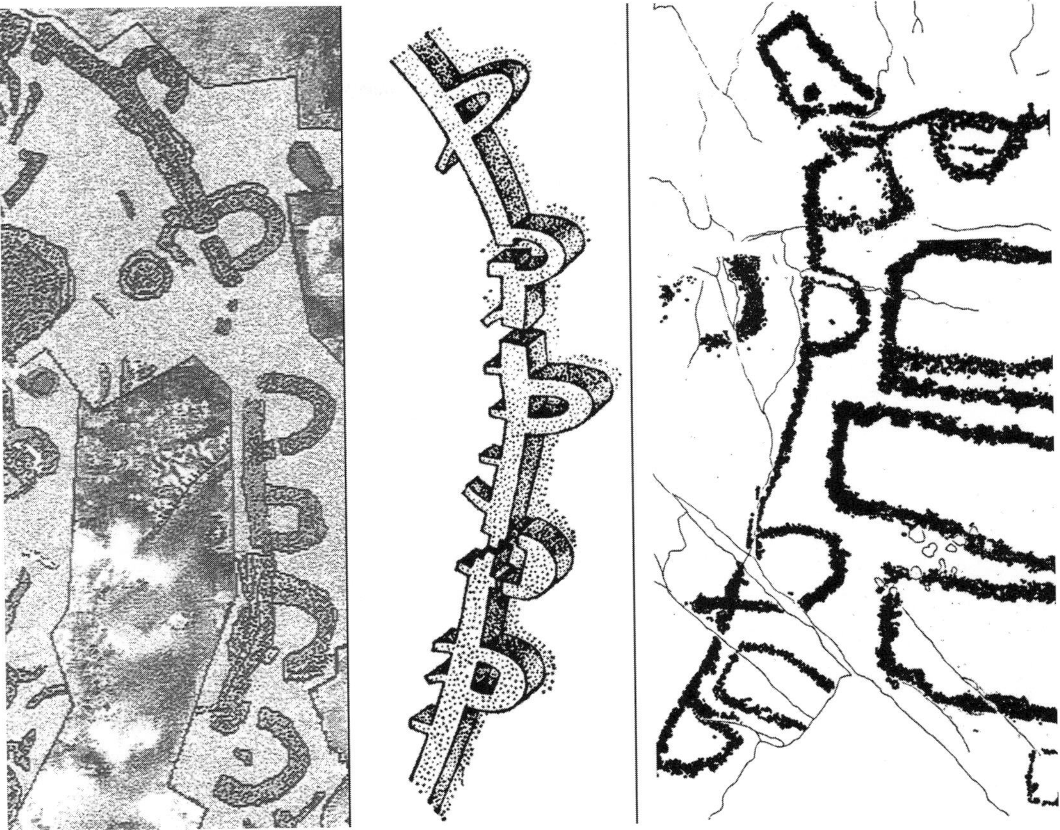

Fig. 15.10. External walls with perimeter line.
(a) Leceja, Portugal: Copper Age external wall. From Cardoso 1997.
(b) Los Millares, Spain: Copper Age external wall. From Renfrew 1973.
(c) Vite rock 20, Valcamonica: perimeter line with 'eyelets'.

wide panoramic view, particularly over the bottom of the valley about 400–500 m below, and over the opposite right slope. On the opposite slope, the site of Le Crus is particularly rich in topographic engravings (seven rocks, twenty sectors). The Vite slope is quite steep, so uncomfortable to work – whether for rock-art study or other purposes. Its land has been abandoned during the last forty years: this is probably the reason it has not been studied in the past. More than fifty rocks (thirty with topographics), have been completely traced; these remain mainly unpublished.

The first phase of topographic engravings at Vite is made up of *maculae*, totally pecked pseudo-rectangular areas on which double-based rectangles and alignments of pecked dots are sometimes superimposed (VIT6, VIT29). Other morphological elements are: contoured figures filled with dots (the 'common module', VIT3, VIT20); contoured oval figures (VIT8), often with a central point; grid rectangles (VIT13); filled rectangles and perimeter lines with eyelets (VIT20, VIT21). The same shapes are found in the zone of Dos dell'Arca, a hillock of the valley floor below. The peculiarity of the Vite

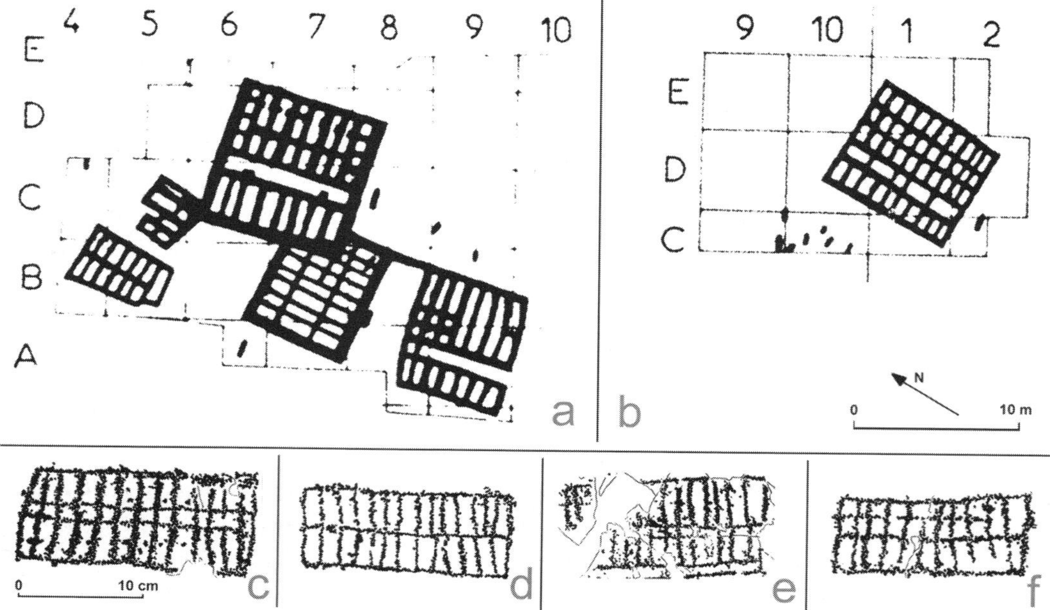

Fig. 15.11. Buildings and grids compared.
(*above*) Box-building structures (aceramic Neolithic to early Copper Age) at Mehrgarh, Pakistan. Drawing from Samzum 1987.
(*below*) Grids on Vite rock 13, Valcamonica.

area is the presence of some complex compositions (VIT13, VIT20, VIT29) which could recall a human settlement, like a 'village-map' (Figs. 15.12 and 15.13). Perimeter lines are quite common, while in one case (VIT20) four concentric rounded squares seem to depict a defensive unit.

It remains to decide whether we should refer the Vite engravings to the Neolithic or to the early Copper Age. For the moment, this aspect is strictly related to the interpretation of the figures. In fact, we can interpret them both as cultivated fields and as village-maps. The interesting idea is to try to merge them into the definition of an 'agricultural settlement', a complex structure of a human landscape with a series of fields organized as a village and protected by a common enclosure.

Following the agricultural interpretation makes a Neolithic date-range possible on Mount Bego, where early Neolithic pottery is well represented (e.g. at Gias del Ciari). On some more complex village-maps, such as those at Vite, perimeter walls and bastions indicate a protected settlement, more probably dating to the early Copper Age. It is quite probable that we are dealing with a long time-range, where different phases are to be better defined. The possibility of some very ancient origin is testified by the comparison with the oldest Neolithic elements of Anatolia and the Indus Valley.

Neolithic to Copper Age topographics: Mount Bego

Henry de Lumley's great team-work (Lumley *et al.* 1995) interprets the topographic engravings, in accordance with Bicknell, as the 'symbol' of the cultivated fields or the enclosures for animals,

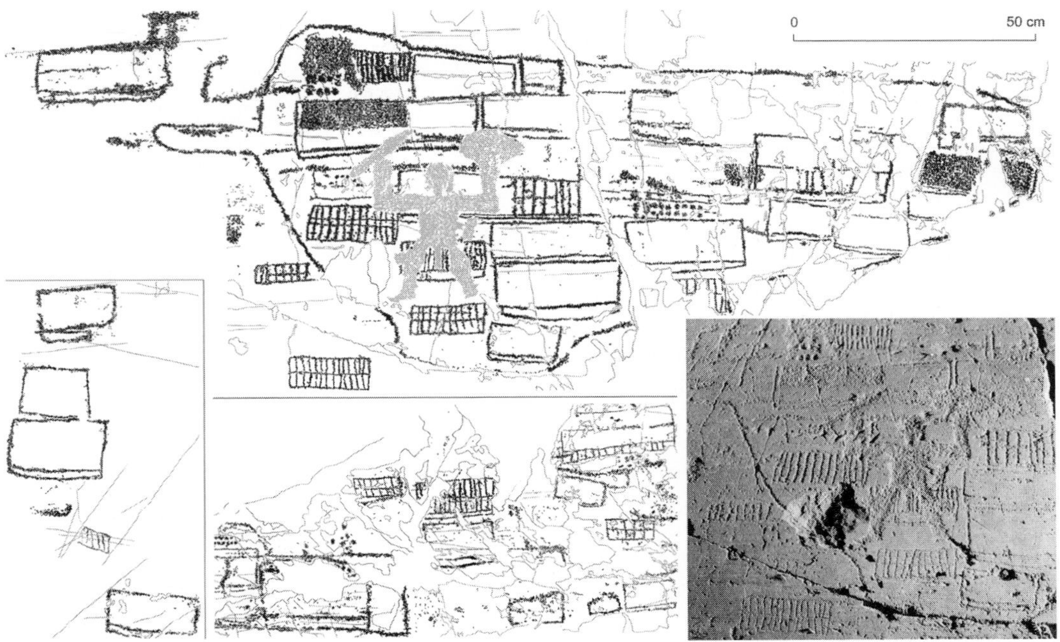

Fig. 15.12. Vite rock 13, Valcamonica: tracing and photograph taken with grazing light which makes the relief clearer. The warrior figure (Iron Age IV2 style), drawn in grey, superimposes the topographic composition, drawn in black.

with the infilling by dots symbolizing the fertilizing rain.

Lumley's general interpretation of the Bego engravings is based on a theory of the expression of the divine. In this context, the topographic engravings appear to represent both an earth divinity and a female divinity at the same time (the God Earth, the Goddess Mother). Lumley's chronology, amplified recently, concentrates the Bego engravings in a Chalcolithic to early Bronze Age time-range (2500–1700 BC), in which a greater antiquity is suggested for the Fontanalba area figures than for those of the Meraviglie.

The Fontanalba figures of the compound geometric type are identical to the pre-Remedello topographics of Valcamonica. Archaeological excavations at the Gias del Ciari shelter (Conti 1942) revealed a human presence on Mount Bego from the Cardial early Neolithic to the Chalcolithic and the early Bronze Age. So one can hypothesize here, as well, a pre-Remedello engraving phase (Neolithic or early Copper Age), originating in the fourth millennium. This anticipates by many centuries the beginning of engraving at Mount Bego, which is for following phases otherwise dated by the depiction of metal objects largely of Bronze Age form.

It seems that both Valcamonica and Mount Bego engravings are well preserved. Damage is mostly caused by exfoliation of the external layer of the rock, badly affected by repeated natural temperature changes and freezing. In the Mount Bego area, exfoliation is greater than in Valcamonica. But where the engraved dots survive the conservation is very good, particularly on vertical surfaces. In Valcamonica we can clearly discern Copper Age figures at the dot-by-dot scale, which have been executed with very fine

Fig. 15.13. Vite rock 29, Valcamonica, in three images: panoramic view from the surface, photograph taken with grazing light, and tracing.

pecking. In the same way we can discern superimpositions: it is often clear when a figure superimposes another, because the weft of its dots is different, mostly in the edges, where it is deeper.

On Mount Bego, the situation is not so clear. The good preservation of the figures is due to an optical effect: pecked areas are still paler than the unpecked surface. If we look closely at the engraved dots, we find them smoothed as if they were made in butter: the appearance is similar to a partially melted polystyrene surface. It means that the edges (the ridges between each pecked hole) have been smoothed by weathering, as if sand-blasted (G. Bresso, pers. comm.). Where this is the case, recognizing superimpositions is obviously more problematic.

Sequence in the Mount Bego figures: topographics and plough-teams

Here, perhaps, we can find the reason why it is so hard to define a chronological sequence in the Mount Bego rock-art. The evidence of subsequent engraving phases seems poor. Also the conventions used in making the record tracings does not make it possible to distinguish superimpositions; there is a risk of compressing into a restricted chronological and interpretative frame motifs that actually belong to very distant periods. So we might ask ourselves: were the different Bego subjects executed at the same time? Or does each distinctive type mark a different period, as it does in Valcamonica? From their similarity we can

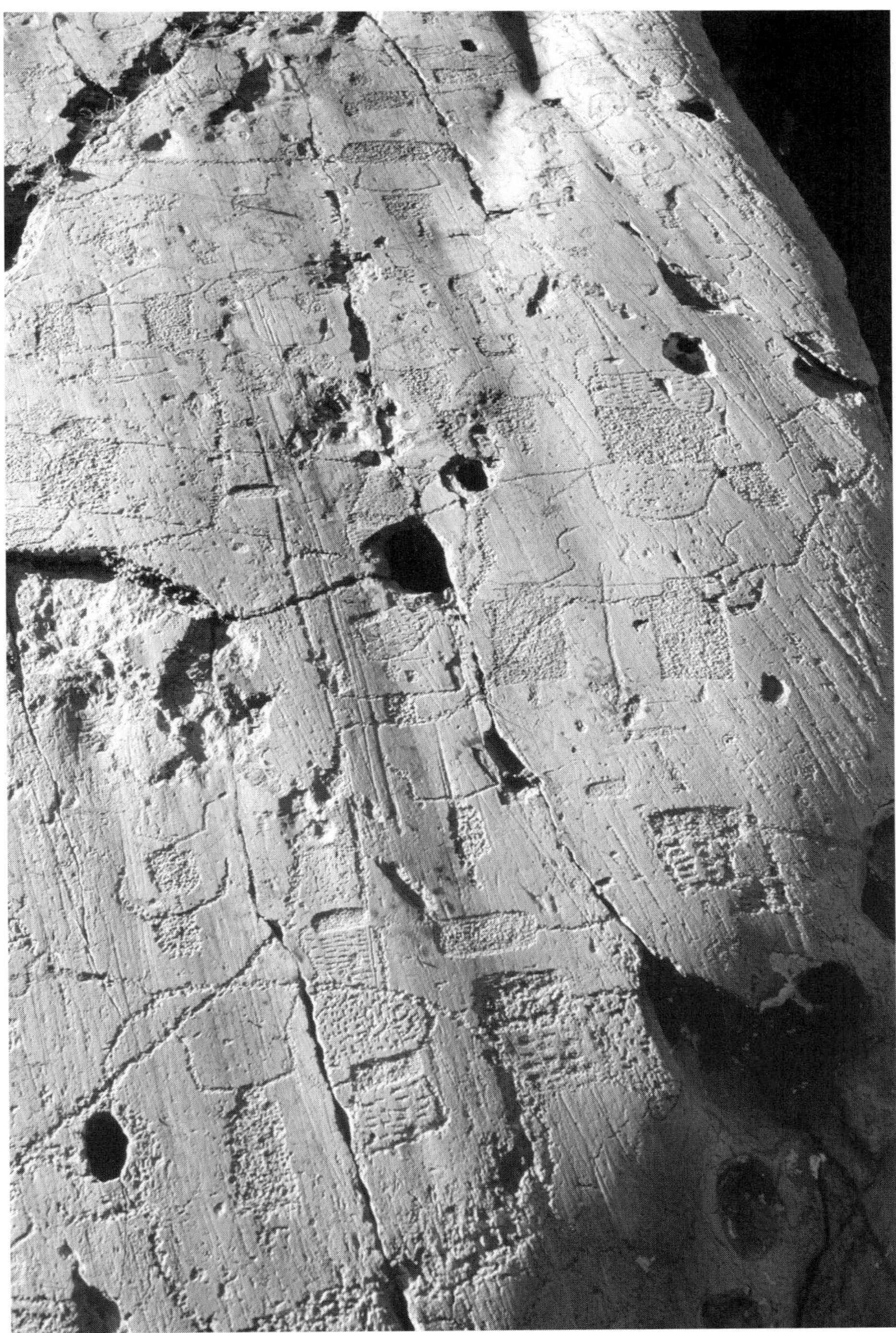

Fig. 15.14. Fontanalba, Mount Bego: the '300 Rock' (ZXIX GIV R21α): topographic composition, oxen and ploughing scenes.

argue for the Mount Bego topographics having the same antiquity as those in Valcamonica; can we validate this by studying superimpositions?

The best place on Mount Bego to do this is the Fontanalba zone XIX, and particularly the '300 Rock', as it was called by Clarence Bicknell (also called the 'Rock of the 26 Ploughing Scenes'; registered as ZXIX GIV R21α). The entire tracing has been published in the *Le Grandiose et le sacré* (Lumley *et al.* 1995). This rock is a large, reddish, flat surface, at an elevation more than 2200 m above sea-level; it is in the middle of a rocky slope facing south-east, where the topographic engravings appear to be more concentrated (Fig. 15.14). The central–upper part of the inclined surface has been filled by an aligned series of completely pecked large rectangles, joined and surrounded by 'path-lines'. In some cases, they are accompanied by rectangular nuclei that are totally pecked, surrounded by curved lines and filled by dots in an orderly arrangement. A large series of ploughing scenes (the '26 Ploughing Scenes' that give a name to the rock) occupies most of the right side of the surface, from the upper to the lower part of the rock, all of the plough-teams facing upwards. These are yoked oxen, depicted with square body and zigzag horns, guided by one or two ploughmen, in the characteristic style of the small Mount Bego anthropomorphic figures (Fig. 15.15). A constellation of single oxen figures (body, horns and tails mainly depicted) seems to fill all the unengraved spaces, while only six weapons (halberds, five of them each held by a man) have been carved in a restricted left part. All the figures, except the human ones, seem to be depicted as if seen from above.

The '300 Rock' is one of the most richly engraved on Mount Bego.[24] Looking at the whole tracing, it seems clear that the figures have not been executed at the same time. Although the ploughing scenes fit well with the topographic engravings, many surrounding rocks have been pecked only with geometric figures; here the absence of ploughing scenes demonstrates that the two subjects do not constitute an association. The 'clean' module in its complex form as a composition of rectangular areas, line-paths and arranged dots can be found on many surrounding rocks.

Another point arises from the arrangement of the figures on the surface, which clearly 'suffocate' one another: this cannot be the consequence of one-off, single-theme execution, nor should it be interpreted as such. A result of this crowding is a series of superimpositions; twenty-six can be counted. In sixteen cases, it is not possible to be certain: the rock is too eroded, or the pecking is too smoothed, or there is a simple contact without superimposition. But in six cases (three of them ploughing scenes), we can find that the body, horns or tail of the oxen cut the line-paths or the pecked rectangles of the larger geometric-topographic composition (Fig. 15.16).

The same fact is shown also by two other examples. A ploughman is depicted in an uncommon position, not in the usual relationship to the plough, but placed so as to avoid a previously pecked rectangle. And in the case of a harrow, the heads and the horns of oxen pulling it have been engraved over a pecked rectangle, as the published tracing shows (Lumley *et al.* 1995: 125, upper left), where it would not be possible to trace the entire figure if it were not superimposed on the topographic.

In four other cases, oxen or ploughing scenes cover topographic engravings, even if in an uncertainly visible way, again owing to erosion. One apparently demonstrates the contrary: a ploughing scene in the lower right part appears cut by a 'path-line'. The line is clearly visible inside the body of the left ox and so seems to cover it. But on looking closely at the edges, we find that the ploughing scene is deeper; what we can see of

[24] It is by no means the largest in terms of the number of engravings.

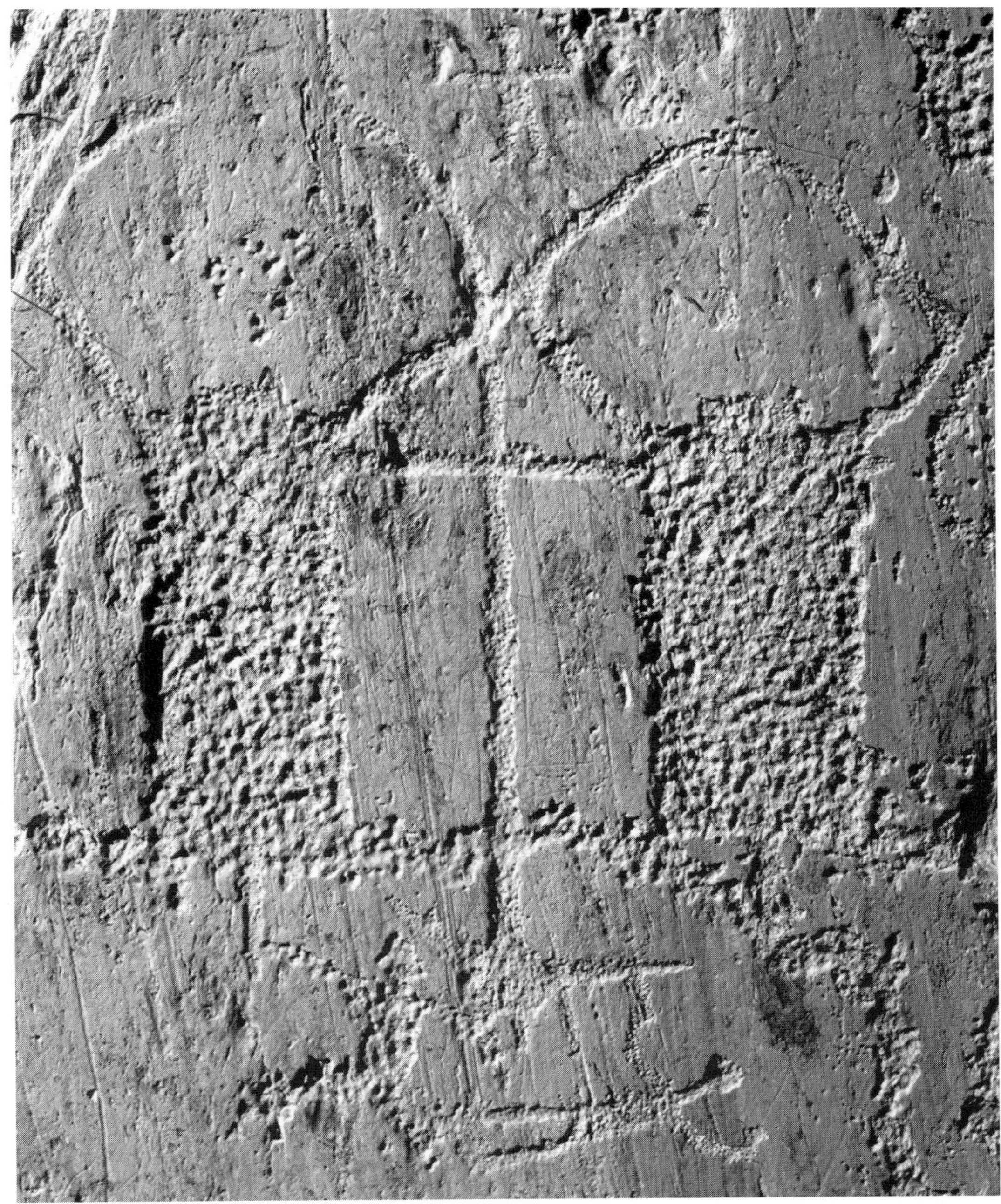

Fig. 15.15. Fontanalba, Mount Bego: the '300 Rock': ploughing scene covering a 'path' in a topographic composition.

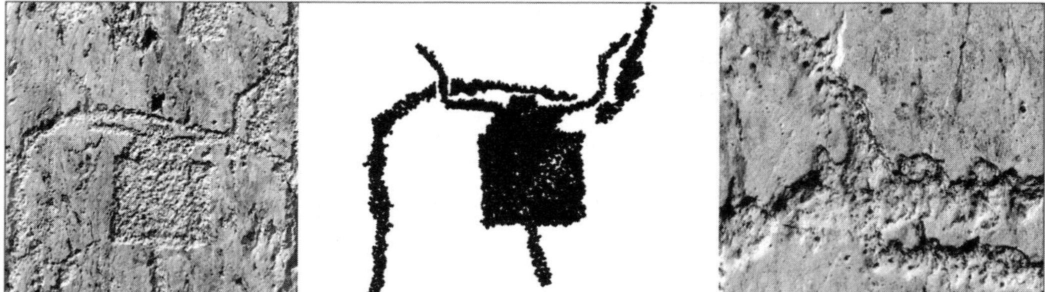

Fig. 15.16. Fontanalba, the '300 Rock': horned figure covering a 'path' in a topographic composition: photograph, tracing and close-up photograph.

the line is only the deeper part, as happens when superimposed pecking does not completely obliterate the previous figure.

This preliminary examination suggests at least two engraving phases, the first constituted by complex topographic compositions, the second by ploughing scenes and oxen. It remains uncertain whether we must assign *all* the oxen to the second phase or only some. Oxen in the plough-teams are of the 'square-horned' and 'multi-segmented' type, and perhaps all oxen of that form should belong to the later phase.

Valcamonica and Mount Bego figures: plough-teams

In Valcamonica, we can find only two rocks with a series of plough-teams, the Dos Cuì rock with thirteen ploughing scenes and Foppe di Nadro rock 22. As in Fontanalba, topographic engravings (large *maculae*) also appear in these Valcamonica rocks, clearly unrelated to the ploughing scenes. These ploughing scenes can be compared with the analogous scenes on the Bagnolo II and Borno I boulders, dated to the Remedello Copper Age. The co-existence of Remedello-type daggers on the same surface, in both Foppe di Nadro and Dos Cuì, confirm that dating. The scene is normally seen from the side. The pair of oxen is depicted with curved horns, yoked at the neck. The ploughman has stick legs and arms, with a slightly enlarged body, as in the typical Mount Bego figures. Another style of ploughing scene is related to the Bell-Beaker Copper Age phase: the body of the ploughman shows a typical triangular body shape. A last case can be found in a rock at Campanine, where we notice the absence of the ploughman. Ploughing scenes appear again in the First Iron Age, but different as the plough is drawn by horses.

The result of this preliminary analysis of the Fontanalba superimpositions on the '300 Rock' clearly matches the Valcamonica situation. It demonstrates that on Mount Bego topographic engravings were executed prior to the ploughing scenes, with a second parallelism constituted by the ploughing scenes, again in the early phases. Comparison with Valcamonica suggests similar dates for Mount Bego: the Neolithic to first Copper Age for the topographics, the Copper Age for the ploughing scenes.

Iron Age topographics: Bedolina (Valcamonica) and Aussois (Haute Maurienne)

Iron Age engraved maps are rare. Two are in Valcamonica, rock 39A at Le Crus (Fig. 15.17a)

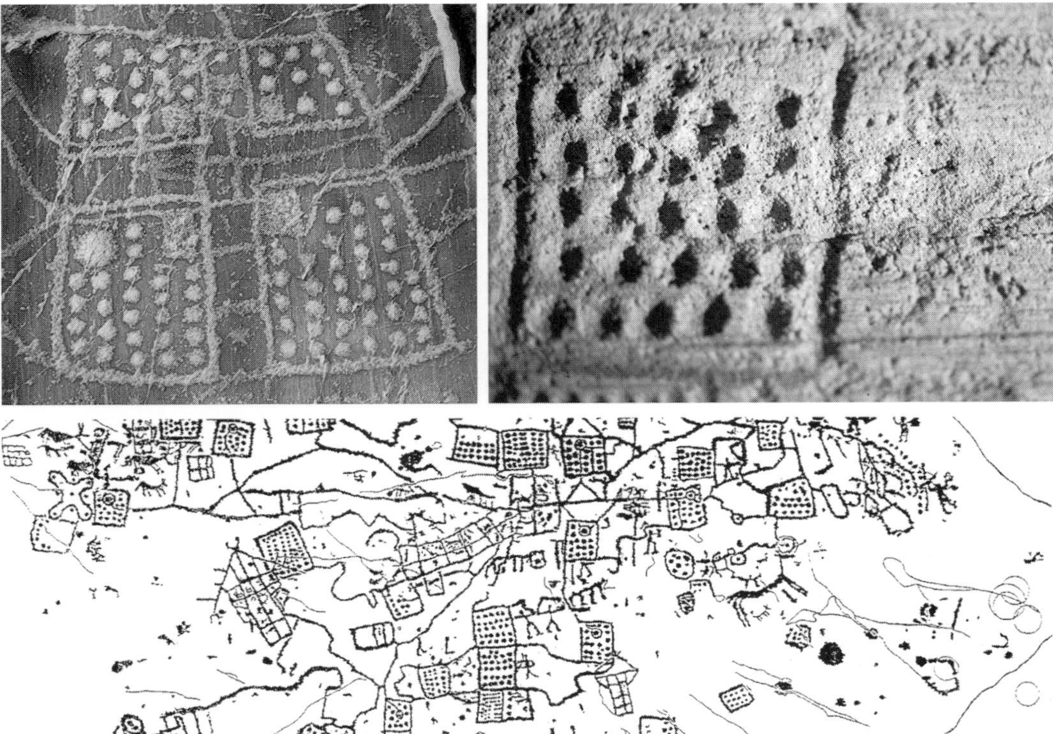

Fig. 15.17. Iron Age topographics, Valcamonica.
(a) Le Crus: rock 39A. Gavaldo 1995.
(b) Bedolina: dotted square.
(c) Bedolina: complex figure in a recent tracing. Turconi 1997.

and the Bedolina map (Figs. 15.17b and 15.17c); the third is in the Haute Maurienne valley (France), at Aussois, some 350 km away (Ballet and Raffaelli 1993; 1996). Curiously, the chronology of all three cases is well testified by the superimpositions. At Bedolina, in the famous 'map of Bedolina' – already placed in the last phase of style III, i.e. the late Bronze Age (Anati 1976) and recently studied by C. Turconi (1997a; 1997b) – the topographical representation covers warriors dating to the First Iron Age (Arcà 1996), and it is covered by late Iron Age huts. The same occurs at Le Crus (Gavaldo 1995), where many warriors are covered by topographical grids. At Aussois a square filled with orderly arranged dots covers a bi-triangular figure of a First Iron Age warrior holding a spear (Fig. 15.18). The warrior resembles figures depicted on Iron Age Italic pottery (Sala Consilina, sixth century BC), clearly related to First Iron Age (eighth century BC) Greek Geometric style. At Aussois at least eight rocks can be counted with contoured squares, often internally dotted. In one case there is a circle, again dotted. From many squares runs out a zigzag line.

In all these cases it is possible to suggest a Middle Iron Age date. In comparing the older topographic figures with the Iron Age ones, we find stylistic difference. In the Bedolina map, the geometric modules are square instead of rectangular. They are always contoured and never totally pecked, and the alignments of dots are much more precise. A central dot surrounded by a ring recurs

Fig. 15.18. Aussois, zone 9: dotted square of a topographic figure of the late type covers a First Iron Age warrior with bi-triangular body, in a digitally grey enhanced photograph.

The main part of the warrior figure is adjacent to the topographic square, without their touching. Notice, however, the long pole or spear held horizontally about the waist of the figure, which is superimposed by the square.

repeatedly. At Aussois the dotted squares often reserve an internal part undotted, as indicating a particular kind of cultivation technique. All the Iron Age maps show a more complex web of lines, like paths, joining the modules, which are more distant from each other. They probably indicate more scattered farm units.

Outlined geometric shapes and series of filling dots are still present in the Iron Age compositions, probably having a similar meaning, despite so long a separation in time. This distance represents a true interruption, as for the moment there is no evidence of topographical compositions from the Bronze[25] and First Iron Ages. In this way Iron Age topographics – completely unaware of the 'ancestors' two millennia and more older, already almost completely weathered and so quite invisible – should represent similar, although evolved, agricultural patterns. This unconscious repetition may be useful to our 'contemporary' interpretation process. It may also relate to a second phase of mountain-slope settlement, possibly permitted by new climatic conditions or by the exploitation of new areas.

The cereal and the granary – key words which seem to emerge from this interpretation of the ancient topographics – also apply to the Iron Age, where not only maps are present, but also depictions of buildings or huts. The Iron Age images of Camunian wooden huts show them often narrow, too narrow to be comfortable as houses, in some cases built over a single pillar. The ethnographical Südtiroler Landesmuseum für Volkskunde (Bruneck, BZ, Italy) gives an overview on the different kinds of Tyrolean Alpine buildings,[26] starting from the thirteenth century AD. The closest resemblance with Valcamonica engraved 'huts' is with a wooden granary.

Interpretation

What is depicted?

The presence of different elements and shapes in the topographics has already been reported. How is one to assign a function to each 'object' and a meaning to the entire iconographic complex? If all the particular functions comply with a general model, that interpretation might be appropriate. I suggest distinguishing four different elements, or 'objects':

Object 1 rectangular, square or round well-defined *geometric areas* (see 'areas' in Fig. 15.1), completely pecked or simply contoured;

Object 2 alignments or arrays of *dots* ('dottings' in Fig. 15.1);

Object 3 square or rounded *grids* ('grids' in Fig. 15.1);

Object 4 *perimeter lines* ('other' in Fig. 15.1), with eyelets or not.

[25] Unless one recognizes as topographic the concentric circle patterns, like those at Carschenna (Switzerland), and common in the rock-art of Galicia and Scotland.

[26] The same wheels that we find sometimes engraved at the extremities of the roofs of the Camunian huts, interpreted as solar symbols, are still now hung as cast-off cart-wheels on the wooden façades.

Fig. 15.19. Fields and maps: (*above*) Tyrol mountain fields and (*below*) Foppe di Nadro rock 23, Valcamonica.

Object 1 bears in its own definition the idea of 'measuring the earth', the meaning of the Greek word γεωμετρια ('geometry'). A shape and a measure are applied to human-modified earth, i.e. to a field, cultivated and previously delimited. Some of these geometric areas can be interpreted as houses, particularly the double-based or subdivided pecked or contoured rectangles; but it seems more suitable to read these as fields, larger and more evident subjects in a mountain landscape (Fig. 15.19). At Mount Bego, Object 1 is present as fully pecked areas, while in Valcamonica it exists also as contoured and subdivided areas.

Object 2 may constitute the core of the problem. It is evident that it represents many identical units. Also evident is the impossibility of depicting in this way animals like cows or sheep, which cannot be trained to stay scattered in regular rows and columns. So we are treating fruit-trees or stooks. The second suggestion seems more appropriate, stooks being the small stacks into which individual sheaves of hay or cereal stalks are gathered when they have been cut. Are they hay stooks or cereal stooks (Fig. 15.20)? The first solution is related to livestock, the second to food-raising. While a mountain landscape dominated by hay-fields and sheaves is surely more common and reaches higher altitudes, the theme of cereals should be more important and strictly connected to the survival of the community.

Object 3 is quite problematic. It occurs at a small size on a few rocks in Valcamonica (e.g. VIT 13), larger in the area of Luine, always orthogonal. On Mount Bego it is mostly found in the Meraviglie area, with large modules variously and often irregularly subdivided. The tiny Valcamonica grids might be compared with some structures to dry and store cereals, like the vertical wooden ones called in the Alps *Histe*, *Casné*, *Rascàn*, *Raschéna*, *Arfa* (Arcà 1999) in various German or Latin dialects. But the most relevant comparison (Fig. 15.11), first suggested by B. Brentjes (1998), is to be made with the grid mud-brick or box-building structures of Mehrgarh (Indus Valley, Baluchistan: Jarrige *et al.* 1995–96) periods IB,[27] II[28] and III[29] (Samzun 1987) and with the cell-buildings of Çayönü Tepesi (south-eastern Anatolia: Schirmer 1988). These kinds of rectangular buildings, made of rammed earth (*pisé*), fulfilled the function of drying and storing cereals (barley and wheat) (Owen 1998), so indicating crop surpluses. They would have been built with wooden or wattle-and-daub upper parts. They appear at Mehrgarh[30] in the early phases

[27] Aceramic Neolithic, 7000–6000 BC.

[28] Neolithic, 6000–4500 BC.

[29] Early Copper Age, 4500–3800 BC.

[30] Mehrgarh, situated at the foot of the Bolan Pass, point of passage between the Indus plain and the Iran and Central Asia mountains, is one of the most ancient agricultural villages in the world.

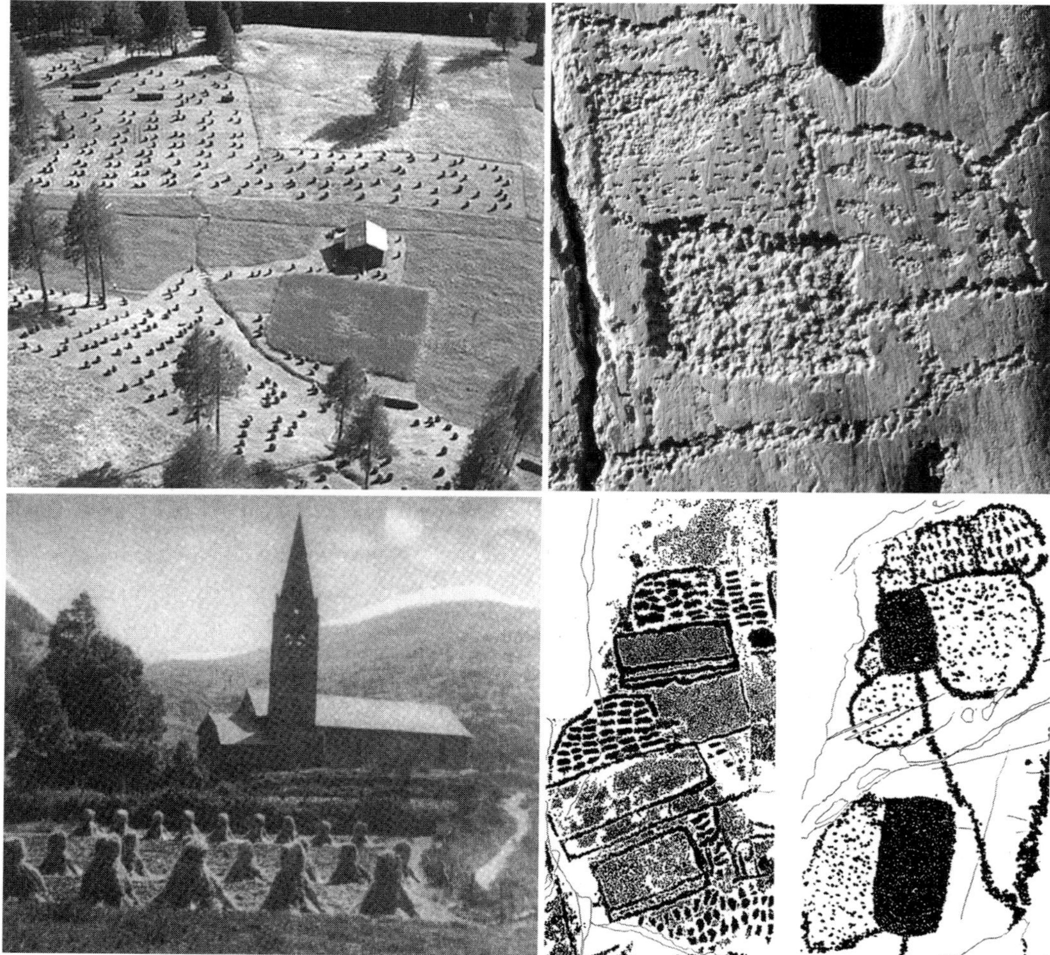

Fig. 15.20. Shapes in the Alpine landscape and in the topographic figures.
(*above left*) Tyrolean mountain fields and hay-stooks, from a Tappeiner – Lana BZ I – 1995 postcard.
(*above right*) and (*below right*) Fontanalba zone XIX topographics, Mount Bego.
(*lower left*) Haute-Provence cereal-stooks. Martel 1983.
(*lower centre*) Vite rock 29, Valcamonica.

of the aceramic Neolithic, lasting till the early Copper Age (phase III), when their architecture becomes more elaborate. At Çayönü Tepesi too they are present in an aceramic Neolithic culture. Both sites show evidence of early copper-working (hooks and awls, 7000 BC),[31] by heating and hammering. The recognition of some granary depictions in Alpine rock-art, with shapes so closely related to architecture of the most ancient world-wide agricultural sites, offers a strong validation for the Neolithic to early Copper Age chronology proposed and to the agricultural interpretation. In the Mount Bego area, as already suggested, there is in addition the possibility

[31] Richard Cowen, http://www-geology.ucdavis.edu/~gel115/115CH3.html.

Fig. 15.21. Bounded settlements and topographic figures.
(*above*) and (*lower right*) The Boussargues Copper Age settlement, France.
(*lower left*) Vite rock 21, Valcamonica.

of comparing the grid figures with stone terracing on slopes or stone enclosures for the herds.

Object 4, apparently incomprehensible and originally named a 'bandoleer',[32] was suggested to be a topographic element by P. Frontini (1994), relating it to megalithic structures. It has a clear resemblance to the perimeter walls and bastions of some Copper Age settlements (Arcà 1998; 1999; Fig. 15.10), already cited above. A more striking resemblance can be found between the 'bandoleer' of Vite rock 21 and the Copper Age structure of Boussargues in France (Coularou 1998). In the Boussargues structure (Fig. 15.21), a stone perimeter wall incorporates six round bastions or rooms and protects two oval–rectangular structures, with traces of food-storing and specialized activities. Four rocks at Vite (VIT13,

[32] The 'bandoleer' element is also present on four Copper Age stelae in Valtellina (Poggiani Keller 1989).

20, 21 (Fig. 15.21b–c), 29) show a bandoleer or perimeter line. It should be interpreted as a protective wall or fence, not only a fortification but a boundary to protect food-stocks or to enclose the herd.

All these functions suggested for Objects 1–4 clearly comply with a general model strictly related to a farmer-shepherd economy – a good base for appropriate interpretation.

The threshing-floor and the sheaves

An image almost never seen in the summer fields of Europe nowadays is that of the reaping and then the threshing of wheat. The modern combine harvester, both reaping and threshing machine, has replaced seasonal manual work that was for millennia the focal point of each sowing-to-harvest cycle. The mowing day was carefully chosen (Comet 1992), paying attention to the weather (a shower could be very dangerous) and to the moon (it must be on the waning moon). The wheat was never left to be fully ripe when cut: by that time, the ripe grains could fall out or be more easily pecked by birds. Ripening was completed in the field, by binding the sheaves and building them into lines of stooks or stacks as protection against rain, in the same way as is done today with hay.

The final job of separating the grain from the ears was done by beating with flails or by trampling by animals – cows testified in ancient Egypt, or horses in typical Mediterranean techniques. A threshing-floor was necessary; it was prepared in an open and windy site, by digging down a few centimetres and making a floor of a ground-clay mix, many times watered and trodden. The threshing-floor was the core of each farm unit, always close to the house. As threshing needed the collaboration of many, it was also a group activity carried out at a communal threshing-floor (Fig. 15.22).

Fig. 15.22. A public threshing floor at Sisteron (Hautes-Alpes), France.

All the steps of reaping and threshing were accompanied by ritual practices: a male or female name was given to the sheaves (depending on the kind of cereal, South Tyrol), a corn dolly or straw-puppet was made by the reaper first accomplishing the job (Veneto region, Italy), the stooks were composed with the 'magic' number of 13 sheaves (Veneto region, Italy), a cock was eaten (Martel 1983: 72), a cross was fixed at the top when the building of the big stack close to the threshing-floor was accomplished (Romagna region, Italy; Haute-Provence, France). At the end of threshing, the wheat was offered to God during the mid-September feast of the cart (Provence, France; south Italy). In the iconography of the calendar, the summer months (particularly June) were traditionally represented by reaping images.

Beginning in the Neolithic, cereals remained the basis of the human diet. Wheat, barley and millet were cultivated in the European Neolithic, while oats are testified in the Roman period. In Europe rye, black corn and maize were introduced in the following period, at the beginning of the Middle Ages. The sequence of reaping then threshing and the leaving of the sheaves in the fields to ripen in aligned stooks is the same for all these cereals.

The common repeated module in Mount Bego and Valcamonica rock-art shows a rectangular (or round) nucleus, totally pecked, surrounded by a curved line(s) and filled by dots (round or rectangular like *macaroni*) in an orderly arrangement. Thanks to a recent suggestion (G. Bresso,[33] pers. comm.), one can interpret this module as the representation of a threshing-floor (the totally pecked area) with a path, surrounded by a regular distribution of stooks (the dots, 'Object 2') or sheaves of cereals, awaiting ripening and protected by enclosures. In the Mugur-Sargol engravings (Tuva, Russia), where we find again the 'common module', the pecked nucleus seems to depict without doubt a house or, better, a granary with small store-rooms inside. This point, a strong key to confirming the 'cereal' interpretation, also offers a link with the Iron Age engravings, two millennia younger, where again the houses in Valcamonica should be granaries, related to the agricultural cycle.

In this way, Bicknell's original suggestion, seeing in some Fontanalba engravings the representation of cattle inside the enclosures around the farm, should be corrected, in recognizing cultivated cereal fields. In the same way it could be important to consider the idea of interpreting the geometric compositions as the symbol of the Earth, of the Goddess Mother. It is indeed the Earth, but a man-worked earth. So which is the focus: the natural entity or the human labour?

Topographic engravings: context and social meaning

Topographic engravings in the Alpine area represent an important constant. In space, they enjoy a vast distribution. In time, they extend, with an interruption, from the Neolithic to the middle Iron Age.

Following the suggested interpretation, topographic patterns represent the land, ploughed and settled. Linked to a process of settlement, they depict concerns of the shepherd-farmer, in contrast to that of the warrior, so well represented by the very long sequence of weapons followed by duelling scenes in the Alpine engravings of the metal ages.

The agriculture theme, of the land becoming possessed in a pioneering way, is a large subject. Barfield and Chippindale (1997) have already identified attitudes to land as a theme uniting the iconography of the Mount Bego engravings. The early date for topographics perfectly matches an economic and cultural era before the metal ages, in which land, stock-breeding and agriculture evidently took the primary role in strategies of sustenance. Certain cereals, and in particular rye, are cultivated within the Alpine area up to relatively high altitudes, and flint blades with use-wear traces from reaping have been found in the Bego zone at over 2000 m altitude (in the Gias del Ciari). It is calculated that wheat can be cultivated in the southern Alps up 1200 m, and barley to 1600–1900 m (Acerbo 1934: 15).

In conclusion, the identification of agricultural patterns in the Alpine rock-art is clear, almost as if it was executed to a formula, diffused from the southern (Mount Bego) to the central Alps (Valcamonica). At high Mount Bego, these landscape elements have their origin in the lower slopes or plain – the farmed land – and so were not engraved in direct sight of it. These conditions make plausible a thesis which sees in the topographics an idealized and conceptual representation of one or more settled units or of farming land – landscape in human charge. These engravings can be interpreted as a topography of the human territory (the *first* topography of territory, we must remember) depicted in an act of

[33] An experienced Mount Bego guide.

ownership or on the occasion of people's first occupation of an area, as in a foundation ritual.[34]

A second, more material interpretation – not distinct anyway from the first – possibly relates to a kind of extensive marking of territory. Not necessarily a totally conscious activity, it is still common in the Alpine pasture areas where it takes a modern form in marking with dates, initials, crosses. It requires a strict relationship with the territory, a daily immersion in the landscape – a matter for shepherds, hunters, camping soldiers, pilgrims, travellers. Even if interpreted as an individual activity (and indeed it is), it always reflects the important cultural aspects of the related period, or – better – the principal topics of the originating human group or clan, mainly young and male. This condition is quite evident in the contemporary phenomenon of urban graffiti, which condenses the self-assertion and often the thoughts and better the dreams of the (mostly male) youth. Thought, mind and dream could be key words to approach the core of this prehistoric problem.[35] Topographic engravings reproduce agricultural landscapes, in some cases distant from the engraving place, relating to the Neolithic-Copper Age economy of the farmer-shepherd. The engraving place, at least at Mount Bego, is today a highland summer pasture, and will have been in prehistoric times. It is still utilized by shepherds[36] coming up from the bottom of the Roya valley or over the watershed from the Italian Piedmont plain, some days of transhumance distant.[37] The marking of the territory with the so important 'common module' could represent for the (young) shepherd, spending hard summer days with the stock in the highest pasture, the recalling of the most important part of his identity, that of the farmer, the one which represents 'home', and at the same time the pride of possessing a territory and the ability to survive in it, probably repeated each new summer. Translated into words, it would say, 'I'm the shepherd. This is my land, like my home down in the valley.'

The identification of the threshing-floor as a grain-related subject opens a wide door to a ritual interpretation. As the wheat is the food and the life, the act of engraving a related iconography in the high mountain at the foot of the sky would be a 'virtual offering' or a 'good-fortune' propitiation in a sort of private or public ritual on the natural 'blackboards' of these beautiful rocky places.

Acknowledgements

Angelo Fossati (Orme dell'Uomo), chronology; Burchard Brentjes, Çayönü Tepesi, Mehrgarh and Tuva comparisons; Elena Marchi and Emanuela Tognoni (Orme dell'Uomo), research and tracings; Giovanni Bresso (Fontanalba guide), 'agricultural' suggestions; Orme dell'Uomo fieldwork participants, tracings; Paola Tirone and Gruppo Ricerche Cultura Montana, ethnographic literature.

References

Acerbo, G. 1934. *La economia dei cereali nell'Italia e nel mondo: evoluzione storica e consistenza attuale della produzione del consumo e del commercio, politica agraria e commerciale*. Milan: Ulrico Hoepli.

Acosta, P. 1968. *La pintura rupestre esquematica en España*. Salamanca: Universidad de Salamanca.

Anati, E. 1976. *Evoluzione e stile nell'arte rupestre camuna*. Capo di Ponte: Edizioni del Centro.

[34] Ritual ploughing was found at the lower level of the Copper Age megalithic complex at St Martin de Corléans (AO, Italy; Mezzena 1982).

[35] A recent case would be that of the shepherds, probably with some sailor experience, engraving ships at high mountain sites – Vallée des Merveilles, Mount Bego (surface ZVII GI R17), and Les Oullas, Ubaye (France), at 2400 m altitude.

[36] Interesting content can be found in the writings of contemporary Mount Bego shepherds (Lumley *et al.* 1995: 398–9): 'In this hell-site shepherds are all suffering like damned souls in the devil's house'; 'In 1882 here there were 60 shepherds in July and the same in August'; 'This year, 1890, wind and misery reign here, hunger for the stock.'

[37] The interpretative idea of the 'sacred mountain', suggested both for Mount Bego (Lumley *et al.* 1995) and for Valcamonica (the 'spirit of the mountain': Priuli 1979), may be contradicted by field evidence: the areas of engraving quite perfectly match the distribution of suitable rock surfaces (mainly sandstone, or limestone, polished by the glaciers); and such extensive areas of engravings obviously refer to an extensive and economic use of the territory, in contrast to sanctuaries which are always situated in well-delimited and restricted sites.

1979. *I Camuni, alle radici della civiltà europea*. Milan: Jaca Book.

1982. *Luine: collina sacra*. Capo di Ponte: Edizione del Centro. Archivi 8.

Arcà, A. 1992. La roccia 13 di Vite Paspardo, elementi per un archivio di archeologia rupestre, *Appunti* 19: 25–31.

1994. Vite, incisioni topografiche: prima fase dell'arte rupestre camuna, *Notizie Archeologiche Bergomensi* 2: 91–8. Bergamo: Civico Museo Archeologico di Bergamo.

1995. La roccia della fata e i segni topografici nell'arte rupestre alpina, in *Immagini dalla preistoria: incisioni e pitture rupestri: nuovi messaggi dalle rocce delle Alpi occidentali*: 96–9. Boves: Corall.

1996–97. The settled ground in the 'topographic engravings' of the Alpine arc, *TRACCE On line Rock Art Bulletin* 2–3–4–6, http://rupestre.net/tracce/topo4.html.

1998. Settlements in topographic engravings of Copper Age in Valcamonica and Mt. Bego rock art, in *Proceedings of the XIII International Congress of Prehistoric and Protohistoric Sciences – Forlì 1996* 4: 9–16. Forlì: ABACO.

1999. Fields and settlements in topographic engravings of the Copper Age in Valcamonica and Mt Bego rock art, in Philippe Della Casa (ed.), *Prehistoric Alpine environment, society and economy: papers of the international colloquium PAESE '97 in Zurich*: 71–9. Bonn: Rudolf Habelt.

Arcà, A., G. M. Cametti and P. Meirano. 1996. Gravures rupestres de l'Age du Fer en Valcenischia (Alpes Occidentales), *International Newsletter on Rock Art* 14: 7–9.

1999. Iron Age petroglyphs found in Valcenischia (Italy), in *News 95 proceedings*. Pinerolo: CeSMAP.

Arcà, A., C. Ferrario, A. Fossati and M. G. Ruggiero. 1996. Paspardo, localita de Plaha, in Ministero dei Beni Culturali ed Ambientali, Soprintendenza Archeologica della Lombardia, *Le vie della pietra verde: l'industria litica levigata nella preistoria dell'Italia settentrionale*: 256–8. Turin: Omega.

Arcà, A., A. Fossati, E. Marchi and E. Tognoni. 1995. *Rupe Magna, la roccia incisa più grande delle Alpi*. Sondrio: Ministero dei Beni Culturali e Ambientali, Soprintendenza Archeologica della Lombardi, Consorzio per il Parco delle Incisioni Rupestri di Grosio. Quaderni del Parco 1.

In press. Le ultime ricerche della Cooperativa Archeologica Le Orme dell'Uomo sull'arte rupestre delle Alpi, in *Proceedings of the 2nd International Congress of Rupestrian Archaeology*. Milan: Civiche Raccolte Archeologiche e Numismatiche di Milano.

Ballet, F. and P. Raffaelli. 1991. Gravures figuratives et abstraites des âges des métaux dans les Alpes de Savoie, in *Le Mont Bego, une montagne sacrée de l'Age du Bronze, prétirage des actes du Colloque de Tende 5–11 juillet 1991* 1: 162–91.

1993. *L'Art rupestre de Maurienne*. Chambéry: Mémoires et Documents de la Société Savoisienne d'Histoire et d'Archéologie 95.

1996. Un exemple remarquable: Aussois, *L'Histoire en Savoie* 31, numéro spécial.

Barfield, Lawrence and Christopher Chippindale. 1997. Meaning in the later prehistoric rock-engravings of Mont Bego, Alpes-Maritimes, France, *Proceedings of the Prehistoric Society* 63: 103–28.

Battaglia, R. 1934. Ricerche etnografiche sui petroglifi della cerchia alpina, *Studi Etruschi* 8: 11–48.

Beltrán Martínez, A. 1983. El problema de la cronología del arte rupestre esquemático español, *Caesaraugusta* 39–40. Saragossa.

Bicknell, C. 1913. *A guide to the prehistoric rock-engravings in the Italian Maritime Alps*. Bordighera: Giuseppe Bessone. (Italian translation: *Guida alle incisioni rupestri preistoriche nelle Alpi Marittime Italiane*. Bordighera: Istituto Internazionale delle Studi Liguri, 1972.)

Blain, A. 1975. Des gravures sur les menhirs du Chemin des Collines à Sion, Valais, Suisse, *Bollettino del Centro Camuno di Studi Preistorici* 12: 154–156.

Borgna, C. G. 1980. *L'arte rupestre preistorica nell'Europa Occidentale*. Pinerolo. Privately published.

Brentjes, B. 1998. Orientalizing motives in Alpine rock art, *TRACCE On line Rock Art Bulletin* 9, http://rupestre.net/tracce/anatol.html.

Breuil, H. and M. C. Burkitt. 1929. *Rock paintings of southern Andalusia: a description of a Neolithic and Copper Age art group*. Oxford: Clarendon Press.

Briard, J. 1990. *Dolmens et menhirs de Bretagne*. Luçon: Jean-Paul Gisserot.

Bueno Ramirez, P., F. Piñon Varela and L. Prados Torreira. 1985. Excavaciones en el Collado de Sejos (Valle de Polaciones, Santander), Campaña de 1982, in *Noticiario Arqueológico Hispánico*. Madrid.

Cardoso, J. L. 1997. *O povoado de Leceia (Oeiras), sentinela do Tejo neo terceiro milénio a.C.* Lisbon: Museo Nacional de Arcqueologia.

Comet, G. 1992. *Le Paysan et son util: essai d'histoire technique des céréales.* Rome: Ecole Française de Rome. Collection de l'Ecole Française de Rome 165.

Coularou, J. 1998. L'habitat calcolithique de Boussargues (France), in L. Castelletti and A. Pessina (eds.), *Introduzione all'archeologia degli spazi domestici*, atti del seminario, Como 4–5 novembre 1995: 57–62. Como: New Press/Museo Civico Archeologico Giovio.

Courboud, P. 1986. Saint Léonard, Crête des Barmes, in *Le Valais avant l'histoire, 14000 av. J.-C.–47 apr. J.-C.*: 286–91. Sion: Musées Cantonaux.

De Marinis, R. C. 1994a. La datazione dello stile IIIA, in *Le pietre degli dei: menhir e stele dell'età del Rame in Valcamonica e Valtellina.* Bergamo: Centro Culturale Nicolò Rezzara.

1994b. Problèmes de chronologie de l'art rupestre du Valcamonica, *Notizie Archeologiche Bergomensi* 2: 223–34. Bergamo: Civico Museo Archeologico di Bergamo.

1997. The Eneolithic cemetery of Remedello Sotto (BS), and the relative and absolute chronology of the Copper Age in northern Italy, *Notizie Archeologiche Bergomensi* 5: 33–51. Bergamo: Civico Museo Archeologico di Bergamo.

Devlet, M. A. 1976. *Petroglify Ulug Khema.* Moscow.

Ferrario, C. 1992. Le figure di oranti schematici nell'arte rupestre della Valcamonica, *Appunti* 19: 41–3.

1994. Nuove cronologie per gli oranti schematici dell'arte rupestre della Valcamonica, *Notizie Archeologiche Bergomensi* 2: 235–48.

Fossati, A. 1992. Alcune rappresentazioni di oranti schematici armati del Bronzo Finale nell'arte rupestre della Valcamonica, *Appunti* 19: 45–50.

1994a. Le rappresentazioni topografiche, in *Le pietre degli dei: menhir e stele dell'età del Rame in Valcamonica e Valtellina*: 89–91. Bergamo: Centro Culturale Nicolò Rezzara.

1994b. Le scene di aratura, in *Le pietre degli dei: menhir e stele dell'età del Rame in Valcamonica e Valtellina*: 131–3. Bergamo: Centro Culturale Nicolò Rezzara.

1994c. Ossimo 8, in *Le pietre degli dei: menhir e stele dell'età del Rame in Valcamonica e Valtellina*: 189–92. Bergamo: Centro Culturale Nicolò Rezzara.

1995. I Cervi al castello, in *Immagini dalla preistoria: incisioni e pitture ripestri: nuovi messaggi dalle rocce delle Alpi Occidentali*: 117–23. Catalogo della mostra in occasione della XXXII Riunione Scientifica dell'Istituto Italiano di Preistoria e Protostoria. Boves: Corall.

Frontini, P. 1994. Il masso Borno 1, *Notizie Archeologiche Bergomensi* 2: 67–77. Bergamo: Civico Museo Archeologico di Bergamo.

Gambari, F. M. 1992. Le pitture rupestri della Rocca di Cavour (TO) e le influenze mediterranee nell'arte rupestre dell'Italia nord-occidentale, in *Atti della XXVII riunione scientifica, l'arte in Italia dal Paleolitico all'età del Bronzo*: 399–410. Florence: Istituto Italiano di Preistoria e Protostoria.

Gavaldo, S. 1995. Le raffigurazioni topografiche, in U. Sansoni and S. Gavaldo, *L'arte rupestre del Pia' d'Ort: la vicenda di un santuario preistorico alpino*: 162–8. Capo di Ponte: Edizioni del Centro. Archivi 10.

1999. Le raffigurazioni topografiche, in U. Sansoni, S. Gavaldo and C. Gastaldi, *Simboli sulla roccia: l'arte rupestre della Valtellina centrale dalle armi del bronzo ai segni cristiani*: 99–101. Capo di Ponte: Edizioni del Centro. Archivi 12.

Geist, H. 1995. Fontan, Cime de Causéga, in *Direction régionale des affaires culturelles Provence–Alpes–Côte d'Azur bilan scientifique 1994*: 91–3. Aix-en-Provence: Ministère de la Culture et de la Francophonie.

Hameau, P. 1989. *Les Peintures postglaciares en Provence.* Paris. Documents d'Archéologie Française 22.

Jarrige, C., F. Jarrige and G. Quivron. 1995–96. *Mehrgarh: field reports 1974–1985: from Neolithic times to the Indus Civilization.* Karachi: Department of Culture and Tourism, Government of Sindh.

Lumley, H. de *et al.* 1995. *Le Grandiose et le sacré: gravures rupestres protohistoriques et historiques de la région du Mount Bego.* Aix-en-Provence: Edisud.

Martel, P. 1983. *Les Blés de l'été: l'été des paysans en Haute-Provence.* Les Alpes de Lumière 77/80, 82/83. Gap.

Mezzena, F. 1982. La Valle d'Aosta nella preistoria e nella protostoria, in *Archeologia in Valle d'Aosta*: 14–50. Aosta: Regione Val d'Aosta.

Nehl, G. 1989. Aperçu sur l'art rupestre de l'Haute Maurienne, *Les Cahiers du GERSAR* 2: 13–18. Milly la Forêt: Gersar.

Nisbet, R. 1994. Alcuni aspetti dell'ambiente umano nelle Alpi Cozie fra quinto e quarto millennio BP, in P. Biagi and J. Nandris (eds.), *Highland zone exploitation in southern Europe*: 259–71. Brescia: Museo Civico di Scienze Naturali di Brescia. Monografie di Natura Bresciana 20.

Owen, B. 1998. *Harappan civilization in the Indus valley*, notes of Class 23 Anthropology 325 – Word Prehistory S '98, Sonoma State University, http://members.aol.com/wph-c23.html.

Pace, D. 1972. *Petroglifi di Grosio*. Milan. Privately published. Tellina Opuscula 2.

Pace, D., M. G. Simonelli and L. Valmadre. 1985. *Escursione nell'antichità della Valtellina da Teglio a Grosio*: 116–17. Tirano: Sistema bibliotecario di Tirano.

Piombardi, D. 1989. Le figure di aratro nelle incisioni rupestri della Valcamonica, *Appunti* 8: 7–12.

1992. Cinque nuove scene di aratura nelle incisioni rupestri della Valcamonica, *Appunti* 19: 18–24.

Poggiani Keller, R. 1989. Le stele dell'età del Rame, in *Valtellina e mondo alpino nella preistoria*: 40–6. Modena: Edizioni Panini.

Pons, S. 1938. Preistoria Valdese: di un antico disegno a calcina della Valle Germanasca (Alpi Cozie) e di alcune ricerche affini, *Bollettino della Società di Studi Valdesi* 70: 3–17.

Priuli, A. 1979. *Preistoria in Valle Camonica: itinerari illustrati dei siti e dell'arte rupestre*. Capo di Ponte: Museo Didattico di Arte e Vita Preistorica.

Renfrew, A. Colin. 1973. *Before civilization: the radio-carbon revolution and prehistoric Europe*. London: Jonathan Cape.

Samzun, A. 1987. Die frühe Kupferzeit: Mehrgarh, Periode III, in *Vergessene Städte am Indus*: 74–80. Mainz: P. von Zabern.

Sansoni, U., S. Gavaldo and C. Gastaldi. 1999. *Simboli sulla roccia: l'arte rupestre della Valtellina centrale dalle armi del bronzo ai segni cristiani*. Capo di Ponte: Edizioni del Centro. Archivi 12.

Schirmer, W. 1988. Zu den Bauten des Çayönü Tepesi, *Anatolica* 15: 140–60.

Seglie, D. and P. Ricchiardi. 1988. Pitture rupestri di Ponte Raut in Val Germanasca, *Survey* 3–4: 71–3.

Sluga, G. 1969. *Le incisioni rupestri di Dos dell'Arca*. Capo di Ponte: Edizioni del Centro.

Turconi, C. 1997a. The map of Bedolina in the context of the rock art of Valcamonica, *TRACCE On line Rock Art Bulletin* 9, http://www.rupestre.net/tracce/TURCONI.html.

1997b. La mappa di Bedolina nel quadro dell'arte rupestre della Valcamonica, in *Notizie Archeologiche Bergomensi* 5: 85–113. Bergamo: Civico Museo Archeologico di Bergamo.

Part Four

Pictures of pictures

In a book which otherwise approaches pictures largely through the contrary medium of words, a closing essay approaches pictures instead through pictures.

16

Walking through landscape: a photographic essay of the Campo Lameiro valley, Galicia, north-western Spain

George Nash, Lindsey Nash and Christopher Chippindale

When describing rock-art and landscape, one usually reports what can be seen, without mention of light conditions and temperature. Moreover, descriptions are usually assigned to a single moment in time. The words that describe the sight are usually devoid of emotion, although we as archaeologists are sometimes overawed by what we see. Using the old adage that 'a picture is worth a thousand words', we here 'walk' the reader through a landscape, in this case, the rock-art landscape of the Campo Lameiro valley, southern Galicia (north-west Spain).

Sorting and arranging

This photographic essay, like a wide-angle lens on a camera, focuses first on an open landscape; this introduces the viewer and reader to a series of open and focused perspective shots which presence both the rock-art and the on-looker. This chapter also moves through the landscape temporally; starting in full daylight, followed by dusk shots, then moving through into night time, and on to dawn. The technicalities of each shot are not important, nor is any discussion concerning the standpoint of the onlooker. There are no captions to instruct the viewer what to look for. A brief technical note by the side of each image reports where it is from, and what the viewer might see; each has a number for reference. What is important is that each photograph tells a story based on emotion and mood; creating a visual rather than a textual phenomenology.

This photographic essay was created not within the Galician landscape but in a small basement in Cambridge. Until then, for many years over 300 pictures and colour transparencies had remained sorted, filed and forgotten. This visual narrative, deriving from a series of visits to the Campo Lameiro valley in 1992, focuses on the aesthetic mechanisms of viewing rock-art within a landscape.

Using a landscape approach, research in this area of Spain had been undertaken by Peña Santos and Vazquez Varela (1979), García Alén and Peña Santos (1980), Costas and Novoa (1993), Bradley (1997) and Nash (1997; 2000). These surveys were based on earlier research work by Obermaier (1925) and Sobrino Buhigas (1935). This corpus of research has concentrated mainly on recording techniques and spatial distribution.

Recently, Richard Bradley with Felipe Criado Boado and Fádregas Valcarce (1994a; 1994b; 1994c) have provided a series of discussions on landscape narrative which organize the rock-art into a wider pan-European spatial assemblage.

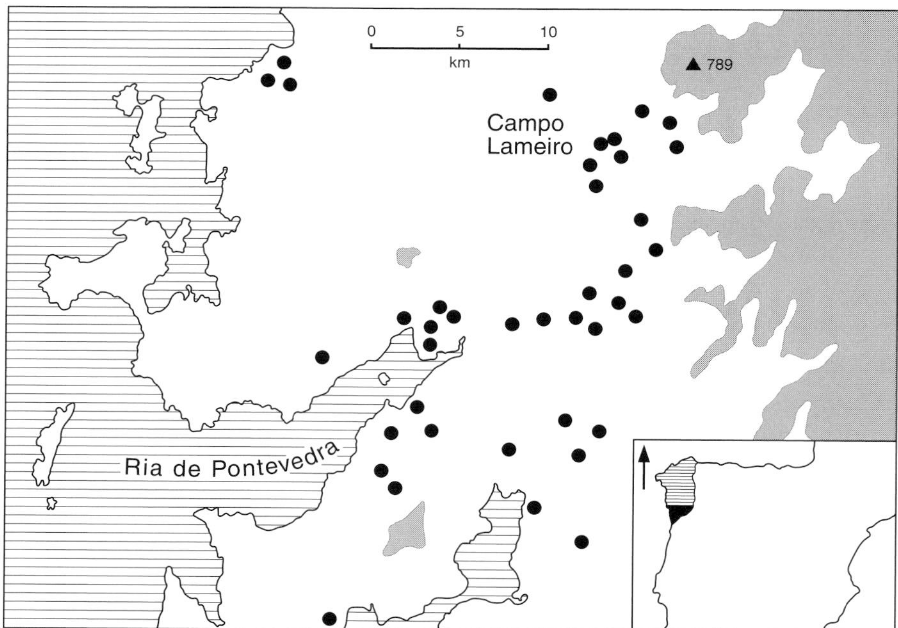

Location of the Campo Lameiro valley, and distribution of Bronte Age rock-art sites.

Bradley (1993; 1997) has discussed stylistic and location similarities between rock-art areas in Galicia, France, northern Britain and Ireland.

Walking the landscape

The rock-art of the Campo Lameiro valley falls into five generic groups: zoomorphic and anthropomorphic figures; spirals (and concentric circles); cup and hoof marks; crosses; and wheeled-crosses. Each group is subdivided into distinct stylistic forms. Survey recognized thirteen rock-carving panels, part of a much larger rock-carving area within the valley. If defined by style, the spatial distribution of the Campo Lameiro group may be extended 40 km westwards to either side of the Rio de Ponteverdra (see map). The northern part of the valley is surrounded by a small, but dominant mountain range – Monttillon de Arriba, Monte Cregos.

Nearly all the panels are sited on open, rocky outcrops within the valley slope areas (or what can be termed the intermediate slope zone). However, at the Fentáns station, five large panels are located on a small valley plateau and away from the northern part of the Campo Lameiro valley. Generally the position of each panel within the intermediate slopes segregates the rich fertile valley floor from the hostile environment of the uplands (Nash 1997).

At present, the valley has been allotted into small field systems; the predominant crop grown within the valley, indeed the whole region, is grapes. On the intermediate slopes, recent eucalyptus plantations intrude on the deeper, more fertile soils. In addition to eucalyptus planting, small herds of goat and cattle are grazed, especially on the poorer soils on the valley slopes, usually during the summer months (in an annual rhythm similar to that of the Alpine grazing system). The soil structure within the slope zone is predominantly thin and well drained. In many cases, the soil has been completely eroded to expose smooth-rock granite outcrops. Rock outcropping occurs throughout the intermediate slopes and highland zones. The slope areas, the mountains and the valley floor constitute three very distinct geographic zones.

The photographic essay includes the following sites: the De Laxe de Rotea de Mende, Caneda, Chan de Lagoa, Fentáns, Parada and Paredes stations.

Pictures are pictures!

We do not further explain, justify or annotate the pictures with yet more words. The force of academic habit has already made us, probably clutter them already too much. Place and time are the elements instinct has us report.

References

Bradley, R. 1993. *Altering the earth: the origins of monuments in Britain and continental Europe*. Edinburgh: Society of Antiquaries of Scotland. Monograph Series 8.

1997. *Signing the land: rock art and the prehistory of Atlantic Europe*. London: Routledge.

Bradley, R., F. Criado Boado and R. Fádregas Valcarce. 1994a. Rock art research as landscape archaeology: a pilot study in Galicia, north-west Spain, *World Archaeology* 25(3): 374–90.

1994b. Petroglifos en el paisaje: neuvas perspectivas sobre el arte rupestre gallego, *Minius* 3: 7–28.

1994c. Los petroglifos como forma de appropiación del espacio: algunos ejemplos gallegos, *Trabajos de Prehistoria* 51(2): 159–86.

Costas Goberna, F. J. and P. Novoa Alvarez. 1993. *Los grabados rupestres de Galicia*. Coruña: Museu Arqueolóxico e Histórico.

García Alén, A. and A. Peña Santos. 1980. *Grabados rupestres de la Provincia de Pontevedra*. Pontevedra: Museo de Pontevedra.

Nash, G. H. 1997. Dancing in space: rock art of the Campo Lameiro Valley, southern Galicia, Spain, in G. H. Nash (ed.), *Semiotics of landscape: archaeology of mind*. Oxford: British Archaeological Reports. International Series 661.

2000. Conceptualising a landscape: discovering and viewing on Bronze Age rock art of the Campo Lameiro Valley, southern Galicia, Spain, in K. Sognnes (ed.), *Rock art in landscapes – landscapes in rock art: VITAK*. Trondheim: University of Trondheim.

Obermaier, H. 1925. Die bronzezeitlichen Felzgravierungen von Nordwest Spanien (Galicien), *IPEK (Jahrbuch für prähistorische und ethnographische Kunst)* 1: 16–22.

Peña Santos, A. and J. M. Vazquez Varela. 1979. *Los petroglifos gallegos*. La Coruna: Edicios do Castro.

Sobrino Buhigas, R. 1935. *Corpus petroglyphorum gallaeciae*. Santiago de Compostela: Seminario de Estudos Galegos.

1 Looking north: afternoon, 2 p.m.

Campo Lameiro Valley.

2 Looking east: afternoon, 2.30 p.m.

Farmstead below the Parades petroglyph.

3 Looking north-east: afternoon, 3.15 p.m.: Parada 5b

Main visible designs include curvilinear designs with cup-marks and red deer.

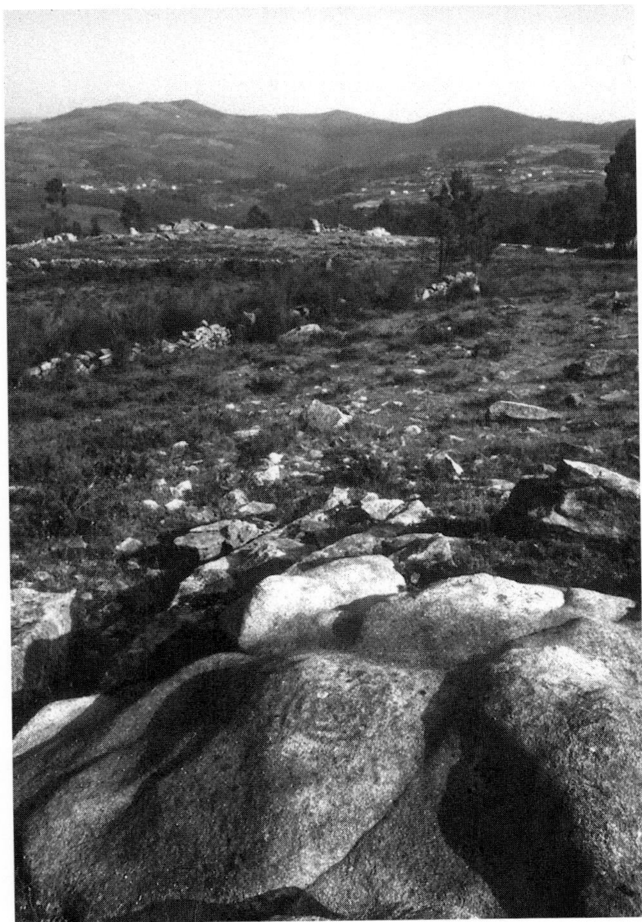

4 Looking east: afternoon, 4.30 p.m.: Parada 5a

Main visible designs include curvilinear designs.

5 Looking south-east: afternoon, 4.40 p.m.: Fentáns 6c

Main visible designs include a row of red deer stags, curvilinear designs with cup-marks.

6 Looking north: afternoon, 4.55 p.m.: Fentáns 6c

Main visible designs include female red deer, curvilinear designs with cup-marks.

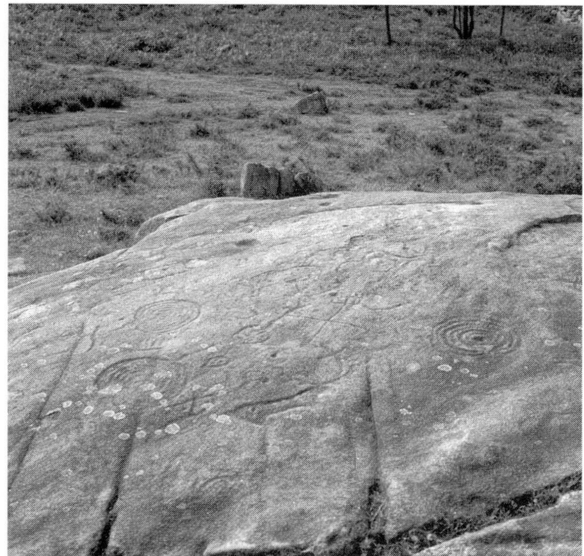

Main visible designs include curvilinear designs, red deer, open crosses, wheeled crosses and stick anthropomorphs.

7 Looking south-east: afternoon, 5.20 p.m.: Chan de Lagoa

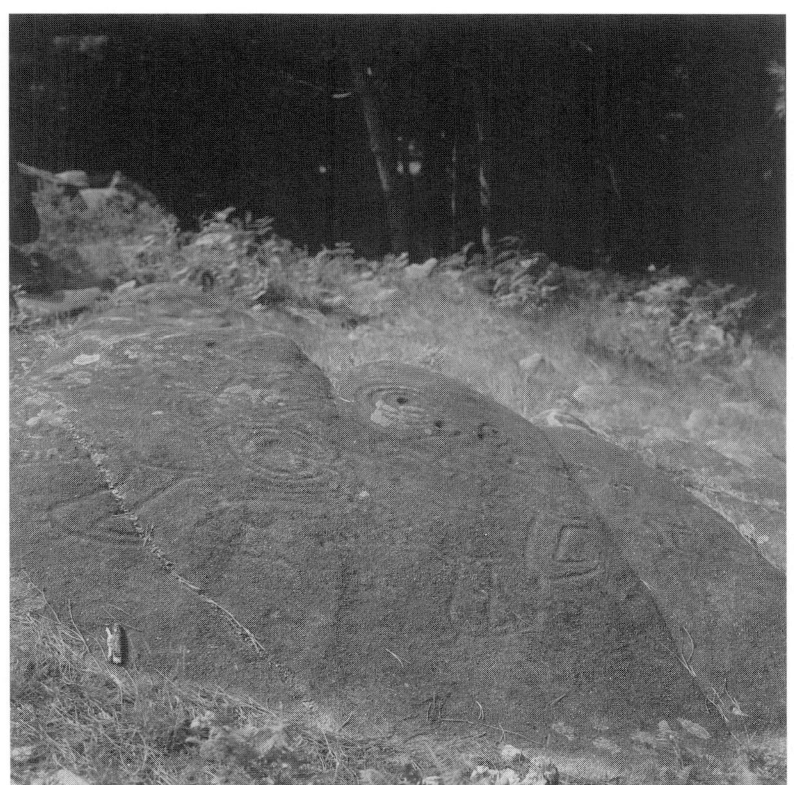

Main visible designs include a row of red deer (stags), curvilinear designs with cup-marks.

8 Looking south-east: late afternoon, 6.10 p.m.: Fentáns 6c

Main visible designs include a single red deer (stag).

9 Looking east: late afternoon, 6.30 p.m.: Parada 5c

Single red deer (stag).

10 Looking north-east: late afternoon, 6.35 p.m.: Parada 5c

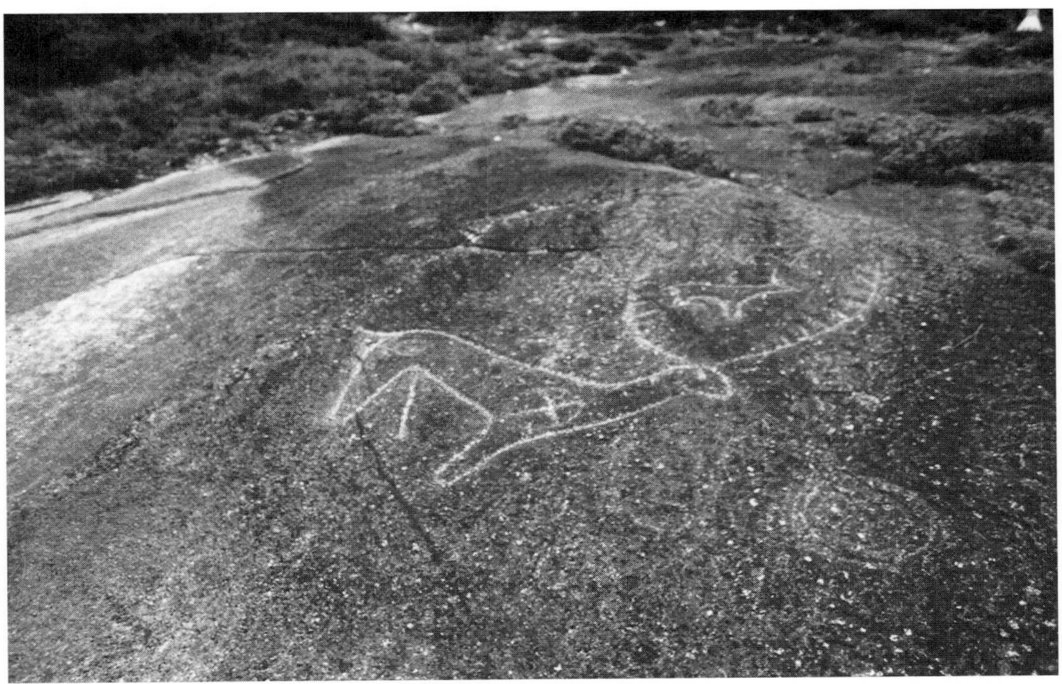

11 Looking north-west: dusk, 7.50 p.m.: De Laxe de Rotea de Mende

Main visible designs include a red deer (stag) with inverted barbed antlers, female deer, curvilinear designs.

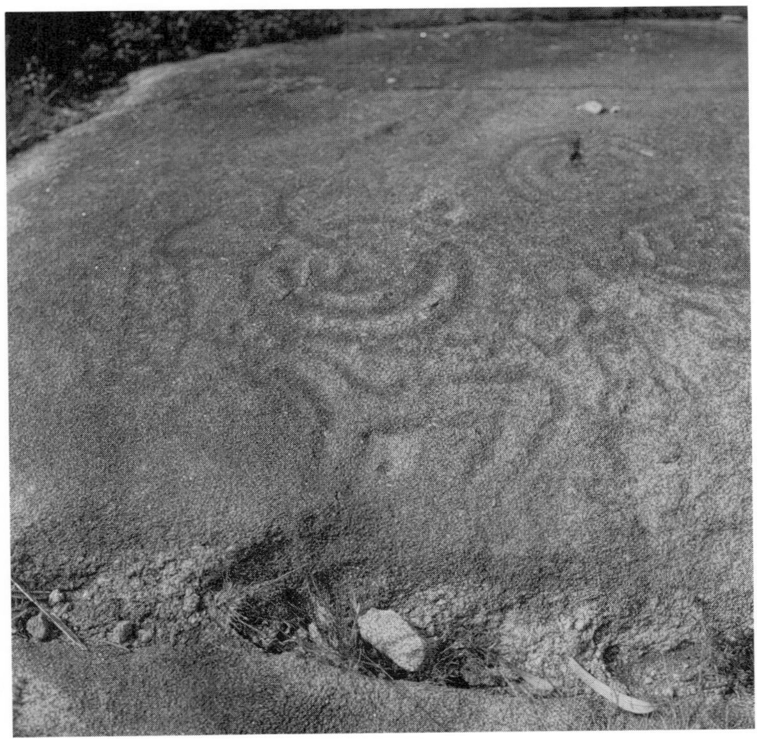

12 Looking north: dusk, 8.20 p.m.: Fentáns 6c

Main visible designs include female red deer, curvilinear designs with cup-marks.

13 Night , 11.30 p.m.: De Laxe de Rotea de Mende

Main visible designs include a red deer (stag) with internal wheeled-cross. Between the barbed antlers are a further two red deer (female).

Shot using 50 watt video light and high-speed 1600 ASA transparency film.

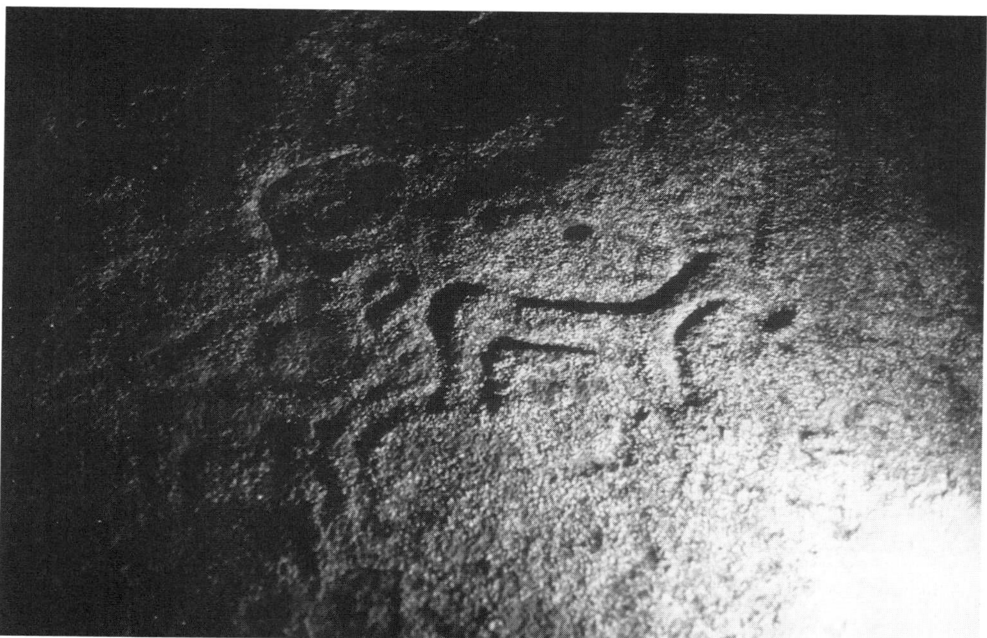

14 Night, 1.30 a.m.: Fentáns 6a

Site also known as Pedra das Ferraduras: main visible designs include red deer with antlers and cup-mark.

Shot using 50 watt video light and high-speed 1600 ASA transparency film.

15 Night, 1.50 a.m.: Chan de Lagoa

Main visible designs include curvilinear designs (horned spirals – showing possible stylised face, eyes are represented by two cup-marks).

Shot using 50 watt video light and high-speed 1600 ASA transparency film.

16 Night, 2.20 a.m.: Fentáns 6a

Main visible designs include curvilinear design incorporated into a 'field system'. To the left are red-deer hoof-carvings.

Shot using 50 watt video light and high-speed 1600 ASA transparency film.

17 Night, 2.30 a.m. Fentáns 6b

Site also known as Laxe dos Cebos: main visible designs include curvilinear designs. Shot using 50 watt video light and high-speed 1600 ASA transparency film.

18 Night, 3.50 a.m.: Parades 3a

Main visible designs include horse and rider. This panel is intervisible with the Caneda Station (Nash 1997: 48).

Shot using 50 watt video light and high-speed 1600 ASA transparency film.

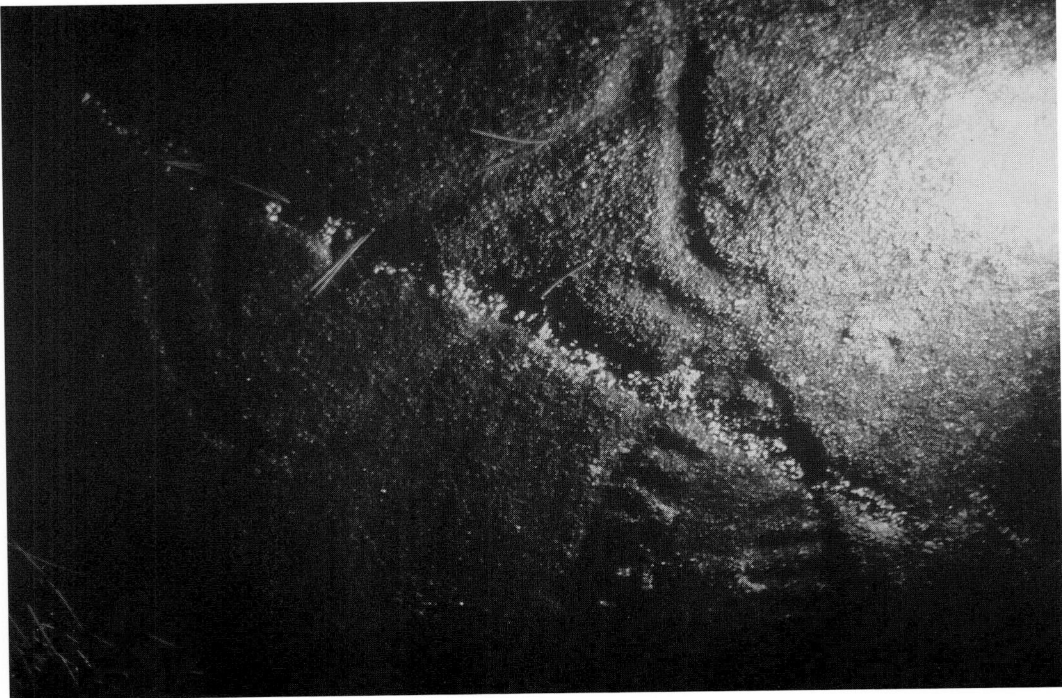

19 Night, 4.05 a.m.: Parada 5b

Main visible designs include a red deer (stag) cut by natural fissure.

Shot using 50 watt video light and high-speed 1600 ASA transparency film.

20 Night, 4.25 a.m.: Chan de Lagoa

Main visible designs include a double curvilinear design, wheeled-cross, single and multiple lines and possible stick anthropomorph.

Shot using 50 watt video light and high-speed 1600 ASA transparency film.

21 Night, 4.55 a.m.: Caneda 4b

Main visible designs include a curvilinear circle design.

Shot using 50 watt video light and high-speed 1600 ASA transparency film.

22 Looking north: dawn, 6.15 a.m.: De Laxe de Rotea de Mende

Main visible designs include a red deer (stag) with inverted barbed antlers, wheeled-cross. Possible erect penis or rear leg. Bradley (1997: 197) records superimposed designs over and above the stag.

23 Looking north: morning, 6.25 a.m.: De Laxe de Rotea de Mende

Main visible designs include a stylized female(?) red deer and curvilinear design.

24 Looking east: morning, 7.00 a.m.: Fentáns 6b

Main visible designs include red deer (stags) with barbed antlers and female red deer, curvilinear designs with cup-marks.

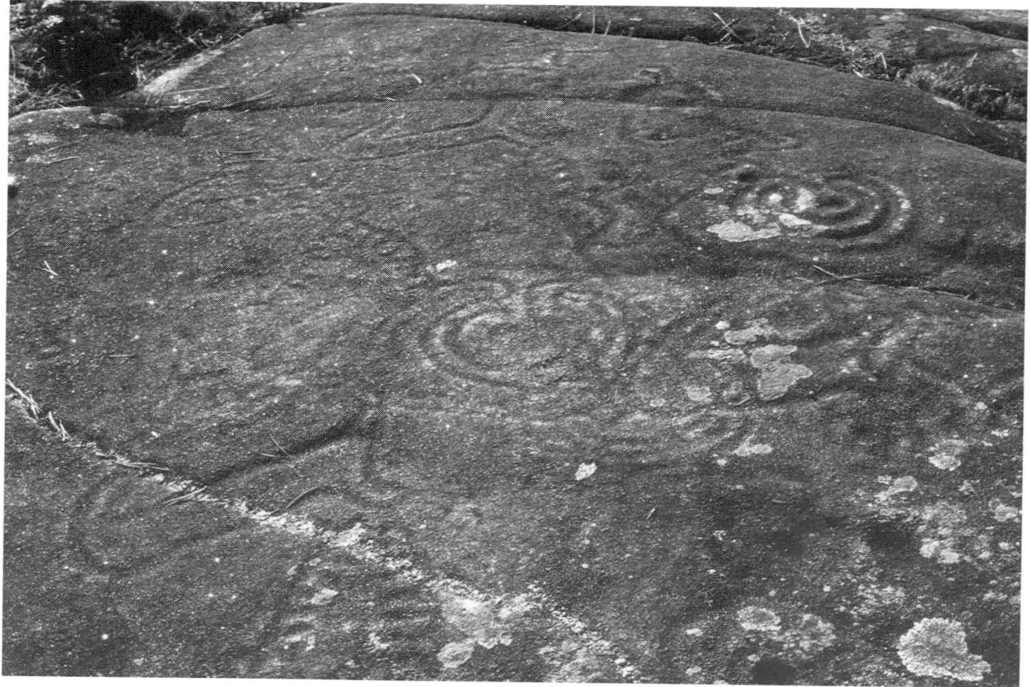

25 Looking east: morning, 7.10 a.m.: Fentáns 6b

Main visible designs include red deer (stags), curvilinear designs.

26 Looking south-east: morning, 7.30 a.m.: Fentáns 5b

Main visible designs include a red deer (stag).

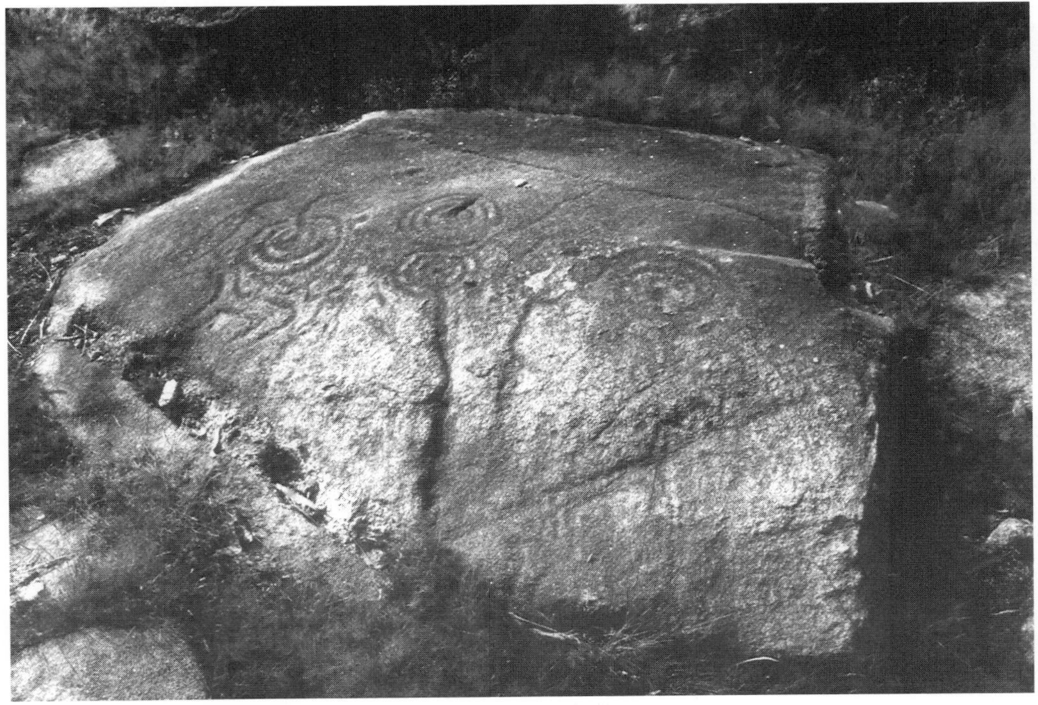

27 Looking west: morning, 7.50 a.m.: Fentáns 6c

Main visible designs include red deer (female), curvilinear designs with cup-marks.

28 Looking north: morning, 9.05 a.m.: Chan de Lagoa

Main visible designs include curvilinear designs, red deer, open crosses, wheeled-crosses and stick anthropomorphs.

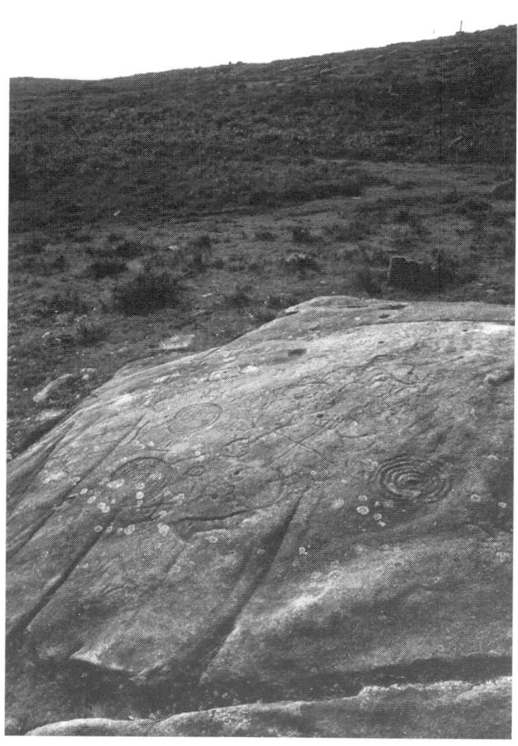

29 Looking south-west: morning, 9.15 a.m.: Chan de Lagoa

Main visible designs include curvilinear designs, red deer, open crosses, wheeled-crosses, and a stick anthropomorph.

30 Looking south-east: morning, 10.50 a.m.

Farmstead below the Parades petroglyph. Intervisible with the Caneda Station. In the background, within the valley zone are fertile field systems, whilst on the intermediate slopes are eucalyptus trees.

31 Looking south-east: morning, 10.55 a.m.

Farmstead below the Parades petroglyph.

Index

In mention of figures and tables, the page where the figure or table is to be found follows within brackets, as: 'fig. 2.13 (59)'.

The index is largely of proper names, especially sites and places, and of more specific subjects.

Authors are indexed where there is discussion of their work beyond simple references.

Broad subjects of the book, such as 'landscape' are not indexed; they are better traced through the detailed Contents (pages vii–x).